Canadian Literature
and Cultural Memory

Edited by Cynthia Sugars and Eleanor Ty

OXFORD
UNIVERSITY PRESS

OXFORD
UNIVERSITY PRESS

Oxford University Press is a department of the University of Oxford.
It furthers the University's objective of excellence in research, scholarship,
and education by publishing worldwide. Oxford is a registered trade mark of
Oxford University Press in the UK and in certain other countries.

Published in Canada by
Oxford University Press
8 Sampson Mews, Suite 204,
Don Mills, Ontario M3C 0H5 Canada

www.oupcanada.com

Library and Archives Canada Cataloguing in Publication

Canadian literature and cultural memory / Cynthia Sugars
and Eleanor Ty.

Includes bibliographical references and index.
ISBN 978–0–19–900759–2 (bound)

1. Canadian literature (English)—History and criticism. 2. History
in literature. 3. Collective memory in literature. I. Ty, Eleanor, 1958–,
editor of compilation II. Sugars, Cynthia, 1963–, editor of compilation

PS8101.H58C35 2014   C810.9'35871   C2014-900752-3

Cover image: From "Floating House" (2002) by Paulette Phillips

Printed and bound in the United States of America

1 2 3 4 — 17 16 15 14

CONTENTS

PART III: RE-MEMBERING HISTORY: MEMORY WORK AS RECOVERY

Contributors

Jennifer Andrews is Professor of English at the University of New Brunswick. She is the co-author of *Border Crossings: Thomas King's Cultural Inversions* (U of Toronto P, 2003), the author of *In the Belly of a Laughing God: Humour and Irony in Native Women's Poetry* (U of Toronto P, 2011), and has published over twenty articles and book chapters in the areas of English-Canadian, American, and Native North American literatures.

Jesse Rae Archibald-Barber teaches Indigenous literatures at the First Nations University of Canada. His publications include articles on cognitive theories of oral and written traditions in the *International Journal of Canadian Studies* (2004), the use of Aboriginal symbolism in Leonard Cohen's *Beautiful Losers* in *Selves and Subjectivities: Reflections on Canadian Arts and Culture* (Athabasca UP, 2012), and the poetics of place in early Métis and English Canadian poetry in *Indigenous Poetics in Canada* (Wilfrid Laurier UP, 2014). His recent interests involve blending digital humanities with Indigenous literature, film, and popular culture.

Joel Baetz is an Assistant Professor at Trent University. He is the editor of *Canadian Poetry from World War I: An Anthology* (OUP, 2009), and the author of several articles on early and contemporary Canadian poetry and fiction, including ones about Robert Service's war journalism and poetry, Anna Durie's elegies, Rohinton Mistry's rendition of cricket, and Ann-Marie MacDonald's formulation of cultural pluralism. His work has appeared in *Canadian Literature*, *Canadian Poetry*, *Studies in Canadian Literature* and various edited collections, including *The Ivory Thought: Essays on Al Purdy* (U of Ottawa P, 2008) and *Home Ground, Foreign Territory* (U of Ottawa P, 2014).

Pilar Cuder-Domínguez is Professor of English at the University of Huelva (Spain), where she teaches British and Canadian Literature. Her research interests are the intersections of gender, genre, nation, and race. She is the author of *Margaret Atwood: A Beginner's Guide* (Hodder & Stoughton, 2003), *Stuart Women Playwrights 1613–1713* (Ashgate, 2011), and *Transnational Poetics: Asian Canadian Women's Fiction of the 1990s* (TSAR, 2011), and the co-editor of six essay collections. Her latest publications have discussed works by writers of Black and Asian ancestry in the UK and Canada.

Eva Darias-Beautell is Associate Professor of American and Canadian literatures at the University of La Laguna (Spain). Her books include *Shifting Sands: Literary Theory and Contemporary Canadian Fiction* (Mellen, 2000) and *Graphies and Grafts: (Con)Texts and (Inter)Texts in the Fictions of Four Canadian Women Writers* (Peter Lang, 2001). She has co-edited *Canon Disorders: Gendered Perspectives on Literature and Film in Canada and the United States* (with María Jesús Hernáez Lerena; U de La Rioja P, 2007), and edited *Unruly Penelopes and the Ghosts: Narratives of English Canada* (Wilfrid Laurier UP, 2012). She currently directs an international research project on the representation of the city in Canadian literatures in English.

Dennis Duffy (Emeritus/English/UofT) is the author of *Gardens, Exiles, Covenants: Loyalism in the Literature of Upper Canada/Ontario* (U of Toronto P, 1982); *Sounding the Iceberg: An Essay on Canadian Historical Novels* (ECW, 1987), and *A World Under Sentence: John Richardson and the Interior* (ECW, 1997). In the last ten years, he has published major articles on such iconic Canadian structures as Algonquin Park and the Vimy Memorial, the cultural politics of Mackenzie King, and close readings of stories by Alice Munro. His current project involves attempts to engage with Munro's later fiction.

Marc André Fortin is Assistant Professor of English and comparative literature at l'Université de Sherbrooke. His research focuses on representations of science in Canadian and international literatures, and the connections between scientific thought, faith, and poststructuralist and postmodern theory. His work also includes research on early ethnography in Canada, modernism, and Indigenous representation in ethnographic archives and museums. His work has been published in *Studies in Canadian Literature, Canadian Literature*, and *ESC: English Studies in Canada*.

Marlene Goldman is a Professor in the Department of English at the University of Toronto. She specializes in contemporary Canadian literature. Her recent research focuses on the intersection between narrative and pathological modes of forgetting associated with trauma, dementia, and Alzheimer's disease. She is the author of *Paths of Desire* (U of Toronto P, 1997), a book on apocalyptic discourse in Canadian fiction, *Rewriting Apocalypse* (McGill-Queen's UP, 2005), and *(Dis)Possession* (McGill-Queen's UP, 2011). She is currently writing a book entitled *Forgotten: Age-Related Dementia and Alzheimer's in Canadian Literature*.

Robyn Green is a doctoral candidate in the School of Canadian Studies at Carleton University. Her doctoral project explores the "economics of reconciliation" by employing a political economy analysis of the Indian Residential School Settlement Agreement. Previous and forthcoming publications can be found in the *Canadian Journal of Law and Society* and the *Journal of Genocide Studies*.

Peter Hodgins is an Assistant Professor in the School of Canadian Studies at Carleton University. He is currently serving as the Acting Director of Carleton's Institute of Interdisciplinary Studies. His research has primarily focused on the politics of public memory in Canada. He is the co-editor of *Settling and Unsettling Memories: Essays in Canadian Public History* (U of Toronto P, 2011) as well as book chapters and articles on the subject. More recently, he has been researching the relationship between civil servant scientists, writers, and artists; the Canadian culture of extraction; and the formation of a national and local cultural infrastructure in late Victorian Ottawa.

Renée Hulan teaches Canadian literature at Saint Mary's University in Halifax, Nova Scotia. She is the author of *Northern Experience and the Myths of Canadian Culture* (McGill-Queens UP, 2002) and editor of *Native North America: Critical and Cultural Perspectives* (ECW, 1999). With Renate Eigenbrod, she edited *Aboriginal Oral Traditions: Theory, Practice, Ethics* (Fernwood, 2008). From 2005 to 2008, she served with Donald Wright as editors of the *Journal of Canadian Studies/Revue d'études canadiennes*.

Shelley Hulan is an Associate Professor in the Department of English Language and Literature at the University of Waterloo. She specializes in early Canadian literature, with a particular interest in nineteenth-century Aboriginal and Euro-settler rhetorics. Her work has appeared in several essay collections and journals, including *Canadian Poetry: Studies, Documents, Reviews*; *Essays on Canadian Writing*; *Journal of Canadian Studies*, *Mosaic: A Journal for the Interdisciplinary Study of Literature*; and *National Plots: Historical Fiction and Changing Ideas of Canada* (Wilfrid Laurier UP, 2010). With Randy Harris and Murray McArthur, she is the co-editor of *Literature, Rhetoric, and Values.*

Tanis MacDonald is the author of *The Daughter's Way: Canadian Women's Paternal Elegies* (Wilfrid Laurier UP, 2012) which was a finalist for the Gabrielle Roy Prize for Canadian literary criticism. She has published articles on the work of Thomas King, Gregory Scofield, Sky Lee, Anne Carson, George Grant, and Dennis Lee, and on the films of Bruce McDonald and Terrance Odette. She is a well-known reviewer and the author of three books of poetry, the most recent of which is *Rue the Day* (Turnstone, 2008). She is Associate Professor in the Department of English and Film Studies at Wilfrid Laurier University in Waterloo, Ontario.

Kimberly Mair is Assistant Professor of Sociology at the University of Lethbridge, Alberta. Her research is concerned with space, aesthetics, and communicative formations. She has work published in edited collections as well as in journals such as *Third Text: Critical Perspectives on Contemporary Art & Culture*, *The Journal of Historical Sociology*, and *The Senses and Society.*

Sophie McCall is an Associate Professor in the English department at Simon Fraser University where she teaches contemporary Canadian and Indigenous literatures. She is the author of *First Person Plural: Aboriginal Storytelling and the Ethics of Collaborative Authorship* (UBC P, 2011), which was a finalist for the Gabrielle Roy Prize for English Canadian literary criticism and the Canada Prize for scholarly work in the Humanities. She is the editor of a new publication of Anahareo's *Devil in Deerskins* (U Manitoba P, 2014), and co-editor, with Christine Kim and Melina Baum Singer, of a collection of essays, *Cultural Grammars of Nation, Diaspora, and Indigeneity in Canada* (Wilfrid Laurier UP, 2012).

Marissa McHugh completed her PhD in the Department of English at the University of Ottawa in 2013. Her dissertation focuses on contemporary Canadian plays about the First World War. Other research interests include Canadian drama, Canadian adaptations of Shakespeare, and theatrical representations of war. She co-edited *Shakespeare and the Second World War: Memory, Culture, Identity* (U of Toronto P, 2012) with Irena Makaryk.

Farah Moosa is a doctoral candidate in the Department of English and Cultural Studies at McMaster University. Her research focuses on representations of cultural inheritance in contemporary Canadian literature by writers such as Hiromi Goto, Larissa Lai, Fred Wah, David Chariandy, and Renée Sarojini Saklikar. She has published in *Chimo*.

Robyn Morris (PhD) lectures in the English Literatures and Cultural Studies Program at the University of Wollongong, Australia. Her areas of interest include diaspora studies, trauma and memory studies, and the politics of citizenship and belonging. Her focus is contemporary diasporic Asian writing. She has published widely on the work of writers such as Larissa Lai, Joy Kogawa, Hiromi Goto, Evelyn Lau, Lillian Ng, Simone Lazaroo, Hsu-Ming Teo, Madeleine Thien, and Alice Pung in articles, book chapters, interviews, and reviews. She is the Editor of *Australasian Canadian Studies* and President of the Association for Canadian Studies in Australia and New Zealand (ACSANZ).

Alexis Motuz is a doctoral student in the Department of English and Film Studies at Wilfrid Laurier University in Waterloo. Her dissertation explores notions of ethical global citizenship in Canadian women's ecological poetry, specifically in works by Pat Lowther, Erin Mouré, Sina Queyras, Di Brandt, and Dionne Brand. She has published in *Memory Studies*, *Arc Poetry*, and *Canadian Review of American Studies*.

Brooke Pratt has a PhD in English from Western University. Her research focuses on representations of abandoned space in Canadian writing. She also has an interest in Canadian literary landmarks in the context of heritage tourism and public culture. Her published work, which appears in *Canadian Literature*, *Canadian Poetry*, *English Studies in Canada*, and *Re-exploring Canadian Space / Redécouvrir l'espace canadien* (Barkhuis, 2012), includes articles on Margaret Atwood, Sara Jeannette Duncan, Hugh Hood, and Duncan Campbell Scott.

Candida Rifkind is an Associate Professor in the Department of English at the University of Winnipeg. She specializes in Canadian popular and political writing, modernisms, and non-fiction comics and graphic narratives. Her award-winning book, *Comrades and Critics: Women, Literature, and the Left in 1930s Canada*, was published by the University of Toronto Press in 2009. Recent and forthcoming publications include articles on 1930s Mountie serial fiction and kitsch, Mazo de la Roche and the middlebrow, the bio-topographies of Seth's "picture novella" *George Sprott*, and metabiography and black visuality in Ho Che Anderson's graphic biography *King*. She is currently co-editing a scholarly collection with Linda Warley, *Canadian Graphic Life Narratives*, and working on a book project about contemporary graphic biographies.

Cynthia Sugars is Professor of English at the University of Ottawa. She is the author of *Canadian Gothic: Literature, History and the Spectre of Self-Invention* (U of Wales P, 2014) and is the editor of *Unhomely States: Theorizing English-Canadian Postcolonialism* (Broadview, 2004), *Home-Work: Postcolonialism, Pedagogy, and Canadian Literature* (U of Ottawa P, 2004), *Unsettled Remains: Canadian Literature and the Postcolonial Gothic* (with Gerry Turcotte; Wilfrid Laurier UP, 2009), and the historical anthology, *Canadian Literature in English: Texts and Contexts* (with Laura Moss; Pearson/Penguin, 2009). She is currently editing *The Oxford Handbook of Canadian Literature* (forthcoming with OUP in 2015) and is the co-editor, with Herb Wyile, of the journal *Studies in Canadian Literature*.

Tony Tremblay is Professor of English at St. Thomas University and Canada Research Chair in New Brunswick Studies. He is founding editor of the *Journal of New Brunswick Studies/Revue d'études sur le Nouveau-Brunswick* and general editor of the *New Brunswick Literary Encyclopedia*. His recent work includes the digital critical edition, *Fred Cogswell: The Many-Dimensioned Self* (New Brunswick Studies Centre, 2012), the documentary film *Last Shift: The Story of a Mill Town* (2011), and the critical biography *David Adams Richards of the Miramichi* (U of Toronto P, 2010). His current research examines New Brunswick's modernist cultural workers—A.G. Bailey, Elizabeth Brewster, and Desmond Pacey.

Eleanor Ty is Professor of English at Wilfrid Laurier University. Her research areas are in Asian American and Asian Canadian literature, as well as eighteenth century British women novelists. Author of *Unfastened: Globality and Asian North American Narratives* (U of Minnesota P, 2010) and *The Politics of the Visible in Asian North American Narratives* (U of Toronto P, 2004), she has co-edited *The Memory Effect: The Remediation of Memory in Literature and Film* with Russell J.A. Kilbourn (Wilfrid Laurier UP, 2013) and *Asian Canadian Writing Beyond Autoethnography* with Christl Verduyn (Wilfrid Laurier UP, 2008).

Linda Warley is Associate Professor in the Department of English Language and Literature at the University of Waterloo. Her research focuses on Canadian life writing, including texts by Indigenous peoples, and life writing in visual, digital, and graphic forms. She has co-edited two books, *Tracing the Autobiographical* (Wilfrid Laurier UP, 2005) with Marlene Kadar, Jeanne Perreault, and Susanna Egan, and *Photographs, Histories, and Meanings* (Palgrave Macmillan, 2009), also with Marlene Kadar and Jeanne Perreault. She is currently editing *Canadian Graphic Life Narratives* with Candida Rifkind.

J.A. Weingarten lectures at McGill University, where he received his doctorate in 2013. His research focuses on the function of lyric in historically conscious Canadian poetry, as well as on cultural memory and recovery in Canadian literature, visual art, and media. He is also the co-founder and co-managing editor of *The Bull Calf: Reviews of Fiction, Poetry, and Literary Criticism*. His critical work has appeared in *English Studies in Canada*, *Canadian Poetry*, and *Studies in Canadian Literature*. Currently, he is completing the manuscript of *Ad Astra: The Selected Letters of John Newlove*.

Doris Wolf teaches in the Department of English and Community-Based Aboriginal Teacher Education Program at the University of Winnipeg, where she is also the Director of the Centre for Research in Young People's Texts and Cultures. She currently researches and publishes in the areas of YA novels and memoirs about German childhoods in the Second World War and Canadian Aboriginal picture books and graphic narratives.

Robert Zacharias is a Banting Postdoctoral Fellow in the Department of English Language and Literature at the University of Waterloo, and Visiting Scholar with the Centre for Diaspora and Transnational Studies at the University of Toronto. His primary research interests are in Canadian literature, migration writing, and Mennonite studies. He is the author of *Rewriting the Break Event: Mennonites and Migration in Canadian Literature* (2013), and co-editor, with Smaro Kamboureli, of *Shifting the Ground of Canadian Literary Studies* (2012). He is a contributing member of the Canadian Consortium for Performance and Politics in the Americas, and is the Associate Editor of the *Journal of Mennonite Studies*.

Acknowledgements

We would like to thank our contributors for their excellent essays and their timely responses to our many requests. We are especially grateful for the help and contagious enthusiasm of our editor at Oxford, Jen Rubio. Thanks are also due to Leslie Saffrey for her careful copyediting and to the two very supportive anonymous readers of the manuscript. We would like to acknowledge the Social Sciences and Humanities Research Council of Canada for its financial assistance over the years. Shannon Maguire, our student assistant, provided us with efficient and judicious help with our bibliography. Thanks to the Association for Canadian and Quebec Literatures (ACQL) for allowing Cynthia to organize a series of panels on "Canadian Literature and Collective Memory" at the annual Congress in Fredericton in 2011. Finally, this work would not have been completed without the support and love of our families and the encouragement of our colleagues and friends.

Cynthia Sugars and Eleanor Ty

INTRODUCTION

·◆·

Thinking Beyond Nostalgia: Canadian Literature and Cultural Memory

Cynthia Sugars and Eleanor Ty

From here it's easy to see the border between memory and history; everything is forgotten and resurfaces in another's hands.
Paul Tyler, "A Short History of Forgetting" 29

Literature fills a niche in memory culture, because like arguably no other symbol system, it is characterized by its ability [. . .] to refer to the forgotten and repressed as well as the unnoticed, unconscious, and unintentional aspects of our dealings with the past.
Astrid Erll, *Memory in Culture* 153

THEORETICAL CONTEXT

The last two decades have seen what many have called a "memory boom" in the fields of sociological and cultural studies. The phrase was coined by Andreas Huyssen to describe "the emergence of memory as a key concern in Western societies, a turning toward the past that stands in stark contrast to the privileging of the future so characteristic of earlier decades of twentieth-century modernity" (21). This shift has been marked by a concern with the ways the past continues to infuse the present—sometimes through intangible or unconscious means, but also in self-consciously manufactured and consumable forms. This is not to say that memory discourse is necessarily nostalgic in impetus, though in some cases it may be, but rather that a concern with the cross-over, transmission, and utilization of "memory" as a vector of signification has become a central concern in contemporary cultural discourse. In many ways, contemporary Western societies are immersed within what Jan Assmann has termed "a culture of memory" (Erll 33) or what David Lowenthal has termed being "possessed by the past," though, as these critics acknowledge, this memory overlay manifests itself in divergent ways. According to Assmann, "The concept of cultural memory comprises that body of reusable texts, images, and rituals specific to each society in each epoch, whose 'cultivation' serves to stablise and convey that society's self-image" (132). The predominance of memory discourse within the academy and without is evident in the increasingly widespread interest in a variety of interrelated topics—themes such as heritage, antiquity, nostalgia, elegy, ancestry, haunting, trauma, affect, aging, authenticity, commemoration, public history, etc. The surge in the popularity of the genre of historical fiction in recent decades is one part of this trend toward historical commemoration and (post)colonial nostalgia. Outside the academy, the interest in relics of cultural memory is evident in such phenomena as the rise of historical reenactments (see Agnew; McCalman; Sturken); a growing popular interest in ancestry and origins; a fascination with heritage regalia (as marketing tools and cultural motifs) and "retro" collectibles; the advent of heritage tourism (evident, for example, not only in the commemoration of the War of 1812 in 2012 Canada, but in the tourism industry's plans to capitalize on the anniversary of Vimy Ridge in 2017); and a general obsession with notions of antiquity, origins, and authenticity, explored very piercingly in David Lowenthal's *Possessed by the Past* (1996) and Andrew Potter's recent bestseller *The Authenticity Hoax* (2010). Critical attention to ideas of memory, commemoration, and identity, then, represents not a turning away from the concerns of the present, but a means of exploring how the past continues to inform the present, and how the present manipulates the past, in material and intangible ways. As Paul Tyler expresses it in his beautiful poem "A Short History of Forgetting," there is a precarious continuum between history and memory, which is in danger of both erasure and repetition, and yet which never disappears without some after-effect.

Since the work of Maurice Halbwachs in the 1920s, it has been a widely held assumption that cultural memory is necessarily a form of social memory—both emergent within social contexts and constructed by social networks. It is in this sense that any notion of individual cultural memory is implicitly social in nature. It has also become customary to speak of the ways cultural memory is typically linked to notions of place or things—the *lieux de memoire* that Pierre Nora speaks of—whether in the form of a concept of homeland (nation) or merely "home" (familial or communal space). For Nora, a site of memory need not refer only to a place, however; it can be a person, an author, a book, an event, a ritual—in short, "any cultural phenomenon [. . .] which a society associates with its past" (Erll 25). Nora's work has come under a fair deal of criticism for its inherently nostalgic sense that people's "authentic" relation with the past has been increasingly eroded in recent decades, hence the need for artificially bolstered "*lieux de memoire*" which have a compensatory function. As Nora famously puts it, "We speak so much of memory because there is so little of it left" (146). In his view, the construction of obvious memorial "sites" covers over the fact that authentic "*milieux*" of memory are no longer available on a communal level. According to Nora, these *lieux de memoire* are the embodiments "of a memorial consciousness that has barely survived in a historical age that calls out for memory because it has abandoned it" (149). Peter Hodgins rightly identifies Nora's and many others' expressions of cultural memory as being steeped in what he terms a "nostalgia for memory" ("Our Haunted" 100), a sense that "we have fallen from an authentic relationship to memory that can only be retrieved through a 'return to our roots'" (101).

Hodgins's analysis picks up on discussions of the fabricated nature of heritage and memory, such as those articulated by the British Marxist critics Eric Hobsbawm and Terence Ranger in their influential collection, *The Invention of Tradition* (1983). The essays in their collection explore the ways nation-states build their discursive and symbolic identities by establishing an often-invented "continuity with a suitable historic past" (1). Following in their wake, British and American cultural theorists have been expanding this work into examinations of cultural heritage, antiquity, commemoration, and national identity, including such influential texts as Benedict Anderson's *Imagined Communities* (1983), David Lowenthal's *The Past Is a Foreign Country* (1985), Patrick Wright's *On Living in an Old Country* (1985), John Gillis's *Commemorations: The Politics of National Identity* (1994), and Lois Parkinson Zamora's *The Usable Past: The Imagination of History in Recent Fiction of the Americas* (1997). These works explore the ways contemporary nations have manufactured a sense of antiquity in order to forge a sense of national cultural memory and community. Such skeptical takes on the constructed nature of cultural memory and tradition have themselves come under critique in an important essay by Mark Salber Phillips, who assesses the different responses to what he calls the "politics of disenchantment" that motivates both Nora's and Hobsbawm's approaches (8). Phillips takes issue particularly with the widespread debunking of "tradition" and "memory" that this discourse has set in motion, the sense that one can only speak of tradition in tones of irony (4). Hobsbawm's distinction between "'genuine' and 'invented' traditions is unworkable," Phillips asserts, since cultural phenomena are inherently variable over time, which means that the notion of an authentic tradition that is "involuntary and unconscious" is nonsensical. Phillips's concern is that the notion of "invented tradition" or memory has inadvertently "become defining for the category of tradition as a whole" (6): "This blurring together of tradition as such with a (putatively) bogus traditionalism lends itself to a notion that tradition is necessarily static or reactionary, never adaptive, constructive, or creative" (6). Hodgins gestures in a similar direction when he notes the impasse that memory theory risks setting up: an outright debunking of memory projects or an embrace of them as a safeguard against a fallen, commodified world. As he puts it, "the nostalgia for memory is easily co-opted for hegemonic ends but, following the same line of reasoning, it can just as easily be the spur for cultural resistance and/or the resuscitation of more authentic practices of remembrance" (106).

Articulations of a retrievable or "forgotten" authentic memory, often linked to ideas of national commemoration, have in more recent years been supplemented by critical attention to instances of counter-memory or "memory from below," which considers communities that have been omitted from official discourses of historical commemoration. In part, this shift has emerged since the 1960s with the advent of feminist and postcolonial interventions and the more general shift in historical studies into the fields of social history and civil rights activism. In the 1970s, Michel Foucault's conceptualization of "counter-memory" and "counter-history," in such texts as *The Archaeology of Knowledge* (1972) and *Language, Counter-Memory, Practice* (1977), was extremely influential, contributing to discourses of memorial recovery in a range of contexts, from subaltern studies, to an interest in postcolonial, migrant, and diasporic communities, to Indigenous studies. As José Medina puts it in his analysis of Foucault's method, counter-histories are possible "because there are people who remember against the grain, people whose memories do not fit the historical narratives available. Counter-histories feed off such counter-memories and at the same time transform them, revitalizing practices of counter-memory and offering them new discursive resources to draw on" (12). According to this view, Medina writes, "alternative memories are not simply the raw materials to be coordinated in a heterogeneous (but nonetheless shared) collective memory; rather, they remain counter-memories that make available multiplicitous pasts for differently constituted and positioned publics and their discursive practices" (24). Foremost among these offshoots of memory theory has been a growing interest in trauma theory and traumatic memory (see Caruth; Felman and Laub; Sturken), particularly in the context of the Holocaust, slavery, indentured labour, and other experiences of genocide, violence, human rights violations, and social rupture. Critics have also been exploring the ways memory functions across generations, leading to instances of what has been termed "postmemory" (Hirsch) or "prosthetic memory" (Landsberg) to refer to memories that do not arise from an individual's lived experience but through some form of cultural or intergenerational inheritance and transmission. In this sense, communal memories emerging out of histories of generational trauma, explored particularly with reference to the Holocaust, can be passed down to second- or third-generation descendants and structure the identity and cultural expressions of a much later generation.

CANADIAN LITERATURE AND CULTURAL MEMORY

Nora's nostalgic lament for the erosion of French collective memory takes on an interesting, and more self-conscious, inflection in Canadian cultural studies in which the sense of a unified "collectivity"—not to mention an identifiable "culture"—has always been a problematic and unstable concept. Although this has not always been the way Canadian national identity has been expressed in the past, as many of the essays in this collection demonstrate, it may be that the *lieux de memoire* in Canada were only ever that: *lieux de memoire* that did not reach back to an identifiable *milieu* (or at best to an invented *milieu*). This may have been the case in feudal France as well, but Canadian critics have long been attentive to the ways that the Canadian nation-state is internally informed by a diversity of often contesting and sometimes overlapping rememberings from heterogeneous inter-communal perspectives. In this sense, Canadian literature as a site of memory is an extremely resonant field, for it attends to the ways that the "idea" of Canada (and Canadian culture) is informed by interacting frameworks of memory. To speak of Canadian culture as a consciously constructed "culture of memory" may

be an accurate way of designating the tentativeness of the Canadian project since its foundations.

An awareness of the interconnections between cultural memory
and identity, even as these apply to understandings of national identity, has a long history in Canadian literary expression, as the essays
in this collection reveal. Early Canadian authors and critics were in-
sistent on the integral links between a national literature and nationhood, and these assertions were often phrased in terms of a required
historical recuperation of an invigorating past. In April 1833, the editor
of *The Canadian Literary Magazine*, John Kent, asserted the importance
of cultural memory in the Canadian colony. The Canadian settler, he
observed, "I cannot believe to be forgetful of the past. [. . .] on the contrary, I believe that he will welcome with pleasure any honest chronicler
who [. . .] will rescue from oblivion's stream those floating fragments,
which some Canadian Hume or Robertson will hereafter search for,
when composing the annals of his country" (1). In *A Purer Taste*, Carole
Gerson explores the ways early Canadian readers and writers favoured
the genre of historical romance, believing that literature would contribute to Canada's emergent self-definition and consolidate a national cultural memory. Whether phrased as a recuperation of Canadian
political history, as Kent goes on to assert in the context of both the
United Empire Loyalists and the veterans of the War of 1812, or in terms
of metaphors of indigeneity, which one finds in early authors' articulations of the ways the spirit of the Canadian landscape was infused with
an Aboriginal presence which would in turn enter into the verses of
settler Canadian authors, Canadian writers have been engaging with
ideas of cultural memory for well over a century. As Gerson reveals, the
"romance" of Canadian history mediated a particular version of cultural
tradition that was anglocentric and imperialist in nature.

The period of European Romanticism, which heralded the beginnings of theories of mind and subjectivity, immediately preceded the
foundation of the Canadian nation-state and its coinciding expressions
of national cultural identity and historicity. Such well-known Canadian
poems as Charles G.D. Roberts's "Tantramar Revisited" and Bliss
Carman's "Low Tide on Grand Pré," building on British Romantic precursors, applied Romantic theories of mind and memory to an explicitly
Canadian location as a way of forging an "authentic" Canadian cultural
expression founded in first-hand experience of local landscapes. The

burden of memory that concludes Roberts's "Tantramar Revisited"—
"rather remember than see"—expresses a Romantic belief in the power
of memory to override personal experience of "chance and change" (and,
one could argue, colonial conquest), which in turn infused the Canadian
locale with a kind of permanence as a site of memory commemorated in
works of literature. The same might be said of a poem such as Duncan
Campbell Scott's "Indian Place Names," in which the dim "memory" of
Aboriginal presence lingers on the edges of settler consciousness, in a
kind of colonial mnemonics that settlers use to assert the authenticity of
commemorated space. The Canadian Romantics saw themselves to be
engaged in the foundational work of both commemoration and enunciation of a new nation through the invention of identifiable Canadian
traditions of national history and place, though like their British counterparts, they did so with an awareness of the ephemerality of memory
as a consolatory substitute. This interest in authenticating Canadian
historical origins found its prose counterpart in the many historical
novels of the nineteenth century which were propelled by an interest in
national consolidation. Texts such as Catharine Parr Traill's *Canadian
Crusoes* (1852), Phillipe Aubert de Gaspé's *Les Anciens Canadiens* (1863),
William Kirby's *The Golden Dog* (1877), and Gilbert Parker's *The Seats of
the Mighty* (1896) testify to an early use of Canadian historical fictions as
a means of representing Canadian French and English reconciliation as
foundational to the national imaginary.

Given this long tradition of historical reclamation in Canadian literary history, it is ironic that by the 1960s, Canadian authors and activists were seeking to "de-colonize" Canadians' sense of themselves as a
people lacking in cultural memory. Dennis Lee's 1968 long poem "Civil
Elegies" and his 1973 essay "Cadence, Country, Silence" lament the
ways Canadians have been deprived of a grounding sense of historical
memory and hence have found themselves rendered voiceless. Lee terms
this the "civil inauthenticity" that characterizes Canadians' occupation
of "colonial space" (471, 475). Such laments for the Canadian colonized
consciousness gave way to a recuperative movement that sought to revive (or invent) symbolic ancestors as a way of establishing a Canadian
consciousness grounded in what we might today consider "invented"
memories and ancestors. The best-known of these fictional precursors is
Margaret Atwood's 1970 series of poems *The Journals of Susanna Moodie*,
which looks to the nineteenth-century Canadian settler Susanna Moodie

as a paradigmatic and foundational Canadian ancestor. Atwood's work found echoes in texts such as Margaret Laurence's *The Diviners* (1974), which charts the life of its protagonist Morag Gunn as she must find ways to "remember" the ancestors that ground her as a Canadian. Similar claims have been made about other texts from this period, including Leonard Cohen's *Beautiful Losers* (1966) and Rudy Wiebe's *The Temptations of Big Bear* (1973), both of which look to Aboriginal precursors as part of a Canadian cultural consciousness that had been eradicated. This concern with instances of ancestral resuscitation and continuity acquired a postmodern inflection in the seminal writings of Robert Kroetsch, whose influential poems "Stone Hammer Poem" (1975) and *Seed Catalogue* (1977) read the text of communal memory as a series of disruptions. "The authorized history," Kroetsch writes in his 1983 essay "On Being an Alberta Writer," "was betraying us on those prairies" (329), suggesting that it is only through discontinuities that one can even conceive ideas of memory and inheritance. *Seed Catalogue*, Kroetsch stated, was to be a kind of archaeological palimpsest that would bring together "the oral tradition and the myth of origins" as a way of demonstrating the ways "even abandonment gives us memory" ("On Being" 331, 329). For Kroetsch and many others, memory is by definition fragmentary, which is not to say that the memories are not "real" in their affective and conceptual power.

The postcolonial turn in the 1980s and 1990s, evolving from the climate of 1960s and 1970s liberatory politics and counter-culture, contributed to the growing emergence of what would become the more profound attention to acts of memorialization and recuperation that we see in the 1990s. With the introduction of the Canadian Multiculturalism Act in 1988, there was increased attention to experiences outside the national mainstream but still clearly rooted *within* a national Canadian context. Attention to alternative histories forgotten within the metanarrative of institutionalized history became of central concern in many of these works. Some of the best-known Canadian novels in the "counter-memorial" tradition are Joy Kogawa's *Obasan* (1981), Michael Ondaatje's *In the Skin of a Lion* (1987), Sky Lee's *Disappearing Moon Café* (1990), and M.G. Vassanji's *No New Land* (1991). These and other works provide powerful counter-discursive accounts of the Canadian national metanarrative, ranging from the perspective of immigrant workers in 1930s Toronto who contributed to the building of the metropolis to that of the longstanding Vancouver Chinese-Canadian community in Lee's novel, which reaches back to the often obscured Chinese-Canadian presence in the "foundations" of the Canadian state. Kogawa's *Obasan* has probably been the single most influential novel in Canadian literary history for its influence on the nation's reassessment of its remembered past. Through this text, which follows the fate of the Japanese-Canadian Nakane family during the Second World War as they are forced into a series of internment and labour camps, Kogawa achieved a national apology on the part of the Canadian government for its treatment of Japanese Canadians during and following the war. The novel takes the form of an extended memory recuperation, as Naomi's Aunt Emily tries to bring the family (and the Canadian government) to a recollection of what occurred during those years. For Naomi, this involves piecing her fragmented memories, dreams, and repressions of that period into a storyline that recovers a silenced history, emblematized through the proud silence of Naomi's elderly aunt, Obasan. The traditional commemoration of Canada's war legacy in terms of courage and peacekeeping was thus opened up to counter-memorial interrogation and critique, and indeed has spurred a wealth of material devoted not only to the redress movement in Canada, but also to a re-engagement with Canada's war legacy more generally.

Canadian writers' interest in counter-history has not abated in recent decades; on the contrary, there has been a steadily increasing interest in themes of memory, nostalgia, recovery, and amnesia in Canadian writing. This has developed into several identifiable areas of interest. One of these includes what might be termed settler postcolonial revisionary treatments of Canadian history, a genre of historical fiction which assumes, at its base, a form of memorial recuperation and postcolonial atonement for past wrongs on a national-cultural scale. These include numerous contemporary postcolonial fictions such as John Steffler's *The Afterlife of George Cartwright* (1992), Rudy Wiebe's *A Discovery of Strangers* (1994), Guy Vanderhaeghe's *The Englishman's Boy* (1996), Fred Stenson's *The Trade* (2000), and Michael Crummey's *River Thieves* (2001). There has also been a spate of Gothic accounts of memory loss, trauma, and testimony, as in Ann-Marie MacDonald's *Fall on Your Knees* (1996), Shani Mootoo's *Cereus Blooms at Night* (1996), and Margaret Atwood's *Alias Grace* (1996). In response to the nation- and period-based postcolonial interventions of these writers and earlier ones, there is another stream of contemporary memory writing that has emerged from a growing awareness of what Diana Brydon and Marta Dvořák term the "shifting relations between national and global imaginaries" (2). Authors and critics in the twenty-first century have turned their attention to fluid collectivities that attend to variously interconnected "glocal" locations, particularly in the context of the gathering force of transnational neo-liberal ideologies. This body of work has demonstrated a growing focus on diasporic communities, global interconnections and circulation, and experiences of collective and/or disrupted memory, often through a concern with histories of transnational displacement, violence, and amnesia. Included in this group are such works as Anne Michaels's *Fugitive Pieces* (1996), Kerri Sakamoto's *The Electrical Field* (1998), Dionne Brand's *At the Full and Change of the Moon* (1999), Austin Clarke's *The Polished Hoe* (2002), Madeleine Thien's *Certainty* (2006), Lawrence Hill's *The Book of Negroes* (2007), David Chariandy's *Soucouyant* (2007), Marlene NourbeSe-Philip's *Zong!* (2008), Johanna Skibsrud's *The Sentimentalists* (2009), Brand's *Ossuaries* (2010), and Esi Edugyan's *Half-Blood Blues* (2011). One of the richest areas in current Canadian writing includes Indigenous treatments of buried memory, witnessing, and recuperative healing, such as one finds in Tomson Highway's *Kiss of the Fur Queen* (1998), Joseph Boyden's *Three Day Road* (2005), and Richard Wagamese's *Indian Horse* (2012), all literally about the lifting of repressed memories related to the residential school legacy. Many of these works have emerged since the creation of the Aboriginal Healing Foundation (1998) and the Indian Residential Schools Truth and Reconciliation Commission (2008), both of which were established to address the experiences of those who were affected by residential schools. Armand Ruffo's award-winning film, *A Windigo Tale* (2010), and Kevin Loring's Governor General's award-winning play, *Where the Blood Mixes* (2009), both take the transgenerational effects of the residential school legacy as a central and powerful theme. Many other works by Indigenous authors engage with the recuperation of buried ancestors and ancestral voices, such as one finds in Louise Bernice Halfe's *Blue Marrow* (2004) and Gregory Scofield's *Singing Home the Bones* (2005).

Another group of literary works explores the interconnections between cognition, neuropsychology, and memory as a way of engaging with questions of subjective experience. If identity has traditionally been aligned with a particular definition of continuous memory, these authors demonstrate that the divide between remembering and identity is not so easily established. The stigmatization of memory loss, as Marlene Goldman explores in her contribution to this collection, has contributed to a widespread fetishization and fear-mongering related to memory and forgetting. Some extremely evocative works, including Jane Rule's *Memory Board* (1987), Michael Ignatieff's *Scar Tissue* (1993), Jeffrey Moore's *The Memory Artists* (2004), John Mighton's *Half Life* (2005), Gail Anderson-Dargatz's *Turtle Valley* (2007), and films such as Sarah Polley's award-winning *Away from Her* (2006, based on a short story by Alice Munro), consider the theme of memory loss and Alzheimer's disease as a way of exploring a larger societal and cultural concern with the uncertain boundaries between memory, history, and selfhood. Indeed, the boundary between remembering and forgetting, as many critics note, is not altogether self-evident (or desirable). Roxanne Rimstead expresses this succinctly in her explanation of the inherent "double take" that constitutes memory, which is in a sense always self-reflexive as it has built within it a determining delay or gap (2). This is a key theme in David Chariandy's *Soucouyant* (2007), which moves through a processual paradox as the mother in the story reclaims the memories of the past through a process of *memory loss*. As the narrator evocatively puts it, she "*forgets to forget*" (32).

CANADIAN LITERATURE AND MEMORY STUDIES

The past two decades have seen a growing interest in themes of memory and commemoration in Canadian cultural discourse, from the foundation of the Cultural Memory Group at the University of Guelph in the late 1990s to a series of major books and conferences since then. Much of this material has focused on public history, historical fiction, and historiography (see Wyile; Cabajsky). The two-volume collection edited by D.M.R. Bentley, entitled *Mnemographia Canadensis: Essays on Memory, Community, and Environment in Canada with Particular Reference to London, Ontario* (1999), was followed in 2003 by Roxanne Rimstead's edited special issue of *Essays on Canadian Writing* devoted to the topic of "Cultural Memory and Social Identity." The 2011 conference on "Memory, Mediation, Remediation," organized by Russ Kilbourn and Eleanor Ty at Wilfrid Laurier University, resulted in the volume *The Memory Effect: The Remediation of Memory in Literature and Film* (2013). In the summer of 2012, the L.M. Montgomery Institute in Charlottetown, PEI, hosted a conference devoted to the topic of

"L.M. Montgomery and Cultural Memory." Critical studies on the related topic of elegy and haunting in Canadian writing, such as Priscila Uppal's *We Are What We Mourn: The Contemporary English-Canadian Elegy* (2009), Cynthia Sugars and Gerry Turcotte's *Unsettled Remains: Canadian Literature and the Postcolonial Gothic* (2009), Tanis MacDonald's *The Daughter's Way: Canadian Women's Paternal Elegies* (2012), Marlene Goldman's *DisPossession: Haunting in Canadian Fiction* (2012), and Peter Hodgins and Nicole Neatby's *Settling and Unsettling Histories: Essays in Canadian Public History* (2012) highlight a growing critical interest in themes of commemoration, remembrance, and haunting. Likewise, the important body of work devoted to transnational critical methodologies, such as Kit Dobson's *Transnational Canadas* (2009), Brydon and Dvořák's *Crosstalk* (2012), and Christine Kim et al.'s *Cultural Grammars of Nation, Diaspora, and Indigeneity in Canada* (2012), point to the ways memory discourse is moving away from nation-based models toward fluid conceptualizations of cultural cross-over and shifting collective imaginaries.

The essays in this collection are concerned primarily with forms of counter-memory and re-membering as opposed to national commemoration. These essays engage with a number of intersecting topics that bear on the ways memory has been invoked, constructed, and imagined in a Canadian cultural context. Specifically, these essays explore

- formulations of literary sites of memory
- instances of forgotten, traumatic, or eradicated histories
- re-visionings of canonical works as sites of amnesia
- engagements with diasporic and Indigenous re-membering
- transnational memory and the possibilities of cultural memory in a global era

Running through all of these topics is the underlying point that memory must be conceived not as a harmonious scene of transmission but as the site of struggles between competing perspectives reflecting a range of social asymmetries. Memory approached from this perspective constitutes one of the most powerful cultural locations where these often competing perspectives are brought into active engagement with one another.

The goal of this volume is to take the discussion of cultural memory beyond discourses of nostalgia and nation-based commemoration into investigations of alternative forms of historical remembering. In many of these essays, one finds a concern with the dialectical relation between memory and forgetting. Stephen Scobie eloquently expresses the continuum between personal memory and forgetting in his 1981 collection of poems *A Grand Memory for Forgetting*:

> the opposite of forgetting
> a shadow in no sunlight
> a ghost of the future
> a space to be filled
> a name on the tip of your tongue
> the opposite of memory (111)

Here, there is no place for nostalgia, since the memory is dependent upon the omissions; indeed, it is understood only in terms of the relation between them. Just as memory and forgetting are reducible neither to their opposites nor to one another—although they only make sense in relation to what they are not—so it is that cultural memory signifies in a myriad of ambivalent and encrypted ways: whether in connection to affective memories of place, or in terms of transgenerational occurrences of postmemory, or in relation to processes of historical re-visioning, or in response to historical trauma and/or global transplantation. The uncovering of buried memories, as one finds in many of the discussions included here, invites attention to the inevitable spectrality of historical and cultural memorialization.

The five essays in Part I, "Sites of Memory," focus on the complexities of using location and place as sites of memory. Tony Tremblay's "Globalization and Cultural Memory" argues against the idealization of post-national *placelessness* and de-territorialization, which the media and the intellectual class see as progressive, while non-urban "folk" are represented nostalgically, infantilized, and marginalized. Tremblay's essay seeks to unpack the politics of post-nationalism as it relates to place, and to show "how an ethos of place is central to overcoming the trauma of forgetting." Using the second Acadian Renaissance of the 1960s as an example, Tremblay considers the reclamation of Acadian identity and homeland through poetry and song, valorizing *placeness* and situated knowledge rather than globalized homogenization. Kimberly Mair's "Putting Things in Their Place" carefully examines the production of place and historical memory in the Syncrude Gallery of Aboriginal Culture, housed at the Royal Alberta Museum in Edmonton. In spite of consultation with First Nations and Indigenous communities in the "planning, design, and realization" of the gallery, the ordering and spatial distribution of objects result in presenting what James Clifford calls a "majority History," which "neutralizes the discomfort" for non-Indigenous visitors "in relation to the colonial and genocidal aspects of the history addressed in the gallery's content."

Renée Hulan's "*Lieux d'oubli*" and Candida Rifkind's "Design and Disappearance" are concerned with the significance of forgotten places and different ways to remember them. Hulan points out that the repressed memory of colonization makes some places, like the North, forgotten places and, conveniently, territory to be staked and claimed for economic exploitation. Examining a series of poems representing the northern landscapes by Aboriginal and non-Aboriginal writers—Margaret Sam-Cromarty, Armand Ruffo, Paulette Jiles—Hulan argues that they become counterhegemonic acts that honour the past and give these locations material, symbolic, cultural, and spiritual meaning. Rifkind's "Design and Disappearance" looks at the inscription of memories and nostalgic emotions that are found in Pascal Blanchet's comic book and Michael Simons and Paul Shoebridge's interactive web documentary about two company towns, White Rapids and Pine Point, that are "symbols of industrial modernity" which have now disappeared. Paying close attention to the aesthetics and visual design of the works, Rifkind reads the postmodern projects as "archives" that, according to Jacques Derrida, are found "at the place of originary and structural breakdown" of memory. The gap between institutional perspectives and the memories of people who lived in the towns is evident in the latter's commitment to commemorate the towns long after their capitalist *raison d'être* has passed, even though the acts of commemoration are marked by equivocation. Also about the conflicted remembrance of place, Brooke Pratt's "Preserving 'the echoing rooms of yesterday'" is about the collective cultural heritage project of preserving Al Purdy's iconic A-frame house. Pratt's sophisticated analysis examines the way the house that shaped Purdy's poetry has been valued as a gathering place for writers and subsequently has attained a kind of folkloric, celebrity status. All of these essays consider the ways Canadian spaces are figured beyond nostalgic discourse as places that are imbued with simultaneous resonance and ambivalence.

Part II, "Memory Transference," includes six essays that explore the transmission of memories across generations, particularly the ways sometimes dark, traumatic, or confused recollections are reworked and relived by the next generation. Robert Zacharias's "Learning Sauerkraut" employs insights from food studies and memory studies to discuss how "the foodways of the Russian Mennonite community in Canada bears witness to the serial migrations of their past." Zacharias examines the ways food enables "the consumption of Mennonite history" and is a means to "experience a historicized form of cultural belonging," which always remains partially elusive. Marlene Goldman's "'Their Dark Cells'" explores the impact of transference and postmemory on individual, familial, and national levels using John Mighton's *Half Life*. The play, set in a nursing home for the elderly, highlights the human capacity for remembering and forgetting as these are figured as both part of and beyond the experience of dementia. Linda Warley's "Remembering Poverty" looks at a different kind of inheritance, that of the guilt, shame, and anger connected to a history of childhood poverty in PEI. Written and illustrated by father and son, *Bannock, Beans, and Black Tea* is a conflicted narrative about the postmemory of poverty, and "exposes the difficulty—perhaps the impossibility—of the privileged ever really understanding and feeling solidarity with the poor, even when they are members of the same family."

In "Postmemory and Canadian Poetry of the 1970s," J.A. Weingarten argues that, following the 1967 centennial, Canadian historical writing shifted from grand narratives to microhistories that focused on familial, regional, and social history. Weingarten reads the poetic text and photographic images in Barry McKinnon's influential long poem, *I Wanted to Say Something*, as an example of the way the personal story of his grandfather intersects with national history through "what Marianne Hirsch calls 'postmemory.'" Tanis MacDonald's "'Exhibit me buckskinned'" reads Joan Crate's poems, *Pale as Real Ladies*, as a tribute to the life and literary works of E. Pauline Johnson. According to MacDonald, Crate discomfits "the practice of rememory through poetic ventriloquism," exploring Johnson's political subversiveness and her "often-difficult personal life as a counterpoint to her artistic life." In "Scrapbooking," Cynthia Sugars looks at the use of evocative objects of memorabilia in Gail Anderson-Dargatz's two interlinked novels, *The Cure for Death by Lightning* and *Turtle Valley*. Instead of illuminating the past, "mementos underscore the intangibility of memorialization." Together, the novels illustrate the simultaneous failure and liberation of memory as the protagonists, through their meditation on inherited objects, learn to accept the incompleteness of memory as a condition of its resonance.

The seven essays in Part III, "Re-Membering History," explore omissions from, inconsistencies in, and problems with official histories and collective memories. Marc Fortin's "Ethnography, Law, and Aboriginal Memory" explores notions of memory and ethnographic documentation by looking at textual representations of the Gitxsan. Fortin argues that the Gitxsan have "not only recently challenged the court in their pursuit of self-government and land rights, but have forced us to question the nature of memory and truth." While remembering usually involves recollecting something that happened in the past, Peter Hodgins's "Between Elegy and Taxidermy" discusses a curious contradiction in the Confederation poet Archibald Lampman's writing, when Lampman "was grieving a traumatic loss that had not yet occurred," at the same time as he was compelled to actively destroy that which he elegized. Hodgins reads Lampman's works as "ecological elegy," a melancholic mourning over an element in nature that will disappear. In contrast to this elegiac tone, Jesse Rae Archibald-Barber reads E. Pauline Johnson's nature lyrics positively in "Under Other Skies." Comparing Johnson's view of nature, of Indigenous people, and of Canada with early English-Canadian poets such as Isabella Valancy Crawford, Charles G.D. Roberts, and Oliver Goldsmith, Archibald-Barber argues that Johnson expresses a more conciliatory and inclusive attitude. Her nature lyrics, he argues, are central to her memorial odes, "as her form of cultural memory aims to overcome the colonial image of Aboriginal peoples as disappearing cultures."

Another essay on Aboriginal collective memory that considers a previously neglected aspect of Indigenous history is Sophie McCall's "Indigenous Diasporas and the Shape of Cultural Memory." McCall examines the two memoirs written by Anahareo, the wife of Grey Owl, through the theoretical lenses of diaspora and postmemory to show how Anahareo is able to continue, renew, and adapt Aboriginal traditions in spite of "multiple displacements—through conflicts with settler populations, loss of ancestral territory, religious schooling, loss of language, property laws, and other colonial regulatory systems." Shelley Hulan's essay "Yours to Recover" poses interesting questions about fictions that derive from the memories of first-person narrators who resemble the

author. If counter-memory attempts to recover what "memory, conflated with history, conspires to forget," Hulan notes that in Alice Munro's
stories, "the task of forging a counter-memory falls to readers who may
choose to recover the traces of another past detectable in these narratives." Specifically, Hulan looks at references to First Nations in Munro's
stories, remarking on the way the non-Aboriginal narrators in Munro's
stories often allude to the presence of First Nations people or culture,
only to subsume them into a more personal concern. Dennis Duffy's
and Marissa McHugh's essays focus on cultural memories of Quebec
in the first half of the twentieth century. In "Romancing Canada in
Bestsellerdom," Duffy traces changing attitudes to Quebec in anglophone Canada from the late nineteenth century to the end of the First
World War by examining two bestsellers, *The Seats of the Mighty* (1896)
and *Jalna* (1927). Duffy reads the historical romance plots in these novels
as indications of Canadian national feeling for Quebec, and discusses the
collective memories and myths about Canada that these novels engendered and perpetuated. Marissa McHugh looks at a dramatic representation of the Easter Riots of 1918 which occurred in Quebec at the end of
the First World War, the historical event that supposedly transformed
Canada from "colony to nation," and analyzes the "active remembering
and selective forgetting" of the riots by English Canada and Quebec. The
courtroom drama, *Québec, Printemps 1918,* produced in the wake of
the 1970 invocation of the War Measures Act, recounts the unjust "war"
waged on innocent Québécois civilians by English-Canadian soldiers,
inviting comparisons between 1918 and the October Crisis of 1970.

Part IV, "The Compulsion to Remember," considers different kinds
of trauma and forgetting. Employing trauma, postmemory, and visual
theories, Robyn Morris's "Under Surveillance" discusses the links between vision, surveillance, and power in Madeleine Thien's novel about
the Cambodian genocide, *Dogs at the Perimeter.* Morris points out that
Thien's writing is characterized by two cultural or political affects: by
what Dominick LaCapra terms "empathic unsettlement" and by what Jill
Bennett calls a "politics of empathy." The novel encourages us to "rethink
assumptions about refugees, about coercion, and about the need for
humankind to resist and take responsibility for such acts." In "'I didn't
want to tell a story like this,'" Farah Moosa argues that the protagonist
of David Chariandy's *Soucouyant* is not only "burdened" by having to
recall his mother's harrowing past but also has to "perform" this cultural

memory. Moosa explores the tension between the desires to remember and to forget for second-generation diasporic subjects, especially where traumatic histories are concerned.

Doris Wolf's and Robyn Green's essays focus on Aboriginal memories and Canada's history of Indian residential schools. Wolf argues that David Alexander Robertson and Scott B. Henderson's *7 Generations* graphic novel series "challenges old ideas of Canada as a settler nation" by insisting on "radical change for Aboriginal peoples as related to land, rights, and sovereignty." Looking closely at the textual and visual techniques of the graphic novel, Wolf demonstrates how the narrative devices reconfigure national conceptions of Aboriginal "savagery" and criminality by restoring an intergenerational focus on the "warrior spirit." The depiction of the warrior spirit in *7 Generations*, she argues, is connected to politics and not simply to culture, a shift that has profound implications for Aboriginal and non-Aboriginal readers. Robyn Green's "Recovering Pedagogical Space" reads Richard Van Camp's novella *The Lesser Blessed* as a narrative that reveals the intergenerational trauma of residential schooling and documents "ongoing systemic disparities that continue to racialize and colonize Indigenous peoples in institutional settings." Green uses a spatial analysis, focusing on various pedagogical locations to show how cultural memory and policy are transmitted and imbricated.

The five essays in the final section, "Cultural Memory in a Globalized Age," demonstrate the increasingly transcultural and global nature of Canadian subjects. Alexis Motuz's and Joel Baetz's essays look at two works by Caribbean-Canadian Dionne Brand. In "'I have nothing soothing to tell you,'" Motuz argues that in *Inventory,* instead of presenting the reader with a lament and ending with a consolation as other elegists do, Brand claims the role of the "informer" and shifts "the burden of mourning" to the reader. Readers are made to consider "the ethical impossibilities of mourning mass death in the globalized and heavily mediated society of twenty-first-century North America." Baetz argues that in *What We All Long For* the young people long to escape home and the burden of memories, but what they get is "a version of Toronto that is full of [. . .] recurring nightmares, familiar haunts, unacknowledged memorials, and repurposed artifacts." He reads the novel not as a simple celebration of the diversity of the city, but as an archive of traumatic stories and developing histories.

The essays in this section demonstrate Anh Hua's contention that cultural memory is a political field in which different stories contend for their place in history (199). Eva Darias-Beautell's "Haunted/Wanted" uses Derrida's notion of hauntology, "tied to memory and historicity, on one end, and to a notion of future justice, on the other," as a trope to investigate questions of cultural memory in Canadian literature. She reads Jen Sookfong Lee's *The End of East* through spectrality to discuss the relationships between East and West as paradigmatic of a process of diasporic cultural memory "that rewrites and reopens the question of the collective imaginary." Jennifer Andrews's essay looks at the gaps in memory present in Helen Humphrey's novel *Afterimage*. Set in nineteenth-century England, the book is concerned with attempts to memorialize the experience of diasporic displacement and childhood loss through the creation of "objects of remembrance that also function as visual markers of colonial conflict." The novel considers both English–Irish relations and the imaginative domain of the Northwest Passage on the eve of Confederation. Pilar Cuder-Domínguez's "Transnational Memory and Haunted Black Geographies" examines Esi Edugyan's first novel, *The Second Life of Samuel Tyne*, which performs an "act of critical memory" in its excavation of the history of Black people in Alberta. Edugyan's approach to Canadian cultural memory relies on the global trajectories of Black subjects, and entails the incorporation of what is inescapably a transnational memory.

All of the essays in this collection demonstrate the ongoing, revisionary processes of cultural memory, the entangled links between what we desire to remember, what we choose to forget, what is elided when we reconstruct the past, and what is recorded for others in official documents and personal papers. Understanding how we remember, and the roles played by literary and cultural representations in shaping our memories, is vital to comprehending ourselves as subjects and communities, and is central to mediating our place in the world. The essays in this volume explore not only the complicated ways our cultural memories shape the contemporary moment, but also how the present continues to rework and reshape our understanding and views of the past.

PART I

.-.

Sites of Memory: Cultural Amnesia and the Demands of Place

CHAPTER 1

•◆•

Globalization and Cultural Memory: Perspectives from the Periphery on the Post-National Disassembly of Place

Tony Tremblay

Should we give away the state—which is a still working, if sometimes creaky, set of social agreements—because some people are impatient with it and others are ill-informed?

W.H. New, *Borderlands* 17

On 8 January 2010, CBC News broke the story that Atlantic Wholesalers, a Loblaw Companies division, was withdrawing a statement of claim filed on 22 December 2009 against Wayne Lord and Bathurst Van Inc., the principals involved in the accident that claimed the lives of seven high-school basketball players and their coach's wife near Bathurst, New Brunswick, on 12 January 2008. The 15-passenger Ford Econoline van that Lord was driving skidded out of control in stormy weather and swerved into the path of a Loblaw transport truck, which had to be towed from the scene two days later. The claim alleged negligence on the part of Wayne Lord, driver and coach, and sought $41,515.36 in damages, which included towing and clean-up costs. The claim cited Lord's failure to keep the van under proper control and lack of reasonable care for his passengers, neither of which was substantiated by the RCMP's Collision Reconstruction Report that had been released on 28 July 2008. Though Loblaw withdrew its lawsuit after widespread public outrage, the corporation apparently saw nothing wrong with initiating the action in the first place, nor with delivering the summons to the widower Lord three days before Christmas. From the action taken we can only surmise that Loblaw and the Weston family, its majority shareholder, considered it appropriate to attempt to extract $41,515.36 from the people who had suffered the most in this tragedy.

When pressed for a statement, Allan Leighton, president of Loblaw, said, "While it is normal legal practice to look for reimbursement from the parties deemed to be at fault, this decision was clearly made without consideration of the specifics of the accident" ("Loblaws backs off"), a quasi-retraction that, in its aloofness, seems exactly aligned with the emotion that must have propelled the lawsuit initially. What "specifics," one wonders, would have brought the Loblaw corporation to a different decision?

The obvious question in the face of Loblaw's action is, *What are the conditions that have to be in place for such an undertaking to occur?* Do we attribute their breach of reasonable conduct and simple decency to corporate amorality, institutional indifference, or the dictates of a litigious culture? It would be tempting to do so, especially given Mr. Leighton's tepid admission of misjudgment, but I would suggest that the cause lies elsewhere: that it is part of a fundamental shift in spatial ethos that has resulted in an epidemic of devaluation, both of "place" and of people. The episode, then, is more indicative of systemic amnesia than of corporate malfeasance, though of course one condition feeds the other. When place, especially rural or marginal place, is devalued to the extent that it has been in recent years, then the abuse of persons within that place follows easily. Loblaw took the action that it did, then, because rural New Brunswick and the people that reside there are remote, disembodied abstractions to its corporate consciousness. And as abstractions, they are easily devalued, easily reduced to material reserve in a boardroom game of litigation. That lives were lost and families forever altered did not figure in Loblaw's calculations. Instead, the numerical imperative— slight though it was—took precedence. Stark in that regard is the fact that $41,515.36 represented 0.021 percent of the $189 million *third-quarter* profit Loblaw reported in 2009 ("Loblaw reports"). That's profit, not sales, and profit reported at the time (autumn 2009) when the lawsuit was being contemplated.

In this chapter I use Loblaw's action as a bridge to thinking in more depth about the changing notion of place in our midst. Does place matter? Or, more appropriate to the context at hand, *should* place matter in an increasingly neo-liberal world that tacitly nudges us toward the efficiencies of the immediate at the expense of our rootedness in history? Is place merely a trope, a sentimental attachment we're meant to outgrow on our way to a more fashionable urbanity? And can we think of place, post–Benedict Anderson, as still significant and formative, or does that render us wistful and naive, citizens of a typographic rather than a post-national commons? Moreover, if place is indeed imagined by narrative and shaped by media, what are the politics behind the shift from local identification to global citizenship, whose interests does *placelessness* ultimately serve, and what are the consequences of systemic amnesia on not just cultural memory but also personal agency and political action? Finally, and perhaps most profoundly, can humans exist as the deracinated beings that Marshall McLuhan envisioned, figures without ground?

In posing those questions from the periphery—specifically from New Brunswick, where the Acadian Renaissance continues to be one of the most vigorous place-based identity projects of the last century—I will show how the bias of "place" is foremost ecological, a bias inflected by media that intervene, destabilize, and reconfigure; in short, a bias that never is or was stable. Understanding that bias in ecological terms provides insight into how the idea of place, as spatial narrative, might be resuscitated for the preservation of local identities, thus offering ways to counter the various dismantling projects being undertaken in the interests of globalization and post-Keynesian, neo-liberal economics. My intent is both to untie the politics of post-nationalism as it relates to place, and to show how an ethos of place is central to overcoming the trauma of forgetting—of the "rhetorical violence," as Barbara Godard sees it ("The Politics" 120)—that globalization instills. By twinning place and memory in this way I am responding to Terry Cook's call for the examination of "our own politics of memory" (19), an examination particularly germane to the reconstituted definitions of citizenship and federalism in Canada.

I proceed by reflecting on "place" not as signifier, for the actual iterations of place are multiple and shift according to locus and relations under consideration, but as signified. I am interested, then, in considering the abstract referent, that site of power, said Michel Foucault, that "is no longer substantially identified with an individual [. . .] [but] becomes a machinery that no one owns" (*Power* 156). What Foucault meant, of course, was that even though no one owns these referents, many live by their dictates. I refer to this more abstract referent as the bias of place, or *placeness*, an odd term, I realize, but my objective in using it will become clear below.

I

For a deeply ambiguous and always relational concept, "place" and the inherent biases associated with it attract an array of attentions from economists, futurists, post-nationalists, and critical theorists that are disproportionate to their claims of its importance. In other words, those who speak loudest about the excitements of global villages (Appadurai, Negroponte, Logan, Tapscott, and Federman and De Kerckhove) also spend inordinate time dismantling the bias of place, calling it, as Joshua Meyrowitz does in *No Sense of Place*, archaic, nineteenth century, typographic, and irretrievable, a relic of a different era and relations of production (307–13). Considered discursively, there seems to be something afoot in what clearly is defensiveness, something behind the poorly disguised condescension through which these speakers view the place bias, not to mention the histrionic of their dismissals of it. That histrionic suggests that, though under duress by the maligning it receives from those who seem to want to theorize it out of existence, the bias of place, or *placeness*, still threatens and destabilizes. *But what does it threaten and destabilize, and how are those threats addressed?*

The answer comes into focus when place, as signified, is situated in the social and historical context from which it first emerged, namely the early modernist Enlightenment project. With only slight variations in the emphasis they give to Karl Marx or Foucault as originary theorists of social space, cultural geographers Derek Gregory (272–313), David Harvey (240–59), Neil Smith (*Endgame* 25–29), and Don Mitchell (60–64) suggest that the Western *place* referent had its provenance in social philosophy's contemplation of "nature." For Jean-Jacques Rousseau that contemplation concluded that "nature," as a social construct manufactured in response to technology and urbanism, is always a highly mediated space that serves the interests of the dominant in culture. It was but a small step from there to the view that the "civil state," too, particularly as manifest in the fifteenth-century nation-state (the democratic ideal of place), was configured to serve the needs of the powerful (*The Social Contract* 1:8, 3:1). In his influential essay on the birth and death of the nation-state, our own Pierre Elliott Trudeau identified this configuration as the construction of "popular sovereignty" (160), contrasting it with earlier designations of place. His point was that though the *idea* of place as mapped locus was certainly evident in Homer, especially when his voyagers undertake sea-borne navigation (a navigation as "periplum, / [. . .] as sea bord seen by men sailing" [Pound 324]), the *bias* of place as figurative trope signifying rootedness, stability, and personal attachment to "popular" democratic values emerged only at a point in history when imperial persuasions *needed to become* manifest in national loyalties.

The bias associated with place, then, surfaced as a social trope when economic mercantilism cultivated the necessity for a broader-based nationalism in newly federated European states that were faced with the challenges of competition in newly opened markets. In those post-feudal free-market environments, nationalism was marshalled to reinforce identifications that, in celebrating and often reifying place, prejudiced locals against foreigners while domesticating loyalties to familiar ethnicities and social practices. Loyalist poet Jonathan Odell imprinted this bias on the New Brunswick wilderness in 1785 in an attempt to claim place from the possession of others, namely the unruly Americans. His "Ode for the New Year" is a good example of the cultivation of place-based loyalty, the kind of jingoistic loyalty that rightly fuels the animus of post-nationalists:

> When rival Nations first descried,
> Emerging from the boundless Main
> This Land by Tyrants yet untried,
> On high was sung this lofty strain:
> Rise Britannia beaming far!
> Rise bright Freedom's morning star! (1–6)

> The shoots of Science rich and fair,
> Transplanted from thy fostering Isle
> And by thy Genius nurtur'd there,
> Shall teach the Wilderness to smile.
> Shine, Britannia, rise and shine!
> To bless Mankind the task be thine! (13–18)

The poem aims directly at what Walter Benjamin famously called "aestheticizing the political" (241), in this case transforming a presumably amorphous space from "Wilderness" (16) to inhabitable place.

A more recent example of marshalling the place-based referent in a competitive environment is the manufacture of American ruralism to sell domestic trucks. Chevrolet's "Like a Rock" campaign is as narrowly *mon pays* as one can get, a nationalist yearning for *placeness* that is constructed out of the nostalgia of rurality, masculinity, belonging, and "whiteness"—biases that are otherwise treated as anachronistic (literally "redneck") in a predominantly postcolonial world in which urbanism, alienation, and syncretism form the more dominant social ideology.

A good deal of coercion is required to neutralize the contradiction that "redneck" evokes, and that coercion is the work of media and the intellectual class. Both bodies must attend carefully to shaping language and its meanings, because all social biases require constant tweaking to continue to serve the dominant interest. Which is why a notion like *place*, however abstract, is a site of such potency, and why it must be brought into line by narrative lest it threaten and destabilize.

The necessity of coercion in the manufacture of consensus recalls the pioneering work of Kenneth Burke, who argued in *Language as Symbolic Action* that the circumference of our reality is extremely small, limited to the sphere of our immediate sense experience. The notional reality that extends beyond that sensory sphere must therefore be constructed symbolically, an action involving complex cultural and linguistic operations that educate people for socio-economic citizenship.

Burke usefully reminds us of the ideological affinity that social designations such as *nature* and *place* share: that, despite minor differences— *nature* manufactured as a reaction to technological urbanism and *place* as an addendum to free-market capitalism—both acquire functions *through* culture and the labour of intellectuals. Both therefore inhabit larger ecological systems, systems in which the relations between humans and their locales are dependent on dominant modes of production and the social roles that follow from those. As part of a larger ecology, then, the bias of place is organic, given to change when change is demanded. When the locus of economic power (namely, labour and industry) was concentrated in nations, the bias of place served the dominant cultural interest of states, thereby legitimizing identifications with home, region, and country that people learned for the last four hundred years. However, when economic power subsumed the state for cheaper labour and even larger trading blocks, many now skirting the globe, place and the micro-economic exchange that served mercantilism became cumbersome, necessitating a recalibration of local identifications that no longer served the dominant interest. In short, the referent had to be modified.

We now exist under the dictates of a new "place" referent—in a time of *place*<u>*less*</u>*ness* when media and the intellectual class actively abet strategies of de-territorialization, championing that which is deracinated, nomadic, and non-material. In the view of Nicholas Negroponte, this era of "[d]igital living will include less and less dependence upon being in a specific place at a specific time, and the transmission of place itself will become possible" (165). Such possibility, says Pierre Lévy, is tantamount to the desire for freedom because *placelessness* reflects "an *ideal* of deterritorialized human relationship[s]" (111; italics added). Indeed, today, multiply distributed citizenship across a variety of digitized social networks is encouraged and rewarded, especially among the young, while citizens who cling slavishly to place, without DSL or iPhone, are considered to be the anachronistic adherents to what Don Tapscott calls an "old paradigm" (138).

Acting (usually unwittingly) as functionaries of the corporate ideology of globalization, some intellectual workers have turned the "leaders of the old" (Tapscott 138) into "the folk," recalibrating their use-value to the economics of cultural tourism. These "folk" have, in effect, been symbolically re-made: infantilized into the passive casualties of a fundamental shift in spatial ethos, and, more importantly, reshaped into the functional "others" against whom the classical liberal tenets of individual and corporate power are advanced. Thus reduced to what Marx called "the already determined" (*Grundrisse* 248), they become, in the parlance of Dale Spender, the "'dinosaurs' who do not want to change" (116–17). Their memories hailed by marketers who feed them the pabulum of nostalgia to sell trucks, their trucks then become a symbol of their dysfunction—"ersatz nostalgia," writes Arjun Appadurai, "nostalgia without memory" (82). As David Adams Richards has observed rather provocatively about the presumption of his characters' amnesic attachment to place, "If one of my characters had a car up on blocks in his back yard, he must be *illiterate*, and probably *slept* with his sister" (78). Because of a presumed powerlessness to change their condition, these "dinosaurs" are easy to devalue. In fact, ridicule has become one of the unwritten rules of the intellectual game as practised by those excited by the potentials of a global citizenship that is delocalized. In short, the recent effort of powerful voices in the intellectual class to rewire our thinking about place and actively denigrate those in the epistemic barrens has become relentless—and has resulted in unusual instances of erasure, as the Loblaw episode illustrates.

Which begs a very important question about self-determination: *Can* placeness *have agency outside the terms of its socio-economic necessity?* I pose that question not to attempt to reverse the systemic shift in spatial ethos that has altered the condition of *placeness* in the last twenty-five years, but to challenge the certainty of those whose enthusiastic defence of this change has assumed that, being structural, it is largely benign—an attitude that results in indifference to the fact that change, when it erases or denigrates, is an instrument of harm, especially for people already marginalized, and increasingly oppressed, by remoteness. (The problem with this indifference is that it comes with the view that those people who do not, or cannot, embrace or adapt readily to change are backward or intransigent, thus *deserving* of being devalued. The pathology seems built-in.)

What is especially important in the midst of fundamental social shift is the response of intellectuals to it, a response that, to my mind, must acknowledge the dominance of the socio-economic imperative while not being cowed or turned toward complicity in the face of it. To put it more directly, I believe intellectual workers have a responsibility to unpack some of the ideology informing the notion of *placeness*—recognizing, to echo Henri Lefebvre, "what 'takes place' there and what it is used for" (17)—so as not to be bound by the neo-liberal project that much of that ideology serves.

It is not sufficient to conclude, as many structuralists have, that nationalism and the bias of place that derived from it were the result of typography (McLuhan 170–78) and particular social roles accruing from typographic culture (Innis 128–29). Print indeed was one of the ways that place-based nationalism was inculcated, both as content/idea and habit/form, but the understanding of that operation is an understanding only of apparatus, an understanding, cautions Sara Blair, "that masks the conditions of its own formation" (544). As Blair and Lefebvre imply, we need to inquire further, asking what social forces lie behind the structural changes that impact directly upon people's lives. Not to do so is to accept the authority of the apparatus and its amnesias over the lives that are defined and changed by it.

Toward that end, and on precisely the ecological terms I have outlined, I suggest that the answer to the question posed above is "*Yes,* placeness *can have agency outside the terms of its cultural necessity if we as intellectual workers wish it to have*." If monopolies of space are sites of constant high-stakes mediation—in effect, imagined and narrated into existence for precisely the purpose of negating amnesia (Anderson 204)—then our own intellectual labour, debate, and resistance is key to that construction, for it is part of a larger ecological system in which meaning is contested. In that sense, place is claimed in its affirmation, and the *bias* of place can be reclaimed discursively in the same way. Merely to speak of place, in other words, is to create and validate it.

The second part of this chapter examines how *place* has been re-claimed from the determinism of post-Keynesian economic necessity on precisely those terms.

II

To underscore the necessity of reclaiming place as an act of personal freedom and political defiance, I turn to a well-known but still poorly understood program of strategic localism that took root in southeastern New Brunswick in the late 1960s. I am speaking, of course, of the second Acadian Renaissance.

Populated by people who speak a dialect extracted from the fifteenth-century French of François Rabelais, the area is defined by outsiders as a site of deportation, literal *dis*placement. Acadians, as we know from history, were expelled from their lands from 1755 to 1762 as a consequence of the European colonial wars between the French and the English. Our rather thin knowledge of expulsion, however, provides only causal perspective. Antonine Maillet, one of the region's preeminent literary speakers, offers the more nuanced affective view. Acadians, she says, were not just geographically exiled, but exiled into silence, a key piece of information that tells us much about the vital connection between *placelessness* and alienation.[1] With the loss of place, she says, came the corresponding loss of speech, for "the only survivors in the Massacre of the Holy Innocents were the Innocents who knew enough to hold their tongues" (*Pélagie* 7). To survive *placeless*, then, was to live in one of three ways: in abject silence, in hegemonic allegiance to colonial masters, or in the grips of a self-imposed amnesia. Those conditions, she asserts, perpetuated a

---

1 The history of forced dislocation—of Aboriginal cultures in settler societies and African-Americans in the United States and Nova Scotia—provides further proof of the relationship between displacement and alienation. What all displaced peoples yearn for is land. Land and ancestral place restore wholeness and memory.

fundamental absence of "deeds" [history] and therefore "nationality" (*La Sagouine* 167). Without place her people had no narrative; and without narrative, no nationality. Kept *placeless* on the margins of English society, silenced Acadians were thereby defined by others, leaving them with no knowledge of themselves. La Sagouine, Maillet's famous washerwoman, makes the point emphatically: "[A]in't easy earnin yer living when you ain't got a country of your own, 'n when you can't tell yer nationality [. . .] Cause you end up not knowin what the hell you are" (166).

When the conditions of this amnesia finally broke and Acadians "return[ed] from exile" to "sniff what the weather was" and to see "all the creeks and all the bays and all the islands" (*Pélagie* 257), they did so discursively, using narratives of place to *reclaim* lost lands. What we call their Acadian Renaissance was foremost a renaissance of language that both re-imagined and revivified place *outside* the domesticated metaphors of occupation, thus reconfiguring (and often unsettling) their relationship with the larger world. Their "literary" turn from silence to speech created the conditions for their re-emergence as a people lost to conquest, and therefore for their legitimacy as global citizens. Revolutionary nationalist Hubert Aquin traced the same pattern of emergence when writing about Quebec's parallel history of national selfhood, stressing that only "that which is typical [meaning local] is profound" ("Cultural Fatigue" 40). Only such "cris de terre," wrote founding Acadian poet Raymond Leblanc, "abolishes the hard lie / The shameful caverns of our silence" (qtd. in Cogswell and Elder 120).

To come out of exile, agreed Acadian songwriter Calixte Duguay, was to sing a homeland, a place, into existence: "To clench in your fists the gravel / Of the road that leads / To the top of the orchard. [. . .] To get your toes wet / In the green water of the Restigouche. / That is what is meant by having a homeland" (qtd. in Cogswell and Elder 82–83; used with the permission of Calixte Duguay). About the same affinity between place and reclamation, Acadian poet Gérald Leblanc wrote,

> Bouctouche awakes in me
> with my father's speech
> (my country is a chain of villages
> or a drunken jig or a clothesline)
> I love you
> in the dawn of images to be born

in a poem
at the bootlegger's
to the rhythms of a mad violin
on the road to Tracadie
in a field of clover
in the dirty streets of Moncton
you are there
and my roots are singing (from "acadielove"; qtd. in Cogswell and Elder 114)

Only when a place is taken back from the possession of others—literally renamed and relocated (fixed, however personally and temporarily) "in the dawn of images [. . .] born / in a poem"—is that place awakened from the silence and amnesias that attend occupation. Without place at the centre of the reclamation project, writes Raymond Leblanc in "Acadie," only two realities exist: "Gens de mon pays / Sans identité" and "Enfants sans langage," people without identity and children without speech (41).

Acadian New Brunswickers knew that instinctively. They mobilized a language fixed firmly to place to move them from what Ottawa bureaucrats in the 1960s had called "Kent [County]: Unproductive Setting, Unfavourable Site" (qtd. in Wilbur 224)—Kent County is the heart of Acadie—to the redefinition of Acadie as a land newly buoyant with history, myth, and promise. Writes Raymond Leblanc,

Voici l'heure de l'histoire voulue
Pour changer la misère des esclaves
Dans la réalité des hommes nouveaux et libres
Cette heure désormais nous appartient. ("Projet" 45)

(This is the long-awaited hour of history
To change the misery of slaves
Into the reality of new and free men
This hour from now on belongs to us.)

The affirmation of place became their great resistance. That affirmation contested the post-national consensus that told them to look beyond themselves for legitimacy, and it contested the abstractions of occupation that put their Acadian identities under self-hating erasure. Their affirmation was therefore an act of *dis*identification that "[took] as its starting point the radical fact of its present situation" (Aquin, "The Politics" 130). To mount a resistance, then, was to write place into action. And to write place into action was to counter the theoretical insinuations that dislocated them.

John Ralston Saul concurs: "To accept a language that expresses neither our true selves nor our true mythologies is to disarm our civilization," he says. "It is to cripple our capacity to talk and to act in a way that reflects both our collective unconscious and our ethical standards" (ix). Without our openness to (indeed, active defence of) avowals of the centrality of place and community in the construction of identity, we would have no reason to disbelieve the more ideologically topical views that "the nation-state is near its end" (Appadurai 9) and "people are living in [an] [. . .] information-system rather than a local town and city" (Meyrowitz 146). Such views are nothing less than *radical acts of emplacement*: they seek to move people from one kind of locale to another, from national to global villages. Those interventions, however, are *never* benign, disinterested, or amoral. Rather, they are best understood as part of a larger ecology of space that moves people for socio-economic ends. We must learn to recognize those strategies for what they are, lest they continue to dislocate and erase.

The struggle of New Brunswick's Acadians to use place to speak against what negated them reminds us that people still stand on firm ground and still are the products of multiple and intersecting histories. The point seems almost too simplistic to make, but it is worth making, for most of us inhabit not just postmodern *space* but physical *place* as well, places from which we create symbolic identities from the complex of narratives that pre-figure, surround, and define us. If we are dislocated, so are we embedded—that is the real and productive dialectic of our lives.

III

Part of the fallout from the theory wars—which, to my mind, signals a troubling complicity between first-world urban theorists and the postnational neo-liberal project—has been the rhetorical re-manufacture of *placeness* out of all proportion to its normal experiential attachments. *Placeness* has been systematically denigrated or fetishized (made backward, anachronistic, or touristic) in order to move symbolic identifications from communities and regions to zones and trading blocks. To be at home in amorphous space—"decoupled from geography," as Negroponte put it (166)—is the latest persuasion *against* being rooted in place. It is a persuasion that denies any situated knowledge, thus replacing "thick" citizenship with "thin," an alteration that raises legal and rights-based imperatives over moral and compassionate actions (*vide* the Loblaw decision).

More difficult to predict is how that decoupling will work to foreclose arguments, in effect writing history in advance. How will normative de-territorialization, for example, affect food security and community sustainability, both integrally land-based?[2] What effect will geographic decoupling have on emerging models of co-operative micro-economic development; on the demographic challenges of still largely rural provinces; and on the balance of power between resource-extraction corporations and their environmental watchdogs? Who benefits when the place bias is absent from discussions of environmental stewardship? Moreover, how will intellectual workers in Canada support First Nations' self-determination, much of it rooted in land- and place-based spirituality and treaty rights, if we accept or are complicit in strategies of de-territorialization? The argument is closed even before it begins, the dependency of Aboriginal peoples on their lands either an expensive bit of nostalgia we have to accept or, worse, a marker of pathology that sets them apart from us, thus easier to ignore or infantilize. Finally, if history and culture, as the Acadian example made clear, are acts of narration that are always "*situated and grounded*" (Derksen 10), then what becomes of history and culture in a post-national commons? Will literature cease to be a force of contestation? And will cultural memories be only those of the dominant, thus reflecting a new era of Soviet-style social realism? Will Loblaw write the national narrative, or will it be Walmart? And what will they know about Bathurst or Acadian New Brunswick?

When theorists such as Appadurai, Meyrowitz, and Negroponte attempt to attract people to deracinated forms of post-national and digital

---

2   The Loblaw corporation, of course, is again implicated here. The so-called "superstore" is an emblem of *placelessness*, a food warehouse where people in any community can go to buy food that is de-localized—grown, purchased, chemically or mechanically preserved, and shipped from remote locations. In what is both an ironic and insulting concession to the local, these warehouses, all of which look alike, flaunt the name "[insert place name] Market" on the front, asking locals to pretend the market is theirs. The gesture, a zero-sum game that relies on the absence of memory, demands that locals will not question the absence of indigenous food or the absence of the local grocers that Loblaw put out of business.

citizenship, promising, as Tapscott does, that that citizenship alone leads to a "productive life" (136), they are hiding the fact that *no* place is or ever was fixed, static, and comprehensible. Rather, each place *at all times* is manufactured "in the dawn of images [. . .] born / in a poem." Narratives of every type and era have always altered the notion and representations of place, shaping its bias to the dictates of the dominant.

But an important aspect of this operation is being hidden: that post-national citizenship is *also* deeply political, it too following the dictates of power. To herald new frontiers for the ways they "undermine [. . .] traditional relationship[s]" (Meyrowitz 7)—"lead[ing] to a nearly total dissociation of physical place and social 'place'" (115)—is a clear indication of that politics, one that seeks to destroy previous identifications with place in order to erect and homogenize them elsewhere. "What is fundamentally at issue," observe Robins and Webster, "is the global po-litical economic logic that is mobilising new information and communi-cations media to create an external space of enterprise in defiance of the cultural and political realities of the actual world most of us are living in" (225). The result, agrees Marxist geographer Neil Smith, is a planned, not inevitable, "uneven development," a new economic geography that sub-ordinates place in an effort of forced dependency (*Uneven* 4). As Aquin insists, however, that new geography never involves a merger of equals, especially for people already marginalized by conquest or remoteness: "There is no possible short cut for moving from a position of inferior-ity [. . .] to a position of co-operation among equals, unless perhaps this short cut simply involves the complete suppression of the minority group in question" ("Cultural Fatigue" 25).

The shift in spatial ethos, then, while made to look inevitable and desirously *avant-garde*, is in fact a carefully orchestrated contestation of space: an age-old fight for territory, one of the tactics of which is an ag-gressive disavowal of history. In this regard, the politics of globalization mimics that of the nation-state almost exactly.

Only when that rhetorical re-manufacture of human geographies is understood by citizens can *placeness* be used as Acadians used it, to unsettle occupation and reclaim the self-defining agencies of history, culture, and language. Accepting citizenship in abstract federations of post-national cosmopolitanism at the cost of local identity merely in-stitutionalizes inequality, trading one kind of occupation for another. For those people already on the margins, provincialism can be the only result, and with it a widening of the gulf between the local and the global that reduces the local to folklore—specifically, to the commodification of local symbols (such as Anne of Green Gables) that signals Frantz Fanon's second stage of colonization (51). Instead of accepting the loss of *placeness* and the loss of the authority of heritage as inevitable, the Acadian example is evidence that the reclamation of place "by users who are not [. . .] makers" (Certeau xiii) is a key to self-determined rescue from the constraints and narratives of the strong.

In her introduction to *The Geography of Identity*, Patricia Yaeger goes further, suggesting that the places we reclaim in our making are "the hidden places of power" (qtd. in Blair 555), the only places where social transformation can occur. Transformation occurs there, agrees John Rajchman, because those "places" are the sites where we "[endow] ourselves with significance" (16). Those places are not just the sites of our being, but also of our becoming, thus integral to both personal agency and political action. Reclaiming place is therefore refusing that it (and we) be reduced to folklore.

As intellectual workers who understand these relational ecologies—who understand that place in the twenty-first century is *both* noumenal/embedded and palimpsestic/dislocated, its meaning altered by necessity and abetted by narrative in large macro-economic systems—we can assist in the reclamation of the positive aspects of place by exposing the tactics of those forces that demand silence or capitulation in their dismantling of our places for monolithic citizenship elsewhere. We must speak openly about the motives of post-nationalists and not be cowed by their complicity in post-Keynesian, neo-liberal economics or their carelessness in de-legitimizing localisms in a larger attempt to abolish the nation-state. Nationalist Hubert Aquin was especially attuned to this necessity, altering his earlier views of nationalism as a result of what he saw as globalization's encroaching hegemony. "*Universalism*," he concludes, "must never be built on the corpses of 'national' cultures any more than of men" ("Cultural Fatigue" 45).

A Canadian post-nationalism that, in attempting to be worldly or accommodating, denies the non-urban realities of dispersed and place-based ruralisms is a regressive post-nationalism, one of "forced and sterile totalization" ("Cultural Fatigue" 45). This seems a particularly apt warning to those theorists in Canada whose discomfort with nationalism has spawned alliance with far more sinister forces of homogenization, forces that, in their turn, writes Masao Miyoshi, use "'postcoloniality' and multiculturalism [. . .] [as] another alibi to conceal the actuality of global politics" (728).

"We have no business, any longer," writes Wallace Stegner, "in being impatient with history":

> History was part of the baggage we threw overboard when we launched ourselves into the New World. We threw it away because it recalled old tyrannies, old limitations, galling obligations, bloody memories. [. . .] Neither the country nor the society we built out of it can be healthy until we stop raiding and running, and learn to be quiet part of the time, and acquire the sense not of ownership but of belonging. (206)

As intellectual workers we can assist in disrupting the homogenization of globalization's geopolitical consciousness by applying the strategies of our own reading practices (which are radically dispersive, yet still productive) to the creation of similar strategies by which the rural, rooted, and marginal are able to speak and are legitimately heard, thus reversing the progression of their anonymity and their devaluation, both of which are as damaging to us as to them. "No natural laws can be done away with," wrote Marx. "What can change, in changing historical circumstances, is the *form* in which these laws operate" (*Correspondence* 246). What the rural, rooted, and marginal say of place will be their own productions; clearing the way to them saying it (in other words, legitimizing the forms) should be ours.

CHAPTER 2

•◆•

Putting Things in Their Place:
The Syncrude Gallery of Aboriginal Culture
and the Idiom of Majority History[1]

Kimberly Mair

In *The Practice of Everyday Life*, Michel de Certeau distinguishes between the concepts of place and space. For de Certeau, place is governed by a stable and "proper" distribution of elements relative to each other so that simultaneous and paradoxical relations of positioning are discouraged or disavowed. The order of place that de Certeau describes has epistemological implications, since the location of an element defines it in relation to other elements. In contrast to the stability and order of place, de Certeau posits that space is infused with mobile elements. Further, space is an effect of numerous operations of orientation, situation, and temporalization. Space is both ambiguous and dependent upon divergent, even contradictory, contexts.

The task of this chapter is to consider the spatial story of the Syncrude Gallery of Aboriginal Culture, opened in 1997 and named for Syncrude Canada Ltd., a joint venture producer of crude oil that funded approximately a third of the gallery's cost of $2.6 million, and housed at the Royal Alberta Museum in Edmonton. My emphasis will be on the production of place rather than on the public reception of gallery space to argue that the production of place and communal memory within the Syncrude Gallery reiterates an idiom of majority history by elaborating its distribution of material elements, its preferred positioning of visitors at various points of passage and stasis, and the epistemological and social implications of these aspects.

The Syncrude Gallery of Aboriginal Culture is a significant case because it was realized five years after the publication of a national

1   The author gratefully acknowledges support from the University of Lethbridge Research Fund, which made possible two papers addressing place and space in Western Canadian museums, of which this chapter is one.

task force report, *Turning the Page: Forging New Partnerships Between Museums and First Peoples*, and almost a decade after the debates about museum practices that were initiated by the Lubicon Lake Cree boycott of the Glenbow Museum's *The Spirit Sings: Artistic Traditions of Canada's First Peoples* exhibition. *The Spirit Sings* exhibition was a key highlight of the 1988 Winter Olympics Arts Festival in Calgary, Alberta. It was sponsored by Shell Oil, whose drilling explorations directly impacted Lubicon Cree lands and ways of life.

Following *The Spirit Sings* exhibition, the two years of formalized dialogue forged between First Peoples and cultural institutions across Canada that culminated in the report *Turning the Page* aimed to arrive at ethical strategies to present Aboriginal histories and cultures. The task force's consultation process demonstrated the crucial need for greater involvement of First Peoples in museum practice and interpretation. The emphasis in the present work is on interpretation of First Nations and Indigenous peoples' culture in the Syncrude Gallery. Despite the apparent implementation of task force recommendations exemplified through the significant contributions of First Nations and Indigenous communities and consultants in the gallery's planning, design, and realization, consideration of the production of place in the Syncrude Gallery suggests that deeper, or even a-disciplinary, interventions into museum practice are imperative.

To consider the force of this gallery, attention will be given to a number of operations that are significant to the constitution of the exhibition and primarily to stopping points, such as dioramas and constructed spaces, that together contribute to the resolution of several disparate elements through an idiomatic production of place. Despite the inclusion of soundscape stories that accompany many of the displays, analysis will illustrate that the Syncrude Gallery produces what James Clifford has called a "majority History" ("Four Northwest" 240) in museum practice, one that is non-oppositional and neutralizes the discomfort that non-Indigenous visitors may experience in relation to the colonial and genocidal aspects of the history addressed in the gallery's content.

AND THE VOICE SAID: "IN THE BEGINNING . . ."

A small foyer at the gallery's entry contains five darkened glass encasements in a horizontal row flush to the curved wall. The lighting is appropriately dim for a multimedia presentation. The presentation,

"500 Generations," is alternately illuminated by large television screens located behind the dark glass of four of the encasements. This presentation plays a crucial role in the construction of authority and the establishment of the gallery's voice—if such a thing can be posited—as it implicitly lays the ground rules for the visitor's interpretation of the exhibition to come. The presentation contrasts different origin stories, each on their own terms. Two Indigenous stories of creation are given, each accompanied by colourful animations. These creation stories are juxtaposed with a scientific account and its visual accompaniment, which follow the systematic steps involved in an archaeological project. The scientific account opens with an archaeological dig, during which an artifact or piece of "evidence" is removed from the site. The artifact becomes the subject or protagonist of the scientific story, and the viewer is brought along as a witness to its journey from the archaeological site, to its study in a laboratory setting, and to its final and singular presentation on the fourth screen for the viewer to observe. It is a spear point; the fifth encasement is then illuminated to reveal that it contains the very spear point (or its construction) that the visitor saw on the fourth screen.

The gallery makes an implicit claim to the absolute authority of science by offering the physical presence of the object of its inquiry. Operating metonymically in relation to the opening audio-visual presentation at the gallery's entrance, the spear point is produced as an alibi for the account of the origins of Aboriginal peoples in North America as proposed by the archaeologists and testifies to the efficacy of the methods of scientific discovery to arrive at the "truth." The presentation of the spear point in the glass encasement has configured the visitor for entry to the gallery proper, as the multimedia presentation and its denouement offering of the physical spear point suggest that *some* of the gallery's contents are fictions, but the products of scientific discovery will provide the last word.

While the Syncrude Gallery is remarkably polyphonic in its combination of several different representational genres, it is produced and consumed within a much larger discursive field, constituted within the hegemonic discourse of scientific discovery and linear temporality. Both of the latter aspects of hegemonic discourse are reinforced by the sequential in-context displays of fragments, such as the spear points. Hegemonic discourse is the "common sense" of a given society and its institutions. When the "common sense" of scientific discourse is considered, the genesis presentation ultimately undermines the given Indigenous accounts of origins to privilege the scientific account.

The narrative approach of the highlighted Aboriginal accounts of creation presented in animated form is juxtaposed with the archaeological dig and, although the archaeological account is equally narrative in form, it will not be visible as itself a story in the context of hegemonic discourse. Rather, in the context of hegemonic discourse, the authority of the archaeologists is reinforced as factual, while the Indigenous accounts may appear to be "merely cultural" stories.

Yet, within the gallery are many cultural stories—including ones that are shaped by scientific genres, such as taxonomy or evolutionary progression. Although some cultural critics have observed a shift in consciousness toward the relativity of knowledge claims and greater epistemological pluralism, many nevertheless concede that the hegemony of the scientific method of discovery and the privileging of linear chronology remain predominant within contemporary consciousness. In the context of the discipline of history, Dipesh Chakrabarty has acknowledged that where relevant epistemological assumptions are incommensurable, "subaltern pasts" are encountered that themselves present explanations that are not widely accepted because they are inconsistent with what can be taken as fact within the limits of the discipline. Chakrabarty draws a distinction between minority histories that address identities, events, and interpretations that have been neglected in majority histories but adhere to the latter's epistemological assumptions and subaltern pasts that cannot be incorporated due to those assumptions. The predicament of the subaltern past is realized in the "500 Generations" audio-visual presentation in the insistence of the juxtaposition between the creation stories and the archaeological dig.

Hence, the introductory origins presentation orients the viewer in relation to hegemonic epistemological assumptions that underlie the ethnographic approach to museum display, which promise to assign generalizable meaning to objects of material culture. In the context of majority history conjoined with hegemonic conventions of display, the transformative limits of one of the key principles derived from the national task force *Turning the Page,* which calls for "[a]n equal partnership [that] involves mutual appreciation of the conceptual knowledge and approaches characteristic of First Peoples, and the empirical knowledge and approaches of academically trained workers" (Hill and

Nicks 7), become palpable, since academic, disciplinary practice itself undercuts subaltern epistemologies. In the case of the Syncrude Gallery, temporal precision, systematic discovery, and textual communication are juxtaposed with orally based communication that is not concerned with fixing temporality and does not conform to the hegemonic chronological imperative. The force of this juxtaposition is illustrated in the introductory presentation when, for example, an Indigenous narrator observes that humans have been living in North America "for a long time" and, immediately following that, a voice-over interrupts by asserting: "11,000 years."

PLACE AND THE PERPETUAL PAST TENSE

The ordering and spatial distribution of objects actively produce meaning, which is sometimes explicitly articulated in the textual panels that accompany various objects, arrangements, and encasements. Implicit connotations cannot be disregarded, however, even in the absence of explicit interpretation or decoding of displays. In the context of the emphasis on the ethnographic approach to display, the diorama (or in situ display) is one of the preferred modes of presentation. For instance, there is a diorama entitled "An Ingenious Bison Kill," documenting prehistoric bison hunting as an Alberta Plains adaptation through the construction of an important hunting site and two hunters with spears, *ambushing* (to use the gallery's chosen word) an ancient bison. The indexed location is the famous Fletcher Site, situated southeast of Taber, Alberta, assumed to be the oldest bison-hunting site discovered in the region thus far and dated at over 9,000 years. Despite the elaborate efforts of "reconstruction" mobilized to produce this simulacrum ostensibly as a testament of means of material subsistence among the Plains people over 9,000 years ago, the accent of emphasis is a celebratory demonstration of the archaeological mastery of the site and the artifacts that it offers. It is unclear what the main subject matter or thesis of the diorama is: Is it related to prehistoric hunting practices and environment or to the mastery of "reconstruction" through archaeology, paleontology, and paleobotany?

As a venue that aims to educate the public and to collaborate closely with provincial primary education curricula, the Royal Alberta Museum's use of more traditional dioramas to depict humans in the Gallery for Aboriginal Culture is problematic in a number of ways. Given the profound subjection of First Nations and Indigenous communities to complex and intractable stereotypes, which are closely tied to concretely negative impacts on opportunities and the uneven distribution of political recognition, the lack of cultural contextualization of the bison hunting and the fishing scenes both historically and in relation to the realities of industrial commercial food production and consumption today, the dioramas naturalize and singularize Aboriginal cultures and peoples, while producing Aboriginality as a spectacle for non-Aboriginal visitors. When the passing comments of gallery visitors in reaction to these dioramas are considered, it is evident that such contextualization is crucial. An active anticipation of how these depictions work to invoke and reinforce stereotypes along artificial nature–culture distinctions would neutralize the spectacular character of the dioramic scenes. Indeed, the extent to which the depictions themselves could be informed by prevalent stereotypes and mediated images already circulated in repetition throughout popular culture over the past century needs to be considered more reflexively and incorporated into the textual aspects of the exhibits.

Frits Pannekoek observes the troubling connotation associated with the use of dioramas as a mode of representation in the Syncrude Gallery. Pannekoek notes that dioramas are primarily used in the display of natural history: "Dioramas separate the exhibit from the visitor/scholar and construct reality as stuffed or inanimate 'curiosities.' It is a technique rarely used to interpret 'modern' cultures" (349). The depiction of humans simultaneously as life-like and inanimate, sometimes in a glass encasement as object, produces Aboriginality in the past tense. The gallery as a whole produces both a truncated modernity and a contemporaneity that is too silent and too ambiguous. The twentieth century was a long one in terms of its relevance for understanding Aboriginal cultures and experiences as they are situated within the political and economic regions of Alberta, Canada, and North America.

In the Syncrude Gallery, there is a noted lack of elaboration of the full political significance of treaty-making in Canada and Indigenous nations' rights and responsibilities that pre-date, and are not negated by, signed treaties.[2] Popular and majority histories that hint at the protective subordination of several autonomous nations under the Crown

---

2   I acknowledge that not all Indigenous peoples are party to treaties, but the popular assumptions about what the treaties signify politically are of widespread material consequence to the lives of Indigenous peoples.

and shape images of their citizens as dependent on the state for "special" rather than *constitutional* rights, obscures Patricia Monture's crucial observation that "all parties to a treaty are assumed to have prior rights. This means that it is not just First Nations who have treaty rights and responsibilities. Various Crowns, including the British, Dutch, French, and Canadian, as well as the United States government, were also a party to those treaties and were accorded both rights and obligations under various treaties" ("What Is Sovereignty" 255). While the gallery does not adequately address the importance of a clear understanding of federalism and the consequences of its misrepresentation and relegation to collective forgetting, it does not avoid *some* of the difficult issues that are associated with what has been, in practice, the colonization of Aboriginal peoples: the systematic devastation of Indigenous peoples' economic activity and institutionally administered genocide (although this word is not used in the gallery); these strategies and their consequences are presented often in the passive voice and always in punctuated time.

For instance, the corridor "Loss and Survival: Effects of Assimilation Policies" presents mortality statistics and audiotaped personal accounts of racism, illness, and the questionably prolonged and differential treatments and hospitalizations of Indigenous peoples diagnosed with tuberculosis. It is a dark and narrow space bordered with a chain-link fence. It is designed to elicit an affective response, and the imposing impacts of the narrow and confining space and its lighting are successfully powerful. The language used in the textual and audio elements, in combination with the visual representations of people, gives the impression that the reverberations of assimilation strategies are specific to the mid-twentieth century. Further, the statistics presented in this section do not go beyond 1976. These conditions are presented as though they are particular to the past and have reached their conclusion. The present, as it is represented beyond the corridor, in a bright and open space, is a time of cultural and spiritual renewal, but the visitor is not given comparable measurements for material well-being in the period since the documented decades.

While there is brief treatment of obstacles to forms of material reproduction, such as the decline of subsistence fishing, the didactic panels present this in the passive voice, so that agents or processes contributing to these obstacles are unattributed. As most of these processes are tied to struggles around land use in Alberta, a province whose wealth is largely dependent upon the extraction of natural resources, the corporate sponsorship of a museum project dedicated to the interpretation of the histories and cultures of First Peoples likely contributes to compromise and self-censorship. Indeed, only one brief sentence in the whole of the gallery was given to the impacts of oil production or logging and mining activities combined.

The latter portion of the "Loss and Survival" corridor suggests an end to these injustices through the work of grassroots movements of the 1960s and 1970s. The gains made by First Nations and Indigenous activist struggles, which in practice have often been treated in Canada as criminal rather than political (indeed, Indigenous political organization was explicitly outlawed in Canada for much of the twentieth century), are incorporated into the national myth of inclusion and fixed by the open space at the end of the corridor, where there are quotations regarding the meaning of spirituality and official letters of support for the gallery on the wall, and the sights and sounds of the Learning Circle are perceptible through a large opening.

The audiotaped stories that are audible in the corridor are effective in establishing a narrative identification that potentially breaks down affective barriers and creates a sense of familiarity and communion. This particular testimonial approach, however, conceals the use of institutional power that selects and frames the prompting questions and edited responses to shape a preferred production of reality. While that reality is at times brutal, it is assigned solely to the past. Likewise, the photographs, charts, and official documentation reinforce that this discussion is specific to the past.

In terms of the positioning of "Loss and Survival: Effects of Assimilation" within the gallery's layout, it is notable that its narrow entryway is located past the back wall of "Suppression and Resistance" and appears to be a dead end. This layout likely discourages many visitors from discovering and entering the corridor at its point of departure. Although the "Loss and Survival" corridor is quite visible from the other side, it is also less effective if experienced in its reverse because it loses some imperative aspects of contextualization in relation to what is presented in "Suppression and Resistance" (e.g., policies for assimilation to eliminate the "Indian question" by eliminating the "Indian").

The spatial distribution of the gallery according to uneven historical time, the address of impacts of colonization relevant to the present in the linguistic and figurative past tense, in conjunction with the heavy use of ethnographic classification and the diorama as a mode of representation, contribute to the problem of place produced as race, as described by Sherene Razack:

> Mythologies or national stories [. . .] enable citizens to think of themselves as part of a community, defining who belongs and who does not belong to the nation. The story of the land as shared and as developed by enterprising settlers is manifestly a racial story. Through claims to reciprocity and equality, the story produces European settlers as the bearers of civilization while simultaneously trapping Aboriginal people in the pre-modern. (2)

Curatorial practice tends to obscure the extent to which museums are often telling a racial story that is a key device in racialization, the process of systematically producing differences and similarities and their meanings. The tendency to treat Indigenous cultures and peoples in the past tense is a subtle but significant one in the Syncrude Gallery, though it is disavowed through a recurring emphasis on Aboriginal culture—in the singular form—as a living culture. "The Culture Lives" is one of the gallery's themes (Gallery Tour), and the exhibition itself is presented as a "living" gallery, with intermediated interactive sites, built environments, and soundscapes that directly deliver personal stories from those who experienced them—from stories of traplines to the stories of hospitalization for tuberculosis.

AUTHORITY AND THE SPECTRAL INTERRUPTION

A crucial and urgent set of problems arises when the predicament of *living* peoples and *living* cultures is in fact taken seriously. The facticity of livingness haunts the Syncrude Gallery, a gallery that simultaneously avows itself as a living one but repeatedly attempts to put to rest—to bury in place—that which is not dead. At the dense intersection between history and subjectivity resides what Avery Gordon has called the social figure of the ghost. Gordon insists that this spectral figure is not the restless figure of superstition. This social figure is very much alive and it interrupts and troubles the smoothly ordered stories that we tell and that are told to us through the use of abstractions, in this case the abstractions of cultural evolution, adaptation, and racism that nest countless other sub-abstractions. These abstractions do not capture "the ensemble of social relations that create inequalities, situated interpretative codes, particular kinds of subjects, and the possible and impossible themselves" (4), especially to the extent that the events depicted are actively produced as the dead events of the completed past. The abstractions seem to urge: Let us bury our dead events and all of the knotted arteries of complicity and temporality too.

In the promise to take livingness seriously—"The Culture Lives"—it is not enough to have the voices of individuals telling their stories in a mediated soundscape (not only because the stories are neutralized by the larger strategies of place within which they are produced and situated), when the messy, intertwined livingness of events, peoples, and cultures is so blatantly displaced and denied. Gordon tells us that haunting is signalled by a charged strangeness that makes palpable that which is missing from the scene or place being haunted. The ghost unsettles "the propriety and property lines that delimit a zone of activity or knowledge" (63). With respect to the Syncrude Gallery as a *living* place, what is inherent to Gordon's conception of haunting is the stress on the profound relationality of all of the subjects, cultures, and knowledges that are simultaneously brought into being and brought to bear by and in the place that is haunted.

The *in situ* First Contact site in the Syncrude Gallery places the visitor under what is presumed (but not confirmed) to be the tipi of a former leader of the Blackfoot Nation (Figure 2.1; see colour insert). This site is significant to the effective production of place and it provides support for the construction of a majority history. Under the tipi, the setting is a meeting described in Anthony Henday's journal as having taken place in 1754 with a people Henday designated in his journal as the Archithinue. Henday was employed by the Hudson's Bay Company to expand the network of fur traders on the prairies. This *in situ* display has, on the one side, Henday and his host seated and engaged in a set of ritual exchanges. On the other side, there is a vast mural that depicts the view of the Archithinue camp from Henday's point of view.

The mural is of great significance in the ordering of place, fixing the authority of the First Contact display and working as a device of identification through deference to a constructed copy of Henday's journal. Since the mural is not contained within the spatial confines of the constructed tipi, it can be viewed in its entirety from only one specific vantage point that places the visitor directly in front of the copy of the journal, uniting both textual and visual records of the event of Contact, as though it were both singular and completed.

E. Hecht's 1903 concept of stopping points, which refers to reconstructed sites in museums that can bring the visitor's mind from a single concept or event "to larger ideas, to a general conception" (qtd. in Griffiths 167), and Avery Gordon's notion of haunting together enable the proposition of the concept of *spectral stopping points* in the production of place. I will briefly describe how the First Contact diorama constitutes a spectral stopping point. First, the First Contact *in situ* display attempts to exorcise the meeting between the Archithinue and Henday by delimiting the event of Contact to the exchange of communication, pipes, and gifts depicted in the scene. Yet, this ongoing process, though produced as discreet event, is not effectively integrated into the After Contact elements in the gallery. Rather, the event of Contact is excised through the ordering of place apart from its consequences.

Second, the production of place in the First Contact site produces and animates imagined human subjects as effects of place. In particular, Henday, while a historical figure, is animated as the protagonist of Contact, since the order of place in the display is oriented toward giving the visitor *his* impressions and, hence, dramatizing his connoted emotions. This is most forcefully exemplified by the mural, which grants the visitor Henday's fictionalized sight of the Archithinue.

Third, and in dramatic contrast to the previous point, the visitor is not offered a mode of identification with the Archithinue at this very significant juncture, and this disavowal contributes to the haunting character of the production of place in the First Contact site, because real subjects of the past and present, who have felt and feel the reverberations of the ongoing *process* of Contact, have been exorcised from the scene. The real historical and contemporary subjects who have existed or do exist but who either cannot be contained or are refused by the gallery's production of place are spectral in this context because they have been made absent. Thus, the spectral stopping point paradoxically both disavows and indexes its absences.

THE ORDER OF PLACE

Beyond the First Contact site, the production of place in the gallery ensures that the flow of visitors from the First Contact site will delay their encounter with the longer-term institutional consequences of Contact,

On the other hand, the defunct presentation at the gallery's entrance, which remains darkened all day, gives the impression that the gallery is closed. Indeed, of the four galleries housed within the Royal Alberta Museum, the Syncrude Gallery is the only one that does not have a lit entry. The darkened entryway, the inoperative multimedia presentation, and the lack of a gallery interpreter together signal the structural disinvestment of the Syncrude Gallery of Aboriginal Culture, which unintentionally becomes a dramatic aspect of the story it tells through the order of place. With a new home for the museum in the downtown arts district of the city of Edmonton anticipated for 2016, there is an emergent opportunity for the Royal Alberta Museum to indeed turn the page by opening a new space of possibility dedicated to the living cultures of the First Peoples on the lands now called Alberta.

CHAPTER 3

•◆•

Lieux d'oubli: The Forgotten North of Canadian Literature

Renée Hulan

In the varied field of cultural history, there are many kinds of memory and of forgetting. There is the kind of forgetting evoked by Paul Ricoeur at the end of *Memory, History, Forgetting*: the forgetting that liberates care and permits forgiveness, and the forgetting that prevents forgiveness by forbidding memory. The first acknowledges memory; the second denies it. There is also the kind of forgetting that is brought about by distraction where the gaze fixes on one historical object and ignores others. This is one of the prominent types of forgetting we are witnessing in Canada now as cultural memory is being shaped by distraction and denial. Like the bicentennial of the French Revolution, whose imminent celebration generated a critique of commemoration in the shape of Pierre Nora's seven-volume *Lieux de mémoire*, the recent celebration of the bicentenary of the War of 1812 should give Canadians pause to consider how we remember the past. For the past two decades, Canadian historians and writers have analyzed the representation of the past in all its forms, from the public history presented in museums, parks, and celebrations to history taught in schools, historiography, and visual culture. This extensive body of work brings to light the ways in which a nationalist narrative of Canadian history is produced, received, and challenged. The history debates arising from a perceived crisis in historical representation have contributed to solidifying nationalist narratives and supporting the celebration of isolated events which serve as distractions from the circumstances in which we are actually living. The War of 1812, the sometime symbol of Canadian resistance against American invasion, helps us forget about our growing subservience to the United States. Cultural forgetfulness is less about the scarcity of memories of our colonial past and present than justifying excessive and self-aggrandizing narratives of the nation. Where national celebrations promote escapism

and suffer from policies enacted by governments on their behalf whether they experience these policies directly or not. The development of natural resources is a case in point, with economic benefits but also social and environmental damage resulting from activities in places most Canadians will never see. Along with collective benefits and suffering comes the potential for collective memory which, as Maurice Halbwachs proposed, creates a framework in which the individual mind reconstructs and recollects events whether or not they were directly experienced (*On Collective* 38). Whereas history relies on written sources and artifacts, collective memory, as conceived by Halbwachs, seems closer to lived experience. History can appear remote and specialized, the preserve of trained professionals and academics, but everyone has memories. In part, this false distinction arises from the crisis in historical representation and the history debates of the late twentieth century with their caricature of history, and thus gives further evidence of the distraction such debates can create. As memory studies continue to expand, the idea of collective memory has taken on a greater authority, and as Alon Confino points out, this expansion has created problems of definition and method as collective memory both engulfs and challenges history (see also Connerton). Halbwachs, however, considered history and memory to be mutually supportive activities and gave various examples of how one enhances the other.

This chapter concerns places that serve as sites not of memory but of forgetting—*lieux d'oubli*—to borrow Nora's elegant idea. Like *lieux de mémoire*, these sites generate meanings that have cultural significance because they show us something important about the society in which we live. Ironically, forgotten places remind us that collective memory is shadowed by forgetting. The effects of our absorption are perhaps most acute in the North, where forgetting operates as the agent of colonialism. There, forgotten places remain discursive territories that are prevented from becoming *les lieux de mémoire*/places of memory by efforts to maintain them as sites of material value whose various symbolic and functional meanings must be denied in order for economic exploitation to continue. As this chapter will propose, the interaction of material, symbolic, and functional meanings that define *lieux de mémoire* is disrupted in representations of the North right at the point where the place potentially ceases to be a territory to be entered, explored, and conquered. By identifying northern places as *lieux d'oubli*, I argue that

Canadian society is revealed, not in the commemorations associated with historical memory, but in the repressed memory of colonization that makes some places forgotten places. Commemorations of national historical events such as the War of 1812 serve to distract members of Canadian society from these sites of repressed memory. Such places fade from collective memory as others gain prominence. In what follows, I examine an example of the cultural production of forgetting: the gradual disappearance of literary representations written in and about northern Aboriginal communities. By tracing the gradual disappearance of particular works from literary culture, especially those produced in and about Cree and Anishinaabe communities, against the media representation of northern communities where environmental and humanitarian crises converge, I will argue that forgetting these works contributes to the maintenance of northern places as material for exploitation.

The idea of a forgotten North may seem counterintuitive given how much writing has been devoted to the North in Canada. Northern studies shelters contributions from the broadest array of disciplines and authors imaginable. In addition to academic and professional research, there are equally vast popular and commercial literatures on northern subjects. More is known about the history, geography, environment, and cultures in the North than perhaps has ever been known, and research on particular northern locations, such as the St. Elias Mountains studied in Julie Cruikshank's *Do Glaciers Listen?*, is transforming historical narratives where they were once "a mere footnote in canonical accounts proceeding from east to west, with only occasional glances north" (12). Two very distinct notions of *place*, real and imagined, compete in representations of the North, which is the subject of the meticulous scholarship found in Shelagh Grant's historical studies. While it is true that "ideas of North" infuse Canadian culture, the imagined North lodged in a collective psyche has never increased knowledge of actual people and local communities in the North.

When the late Inuit artist and author Alootook Ipellie described Canada's colonial administration of his homeland as a "cultural whiteout," he signalled how whiteness comes to signify the dominance of that ethnic category and the exercise of power by those who identify through whiteness. The whiteout experienced by northern peoples has been economic and political as well as cultural, a continued colonization effected through policies of northern development. The material conditions

"At one thousand feet we make quick decisions / about our loyalties, the other engine might fail, / the suitcases of our hearts might be opened with / all that contraband, the jewels and screams, we / might have things to declare" (94). The desperation in the speaker's voice propels the stanza toward the inevitable question "What comes after this?"

In the next and penultimate stanza, end-stopped lines create a feeling of stability:

> What do you mean, what comes after this?
> This is it.
> Attiwapiskat approaches, a Cree village
> on a cold salt coast, flying patchwork quilts in
> several more colours than are found in nature,
> shining with blue-white runway lights. (94)

Attiwapiskat is shining, an image of safety in the dark night sky and hope in the dark moment in the speaker's soul. As it approaches, "everything is as it should be," and "We slide down to the airstrip through salt fogs / from Hudson Bay that slip through the night like / airborne bedsheets" to be greeted by a person from the community:

> Approaching us is an earthman,
> speaking Cree. (95)

Jiles wrote "Night Flight to Attiwapiskat" before the community became synonymous with the crisis in housing on Canadian reserves after the Attawapiskat First Nation declared a state of emergency in 2011. Chief Theresa Spence defended her community against the decision of the government of Canada (GOC) to take over the community's affairs and eventually won an injunction against third-party management. The news media, especially television, represented the housing crisis using the standard conventions of investigative reporting, as journalists with cameras were sent to Attawapiskat to uncover the hidden truth, to bring unseen images of suffering and struggle into view. A year before, Linda Goyette had documented the community's struggle to get a new school in the mainstream magazine *Canadian Geographic*. As Goyette wrote, schools are of crucial importance in the community because "Canada's north country is the territory of the young" with three-quarters of the population of Attawapiskat under the age of thirty-five and more than a third of the population under the age of nineteen. At the time, Goyette observed, the GOC had designated "millions of dollars to build 50 new schools, with 16 already built, and another 27 under construction"—all in Afghanistan (60). "Shannen's Dream," a national campaign for better education on reserves launched by a teenaged student from Attawapiskat, Shannen Koostachin, who died in a car accident that year, continues to draw support, including the passage of a private member's bill in the House of Commons. Linda Goyette promised to remember Shannen and the four other young people lost to the community that year: "I never met Ian, Dakota, Brendon, Dwayne or Shannen, but I will remember that each one died before Canada kept its promise to them" (54). Likewise, I have never been to Attawapiskat, but I will remember how the GOC has treated the people who call it home.

"Night Flight to Attiwapiskat" was written before the development of the Victor Mine by De Beers Canada in the territory of the Attawapiskat First Nation. According to its website, De Beers spent $1 billion on the mine—only $167 million of which went to Aboriginal businesses—and it expects to generate $6.7 million GDP for the province of Ontario (www. debeerscanada.com). The mine was opened in 2008, three years after an Impact Benefit Agreement (IBA) was signed with the Attawapiskat First Nation. To date, the people of Attawapiskat have seen little lasting benefit from this agreement. On 6 February 2009, people from the Attawapiskat First Nation protested the IBA, and demanded that its contents be made public, by setting up a blockade on the winter road near the mine. The ongoing dispute with De Beers and the crisis in Attawapiskat can be followed in *Wawatay News*. On 18 February 2009, it reported that the Attawapiskat chief and council asked to revisit the IBA, especially with regard to racial discrimination, pay equity, and the community's need for a new school and housing.

On 6 March 2012, under the pressure of international scrutiny, the GOC announced that a contractor had been engaged to build a new school in time for the 2013–14 academic year. As Chief Spence told *Windspeaker*, the new school would be "a great accomplishment" for the Attawapiskat First Nation (24). While the members of the community rejoiced at the news, it is important to remember that it had been twelve years since the community's school was condemned and closed due to contamination by diesel fuel and that, for twelve years, the length of a

"Night Flight to Attiwapiskat" appeared at a time when literary critics were beginning to confront the issue of voice appropriation and learning the importance of moving over to make room for Aboriginal authors. In this context, retelling Aboriginal stories by an outsider like Jiles is a violation. Yet if forgetting this poem could be attributed to the rejection of appropriating Aboriginal culture in literature, then one might expect to see poems by Aboriginal authors in its place.[3] While moving over is meant to make way for Aboriginal voices, it also places the burden of understanding and explanation on the Aboriginal people, and frees the outsider, whether the poet or reader, from the responsibility to remember. Ideally, the displacement of Paulette Jiles's poems about James Bay and prose inspired by living and working with the Cree and Anishinaabe of northern Ontario might turn attention to Cree and Anishinaabe poets such as Margaret Sam-Cromarty. Margaret Sam-Cromarty is a Cree poet from Chisasibi and author of poems also written through the 1980s and later collected in *Souvenirs de la baie James/James Bay Memoirs*, poems that are printed in English and translated into French by Jean Ferguson and André Couture and thus have the potential to speak to a broad audience in settler society. Published in the *Racines amérindiennes* series, the collection makes available a voice of Chisasibi, a Cree village across the bay from Attawapiskat. In "James Bay," the speaker begins by evoking images of barren wilderness:

James Bay, my home
is closer than the moon,
its regions so bare,
aloof and remote. (58)

The bay, the coast, the "sights and sounds" evoked in the next three stanzas change from being "aloof and remote" to intimate: "They wrap around me / giving peace" (58). Several poems reflect on the role played by the missionaries and residential school, reliance on the Hudson's Bay store, and other agents of colonialism. Set during the Depression, "A Cree Child" remembers when "the price of furs / was at its lowest" and "both governments didn't care" (40). With credit denied by the Hudson's

---

3   Bennett and Brown's *A New Anthology of Canadian Literature in English* does include a short story by Eden Robinson as a new addition, and Thomas King is one of the authors retained from the earlier edition.

Bay Company, and a church determined "to save souls" not bodies, the Cree are left to suffer:

> I recall small steps
> in the Northern snow,
> a sweet life taken,
> a little boy with no shoes.
> Deeply moved I weep.
> He was my brother. (40)

Decades later, Cree children on the shores of James Bay remain neglected, freezing in portable classrooms or a renovated trailer provided by De Beers.

Read together, the poems in *Souvenirs de la baie James/James Bay Memoirs* follow the speakers as they collectively return to the ways of the past. The "history / Of Indians," turns the speaker in "Written in Story Books" away from "printed words" to "The often tragic people / not written in story books" and to "search for truth / from old songs" (90). In "Dream," the sun connects the speaker to the past, particularly to the elders who have passed on the traditional knowledge and "knew and read / the weather like a book." In the dream, the speaker feels appreciation for their teaching: "I felt the joy of seasons, / followed my nomad elders. / Looked to the circling sun" (18). The "circling sun" returns the speaker to the land and the poem becomes an honour song to the Cree narrative memory (see McLeod). As Jeannette Armstrong explains in "Aboriginal Literatures: A Distinctive Genre within Canadian Literature," Aboriginal authors write from knowledge of specific oral narrative traditions (180) and these traditions have a profound influence on the poetics and aesthetics embraced by poets like Sam-Cromarty.

In "A Tribute to My Father Lifetime Trapper and Hunter," the speaker recalls being a child out on the land. The first eight stanzas remember waiting patiently as the father "would answer the geese / their voices blending together" (30). The child "was taught never to make a noise, or to call out" but to "stop and watch and wait" (30) until the father raises the gun "like a shadow" and takes down a goose:

> Throbbing with emotion,
> his hollow cheeks trembling,

CHAPTER 4

•◆•

Design and Disappearance: Visual Nostalgias and the Canadian Company Town

Candida Rifkind

In his 2006 literary travelogue, *This Is My Country, What's Yours?*, Noah Richler implies that Canada's beginnings in the trading posts of the Hudson's Bay Company established a set of enduring attitudes: "'The Company' established the very foundations of this country on the back of its lucrative hat and felt business, and some of Canada's worst social and political habits too. [. . .] Sobey's, Irving, Air Canada, liquor stores, cable providers, or the Liberal Party—our crippling propensity for monopolies and the habit of dependence they encourage stretch all the way back to the Hudson's Bay Company's system of trading posts— and before" (179). This idea that the nation continues to embody the structures and ideals of the company town that was its European commercial and colonial origin fits with longstanding clichés of Canadian culture as dependent, subordinate, and deferential. Certainly, the established writers to whom Richler speaks, including Fred Stenson, Alistair MacLeod, Michael Crummey, Alice Munro, and Michael Turner, have mixed feelings about life in the company towns they recall and imagine, even as they celebrate the working-class cultures of these communities. In Canada, notwithstanding the long history of fur trade, railroad, and logging towns, industrial company towns, most of which were owned by mining and smelting companies, were a largely twentieth-century phenomenon. The majority were built after the Second World War and then abandoned, consolidated, or restructured

Acknowledgements: I would like to thank Peggy Burns at Drawn & Quarterly and Mike Simons of The Goggles for permission to use images in this article. As well, I am grateful for the feedback I received on an earlier version of this paper from the organizers and attendees of the panel, "Work, Workers, and Community," at the 2012 meeting of the Association for Canadian and Québec Literatures in Waterloo, Ontario.

by the 1990s.[1] Although it may be in general use as a term to designate a variety of single-industry communities, I am using the term *company town* here to refer specifically to a planned community built by a single corporation to house its workers in a remote location. Laurie Mercier's study of Cold War–era Canadian and American mining towns offers a helpful summary of how these towns operated: "Companies controlled the workforce through a combination of paternalism and intimidation, which often included spatially arranging worker housing near mines or the smelter, maintaining political power, creating corporate welfare programs, sustaining local institutions, and busting unions, as well as controlling jobs" (158). They were, as Oliver Dinius and Angela Vergara point out, "powerful symbols of industrial modernity" and manifestations of labour control through welfare capitalism, since the corporations' various investments in workers' social welfare (housing, education, recreation) was undertaken in order to increase profit (5).

At the same time, workers often organized in these communities, and some company towns were as much union towns, nurturing alternative politics and cultures. So, while the idea of the company town might seem like a relic of the age of monopoly capitalism best forgotten, labour historians, folklorists, writers, and artists continue to seek out and inscribe memories of these places in ways that negotiate experiences of exploitation and entrapment on the one hand and feelings of community and identification on the other. As a result, the company town is often a fraught memory site in Canadian literature and culture, a space of belonging and non-belonging that, given the rapid disappearance of its physical traces due to global economic restructuring and cultural homogenization, is re-emerging in contemporary memory projects in surprising ways.[2]

One of the problems of remembering such a complex social space as the company town is that such cultural memories risk being perceived

---

1   For specific studies of Canadian company towns, see Mercier, Rollwagen, Saarinen, and Neil White.

2   Richler's conversation with Michael Crummey illustrates the extent to which many company towns exist more in memory than in reality. Speaking of Buchans, Newfoundland, Crummey explains, "What affects me most . . . is not what's left but what's gone. Every time I come back something else has disappeared, some other building has been torn down. Driving into Buchans is driving into a place I don't recognize" (191).

labels, as well as floating text that integrates into the compositions as spoken words, narrative text, and directional cues" (Badman). This unique form allows Blanchet to develop the town as protagonist by subordinating individual characters, who are nameless typifications, to represent various stages in its development. As he comments in an interview, "I wanted the village as the main character and wanted to represent it in a broad way to express the fact that Rapide Blanc was just a little town that was born and died without leaving a trace, to try to give a bit of a cold look on the story—the same kind of look that [the] big boss must have had on that village at the time, thinking of everything but the people for whom that little place was home" (Blanchet, Interview). Although the sepia tones and lack of character individuation may reproduce that austere gaze of the CEO, Blanchet lingers on scenes of community harmony. For example, he depicts the joyful scene of a summer evening dance as part of a series of images of happy village life (see Figure 4.2): the Co-op store as the space of community conversation and gossip; the company shuttle bus that takes residents out to the company beach at the lake; the weekly film screenings of reels brought in on the train; the baby boom leading to the building of the bilingual school; staying up until midnight on 24 December, and so on. Work itself is represented as clean and white collar: the men who work in the dam control room get authorization from head office in Shawinigan Falls to open the floodgates every spring. Indeed, the work of this town that is its reason for being is much less significant to the narrative than leisure and community pursuits, in particular hunting and fishing.

Blanchet's Art Deco aesthetic borrows as much from comic books as it does from illustration and film. At the beginning of the story, Blanchet draws 1930s downtown Montreal like the Gotham of Batman, while the character of the modern architect appears as a superhero leading us into the modern future. In these visual echoes, Blanchet hints at the darker side of company town optimism: the CEO making his decision is drawn in an Expressionistic style, his shadow an ominous presence in a frightening, disorienting office space atop a new skyscraper (Figure 4.1).

However, as the narrative progresses, this darkness at the top of the company is quickly surpassed by the brightness of the small town. Once the timeline moves forward, Blanchet shifts his visual references from 1920s Expressionism to 1950s Space Age design, specifically the Populuxe aesthetic of mid-century modernism and the Googie architectural design motifs that symbolize motion and speed (boomerangs,

4.1. "The Board Members Are Waiting." From *White Rapids* by Pascal Blanchet (greyscale reproduction of colour original). Courtesy Drawn & Quarterly.

parabolas, atoms, arrows, and so on). Despite being separated by several decades and fractured into sub-movements, in general Art Deco and Space Age design share an excitement about technology and a passion for reorganizing social relations through architecture and design. They are also both visual fields that have come to stand for various forms of retro-futurism in that they signify how the past imagined the future that is now the present. The visual optimism of this mid-century design aesthetic shapes Blanchet's narrative content and idealizes the town of White Rapids as a modern workers' utopia, in which labour is the organizing principle of the place but leisure is the meaningful activity that transforms it into a civil space (Figure 4.2).

Ironically, the very modernity that the form of the book celebrates is the cause of the town's disappearance. Blanchet returns to 1920s Expressionism, mixed with a bit of Social Realism, to represent the impact of nationalization on the town. The smashing fist of Quebec nationalism is paired with the architectural monolith of Hydro-Québec in a violent interruption of the story of the rural idyll of White Rapids (Figure 4.3).

The remainder of the narrative shifts from optimism to melancholy, as nationalist corporate takeover leads to the town's closure and the

years, The General became a local legend" (Blanchet n.pag.). Blanchet juxtaposes the bright modern idealism of the town-as-character to this murky mythological creature that represents the ancient and threatening character of the northern wilderness. The final pages of the story depict The General swallowing a house key the last resident throws over the bridge on his way out of White Rapids. In this way, Blanchet's book represents emplaced memory through juxtaposing culture to nature and the ephemeral to the eternal. The residents who strive to catch The General never will succeed, and indeed he outlives them all. In this poignant conclusion, Blanchet juxtaposes the ephemeral time of the company town, itself represented in mid-century design ephemera, to the enduring and even eternal time of the prehistoric fish whose dark sublimity contrasts with the bright beauty of the town.

White Rapids was a middle-class company town built according to the principles of "enlightened capitalism" that shaped the Garden City movement, popular in Canada during and shortly after the First World War. According to this ideology, company towns should be simple, practical, and provide for the workers' and their families' recreational needs to maintain a stable and content workforce.[4] Pine Point, in the former Northwest Territories, was built in 1963 as a typical Cold War-era company town defined by corporate control registered through spatial arrangement of houses close to the mine. It was funded by a partnership between the federal government and Cominco (the Consolidated Mining and Smelting Company of Canada) to house workers at the nearby open-pit lead and zinc mine on the south shore of Great Slave Lake. At its peak in the 1970s, Pine Point was home to 1,200 people, all of whom relocated when the mine closed in 1988 and all the town buildings were relocated or destroyed. In 2011, as part of the NFB's interactive web project initiative, The Goggles released *Welcome to Pine Point*.

This is a different sort of company town from White Rapids. While Blanchet draws the cheerful lives of middle-class, middle-aged workers, The Goggles focus on the more rough-and-tumble experiences of working-class young people, for whom the company town is a space of youth

---

4   Neil White's study of Corner Brook, Newfoundland, begins with a helpful historical survey of the Garden City movement in Canada, from its late nineteenth-century origins in Britain to its heyday in Canada during the First World War.

culture on the edges of the wilderness. As the narrator explains, "Most Pine Pointers think their home town was the best place on earth to have lived." The Goggles combine the visual and auditory textures of photo albums, high-school yearbooks, cassettes of cover bands, home videos, oral testimonies, and a commissioned soundtrack in their exploration of Pine Point at its height in the 1970s and 1980s. The nostalgic affect of this virtual scrapbook is evident throughout their self-reflexive commentary, such as when they say it was a great time to be young in the North, a "time before seatbelts and sunscreen." For the narrator, it was "maybe the last truly iconic era. The last time when we more or less went through the motions of change together, everyone excited by the same things at the same time." This nostalgia for a coherent community, a shared time on a shared territory called Pine Point, takes aesthetic form in the project's combination of archival artifacts and simple drawings that reproduce the colour schemes, film and photographic textures, and high-school yearbook design of the 1970s. The hairstyles and clothes of the many people we see signify this period as well, and so, like *White Rapids*, *Welcome to Pine Point* is a highly stylized memory object and a formal re-enactment of both the period and its visual periodization.

Like Blanchet, The Goggles use strips of text as visual elements themselves, although in this case there is a clear narrator: Mike Simons, one-half of the design team, who tells us in the Introduction that he visited Pine Point when he was nine. Simons's narration continues in textual strips layered over images, both static and moving, as the viewer navigates through the chapters and pages of the website. Also like Blanchet, this memory project depends on types of characters, although here they are living people whose oral testimonies are layered over images and sounds from their pasts: there is "the Beauty," Kim Feodoroff; the two Hryniuk brothers simply called "the Brothers"; and "the Bully," Richard Cloutier. Throughout the project, Simons comments self-reflexively on what his archival project means to him and those of his subjects who participated in the virtual reconstruction of their former home (Figure 4.5; see colour insert).

Just as Blanchet's book invites non-linear reading, both on individual pages and back and forth between them, in this interactive web documentary (i-doc) users can go to previous and next pages but also click on series of photographs and other documents within certain

town. A committee of members of the local chalet community around the village of White Rapids maintains this virtual local history museum and posts photos of former residents' reunions (see LaRochelle). In a poignant reversal of fortunes, the "bully" of Pine Point, Richard Cloutier, has become its most passionate protector (see Cloutier). Simons explains that he stumbled on Cloutier's website, *Pine Point Revisited*, and was hooked. A much more basic site than the interactive web documentary, Cloutier's virtual museum uses many of the same archival images and objects without much narrative, except that under "Rick's messages" he gives technical instructions for how to submit your own photos of Pine Point, situating himself as the centre of the dispersed community of Pine Pointers. Cloutier's transition from bully to protector is made all the more discordant when Simons reveals in *Welcome to Pine Point* that Cloutier is now paralyzed due to multiple sclerosis and uses voice recognition software for the laborious process of maintaining *Pine Point Revisited* (Figure 4.6; see colour insert).

The Goggles use the metaphors of sifting and burial to describe Cloutier's painstaking work of electronically editing his own and others' visual memories of Pine Point, implying that for every image recovered another is covered over, that for every new life an image gains on the Internet another is lost in its depths. This spatial image of the temporal work of visual memorials also operates in their own project's web design. Only if viewers navigate through The Goggles' site to reach a web chapter titled "Remains" can the voice-over we hear in the Introduction make sense: it is Cloutier's voice giving the computer commands: "mouseclick, tab, 579, click." The Introduction plays these words over grainy footage of a small plane landing in the tundra as the hand-scrawled question appears: "Imagine your home town never changed [. . .] would it be so bad?" Not only has the bully become protector of the memories of Pine Point, but, the documentary implies, this emotional and physical labour to curate and memorialize the place he terrorized in his youth is both individually and collectively redemptive. Cloutier's body is changing over time, but his intellect and feelings work to provide a stable memorial for a town that has disappeared. The metaphors of sifting and burial seem particularly apt to Pine Point, as they echo the images of digging, moving, and piling earth central to the mining labour of Pine Point. The language The Goggles use to describe a generalized desire to shape how we are remembered thus draws on the specificities of this company town's history of the violent disruption of a northern landscape and the town's subsequent burial in individual and collective memories.

The Goggles represent the industrial work of Pine Point in a way that ties it to Cloutier's emotional labour and their own artistic labour. In the web chapter about the mine, Simons asks, "Did the fact that their task was so intensely primal—digging raw materials out of the earth—sharpen their memories of the place? Did anyone ever pause to think that the work of Pine Point was a metaphor for the future of the town? It would live on only for those willing to dig into history, into memory." Pine Point closed in 1988 due to a combination of economic factors, including extended hauling distances, a plunge in deposits, and the high maintenance costs of the townsite. If the work of memory is like the work of digging in the mine, then we need to consider the consequences of this activity. Neither text addresses the ways Canadian company towns exploit natural resources, alter the landscape, and displace First Nations from traditional territories.[7] So, in their narratives that refuse the image of the company town as site of worker exploitation, both texts neglect these other types of exploitation. This is hardly surprising for, as Jacques Derrida and others remind us, every institution of the archive is also an institution of forgetting, at once "revolutionary and traditional" in its work to conserve the past and institute memory (Derrida 7). The emotional labour of both *White Rapids* and *Welcome to Pine Point,* and the aesthetic labour to visualize nostalgia and periodize places, renders two quite different versions of the company town that share this Derridean contradiction: they are at once radical for their playful attention to workers' community and traditional in their nostalgia for a coherent collective organized by industrial capitalism.

The play of these texts occurs in their slips between presence and absence, their memorialization of places in visual archives that become signs without referents, reproductions of reproductions. As a result, both projects display Derrida's notion that "the archive takes place at the place

---

7   For such a self-reflexive project, *Welcome to Pine Point* is surprisingly silent on the negative consequences of the company town on the environment or local First Nations, who remain largely absent in the documentary. One ironic trace of their presence and erasure in this company town is that the Pine Point high school was called Matonabbee High, presumably after the eighteenth-century Chipewyan leader who acted as a guide for Samuel Hearne and became a mediator between First Nations people and the Hudson's Bay Company. Contemporary and living First Nations people, however, are not part of this project's cultural memory of the company town.

of originary and structural breakdown of the said memory" (11). The archive is an "*external place* which assures the possibility of memorization, of repetition, of reproduction, of reimpression," yet that compulsion to repeat is always indissociable from the Freudian death drive, "and thus from destruction" (italics in original, 12). For Derrida, via Freud, the "archive fever" we are experiencing today is a burning passion to locate the archive right "where something anarchives itself" (91). To search for the archive at the point where it slips away is to experience a "nostalgia for the return to the most archaic place of absolute commencement" (91). Beginnings and endings, building and destruction, life and death, the archive and anarchive are central themes to both *White Rapids* and *Welcome to Pine Point*. The narrator's final comment on the demise of White Rapids marks the point where the lived experience ends and the archival memory begins: "From now on, the train would no longer stop at the Rapide Blanc station. The priest would stop coming and the pleasant murmur of summer evenings would be silenced forever" (Blanchet n.p.). The conditional grammar of these sentences reinforces the melancholic tone of the book's conclusion by imagining a probable future which has now become the past. *White Rapids* becomes a textual archive of what might have been but never was, a memory text of the life cycle of a town whose birth was as sudden and deliberate as its death. Similarly, the web page about the Pine Point Hotel Dining Room registers the visual archive as both a desire to return to origins and to reproduce the moment of forgetting (Figure 4.7; see colour insert).

Here, Simons goes underground into the basement of the town hotel to record it as a scene of decay. Its surprising survival, beneath the abandoned surface of the townsite, reminds the narrator of several Pine Pointers' competition to claim final possession of the place, to have been "the last person to. . . ." The photograph, overlaid with Simons's commentary, functions as an archive of the death rather than the life of the town, in itself archiving the residents' desires to have been present at the moment the place became non-place.

Company towns in the twentieth century were "powerful symbols of industrial modernity" that integrated remote regions into the ideal of the nation-state (Dinius and Vergara 4). As Dinius and Vergara, the editors of the collection *Company Towns in the Americas*, observe, "Not unlike trading posts or military forts in earlier stages of the colonization of the Americas, they brought more land, more natural resources, and more people (i.e., workers and consumers) under the control of the European colonizers and their descendants" (4–5). As postmodern projects about industrial modernity, both *White Rapids* and *Welcome to Pine Point* are quite self-reflexive about the failures of monopoly capitalism and its (neo-)colonial ideologies. As much as they long for the good feelings of belonging to these places, and the workers' communities they harboured, these projects highlight the ephemerality of company towns. Nature grows back at the end of both texts: in *White Rapids*, the General swallows the house key of the final departing resident, while in *Welcome to Pine Point*, split screens contrast old photos of buildings with recent images of the forest taking over the abandoned townsite. Ironically, the very profit drive that founded these towns led to their demise. Therefore, their disappearance from the Canadian industrial landscape is the condition of possibility for these artists to construct documents of longing for the era of designed communities in works that draft visual memory as a crucial part of the Canadian cultural landscape. In his *Canadian Encyclopedia* entry on company towns, Allan Seager writes that "Life in the company town could often be fulfilling, but never certain." As these projects suggest, the company town is a site of lived transience and uncertainty, yet the power of these places resonates over generations, even more so because the places are now gone and have entered the narrative spaces of mythology and the affective visual forms of nostalgia. These workers' communities that arose through and in spite of corporate design signify less Richler's "habit of dependence" in Canadian culture than a desire for a habit of community.

CHAPTER 5

•◆•

Preserving "the echoing rooms of yesterday": Al Purdy's A-Frame and the Place of Writers' Houses in Canada[1]

Brooke Pratt

"I can assure you that the preservation of this home is akin to the preservation of Canadian literary history. Should the plan to establish a poet-in-residence program be successful, the home will then also have a part in the future of Canadian literature."
Margaret Atwood, "Support" 152

The A-frame cottage built by Al and Eurithe Purdy in 1957 is an unassuming structure on the shores of Roblin Lake in the tiny community of Ameliasburgh, Ontario. Constructed largely out of salvaged materials with a view to economy and a pressing need to set down roots, the A-frame became Purdy's home for the bulk of his writing career. From the beginning, the house was a place of pilgrimage for a "CanLit" crowd of writers and academics. Although I was more than a decade too late to meet the man himself (Purdy died in 2000), I can now count myself among this list of devotees, having personally made the trek to the A-frame in the fall of 2011. Imagine my surprise when, after driving across the province in search of the house, I arrived to find none other than Margaret Atwood emerging from what I would soon discover to be Purdy's erstwhile writing workshop—a small outbuilding that sits

---

1 The phrase "the echoing rooms of yesterday" is a line from Purdy's poem "Method for Calling up Ghosts" (1965) in which he presents the process of artistic expression and the ability to imaginatively access the past in explicitly architectural and spatial terms (*Beyond* 92). His speaker walks through the streets of the town in which he resides in a deliberate effort to conjure up "all the people who / lived here once and fill the space I fill" (91). This "method" of imagining the past is a decidedly active one; Purdy employs the imperative *must*—"this method *must* be used to think of them"—to issue a warning to the reader: if we in the present are unwilling to envision the traces of those who came before us, such ghostly figures will inevitably—perhaps permanently—"disappear" (91, emphasis added).

adjacent to the house itself. I had just come from visiting his gravesite and the old mill pond that lies next to it; my plan was to have a quiet look at the A-frame before leaving town. I knew that Atwood was in the area: I had attended a public lecture she gave in Picton the previous night on the value of cultural and rural heritage, with some of the proceeds from ticket sales going to the Al Purdy A-Frame Association, a non-profit organization that has purchased the house from Eurithe Purdy with the aim of establishing an A-frame writer-in-residence program; yet, the last thing I expected when I finally pulled up next to the tucked-away property on Gibson Road was a face-to-face encounter with the famous "Ms. Atwood" herself.[2] I begin with this personal anecdote, not to paint myself as some kind of awestruck literary tourist or overeager "CanLit" groupie, but because I think it aptly demonstrates the continued allure of the A-frame as an iconic yet welcoming space whose lasting resonance is intimately connected not only to literary celebrity but also to Canadian cultural memory, built heritage, and the enduring power of place.

The Al Purdy A-Frame Association functions as a fascinating case study for investigating some of the key issues pertaining to literary community and cultural heritage in Canada today. In what follows, I consider the A-frame in relation to cultural memory—and to Purdy's own interest in fostering a sense of historical connection through place—by examining the discourse of inheritance and preservation that characterizes the public campaign to protect Purdy's house as a valuable site of Canadian literary history, using the association's official website and *The Al Purdy A-Frame Anthology* (2009) as my primary resources. Beginning with a closer look at Purdy's celebrity as a writer who has been given what D.M.R. Bentley deems to be "the dubious honour of being described as the 'most,' 'first,' and 'last' Canadian poet" ("Conclusion" 239), I then go on to explore the notion of place as celebrity in relation to national literary heritage through the example of Purdy's renowned A-frame.

In order to safeguard the house as a celebrated space that, for W.H. New, "holds a special place in Canadian cultural memory" ("Support" 155), the Purdy A-Frame project aims to raise enough funds to be able to "preserve it, create an endowment and establish a poet-in-residence

---

2   See Purdy's "Concerning Ms. Atwood" (1988) for his hyperbolic take on Atwood's boundless fame (*Beyond* 496–97).

program" (*Al Purdy*).[3] Only after the house has been fully restored will the association "apply for Heritage Designation under the Ontario Heritage Trust and the Prince Edward County Heritage Advisory Committee" with a view to "protect[ing] the building and its site for future generations" (*Al Purdy*). Because "Al was fascinated by the history of the county, and the country" and was himself "a chronicler of local and national history," the A-Frame Association feels it is only "fitting that the house become a permanent part of Canadian history" (*Al Purdy*).[4] Conserving Purdy's A-frame is less about maintaining the physical space itself exactly as it exists in the present moment (given that the building is in need of significant upgrades) than it is about ensuring that the house and its history do not go unremembered. To my mind, architectural preservation of this sort is as much an attempt to forestall the deterioration of collective memory as it is an act of memorialization. As Bentley convincingly suggests of the demolished and forgotten stone church that appears in Stephen Leacock's *Sunshine Sketches of a Little Town* (1912), "more is at stake here than a mere building" (*Mnemographia* 6). For Bentley, "the destruction of a familiar and historied edifice"—whether in Mariposa or Ameliasburgh—"amounts to the creation of a memory hole into which psychic energies and entities are irretrievably drawn, to the considerable impoverishment of what remains behind" (6). Judging by the materials presented on the Al Purdy A-Frame Association website and in *The Al Purdy A-Frame Anthology*, it is safe to say that one of the central goals of the Purdy project and its supporters is to prevent this kind of damaging "memory hole" while also furthering the development and dissemination of Canadian poetry through the creation of a poet-in-residence program.

"THE VOICE OF THE LAND"

As one of Canada's best-loved and most prolific poets, the literary celebrity of Al Purdy is difficult to deny, both within the academy and

---

3   The Al Purdy A-Frame Association (formerly known as the Al Purdy A-Frame Trust) successfully acquired the property in October 2012 and announced the inaugural call for applications to the A-Frame Residency Program in the spring of 2013; however, given the high cost of upgrading the house and setting up an endowment fund, the fundraising campaign remains ongoing.

4   It is worth noting that the Al Purdy A-Frame Association has the generous "blessing and support"—not to mention the active participation—of Purdy's widow when it comes to restoring the property, developing a writers' residency program, and eventually seeking official heritage designation for the house (*Al Purdy*).

beyond. Dubbed the "unofficial Canadian poet laureate" (Lynch et al. 1) by the editors of *The Ivory Thought: Essays on Al Purdy* (2008), he has achieved, in Bentley's words, "near-mythogenic status" ("Conclusion" 239). Winner of two Governor General's Awards for Poetry, Purdy was also awarded the Order of Ontario and the Order of Canada. His work has been adapted for radio and film; he was promoted as a finalist on the popular CBC competition *Canada Reads*; a larger-than-life Purdy statue graces Queen's Park in the city of Toronto; annual "PurdyFests" take place in Marmora, Ontario; and 21 April has been declared National Al Purdy Day by the League of Canadian Poets.[5] Although some of these honours were granted posthumously, John Bemrose maintains that Purdy "clearly enjoyed a poet's celebrity" during his lifetime as well, what with "the readings, the grant-assisted trips abroad and the literary friendships."

Based on this list of accomplishments and accolades, Purdy's celebrity status is unequivocal. Lorraine York reveals in *Literary Celebrity in Canada* (2007) that the "star image[s]" of some of Canada's best-known writers achieve their longevity, in part, through various extra-literary sites, including "festivals named in their honour, literary homes turned into thriving tourist sites, television and film adaptations, and many other representations in popular and educational culture" (37). Purdy's stardom is confirmed by some of the other conditions for literary celebrity that York identifies as well. Her suggestion that celebrity writers must "constantly negotiate the seemingly exclusive worlds of popularity and literary prestige" (31), for example, fits nicely with David Stouck's assertion that "[o]ne of the distinctive features of Purdy's career is that he has both a serious and a popular audience" (229). According to Stouck, "[n]o other Canadian poet has quite so successfully bridged the span between an intellectual and a popular readership" (229).

---

5   Details of Purdy's various awards and honours are as follows. He won the Governor General's Award in 1965 for *The Cariboo Horses* and again in 1986 for his *Collected Poems*. His well-known poem "At the Quinte Hotel" (1962) has been transformed into a short film starring Gord Downie of the Tragically Hip (2002) and an award-winning animated short produced by Bruce Alcock (2005). He has been portrayed (on both CBC radio and television) by the formidable Gordon Pinsent. In 2006, his *Rooms for Rent in the Outer Planets* (1996) was championed by Susan Musgrave for CBC's *Canada Reads* (making it one of the few books of poetry selected for the program to date). The Al Purdy memorial statue was installed at Queen's Park in 2008 at the behest of Scott Griffin (of the Griffin Poetry Association) as the country's first full-sized statue of a Canadian poet.

What is particularly interesting about Purdy is the extent to which his importance as a celebrated poet is couched in explicitly national terms. As Mark Silverberg observes, Purdy's "canonization" was "simultaneously a process of Canadianization" (226)—one that "has had the paradoxical effect of ensuring his centrality" within Canada "while limiting his power" on the international stage (233). Where Silverberg is wary of "reductively Canadianizing Purdy" (228), Sam Solecki is far more comfortable with Purdy's national status; he regards Purdy in decidedly effusive terms as "the major or central poet of our experience, the one who has given the strongest, most comprehensive, and most original voice to the country's cultural, historical, and political experiences and aspirations that have been at the heart of our various nationalist discourses since Confederation" (10).[6] Yet Purdy is a writer who is very much associated with *local* place, as his intimate connection to the A-frame readily attests.

Solecki attempts to reconcile this tension between the local and the national by arguing that Purdy's poetic "vision" adopts the "local" or "regional" as "the point of departure and as synecdoche for the national and universal" (12). Dennis Lee makes a similar move in describing the "incomparable poetic universe that grew from the house, the patch of ground, the neighbouring village, to take in all of Canada" (11). Understood in these terms, the A-frame itself can arguably be read as a local space that effectively stands in for the nation as a whole. The language surrounding the campaign to protect Purdy's house is a case in point: nearly all public expressions of support for the preservation of the A-frame—including the epigraph from Atwood that prefaces the present discussion—equate its potential destruction with the destruction of Canadian culture more broadly. In the same way that Purdy is rendered in national terms as "The Voice of the Land" (an honorary title bestowed upon him by the League of Canadian Poets that also forms the inscription along the spine of his book-shaped gravestone), his house is frequently portrayed as a crucial venue for Canadian cultural expression. In light of David Lowenthal's observation that "[c]onservation efforts are

---

6   Of course, not everyone agrees with perpetuating this portrait of Purdy as *the* national poet. See, for example, Frank Davey's "Al Purdy, Sam Solecki, and the Poetics of the 1960s" (2002) or David Solway's "Standard Average Canadian" (2003). In his comments on the critical debates over Purdy's canonical status, Tracy Ware rightly suggests that, '[d]epending on the critic, the glass is either overflowing or almost empty" ("Al Purdy" 229).

commonly couched in terms of some national legacy at risk" (*Possessed* 25), perhaps this portrait of Purdy's house as a Canadian cultural treasure is simply par for the course, although the extent to which promoters of the A-frame consistently tout its status as a national icon remains remarkable. Lee's description of the house as "a landmark in the country's imagining of itself" (13) provides a representative example. "[B]ecause so many of the poems written here explore the length and breadth of the country," writes Lee, "the house itself has become a living password, a concrete reminder of who and what we are. It would be folly to lose a totem of such power; we can't afford such cultural amnesia" (17). By couching the A-frame in the language of national symbolism and access to collective identity, Lee lends it a quasi-mystical quality that both positions the house as an irreplaceable entity and makes its place in Canada's national narrative appear indisputable.

HOUSING PURDY'S POETIC IMAGINATION

More than a few critics have commented on the overt correlation in Purdy's poetry between his struggle for successful poetic expression and the construction of his now legendary A-frame cottage.[7] George Bowering describes it as "the site where a pretty bum rimester turned into a masterful national poet" (118). For Bentley, "Purdy's A-frame corresponds in enough ways to his poetry to qualify as its architectural equivalent and commentary" (*Architexts* 296); Owen Percy even goes so far as to suggest that "[t]he A-frame has itself become a poem" ("Support" 155). Purdy, too, directly aligns the process of building the A-frame with his own poetic development. He recalls in *Reaching for the Beaufort Sea* (1993) that his "deficiencies as a house-builder were very obvious" (168):

> Sometimes all the studding, fibreboard, planks and nails danced in my head, like those ephemeral little flies that dance in bright sunlight. A dance of nothingness it seemed to me. And I felt dubious about the house ever being built. And I must do the things I do for their own sake, their own worthwhileness. Anything else was illusory. The poems

---

7   See especially Bentley (*Architexts* 276–98) and Solecki (136). See also Robert Stacey's essay in *The Ivory Thought* in which he argues that, in the case of Purdy's A-frame, "the erection of a dwelling prefigures and possibly enables the construction of a career-making poetic persona" (108).

I wrote must live in themselves, exist as entities and dance in their own sunlight. Without an audience, minus acclaim, even from a few. Thinking such things is treading gingerly close to a fifty thousand gallon tank of bullshit, teetering even. I wallow and rejoice in self-pity, my stiff upper lip is a dirty dishrag. In short, we built a house. (160)

The house provided Purdy with a space in which to write and gave him a much needed "place to stand on" (*Beyond* 157). Assembled from used lumber and other reclaimed construction materials, the A-frame is closely connected to both local place and local history. Not only was it put together with bits and pieces purchased from a demolished building in Belleville and scrap wood taken from a nearby Canadian Pacific rail yard, but its location on the shores of Roblin Lake also acted as a catalyst for Purdy's explorations of the surrounding landscape and its history— subjects that sit at the heart of so many of his best-known poems.[8] In Russell Brown's estimation, "Purdy's poetry really is a poetry of place— and also of placement," in part because it frequently strives to ground both the poet and his audience in a specific locale (61).

When it comes to fostering a sense of personal and historical connection, Purdy often stresses the importance of local place, especially in the poetry that grew out of his early years at the A-frame, including his "Roblin's Mills" poems (1965; 1968) and the oft-cited "The Country North of Belleville" (1965). In "Winter Walking" (1962), for example, Purdy's contemplative speaker reveals that "Sometimes an old house / holds me watching, still, / with no idea of time, / waiting for the grey shape / to reassemble in my mind" (*Beyond* 56). This disclosure of an attraction to spaces with an obvious sense of history, and of the concomitant desire to imaginatively "reassemble" the fragments of the past, speaks to a larger pattern that informs much of Purdy's poetry. As Bentley observes, "Purdy's faith in the historical imagination" is evidenced by "his perception of ruined houses and old plantations as the residue of the individual and collective characteristics of their creators" (*Mnemographia* 367). The

---

8   See, for example, Purdy's overtly autobiographical long poem *In Search of Owen Roblin* (1974) in which he readily confesses that, "In the midst of my own despair and failure / I wrote it all down on paper / everything I learned about Roblin's Mills / and the 19th-century village now called Ameliasburg / in a kind of fevered elation at knowing / the privilege of finding a small opening in / the past" (*Beyond* 247).

past is lost to us, in other words, without continued access to historic spaces as material artifacts. According to Lowenthal, "[m]emory and history both derive and gain emphasis from physical remains" (*Foreign* xxiii). Pierre Nora similarly argues that memory "relies entirely on the materiality of the trace" ("Between" 13) as does Gaston Bachelard, who contends that memories become less tenuous "the more securely they are fixed in space" (9).

As a prime illustration of a material space that "protects the dreamer" and "allows one to dream in peace" (6), the house is an essential form of shelter for the artist's imagination or what Bachelard terms the "creative psyche" (65). Unsurprisingly, the house is also an especially important image for Purdy, in terms of both its historical resonances and its role as a protective and productive refuge for the poet himself. In *Writers' Houses and the Making of Memory* (2008), Harald Hendrix explores "the significance of the writer's house as a medium of expression and of re-membrance" (2). He proposes that these two fundamental elements—ex-pression and remembrance—"fuse most in houses created by authors as a work of art, as a parallel or an alternative to their poetry or narrative" (1). In this way, "writers' houses are instruments of self-fashioning" that "may well be read as alternative autobiographies or self-portraits" (4)—a sentiment that nicely corresponds to Purdy's A-frame cottage. As a re-flective yet characteristically playful Purdy puts it in his autobiography: "I thought the projected [A-frame] house was something marvellous, a factual dream of solidity. I think, therefore I am: I think a house and ergo the house am?" (*Reaching* 159). Of course, in addition to "being shaped by writers," Hendrix continues, "houses shape the writers dwelling in them" (4). I have already rehearsed the impact that the A-frame had on Purdy's poetry, but the notion that "houses shape the writers dwelling in them" has significant implications for the house's future occupants as well, should it be successfully transformed into a retreat for resident po-ets as per the mandate of the Al Purdy A-Frame Association.

For Hendrix, a writer's house is a special kind of place: "[b]esides being a product of a writer's imagination or ambition, his house may also be a source of inspiration in its own right, or a material frame necessary for the production of literature" (4). Like Hendrix, Diana Fuss is interest-ed in the "powerful guiding influence" of writers' houses "on the creative lives of their famous inhabitants" (1). She maintains, in *The Sense of an Interior* (2004), that "[t]he theater of composition is not an empty space but a place animated by the artifacts, mementos, machines, books, and furniture that frame any intellectual labor. These material props, and the architectural spaces they define, are weighted with personal significance, inscribed in equal measure by private fantasy and cultural memory" (1). Hendrix arrives at a similar conclusion: for him, "[t]he captivating thing about writers' houses is not primarily their architectural quality or their grandeur as monuments that celebrate literary giants"; rather, it is the "simple objects that relate to the author's everyday life" (237) and appear to offer "material contact with the author" (1) that make a writer's house so appealing to visitors.

In his work on literary tourism more broadly, Hendrix demonstrates that "[p]laces associated with writers and their writings have attracted special attention since ancient times, both from fellow writers longing for some kind of intellectual exchange or simply keen on expressing their admiration, and from other persons eager to honour poets, their works, or literature as such" ("Early" 14). Anne Trubek also speaks to the cen-turies-old fascination with literary places in *A Skeptic's Guide to Writers' Houses* (2011), in which she examines the history of writers' houses and house museums in an American context in an effort to better understand what she calls, in the title of her opening chapter, "The Irrational Allure of Writers' Houses" (1). Despite her own prevailing skepticism, Trubek acknowledges that the act of preserving and visiting writers' houses can be motivated by a variety of factors, including everything from "celebrity lust" to "literary voyeurism" to the desire for "a secular form of paying homage" (3). Interest in Purdy's house is arguably driven, at least in some measure, by all three of these elements, although the Al Purdy A-Frame Association is careful to single out the latter as a primary influence on (and justification for) its fundraising campaign. Visitors to the official Purdy project website are explicitly told that the A-frame is worth pre-serving because it "draws people in. It's a pilgrimage to see the country, search out the places Al mentions in the poems, find the church spire and the site of Roblin's Mills, visit the Purdy Library in Ameliasburgh, cross the street to stroll down Purdy Lane to the graveyard where Owen Roblin and Al Purdy are buried along with the other pioneers of Prince Edward County." In this respect, Purdy's house both derives and retains a portion of its significance as a cultural icon from the assorted literary pilgrims who have been making their way to the area for more than half a century.

COMMEMORATING WRITERS' HOUSES IN CANADA

For all of these reasons (and more besides), writers' houses have become banner destinations for heritage tourism; yet while the transformation of such spaces into museums and other public institutions has blossomed in Europe and the United States, this trend has met with far less success in Canada where officially recognized sites and monuments specifically dedicated to Canadian writers remain relatively rare. With the notable exception of L.M. Montgomery's invented Avonlea and the thriving tourism industry based out of Cavendish, Prince Edward Island, literary houses in Canada have received little public attention; in fact, fewer than 1 percent of the more than 950 National Historic Sites listed in the official Parks Canada directory commemorate places of literary significance. The country has a total of eight National Historic Sites associated with Canadian writers, a full half of which are in the province of Ontario and two of which pay homage to the same writer. In addition to the ultra-famous Green Gables site, the other seven National Historic Sites that honour Canadian writers are the Leaskdale Manse in Uxbridge, Ontario (where Montgomery lived for the better part of her literary career); the Stephen Leacock Museum in Orillia, Ontario; Chiefswood (the former home of Pauline Johnson on the Six Nations Grand River Reserve near Brantford, Ontario); McCrae House in Guelph, Ontario (preserved in honour of John McCrae); Maison Gabrielle-Roy in St. Boniface, Manitoba; Ralph Connor House in Winnipeg, Manitoba; and Emily Carr House in Victoria, British Columbia. The Robert Service Cabin could also be added to this list, although it represents only one small part of a larger cultural landscape in Yukon Territory known as the Dawson City Historical Complex.[9] The Berton House Writers' Retreat in Dawson City and Historic Joy Kogawa House in Vancouver (neither of

---

9   There are several writers' houses in Canada that have received provincial or municipal heritage designations even if they have not been granted official status as National Historic Sites at the federal level. See, for example, Elizabeth Bishop House (Great Village, NS), Bliss Carman House (Fredericton, NB), Clifton (the former home of Thomas Chandler Haliburton in Windsor, NS), Haig-Brown Heritage House (Campbell River, BC), Margaret Laurence House (Neepawa, MB), Nellie McClung House (Calgary, AB), Montgomery Birthplace Museum (New London, PEI), Wallace Stegner House (Eastend, SK), and Stephansson House (Markerville, AB). Many of these sites operate as registered charities, some are open to the public as museums or interpretive centres, and others support active writers' residency programs.

which has received a heritage designation at the federal level) offer writer-in-residence programs similar to the one that the Al Purdy A-Frame Association hopes to provide, but they are located in the childhood homes of Pierre Berton and Kogawa—homes that arguably have far less resonance as sites of lively literary community than Purdy's A-frame cottage, which provided a regular meeting place for so many of his fellow writers. Purdy's house is also unique in that he designed and built it himself (with the help of family and friends).[10]

In *Mnemographia Canadensis* (1999), Bentley investigates "what happens when an old house and its grounds are simply too big or too costly to be maintained by a single family" (362), as is the case with Purdy's A-frame cottage: a threatened building of this sort can either be "demolished," "adapted" for alternative use, or officially "preserved as a monument" (362). Thankfully, the Al Purdy A-Frame Association has managed to save Purdy's house from the former fate with a view to maintaining its status as a productive space for writers and emphasizing its value as a site of Canadian cultural heritage. Yet, cultural preservation is never a simplistic undertaking; as Hendrix rightly points out, writers' houses that have been (or are in the process of being) commemorated as heritage destinations "not only recall the poets and novelists who dwelt in them, but also the ideologies of those who turned them into memorial sites" in the first place (*Writers'* 5). A writer's house thus goes from being a private source of "personal and individual" recollection to a shared space of "collective and cultural memory" (5). The caveat in Purdy's case is that his house has always been steeped in collective memory, in part because of its reputation as a convivial space for Canadian writers. Although "[t]here are many forms of literary worship other than homes" when it comes to commemorating celebrated writers, part of the appeal of writers' houses, according to Trubek, is that they are, by definition, "both private and

---

10 Like Purdy's A-frame, the significance of Historic Joy Kogawa House reaches beyond its connection to Kogawa as a Canadian writer (although the two spaces have decidedly different roles to play in the country's larger national narrative). As stated on its official website, Historic Joy Kogawa House "stands as a cultural and historical reminder of the expropriation of property that all Canadians of Japanese descent experienced after the bombing of Pearl Harbor in 1941." The Al Purdy A-Frame Association itself is reminiscent of the grassroots committee that successfully fought to save Kogawa's childhood home in 2006 (along with the help of the Land Conservancy of BC). Not only is the Historic Joy Kogawa House Society a useful model for what the A-Frame Association is trying to achieve, but they have also made a generous donation to the cause.

public" (5). The concept of literary celebrity itself rests on a similar combination of privacy and publicity, albeit a slightly less comfortable one; for York, "it seems anomalous even to consider a cultural job that is [. . .] most frequently performed in privacy as a likely basis for the sort of publicity-driven celebrity that is so pervasive today" (12), and yet this is exactly the sort of anomaly that writers' house museums inevitably represent.

CELEBRATING LITERARY COMMUNITY

In contrast to the general lack of official enthusiasm for literary heritage sites in Canada, proponents of conserving the A-frame have been unabashedly vocal in their praise for Purdy and his unconventional house as a site that has come to represent something much more than one poet's biography. Variously labelled as "the most significant writer's residence in the country" (Howard White 9), "the most storied writer's house in Canada" (Lee 17), and "the de facto epicentre of English Canadian poetry" (Vermeersch, Afterword 149), the A-frame is valued by many for its historic—and hopefully continuing—role as a gathering place for writers and a stimulating source of literary creativity. The A-Frame Association's projected poet-in-residence program (as outlined in detail on its website) also includes a community outreach component that highlights the significance of both Purdy and his house to the cultural and literary life of Ameliasburgh and surrounding area.

A large part of Purdy's status as a national celebrity has to do with his lifelong interest in artistic conversation and literary community. That there have been more tributes and appreciation pieces composed in Purdy's honour than have been dedicated to almost any other Canadian poet testifies to the scope of his influence as a generous (if sometimes irascible) mentor to generations of up-and-coming writers.[11] In a 2011 article on the A-frame written for *Cottage Life* magazine, Bowering observes that "[t]here was a time when the Purdys could toil in anonymity on their side of the lake [. . .]. But the poetry kept getting better, and the village kept

---

11 *The A-Frame Anthology* is filled with both original and reprinted tributes to Purdy's life and work from such writers as George Bowering, Steven Heighton, and F.R. Scott (among others). Other examples of poems or stories written in Purdy's honour include Kildare Dobbs' "Remembering Al Purdy," Susan Musgrave's "Thirty-Two Uses for Al Purdy's Ashes," poems by Stephen Brockwell and Gwendolyn Guth in *The Ivory Thought*, and selections from bp nichol, John Steffler, and Bronwen Wallace published in the Al Purdy special issue of *Essays on Canadian Writing* (1993).

getting more famous, and the cars full of poets kept coming through the village looking for the cottage on Gibson Road" (118). Tales of numerous literary visitors to the A-frame over the years have now become, in themselves, a significant part of its folkloric status. The Al Purdy A-Frame Association website reveals that even a partial tally of these visitors "reads like a who's who of Canadian letters—Margaret Atwood, Earle Birney, George Bowering, Lynn Crosbie, Dennis Lee, Steven Heighton, Patrick Lane, Margaret Laurence, Jack McClelland, John Newlove, Anna Porter, Elizabeth Smart, and the list goes on and on." Al and Eurithe Purdy welcomed a variety of other visitors to the A-frame as well, including "publishers, booksellers, academics, pool players, students, radio broadcasters, journalists, photographers, painters, and readers" (*Al Purdy*). John Robert Colombo remarks in *Canadian Literary Landmarks* (1984) that "[t]here is something surprising about seeing a site that has been written about; it is rather like meeting a celebrity" (10). The house itself, it seems, was (and is) a celebrity in its own right.

Given the history of Purdy's house as a hotbed of poetic discussion for a wide range of illustrious guests, the use of celebrity endorsement in the A-frame benefit campaign is not all that surprising. Produced at the publisher's expense as a fundraiser for the house, *The Al Purdy A-Frame Anthology*—replete with photographs of Purdy, the A-frame, and its many visitors—contains entries by several of the "who's who" contingent listed above (most of which consist of recorded anecdotes and memories), along with numerous poems and reflection pieces written by Purdy himself. His prominent place among this group of contributors—nearly half of the book's content comes from Purdy's own hand—almost makes it seem as though he too has become an advocate of the project, although his looming presence within the collection is also a testament to the volume of material that he wrote about the A-frame and its environs. On the whole, the anthology privileges the A-frame as a space that deserves to be remembered. In this context, it can fruitfully be read as an example of what Bentley describes as "architextual resistance to amnesia" of the sort that so much of Purdy's poetry itself embodies (*Architexts* 293).[12]

---

12 The editors of *The Ivory Thought* similarly position their book and the Purdy symposium that preceded it as explicit attempts to prevent "Canadian cultural amnesia, that blighting of the very literary past that feeds us, whereby eminent writers are soon forgotten following their deaths or a change in literary fashion and cultural politics" (Lynch et al. 4).

Support for the A-frame in its capacity as what New labels "a centre for the meeting of minds" ("Support" 155) has come in various
other forms as well: in addition to the assorted local fundraisers that
have cropped up since the Purdy project's conception,[13] Canadian literary celebrities as diverse as Leonard Cohen, Yann Martel, and Farley
Mowat have made individual financial contributions to the campaign (*Al
Purdy*). Beyond the realm of literary celebrity, there is an "academic campaign" to save the A-frame, initiated by David Bentley in the form of an
open letter of support signed by forty of his colleagues at postsecondary
institutions across the country (*Al Purdy*). The A-frame has also received
ample media attention. Writing for the *National Post*, Dave Bidini places
Purdy and his house in eminent literary company: "[f]or Canadian writers and poets, being able to work where their greatest did would provide
them with an unprecedented opportunity. It is the equivalent of putting
an Italian in Dante's villa, an Englishman sitting by candlelight at Keats's
desk." Jean Baird, who heads the Al Purdy A-Frame Association, has also
made attempts to advance the cause by likening the house to another
well-known literary landmark: "[i]t's a wonky little building, but I can't
imagine the Americans would let [Thoreau's cabin at] Walden Pond
[. . .] be torn down because it needs electricity upgrades" (qtd. in Emily
Jackson).[14]

In "The Culture of Celebrity and National Pedagogy," Smaro
Kamboureli argues that "one of the effects of the globalization of culture
[. . .] is that both literature and the humanities have achieved a visibility
and circulation they never enjoyed before" (38). Canadian culture, she
concludes, "has become a culture of celebrity" (38). For Kamboureli, the
"fundamental function" of Canada's so-called culture of celebrity is the
"manufacturing of public memory" in the service of hegemonic national

---

13 The most high profile of these events to date was the Al Purdy Show, a gala fundraiser and silent
auction that took place at Toronto's Koerner Hall on 6 February 2013 and included appearances
by Canadian celebrities ranging from Gord Downie to Gordon Pinsent.
14 Baird seems to have overestimated the American zest for (proactive) literary heritage: Henry
David Thoreau's cabin at Walden Pond was moved from the site (and eventually dismantled)
only a short time after he closed it up for good in the fall of 1847, several years before the publication of *Walden* (1854). The spot where his cabin once stood is now marked by a memorial
cairn and a series of granite posts, while a replica of the original building sits next to the Walden
Pond State Reservation parking lot. Despite the absence of Thoreau's original cabin, "Walden
Pond still receives the most visitors of all the literary sites in Concord" (Trubek 51–52). For
more on the history of this site, see Trubek (51–54).

identity (46). Although Kamboureli stops short of linking celebrity and the manufacture of public memory to the country's built heritage, I think it is a connection worth making. Read in the context of Kamboureli's efforts to tie together celebrity and collective memory, along with York's suggestion that celebrity is "crucially related to the social and historical construction of the self" (16), Purdy's position as a celebrated national poet and the A-frame's reputation as a significant literary landmark have considerable implications for the formation and expression of Canada's national selfhood in relation to both poetry and place. As I have been suggesting throughout this chapter, much of the critical and popular discourse surrounding Purdy's house explicitly relies on a narrative of national development and cultural inheritance. Take, for example, Marni Jackson's 2012 article in *The Globe and Mail*, in which she recounts how "[t]he A-frame, built with its scavenged lumber and paint, became one of the weight-bearing beams of a young culture still under construction." In the words of Stan Dragland, the house remains a place worth cherishing, both because "[i]t's packed with stories" and because "[a] dear shaggy spirit haunts it. For the love of that huge, indelible presence, and for the good of our collective soul, let's make damn sure it's preserved" (19). But the campaign to save Purdy's A-frame is about more than preservation alone: the Al Purdy A-Frame Association's proposed poet-in-residence program envisions the house not simply as a marker of literary history but as a vibrant site of cultural continuity as well.

The conversation around Purdy's A-frame house reveals a great deal about the nature of his status as a celebrated Canadian poet and the complexity of literary celebrity more broadly as it relates to place, cultural heritage, and collective memory. In addition to the various contradictions that can be found in Purdy's life and work (between the popular and the prestigious, the public and the private, the local and the national, the mundane and the profound), there is a certain irony in the attempt to make permanent a ramshackle house that was built with salvaged materials by a poet who was a traveller for much of his life. And, as Anne Trubek reminds us, writers' houses might well be "venerated places" but they are also "expensive to own" (8). Yet the A-Frame Association and its many supporters make a compelling argument for Purdy's house as a special case, given what Dennis Lee fondly refers to as its "hospitality to other writers" (12)—a hospitality that could continue in perpetuity when (and if) the house becomes host to a writer-in-residence program.

Al Purdy is remembered by many of his peers as a poet who taught other writers how to be at home in Canada; the extension of this appreciation to Purdy's house at once confirms the A-frame as a vital site of artistic community and solidifies Purdy's consecration as a national literary celebrity.

PART II

·—·

Memory Transference:
Postmemory, Re-memory,
and Forgetting

CHAPTER 6

•◆•

Learning Sauerkraut: Ethnic Food, Cultural Memory, and Traces of Mennonite Identity in Alayna Munce's *When I Was Young and In My Prime*

Robert Zacharias

"What remains of what does not remain?" asked Hildi Froese Tiessen recently, borrowing a line from Robert Kroetsch to contemplate what will be "Mennonite" about tomorrow's Mennonite literature ("Homelands" 21).[1] Five years after declaring literary authors the primary forces "shaping [. . .] the new cultural memory of the Mennonites" ("Mennonite/s" 48), Froese Tiessen now worries that the disappearance of the most recognizable vestiges of the distinct Mennonite heritage that nurtured the surprising explosion of the field in the 1980s means that the "new Mennonite writing" may not be recognizably Mennonite at all. "In the new Mennonite writing, history and tradition are no longer authoritative," she writes, noting that it seems "less concerned [. . .] with group history than with individual becoming; less compelled by essential identity than by multifaceted identifications" (14–15). In this paper, I want to trace the shifting role of "Mennonite food" in Alayna Munce's remarkable first novel *When I Was Young and In My Prime* (2005), where it moves from a transparent marker of a migrant Mennonite identity to a form of what Smaro Kamboureli has called "diasporic mimicry," as an invitation to consider food as a key but ambivalent component in the cultural

Acknowledgements: A version of this essay was first presented at the conference *Foodways: Diasporic Diners, Transnational Tables and Culinary Connections*, held at the University of Toronto in 2012, and I am appreciative of the valuable feedback it received. I would also like to acknowledge and thank the Banting Postdoctoral Fellowship program and the Social Sciences and Humanities Research Council of Canada for generously supporting this research.

1   This is also the title of an earlier, shorter draft of the *Mennonite Quarterly Review* essay, published in *Rhubarb* 30 (Summer 2012): 12–15.

memory and collective identity of Russian Mennonites in Canada. What
"trace" will remain in Mennonite writing (22), Froese Tiessen wonders,
to enable readers to mark a cultural identity that is losing its clear ties
to the past and, with it, its claims to normativity (19)? One answer, suggested by Munce's novel and less surprising than it might initially appear,
is *the smell of sauerkraut*.

When I Was Young and In My Prime tells the story of Helena
Friesen, a young woman of Mennonite descent living in the Parkdale
area of Toronto at the turn of the millennium. Much of the novel involves Helena learning, and coming to grips with, the dramatic history
of her grandparents, Peter and Mary Friesen, who fled to Canada when
the once-prosperous Mennonite colonies of Ukraine violently collapsed
in the wake of the Russian Revolution. Helena's self-conscious efforts to
live an ethical life come to centre on her relationship with her grandparents as they transition through the various stages of old age, including
her grandmother's descent into the disorientation of Alzheimer's and her
grandfather's rapidly declining health. Originally written as a collection
of poems, Munce's revised prose narrative hangs loosely over a structure
that retains much of its original poetic form; the result is a deeply affective meditation on aging and contemporary urban life, one that contains
a relatively brief but poignant commentary on the shifting structure of
Mennonite cultural identity, mediated at key moments through a deep
concern with Mennonite food and foodways.[2]

While the cultural significance of food has long been a topic of interest in such fields as anthropology and ethnography, the past several
decades have seen a surge of interdisciplinary interest in the field. In
the introduction to their second edition of *Food and Culture: A Reader*
(2007), Carole Counihan and Penny Van Esterik note the explosion
in the field since the first edition a decade earlier, claiming to be "as-
tounded at how food has permeated almost every scholarly field" (1).
The 2005 establishment of the interdisciplinary *Canadian Association for
Food Studies*, the 2012 publication of two Canadian readers in the field,
Critical Perspectives in Food Studies and *Edible Histories and Cultural
Politics: Towards a Canadian Food History*, along with books like Lily

---

2 *Foodways* is a critical term in the field "encompass[ing] the eating habits and other food-relat-
ed cultural and social practices of a particular group, region, or historical period" (Iacovetta,
Korinek, and Epp 5–6).

Cho's *Eating Chinese: Culture on the Menu in Small Town Canada* (2012) and conferences like *Foodways: Diasporic Diners, Transnational Tables and Culinary Connections* (2012), illustrate the expanding interest in the field in Canada.[3] While one might expect the rise of food studies to overlap with the contemporary "boom" in cultural memory studies on the question of cultural identity, the two fields appear to have drawn on surprisingly distinct critical genealogies.[4] In Munce's novel, by contrast, food and cultural memory are intimately connected, serving not only to connect Peter with his Ukrainian and Mennonite pasts, but also as the primary site through which Helena attempts to forge a connection, through a larger Mennonite heritage, to her grandfather.

The Mennonites in Canada are the descendants, either by blood or by faith, of a sixteenth-century movement of religious dissenters collectively known as the Anabaptists. With its earliest roots in present-day Switzerland, Germany, and the Netherlands, the Anabaptists became loosely organized around the writings of a Dutch convert named Menno Simons, as part of what is sometimes referred to as the "radical wing" of the Protestant Reformation. Over time, the widespread persecution of what was initially a diverse group of religious dissenters worked to reorient the Mennonites into small and tightly knit communities. Swiss Mennonites were among the religious communities immigrating to Pennsylvania as part of William Penn's "holy experiment" during the seventeenth century, while many of the Dutch Mennonites fled first to the Prussian Vistula delta (present-day Poland), then on to Southern Russia (now Ukraine). In Ukraine, the Mennonites built a remarkable network of agricultural, religious, educational, and economic institutions sometimes referred to as the "Mennonite Commonwealth," which collapsed in the chaos that followed the Russian Revolution. Through a series of three mass migrations (1870s, 1920s, and 1940s), tens of thousands of these so-called "Russian Mennonites" immigrated to North and

---

3   An interesting precedent for such work is Margaret Atwood's 1987 anthology, *The CanLit Foodbook: From Pen to Palate, a Collection of Tasty Literary Fare* (Toronto: HarperCollins). Compiled as a fundraiser for PEN Canada, the anthology is a selection of Canadian literary texts engaging with food.

4   To take a superficial but telling example of these distinct critical traditions, it is worth noting that neither *The Collective Memory Reader* nor *A Companion to Cultural Memory Studies* have an index reference for "food" or "foodways," while *Food and Culture: A Reader* and *Food: The Key Concepts* have no index references for "cultural memory" or "memory" (although each of these latter texts do briefly engage with memory).

South America. Many contemporary Mennonite churches continue to stress a number of the early Anabaptists' primary concerns, including adult baptism, pacifism, the separation of church and state, and a commitment to simple living.

Today, the term *Mennonite* is primarily a religious designation referring to the 1.6 million baptized members of Mennonite churches worldwide, two-thirds of whom live in Africa, Asia, and Latin America. Within the context of Canadian literary studies, however, *Mennonite* refers, almost exclusively, to the direct descendants of the Russian Mennonites. As I've argued elsewhere, Canadian literary studies have largely disavowed the religious/theological aspects of Mennonite literature, part of the field's larger misrecognition of religious difference in ethnic or racialized terms. Although the notion of any split between an ethnic and a religious identity has been deeply contentious in Mennonite circles, it is worth noting that in this sense, *When I Was Young* is entirely in keeping with the position of Mennonite identity within the critical discourse in Canadian literature: in Munce's novel, where none of the characters attend a Mennonite church or practise anything recognizable as a Mennonite faith, there is little question that the proper referent for Mennonite foodways is ethnic, rather than religious. What is more, Munce's engagement with food and identity relies heavily on the Russian Mennonite 1920s migration story, a key narrative that has long served as a privileged site of debate in the larger negotiation of Mennonite cultural memory in Canada.[5] The relationship between writing, ethnic foodways, and Mennonite cultural identity in Canada is neatly captured in a recent special issue of *Rhubarb* magazine (a publication of the Mennonite Literary Society that lists its past issues under the heading of "preserves") entitled "The Food Issue: Writing that Really Schmecks" (Summer 2010).

When I Was Young begins its engagement with food as a marker of cultural identity early, tightly weaving it into Helena's growing interest in reconnecting with her grandparents. In one of the novel's first sections, for example, Helena wanders the aisles of a No Frills supermarket in Toronto while contemplating their relationship. "I find myself thinking more and more about my grandparents," the section begins, moving

---

5   On this point and the claims of this larger paragraph, see my study, *Rewriting the Break Event: Mennonites and Migration in Canadian Literature* (Winnipeg: U of Manitoba P, 2013).

quickly to make clear the implicit link between the supermarket and the direction of her thoughts:

> I think about their garden and preserves. Their secret recipe for goose-berry jam. Their plastic milk bags of frozen green beans. How they pickled everything from plum tomatoes to asparagus to carrots, the jars lined up on shelves in their basement, an inconceivably intimate grocery store. How, when I was a child, the jars were a lovely quirk particular to my grandparents: no one else I knew grew and preserved their own food; it seemed an elegant and ingenious enterprise. How it took me years to realize it was simply the remnants of a mode of sur-vival, universal, obsolete. (9)

Helena's juxtaposition of a Toronto supermarket with the "inconceivably intimate grocery store" of her grandparents' pantry constructs a common but important binary between an anonymous and corporatized urban space against the intimate (and implicitly more "authentic") world of her grandparents' basement. The novel complicates this notion of authentic-ity as it progresses, but here I want to underline how this early passage not only introduces Helena's connection to her grandparents through the frame of food and foodways, but that it does so while emphasizing how time and comfort can render "the remnants of a mode of survival" of a migrant experience—recognizable as the "traces" of a key period of Mennonite history—into "a lovely quirk" in contemporary Canada. By the end of the scene, we are given her grandfather's first words in the novel, a brief message left on Helena's answering machine that fore-shadows what is, for me, the key scene in the novel: he has, we are told, "bought the cabbages for sauerkraut" (9).

While food and identity are arguably always in close proximity, the conceit of "ethnic food" reveals the ties between food and identity to be particularly explicit for migrant or diasporic communities. In an essay tellingly entitled "You Are Where You Eat: Ethnicity, Food and Cross-Cultural Spaces," Enoch Padolsky suggests that "food in literature pro-vides a terrain [. . .] for sorting out what is happening in the complex relationship between ethnicity and Canadian cross-cultural spaces" (21). Padolsky's claim about the intersection between food and ethnicity in Canadian writing, along with its cartographic language, holds true in Munce's novel, where Peter's memories of Ukraine are consistently routed through his former village's lush communal orchard, a staple of the Mennonite colonies in this period. One early passage, for example, not only shows Peter using the orchard as a means to link himself to earlier generations of Mennonites, it also reiterates an ethnicized class division that marked the Mennonite experience in Ukraine:[6]

> We Mennonites—the settlers I mean, my forefathers—they planted it. First thing they did when they arrived. The Ukrainian peasants, they were jealous as Judas over that orchard but, as Father used to say, it didn't just appear from nowhere. Apples, peaches, pears, apricots, cherries, plums. [. . .] Zwieback buns with stewed plums. Or pluma moos with cream. Or plum plauts hot from the oven. [. . .] Even now, the insides of my cheeks water just thinking of the place. (49)

It is precisely the remembering of this former homeland through food, rather than through, say, the landscape, or through its farmyards or religious institutions, that allows Peter to reconstruct something of that home in southern Ontario by planting his own small fruit garden. Pamela Klassen has referred to this process of reconstruction as a key component in the "Mennonite romance with food," whereby "continuing traditions from the old country gave Russian Mennonites [. . .] a visceral (and perhaps romanticized) connection with a way of life [in Ukraine]" (242). For Peter, this "romance" means that his migratory memories are so invested in Mennonite foodways that his mouth waters "just thinking of the place" that he once called home (49).

Peter's description of the Mennonites' communal orchard in Ukraine is worth dwelling on slightly longer. Traced through a resource like Norma Jost Voth's *Mennonite Foods and Folkways from South Russia,* which carefully catalogues the "remnant traces" that reveal how "Russian Mennonite cuisine follows these people's migrations" (30), Peter's brief list of "Mennonite foods" becomes a map of Mennonite history: the zwieback, or doubled buns, are a vestige of the Mennonites' time in the Netherlands; the pluma moos and plauts were adopted during their century in Poland; the orchard's many fruits are grown in

---

6   Similarly, Helena's grandmother's favourite story of life in Ukraine recounts the poor table manners of the fiancé of their best farmhand, which were so poor that her grandmother would refuse to eat at the same table (99; 110).

Ukraine, and so on. Indeed, the passage offers what the anthropologist Lidia Marte has called a cultural "foodmap," which "trac[es] the boundaries of 'home' through [. . .] food-place connections" (261). "Through food mapping," Marte continues, "we can get a glimpse at the way migrant memory work helps produce a sense of place through food roots and routes" (262). Where Marte is interested in maps in the most literal terms— in "producing a graphic depiction" of food routes (261)—her work offers a concise term for the way in which the foodways of the Russian Mennonite community in Canada quietly bears witness to the serial migrations of their past. Indeed, drawing on Marte's term and Roland Barthes' well-known argument about the function of food more generally—that "all food serves as a sign among the members of a given society" (21)—we can say that Peter's list signifies not simply as *other places*, but as former homelands that span centuries into the past. It should be clear from this list that the construction of cultural identity is an aggregative process, one marked by change, adaptation, and transformation (although, as we will see, the fluidity and complexities of such identities are often forgotten). From this perspective, eating zwieback or pluma moos becomes both the consumption of Mennonite history and a means to quietly express and experience a historicized form of cultural belonging.

What is more, the larger context for Peter's list of Mennonite foods further abstracts the role of food in the novel. In the violent aftermath of the revolution, food becomes temporalized, at once a marker of hunger and a measure of the community's decline. The Mennonites, Peter recalls, became constantly "aware [of] how many days worth of bread we had left, how much dried fruit. We measured food in days," he says, "and let me tell you we were experts" (55). The passage begins with the murder and burial of Peter's father; notably, he is buried in the very orchard that Peter identifies so strongly with his time in Russia, rather than in one of the graveyards that typically lay on the outskirts of such villages. When, in the section's closing image, the soldiers are shown cutting down the communal orchard for firewood, they are destroying the source of the fruit that Peter's list links closely to Mennonite foodways, as well as a final source of food for the family. More than this, however, they are also, quite literally, setting his father's graveyard on fire. It is in this context, where "Mennonite food" signifies well beyond its value as bodily nourishment and into the realms of communal history, genealogical memory, and cultural identity, that the novel's engagement with Mennonite food-ways must be located and understood.

OF MIMICRY AND MENNONITES (WITH RECIPES!)

While the most traditional of Canada's Mennonite communities still self-consciously mark their cultural difference through conserva-tive dress and modes of transportation, few of today's urban-dwelling Mennonites retain the most visible markers of Mennonite identity. Similarly, the vast majority no longer speaks Low German, the distinc-tive Mennonite dialect. As descendants of White, European immigrants living in a country historically dominated by White, European immi-grants, Russian Mennonites can—and largely have—slipped easily and often eagerly into the conventional mainstream of Canadian society. For those interested in maintaining the parameters of the community's distinct cultural identity, then, Mennonite foodways have become exag-gerated in their importance, as "one of the last vestiges of ethnic distinc-tiveness for people who are otherwise fully assimilated into mainstream culture" (Bailey-Dick 175). Or, as Voth rather starkly puts it, "Who are the Russian Mennonites today? [. . .] In many cases only our ethnic foods still bind us together" (17).

In the quarter-century since Voth identified food as the sole binding element for the community, Russian Mennonite food has only grown in its prominence. There are a number of well-known older Mennonite cookbooks that continue to sell well, for example, including *More-with-Less* (now in its forty-seventh printing with sales of over 800,000 cop-ies worldwide) and Edna Staebler's *Food That Really Schmecks* (recently reissued by Wilfrid Laurier UP with a foreword by Wayson Choy), and newer books like *Mennonite Girls Can Cook* (2011) have become sur-prise bestsellers.[7] Many of these cookbooks actively blur the line between what might appear their primary utilitarian purposes—recipes, mea-surements, etc.—and the construction of a distinctly "Mennonite" lens through which the recipes are to be understood. The subtitle of the twen-ty-fifth anniversary edition of Doris Janzen Longacre's *More-with-Less*

---

7   *Mennonite Girls Can Cook* focuses on food in the Russian Mennonite tradition, while *Food That Really Schmecks* focuses on the Swiss Mennonite tradition. *More-with-Less*, by contrast, presents itself as a "world community cookbook."

makes this dual purpose clear: "Recipes and suggestions by Mennonites on how to eat better and consume less of the world's limited food resources." Similarly, Lovella Schellenberg et al.'s *Mennonite Girls Can Cook* divides its pages of recipes with regular "Bread for the Journey" sections, complete with Bible verses and brief commentaries.

While the popularity of such books surely reflects a widespread interest in Mennonite culinary arts, it is also readable as evidence of the ongoing exoticization of Mennonite cultural identity. In a recent piece published in the American journal *Mennonite Life,* Kirsten Beachy offers a caustic assessment of this process at work, in the form of a faux-letter from a Mennonite academic to an editor at a publishing house.[8] Beachy's critique extends to what she suggests are the gendered and neo-colonial connotations of an uncritical celebration of Mennonite cookbooks: a patronizing editor requests that she "add a chapter of recipes to [her] book of essays on Mennonite theopoetics and literary history" and rename it *"Mennonite Girls Can Read (With Recipes!),"* presumably because she is a "Mennonite girl"; the cultural colonialism of "world community cookbooks" is parodied by the adoption of foods like "Bhati Stew"—originally prepared for the hopelessly naive narrator by an impoverished nomadic family from "Arvedistan"—as a distinctly Mennonite dish. For Beachy, the emphasis on distinctly Mennonite foodways has troubling implications that extend into the field of literary studies.

While a firm link between food and identity is often assumed through the straightforward logic that holds "you are what you eat," Beachy's article is part of a wider interrogation of such claims. In fact, a strong countervailing argument has been made by critics exploring the exoticization of "ethnic food" as the construction and consumption of *otherness*, in which cultural, ethnic, and racial differences are depoliticized and commodified as a form of culinary tourism, or what one critic calls "cultural food colonialism" (Heldke xv).[9] In such a model, "ethnic food" becomes less the bearer of distinct cultural memories and more the locus of a hegemonic imagination, wherein the foodways of the

---

8   I thank Julia Spicher Kasdorf for alerting me to Beachy's article.
9   For an exemplary case of such an argument, see Heldke's "Let's Cook Thai: Recipes for Colonialism," in Counihan and Van Esterik. For a trenchant response, see Uma Narayan's chapter "Eating Culture" in her study *Dislocating Cultures: Identities, Traditions, and Third-World Feminism* (New York: Routledge, 2005).

dominant culture are normalized, and the foodways of minoritized communities are tokenized and consumed as reified markers of "authentic" cultural difference. Beachy's critique of Mennonite cookbooks adds to this critical conversation by reminding us of the ways in which the active promotion of cultural foodways may unwittingly participate in the process of their own exoticization. Munce's novel, I want to suggest, presents a fascinating variation on this critique, for Helena's primary concern in engaging Mennonite foodways is not to perform her Mennoniteness for an appreciative host community, but rather to learn to perform a cultural identity she already imagines to be her own.

I want to turn now to a final passage from *When I Was Young*, in which the novel's brief but consistent engagement with Mennonite foodways comes to a head. Peter, we discover, has been trying to teach Helena how to make sauerkraut, traditionally a favourite dish among Russian Mennonites (Voth 274). Helena has brought a pail of the salted cabbage back to her apartment, where she has left it to ferment in a back room. When a plumber knocks on the door asking to get at the building's water lines, Helena balks, realizing they are beside the pail. "I'm instantly aware that his nose won't be adjusted to the stink of out-of-control sauerkraut," she thinks (135). When the worker is finished, an embarrassed Helena decides to try and deal with the smell, only to overhear the plumbers talking in the apartment below. "[T]he one workman [is] telling the other how my place stinks," she says, "how disgusting it is, how there's definitely something rotting up there" (135). Given the importance of Mennonite foodways in the novel's larger construction of Mennonite identity, and given that Helena is using the sauerkraut as a means of connecting with her grandfather, we might expect her to simply dismiss the plumber's concerns. Instead, she responds with a three-page stream-of-consciousness monologue that reveals how thoroughly her engagement with the food has been overdetermined as a marker of cultural and familial identity. "I'm working up my courage," she says, to go downstairs and "explain about the sauerkraut":

> how I hate the stink too, how I wish I could just dump the whole fuck-ing crock into the compost except I don't have a compost so it would have to be the garbage, but that I can't because, you see, because of my grandfather.

Because—how to explain—because of the small messages he leaves to himself [. . .] and because of the shaky hand he writes them in.

Because his house is for sale and I'm guessing this was the last time we'll ever make sauerkraut together. [. . .]

Because the first year I made sauerkraut with him I told everyone, *Did you know there's no vinegar in sauerkraut.* [. . .]

Because we have the same taste for vinegar. Because I don't speak Low German or German or Ukrainian or Russian or Dutch.

Because the lantern that used to light his way to the barn for morning chores now hangs unlit in my living room.

Because he bought thirty cabbages and bragged to the Mennonite woman who sold them that his granddaughter wanted to learn sauerkraut.

Because she was impressed. (135–36)

As the passage makes clear, any identity-forming function played by the sauerkraut has already been mediated through, and complicated by, a more intimate network of familial ties. At the same time, Helena clearly understands the food as enabling a vague but vital connection between herself and a larger cultural community, represented here by an anonymous Mennonite woman who is apparently pleased by second-hand news of Helena's efforts. If it is true, as Marlene Epp has suggested, that "in immigrant experience across generations, language is the first to disappear and food is the last" ("Memories" 33), then we can see Helena's efforts to "learn sauerkraut"—a project undertaken at least in part because of her inability to speak five of the six languages spoken by her grandfather—as an effort not only to connect with her grandparent, but also to lay claim, in however small and conflicted a manner, to a larger and longer Mennonite cultural memory.

To better understand the complex interplay between identity and food in this passage, it is worth turning to Kamboureli's influential study *Scandalous Bodies*, which introduces the concept of "diasporic mimicry" in reference to the heritage displays commonly supported by Canadian multiculturalism. Differentiating diasporic mimicry from Homi Bhabha's seminal discussion of mimicry in the colonial context, Kamboureli suggests that in the diasporic subject's self-conscious invocation, or imitation, of the most reproducible elements of her own heritage, the "subject and object [. . .] are one and the same" (110). Although "the operative trope is a discourse of authenticity" in such moments, Kamboureli insists that it "functions ironically, at the expense of the ethnic subject herself" (110). In diasporic mimicry, she concludes, "the ethnic subject" ultimately "experiences a loss of identity," rather than its affirmation (111). Although Kamboureli acknowledges the positive potential inherent within certain modes of mimicry, she stresses its dangers because, as she points out, "there is always something disfiguring that survives the performance" (110). Turning to Lacan, she identifies this "something" as "the stain [that] leaves a 'track', 'a trace'" that can be located in "a desire whose performative function often reveals that desire and reality to be at odds with each other" (112). Here, then, is a very different ethnic "trace" than the one proposed by Froese Tiessen at the outset of this essay. What remains in diasporic mimicry is not the vestiges of distinct community, identifiable by the Mennonite reader in search of a text to "identify [her] to herself" ("Homelands" 22), but rather the "stain" of a community attempting to hold on to those vestiges by imitating itself under the aegis of cultural difference.

Much as Kamboureli's discussion of mimicry focuses on a highly mediated performance of ethnicity, Helena's engagement with "Mennonite food" is routed through her self-conscious attempt to learn and perform the process—or, better, the *ritual*—of its production. In much the same way that she has propped up her grandfather's farmlamp, left unlit, as a decorative item in her living room (136)—this is the lamp that "used to light his way to the barn for morning chores" (136)—the sauerkraut has, for Helena, effectively detached from its function as food, and now stands simply as a reified and decontextualized identity marker she is attempting to claim as her own. While diasporic mimicry may operate, by definition, within the context of a normalized dominant society, Munce's novel reminds us that that society need not be the intended audience of its performance. After all, neither the non-descript plumbers nor her non-Mennonite husband have any interest in Helena's performance. In fact, the primary function of Mennonite food in the novel is not to endear the minoritized community to a skeptical majority at all, but rather precisely the opposite: Helena's efforts to "learn sauerkraut" is a self-conscious deployment of a distinct cultural identity in an effort to enable, affirm, and protect a unique familial connection across ages and generations. "Even while Mennonites were increasingly assimilating into Canadian middle-class society," writes Marlene Epp, "the retention of traditional foods was a relatively benign way to signify an identity that made them *not completely mainstream*" ("Memories" 37; emphasis mine). For Helena, the aim is not to create bridges to a larger host community, but rather to create an intentional distance from it—to not be "completely mainstream"—as a means of establishing an enduring connection to her grandfather that is encased within the performance of a distinct cultural identity.[10]

But why sauerkraut? Why not have Helena learn how to make a dish with more obvious and distinct ties to the Russian Mennonite tradition, such as zwieback? In order to understand the particular role played by sauerkraut in the novel, we must keep in mind the above discussion of the distancing function of mimicry, as well as Kamboureli's discussion of mimicry as something which, taking up the language of Canadian multiculturalism, aims at the "'preservation' . . . of ethnic traditions" (110). The most obvious element of sauerkraut in such a context is implied in Norma Voth's suggestion that the "reward" for the challenges of making sauerkraut is "a constant supply throughout the winter" (274). As a preserve, sauerkraut can be left on a shelf for months without spoiling, making it a useful metaphor for Helena's desire to retain a connection to her grandfather as his health rapidly declines.

It is Helena's attempts to learn/perform sauerkraut specifically as a *distancing gesture* that will mark her Mennonite identity while maintaining its separation from a mainstream Canadian one, however, that proves the key to understanding her frustrations with the food. In a section

---

10 For related and valuable discussions of self-imitation in the context of multiculturalism, see Fred Wah's work on "faking it" in *Faking It: Poetics and Hybridity* (2000) and Rey Chow's critique of "coercive mimicry" in *The Protestant Ethnic and the Spirit of Capitalism* (2002). While both Wah and Chow discuss the self-imitation of the racialized or ethnic subject, Wah's work emphasizes the strategic and subversive possibilities of self-mimicry, while Chow emphasizes the political pressures that coerce the ethnic subject into such a performance. For a useful review of Wah's and Chow's work, see Carrie Dawson, "The Importance of Being Ethnic and the Value of Faking It."

entitled "That Sauerkraut Smell," Edna Staebler offers some suggestions on how to deal with the distinct and powerful smell of fermenting sauerkraut. "I don't know any way that you can prevent the smell of cooking sauerkraut from permeating the house," she writes. "Because it can be rather overpowering I open the draft of my fireplace, light a bayberry-scented candle, and occasionally open a door to let in a breeze. After a while I get used to the sauerkraut smell and let it take over, assuring myself that on a cold winter's day no aroma could be more warmly inviting" (89). Helena, however, is never able to embrace the smell, its taking over of her apartment, or even its taste. Rather, she openly admits her sauerkraut is "out-of-control"; it "stinks"; it is covered in "scum"; she "hates it" and wants to "dump the whole fucking crock" (135). If Susan Miller is correct in arguing that disgust is the "gatekeeper emotion," with a primary function of affectively distancing the self from the foreign or *other*, we can say that Helena finds herself on the wrong side of what she not only recognizes but is attempting to deploy as an ethnic shibboleth. Here, then, is the spectre of Kamboureli's notion of the ethnic trace as "stain," as the mark of "a desire whose performative function [. . .] reveals that desire and reality to be at odds with each other" (112). The scene ends with Helena, acutely aware of her failure to perform what Kamboureli calls a "discourse of authenticity" (110), on her knees in front of the pail of sauerkraut, weeping openly as she holds her breath against the stink.

When I Was Young and In My Prime reveals the complexities of reanimating the vestiges of cultural memory, offering an intimate portrait of how and why such projects become deeply necessary. And yet if Helena is frustrated by her inability to fully "learn sauerkraut," the broader novel ultimately affirms her efforts, for it is her difficult engagement with the particulars of a cultural memory—quite apart from whether or not she is able to ritualize it and perform it "accurately"—that succeeds in establishing the freshly historicized, intergenerational relationship at the core of the novel.

What remains of what does not remain? Even as I am much less concerned than Froese Tiessen that the current moment suggests anything like an end to writing that directly engages Mennonite identity—strong recent work by emerging authors like Munce, Darcie Friesen Hossack (Mennonites Don't Dance), and Carrie Snyder (The Juliet Stories) seem to me convincing evidence to the contrary—her article serves as a valuable reminder of the quickly shifting form and function of Mennonite cultural identity in Canada. *When I Was Young* is a compelling example of the way that fiction can reveal the friction behind such shifts, between, as Froese Tiessen suggests, the "group history [and] individual becoming," and between "essential identity [and] multifaceted identifications" ("Homelands" 15). More specifically, it reminds us of the key but ambivalent role that food continues to play in the ongoing negotiation of Mennonite cultural memory, where it is conceptual foodmaps, rather than the geopolitical maps, that reveal a difficult but fruitful cartography of belonging.

CHAPTER 7

•◆•

"Their Dark Cells": Transference, Memory, and Postmemory in John Mighton's *Half Life*

Marlene Goldman

The role of those with a part "is to take the part of those with no part"
Jacques Rancière, qtd. in Faulkner 83

Another advantage of transference is that in it the patient produces before us with plastic clarity an important part of his life-story, of which he would otherwise have probably given us only an insufficient account. He acts it before us, as it were, instead of reporting it to us.
Sigmund Freud, "An Outline of Psychoanalysis" 174–76

Set in a nursing home for veterans and their families, where many of the residents are celebrated for their heroic participation in the Second World War, John Mighton's play *Half Life* (2005) underscores the vagaries of memory by drawing attention to the connections and conflicts between individual, familial, and national imaginaries. *Half Life* portrays the amorous relationship between two residents of the nursing home—Patrick, a brilliant mathematician who worked with Special Services as a code breaker during the Second World War, and Clara, a woman suffering from dementia of the Alzheimer's type. In addition to tracing Patrick and Clara's affair, the play focuses on how this relationship affects their respective divorced and middle-aged daughter and son. Clara claims to have met Patrick during the war, but her son, Donald, who has only second-hand knowledge of his parents' wartime experiences, can neither verify nor discredit her memory of their encounter. Donald's relationship to his parents' wartime past recalls Marianne Hirsch's observations in her essay "The Generation of Postmemory." Hirsch coined the term "post-memory" to describe the relationship that "the generation after those who witnessed cultural or collective trauma bears to the experience of those who came before, experiences that they 'remember' only by means of the stories, images, and behaviors among which they grew up" (106). As she explains, the "formative events of the twentieth century have crucially informed our biographies, threatening sometimes to overshadow and overwhelm our own lives. But we did not see them, suffer through them, experience their impact directly" (106). Postmemory's "connection to the past is thus not actually mediated by recall but by imaginative investment, projection, and creation" (107). In keeping with Hirsch's research on the conjunctions between the family and memory, my analysis of *Half Life* explores the transmission of memory across the generations. Whereas Hirsch emphasizes the roles of projection and photography, I concentrate on the impact of transference on individual and collective remembrance.

None of Freud's epochal discoveries, argues Aaron Esman, has proved more heuristically productive or more clinically valuable than his account of transference: the demonstration that humans "regularly and inevitably repeat with the analyst and with other important figures in their current lives patterns of relationship, of fantasy, and of conflict with the crucial figures in their childhood—primarily their parents" (1). Initially, passionate eruptions of transference took Freud by surprise since these childhood figures reappeared and were projected onto the physician without awareness on the part of his patients. Owing to its origins in the unconscious, Freud felt that transference narrows the scope and efficacy of the ego because it instigates the "transfer of powers from the subject to the Other" (Lacan, "Presence" 486). In the grip of transference, the individual's unconscious—the Other within—holds sway. In Freud's initial remarks regarding transference, he stresses its powerfully deceptive features. The patient, he asserts, makes "a false connection" to the person of the analyst when "an affect became conscious which related to memories which are still unconscious" (Freud, *Fragment* 139).

Freud also insisted that the spectral phenomena associated with transferences do not arise as a result of the analytic context; instead, they are merely "new editions or facsimiles of the impulses and fantasies that are aroused and made conscious during the progress of analysis; but they have this peculiarity that they replace some earlier person by the person of the physician" (Freud, *Fragment* 116). As James Strachey explains, it was suggested "that in everyone there existed a certain number of unsatisfied libidinal impulses, and that whenever some new person came upon the scene these impulses were ready to attach themselves to him"

(52). These impulses, however, remain unconscious if left unanalyzed. As the epigraph from Freud cited above suggests, the patient in the grip of transference inevitably "acts it out before us," rather than consciously "reporting it."

I offer this brief introduction to transference because *Half Life* portrays the workings and affective resonance of transference, and their impact on memory and postmemory on the individual, familial, and national levels. In accordance with Freud's emphasis on acting out, the cast of *Half Life* literally "acts" transference phenomena out before us, implicating the audience in the repetition of "patterns of relationship, of fantasy, and of conflict with the crucial figures in their childhood" (Esman 1).[1] Moreover, as August Aichorn insists, transference is not restricted to individual and familial contexts since it informs broader forms of political and national organization and memory. "Our attitude to society and its members," writes Aichorn, "has a certain standard form. It gets its imprint from the structure of the family and the emotional relationships set up within the family. Therefore the parents, especially the father, assume overwhelming responsibility for the social orientation of the child. The persistent, ineradicable libidinal relationships carried over from childhood are facts with which social reformers must reckon" (96). By repeatedly highlighting the workings of transference and the operations of remembering *and* forgetting on which transference phenomena depend, *Half Life* illustrates "the transfer of powers from the subject to the Other"—what psychoanalyst Christopher Bollas describes as "the shadow of the object as it falls on the ego," which leaves "a trace of its existence in the adult" (3). In essence, Bollas is referring to the shadows cast by both paternal and maternal objects—not the actual father and mother, but their received impressions in the child's psyche—impressions that "fall" upon the ego of the child, and thus shape the child's memory and postmemory. As R. Emde observes, "what we reconstruct, and what may be extraordinarily helpful to the patient in 'making a biography,' may never have happened. Reality is neither given nor necessarily registered in an unmodifiable form" (Emde, qtd. in Arnold Cooper 517). In *Half*

---

1 My use of the term *transference* exceeds but is not antithetical to the psychoanalytic paradigm since I explore its relevance and impact beyond the clinical context to which discussions of it are most often limited and investigate the impact of transference on broader socio-political relations.

Life, the shadow of the object also falls on the nation-state—a shadow largely associated in the play with society's preoccupation with male heroes and heroism.

Transference operations explicitly define the central question in *Half Life*—namely the veracity of Clara's insistence, after encountering Patrick at the nursing home presumably for the first time, that she met him earlier, during the war, and that she has loved him ever since. Rather than unconsciously bringing to bear the early emotions associated with a parental relationship on an entirely new relationship, Clara consciously insists that the past and present objects of her affection are identical, and she names them both Patrick. While this is not a typical example of transference, and it could be argued that Clara suffers from delusions associated with dementia, I would suggest that even if this were the case, her delusions are a subset of transference. Her son, Donald, maintains that Clara's memory is unreliable and that his mother—like a patient in full transference—is deceived. Yet Donald's denial of his mother's memory of Patrick serves to shore up an idealized image of his father, whom, in Donald's fantasy, his mother eternally adored, and by extension, Donald himself, as their cherished son. In keeping with the affectively and temporally disruptive nature of transference, *Half Life* explores how our understanding of the past impacts our experience of the present: were Patrick and Clara lovers many years before or is this a recent fiction—what Freud might term "a compulsion and a deception"? (Freud, *Studies* 230). Rather than focus solely on Clara, the play emphasizes that no one's memory, including that of the audience, is free from the operations of transference and projection and, by extension, from the ethical implications of acting in the half-light of its shadows. Due to the effects of transference, virtually all of the characters in the play and the audience see through the proverbial "glass darkly" (I Corinthians 13:12). The operations of transference structure both the experiences and responses of the patients in the nursing home to the staff and *vice versa*. The ethical complications arising out of the ambiguities associated with memory and postmemory are starkly rendered because Donald must decide whether or not to credit and honour Clara's memory—which Patrick never contradicts—and her passionate attachment to Patrick. Due to Donald's need to affirm his fantasy of his parents' supposed eternal fidelity, he is tempted to discredit his mother's story of having met and fallen in love with Patrick during the war. But dismissing Clara's story of Patrick to shore up Donald's preferred story constitutes a potentially unethical act of appropriation and revision. At bottom, his dilemma raises a fundamental question posed by Hirsch: "How can we best carry stories forward without appropriating them?" (104).

What is perhaps most striking in the play and what I focus on in this paper is how *Half Life* links individual and cultural transference phenomena to the workings of national memory and postmemory. The play repeatedly juxtaposes Donald's obsessions with his mother's fidelity and his father's heroism to the communal investment in these roles as manifested in public rituals such as marriage and Remembrance Day. By portraying the agonistic struggle between individuals such as Donald, whose memories serve and reflect personally and culturally iconic interests, and individuals such as Clara and Patrick, whose memories transform and decay, and who resist the discourses of heroism and fidelity, and by literally juxtaposing Alzheimer's disease with Remembrance Day, *Half Life* interrogates our construction of and investment in personal, familial, and national memory.

On the one hand, *Half Life* illustrates how individual and communal transferences legitimate and reify the state's valorization of the adult, masculine citizen—the hero. On the other hand, the play simultaneously highlights the proliferation of alternative figures that have haunted the image of the hero since classical times—the subordinate, liminal, and related categories of the child, the machine, and the animal. These intercalated categories both define *and* uncannily disrupt the integrity of the officially sanctioned category of the heroic masculine citizen. In what follows, I trace the metaphor of the child to show how individual transference remains linked to, yet exceeds, the Oedipal triangle. The elderly citizens confined in the nursing home—Clara, Patrick, and Agnes—both engage in transference and are themselves forced to bear a set of affectively charged cultural metaphors that are repeatedly displaced onto them by their children and the staff at the nursing home. In *Half Life*, these categories hauntingly surface because instances of pathological memory loss in the very old and the attendant spectres of decay and death trigger broader cultural anxieties concerning the fundamental categories on which the idea of the hero/human depends.

Although the focus of my paper is transference, it is worth noting that in *Half Life*, the threat of memory loss forcibly recalls John Locke's powerful contribution to Western society's understanding of the relationship between memory and human identity. In his *Essay on Human*

Understanding, John Locke famously distinguishes between human identity, which corresponds to substance and is dependent on bodily or physical continuity, and personal identity, the identity of the self, which is a function of the continuity of consciousness. For Locke, personal identity is identical with remembering one's own actions and the ability to narrate past experiences in the present (see Whitehead 53–58). As Ian Hacking puts it, for Locke "the person is constituted not by a biography but by a remembered biography" (81).

Whereas scholars focus primarily on Locke's valorization of memory, *Half Life* sheds light on Locke's often elided account of the challenges to memory posed by forgetting, interruption, and passionate eruptions of turbulent emotions. As Locke maintains, consciousness itself is susceptible to "being interrupted always by forgetfulness" (302). For Locke, memory is inherently entropic: "there seems to be a constant decay of all our ideas, even of those which are struck deepest, and in the minds the most retentive" (149). Whether interrupted by sleep, forgetfulness, or an inability to attend to all of a given memory at one time, for Locke, consciousness is always/already interrupted. This awareness prompted Locke to question how such moments of oblivion can be accounted for in an understanding of the self. Ultimately, Locke determined that remembering and forgetting provide the foundation for human identity.

In addition to remarking on the inevitability of interruption and, hence, forgetting, Locke also recognized that memory is not solely the product of voluntary cognitive activity since memories and remembering are activated and disrupted by passion. Memories, Locke writes, are "roused and tumbled out of their dark cells" by "some turbulent and tempestuous passion" (150). In contrast to that of Aristotle, Locke's conception of memory is, as Anne Whitehead observes, "non-intentional and seems to initiate a chaotic, if not threatening chain of activity which releases memories from the 'dark cells' within which they have hitherto been secured and confined" (55). The disruptive effects of interruption and passion, elided features of Locke's writings on memory and identity, are foregrounded in *Half Life*, and are signalled from the start by the play's title, since the term "half life" measures exponential decay (*Oxford English Dictionary*). Viewed in this light, the title of Mighton's play implicitly posits decay as integral to identity, and suggests that forms of decay including forgetting are the property of all matter.

Before turning to the interruptions and passionate instances of transference in *Half Life*, I want to begin by offering some observations on the evolution of the concept. Following this, I offer a reading of *Half Life*'s central depictions of transference—ranging from Clara's sudden passion for Patrick, to the staff's infantilization of the residents—and explore the implications of these depictions in the context of the connections I have been tracing between familial and societal structures and the role of memory in transmitting and maintaining them.

Freud's observation in passing is that transference flourishes when an individual's libido has been driven along a regressive, unconscious path because "the attraction to reality has diminished" ("Dynamics" 30). Drawing on Ida Macalpine's insights that the analytic context itself creates an infantile setting that exacerbates the patient's already diminished attraction to reality, I argue that the impoverished and isolated context of the nursing home similarly triggers the residents' transference and regression. In addition to exploring the context for the residents' transference—essentially an adaptation to their infantilization—I wish to argue that Donald's adamant belief that Clara is deceived and his insistence that his mother remain faithful to his dead hero-father represent a powerful illustration of the ethical quandaries associated with postmemory. *Half Life* contrasts the figure of the national hero, who performs deeds of valour in the political realm, with the abject, elderly female residents confined to the nursing home.

Rather than resolve the multiple, intersecting levels of projection and transference or attempt to separate illusion from reality, *Half Life* insists on the necessity of living in a world shaped by the imagination and our human capacity for both remembering and forgetting. In the final section of my paper, I demonstrate how the play's central formal strategy of interruption underscores Locke's insight into the limits of human memory. Ultimately, in *Half Life* the constant interruptions deny the characters and the audience alike access to a singular Truth and the related illusion that we can ultimately know and therefore master the Other.

TRANSFERENCE

As Freud's comments cited above indicate, early analysts presumed that transference was an erroneous and autogenous product of the patient's unconscious. In addition, for Freud, transference's temporal vector pointed unequivocally toward the past. By the mid- twentieth century, however, these foundational presumptions were increasingly challenged. Roy Schafer argues, for example, that transferences are not merely repetitions, but are entirely new experiences. Schafer likens transference phenomena to "metaphoric communications" that are "multidirectional in meaning rather than simply regressive or repetitive" (419). Schafer suggests that transference produces artistic or "creative" memories that depend as much on the imagination as on any accurate recall of past events. Traditional analysts viewed the interpretation of transference as a teleological quest, "an intellectual journey, emotionally loaded of course, but basically a trip back in history, seeking truth and insight" that resolves the deception (A. Cooper 518). By contrast, many contemporary analysts insist on the impossibility of ever arriving at the Truth about the past. Lacan insists that we can't "isolate reality and separate it from illusion," and he argues forcibly against any model of transference that appeals to the real. Rather than appeal to the Truth—which Lacan famously dismisses as merely "an effect of speech, which even when it consists of lies, appeals to it and gives rise to it"—he argues that contact with the Other, what he terms "the beauty," remains paramount: "it is to the beauty one must speak" (487). Viewed in these terms, Clara's poignant memories of the earlier selves and unrealized potential of her son, Donald, in addition to her passion for Patrick, which may be "creative" rather than empirically based, facilitate this type of contact with the Other. Of all the characters, Clara and Patrick alone are seemingly able to "speak" to this form of "beauty."

ELDERLY WOMEN AND SOCIETAL TRANSFERENCE OF THE FIGURES OF THE CHILD/ANIMAL

Whereas contemporary analysts including Lacan promote attenuating the spectral encounters associated with transference, in my reading of *Half Life*, I remain somewhat skeptical of Lacan's tendency to romanticize the flight from reality. As noted earlier, the setting of the nursing home, like the context of analysis, has an iatrogenic impact on the residents and encourages transference and regression. In contrast to Freud, who famously insisted that analysis does not instigate transference but merely "unmasks" it (Freud, *Autobiographical* 67), contemporary analysts recognize that the classical psychoanalytic technique forged an environment that was ripe for transference and regression. Classical psychoanalytic technique, argues Macalpine, creates "an infantile setting to which the analysand . . . has to adapt, albeit by regression" (205). She lists fifteen factors that constitute the infantile setting, including the curtailment of the object world, constancy of environment, fixed routine, not receiving a reply from the analyst, authority of the analyst, and the frustration of every gratification. *Half Life*'s depiction of the veteran's nursing home, in which the residents are confined—some forcibly—mirrors the infantile environment of classical analysis.

In *Half Life*, "the attraction to reality" wanes largely because patients' object world and object relations are severely diminished. The residents are parked for hours in the games room. News from the outside world is limited to postcards (29, 71) and profoundly out-of-date magazines, and residents such as Clara understandably prefer sleep to waking. During the brief periods in which she is awake, Clara appears content to play the role of the child. As she says to the Reverend while playing with clay, "It's like when you were little. And you could put your hands in the mud" (43). Even when Patrick and Clara attempt to make love, they are treated like children. Rather than offer the couple a modicum of privacy, the nurse, Tammy, intervenes and sets the agenda; she literally forces them to act out *her* fantasy of their meeting long ago. Taking hold of Patrick, she dances with him and, like a director, narrates her version of his first encounter with Clara. In this case, the residents are treated as puppets (54–55).

In contrast to Clara, who acquiesces to the whims of authority without complaint, her foil, Agnes, repeatedly makes it clear that she loathes being forced to engage in meaningless activities and she often balks at the nursing home's enforced regression. "I'm a senior citizen," she insists, "and I'd like to be treated like one" (42). Deprived of autonomy and forced to submit to the whims of authority, some of the residents understandably begin to behave like children. At one point, Tammy forces Clara to sit for hours in a urine-soaked diaper because she is too busy to change her (25). Donald also suspects with good reason that Tammy is stealing money from Clara (58).

In *Half Life* the figure of the child—the shadow borne of transference that falls on the female senior citizens—sheds light on both the individual and the political unconscious—a shadow whose range extends beyond the nursing home and, as noted above, includes the powerful affect associated with society's veneration of the hero. As Joanne Faulkner explains, within Western society, the child is frequently conceived of as "an underdeveloped, nascent human being—the animality that adult humanity leaves in its wake . . . in order to create a better humanity" (74). As she observes, both children and animals "furnish the coordinates for the human but are thereby rendered invisible in themselves" (75). Faulkner traces the separation between the properly human and the child back to Aristotle, who "initiated (or at least formalized) the conceptual separation of the 'political life' of the city from the *oikos*, or home, which contains 'simple natural life, the life of 'daily needs'" (76).

In *Half Life* the "bare lives" (see Agamben) of elderly people, filled with meaningless, childish games and puzzles, are likewise separated from the political life of the city, and ruthlessly contained in the "oikos" of the nursing home. I use the term *ruthless* because, as Faulkner, citing Agamben, maintains, the disavowal and misrecognition that secures the category of the human entails that there is an aspect of the self that "is akin to meat, and accordingly is available for others' use" (74). The self "akin to meat," in essence the corporeal self, renders humans vulnerable to exploitation and harm. As Faulkner states, this form of bare life haunts political relationships "as a threat of violence" (74)—a threat that is realized in the unethical treatment of the residents at the nursing home, who are the targets of theft as well as physical and possibly sexual abuse.

THE AMBIGUITIES OF TRANSFERENCE, MEMORY, AND POSTMEMORY

It is under these dehumanizing conditions that Clara's attraction to Patrick flourishes. Ensconced in the games room for the umpteenth time, Clara informs the newcomer, Patrick, that he looks familiar: "I knew a Patrick once," Clara begins. "During the war. He used to take me dancing" (23). After Patrick wins the hand, Clara repeats her previous statement verbatim, but adds the following detail: "In his spare time he [Patrick] made models of sticks and plasticine. I believe he called them polyhedra. [. . .] He said they were shadows of something [. . .] in the fourth dimension. I didn't understand how they could be shadows of anything" (26). Patrick's illustration of polyhedra and the model of the tesseract—the "four-dimensional cube" that he later constructs from modelling clay and popsicle sticks (43)—forcibly recalls Bollas's description of transference, "the shadow of the object" (3). In keeping with Bollas's conception of transference, the language of shadows pervades this scene. After Patrick's demonstration of the tesseract, Clara muses, "We would walk [. . .] in the shadows. By the river. Do you remember those days Patrick?" (27). Rather than directly affirming or negating her recollection, Patrick offers an enigmatic reply: "Barely," he says.

In fact, the veracity of Clara's memory of Patrick is never affirmed by him. Both Patrick's response and this central ambiguity concerning the origins of Clara's passion maintain *Half Life*'s insistence on the powers of transference and the vagaries of human memory. Viewed in light of transference, it is possible—as Donald suspects—that for Clara, every Patrick may be the same: a shadowy, romantic, paternal image projected onto the man whom she has just met. The ambiguity concerning Clara's memory and, by extension, all memory, highlights the ethical dilemmas surrounding the appropriation and use of postmemory.

In addition to recalling transference or "the shadow of the object," and its demonstration of Clara's passionate response to Patrick, *Half Life* comments directly on the infantile impulses at the core of transference. The fact that both the younger generation—Anna and Donald—and the aged residents—Clara and Agnes—remain emotionally tied to their parents, and that society as a whole reveres the heroic father figure in Remembrance Day ceremonies, affirm the socially pervasive nature of transference (see Aichorn). Indeed, *Half Life* underscores the power associated with the figure of the paternal hero from the start. For example, Donald's opening lines refer directly to his father's heroic exploits in the war, and he later returns to the topic of his father when he admits to Anna that the latter's heroic conduct during the war provided him with "the moral centre" of his life: "He endured things that would have broken my spirit. The world doesn't have heroes like my father anymore" (40). In this way, *Half Life* establishes the primacy of the figure of the masculine hero—the citizen *par excellence*. For Donald, however, his mother's relationship to his father is equally paramount in shoring up his sense of safety. As he tells Anna, despite the fact that his mother was married only a week before her husband was shipped overseas and she did not receive a letter from his father "for two years and did not know if he was alive or dead," Donald insists his mother "never lost hope" (57). As Donald says, his parents' marriage "was the most consistent thing in my life" (57). Donald's reliance on his parents' memories recalls

Hirsch's account of the second generations' affective dependence on postmemory. Hirsch cites Eva Hoffman's account of the vivid yet fragmentary nature of the memories passed down to her thus: "I took in that first information as a sort of fairy tale deriving not so much from another world as from the center of the cosmos: an enigmatic but real fairy tale" (109). Hoffman's description of the tales' origin at "the center of the cosmos" echoes Donald's view of his father's place at "the moral centre" of his life. The role played by these fragmentary postmemories is so fundamentally constitutive of the second generation and, hence, so sacrosanct that any challenge to them constitutes a profound threat to the identities of both the parent and the child as well as to the larger construction of society and, indeed, the very "cosmos" in which human interaction is given context and meaning.

Due to the intersubjective foundation of identity and the centrality of parents, "especially the father" (Aichorn 96), in *Half Life* paternal figures remain a source of anxious rumination. With the exception of Patrick, the nursing home's elderly residents likewise remain preoccupied with and, in some cases, haunted by their childhood relationships to their fathers. Agnes's reminiscences include an ominous revelation: "My father took away my childhood. When I was eight, he decided I was the love of his life. I've never told anyone" (17). Following this startling confession of incest, Agnes weeps. Rather than comfort her, Tammy changes the subject and reminds the residents that a number of them, including Patrick, will be honoured at the Remembrance Day service (17). As Tammy's response indicates, only heroic events have a place in communal memory; suggestions of pedophilia and incest at the hands of the father are another matter.

THE ETHICAL AND EPISTEMOLOGICAL LIMITS OF MEMORY AND POSTMEMORY

In keeping with Freud, who infamously remained uncertain of whether memories of incest represented his patients' repressed desires or memories of actual abuse, as noted above, neither Donald nor the audience has any way to resolve the veracity of the residents' memories. This epistemological cul-de-sac is pivotal to the play's ethical concern with the second generation's reliance on postmemory for potentially morally dubious ends. More specifically, the elderly—the actual bearers of memories of the war—are infantilized and, in some cases, victimized by the staff and, in some instances, by their own children. After Patrick attempts to escape, the staff put him in a straitjacket. By the end of the play, Clara and Patrick have been forcibly separated, and Patrick is confined to the locked ward. Under these conditions, it is understandable why both of the elderly female residents identify with the figure of the helpless, abused child.

The banality of the transgressions against the residents in *Half Life* demonstrates further that evil individuals are not restricted to historical or foreign enemies such as the Japanese during the Second World War. Instead, ostensibly well-meaning, responsible citizens—reverends, nurses, sons, and daughters who uphold the values of the nation-state—are revealed as contemporary doubles of the historical villains who starve and imprison inmates. It is significant in this regard that on several occasions, Anna and Patrick explicitly voice their concerns that their parents are starving (3, 74). At one point, the Reverend makes a direct comparison between prisoners of war in the Second World War and the residents of the nursing home (47), but no one attends to his analogy and he himself does not understand his complicity in the residents' imprisonment. At one point, Donald even assumes the role of the interrogator of a prisoner of war when Patrick is captured after trying to escape the home. In this perverse interrogation scene, which links familial and national wars, the prisoner is willing to talk but his words threaten his interrogator, who therefore refuses to listen.

Just as the play never resolves whether Agnes was abused in the past, *Half Life* never unequivocally determines if Patrick is Clara's courageous and tender lover or an opportunist taking advantage of an elderly woman's frailty. Rather than offer the Truth or, in the case of the agonistic battle between Patrick and Donald, effect a mere reversal between hero and villain, the play demands that we reconsider the transference figures that structure the dynamics of power between individuals and, more broadly, within families and the nation-state.

What makes *Half Life* remarkable is its ability to suspend revelation while exposing the relationship between individual transference and more widespread analogies that shape our understanding of human identity. At the core of the play lies a familiar, haunting question so memorably posed by Plato, who likewise used the language of projected shadows: Is it possible that what we believe to be true about someone or about a group of people (in this case, senior citizens) are merely shadows that prevent us from grasping the complexity and wonder of the world and its diverse inhabitants? What if the metaphors—human, child, animal, and machine— that we have inherited and that currently structure our thinking do not help us to make sense of ourselves or the changes that we experience throughout the life course, particularly in old age?

Throughout the play, clichéd metaphors and ossified familial and societal roles are repeatedly rendered suspect. In the final scene, Patrick briefly escapes from the home's locked ward to visit Clara, and together they fabricate a story that deconstructs Donald's account of his parents' marriage; the formers' story continues to highlight the complex relationship between remembering and forgetting:

CLARA: You don't really remember me do you, Patrick?
PATRICK: Yes. I do.
CLARA: But I didn't mean anything to you.
PATRICK: You meant everything.
    Pause.
CLARA: Do you remember when we first met?
PATRICK: Yes, I was on leave.
CLARA: But you were wearing your officer's uniform.
PATRICK: You were in a blue dress.
CLARA: You were another person's date.
PATRICK: I didn't care about my date. You were so beautiful.
    Pause.
CLARA: A week later you were gone.
PATRICK: I'm sorry. I had to.
CLARA: And I never heard from you again.
    Pause.
You'll find people never do what you think they should do.
PATRICK: I'm sorry. For everything.
CLARA: I forgive you [. . .] Now we can start over. (78–79)

In keeping with the atemporal nature of transference, this encounter ranges from the past to the future and ends in the present, where it is interrupted again by a nurse. Clara's future life with Patrick, like their past, may only exist in their imagination. Whereas Donald's story condemns Clara to limbo and a second childhood, Patrick and Clara's story allows them to envision a future.

THE LIMITS IMPOSED BY INTERRUPTION

Despite the fact that virtually all of the characters' memories and motivations remain opaque, *Half Life* repeatedly stresses the material consequences of the analogies and the labels that we use to determine people's identities. Donald's beliefs about his mother and his role as caregiver are thus not merely abstract philosophical problems requiring more profound contemplation. Instead, as the play repeatedly illustrates, Donald must act, and he does, for good or ill. On both thematic and formal levels, *Half Life* engages in the ethical work of highlighting both the necessity of acting (pun intended) and the limits of our ability to comprehend the Other—limits that are, not surprisingly, foregrounded by a host of interruptions.

On several occasions, Tammy interrupts Donald's conversations with Anna and the Reverend. The latter repeatedly interrupts Patrick and Clara's privacy. In the scene cited earlier in which Tammy and the Reverend treat the couple like puppets, forcing them to dance, Agnes interrupts them further. "Would you mind keeping the noise down in here?" she says. "I'm trying to sleep" (55). Her comment is significant because, as noted earlier, sleep is one of the central interruptions of consciousness that Locke identifies in his writing. Taken together, the interruptions have an impact on events that befall the characters and the audience. In the case of the latter, the repeated interruptions might cause some audience members to forget information and events that occurred prior to the interruption. Thus, in addition to portraying the inescapable workings of transference, *Half Life*'s formal structure implicates us in the challenges associated with remembering and forgetting.

Rather than viewing the tactic of interruption solely as a trap that demonstrates our compromised ability to remember—shattering the myth of the autonomous, fully functioning citizen—the technique can also be interpreted as an attempt to demonstrate the pitfalls associated with our attempt to master the Other—both the external Other and the Other within, as evidenced by Donald's earlier and unrealized potential selves. With respect to the former, by strategically introducing obstacles to communication, *Half Life* frustrates the hermeneutical impulse to cross barriers and merge self and other, particularly when this impulse is directed at vulnerable or marginalized groups. The various obstructions, including the repeated use of curtains that preclude our vision and the instances of interruption, prompt readers to relinquish "the exorbitant (and unethical) but usually unspoken assumption that we should know others enough to speak for them" (Sommer 206).

Half Life does not inscribe new and better metaphors or more accurate postmemories that we can project onto the bodies of senior citizens; nor does it attempt to resolve the challenges posed by transference. As Joanne Faulkner suggests, "the moment of human 'salvation' is not its recuperation to divinity or to its proper place, but rather an embrace of abandonment or displacement" (79). Ending as it does with an anti-revelation—Clara, obscured behind a curtain, alone in bed, falling asleep—*Half Life* bids us to confront and accept interruption and decay as integral to our humanity, and to risk ourselves in this emptiness: the suspension of the relation between human and non-human—the moment of interruption, to paraphrase Lacan, when the subject transfers its powers to the Other.

CHAPTER 8

• ◆ •

Remembering Poverty: *Bannock, Beans, and Black Tea*, a Tale of Two Lives[1]

Linda Warley

Bannock, Beans, and Black Tea is a co-authored book by John Gallant and his son Gregory Gallant, otherwise known as Seth, one of Canada's most accomplished and well-known graphic authors and illustrators. John Gallant wrote most of the content of the book, which focuses on his childhood experiences of growing up in abject poverty in rural Prince Edward Island in the 1930s. Over a decade Seth illustrated, designed, and published the collection of stories as a book. It is a "poverty narrative," a category developed by Roxanne Rimstead in her 2001 book *Remnants of Nation* to describe narratives both *about* those living in poverty in Canada and those that are produced *by* poor people themselves. But the book is also more complex and more ambivalent than the term *poverty narrative* implies, for it is also the story of John Gallant's son Seth and his artistic engagement with his father's stories. In this sense *Bannock, Beans, and Black Tea* is a story of two lives, and the memory work it enacts is multifold. In part, this is a book about a son trying to understand and honour his father's difficult life. It is also a text that reveals a tension not just between generations but also between class positions. John Gallant, despite faring materially better later in life, constructs his subjectivity in the text as a poor boy[2] who feels only shame and anger because of his poverty. This story of childhood poverty is, to be sure, important. But *Bannock, Beans, and Black Tea* is as much about the son's anxiety about his own decidedly middle-class privilege

---

1   An early version of this paper was presented at the "Canada and Beyond" conference at the University of Huelva, Spain in 2010.

2   The phrase *the poor* can be thought of as a disrespectful naming of people who live in poverty; however, in this essay I have chosen to retain terms such as *poor people* and *a poor boy* to indicate that these are subject positions not descriptors.

and comfort as it is about his father's terrible past. This doubled life story produces a text characterized by subtle but nonetheless disturbing tensions and anxieties, feelings of guilt, anger, shame, and disappointment that can be attributed not just to the father but also to the son. Poverty is part of Seth's formation as a subject too. It is not his experience as *lived*, but his experience as *known*. He has both internalized and distanced himself from that knowledge, but in doing so he creates a text that reveals something about how social class positions work in contemporary Canadian society. Through word and image, through the shifting of narrative modes from comic strip to prose and illustration, through representations of two different childhoods and adulthoods experienced from the perspectives of poverty and relative wealth, *Bannock, Beans, and Black Tea* exposes the difficulty—perhaps the impossibility—of the privileged ever really understanding and feeling solidarity with the poor, even when they are members of the same family.

Life-writing texts such as this one reveal how Canadians remember—or forget—the past. They can be understood as performances of cultural memory because, although life-writing texts generally focus on individual lives, in telling their personal stories authors draw on models of identity that are culturally available to them (Smith and Watson 39). These models are discursively constructed—in terms of family, religion, gender, ethnicity, social class, and so on. They shape the kinds of narratives life-writers construct, and they, in turn, are shaped by specific cultures, historical periods, and geographies. In *Bannock, Beans, and Black Tea*, one dominant discourse is the Great Depression, which produces a model of identity—the poor boy—that John Gallant takes up. As Alice K. Hale and Sheila A. Brooks note in their introduction to the anthology *The Depression in Canadian Literature*, "The literature produced during the Depression was most often concerned with social and political criticism" (2). Whereas much of that literature was written by middle-class authors (such as Morley Callaghan, Dorothy Livesay, and F.R. Scott), John Gallant's narrative is a first-hand account. He bears witness to what poverty really meant to those who endured those years, and he is certainly critical of the social and political realities that informed a large part of his childhood.

Bannock, Beans, and Black Tea narrates the past, yet its relationship to that past is rather more ambivalent. While the stories that John Gallant tells are certainly set in those years, the Depression itself is not the dominant theme. Instead, John Gallant represents his circumstances as deriving from adult and institutional neglect. All those who had a duty to secure a child's welfare are either absent or fail him. John Gallant's own father—through idleness, selfishness, and moral laxity—fails to provide even the basic necessities of life for his wife and eight children. His mother, a shadowy figure, who is cowed by her devotion to the Catholic Church, seems defeated. The Roman Catholic Priest preaches charity but denies food, money, or any other material help when he is directly asked for it. Apparently there were no community or governmental organizations that helped those living in dire poverty during those years, or at least none that John Gallant names.[3] Because of this thematic focus on adult and social neglect, and because of the angry, resentful tone in which most of the text is narrated, *Bannock, Beans, and Black Tea* could also be understood as a memoir of childhood trauma, possibly even child abuse.

In the Canadian literary context, poverty narratives are often valued for their depiction of a stoic, survivor protagonist who triumphs over his or her miserable circumstances (think of *The Diviners* and Morag's escape from the shame associated with her stepfather Christie's job as the town garbage collector). Being able to rise up from below is one dominant cultural narrative that shapes the national imaginary. Meagre economic circumstances can also be equated with a simple but moral life, especially in rural contexts. As Herb Wyile examines in his book *Anne of Tim Hortons: Globalization and the Reshaping of Atlantic-Canadian Literature*, the Atlantic region as a whole is often stereotyped as a folksy, friendly, conservative region where people live simple but happy lives close to the land and the sea. As one response to shifting economic realities (including the collapse of the fishery in the twentieth century), the tourism industry, an increasingly important sector of both regional and local economies, has exploited this stereotype. This view represents Atlantic Canada as underprivileged in economic terms but pastoral and attractive nonetheless. It is as if the region exists in a perpetual past. Candida Rifkind also comments that *Bannock, Beans, and Black Tea* and

---

3   Heidi Macdonald acknowledges that PEI had fewer government health social services than other parts of Canada during the Depression years; however, there were other sources of support and aid. She explores the key role that Roman Catholic women's religious groups played in providing social services, focusing on the Sisters of St. Martha. The order was (and is) based in Charlottetown, the capital city, so it is unclear how far they reached out to the more remote rural communities. Certainly in Gallant's narrative there is no mention of such a group.

other "popular auto/biographies of childhood poverty, notably Frank McCourt's *Angela's Ashes* [. . .] [are set] in a region frequently imagined in the dominant culture as a site of the pre-modern, even bucolic, folk" (409). But like McCourt's memoir, in Gallant's narrative the past is not at all folksy or pastoral. In this story of growing up as a poor boy, the protagonist keeps his and our focus on the experience of lived poverty: of being hungry, of lacking clothing and footwear, of being forced to perform manual labour or to scrounge and scavenge to sustain self and family. As the adult son Seth later realizes, his father's stories of his childhood, while seemingly amusing when he was young, are really "tales of awful desperation" (2). This book, then, is less easily assimilated into the literary canon (either national or regional) because the protagonist refuses to be stoic, because his poverty is partly his father's and other adults' fault and not just a circumstance of larger economic forces, and because the plot does not follow the rags-to-riches template.

Characterized by Seth as a natural-born Maritime storyteller (which is, of course, a stereotype), John Gallant orally told stories of his past to his son generally to entertain the boy. After John Gallant retired (and much to his son's surprise) he moved back to PEI, where, presumably, memories of his childhood gained extra sharpness. Seth encouraged his father to write his stories down, which he did, and Seth turned them into the book. Seth writes: "I wanted the stories to feel as much like the spoken word as possible," but, "sadly, some stories were cut (or never even written down) because they depended too heavily on dialect or physical humour. These were among the stories I liked best as a child" (5). It makes sense that the humorous stories would be his favourites; the harsher stories are more difficult to hear, especially when you know that your own father is talking about what really happened to him. While it is important to be cautious about the so-called authenticity of any life narrative, poverty narratives seem to require our respectful attention. We might generalize about "the poor" (as a disembodied merely demographic group) in Canada but never really listen to a poor person's account of his or her own experiences. Personal narratives matter, for they particularize life experiences and the ways in which those experiences shape human subjectivities. Gathered together in *Bannock, Beans, and Black Tea*, John Gallant's anecdotes become memoir, a genre of life narrative that situates the human subject in relation to particular historical moments and contexts. Helen M. Buss argues that memoir is valuable partly due to its accessibility. While her subject is women's memoirs, her comments can also pertain to texts written about the lived experience of poverty: "memoir's accessibility as a form that is associated with both literature and history is an important part of its ability to represent human subjects who are not normally represented by the central discursive form of our [Western] culture" (11). Memoir can also facilitate a shift in attention away from national memory—which is broad, institutionalized, and dominant—to cultural memory, which is shaped by institutions to be sure, but which can expand to incorporate individual memories that don't fit easily within national scripts. Such acts of narrative are potentially transgressive, for they are not merely personal, located in the psyches of individuals; they illuminate how culturally specific discourses, including social class, impact human subject positions.

Rimstead argues that poverty narratives "often unfold a national imaginary which locates the poor outside the imagined community on the fringes as fragments of nation" (*Remnants* 7). It is not that there are no stories about poverty in Canada, including Canadian literary works as well as other genres such as oral narratives and autobiography; rather, discourses of poverty, especially those engaged with by poor people themselves, are marginal to the national literary project, not an integral part of it. Critics of Canadian literature have, frankly, not done much to address what Rimstead identifies as a consistent failure of criticism to remember poor people as living, thinking, speaking, agential subjects. She writes in a 2008 article that "while critical expertise [specifically Canadian criticism] has recovered the history of institutionalized racism, exploited immigrant labour, and accompanying social movements for redress, we are still avoiding the stories of class, conflict, and poverty that undermine a national discourse based on progress and wealth" (44). Regional differences are part of this equation too, for lived experiences of poverty and deprivation vary from place to place within the nation.

Seth's working with his father's memories of the past is an act of "exchange between first and second person that sets in motion the emergence of narrative" (Bal x). As Mieke Bal remarks, there can be a special relationship between storyteller and witness if that witness happens to be, like Seth, an artist. Bal argues that the resulting "account [can] perform an act of memory that is potentially healing, as it calls for political and cultural solidarity in recognizing the traumatized party's predicament" (Bal x). This outcome, I suggest, is much less clear in relation to *Bannock,*

Beans, and Black Tea. How does this text provide access to a difficult past? And how does witnessing that past shape the present? Does it call for "political and cultural solidarity" on the part of readers/witnesses? To John Gallant the past was awful. He writes his stories down because his son asked him to: the son was the coaxer/coercer who elicited the narrative (Smith and Watson 64). But there is little evidence that doing so produced any therapeutic or healing effects for John Gallant. Nor does the son, Seth, necessarily feel solidarity with his father's predicament. On the contrary, for Seth there is something appealing, even exotic about his father's past. This intergenerational auto/biography[4] brings to our attention just how complicated performances of cultural memory can be.

For in this text there is not one life narrative but two: John Gallant's childhood memoir, the poverty narrative, and a six-page comic strip that functions as a Foreword. The comic strip describes how the book came into being, and in it Seth depicts his father but also (and more importantly) himself in relation to his father. Seth draws himself numerous times, sometimes as a child listening to his father's stories, but also as the adult now working intensely with his father's written texts. I have already quoted the words from the comic strip above, but it is crucial to take into account the visual elements of the comic strip as well. The comic strip is very structured with six frames per page, all of equal size and almost perfectly square. The rigid design seems to indicate a desire to control the narrative. Seth's Foreword is tidy, orderly, visually comforting. By contrast, his father's stories, while also short, are more upsetting to read both because of their content and because of the bitter tone in which they are narrated. Time shifts in these frames in the Foreword, moving from Seth being depicted as a boy of about six or seven years of age eagerly listening to his father while sitting across a table from him, while in the car, or while walking in the woods. Interwoven with these frames of the past are moments from the present: Seth depicts his father as an old man with white hair, located back in PEI, working on his stories, mailing them to his son and himself reading them, working on them, making the book.

---

4   I have borrowed this phrasing from Candida Rifkind, who has also written on *Bannock, Beans, and Black Tea.* Her essay examines the father–son relationships explored in three works of intergenerational graphic auto/biography. She focuses on how the collaborative nature of the texts, as well as their tendency to "gravitate towards an aesthetic of smallness" (401), engage issues of masculinity and fatherhood.

There are so many ways in which this book embodies binaries, para-doxes, contradictions, and ironies, each representing a site of tension or anxiety as two subjectivities—father and son, now and in the past—are negotiated in relation to one another. Some of these are obvious. For ex-ample, every autobiographer represents him or herself as an earlier self, including, often, a childhood self. Here that happens twice: we have both Johnny Wilfred the boy (as his father was then called, the tradition in PEI at that time being to name the son after the father's first name rather than surname) and John Gallant the older narrator. We also see Gregory Gallant as a child and Seth as the adult artist. There are also the binaries of the oral and the written and the written and the visual, issues that Rifkind has analyzed in some detail. But more subtly there are elements that when placed beside one another speak to the thematic subtext of the book: the narrative of class mobility that was struggled for but not cele-brated in the text by the father, and the situation of middle-class comfort and privilege that the son enjoys but did not have to work to attain.

In the "Conclusion" of the book John Gallant reveals that joining the army was his ticket out of his impoverished childhood and away from PEI. After leaving the military after a thirty-year career, he was able to upgrade his education (as a child he only reached grade two) and become a high-school teacher of technical studies. This sixty-odd year period of his life is covered in a scant two and a half pages at the end of the text and is narrated in a factual, monotone voice. The ear-lier part of the narrative of his childhood is where all of the drama and play with narrative voice takes place. He is obliged to acknowledge that he did not live his whole life in poverty, but John Gallant's purpose is not to celebrate his success. Rather, his purpose is to reprimand "young people" for not thinking about and not appreciating the hard work his generation had to do to provide "nice homes, clothes, telephones, radios, televisions, cars, school buses, beautiful schools, well-trained teachers, central heating, skating rinks, swimming pools, ball fields [. . .] I could go on and on" ("Conclusion").[5] As the reader has learned by this point, Gallant had none of those things—including the basics of sufficient food, shelter, heat, and clothing—when he was a boy. Thus the life narrative

5   Except for the six-page comic strip Foreword there are no page numbers; therefore I have in-cluded brief chapter titles as references.

offers not just a story of growing up in a family of "a class lower than poor" ("Introduction"); it also functions as a critique of contemporary Canadian capitalist society and its citizens' expectations of comfort, care, and privilege. Or to put it more bluntly: contemporary Canadians' unquestioned belief that what to some are privileges are for "us" normal. In this sense, *Bannock, Beans, and Black Tea* is not a therapeutic life narrative that heals personal trauma. Instead it takes readers through stories of one poor boy's past in the hope that issues of social class relations might at least be brought to the foreground and recognized as shaping the circumstances and identities of poor people in the past *and* in the present, on the margins of the nation and at its centre. The critique of being blind to how class works in Canada is also implicitly aimed at his son, one of those "young people." It seems to me that Seth internalizes that criticism and represents his complex feelings about it in the comic strip. Seth's access to mobility, technology, good food, nice clothes, and other accoutrements of a middle-class life are visually represented, though not directly commented upon by Seth.

For example, on the first page, five of the six frames depict Seth as a child listening to his father telling his stories (Figure 8.1). The older and younger versions of both men are juxtaposed and contrasted. The very first frame is of the present, showing the adult Seth sitting at a drafting table, working at what some would see as a leisured or even trivial job. He is an artist. Contrast this to what comes later in the book, his father's accounts of the extremely hard physical labour that he had to perform as a child. John Gallant was frequently taken out of school in order to work. He worked in a lobster factory when the harvest was in season; he picked potatoes by hand from fields and did all sorts of other manual labour for farmers and villagers; he fished, hunted small game, and picked berries. He worked hard and with his body. He worked outside and often in inclement weather. He worked like a man even when he was just a child. And he worked hard because most of the time his lazy father wouldn't.

In the second frame we are transported back to the past where father and son sit at a table. There is food and drink on the table: the remains of sandwiches perhaps, some fruit in a bowl, a glass of something for the boy and maybe a bottle of beer for his father. Again, once we have read the entire book we must acknowledge the contrasts. In John Gallant's life narrative the *scarcity* of food is a dominant theme. How many Canadians have known real hunger? Yes, during the Depression years many did and many in our communities still do. But in this narrative, the scarcity of food is a direct consequence of his father's unwillingness to find work to support his family, the absence of food banks or other social services,

8.1 Copyright 2004 G. (Seth) Gallant. Image courtesy of Drawn & Quarterly.

as well as the Priest's appalling lack of charity. Most of the time if there was food it was meagre fare: "Breakfast would be plain at best: porridge or beans, bannock and tea. Lunch, if any, was likely beans with bread. Dinner: fish and potatoes. Your choices to drink were tea or water" ("House and Home"). At times there are interruptions in the stories that collectively form the memoir of child poverty. In those sections John Gallant makes lists that often compare the present with the past. Here the tone becomes ironic, even sarcastic, and the humour is grim. For example, in a section titled "More Lucky Breaks" the list begins and ends with references to hunger:

1. We didn't have to fast for lent (we were already fasting).
2. No one forcing you to have a bath (you couldn't bathe in the winter until the bay warmed up).
3. If the bathroom (backhouse) was occupied you had the whole world at your disposal.
4. No worries about putting your clothes away. If you'd put them away you'd have nothing to wear.
5. No garbage to take out—you'd eaten it.

In this context, then, that simple scene in the comic strip of father and son sitting at a table eating and drinking acquires extra significance.

In the next few frames the oral storytelling scene is set in a car. Again, the contrast with the past becomes acute when we read about the numerous times John Gallant remembers walking very long distances, with inadequate footwear, often in unpleasant weather conditions. In the story titled "Going to the Priest for Help," for example, he walks two hours "in the cold snow and wind" on a late fall morning to the Priest's house to ask for help. The Priest refuses: "He told me he had no money for the poor." Starting back home but fearing his father's anger at him coming home empty handed, he decides to beg again. This time he is given "a roll of nickels—one dollar's worth." The boy walks home, only to be sent out again to the store to buy supplies. "I got my exercise that day. At least five miles to the priest and back and then two miles to the store and another two miles back." Eventually Gallant does acquire a vehicle—"an old wreck of a car—a 1927 Model T Ford with no hood" ("Part Three—Blueberries"). The sedan pictured in the comic strip Foreword is by comparison luxurious. When we think of the car culture of contemporary

Canada, where families often have not one car but several, we must pause to remember that not having access to transportation (even, possibly, public transportation) situates Canadians who live in poverty at the very margins of our society.

Later in the comic strip Seth draws his father hand writing his stories. By contrast he draws himself writing at a typewriter or drawing at a drafting table. Seth has greater access to the technologies of his art, and as a professional comics author and illustrator he has years of expertise behind him. While his father is an amateur author his son makes his living as an author and artist. Seth's reputation is such that his publisher worked with him in making what is known as the "Seth font" (Devlin). So while the font resembles handwriting it is actually a carefully designed professional font that only Seth can use. The artist makes art out of his father's craft.

More contrasts and tensions emerge the closer one looks. In the comic strip Seth's elderly father is shown in a constricted world of the house or alone in a rural Maritime setting in PEI—a province that is literally on the periphery of the nation. By contrast, Seth is shown in an urban environment in Southwestern Ontario (Seth lives in Guelph). John Gallant chose to return to the place of his childhood and youth, but he did not choose to return to its main feature: deprivation. Rather, as a retired teacher (presumably with a pension), he now has choices and returns "home" like "any refugee" (3). Seth's world is "the rolling hills and rural farmland of south-western Ontario" (3), a bucolic (if brief) representation of the region. Interestingly, in the memoir of his father's poor childhood, Seth includes illustrations both within the stories and as headers for each chapter. Many of the illustrations at the heads of chapters also depict a pastoral representation of island life. There are pictures of the waves of the sea, small houses, fishing boats, lines of trees or fences (some with barbed wire), haystacks, clouds, and so on. Larger two-page illustrations, as well as the front and back covers and the inside front and back covers, are even more pleasing (Figure 8.2).

The colours are muted. The lines are crisp. There is a certain quietness to the illustrations as if time has stood still and nothing is happening to disturb the scene. But the illustrations are in sharp contrast to the plot. In the story "I walked all the way to the lobster factory just to get fired," for example, father and son are shown setting out on their long walk (of ten to twelve miles) to the lobster factory (Figure 8.3). While

8.2 Copyright 2004 G. (Seth) Gallant. Image courtesy of Drawn & Quarterly.

8.3 Copyright 2004 G. (Seth) Gallant. Image courtesy of Drawn & Quarterly.

John Gallant's father here displays a rare desire to work, his son, John Gallant, is a child who has probably been taken out of school (yet again) in order to work. This is child labour of the kind one associates with the nineteenth century not the twentieth, and rarely in Canada.

Notice how the "long walk" is drawn. They walk through a pastoral rural landscape. It is peaceful and pretty. There is almost an air of measured excitement as they embark on an adventure together. But this too is dashed by the story itself: his father picks a fight with the boss and they are both fired before they can even begin. As Rifkind remarks about the same example, "Here, the visual image references not the father's [John Gallant, not his father] physical performance but rather a history of illustration, in order to draw on an iconography of bucolic childhood" (417). The "collision of sign systems" reveals "competing epistemologies" (Rifkind 417). They also reveal the distance between John Gallant's status as an amateur author and his son's career as a professional artist. Seth can *shape* what Gallant can merely *remember*.

There is nothing funny, gentle, or innocent in the stories John Gallant has to tell. And yet these stories, when under the editorial and design control of his son, are published in a book that hearkens back to a nostalgic past. It is not the romanticized past of that other story of childhood lived in rural PEI—*Anne of Green Gables*—but it is a gesture towards a past that the artist Seth has made aesthetically pleasing. If John Gallant had perhaps written his stories down in order to present a "counter (cultural) memory" (Rimstead, "Introduction" 6) to dominant narratives of Canada as a prosperous and peaceable nation, then the aesthetic beauty of the finished product works to undermine that intention. Is the poverty narrative usable as a corrective to amnesia concerning classed relations and experiences of poverty (in the past and in the present) if the packaging of that narrative is so clearly aligned with middle-class tastes? With Seth's tastes?

In his self-presentation as Seth, the author adopts a 1930s and 1940s fashion aesthetic, and he is known for surrounding himself with collectibles from the past, as well as doing most of his comic booking about earlier times (see Miller interview). He has an ambivalent relation to this period: he does not want to be in that past, but he does find it fascinating. In his other work of life-writing, *It's a Good Life, If You Don't Weaken*, Seth explicitly addresses his fascination with a certain period of North American society. In conversation with the character who is the graphic persona of another comics artist, Chester Brown, Seth draws his own persona saying, "I do think life was simpler then [the 1930s] [. . .] easier for people to find personal happiness" (16). At another point in the same book, he admires an old-style diner and looks through the window: "All that beautiful '30s detailing—wood shelves, tile floors, tin ceiling [. . .] and all of it abandoned, crumbling [. . .] forgotten. It kills me" (42). His use of the adjective *forgotten* here gives me pause. Seth knows that for his father the 1930s were not "beautiful." Has Seth forgotten that? In his self-conscious return to a past rendered through the lens of contrived nostalgia—after all, can one feel nostalgic for a past that one has not lived?—Seth forgets his own father's experience of that same time. He quickly corrects himself: "but when I'm truly honest with myself I couldn't stand the attitudes or the social conditions back then. I sure wasn't thinking of living through the Depression" (43). The things that remain in the present from that time period seem to him "like remnants of some ghost world—a vanished world" (43). And now that word *remnants* gives me pause, for it is in the title of Rimstead's book about Canadian women's poverty narratives. It is not just "things" that are remnants, but people. Poor Canadians are forgotten or at least pushed to the edges. They are Canada's "remnants," those scraps of the social fabric that are not valued and often not even seen.

And what about the title of Seth's book *It's a Good Life, If You Don't Weaken*? In the dedication he claims that this is a saying he heard often from his mother. What does *weaken* mean? Does it mean be lazy (like his grandfather, John Gallant's father)? Be less than a man? Be soft? Be too assured of and reliant on your comforts? Or to ask the question the other way: what is his mother's definition of a "good life" and has Seth achieved it? Here the issue of gendered subjectivity comes into view and links back to his father's childhood experiences. One memorable story again reveals the dire poverty of his family's circumstances, but now gendered identity is also a factor. In another year when spring finally arrives and there is work to be had at the lobster factory, John Gallant, ten years old at the time, faces a problem: he has no boots and he cannot walk the ten to twelve miles to the factory barefoot. His grandmother offers a solution: he is to wear her old white button boots. A woman's boots. This is worse than having to wear a shirt made out of a bleached flour sack. This is emasculation. As soon as he arrives at the factory he gratefully dons a discarded pair of rubber boots that are full of holes.

Anything is better than wearing women's boots. Poor people—especially poor children—do not have the luxury of refusing what is given to them in an act of charity, no matter how inappropriate. Those old-fashioned but intact women's boots are more of a sign of the shame associated with poverty than men's rubber boots with holes in them. Gallant as a boy must distance himself as much as possible from the stigma that is both classed and gendered.

In her discussion of "Varieties of Exile," a short story by Mavis Gallant, Rimstead notes that in the story Gallant's main characters, self-described Socialists, "contemplate the poor intellectually from a distance" (*Remnants* 11). "In order to maintain that distance, her characters play out a popular strategy that is familiar in Canadian culture: the strategy is to project extreme poverty elsewhere in time and or geographic space in order to distance it from the here and now and to make it appear anomalous to the wealthy nation rather than systemic" (12). In Mavis Gallant's story, that "elsewhere" is Britain during and immediately after the Second World War; in Seth and John Gallant's book, it is PEI during the 1930s. Seth simultaneously romanticizes that period in Canadian history and distances himself from it. His personal knowledge of his father's terrible childhood opens up a large gap in the text that is not resolved.

When Seth makes a book out of his father's life narratives he makes what is actually a terrible, ugly story into a beautiful object. Here is another contradiction that marks the tension between father and son, between "lower than poor" misery and middle-class comfort and security. As Kate Douglas has demonstrated, in childhood autobiographies nostalgia and trauma are the dominant "memory practices" of recent years, but usually texts would fall into either one category or the other. Here they are confused. How are John Gallant's memories of trauma to be reconciled with Seth's nostalgia? What are the implications of treating this story of childhood deprivation aesthetically? What does it mean that Seth makes a gorgeous and expensive book that his father, at least as a young person, would never have been able to afford to buy?

It seems to me that the aestheticization of Seth's father's life narrative serves three functions. First, the book is a gift from son to father. While the father entertained his son as a child with stories orally told, the adult son uses his considerable creative talents to create a lasting, material work of art. He honours his father by doing so, not only by transcribing and editing his father's personal stories and bringing them before a larger reading public, but also by creating a text that is beautiful. *Bannock, Beans, and Black Tea* is deliberately made to look like a children's book or picture book from the period John Gallant writes about, suggests Rifkind (419). It also evokes other special kinds of books: a personal journal, a prayer book perhaps, certainly a keepsake book. It is small, more square than oblong. It has a hard cover that is made of cardboard and cloth. It has a ribbon place marker. The front and back covers are richly coloured: mossy green and black on the front; rusty reddish brown and black on the back. The paper stock is heavy and cream-coloured, evocative of the yellowed pages of old books. Sepia, muted blue, and grey are important parts of the colour palette Seth uses. These colours evoke the past, but they are also muted colours that cast a warm filter over the harsh black words that tell a more troubling story.

Second, the book represents a counter-discourse to romanticized images of PEI as the "garden province" of Canada, especially as these have been developed by the "Anne industry" based on Lucy Maud Montgomery's novel *Anne of Green Gables* and the tourism industry that promotes PEI as a land of brilliant skies, verdant woods, pristine blue ocean, and red fields and beaches. Whereas PEI is known to be one of Canada's "have not" provinces along with the rest of the Atlantic region, popular representations emphasize its charm and beauty. Along with works by other Atlantic-Canadian authors (authors much better known than John Gallant, such as Bernice Morgan or Michael Crummey) contemporary writing about the past can disturb the romanticized, commodified, touristic images by shifting focus. Wyile reminds us that representations of the past in works of contemporary historical fiction can bring into view "how the region [. . .] was built on centuries of entrepreneurial acumen and more importantly, hard, hard work. But their writing also emphasizes the dangers of forgetting the imbalance of opportunity and privilege running through that heritage—the fact that not everyone had the option to be entrepreneurial or even to work, except perhaps in the most menial, degrading, low-paying positions" (234). Gallant's memoir is not historical fiction but written from his memories of his own life, even though, like any life narrative, it has been edited and shaped. Nevertheless, both the contemporary historical fictions that Wyile discusses and memoirs such as this one that come out of the Atlantic region offer a counter-discourse to more romanticized images that serve both regional and national purposes.

Finally, the text is also an auto/biography of class conflict, and it be-trays a certain guilt associated with class mobility. It seems to me that there's an awful lot of emotional desperation in Seth's engagement with his father's bitter tales. The tension between the generations and their radically different locations within Canada's stratified economic struc-ture is not mitigated by their seemingly close personal relationship, only deferred. There is no suturing the gap between the content and tone of the verbal narrative and the aestheticization of the material object. But perhaps that's the point. Readers cannot help but be aware of the disjunc-tion, which might bring to our attention the stark contrast between those whose subjectivities are shaped by being members of "a class lower than poor" and themselves, for if we know this book, we are probably (at least) middle-class readers.

It is of course important that we recognize and attend to "poverty nar-ratives" in Canadian literature and culture, but what does our encounter with such narratives actually mean? Does this book foster solidarity with the poor as other performances of cultural memory associated with trau-matic pasts might? As Gary Boire has argued, reading such works might raise awareness but it does little to redress the social injustices that are the realities of poor people in our society. Furthermore, the "endowed privilege" in both economic and educational terms that characterizes the student and professorial bodies means that we are able to distance our-selves from those stories. But Seth can't distance himself from his father's childhood stories. They make him sweat. They make him uncomfort-able. They cause him emotional pain. And it is this experience of middle-classedness, born out of the struggles of others, endowed and not earned, that is rather more difficult for readers like us to deny.

•◆•

Postmemory and Canadian Poetry of the 1970s

J. A. Weingarten

In the years immediately preceding and following Canada's 1967 centennial, there was a tremendous outpouring of historically conscious writing. Critics have long observed this body of literature and clarified the links between it and the rise of Canadian nationalism or, alternatively, movements antagonistic toward nationalism. In so doing, scholars have generally focused on writing that celebrates or rejects the concept of a homogeneous Canadian "nation." But by the 1970s such nation-focused literature was beginning to seem passé to historians and creative writers alike. In the 1970s, historically conscious writing branched off into a new direction that privileged "microhistory" (family or local histories) over the grander stories about or postmodernist deconstructions of an ideally coherent concept of "Canada."

The shift in this direction began in the late 1960s, when two historians, Ramsay Cook and J.M.S. Careless, questioned the usefulness of broad narratives of the Canadian past and asked historians to reconsider what qualifies as purposeful Canadian history. Cook and Careless derided wishful narratives of "nation-building" and declared them to be generally ineffective in a country as multicultural as Canada (Careless 1; see also Cook). These were groundbreaking positions to adopt in the late 1960s, and they helped reorient Canadian historical writing toward regional and social history. It became ideal to explore history on a smaller scale, to consider the distinctive social history and cultures of local regions. One result of this shift was that social history gained unique footing in the 1970s. As Carl Berger puts it,

> The growth of the professional study and teaching of history was but one aspect of an upsurge of cultural nationalism and an unprecedented

popular fascination with the past. Inspired by the celebrations of the centenary of Confederation and sustained by a universal search for roots and genealogy, this wave of nostalgia expressed a hankering for direct contact with a visible, tangible "living history." It led to countless private ventures in family history, the vast outpouring of publications on local and regional history, the retrieval of memorabilia and memories, and the creation of many local museums. ("Writings" 295)

The sudden popularity of social history that Berger outlines inevitably led to an upsurge in studies of the family. David Gagan and Herbert Mays were quick to note this shift in 1973. "In increasing numbers," they observed, "historians are turning to [. . .] daily experience" and to "the family unit" (27–28). The family was not, however, always a topic of disinterested scholarship; many writers, scholars, and amateur historians regarded the family as the most "tangible" (Berger's term) history imaginable. The writing that explored this tangible, personal link to history was a continuation, not an abandonment, of centennial-era historical writing. Indeed, "no understanding of the family can be ahistorical, since families have history built into their generational flows" (McDaniel and Mitchinson 13). The historical dimension of family writing is therefore implied, serviceably "built into" a broader historical framework. Ian Underhill, for instance, wrote in the 1970s that Canadian history "has been so recent that our grandparents are scarcely removed from the pioneer generation and are often the spokesmen for 'old-world' values. In this sense, the family portrait may also be a portrait of Canada itself" (7).

Hence, by the end of the 1970s, Canadian history was less about a national metanarrative and more about familial history and memory, and this shift had a massive impact on poetry from this decade.[1] Family history was a "usable past" for seventies writers: it was a generally encouraging search for "acceptable sources of cultural authority, the appropriate intersection of community and individual" (Zamora 5). Rather

---

1   So many familial poems were written during the 1970s that Ian Underhill published an aid for teachers of Canadian literature, *Family Portraits* (1978), which provided lesson plans, classroom questions, and a selection of poems designed to introduce students to this literary niche. Kenneth Sherman edited *Relations: Family Portraits* (1986), an anthology of Canadian family poetry written during the postwar era.

than compelling the writer to mask his or her identity in the name of objectivity (as more conventional approaches to national history had done),[2] the usable familial past is actually achieved and sustained by a writer's subjectivity. This embrace of subjectivism served lyric poets quite well: the personalism of the lyric and the subjectivism natural to familial history proved complementary and led many postwar writers to believe that they had discovered a viable method of convincingly representing history in poetry. They could assert authority over the memories of their family and use them as an analogue for broader episodes of Canadian history. Albertan poet Barry McKinnon was one of the first to adopt this approach in centennial-era poetry, and his long poem *I Wanted to Say Something* (1970)[3] helped inaugurate the voluminous outpouring of family poems that followed during the 1970s.

Poems such as McKinnon's *I Wanted to Say Something* exemplify what Marianne Hirsch calls "postmemory," and this theoretical framework is a profitable methodology for engaging with the familial literature of Canada's postwar era. Postmemory writing is an individual rumination on a historical period that another subject close to the observer can recall as a lived experience. Hirsch specifically uses "postmemory" in the context of trauma theory. Discussing Art Spiegelman's *Maus*, she discerns "the story of the father and the story of the son [. . .] family photographs are documents both of memory (the survivor's) and of 'postmemory' (that of the child of survivors)" (21–22). "[P]ostmemory," Hirsch says, "is distinguished from memory by generational distance and from history by deep personal connection. Postmemory is a powerful and very particular form of memory precisely because its

---

2   The implied subjectivity of history has been the focus of numerous scholarly discussions since the mid-twentieth century (and, in fact, even since the beginning of the profession of history). Such discussions partly form the basis of Hayden White's hugely influential texts, *Metahistory* (1973) and *The Content of Form* (1987). Historiographers have continued this discussion exhaustively; see Michel de Certeau's *The Writing of History* (1988), Ian Haywood's *The Making of History* (1986), Dominick LaCapra's "History and Psychoanalysis" (1987), and Tamsin Spargo's edited collection of essays *Reading the Past* (2000).

3   The first official publication of McKinnon's poem did not appear until 1975; he did, however, circulate the poem quite widely c. 1970. His book began as a short lyric poem, and he radically expanded it during 1969. By the spring of 1970, McKinnon finished *I Wanted to Say Something* and divided it into three parts, only two of which remained in the final version (Email Interview). It was this final version that he photocopied and circulated until an official publication appeared. Red Deer College Press republished the text in 1990.

connection to its object or source is mediated not through recollection but through an imaginative investment and creation" (22). Although one should, as Hirsch does, distinguish postmemory from history, the historical dimension of postmemory is naturally implied, just as the history of Canada, according to Underhill, is implied by the history of the Canadian family.

The connection between nation and family that Underhill observes suggests that literary and historical texts of the 1970s invite an exceptionally compelling application of Hirsch's methodology. The intersection of centennial-era nationalism, nation-building narratives, and family history during that decade palpably demonstrates the cultural relevance and creative possibilities of postmemory writing. There are many ways to assess this relevance and these possibilities. First, the self-reflexive and sharply focused lenses of postmemory writing implicitly prevent any one writer from claiming that he or she has apprehended the whole of the Canadian past. Privileging microhistory over the national metanarrative, seventies postmemory writing found itself in line with the progressive historiographic scholarship of Cook and Ramsay that questioned the sustainability and usefulness of nation-focused histories. Second, the unveiled and unpretentious subjectivism built into familial histories necessarily leads one to assume that one history of the family is as valuable as any other. In other words, postmemory invites any attentive writer to share his or her family history as a fragment of a larger, cacophonous past and, simultaneously, to appreciate any similarly individual recollections of or encounters with the Canadian past on even the smallest of scales. Postmemory writing implicitly encourages *discourse*, the comingling of different readings of Canadian history at the micro level. These narratives are not necessarily the traumatic pasts that Hirsch studies (though, they certainly can be), but they are always the pursuit of familial memories that contribute to and find value in a profitably dissonant story of the nation.

If critics are to mine the great wealth of Canadian postmemory writing, then texts that fully explore the power of photography are a sensible place to begin, especially because Hirsch sees the photograph as integral to postmemory. She values photography because it is "perched on the edge between memory and postmemory" (22), a natural fragment of time, one of "the leftovers, the fragmentary sources and building blocks" that allows the "work of postmemory" to occur. These fragments "affirm the past's existence and, in their flat two-dimensionality, they signal its unbridgeable distance" (23). The photograph is, paradoxically, an un-equivocal insistence on the past as having been real and equivocal in what it relates about that past. Still, the photograph *feels* useful as part of the methodology of postmemory: it is easy enough, one expects, to peruse the family photo album and retrieve some fragment of the past useful to the imagination of the historically conscious writer. But as this imaginative act takes place, the observer inevitably faces the paradox of postmemory that, as Hirsch understands it, the photograph so help-fully epitomizes: discovering a tangible link to history, the observer, still far removed from that time period, can only partially understand the significance and weight of the events and images with which he or she feels associated. There are histories outside the frame of the literal and figurative "picture" of the past that the observer cannot readily perceive. However tenuous the epistemological certainty afforded by the photo-graph, pictures (like postmemory more generally) affirm the existence of events, eras, and people situated in the past and encourage the explo-ration of one's personal past, which was a process of the utmost impor-tance to the centennial-era writers who were eager to locate themselves in Canadian history.

McKinnon's *I Wanted to Say Something* is an ideal case study of post-memory in Canadian literature: he explores the hopefulness and the complexities of postmemory against the backdrop of the centennial era, uses photography to breathe life into historical moments, meditates on the national past as viewed through his family's eyes, and returns contin-ually to the challenges posed by a very focused, subjective historical lens. Much too little has been said about this text, which inspired many of the better-known "postmemory" poems and volumes of the 1970s, such as Andrew Suknaski's *Wood Mountain Poems* (1976). Suknaski fondly ac-knowledged McKinnon's impact on prairie writing:

> There is so much I could try to say about *I Wanted to Say Something*. But I can't articulate it. All I can say is this seminal poem was there before me. And where I went with *Wood Mountain Poems*, Barry's poem was a beacon for me. And I am sure something of Barry's vision of the early west—with all its hopes, dreams and losses—flared in Sid Marty's imagination when he wrote his poems about the Marty family in Southern Alberta [*The Tumbleweed Harvest*]. ("Foreword" n.p.)

Suknaski goes even further and credits McKinnon with seeding the search for family in the minds of Robert Kroetsch and Eli Mandel. Yet, with the exception of Suknaski's introduction to the 1990 reprint of *I Wanted to Say Something*, shockingly little has been said about McKinnon's book. In 1980, Lorna Crozier lamented that the poem had "received very little critical attention, though it has influenced a number of poets who have felt the same need to define their roots." "I offer my analysis as an apology to McKinnon," she wrote, "for the lack of attention paid in the past to a beautiful, well-crafted book" ("Edge" 106). Dennis Cooley likewise speaks rather apologetically about *I Wanted to Say Something* and describes it as "one of the first, one of the best, and one of the least-known of the post-modern long prairie poems" (204)—though he himself declines to discuss the poem in his article. Nonetheless, *I Wanted to Say Something* is a paradigm for postmemory poetry of the 1970s in that it explores and exposes the limits and biases of family narratives, an exposure that challenges the poet's faith in his personal and national history.

McKinnon divides *I Wanted to Say Something* into two parts: (1) "The Legacy," a lyric history of McKinnon's grandparents (especially his grandfather, Fred Dalton), their photographs, and the prairies more broadly; and (2) "The Moving Photograph," which showcases his lyric persona meditating on the usefulness of photography, memory, and history, as well as on the struggle of the lyric poet to retrieve and represent the past. McKinnon bridges these two parts by gradually intensifying the meditative quality of his poem. As the poet pieces together his familial past through the interaction of photographs and text, he celebrates his family. But his attempt to valorize his family history instigates the speaker's conflicted recognition of racism and social injustice. Stories about his grandparents bring to light stories about Aboriginal peoples' displacement. As the persona comes to recognize the existence of many different perspectives on the prairie past, he gradually drifts from a narrative style to a more meditative one: McKinnon's speaker thinks on the successes, failures, and ambiguities of a past that he initially attempts to romanticize. He ceaselessly questions his preliminary urge to rejoice in postmemory and concludes the poem with questions about his ability to understand fully the history of which he and his family are a part.

The persona of "Part 1: The Legacy" initially seems confident in his depiction of history. The poem begins with a look at "the photo album" and the speaker begins to craft a story around the pictures with the help of his family. Here is an instructive example of McKinnon's interpretation of postmemory:

> they thumb thru history and give
> us names to place on the distorted shapes (mothers, uncles and
> those who've died: photos continue   and we all laugh in the
> innocence—that it's all past that nothing lasts once the
> dream ends.
>
> I trace the ignorance / blunt men
>   with plump wives
>   dragging themselves thru prairies
> and dust storms   (15)[4]

Reliant on his family's stories—a reliance made evident by the plural pronoun *they*—McKinnon's persona is hopeful in his quest to piece together a fragmented past: "distorted shapes" seem clarified once they are named, photographs "continue" history, and even the suggestion that "nothing lasts" seems disbelieved by the poet-speaker who decides nonetheless to "trace" the historical narrative. In the photographs he finds a "tangible" history, "frozen" in pictures (42), and waiting to be explored.

In these early sections of the poem, McKinnon's persona relies heavily on the aesthetic power of and information contained in such photographs. The persona's language is noticeably deictic as he confidently guides the reader through pictures. Of the first photograph, for instance, he writes,

> the train ended here right
> by the house. you can see the
> men—and there, the crane just past
> the house (16)

---

4   All citations refer to the 1990 version of *I Wanted to Say Something*.

9.1 From *I Wanted to Say Something* by Barry McKinnon, p. 16. Used with permission.

For Roland Barthes, one of the most important effects of a photograph is its ability to create an inhabitable landscape: "I want to live there, *en finesse*," Barthes writes, "and the tourist photograph never satisfies that *esprit de finesse*. For me, photographs of landscape (urban or country) must be *habitable*, not visitable. [. . .] Looking at these landscapes of predilection, it is as if *I were certain* of having been there or of going there" (38–40). McKinnon's photograph is not only a testament to an inhabitable landscape (epitomized by the pristine home), but his deictic language makes the photograph itself inhabitable. Images, Barthes notes, are always "an antiphon of 'Look,' 'See,' 'Here it is'" and other similarly "pure deictic language" (5). McKinnon adopts such language: "here right / by the house" and "there, the crane just past / the house." The effect is an inhabitable landscape made more compelling by a photograph that readers are explicitly asked to inhabit and navigate. Whatever appears hidden—in the photograph in Figure 9.1, the barely visible figures of labourers behind the house—is made plain to the reader. A comparable elucidation of the photographs occurs when McKinnon's persona observes a picture of his mother:

and here, your mother/your aunt
hidden in the grass, the oats
brushing
        her shoulders

        (who gave this life to me,

the legacy: pictures/and ignorance and love
to look back
            upon: (17)

9.2 From *I Wanted to Say Something* by Barry McKinnon, p. 17. Used with permission.

McKinnon again adopts deictic language ("here"), but he also draws the reader into relation with the photograph by appropriating (presumably) his grandfather's voice and adopting a second-person pronoun ("your mother/your aunt"), which effectively conflates the reader with the poet-persona looking back at his familial past. More importantly, the implicit promise that what is "hidden" can be revealed—one might otherwise miss the near-invisible aunt hiding in the grass—suggests a rather confident lyric persona; though, McKinnon's forward slash ("your mother/your aunt") might actually denote his uncertainty about *who* is in the grass. Still, the scene, like others in the same section, generally seems authoritatively rendered: the picture propels the persona forward, rather than stymieing him. As the inheritor of a "legacy," of a "dream lived in the genetic structure" (19), the persona feels that an authentic apprehension of the past is possible: he can see and articulate an era in Canadian history by mastering his knowledge of his family.

The persona's apparent ability to clarify images, narratives, and histories for the reader contrast with his later realization that his grandparents' experience was one of confusion and "failure." The speaker refers frequently to the "geometry" of the prairie as a means of capturing his grandfather's wish to impose order on a disordered landscape: "they came to conceive the land as enemy and fought / back with god and muscle and stupidity until the first winters / are thru, then spring and the promise enters again, the natural / cycle of trees beginning to bud" (26). Nature is indifferent to Grandfather Dalton's "geometr[ic]" conception of "the land" (28), the "angles / in his head" (31). The farmer imagines the land, but his "meditation lack[s] [. . .] / clarity" (28), his "suffering lack[s] / clarity" (29). Incapable of ordering, shaping, or even understanding their experience, the family exists "amidst the chaos" (32), a chaos that the persona tends to observe both in nature ("trees die on purpose" [34]) and in acts of social injustice: female farmhands and mothers who—unlike male farmers—"never" took breaks from their work (23) and the Aboriginal peoples who were "pushed further east / by the government" in order to make room for new settlers (26). As the persona discovers the correlation between these histories of oppression and the "ignoran[t]" (15, 17) vision of prairie pioneers, he comes to distrust his generally romantic attitude toward family history. He adopts a more skeptical position on the past and proclaims this skepticism about halfway through the collection: "I emerge to destroy my own dreams / and the tricks of / memory" (30). This is a turning point in McKinnon's volume: the initial urge to document a tangible, postmnemonic past evolves into a consideration of the pasts excluded by that very specific perspective on history. For the remainder of the poem, McKinnon's speaker thinks on what stories *others* could tell; he explores the fissures in the narrative he initially thought he apprehended and controlled.

As much as his written lines, McKinnon's photographs invite readers to think outside the frame of his persona's historical perspective. I noted earlier the feeling of textual participation that McKinnon's deixis

engenders for readers. The photograph in Figure 9.3, conversely, produces a different effect. McKinnon's spacing before and after the picture
is substantial, so I have shrunk the structure somewhat for purposes of
reproduction:

then, the man's task: horses, plows, and hired strangers –
and the fields stretched

    natural before him

       (the thick soil. the enemy

lying flat

  and Indians pushed further east

by the government:

9.3 From *I Wanted to Say Something* by Barry McKinnon, p. 27. Used with permission.

it all begins in innocence: the old news reels,
the chronicles. shots of the plow, and
black earth cut deep

    thru the grass

      beneath the roots—earth

split in

  furrows

    a trench for the

seed.   (26–27)

The persona's criticism of colonialism introduces the picture of Fred Dalton via his use of a colon, which indicates that the speaker sees a direct correlation between the displacement of First Nations people and the settlement of the prairie. The photograph that denotes "the innocence" of a farmer's dream also connotes the injustices committed against another people, which made that dream possible. Dalton's pose supports this reading: whereas the persona invites the reader into earlier photographs with deictic language, here Dalton points outside the frame and, with his deictic gesture, asks the reader to see *beyond* the limits of perception. Whatever event or object captures Dalton's attention is outside the frame of the picture; readers must look beyond the edge of the photograph. What lies outside the frame is a story of colonialism, a story to which pictures of prairie farmers can only gesture. The scattered and groundless line structures that follow the photograph speak both to the persona's lack of epistemological certainty and to the uprooted prairie peoples. The speaker's subsequent metaphor reinforces the latter idea, an underlying and obscured narrative of conquest: the farmers destroy whatever is rooted in the land (or, whatever people first occupied prairie spaces) in order to make room for a new "seed." This moment is decisive in McKinnon's text because it marks the abandonment of the tell-all photograph: his persona begins to observe boundaries in pictures, stories, and poems, a realization that leads to his declaration that he will "destroy" his "dreams" and the "tricks of / memory" and "begin to speak only of the failure—and difficult / love" (36). In this vein, Part 1 ends with "whispers," a "scattered history," and a poet who realizes that he is beginning to "counter the mechanical / accuracy" of his family's stories (42). These sections of McKinnon's text evidence a principal tension in postmemory writing: the value an observer places on his or her familial connection to a historical era insists upon the presence of other, equally legitimate perspectives on that same past. This tension helps contextualize the division of McKinnon's poem into Part 1 as primarily an iteration of his persona's familial past and Part 2 as a reflection on the complexity of historical representation by any "I."

Another obvious difference between Part 1 and Part 2 ("The Moving Photograph") is the absence of photographs in the latter: the speaker has come to rethink the effectiveness of literal "images" of history. The persona constantly struggles with this doubt, as he contemplates the "dust / in his lungs" (48) that makes him wonder, "where does he want the poem / to go / (thru angular history, / and names, the dates running as

/ a line / thru our lives," even though "the journey is not simple" (48). History, even one born out of postmemory, cannot be neatly ordered into a straight (or, for that matter, poetic) line.

As a writer, however, McKinnon's persona finds disorderly histories to be valuable poetic material. Part 2 begins,

> with innocence the land
> bore me. the cultivated
>   womb became my
>   skin. images pushed
> inside the eye. the legacy of
>   elevators and angles and
> grass to get lost
> in
>
> hear the wind against his
>   skin
>
> the decay begins as he hears the mystery,
> a whisper thru the trees, and voices
> in the rooms
>   below   (47)

McKinnon's opening line reinforces the fact that the poet-speaker was, of course, born out of his family history. At the same time, "innocence" is, according to the poet-persona, where stories begin. Given the speaker's urge to advance past that beginning, the second line more than likely hints at his "bore[dom]": once one moves past the inaugural images of innocence and observes glimpses of a buried past, a more dynamic, if incoherent, history surfaces. Abandoning the celebration that initially inspired his story, he approaches the limits of subjective history, the edge of the photograph and the postmemory narrative. The returned image of his aunt "lost" in the "grass" may be a metaphor for his consequent disorientation, but this confusion is profitable for the poet fascinated by the challenges of a dynamic and inclusive history. Significantly, his grappling with such issues initiates a section entitled "The Moving Photograph," which carries two meanings related to epistemology and affect: (1) the ultimately unstable photograph that "moves" away from or evades the meaning the speaker expected it to signify; and (2) the affective and "moving" photograph that inspires the speaker's "difficult love" for his family. Both interpretations speak to a fundamental tension in McKinnon's interpretation of postmemory: the tension between what cause for celebration his persona hopes to find in the familial past, and the "decay" of this image, as buried (the obvious connotation of "below") voices "whisper" otherwise unspoken stories and perspectives. The coherent history that began this poem fragments: the lyric persona struggles to comprehend inherited, exposed, and buried histories that underlie or are implied by his familial past. Readers thus engage with the second part of McKinnon's poem by focusing on the poet's more philo-sophical meditation on epistemology instead of on a history conjured up by postmemory. McKinnon's persona deviates from these images and stories and finds himself more compelled by lyrical meditation and the boundaries to which he can push a familial memory.

Speaking to these issues, the conclusion of *I Wanted to Say Something* is not a lament about the apparent "limits" of postmemory; rather, at the end of the poem, the speaker stresses the discursive value of such per-spectives on history. He concludes the poem thinking about the literary possibilities of postmemory. The persona writes of himself,

he will sing before he disappears.
the history, people sustain him. the voice taught
by birds, the meadow lark
                    cutting the air
with a sound/
          he imitates
in his vision requiring the elements
    to balance and cohere

and now he sings again
here

where we reach
          the edge
of the moving photo

graph   (61)

McKinnon's persona continues to use deictic language, but he does so here in order to draw attention to the presence of a poet-figure. The poem and poet, not the photograph, become the focus of the reader's attention: the distinctly prairie bird imagery, like the repeated image of a singer, recalls the "songbird" motif of romantic lyrics (John Keats's "Ode to a Nightingale" or Percy Shelley's "To a Skylark"). Readers are left imagining the "I," the poet-persona who can only bring them to the "edge" of an evasive and emotionally "moving" image, not to its "end"; there is more to be discovered, but the poet's range of sight cannot fully account for the larger past of which his family played a small part. The final and broken word, "photograph," further emphasizes the incompleteness of his historical image, but it also signifies the poet's faith in the process of recording these images: McKinnon "places emphasis on 'graph,' the Greek suffix for writing" (Crozier, "Edge" 108). Perhaps the concluding line, isolated and broken, feels like an image of defeat: the poet giving up on the fragmented past, the broken picture, and the isolating act of writing. But the last line also seems to be an imperative that asks the reader to "graph," to write history, to write and record *anything* that enlarges our perspectives on the past. This reading would indicate that the poet-persona sees the documenting of postmemory as an essential creative act: every familial memory enriches and adds diversity to our understanding of a broader history, no matter how quickly or often the writer encounters the edge of his or her knowledge.

Building on the tradition that McKinnon partly inaugurated, seventies poets pursued similar projects, and some, such as Al Purdy, represented postmemory in similar lights. Take Purdy's *In Search of Owen Roblin*, which fused his early lyrics about the nation and explorer Owen Roblin (such as "Roblin's Mills" and "Roblin's Mills [II]") with those about his grandfather, Ridley Purdy (such as his late 1950s poem, "Elegy for a Grandfather"). This fusion led many reviewers to observe that, despite the title of Purdy's long poem, his "search is not only for Owen Roblin, but for Purdy himself, his identity, and the source of his being" (van Steen 68). As such, his poem denotes the intersection of personal and national history; it is, like McKinnon's poem, an instructive example of postmemory. Purdy's speaker "[o]pen[s] the album," the "cage of ancestors," and thumbs through the past with his "own careless fingers"

(*Beyond* 238);[5] he reads "the well or little-known facts of Canadian history" in tandem with "the dry record of genealogy" (251). Purdy's persona admits that this fusion (and the entire poem) engenders only "wild speculations" and "elusive unverified facts," which are "not very damn much" (270). The speaker, however, still values this inscrutable past; regardless of its contradictions and ambiguities, the past is a "place" for the present "to stand on" (274). Purdy's negotiation of faith in and doubt about authentic or sufficiently inclusive images of history echoes what one finds in McKinnon's poem, and this echo suggests the enduring appeal of projects similar to those of McKinnon throughout the 1970s.

Indeed, what can be said of McKinnon's collection or of Purdy's *In Search of Owen Roblin* could also be said of numerous other seventies volumes. Douglas Barbour's *Visions of My Grandfather* (1976) ends with his persona's admission that "the truth is always hidden" (n.p.), even if he still optimistically constructs a version of his family's history. Andrew Suknaski's *Wood Mountain Poems* is a provocatively divided collection that balances very confident poems about the family (such as his inaugural poem, "Homestead") with self-questioning lyrics that investigate the regional past (such as "Indian Site on the Edge of Tonita Pasture"). Eli Mandel's *Out of Place* (1977)—a volume inspired by *Wood Mountain Poems*—ends with a speaker ruminating on photographs of his relatives' grave markers: "These names I rehearse: / Eva, Isaac, / Charley, Yetta, Max / now dead / or dying or beyond my lies [. . .] / till I reeling with messages / and sick to hold again their bitter lives / put them, with shame, into my poetry" (73).[6] The sense of loss in Purdy's *Owen Roblin* is also observable here; Mandel's persona "shame[s]" himself for his inability to move "beyond [his] lies" about history. The experience of an epistemological impasse in these poems is in keeping with the trajectories of most extended lyric poems about the family.

Unsustainable "nation-building" narratives led poets to wonder from where authentic images of history might emerge. Postmemory and

---

5   As the original "In Search of Owen Roblin" has no page numbers, all quotations are drawn from *Beyond Remembering: The Collected Poems of Al Purdy* (2000).

6   In "Writing West on the Road to Wood Mountain" (1977), Mandel wrote, "I remember how moved I was when last year I first heard Andrew Suknaski read. [. . .] I thought: [*Wood Mountain Poems* is] the book I should have written, its terrible authenticity, its powerful directness, its voices and places echoing in its time and truth" (26). After he read Suknaski's book, he completed work on *Out of Place*.

the family photo album seemed suitable leads to follow: they were personal and therefore empowering because they enabled the poet to claim
superior knowledge of the past. But as writers more deeply probed their
celebratory investigations of the family, they came to realize that "superi-
or knowledge" was not absolute knowledge. Even if postmemory writing
could not offer these writers a vision of history that felt all-encompassing,
it did give them a greater confidence to explore a very personal perspective on history that became part of a larger discourse of equally personal
postmemory narratives.

This confidence was surely the appeal and exciting quality of postmemory writing during the 1970s, which explains why, as a genre, it
had such great reach and range. Poetry that explores the limits of lyric
is only one wave within the vast spectrum of postmemory writing; there
are many alternative interpretations. With regard to poetry from and
after the 1970s, each of Steven Berzensky's (a.k.a. Mick Burrs) ongoing
sequence of poems, "A Document of Secrets," Lorna Crozier's family
poems in *Inventing the Hawk* (1992) and *Angels of Flesh, Angels of Silence*
(1988), Kristjana Gunnars's *Settlement Poems I* and *II* (1981), Stephen
Morrissey's *Family Albums* (1989), and Peter Stevens's *Family Feelings
& Other Poems* (1974) uses family images and histories to engage with
issues such as twentieth-century Canadian immigration, gender dynamics, "old world" history, and so forth. Seventies writers' attraction to postmemory as often guided novelists, as in the case of Margaret Laurence
and *The Diviners* (1974). Laurence's protagonist, Morag Gunn, writes
about photographic memories or imagines the intersection of the history of her ancestors and others' ancestors with the history of the nation.
There are similarly evocative family portraits in Joy Kogawa's *Obasan*
(1981) or Michael Ondaatje's *Running in the Family* (1982), both of
which bring the metonymic family story into dialogue with international histories. At the same time, Canadian postmemory writing may have
nothing to do with the family at all: Daphne Marlatt's *Steveston* (1974)
meditates on the memories and integrates photographs of Steveston (a
small West Coast community) residents in order to draw out a partial
history of Japanese internment during the Second World War. Writers
gravitated toward postmemory and interpreted it so variously because
it provided the means to escape the tired fad of nationally unifying literature that hurried past or altogether ignored theories and histories of
difference. The testimonial impulse of postmemory writing necessitates

the reader's confrontation with the heterogeneity of Canadian writing: every individual story becomes as important as any other. Postmemory writing was an ideal genre to reinvigorate the trope of the Canadian mosaic during a decade in which various cultural groups and activists were posing serious challenges to the long-held ideas of Canadian identity and national history.

In this vein, postmemory reminds readers that the cultural conditions of the 1970s were favourable not just to pockets of romantic nationalists or nihilistic postmodernists but also to those writers who exhibited a conflicted curiosity about the intersection of individual and nation. McKinnon's *I Wanted to Say Something* exemplifies some of the potential of this writing, and an entire generation of his contemporaries saw value in and pursued this genre. The rich body of postmemory writing produced in the 1970s and thereafter allows scholars to bring old texts, mixed genres, and different aesthetics into fruitful, new dialogue with each other and to nuance conventional notions of "the centennial era" as a period of either blind nationalism or uncompromising skepticism. Indeed, as a methodology, "postmemory" may provide inroads into much more dynamic images of the era that brought microhistories to the fore of nationalist discussions.

CHAPTER 10

• ◆ •

"Exhibit me buckskinned": Indigenous Legacy and Rememory in Joan Crate's *Pale as Real Ladies: Poems for Pauline Johnson*

Tanis MacDonald

Bill me as the Mohawk Princess.
Exhibit me buckskinned on a platform,
chanting, my skin bitten
by teeth, quills, clawed.
To have you hear my voice,
I will turn any trick at all.
Joan Crate, "The Naming," *Pale as Real Ladies* 41

Indigenousness is an identity constricted, shaped and lived in the politicized
context of contemporary colonialism.
Taiaiake Alfred and Jeff Corntassel, "Being Indigenous: Resurgences against
Contemporary Colonialism" 597

PART I: TRICKS OF MEMORY

Who has the right to remember? And who determines the appropriate-
ness of using the act of remembering to shape and order a text? We speak
colloquially of a "trick of memory" as that which reveals even as it obscures; a trick of memory need not necessarily be "correct" in terms of
its accuracy, but the phrase suggests that the trick has offered a different
perspective or a new way of recalling. Joan Crate's *Pale as Real Ladies:
Poems for Pauline Johnson* is such a "trick" text in that, like the historiographic metafiction it imitates, the memory it purports to re-animate is
that of a historical person rather the author's personal memory, and uses
the first-person address to offer a constructed confessionality. This way
of re-writing memory through an acknowledged appropriation of the
author's life and memory is a memory trick that readers agree to witness:
in the case of *Pale as Real Ladies*, a deliberate rewriting of a cultural and

literary legacy by a contemporary writer to "re-invent" a literary fore-mother (E. Pauline Johnson, the Mohawk poet and performer) for a contemporary readership (*Pale* 8). Crate's bold statement, in "The Naming," that Johnson's commitment to speaking on behalf of Indigenous people in the early years of the twentieth century is fierce enough to "turn any trick at all" is introduced with the idea of Johnson as a self-conscious but politically aware "exhibit." Crate's understanding of Johnson's risk-taking stage performances combined with her desperation is undoubtedly feminist in its intent. *Pale as Real Ladies* torques time and subjectivity (that of Johnson as subject with that of Crate as author) to speak of the parallel difficulties of being a woman with a mixed-race Indigenous heritage in Canada in two time periods, the late nineteenth and late twentieth centuries, and additionally, to emphasize that the past is actually the present in the bad-faith relations that Canada has had with Indigenous peoples. Carole Gerson notes with chagrin that it is possible to read the critical neglect of Johnson's work in a corresponding critical neglect of Crate's work of reclaiming Johnson, writing in 1998 that "Joan Crate's fine volume, *Pale as Real Ladies: Poems for Pauline Johnson* [. . .] remains virtually unknown, to the undeserved disesteem of both Johnson and Crate" ("Most Canadian" 99).

Concerning the question of who has the right to remember, Avishai Margalit's exploration of an "ethics of memory" provides us with some parameters: "Ethics [. . .] tells us how we should regulate our thick relations; morality tells us how we should regulate our thin relations" (8). Margalit also suggests that memory provides "the cement that holds thick relations together" in families, villages, tribes and nations: what he calls "a community of memory" (8). Part of defining "thick relations" depends upon a shared culture that is at least partly predicated on a shared past, and Margalit comments on the role of responsibility to the past when he notes that "A community of memory is a community based not only on actual thick relations to the living but also on thick relations to the dead" (69). "Thin relations," by contrast, are the relations we have with strangers who may be as united with or as disunited against the community in question as the idea of being "part of humanity" suggests.

Thinking about the Indigenous peoples of Canada as communities of memory that continue to struggle against systems of contemporary colonialism, as well as communities that seek acknowledgement of a past marked by the state-initiated genocide of Indigenous peoples, it is useful to consider Toni Morrison's concept of rememory as it encapsulates the idea that the cultural past—including that past's shaping by colonial violence—is absolutely alive in the minds of the community. Marianne Hirsch glosses rememory's political possibilities when she notes "rememory serves as a ground of resistance and opposition. Rememory is neither memory nor forgetting, but memory combined with (the threat of) repetition" (94). But what is the place of rememory as resistance in reading *Pale as Real Ladies*? Readers have noted that the text reads two ways depending upon whether Joan Crate is perceived to be an author with a mixed-race background or an author without any Indigenous heritage. Does the "trick" of memory in Crate's text turn upon the appropriation of Johnson as an exotic literary commodity? Or does the text return readers to the challenges of establishing legitimacy and authenticity in Indigenous literatures in Canada, something that Lenore Keeshig-Tobias (Chippewa), among others, addresses in her foundational short essay "Stop Stealing Native Stories"? We must acknowledge that the enculturation of "Canadian" literature necessitates a negotiation of memory that is sometimes made over into a commodity by subgenres like historiographic metafiction or documentary poetry, even when it is offered as a feminist re-vision in Adrienne Rich's sense of the term. The ways in which *Pale as Real Ladies* raises questions about how Johnson is "billed" and "exhibited" as a remembered foremother is rich in irony especially when set against questions of Crate's own "billing": her sometimes-ambiguous cultural identification.

Pale as Real Ladies turns upon a particular trick of remembering Johnson as a literary and political icon, and then performs a similar kind of identity trick as the one that Johnson performed for her audiences: the transformation of the author's identity from Indigenous to White, probing at the possibilities of mix in the term *mixed-race*. The series of tricks that Crate embeds in the text act as deliberate manipulations of memory and identity, and these tricks of memory lead the way to deeper issues of community as they appear not only in the content of Crate's text, but also in its context as a text that either resists or re-enacts contemporary colonialism. The work of Taiaiake Alfred (Mohawk) and Jeff Corntassel (Cherokee) on reclaiming Indigenous identity suggests that a thoughtful reading of *Pale as Real Ladies* must include its "constrictions and shaping" by contemporary colonialism. Alfred and Corntassel warn that postmodern imperialist policy "pulls Indigenous peoples away from cultural practices and community aspects of 'being Indigenous' towards a political-legal construction as 'aboriginal' [. . .] representative of what we call being 'incidentally Indigenous'" (599). Is the self-conscious "exhibit" of Johnson in *Pale as Real Ladies* an example of "contemporary colonialism" because Crate may be an "incidentally Indigenous" author who exists outside of an Indigenous community of memory and its attendant cultural practices? Or does the audacity of that exhibit as a literary political act align both Crate and Johnson with Thomas King's refusal of rigid racial denominators that uphold contemporary colonialism's "romantic, mystical, and, in many instances, a self-serving notion" of otherness in Western epistemology (King, "Introduction" xi)? This paper will examine Crate's memory work in *Pale as Real Ladies* as subject to discourses that caution against literary re-colonization even as they assert the need to remember "all our relations" in twenty-first century Canada.

PART 2: REMEMORY: ON BEING PAULINE

Pale as Real Ladies: Poems for Pauline Johnson shows Alberta writer Crate rewriting the life and work of E. Pauline Johnson, the part-Mohawk writer whose popular and culturally subversive public performances of her poems in the early years of the twentieth century were unfortunately denigrated as sentimental by mid-century critics who favoured a cooler modernist literary style. While Johnson was respected and often lauded by her contemporaries, Gerson notes that Johnson's fading reputation among modernists "was largely due to three features that make her especially interesting today: she was female, she claimed a First Nations identity, and she was amazingly popular" (94). Since the mid-1980s, other writers, Indigenous and non-Indigenous, have reasserted Johnson's importance to Canadian, feminist, and Indigenous literatures. George W. Lyon, in "Pauline Johnson: A Reconsideration," writes "Pauline Johnson created poems and stories that strain against the semiotic boundaries imposed by the world she knew. [. . .] And she was also capable of writing lines that ought to be allowed to resonate even in postmodern ears" (158). Mary Elizabeth Leighton, among other critics, has written about Johnson's performances as designedly ironic and shrewdly manipulative of the media coverage of her era. Johnson has been the subject of Gerson and Veronica Strong-Boag's literary biography *Paddling her Own Canoe: The Times and Texts of E. Pauline Johnson, Tekahionwake* (2000) and their edited collection, *E. Pauline Johnson, Tekahionwake: Collected Poems and*

Selected Prose (2002), as well as Charlotte Gray's Pierre Berton Award–winning biography *Flint and Feather: The Life and Times of E. Pauline Johnson, Tekahionwake* (2002). But most tellingly, Mohawk writer Beth Brant declares in her 1994 book *Writing As Witness* that it is time "to recognize Johnson for the revolutionary she was" (6) and that Johnson's position as a literary foremother for Indigenous women writers must be acknowledged, for Johnson "walked the writing path clearing the brush for us to follow" (8).

By commenting on the politics of female Indigenous identity as Johnson performed them in the decades following Confederation, *Pale as Real Ladies* foregrounds some thorny questions about the use of memory as community legacy, about the definition of community in the context of Canadian Indigenous literatures, and about the practical politics of being Indigenous. In the face of these questions, it is not enough to think of "looking back through our mothers" in Virginia Woolf's context, nor to focus primarily on poetry as "re-vision" in Adrienne Rich's sense of that phrase, though the feminist project of recovering forgotten women writers aligns in some ways with the work of Indigenous female writers like Maria Campbell (Métis) who seek to "put the Mother back in the language" (Interview 49). The metaphor of maternal literary ancestors is brought sharply into focus by the concern for Indigenous identity that is rooted in culture rather than in legal governmental-controlled definitions and underscored by the kind of identity tricks offered by Johnson in public performance and by Crate in *Pale as Real Ladies*. Johnson, one of four children born in 1861 to George Johnson, chief of the Six Nations Mohawk Reserve, and his White English-Quaker wife, Emily Howells Johnson, devoted much of her life and writing to parsing the ways that a mixed-race woman could be "read" as a citizen of the Dominion of Canada, as an Indigenous person, as an inheritor of cultural practices, as a cultural ambassador to the "White world," and perhaps most poignantly, as a performer of those cultural codes and their various undoings. Crate's *Pale as Real Ladies* is positioned, at least in part, to view the tensions between these roles as they arose in Johnson's performing life (in poems like "The Censored Life of a Lady Poet" and "The Poetry Reading") and in her personal life, delving into the romantic mishaps and loneliness of her siblings' relationships ("The Party," "To Allen on His Wedding Day," and "Eva, my sister") as well as her own two broken engagements ("Dearest Pauline" and "Charles, what shall I do").

Paying homage to Johnson's performance of racial identities in her dual on-stage personae of elegant Victorian lady and politically assertive "red Indian," Crate's use of first-person narration assumes the biographical voice of Johnson in order to unpack the complex social, cultural, and political constructions of both author and subject as women of mixed racial heritage. When she writes in Johnson's voice, "Exhibit me buckskinned on a platform [. . .] / To have you hear my voice, / I will turn any trick at all," Crate discomfits both the identificatory practice of literary foremothering and the practice of rememory through poetic ventriloquism. Crate also remembers Johnson's politics through the lens of the social abuse of Indigenous women in the twentieth century in poems like "Gleichen" and "I am A Prophet," and in offering an unromanticized portrait of poverty and prostitution, rapidly desentimentalizes Johnson's legacy to remind readers of Johnson's position as an advocate for Indigenous visibility and civil rights in the early years of the twentieth century. In this sense, *Pale as Real Ladies* can be read as a text that strives "to address history and historicity of our present moment responsibly— without, that is, maintaining the illusion of innocence or non-complicity" as Smaro Kamboureli asserts in *Scandalous Bodies* (25).

Modernist assessments of Johnson's work as non-political do not stand up upon even a cursory examination of her oeuvre. Her feminist sensibilities are crystal clear in poems like "Ojistoh," in which a woman kills her abductor and would-be rapist, and appear more subtly but just as intensely in her canoeing poems like "The Song My Paddle Sings" and "The Idlers" in which the female canoeist's athletic independence cannot be separated from her sexual subjectivity. So, too, Johnson's fierce dramatic monologue "A Cry from an Indian Wife," based on the Battle of Cut Knife Creek on 2 May 1885, was published by Charles G.D. Roberts in *The Week* on 18 June 1885, a mere six weeks after the battle itself, and while the Battle of Batoche continued. Johnson not only took up the cause for the Métis, but also recited that poem in her touring performances in later years, making a direct appeal to her mostly White audience members to think about the cost of "making our nation least"—that nation, in the context of "A Cry from an Indian Wife," refers to the Métis. Johnson's was no distanced discourse, but rather an assertion of cultural tradition and racial subjectivity undertaken in circumstances that could not have been more politically audacious. If it is true that her audiences tended to romanticize her "red Indian" persona, and that Johnson let them do so in order to satisfy her larger agenda of having a public voice for Indigenous peoples, she could also be tart in her defence of her culture, famously confronting a reporter for the *Chicago Tribune* in 1897: "If you don't want to hear about the history of my people, what did you come here for?" (qtd. Gray 233). Thinking about "A Cry from an Indian Wife" in the context of Johnson's dismissal by early male modernists in Canada suggests that the prejudice against Johnson may also have roots in regionality; what did F.R. Scott and the members of the McGill Group know about Batoche?

Undeniably, Johnson's political writings went beyond poetry. From her short story "A Red Girl's Reasoning" to her wry but determined humour in "A Strong Race Opinion: On the Indian Girl in Modern Fiction" to her *Legends of Vancouver*, Johnson's legacy is marked by her struggle, often isolated, to situate herself as an inheritor and sometimes as a translator of a rich Indigenous tradition that had survived colonialism and would continue to do so. She sought to educate non-Indigenous peoples about Indigenous cultures and suggest that alliances were possible, even in an era when such alliances were few and far between. In this light, Crate's *Pale as Real Ladies* seems to be a timely and welcome re-imagining, not only because Crate's book explores Johnson's political subversiveness, but also because it offers sensitive insight into Johnson's often-difficult personal life as a counterpoint to her artistic life: the physical challenges of touring, her loneliness, her financial problems, her resistance to assimilation into the White world for which she performed but from which she remained apart: "I never felt it was I, but rather the characters I assumed that the eyes were upon" (Johnson, qtd. Gray 221). Johnson's feeling of separateness from an on-stage "I" finds a literary correlative in Crate's use of a shifting narrative "I" which deliberately blends not only the dual stage personae of "red Indian" and "Victorian lady" that Johnson manipulated to such dramatic advantage, but also questions the distinctions between present and past and between writer and subject. In a poem like "The Society Page," Johnson's intimate backstage admissions of frailty, initially addressed to her absent lover, Charles Drayton, are distracted by an awareness of "someone" from the future, a contemporary writer—who may or may not be Crate—who regards Johnson's successes and sacrifices:

Someone writes poems about me,
words lying on the page, small corpses.
She is afraid of my moist breath under her wrist,
and ink mixing in our veins.
She reels me into the late twentieth century
where I am quaint as the disintegrating
paper lace on the valentine you gave me. (*Pale* 27)

This constructed awareness of the self as an event subject to historical narrative and even subject to "lying"—a pun Crate foregrounds in the
poem—is meant to discomfit the reader as well as Crate's construction
of Johnson as "Pauline": both historical and poetic subject. Pauline notes
that the poems written by the future "someone" will drain words so that
they become "small corpses" and that she herself, reeled like a prize fish
into the future, will be regarded as "quaint" rather than powerful, as a
"disintegrating" object rather than an active agent. Crate's diction in "The
Society Page" seems tailor-made for introducing "the challenge of being
Indigenous" as Alfred and Corntassel outline it, especially as Johnson
may be reread in "the era of contemporary colonialism—a form of postmodern imperialism in which domination is still the Settler imperative
but where colonizers have designed and practised more subtle means
[. . .] of accomplishing their objectives" (Alfred and Corntassel 597–98).
Is rememory at work here, or a "lying" appropriation?

Crate's own racial position—or the position of that "someone" from
the future—becomes especially important by the time the collection
comes to the dramatic and searing "I Am a Prophet," in which the politics of identity are impossible to ignore. This poem is a dramatic monologue spoken by a kind of Indigenous Scheherazade, a mystic dancer
whose stories are written on her body. She declares, "I have been chosen
by Tyee / to speak of the beginning. My flesh / is a series of writhing
tablets" (*Pale* 59). "I Am a Prophet" combines the Judeo-Christian myth
of "lost tribes" with images drawn mainly from Coastal peoples such as
Chinook, Haida, and Haisla cultures: salmon, whales, ravens, eagles, and
totem poles depicting all of these animals appear on her flesh. She is a
living totem pole, a storytelling artifact upon whom the stories of First
Peoples are depicted. The poem takes a grisly turn as the speaker reports
that Tyee has vanished, "Our garden was cleared / and our spirits shrank"
and storytelling collapses into begging:

They will speak to you from my mouth
if you will just buy me a drink.
No, don't go yet!
You haven't seen it all.
For ten bucks I will show you
Every scar on my body.
Another ten, you can make your own.
I will dance for you in a veil
of red waterfalls.
Stay, I am a prophet. (*Pale* 60)

This poem is disturbing in its violence as well as in its implication that female prophets are inevitably sacrificial figures. The echo of Crate's promise to "turn any trick at all" is strong, but the tone of "I Am a Prophet" is nothing if not boldly ironic. In a 2008 introduction to the poem on the website for *The Literary Review of Canada*, Cornelia Hoogland notes that "I Am a Prophet" acts as "the reader's encounter with Johnson on one of her performance tours across Canada in the late 1800s" and that the poem "invites the reader into a striptease of Canada's history of colonization, betrayal and genocide of Native peoples [. . .] and is brilliantly written from a Native perspective." However, it is not certain that the speaker is Johnson, or even an imagined extrapolation of her, particularly because Crate's Johnson is the dying speaker of the "Last Words" poem that immediately precedes "I Am a Prophet" in *Pale as Real Ladies*. The prophecy of the poem is undeniably a warning about the future, but it is also problematically about a present in which a powerful woman is reduced to begging for money and abuse, and—by implication—to prostituting her culture and her body. The implications change if we think of the poem as coming from a master storyteller like Johnson (as Hoogland suggests) who controls the narrative irony as a history lesson, making the poem an indictment of colonialism rather than a re-enactment of it. It is also possible to read the poem as a warning about contemporary colonialism in which culture is co-opted and commodified so thoroughly that not even the woman who carries the stories on her body can access their cultural power. Is the poem a visceral reminder that every story is as "sharp as a knife" as Robert Bringhurst's compilation of Haida stories notes? Crate's "reeling in" of Johnson into the twentieth century could suggest that she could not finish the book without providing a picture

of the violence that has been visited on Indigenous women by the ongoing forces of colonialism. Or is this poem, too, a violent re-colonization,
reducing an Indigenous woman to a cliché of princess-turned-squaw as
Janice Acoose (Salteaux/Métis) has written? Is the poem a literary example of what Alfred and Corntassel would call "colonial power as shape-
shifter" (601)? The answers depend at least in part upon how we read
Crate's racial identity and her definition of alliance.

PART 3: COMMUNITY OF MEMORY:
ON BEING INDIGENOUS

Most scholarly analysis and inclusion of Crate's work in the classroom
or as a text of note relies upon reading Crate as a woman of mixed-race
heritage whose background is a significant factor in her re-matriation of
Johnson. For example, Kimberley J. Verwaayen's work on this text emphasizes the complexity of "consanguinity and sorority—renunciation
and refusal" (220) that describes the dynamics between author, subject,
and author-as-subject in *Pale as Real Ladies*. In her analysis of "identity
as a discursive construction" (217), Verwaayen reads Crate's text "as hy-
perconscious of the jeopardy of appropriation" and of "the epistemic violence" of re-writing another subject (212), and further notes that Crate
"is a woman of mixed-European and Aboriginal heritage (Crate's nation
is Blackfoot/Cree)" (212n) even as she argues against adopting any easy
equivalency between Johnson and Crate, writing that "identification
does not mean identicality" (213n). Verwaayen points to "Crate's careful
positioning of the 'Prairie Greyhound' narrator as an Aboriginal woman"
(213n), but I note that poem is as ambiguous about the narrator's racial
heritage as Crate is about her own. The male bus passengers first call
the narrator "Babe" in the present tense, and then the narrator speaks
to Pauline who watches the scene in the narrator's imagination: "It's still
difficult for a woman to travel alone at night. In the window you watch
me. 'Squaw,' they called on the bus, the train" (*Pale* 8). Switching to the
past tense suggests that the narrator is speaking of Pauline's experience,
but the inclusion of the bus in that past tense suggests the men address
the narrator as "Squaw," having received no reaction to "Babe." Is this a
catalogue of insults to a woman, or do the men actually see the narrator
as Indigenous? It's hard to tell. There is a careful racial positioning going
on here, but Crate's intent appears to be to remain ambiguous about the
narrator's racial heritage.

To be "incidentally Indigenous" in the way that Alfred and Corntassel have described is to claim the legal governmental definition of Aboriginal as a personal identity without a cultural and political commitment to an Indigenous community. In their potent article, "Being Indigenous: Resurgences against Contemporary Colonialism," Alfred and Corntassel define "being Indigenous" as "the struggle to survive as distinct people on foundations constituted in their unique heritages, attachment to their homelands, and natural ways of life" as well as the equally significant "fact that their existence is in large part lived as determined acts of survival against colonizing states' efforts to eradicate them culturally, politically and physically" (597). Crate's racial background—like that of many Canadians—appears to be ambiguous and highly negotiated. It is an open secret in the Canadian literary community that some Indigenous authors believe that Crate is not Indigenous enough to be rewriting the subjectivities and voices of First Nations women. If we look at what Crate says about herself, her brief biographies prove a bit mystifying. Author biographies in *Pale as Real Ladies* and in her next poetry book, *Foreign Homes* (2001), neither state a tribal affiliation nor mention a mixed-race heritage. *Foreign Homes* features a poetry series similar to *Pale as Real Ladies*, titled "Loose Feathers on Stone," in which Crate voices Shawnandithit, the final surviving Beothuk woman who died of tuberculosis in Newfoundland in 1829. However, biographies of Crate in several anthologies of Indigenous literature published between 1990 and 2005 do imply, and in some cases, openly cite an Indigenous heritage for Crate. The "Native Writers and Canadian Writing" special issue of *Canadian Literature* (1990) includes three poems by Crate, including two from the "Loose Feathers on Stone" series, though no tribal affiliation accompanies Crate's name. In *An Anthology of Canadian Native Literature in English* (2005), edited by Daniel David Moses (Delaware) and Terry Goldie, Crate's short biography does not mention an Indigenous background, but tribal affiliation "Cree" appears beneath her name. Cornelia Hoogland, in *The Literary Review of Canada*, refers to the author as "Métis poet Joan Crate."

In the anthology *Native Poetry in Canada: A Contemporary Anthology* (2001), edited by Jeannette Armstrong (Okanagan) and Lally Grauer, Crate fleshes out her autobiography:

being of mixed nations (Cree and about five million other things),
and having been part of different socio-economic groups at different

periods of my life, have made me think of "home" and "belonging" as somewhat transitory, really existing in terms of the spirit within the universe, rather than the physical body at some address or part of some identifiable group. My work with Pauline Johnson and Shawnandithit has allowed me to feel (and hopefully express) the existence of those of the past in our present lives and as part of the landscape which they inhabit(ed), both physical and spiritual. (227)

The biographical statement rings with ambiguity; it stakes a claim on a community of memory partly through a mixed heritage and partly through a spiritual connection forged by literary ventriloquism, even as it casually eschews a traditional claim on inherited culture as a form of belonging ("Cree and about five million other things"). Crate's statement is important to take seriously in 2012, when especially on the prairies, the culture of Métissage has begun to reflect the fact that four generations after the Battle of Batoche, many of the great-great-grandchildren of the Métis have grown up knowing only about the French or Scottish parts of their heritage and must now make a conscious effort to identify themselves as Indigenous, through familial history and through cultural consciousness. At the Symposium for Manitoba Writing in May of 2012, Niigaanwewidam James Sinclair (Anishinaabe) reminded the audience that as an unfortunate legal result of the 1885 action at Batoche, Métis people on the prairies were considered enemies of the state until the 1940s. Given this designation, it is no small wonder that four generations may have chosen to mute or in some cases even hide their heritage in order to raise their children.

Moving from a declaration like Crate's definition of a mixed-nations background to a politically and culturally conscious Indigeneity, what can we say about the role of rememory in such a complex—and so historically colonized—dynamic of identity? Might we read Crate's work with Johnson and Shawnandithit as a way of defining poetic rememory as a "determined act of survival" in Alfred and Corntassel's terms? The problem with demanding proof of any kind of authenticity is the increased inability to "prove" anything at all about the diverse, suppressed, disconnected, or historically denigrated racial backgrounds of people living in Canada at the beginning of the twenty-first century. Crate's ambiguous declarations may be adequate proof for some that she may responsibly write about Johnson as a foremother figure; for others, this may be considered inadequate. There is a real concern with preserving Indigenous community in conjunction with, or in defiance of, the rediscovery of Indigenous backgrounds that is a by-product of the suppression of such identities for several generations. Is the problem with Crate that she is "not Indigenous enough" to be counted as an Indigenous author? Or that she is not Indigenous in the right way? These are discomfiting questions, ones that as a non-Indigenous scholar, I cannot answer; but neither can I responsibly sidestep the need to discuss the historical and cultural complications that have begun to surface around Indigenous identity in Canadian literature, particularly as Indigenous communities consolidate their rights to community practice and against appropriation with movements like Idle No More.

Pale as Real Ladies, with its taunting title proposing many levels of irony about race and gender, sets up "realness" as the grit that abrades the surface of the text, just as Johnson's recitals were set up to rattle her audience's definitions of racial authenticity. It is easy to be presentist and to sit in judgment of early-twentieth-century audiences who asked Johnson—so naively, so earnestly—if she was "a real red Indian," but are we not asking something similar about Crate? Is she "real" enough to inherit the right to "remember" Johnson? Is Crate "Indigenous enough" for her rewriting of Johnson's voice to be an act of rememory and not appropriation?

At the core of this debate, somewhere between the need to "find the Mother" in the language of the Indigenous women writers of the past and the discourse of Indigenous identity and its role in resistance to contemporary colonization, there is a very difficult question indeed: one of authenticity and the claim to an Indigenous heritage. While the assertion of community practice as identificatory in the face of governmental definitions is undoubtedly urgent, I have to wonder about young people who are newly discovering their buried familial legacies and may be at this moment—through no fault of their own—"incidentally Indigenous" because they are not yet involved in cultural practice. Those great-great-grandchildren of Batoche survivors are now young adults, discovering that their own identities as people with Indigenous backgrounds are marginal, or contested, or confronted with possibilities that they had never before considered. "You're not the Indian I had in mind" writes Thomas King (Cherokee/Greek) in *The Truth about Stories*, riffing on non-Indigenous people's responses to his own mixed heritage, his childhood lived outside of an Aboriginal community, and his own thoughts about what exactly establishes Indigenous identity (31). What if, given the long history of mixed relations in Canada, we are not the Indians anyone had in mind, including ourselves?

CHAPTER 11

◦◆◦

Scrapbooking: Memory and Memorabilia in Gail Anderson-Dargatz's *The Cure for Death by Lightning* and *Turtle Valley*

Cynthia Sugars

There is something about objects, *memento mori*, that seem to encapsulate the past. We speak of *lieux de mémoire*, but *objets de mémoire*—especially those associated with familial history and genealogy—acquire the status of memorial time-capsules. They encrypt the cultural memory of a family—and family inheritance—in seemingly tangible yet nevertheless inexpressible ways. We impose on these objects an impossible function, as though transgenerational memory, in some mystical fashion, were embodied and transmitted in the inherited objects themselves. The psychic and emotive resonance associated with ancestral objects appears to capture the "Real" of the past, which in turn initiates an essentially melancholic relation to external objects by asking that they span the gulf between historical generations.

This emotive relation to memorabilia translates into a specific form of postmemory, since it construes the object as a bearer of transgenerational experience. Peter Hodgins makes use of the evocative phrase "nostalgia for memory" ("Our Haunted Present" 100), which could be extended, in this instance, to a "nostalgia for *inherited* memory" as a way of emphasizing intergenerational continuity. In the present, then, heirlooms and memorabilia consolidate a nostalgia for *inherited* memory as it is evoked through the physical object. The allure of the evocative memorial object is a central element in Gail Anderson-Dargatz's two interlinked novels, *The Cure for Death by Lightning* (1996) and *Turtle Valley* (2007). An important concern of both novels is the unravelling of memory and historical continuity—perhaps even the inadequacy of a word such as *unravelling*, which would suggest a memory that has taken hold but is being eroded.

The fleetingness of historical continuity is a recurrent theme in theories of memory and historical fiction. In many of these accounts, the social and the individual are mediated by the idea of transgenerational memory, which can occur through a variety of processes, from psychoanalytic theories of unconscious memory to the commemorative mechanisms that Pierre Nora describes as *lieux de mémoire*. According to Nora, these *lieux de mémoire* are the embodiments "of a memorial consciousness that has barely survived in a historical age that calls out for memory because it has abandoned it" (149). Without "commemorative vigilance," he states, "history would soon sweep [memory] away" (149). Hodgins' reformulation of Nora's account notes how the "assumption that we have fallen from an authentic relationship to memory" initiates a "return to our roots" (101). This perspective is characterized by a simultaneous sense of urgency and melancholy, which "endow[s] memory with a quasi-magical character in which memory is celebrated as the key to rediscovering an authentic being in the world that is obscured in our [. . .] ephemeral present" (101).

The insistence on memory as a link across historical generations informs Marianne Hirsch's concept of "postmemory,"[1] which refers to the transmission of traumatic memory between generations and thus reflects "an uneasy oscillation between continuity and rupture" (106). In Anderson-Dargatz's work, this notion of transgenerational transmission is given a new slant, for her novels explore the *desire* for embodied memory as a means of containing the slippage into ephemerality. Her characters are propelled by a desire for a form of postmemory, a yearning for inherited memory "that preceded one's birth or one's consciousness" (Hirsch 107). As Hirsch puts it, "Postmemory's connection to the past is thus not actually mediated by recall but by imaginative investment, projection, and creation" (107). This process informs what Eva Hoffman describes as the sensation of inheriting a "'deeply internalized but strangely unknown past'" (qtd in Hirsch 108). Anderson-Dargatz's novels describe characters who conjure memorial inheritance through

---

1 I am using Hirsch's concept of postmemory to describe the generalized desire for inherited memory that is present in Anderson-Dargatz's works. However, it is important to note that the large-scale traumas that inform Hirsch's account of the concept yield a different assessment from the willed inheritance of familial memories—even those marked by ancestral trauma—that I am discussing here.

fantasy: her characters want to believe in the possibility of inherited memories. Arguably, a form of heritable transmission is present in the possession by Coyote in *The Cure for Death by Lightning*, yet this phenomenon may or may not be a figment of the protagonist's imagination. Moreover, the "oscillation between continuity and rupture" (106) that Hirsch describes as integral to postmemory becomes contained in *Turtle Valley*, where it is an inherited predisposition for forgetting that is passed down through the generations. Indeed, the characters in *Turtle Valley* exhibit a variety of memory disorders—the mother who apparently suffers from dementia; the husband whose stroke means that he can only speak in poetic approximations; the father who is dying from cancer. In the midst of this unravelling, the focus is on the adult daughter of the family, Kat, who senses a loss of self in the absence of memories that she yearns to acquire. In the novel, Kat searches for genealogical antiquities as a way of assigning memory traces to particular objects, seeking to transform them into commemorative artifacts. This entails a search for the Proustian eureka moment, when memory is conjured wholesale by a serendipitous object. What the novel offers, by contrast, is a de-materialization of memory in what we commonly refer to as mementos (more plainly thought of as willed memory triggers): treasures, letters, possessions, scrapbooks, and documents. Indeed, Kat discovers how objects can function as obstructions to memory because the encodings she seeks are elusive. It may be that the dislocation of memory taps into something more profound than a continuous memory trace, conveying the ephemeral nature of subjective memory *as it is evoked* in the keepsakes that surround us. The paradox is that mementos underscore the intangibility of memorialization.

This essay will consider the connections between memory and memorabilia in *The Cure for Death by Lightning* and its sequel *Turtle Valley*. One of the most famous symbols in *The Cure for Death by Lightning* is the scrapbook that belongs to the protagonist's mother, Maud. Throughout the novel, Beth appeals to the scrapbook as a clue to the events of her fifteenth year, which she describes as "the year the world fell apart" (2). In critical discourse about the book, the scrapbook is often figured as an emblem of female experience and cultural transmission (Lewis; Kelman). The scrapbook is at once Maud's aesthetic creation, her encrypted rebellion, her record of her experience, her almanac of female culture, and her source of solace. Like the damaged tortoiseshell butterfly that is pasted in its pages—which is interpreted as "a reminder to keep going" (1)—the scrapbook as a whole is posited as a testament to continuity and survival.

However, what critics often overlook is the extent to which the scrapbook is in fact a barrier to communication in the novel. While Beth suspects that the scrapbook might offer cultural-historical transmission, in the narrative Maud repeatedly restricts Beth's access to its pages. The desire for female cultural continuity that is seemingly represented by the scrapbook is thus thwarted, since the scrapbook establishes a barrier between mother and daughter; in fact, Maud often uses it to shut Beth out. This is epitomized the night when the father forces Beth to help him remove the cow's ovaries. Maud abandons Beth to the torture, and flees into the house where she is found "sitting at the kitchen table, writing on one of the pages of her scrapbook" (86). Likewise, after the "nylon" incident (the token pay-off after Beth has been raped by her father), Maud becomes almost catatonic and clutches the scrapbook to her breast refusing to speak to her daughter. Maud's obsessive control over the book means that she selects what Beth is allowed to see, forbidding her to consult it in her absence. As Beth points out in the novel's prologue, "I didn't [. . .] touch her scrapbook, at least not when she was in the room" (1). At times, Beth even thinks that her mother tries to tease and chastise her within the pages of the book, inserting new material and commentaries which Beth will stumble upon. Midway through the novel, for instance, we, along with Beth, make the disconcerting discovery that Maud has glued into the scrapbook a square torn from the package of nylons (219). This jarring memento creates a strange metafictional effect—evoking shared memory through a form of uncanny surveillance, in which the reader of the diary is conscious of its creator "speaking" to him/her within the text—as though to destabilize the priority of both scrapbook and memory narrative, so that the very book we've been reading appears to have been a transcription of the scrapbook itself, or vice versa. The uncanny relation of the scrapbook to Beth's narrative means that its mnemonic function is disrupted. Similarly, Maud inserts a reference to the lightning strike that paralyzed Beth's arm "on the space between the cure for death by lightning and the butterfly with its wing torn away" (219); yet this addendum to the scrapbook page is not cited in the novel's prologue (even though the scrapbook the narrator possesses in the prologue is supposedly the most up-to-date version, inherited by Beth after her mother's death). At the conclusion of the novel, Beth begins to fashion a scrapbook of her own, but only "because my mother had refused to buy me one when I pleaded with her" (287).

The failure of memorial objects in *The Cure for Death by Lightning* is emblematic, more generally, of Beth's sense of being out of place in Turtle Valley due to her obscure family origins. If the scrapbook refuses any transparent connection with her past, so does the landscape she inhabits. As a kind of cultural orphan, Beth sees herself to be lacking a coherent genealogical ancestry. Her father, whose mother died in childbirth, is of unknown origin and there are no photographs of his family in the house (16). Her mother, Maud, is a war bride from England whose two sisters live in England and Australia: "I had never met either of them, and my grandparents were long dead" (17). The boys on the Turtle Reserve taunt her with the label "Cockney": "'Go back where you belong, Cockney'" (113). Beth is something of a genetic orphan in this world, which in part is why she is so mesmerized by the larger-than-life presence of Bertha Moses and her extended family. Not only does Bertha's family include generations of women and their children, but the two farmhands who work on Beth's farm are related to Bertha, making the settler family here at once landholders but also people who are culturally and genealogically bereft. In a sense, Maud's scrapbook becomes an overdetermined and encrypted site of cultural memory, as if to fill in for the striking absence of genealogical memory that pervades Beth's history. After Bertha's granddaughter Nora relays to Beth how the "winter house" (111) belonged to her great-grandmother, grandmother, and now to herself, Beth laments, "'My dad wouldn't give nothing to me'" (112). The only ancestral presence in their home is the ghost of Beth's grandmother, but this takes the form of a private haunting. Only Maud can see her, and the two of them are engaged in settling their personal demons (presumably because Maud was molested by her father with the mother's knowledge). The grandmother, then, offers no solace or instruction to Beth; indeed, Beth repeatedly sees her as a sign of her mother's mental instability, for whenever Maud is upset she retreats into an extended argument with her mother's invisible ghost.[2]

---

2   This sense of cultural-genealogical isolation is rectified in *Turtle Valley*, in which the ghosts of Maud and her husband, two generations later, linger on the family property as remnants—and reminders—of the traumatic past.

"'[L]isten to your ancestors,'" Bertha tells her own daughter, "'Even those who've passed over'" (245). The trouble is that Beth does not know her ancestors, nor does she have any sense of cultural transmission or historical connection with them. The closest she comes are the "home-steader's children" (33), whose bodies are buried beneath the rock pile beside the barn. The children are the progeny of the previous owner of Beth's family's house, a Swedish homesteader named Olsen who married a woman from the Turtle Creek Reserve. Rumours abound about the cause of death of the children, since all eight of them died (as a result of either a bear attack or some form of insanity). The homesteader graves are one of the few markers of settlement ancestry in the area, but Beth's father has bought the property following Olsen's death and has covered the graves with a rock pile to obscure them. As Beth recalls, her father "picked rocks from the field and piled them to hide the graves of the homesteader's children and to rid himself of their bad luck" (33). Beth clearly identifies with the homesteader children as settlers who have in-habited the same land grant and who have lived the experience of set-tler trauma. They take the place of family ghosts, as she imagines she hears "their footsteps, the noise of their play, or the sound of a child crying" (34). The children speak to Beth from beyond the grave, becom-ing an emblem of her desire for ancestral spirits that share her habitation and history on the farm. Beth feels a connection to them as victims of her father's violence. In this sense, one might say that transgenerational memory does not necessarily have to occur within a family, and Beth's inheritance of this legacy enables her to forge a sense of historical inter-connection that is initiated through a shared habitation of place (and by the inscriptions—graves, roads, fences—that are etched upon that com-munal space). The comfort she seeks in such transgenerational connec-tions enables her to forge a bond with these earlier settler inhabitants, and in a sense their experience of traumatic violence acts as a warning (and protection) to her.

The link between the children and Beth's present experience comes in the form of Coyote, the voracious spirit that functions as a kind of transgenerational curse in the novel, taking possession of both settlers and Aboriginal people who, in varying ways, have inherited the violence of colonialism. Interestingly, Coyote Jack, the hermit who lives by himself in the woods, is a blood relation of the homesteader's children, since the "Swede," Coyote Jack's father, married one of the children, which makes

Coyote Jack their nephew. The question of genetic inheritance arises, obliquely, in the novel's ambiguous depiction of Coyote Jack. By making Coyote Jack a possible victim of Coyote "possession" (an encoded term for psychotic violence, among other things), the storyline implies that he has inherited a trauma/predisposition from the homesteader's children, which in turn is aligned with a violent settler-colonial history. Coyote Jack is thus a reluctant inheritor of postmemory, which aligns him with both the victims and the perpetrators of a violent past (since he is the mixed-blood grandchild of a White male settler, Olsen, and an Aboriginal woman).

Even though the children's voices remain spectral, and their full history inaccessible, the homesteader's children act as mediators of transgenerational memory. The difficulty for Beth is to decipher their warning. She thus embraces her mother's scrapbook as a repository of memory that she can turn to for corroboration. In the framing text of the novel, Beth has inherited her mother's possessions following her mother's death, which is why the scrapbook "sits inside the trunk that was her hope chest. I sometimes take out the scrapbook and sit with it at my kitchen table" (2). At the outset, Beth wants to establish her mother's scrapbook as a form of authentic cultural transmission that is absent in the world of her youth, yet when Beth looks into its pages she is continually denied access to interpretive transparency. The novel highlights the intensely mediated nature of memory, in this case as it is re-mediated through the format of the scrapbook. The scrapbook thus performs what Jay Bolter and Richard Grusin describe as the "double logic of *remediation*," that is, "the twin logics of immediacy and hypermediacy" (5). As a mnemonic device, the scrapbook is enigmatic and palimpsestic. On the other hand, its hyper-immediacy renders it unreliable and changing. Even in the framing "present tense" of the narrative, Beth continues to "find new entries in the scrapbook, things I've never seen before, as if my mother still sits each morning before I wake and copies a recipe, or adds a new page" (2). She embraces the scrapbook as material evidence for what she can recall *only from memory*, but by highlighting its role as a form of mediation, Beth only renders it more unstable.

Socrates' explication in Plato's *Phaedrus* of the ways that textual records encapsulate the failure of memory echoes the functioning of the scrapbook in *The Cure for Death by Lightning*. According to Socrates, the true effect of writing will be to "implant forgetfulness forever in [men's] souls; they will cease to exercise memory because they rely on that which is written, calling things to remembrance no longer from within themselves" (Plato 27). The fact is that Beth *does not clearly remember* what occurred that summer, which is why she relies on the scrapbook as a testament (perhaps even as the catalyzing sourcebook) of her story. If the scrapbook was Maud's "way of setting down the days so they wouldn't be forgotten" (2), the narrative that Beth writes becomes her way of doing something similar. As works of historiography, and hence of historical continuity, the two texts have similar goals, propelled by a form of personal and collective amnesia. No one can say "it was all a girl's fantasy," Beth insists, because it has now achieved material permanence as an artifact. Like a photograph, the scrapbook and memoir "become surrogate memory and their silences structure forgetting" (E. Edwards 332). And yet, Beth's account of the scrapbook's truth status is telling: "No one can tell me these events didn't happen. [. . .] The reminders are there, in that scrapbook, and I remember them all" (2). The slippage here from *reminders* to *remembering of reminders* is important, as if to say that Beth "remembers the reminders" and not the memories themselves. This is echoed in the *Phaedrus* when Socrates insists that writing "is a recipe not for memory, but for reminder" (27). What Beth "remembers" is her mother's scrapbook, or at least her sporadic glimpses into its pages. This movement from remembering to reminder (or from memory to memento) is confirmed in the novel when we are privy to the mother's mnemonic method. The messages in Maud's scrapbook are neither literal nor metaphorical cues to actual events; they are encrypted, metonymic. For example, Maud puts a pinch of blue flax into the scrapbook from the bunch that Beth has picked for her on the day following Beth's rape by her father. "'Something to remember the day by,'" Maud says enigmatically (195). However, another page contains a blue flax flower to commemorate "the big storm when the flax rained down on us" (219), so even the mementos themselves are duplicated. Another example is the sooty fingerprint that Beth accidentally leaves on the recipe for Honey Cake, which she interprets as a memento of the Swede's barn fire (218). As encryptions of actual events—and hence as evidence of the events of Beth's fifteenth summer—the cuttings in the scrapbook are less carriers of memory than signs of the inevitability of memory loss. Once the creator of the scrapbook is dead, or even after a brief passage of time, the mementos will no longer signify since their referents will be lost, thus embodying the actuality of historical rupture that Beth seeks to hold off.

In Beth's account, then, the scrapbook is sometimes a red herring. There is nothing in the scrapbook to "prove" the validity of Beth's story, to yield up the memory of past events, despite her insistence that it do so. This failure of signification is best highlighted by the "recipe" that opens the novel, the so-called "cure for death by lightning." On the one hand, the syntactical ambiguity of the phrase leaves it unclear whether the recipe is a cure for a lightning strike (cure for *death by lightning*), or whether lightning is a cure for death (*cure for death* by lightning). This confusion is highlighted by the mother's inscription of "*Ha! Ha!*" beside the recipe (1), calling into ironic question the memory that Beth is re-constructing. The scrapbook's mockery of its reader represents a beautiful instance of what Peter Schwenger describes (via Merleau-Ponty) as the "resolutely silent Other" that "holds itself aloof from us and remains self-sufficient" (3). It refuses direct access to its secrets. And yet, there is a positive message that can emerge from this lesson, one that is explored in *Turtle Valley*, in which an acceptance of the transitory nature of memory—even of memory loss or instability—becomes an affirmation of the transgenerational condition. If mementos evoke a psychic state that resides in the perceiver and not in the objects themselves, they nevertheless enable an articulation or narrativization of memorial inheritance: one that is partial and shifting and perhaps often imagined, but which nonetheless addresses the desire for mediation between generations.

In *Turtle Valley* the focus is on memory before it is entrenched *as* memory, or the anticipated failure of this entrenchment taking place (the fear that one will not remember). In this novel, it is Beth's daughter, Kat, who struggles to conjure memory from the material objects in the house that belonged to her parents and grandparents. Through a form of pathetic fallacy, Kat's emotional state (her fear of memory erasure) is paralleled by the forest fire that is rapidly encroaching on the community. The novel constitutes a meditation on the ghostly effects of evocative objects and a lament for memory loss, namely the ways we invest objects as repositories of memory, or as willed connections to the past. When faced with the possibility of the utter eradication of their homes, the local people begin to imbue household objects with forced evocative potential. A newspaper headline in the *Vancouver Sun* reads: "If you have 10 minutes to flee a forest fire, what do you take?" (3). In the process, the novel provides a meditation on the *burden of memory* as the threat of its impending loss plagues all of us. By this I don't refer to the burden of traumatic memory, but rather to the burden of memory more generally, the weight of memorabilia, particularly as it instills a fear of dispersal in the remembering subject. The novel is thus about the inevitability, the necessity, of letting the yearning for the "thingness" of memory go. John Frow, in his critique of Nora's *Lieux de Mémoire*, phrases this in terms of avoiding "the nostalgic essentialism that affirms the reality of an origin by proclaiming its loss" (152). The idea of a willed abandonment of the nostalgia for memory provides an evocative edge to this novel, which is at once about a desire for inherited memory and the need to eradicate the impossible exhortation *to* remember.

This focus is materially highlighted in the novel by its form as a kind of scrapbook, for each chapter is prefaced by a photograph of an antique object that is sometimes only peripherally mentioned in the chapter. The radical independence of the object is both highlighted and obscured in these cases—through a form of scrapbook simulation—for the photographed objects are pasted into the book, inviting the reader to "read" them as evocative objects in the chapters that they preface (see Figures 11.1 and 11.2). Kat finds these objects in the house, but the immediacy she seeks from them is barred, in part because the narratives surrounding the objects have been ruptured and forgotten in the passage of time. Kat is not sure what draws her so emotively to these objects—as though, like her husband and mother, she is compelled more powerfully by a gap in memory than by an active transgenerational connection. The connection is there, but not in the discernible sense Kat yearns for. Although she seeks direct access to the "pastness" of the past as it manifests in the present, the objects offer only a tantalizing promise of memory, which ultimately Kat is unable to tap in any transparent way.

Each object that Kat finds is associated with a particular family member and conjures a bygone era. However, in some cases they receive hardly any notice, as when Kat empties an old carpetbag and finds a collection of objects, including a comb, a lipstick, and a makeup compact (113–14). While an image of the compact heads Chapter Ten (Figure 11.2), its relevance to Kat remains unstated. The reader is thus positioned much like Kat herself, responding to the objects as potential encryptions of memory, and indeed, their appearance as old family photographs enhances the effect. The objects might echo Nora's claim that "there is no spontaneous memory" (149) and thus testify to what Paul Whitehouse terms "a residual compulsion to commemorate [. . .] within the [. . .] amnesiac modern world" (10). As Kat rummages through the items she finds in the house, the objects acquire an evocative resonance, but often of memories that Kat cannot have had (since she would have been an infant, or possibly not even have been born, at the time). As such, the objects embody what Hirsch describes as "not memories" (109), which nevertheless possess real affective force. As Benedict Anderson describes the paradox, there is "a huge modern accumulation of documentary evidence (birth certificates, diaries, report cards, letters, medical records, and the like) which simultaneously records a certain apparent continuity and emphasizes its loss from memory" (204). If Kat turns to the objects out of a yearning for a form of prosthetic memory, it is because she sees this process as a reverse displacement of the memory loss that she has experienced in her individual life.

In the novel, Kat's mother, Beth, now an old woman, duplicates the behaviour of her mother Maud in *The Cure for Death by Lightning*, obsessively recording her daily life in a series of notebooks. "It was her habit to chronicle even the smallest details of her life immediately after they transpired," Kat observes, "but she wasn't present for these moments

11.1 and **11.2** Illustrations from *Turtle Valley* by Gail Anderson-Dargatz, pp. 78 and 112.

any more than tourists who view their vacations through the lens of a camcorder" (20). Kat believes that her mother writes "to remember—as memory was such a mercurial companion, and one not to be counted on" (20), thus echoing Beth's "reading" of her mother's scrapbook in the first novel. In *The Cure for Death by Lightning*, Maud retreats to her rocking chair clutching her scrapbook to avoid the trauma of her married life and abusive husband. In *Turtle Valley*, it is her descendant, Beth, who turns to her texts for similar catharsis. Whenever she is anxious, Beth settles into her chair and scribbles furiously into a notebook. Her daughter Kat resents these moments as a kind of abandonment: "'I didn't like that you disappeared into it,'" she tells her mother. "'But I have the same desire to write everything down, so I'll remember it'" (150). And yet, Kat is mistaken. Fully aware of the failure of writing as a fitful means of preserving the past, Beth turns to it for expressly that function: as *a means of memory loss*. She writes, in other words, in order to forget. As she puts it to her daughter: "'That's not it at all. When I write my mind is *here*, in the present. I don't remember the past. I can forget, then. And there's so much that I want to forget'" (150). Since Beth is by now suffering from dementia, the writing acquires a further level of significance as a metonym for acute memory loss. What Kat fails to see is the force of memorializing—and constant self-inscription—as an obsessive-compulsive form of erasure. Beth does not seek to preserve the past, but to obliterate it in a cascade of words.

The same may be said for the newspaper reports, many of them written by Beth, that are pasted in Maud's scrapbooks. On one level these reports signal the ways any official documentation defeats historical accessibility. But there is more to it than this, since many of the reports function not so much as a way of encoding historical memory—as we are tempted to say of Maud's scrapbook in *Cure*—but as a way of radically obliterating it. Hence, Kat's father tells the story of the shivaree that took place the night he and Beth were married. The newspaper story, written by Beth, tells of a sedate and happy affair in which the couple were heralded with a rendition of "For They Are Jolly Good Fellows" (53). The father reveals the "truth" behind the event, that Beth secluded herself in terror in the outhouse and would not come out until the next morning. She very literally was not present for the event, and so she cannot possibly "remember" it. The official record becomes a facade, which Beth can use not only to maintain her public dignity, but also as a kind of therapeutic letting go. She seeks not so much to rewrite the event as to forget it through a form of scripted remembering (comparable to the process by which the amnesiac, to cover over the initial forgetting, is given memories that he or she is emotionally detached from but which he/she must "claim" in the name of normalcy). In this sense, the scrapbooks are not "an act of faith in the future" (332), which Elizabeth Edwards identifies as the functioning of the commemorative family photograph, but rather an *active* inscription and initialization of memory loss.

Beth's unspoken awareness of the scripted nature of memory contrasts with Kat's insistence on objects as fetishized "bearers of memory" that are somehow "traced off the living" (through having come into physical contact with them) (Edwards 334). Kat's frantic attempts to preserve the objects in the house are matched by her mother's equal fervour in writing it all down as a way of incinerating her life in a fury of words. Compelled by the "resurrectional qualities" of evocative objects (335), Kat searches through family scrapbooks and mementos for a physical memory trace. The ghost of her dead grandparents who haunt the property are not enough for her. Kat wants physical remainders, objective correlatives of their existence. "There were clues here, in this scrapbook. I was sure of it. [. . .] Something of my grandmother was sealed here in ink" (182–83). Responding to the words as material traces, Kat in fact misreads the words her mother and grandmother have set down. A page of her grandmother's scrapbook contains a recipe for preserving flowers: "Dip the whole blossom and stalk in melted wax, coating completely to seal from the action of air and the passage of time" (183). We might pause to think about the paradox of "sealing from the passage of time," a process which might in fact both preserve and bar the distillation of memory. Memory does not exist without the passage of time (in a perpetual present), so a sealing off of something from that passage would obviate its functioning as a memory. The preserved rose would seem to be an evocative object that preserves a moment from loss to an amnesiac history. And yet, the crumbling rose inside the scrapbook says nothing to Kat, who can only speculate on its provenance. This is indicated by the photo that prefaces this important chapter: not of the rose, but of an ink bottle (Figure 11.3). The evocative power encapsulated by the rose is thus undercut by the image at the outset of the chapter, a juxtaposition that underscores the insufficiency of these objects to "speak" to Kat in the present. The ink bottle, as a physical object that Kat finds in the attic (174), evokes nothing in itself—indeed, Kat barely acknowledges it—though as an index of something else, it does. In this case, the ink points, metonymically, to a pivotal discovery in the chapter, in which the written texts inside a newly discovered scrapbook provide clues to the past expressly for what they do not say. The scrapbook contains a newspaper article written by Beth about a wild cougar on the loose the night her father went missing, deflecting attention away from the truth of that evening: that Beth shot her own father and has been involved in a transgenerational cover-up along with her future husband and his father. The act of writing here is key to what Kat is unwilling to accept: that the past can only partially be retrieved, that memory will elude one's grasp even within one's lifetime, not to mention in the space between genera- tions. As Kat thinks to herself, "My recollections of the moment I was in now—which seemed so very sturdy—would shake and shift like this old building, and finally fall. In a decade or two I would remember only this plank under my feet, this nail, but not the whole structure" (198).

11.3 Illustration from *Turtle Valley* by Gail Anderson-Dargatz, p. 172.

Schwenger writes about the ways people surround them- selves with familiar objects as a source of comfort. They are of value, he argues, "because they seem to partake in our lives. [. . .] Their long association with us seems to make them custodians of our memories; so that some- times [. . .] things reveal us to ourselves in profound and un- expected ways" (3). Or as Sherry Turkle puts it, "Objects are able to catalyze self-creation" (9). Anderson-Dargatz's novel explores this resonance of the evocative object through a kind of looking awry, re- vealing more about the object-relation by blurring the edges of desire. What if this evocation of memory is what is desired from the object, but is denied? What if we seek evidence of *inherited memory* as it is car- ried through objects (in the same way it is carried through the genes)? Anderson-Dargatz seems to suggest that this desire can be debilitating.

Significantly, then, as the family is finally fleeing the farm with their possessions loaded in the back of a pickup, a falling ember lands amidst

the packed boxes and they catch fire. Kat manages to rescue her grandmother's carpetbag full of letters and an antique kitchen scale, but that
is all. As they drive off, Kat watches through the rear window "as our
past burned away" (279). The novel ends on a curiously unemotive note.
When Kat returns to the scene of the fire with her mother, they both muse
on how the landscape no longer seems theirs. "'I don't feel *attached* to the
memories I have of this place,'" Beth tells her daughter, "'I wonder, now,
why I chose to live here all those years'" (287). If Beth and Kat are turned
into amnesiacs in the end, the experience is offered as a form of liberation
from the weight of familial history and genetic memory. This is particularly true since the attachment to objects and memories has been clearly
aligned with Maud's clinging to the man who is the source of her abuse—
even in death, their ghosts are tied together. This explains, as well, why
Maud haunts the house (because she is overly attached to her memories
of the place) and equally why her ghost repeatedly tries to burn down the
house (to erase the link between consciousness and memory).

Kat is saddened in the end, not only because she cannot capture the
memories of her ancestors through prosthetic memory triggers, but also
because she has become emotionally detached from her own past. And
yet, there is something in this that enables her to break free: "My memories are so like [a] hat full of butterflies, some already deteriorating the
moment they are collected, some breathed back to life now and again, for
a brief moment [. . .] before drifting away, just out of my reach. How much
of myself flits away with each of these tattered memories? How much of
myself have I already lost?" (289).[3] The characters in *Turtle Valley* must
confront the inevitability of both cultural and personal memory loss, a
loss that is only heightened by the failure of objects to signify. It may be
that amnesia is what grounds personal and cultural selfhood, that the
desired transitional object (between generations, between time periods) only distills the intense melancholy associated with mutability. "We
speak so much of memory because there is so little of it left" (146), writes
Pierre Nora. Or, in Kat's words at the end of *Turtle Valley*: "I knew that at
the end of that day the memory of our time together would already have

---

3   These butterflies recall the preserved butterfly in Maud's scrapbook in *Cure*, which functions
     there as an emblem of perseverance. The single butterfly, like memory itself, is necessarily in-
     complete. This butterfly is mentioned again in *Turtle Valley* (115).

begun to disappear. I'd be left with a crumbling rose and a pot of faded rouge" (290).

Like Martin Heidegger's emblem of the hollow jug,[4] Maud's scrapbook, like the family memorabilia in *Turtle Valley*, masks beneath its bits and patches a void, a hollow space, a blank page. Kat's realization at the end of *Turtle Valley* is that there is no ghost that is animated by the inherited object, much as one might will there to be. Or more precisely, there is no way of embedding ourselves, as part of a genealogical postmnemonic chain, within the object: neither in order to speak with the dead, nor as a way of returning in the future. As Susan Stewart notes, the memento conjures an experience that it "can only evoke [. . .] and can never entirely recoup," which means that it "promises, and yet does not keep the promise of, *reunion*" (136, 139). Schwenger notes how "melancholy attaches itself to everyday objects whenever they slip out of the symbolic system that controls them and so manifest their uncanny otherness" (33). Nevertheless, there is a kind of consolation in the recognition of mnemonic mutability. The scrapbook fragments of a life, compelled by glue and fancy borders and bevelled edgings, are emblems of our own fragility as mnemonic extracts. Trimmed, snipped, glued in place, we inevitably await the day when the ink will fade, the glue will disintegrate, and the generations will trundle on. The scrapbook's pages will then flutter down, like wing fragments of a damaged butterfly, lured by gravity to settle at the feet of the amnesiac descendant.

---

4   See Heidegger's account of the ways the jug, by definition, "shapes the void" in its interior. As he puts it, "The vessel's thingness does not lie at all in the material of which it consists, but in the void that holds" (115). In *The Ethics of Psychoanalysis*, Lacan invokes Heidegger's jug to describe the workings of "the Thing" (120–21).

PART III

·◆·

Re-Membering History:
Memory Work as Recovery

•-•

CHAPTER 12

Ethnography, Law, and Aboriginal Memory: Collecting and Recollecting Gitxsan Histories in Canada

Marc André Fortin

To be an Indian is having non-Indians control the documents from which other non-Indians write their version of your history.
William T. Hagan, "Archival Captive—The American Indian" 135

In cultural theory, "the archive" has a capital "A," is figurative and leads elsewhere. It may represent neither material site nor a set of documents. Rather, it may serve as a strong metaphor for any corpus of selective forgettings and collections—and, as importantly, for the seductions and longings that such quests for, and accumulations of, the primary, originary, and untouched entail.
Ann Laura Stoler, "Colonial Archives and the Arts of Governance" 94

I. THE LAW, ETHNOGRAPHY, AND ABORIGINAL PRESENCE

The rights of Aboriginal peoples in Canada are legally enshrined within the Indian Act, 1985, first enacted in 1876, and section 35 of the Constitution Act, 1982. Together, these documents recognize existing treaty rights, loosely define the term *aboriginal peoples of Canada*, extend treaty rights to future land-claims agreements, and maintain that Aboriginal peoples will be consulted to discuss any future changes concerning land rights in Canada, or any changes to the Charter's recognition of rights and freedoms that derogate from existing rights and freedoms of Aboriginal peoples including those "recognized by the Royal Proclamation of October 7, 1763" (25a). It is from these two Acts that Aboriginal peoples in Canada work within and against the legal system to redress past wrongs, achieve equality of life as human beings, and move towards the future. However, as Dara Culhane points out, law is not necessarily equivalent to justice, and any interpretation of legal rights does not always lead to fair and equitable representation under the guise of rights and freedoms, no matter how powerful the legal documentation in which such rights are contained, nor how lasting the memory of the past as represented by legal precedence (16).

Judge Allan McEachern, Culhane states, openly exposed the disconnection between law and justice in his final judgment of the original *Delgamuukw v. British Columbia* case (1991), a land-claims trial put forth by members of the Gitxsan and Wet'suwet'en communities, when he argued that prior to European colonization of North America, Aboriginal peoples had no system of governance and were "too 'primitive' to have had property laws" (16). Despite the oral testimony of the Elders, and anthropological evidence to the contrary, McEachern ruled that Aboriginal peoples had no claim to the land upon which they have lived since "time immemorial" (*D. v. B.C.* [1991] 10.3a, 21.2). McEachern's bias in this decision was clearly evident, and his ruling controversial because he "gave little weight to the plaintiffs' evidence in the form of oral history of attachment to the land" (Hurley). The negation of oral testimony ended with a "'blanket extinguishment' of all the plaintiffs' Aboriginal rights by colonial or provincial enactments" (Hurley). In legal rhetoric this might be a negation of the rights of the individual, but it is ideologically a negation of the individual's very existence in a democratic society. Culhane points out that even by 1984 "[t]he provincial government of British Columbia still refused to recognize the existence of First Nations" (105). McEachern's response to critics of his judgment was "that he was compelled by historical precedents to repeat the rulings of previous judges that dated back hundreds of years" (16). McEachern's judgment is certainly a case of erroneous legal reasoning, but it does provide a pivotal point of intersection between memory, law, and ethnography, both theoretically and historically in Canada. These three complicated and complex frames of reference—memory, law, and ethnography—often cross over in the examination of notions of truth and fiction, and history and fantasy, and come together under the terms of precedence and the power of written documentation to offer proof of truth against the oral history of Aboriginal peoples; that is, a hierarchy of archival documentation that places the Aboriginal within a conflict of representation in both the personal and political sense of the term.

Both ethnography and law produce a form of memory that is equivalent to Ann Laura Stoler's idea of the archive as "a strong *metaphor* for any corpus of selective forgetting and collections" (269, original emphasis), which encapsulates the difficulty inherent in examining a concept as ephemeral and fleeting as *memory*. This is especially true of the *Delgamuukw* case, as the defendants successfully appealed the decision of McEachern in 1993, and ultimately had their case heard by the Supreme Court of Canada in June 1997. According to the Supreme Court judges involved in the case, McEachern simply "did not accept the appellants' evidence of oral history of attachment to the land" and that "[h]ad the oral histories been correctly assessed, the conclusions on these issues of fact might have been very different (*D. v. B.C.* [1997]). The Supreme Court's judgment clearly has an impact for legal relationships between the Crown and Aboriginal peoples, but it also represents a profound shift in the understanding of memory as legitimate knowledge of the past against dominant archival versions of truth. I will expand on the notion of "selective forgetting and collections" to explore the notions of memory and ethnographic documentation by looking at the connections between ethnography and textual representations of the Gitxsan to show a changing conception of memory in relation to ethnographic, and thus archival, representations of the Indigene. I follow Ann Laura Stoler in thinking of the archive, particularly the colonial archive as it exists in Canada, as "a repository of codified beliefs, genres for bearing witness, clustered connections between secrecy, power, and the law" (270), and consider past representations of the Gitxsan as participating in the work of making the Aboriginal figure an *archived* other. Three texts in particular stand out as important historical points of reference for understanding the nature of the archived Gitxsan and the recovery and repatriation of the of the oral Aboriginal voice: Marius Barbeau's *The Downfall of Temlaham*, Chief Kenneth B. Harris's *Visitors Who Never Left: The Origin of the People of Damelahamid*, and Headlines Theatre's *NO' XYA' (Our Footprints)*. In looking at texts that bring up questions about ethnography, documentation, and memory, I argue that the Gitxsan have not only recently challenged the court in their pursuit of self-government and land rights, but have forced us to question the nature of memory and truth.

Stoler's interpretation of the archive aligns with legal authority at the site of memory. If precedence leads to present and future judgments, archives lead to a similar power of memory invested in the past as a site of authority. The problem becomes apparent when knowledge is used against one's own history, as in McEachern's refusal to accept oral testimony of the Elders. As Perry Shawana argues, in discussing the preservation of Aboriginal knowledge, the archive can lead to fractures within Aboriginal communities that have already experienced intrusions from both government representatives and ethnographers who have used gathered information against Aboriginal conceptions of self, law, and history:

> [A] consequence of adopting a singular objective of "protecting" Indigenous knowledge is its potential to drive all forms of Indigenous knowledge underground. Fear that Indigenous knowledge will be abused and/or misused for personal or financial gain could prevent its transmission, even among members of the Indigenous community. A pressing concern in Indigenous country is the secrecy that has become attached to Indigenous ways of knowing. (122)

The collecting of Aboriginal masks, stories, names, music, and ceremony poles by early ethnographers in Canada at the beginning of the twentieth century has led to an accumulation of Aboriginal "data" held by archives. But the objects and recorded accounts are more than simply material archives; they are the cultural, legal, and political histories of Aboriginal communities that have been taken away and stored for others to research. Such information allows others to recreate history from translated accounts of the past, making archives a site of possible reconstruction rather than truth. Molly Torsen and Jane Anderson, writing for the World Intellectual Property Organization, point out that "Indigenous peoples and traditional communities have not been recognized as rights holders or acknowledged as having legitimate relationships with the material within the collections of such cultural institutions" (12), and thus power is given to those whom William T. Hagan states write "their version of your history" (135), rather than to traditional owners of Aboriginal knowledge.

In 1928, Marius Barbeau, the first Canadian-born anthropologist hired by the Anthropological Division of the Geological Survey of Canada in Ottawa, published the novel *The Downfall of Temlaham*, a version of Gitxsan history that focused on a particular historical event that was sensationally framed by *The New York Times* as the "Skeena River Revolt." Beginning in 1914, Barbeau undertook a number of field trips to the Skeena and Nass Rivers on the Northwest Pacific Coast to study the Ts'msyan, the Nisga'a, and the Gitxsan. As Andrew Nurse has pointed out, Barbeau employed a method of "salvage ethnography" in which "[f]ield research was a work of collection, not of observation or understanding. The aim of effective field research was to record different cultural traits and purchase material objects that could be preserved and later published or kept in museums. In other words, the aim of field research was to create archives and museum collections" (55). Barbeau was highly effective at this form of research, accumulating a massive archive of Aboriginal objects, as well as recorded songs, stories, names, and lineages. In 1923 Constance Cox recorded a story about Gitxsan crests from Charles Mark, a Gitxsan elder, for Marius Barbeau. The narrative ends with a symbolic warning about the nature of colonialism, ethnography, and memory: "It is quite difficult for the informant to repeat these things and makes him very sad. It is because it has all been taken away from them. They are left empty now. It brings tears to his eyes" (Mark 3). The history of the Gitxsan at the turn of the twentieth century could be said to have moved from the Skeena River to Ottawa, the political and cultural centre of Euro-Canada.

The Downfall of Temlaham is very much a product of the archive as defined by Hagan and Stoler. The text of the novel links back to no single document in the archives, but to a multitude of documents that are interpreted by the author to create a vision of history. In this case, that history includes the so-called "Skeena River Revolt" of 1888, three Gitxsan origin stories that follow the historical narrative, and thirteen illustrations of the Skeena and surrounding area by artists such as Emily Carr, Edwin Holgate, and A.Y. Jackson. Barbeau and his publishers were aware of this act of translation, and stated clearly on the dust jacket the novel's layered authority: "The pageantry and inherent poetry in this narrative flow naturally from the native sources, the abundant records being freely interpreted and paraphrased by Marius Barbeau." Coming at a time in which the Canadian government was actively pursuing policies of assimilation (and Barbeau was corresponding with Duncan Campbell Scott, Head of Indian Affairs), the novel is a complex text that is intertwined in theoretical, social, political, and legal questions concerning Aboriginal history, law, and identity.

The Downfall of Temlaham was Barbeau's first foray into creative fiction. He had already published works based on his field research and focused on the Huron-Wyandot in *Huron and Wyandot Mythology* (1915), and on the Cree, Stony, and Kootenay in *Indian Days in the Canadian Rockies* (1923). It is in *Indian Days* that Barbeau offers an understanding of his interpretation of Aboriginal presence in Canada in the early twentieth century:

> The present-day Indians of the western prairies and the Rocky Mountains are no longer what they used to be. They have dwindled in numbers; their ancient customs are gone, their character is lost. They are a vanishing race. In the white man's pageants or in silver screen views of the wild west, they may still appear to us, when garbed in buckskin and feathers, as spectacular personalities dwelling in a sphere apart from the rest of mankind; but when visited at home, on the reserves, they seldom live up to the fanciful expectations we derive from literature and pictorial art. (6)

There is no hint of irony in Barbeau's erasure of the Aboriginal from the physical world, and thus we can see in his understanding of the "vanished" Aboriginal the desire to recreate the "pageantry" of the past from the memory of ethnographic documentation. The historical account of Kamalmuk from the Northwest Pacific Coast, the protagonist of Barbeau's novel and the focus of the historical manhunt, becomes a romanticized, imaginary erasure of the Gitxsan in *The Downfall of Temlaham*. Yet, even in his act of inventing a fictional account of the Gitxsan and Ts'msyan, he took the ethnographic approach to their history. In fact, *The Downfall of Temlaham* is a literal rewriting of Gitxsan stories through ethnographic translation that interprets fragments of field notes pieced together to create a new version of history from a single perspective that has no singular origin. Although seemingly objective in scope, such a translation decontextualizes the individual stories in order to produce a metanarrative outside of the time/space environment from which it was taken. Barbeau's novel is a rewriting of Gitxsan history based upon ethnographic evidence that has been re-imagined as a form of truth. Objectivity and truthfulness arise out of Barbeau's insertion of an index into the back of the text, which lists all the informants, ethnographers, and translators that compiled the stories from which he wrote the novel. The index is an authoritative account of the stories that come before it, marking the novel both as a document of scientific accuracy and Aboriginal authenticity. It is a fiction produced from fact; an origin story created from archival truth.

II. A GITXSAN VERSION OF HISTORY?

In 1974 the University of British Columbia Press published a text focused on the long history of the Gitxsan, *Visitors Who Never Left* by Chief Kenneth B. Harris. As stated on the title page, the text was published *"in collaboration with* Frances M.P. Robinson," a researcher from the Department of Fine Arts at UBC. The text is meant to respond to ethnographic rewritings of Gitxsan history such as Barbeau's in that, as Robinson states, the stories "have not been tampered with in any way and are given exactly as translated by Ken Harris" (xvii), and that the stories "belong to the Indians" (xx). In Harris's work, Stoler's conception of archives and memory, especially related to the terms "primary, originary, and untouched" (94), become visibly troubled, surrounded as they are by issues of translation and authority. The book is ostensibly the "legends" of the Gitxsan, and details a history that dates back to the founding of Damelahamid (Temlaham) along the Skeena River in present-day British Columbia as told in the voice of the Gitxsan. However, the stories are framed by scholarly paratextual material: a glossary, major sources, an introduction by Robinson, and photographs of the Gitxsan communities. Like the images in Barbeau's novel, there is a distinct absence of people in the photographs, with mostly images of the empty landscape and Aboriginal artifacts. And perhaps the most important document in the text comes from the then–prime minister Pierre Elliott Trudeau, whose letter to Kenneth Harris is inserted at the beginning of the text. Trudeau writes:

> This highly important event enables many people to share the wisdom, mystery and memory of the people of the Damelahamid. Through such sharing, we are immeasurably enriched and we are more fully appreciative of the quality and depth of our Canadian heritage. (vii)

The authorial acceptance of Kenneth Harris's work by Trudeau subjects the mythological storytelling apparatus of print publication to the contemporary conditions of Aboriginal identity in Canada. Harris's work is considered national, historical, and ethnographic in its recounting of the history of the Gitxsan people and their past. Harris himself tells the reader this in a more subtle understanding of the politics of colonial appropriation:

> This is Ken Harris speaking. I will attempt to translate the history of our people of *Damelahamid* as it was told by Arthur McDames who was the Chief of *Damelahamid* and my mother, Mrs. Irene Harris, who explained the meaning of the Indian terms to me. I also speak for myself as I am the last source of such information and as I hold the title of *Hagbegwatku*, First Born of our Nation. I feel that this information must be passed on to my relatives and clansmen. Because of the changing times and the fact that our people are now in a transition period, my choice of media, the printed word, is essential. There is no longer the time to tell the myths as we used to in the old days. (xxiii)

Harris's belief in the need to shift the traditional practice of oral storytelling to the printed publication of Gitxsan stories suggests a movement from memory as a social practice wherein community members come together to listen, share, and understand the cultural, moral, and legal questions related to Gitxsan politics, to the ethnographic recording of the present to salvage the history of the Gitxsan before it disappears forever.

Robinson points out that the recording of the stories was distressing for Harris. This is because, she argues, "[o]ral tradition was broken. However, as far as possible, uncontaminated myths were now a written fact. The act of transposing oral tradition into written form was upsetting to Ken. It was an irrevocable changing of the old order" (xviii). There is no doubt that the use of the medium of print to tell traditional oral stories was a major shift in the social structure of Gitxsan culture, but it is evident that the idea behind the necessity of recording the stories is premised on a desire to preserve a culture within the margins of ethnographic archiving of information. The trope of the dying race is used to establish a connection between the present and the past that is based on earlier ethnographic representations of the dying race, such as Barbeau's. Memory will not suffice to keep the Gitxsan culture alive, but must be recorded, shared with those for whom it was not originally intended, and finally authorized by the state as documented proof of the memory of a culture that once existed in Canada, enriches Canadians for its heritage value, but ultimately, once again, signals the downfall of Aboriginal peoples.

Aboriginal cultures in North America share a common history of oral storytelling as a social method of information preservation, genealogical lineage, and epistemological sharing of history from one generation to the next. There is no doubt that Western cultures also participate in oral culture, but the shift from oral to written culture suggests neither an advanced evolutionary moral progression, nor a cultural shift from primitive to civilized technologies. What it does suggest, however, is a radical difference between cultures in how memory is understood and how it functions within different societies, and what memory says about the social, cultural, religious, and ethical processes of such cultures. Drew Mildon makes a comparison between oral culture and the archive by stating how racialized interpretations of the "Indian" have led to false understandings of how the privileged arena of writing over orality upsets the truth-telling process itself. In this instance he points out how courts see "aboriginal tradition" as a form of "frozen rights" in which "change over time within Aboriginal communities is not an important element in their culture and traditions" (82). He states:

> The image of the "natural Indian" has a long and damaging background: from the elegiac painting of Paul Kane, to Duncan Campbell Scott's poetic laments for a "dying race," to Disney's Pocahontas (where the fish cheerily meet their deaths at the feet of industrious "braves"). Daniel Francis has called this racist idealized representation the "Imaginary Indian." [. . .] This representational force has also placed First Nations within the natural order, situating them both individually and collectively in an innocent and fading past—indexed and archived. [. . .] (82)

Despite Barbeau and Robinson's ethnographic perception of the Gitx̱san, or perhaps because of such views, one can level the same accusation of romanticization of the "Indian" based on a perceived view of a lost race that would have offered unimpeded access to a society untouched by modern reality. Both Barbeau and Robinson, most likely in the best interest of preserving the memory of the Gitx̱san, fall into the trap of producing the archived Aboriginal figure in recording the Gitx̱san stories meant to be shared through oral transmission.

Once the Aboriginal figure is archived, through the recording of stories, images, and other apparatuses associated with archival documentation, archival memory produces a form of legitimacy from which it is difficult to extract truth from fiction. The museum archive, which is the traditional site of the ethnographic holdings of cultures, is a space of authority, hierarchy, and reverence. Objects and documents are kept stored in climate-controlled areas, locked in vaulted chambers, and studied, seen, and touched by only a handful of people who are given approval to do so, or who have paid the price of admission to the exhibit if the object is given a spot in the public section of the museum. So, too, are the wax cylinder recordings from Edison phonographs, transcriptions, documents, photographs, and films kept secured and safe in storage chambers, the voices of Aboriginal Elders locked up far from the land and ancestors of those whose stories were taken down decades ago. The ethnographic recording of Aboriginal culture is the *translation* of language, culture, and identity into certain trans-historic models of knowing the other. And any ethnographic documentation of Aboriginal culture is primarily looking back at its own production. It looks back at the culture that produced the perspective of the other through technological, epistemological, and ideological lenses. Knowing this makes it difficult to see such archival documentation as representative of anything more than a mapping of historical anthropological tendencies.

III. RECLAIMING THE VOICE

If *The Downfall of Temlaham* is an ethnographic reflection of early-twentieth century perspectives on Aboriginal culture, and *Visitors Who Never Left* a reflection of the Gitxsan as having moved away from oral culture entirely, then *NO' XYA' (Our Footprints)* is the late-twentieth-century response to the archived image of the absence of the Aboriginal from the land and the reclaiming of the Aboriginal voice. Moving back into the realm of the oral culture of the Gitxsan, this drama performs a historical rewriting of ethnographic translations of Aboriginal culture. It re-imagines the social conditions under which colonialism produced its own skewed history of Aboriginal culture using memories from the Aboriginal communities affected by such forces. It speaks back to the imagined "Indian" of Barbeau's time, and questions the image produced from ethnographic representations of the dying, or dead, Aboriginal culture.

NO' XYA' was written by David Diamond, Hal B. Blackwater, Lois G. Shannon, and Marie Wilson, co-produced by Vancouver's Headlines Theatre and Gitxsan and Wet'suwet'en Hereditary Chiefs, and ran

between 1987 and 1990. The play is both a direct critique of legal interpretations of Aboriginal presence and an allegorical response to ethnographic representations of the archival memory of Aboriginal peoples.
The plot involves events that take place during different historical periods and which chart the relationship between settler and Aboriginal
communities. *NO' XYA'* uses the same four actors to portray the characters in these different periods, and the layering of history through the
use of this device complicates the ethnographic history of the Gitxsan
and Wet'suwet'en, while it opens up a dialogic space for questioning the
authority and continuity of representations of Aboriginal culture across
history. At the same time, the question of truth and memory is considered between settler and Aboriginal accounts of history.

An early scene shows two women picking berries alongside each other, an Aboriginal woman (named Maryanne by the other) and a Scotch
settler (named Helena). Maryanne asks the other to tell her one of her
legends. Helena responds with a start: "They are not legends Maryanne.
They are the truth. From the Bible!" When Maryanne explains that they,
too, have stories about a virgin birth and a flood, Helena asks further
about the Gitxsan and Wet'suwet'en legends. Maryanne responds: "They
are not legends Helena. They are *adawaak*. Histories handed down. They
are the truth." An *adawaak*, as defined by P. Dawn Mills, is "[t]he narrative owned by a particular *wilp* or by Houses denoting their migration
back into the [territories] and the boundaries of their particular territories" (13). This tension between written and oral truth reflects the larger
argument put forth by the drama. *NO' XYA'* challenges colonial conceptions of property ownership, Aboriginal presence on the land, and
the right to resources. Using historical textual documents in dialogue
with songs and speech in the language of the people, *NO' XYA'* directly
responds to the ethnographic representation of Aboriginal peoples as
absent from the land and confronts the divide between written and oral
proof of such a truth. As one of the main characters asks, "is the truth
only the truth if it is written on white paper?"

NO' XYA' details Gitxsan and Wet'suwet'en history in the voice of
Gitxsan and Wet'suwet'en themselves. It tells of the first settlers to the
area, the arrival of missionaries, the effects of residential schools, the destruction of land, the construction of fences, and the loss of identity inherent in colonial policies of assimilation. Because the play was performed
during the years in which the *Delgamuukw* case was before the courts,

during which Judge McEachern refuted the stories of the Elders, it enacts a secondary legal case that is more in line with Git<u>x</u>san and Wet'suwet'en policies of justice. The play allowed the Git<u>x</u>san and Wet'suwet'en to speak in their own voice about a history that was not founded on documented proof of events, but on the memory of the people themselves. *NO' XYA'* is its own form of legal reasoning that responds to the *Delgamuukw* version of justice. It resides outside Western law, but is nevertheless an important alternative to the hierarchical system of justice that is premised on precedence, paper, and proof. As Ginny Ratsoy states, "the play fuses written documentation and First Nations oral testimony" and "[i]n a device that erases conventional barriers between art and audience, audience members are invited to speak and 'act on' the message of the production; the play carries on beyond the script" (302–3).

Reversing the hierarchical order of the primacy of written documentation over oral culture in relation to memory and truth does not produce an answer to the flawed continuities of ethnography and law when it comes to Aboriginal cultures. As Tasha Hubbard argues, "When 'literate' memory is compared to 'oral' memory in Western European thought, colonial superiority, misinformed generalization, and blatant misunderstanding ensues" (139). However, it is also possible to reconsider how the archived history of Aboriginal peoples should be understood within the larger conditions of social, political, and legal representations of Aboriginal peoples in relation to oral tradition as a mode of discourse against legal and ethnographic truth. Hubbard, in critiquing the work of Jeannette Armstrong, discusses "the need for Aboriginal peoples to keep their sacred songs and ceremonies hidden away from the eyes of police, government, and other colonial forces in order to keep them safe" (146). She points out how Armstrong's work seeks to open up a safe space for the Aboriginal voice, and her interpretation can be mapped onto the archived Indigene in relation to legal, social, and political information that responds to colonial ethnographic interpretations of history at the same time that it can be used to further entrench colonial interpretations of indigeneity.

The connection between law, ethnography, and memory exists in both the material and theoretical space of the archive, and the archived Aboriginal. Molly Torsen and Jane Anderson offer an alternative future for archives that contain the history of Aboriginal peoples and a possible theoretical way of moving away from the archived other of legal and ethnographic memory:

As many institutions have discovered, working with indigenous peoples and traditional communities can provide invaluable information
about the collections. Indeed, tradition-bearers can provide contextual
information and personal narratives regarding their accumulation,
explain the alternative meanings embedded within them, and outline
the access conditions that respect the indigenous or traditional community from which those materials derive, as well as those other users
who are keen to learn and understand different cultures and cultural
practices from them. (12)

In other words, the past abuse of the Aboriginal voice goes beyond simple appropriation to the question of archival and legal memory, and how
memory functions within the ethnographic and legal conceptions of the
past to maintain political control over the historical understanding of
Aboriginal peoples. If law is the memory of ethnographic documentation of Aboriginal peoples, the need to begin to listen to other voices
becomes paramount in negotiating an equitable interpretation of history
that can pave the way for better understanding between different conceptions of law and justice.

When the Superior Court of Canada concluded the *Delgamuukw v.
The Queen* case in 1997, the Gitxsan and Wet'suwet'en Nations may not
have immediately won legal rights to be the owners of the lands upon
which they had been living for many thousands of years, but they had
won a decisive victory over Western colonial cultural and legal interpretations of *memory*. For the courts were forced to accept that the plaintiffs
had the right to speak their history to the court of the nation in voices
that spoke truth as real as the privileged written historical documentation
that had meant to deny them their own history and memory of existence
as living individuals and communities. The Gitxsan and Wet'suwet'en
Nations changed the concept of *memory* in Canada in 1997, and thus
that of history, by showing that the communal memory that makes up
the cultural tradition of oral storytelling is built upon a shared system of
verification, authority, assent, and concordance that involves both regulation and evolution as history is told, retold, and unfolds through time
and space. The Gitxsan and Wet'suwet'en reconceptualized the idea of
social and historical memory as distinct from state-sanctioned memory
and the scientific, rational, Enlightenment-era ideology of truth derived
from privileged documented evidence.

Nevertheless, law does not equate to justice, and the archived ethnographic Aboriginal figure still exists in the cultural imagination. The Gitxsan and Wet'suwet'en continue to fight colonial intrusions onto their traditional territories from private companies seeking access to pipeline routes and natural resources. Despite the acceptance of oral history by the courts of Canada as evidence, there still exists a conception of the absent Aboriginal that is implied in colonial memory, literature, and law. There is clearly a need to overcome this nostalgic impulse for the "empty land" theory of early settler imagination. The archived Aboriginal is simply one of the "selective forgettings" that have accumulated from ethnographic and legal thought in Canada, and produces a troubling condition in the imagined history of colonial authority today. What the *Delgamuukw* trial and *NO' XYA'* tell us is that memory is not simply a biological process encoded in human bodies, but a socially mandated conception of truth that is bound by tradition. As P. Dawn Mills states, "[t]he Gitxsan, like all citizens, look to their law as the basis for their relationship with the Crown, yet their concerns are not being heard" (12). Perhaps this is because it is difficult to listen to voices that one already considers only a memory of the past.

CHAPTER 13

•◆•

Between Elegy and Taxidermy: Archibald Lampman's Golden Lady's Slippers

Peter Hodgins

Oak, elm, white pine, hepatica, adder-tongue, squirrel-corn, bloodroot, trillium, blue cohosh, lady's slippers, syringa, clover, marguerite, buttercup, bladder-campion, blue-eyed grass, twin flowers, sanilacina [smilacina], windflower, lillium, alder, water weeds and mosses, bittersweet, loose-strife, goldenrod, purple bone-set, turtlehead, chelone, bed straw, white snakeroot, gentian, asters, arrowhead, purple pickerel-weed, golden lilies, cedar, violets, golden lady's slipper, moccasin flower, song-sparrow, robin, blue bird, vesper sparrow, bob-o-link, white-throat sparrow, thrushes, veery, hermit thrush, wood thrush, brown thrush, catbird, peweet, great highholder or higho, meadow lark, warblers, flycatchers, vireos, passenger pigeons.

CONTEMPORARY CULTURAL MEMORY STUDIES AND THE LOSS OF IMAGINATION

These are the plants and birds that Archibald Lampman, in his entries in "At the Mermaid Inn," reported seeing in his many walks in and around Victorian Ottawa. I, too, have spent much time wandering the forests and fields of Ottawa and the Ottawa Valley. I've seen some of these plants and birds and I know them by the names he gives them. I've perhaps seen others but don't know them by name or I know them by other names. Others I've seen only in garden centres or botanical gardens but never on my walks. Finally, there are others I've only seen in books or museums because they have long since been killed off.

When what has now come to be known as "cultural memory studies" emerged as a central concern in the social sciences and humanities in the late 1980s and early 1990s, it insisted on the ideological, political, and polysemic nature of all forms of cultural remembering. Early research in the field took hegemonic memory projects and/or crass commodifications of the past as its main object, and broad agreement existed among memory scholars that personal and collective pasts were constantly subject to processes of revision, selective remembering, supplementation, and reframing by generic narrative frameworks (Olick and Robbins). The question of the "reality" of the past, however, was more vexatious. Researchers inspired by French theory asserted that the past existed only as a discursively constructed absent presence that comes to be given substance only through rhetorical sleights of hand often backed up by institutional power. What was probably a much larger camp, on the other hand, sought to preserve the possibility that no matter how redacted or revised an act of remembering might be, it could be traced back to some sort of constitutive event always existed (Keith Jenkins).

Freud, whose work has seen a renaissance with the rise of trauma as a central category within memory studies, expressed this realist faith nicely when he wrote that in spite of the fact that traumatic remembering breaks up the linear arrangement of time and introduces imaginary elements into the narrative in order to screen out the most unsettling aspects of the remembered past, "trauma is always an effect of history [. . .]" (qtd. in Lahji 105). As Susannah Radstone has argued, the ethical turn within memory studies with its focus on issues of trauma, cultural haunting, and ethical witnessing has endowed Freud's assertion that history stands behind every act of remembering with an almost sacred character. The irony of this new emphasis on trauma, haunting, and witnessing, she asserts, is that at the same time that its students are well aware of the difficulty, if not impossibility, of representing traumatic memory, they often follow "a literalist and uncritically realist path" that obscures the constructed nature of memory, curtails the play of meaning, and offers only one possible reading position: an empathetic identification with the subject of trauma combined with an unquestioning belief that their suffering was caused by some sort of real historical event (Radstone 34).

In this essay, I want to trouble this realist tendency within contemporary cultural memory studies by examining a series of texts composed by the Confederation poet Archibald Lampman. Like many memory-texts currently being examined under the auspices of memory studies, these texts are infused with a sense of melancholy and mourning.

However, what perhaps differentiates these texts from other similar texts studied by contemporary scholars of cultural memory is that Lampman was grieving a traumatic loss that had not yet occurred. In other words, there was no antecedent constitutive event, no history that led to his sense of loss. There was only an imaginary projection of loss into the future, but this imagined loss still caused him to suffer. What is more, his melancholic disposition seemed to compel him, in both word and act, to actively destroy that which he elegized. As this essay will explore, Lampman's anticipatory mourning troubles any simple linear and causal notion of memory and perhaps even corroborates Thomas Hobbes's observation that "imagination and memory are but one thing, which for divers considerations hath divers names" (Hobbes 89).

"THE TREES MUST ALL GO, MUST ALL PERISH IRRECOVERABLY": LAMPMAN'S HISTORY OF DESTRUCTION

Between the winter of 1892 and the summer of 1893, the Ottawa-based poets Archibald Lampman, Duncan Campbell Scott, and Wilfred Campbell wrote a column for the Toronto *Globe* entitled "At the Mermaid Inn." The majority of the columns were devoted to what one might expect from a group of Victorian middle-class civil servants/poets—book reviews, discussions of literary life in Canada, calls for increased patronage of the arts, social and political commentary, and so on. Each poet had their distinctive prose style—Campbell's was long-winded and pompous and Scott's was didactic and restrained. Lampman's was the most readable, alternating between the poetic and the polemic. Lush depictions of the quality of the Ottawa sunlight in winter or of the diversity of plants growing by a lakeshore in late summer alternated with denunciations of the Canadian elite's failure to invest in Canadian cultural development or celebrations of the rise of the Canadian women's movement.

In two of his last entries for the column in the summer of 1893, the poetic and polemical aspects of Lampman's prose began to bleed together. On 10 June 1893, his section in the column discussed the announcement by the federal government of the creation of a natural preserve around Banff. This announcement, he wrote, raises the subject

> upon which every lover of nature and every one who has interest and
> pride in his mother earth must feel deeply, viz., the rapid and certain

destruction of the primeval pine forests. In the older provinces these noble and irreplaceable forests are already nearly gone. While there are still adequate specimens of them left, ought not some reservation to be made, in order that our children and we ourselves in the years to come may have an opportunity of knowing what our country looked like in its natural condition. (329)

Such pronouncements of the imminent destruction of old-growth forest were already relatively common in naturalist and scientific circles by the time that Lampman was writing his column. So, too, was the conservationist argument which demands that governments take action to conserve parts of what we might now call "our natural heritage." As several entries in "At the Mermaid Inn" reveal, Lampman was an avid reader of such American naturalist writers as Henry David Thoreau, Bradford Torrey, and John Burroughs, some of whom were on the forefront of the American conservation movement (Armitage 535).

Equally unsurprising are the next few lines in which he chastises the extraction-addicted Canadian political and economic elite for its myopic stupidity and greed:

An ancient and close-grown pine forest is a unique and wonderful spectacle, and its effect upon the imagination is something not produced by any other thing in the world. Once gone they are gone for generations; as far as we are concerned, forever. Is it impossible to expect that any light, any gracious impulse, any ray of imaginative ardour, should penetrate the barbarism of our rulers? Could they not be induced, at the small sacrifice of some pitiful gain, to set aside even a moderate space of the unbroken wild in each province as a national or provincial park? (329–30)

For contemporary readers, there is something comfortingly familiar about Lampman's denouncement of the elite of his period and its death-drive to extinguish Canadian nature for the sake of "a pitiful gain." In the final lines of his entry, however, the familiar becomes uncanny: "As I have remarked before, all nature-loving people feel strongly on this point. I never see a sawlog afloat on one of our rivers without a pang, not because I would not have logs cut, but because I know that *the trees must all go, must all perish irrecoverably*" (330; my italics).

The contemporary reader struggles to understand what to make of Lampman's final phrase. (S)he might even ask the mute website in which "At the Mermaid Inn" is now collected: Why *must* the trees go? Why must their loss be irrecoverable? S/he might reel from the abrupt discursive shift from the melancholic and elegiac ("I never see [. . .] without a pang") to a resigned yet forceful declaration of some sort of iron law of historical necessity. What kind of historicity is at work here, (s)he might wonder? What kind of strange pre-emptive mourning are these words expected to provoke?

In his next entry written for the week of 24 June 1893, Lampman returns to the theme of environmental despoliation and rapacious consumption: "The awful destructiveness of the human race is exemplified in small things as well as great. Not only are our magnificent pine forests disappearing, not only is the buffalo practically extinct and the wild pigeon rapidly becoming so, but wherever any wild thing of interest or beauty occurs in rare haunts it is instantly set upon and destroyed" (339). As the first two sentences suggest, Lampman was one of many late Victorians who had grown increasingly skeptical of the Victorian faith in better living through constant economic development and the concomitant destruction of natural habitats. He was also deeply critical of the collecting impulse from its most brutal manifestations in mining and forestry to its most sublimated forms in amateur and professional natural history.

In the final phrase from the 24 June 1893 entry quoted above, his criticism of the collecting/extractive impulse becomes quite pointed when he writes that "wherever any wild thing of interest or beauty occurs in rare haunts it is instantly set upon and destroyed" (339). This short passage powerfully anticipates postcolonial and postmodern critiques of the relationship between the gaze, the Western power/knowledge complex, and the destructive character of the collection and consumption of the beautiful and the exotic. As the myriad studies on the role of anthropologists, archaeologists, folklorists, and so on in their dual roles as the shock troops of colonization and collectors of indigenous "exotica" for Western museums or the ongoing illegal international trades in endangered plants and animals all suggest, the Western quest for the rare, the beautiful, and the exotic often involves destroying the natural and historical conditions which originally produced the object of the collector's desire. In fact, it could be argued that the logic of the market for the exotic demands that destruction because rarity and non-reproducibility are its main criteria for assigning value to the object.

In the middle section of the entry from 24 June, Lampman again equates collection with destruction:

> I have known some out-of-the-way places in my neighbourhood where rare wild flowers could be found not long ago in considerable numbers: now they are gone. People could not be content to look at them, admire them, pluck a few, and leave the rest to renew their kind, and yield us the yearly service of their beauty. They must bear them away in armfuls, pull them up by the roots, and make an end of them in the momentary pride of securing a greater display than anyone else. They have killed the goose that laid the golden egg. (339)

This passage evokes in many ways his previous entry on the need to create national parks. In it, we find once again the mourning of the loss of rare wildflowers and, more generally, the "natural commons" as a result of the rapacity of the collectors, the logic of privatization, and the failure to recognize nature as a shared and renewable spiritual and aesthetic resource.

Similarly, things get a bit odd here in his concluding sentences. He begins by telling of having been "told of a place where I might find the golden lady's slipper, the moccasin flower. The knowledge was imparted to me as a secret. I went there, and found many of them blossoming in bits of deep wood that the crowd had somehow missed. They stood in little companies by the pools in the moist, rocky soil, and shafts of the afternoon sun shining in upon them made them wonderfully beautiful" (339). Based on what we have seen so far, it would not be unreasonable to expect the passage to end there with the naturalist-poet keeping the secret, practising an ethic of "letting-be" and simply imparting to us the beauty of the scene through the non-interventionist medium of the written word. Puzzlingly and even disturbingly, however, it does not end there. Instead, the entry concludes with the following: "I carried only two or three of them away, and neither persuasion nor torture shall draw from me the knowledge of their secret abode" (339).

BETWEEN ELEGY AND TAXIDERMY

The strange temporality of Lampman's anticipatory mourning for a not-yet-lost nature is consonant with what Timothy Morton describes as the peculiar relationship of ecological writing to elegy (251). Ecological elegy, like traditional elegy, is about loss but, unlike the latter, that loss is projected into the future. In this future, there is both nothing left to mourn at the same time that there is no end to mourning. This endless mourning over a nature that will be destroyed, that will become nothing, is a further result of how the ecological elegy differs from the traditional elegy. In the latter, the lost object is delimited (a lover, a homeland, a grey cat) and, through the use of textual strategies such as pathetic fallacy, the projection of loss upon nature begins the process of normal grieving in which the mourner's libido slowly decathects from the lost object. In the ecological elegy, on the other hand, the situation is far more complicated. On the one hand, it is impossible for us to decathect from nature because we literally are nature. On the other, the loss of nature means that we have nothing upon which to project our loss and thus begin the process of putting that loss behind us. As a result, Morton concludes, with the ecological elegy, we have "lost the objective correlative for loss itself, and have slipped away from mourning, which finds an appropriate way of symbolizing loss, back into melancholia, which had no way of redressing woe. We have moved from the work of mourning to the work of sheer suffering [. . .]" (253–54).

Morton's arguments go some way towards explaining Lampman's anticipatory lament for the imminent disappearance of Canada's forests and the ecosystems they support. As Giorgio Agamben explains in *Stanzas*, in so-called "normal" mourning, once the mourner gets past the initial stage of grief for the lost object, (s)he begins to distance her-/himself from that object so that (s)he can eventually come to desire other objects. The melancholic, on the other hand, refuses to let go. Melancholy, Agamben writes, "is a reaction to the loss of a loved object; however, contrary to what might be expected, such loss is not followed by a transfer of libido to another object, but rather its withdrawal into the ego, narcissistically identified with the lost object." Because the lost object is jumbled up with the desires, memories, and fantasies of the narcissistic self, he continues, "not only is it unclear what object has been lost, it is uncertain that one can speak of loss at all [. . .] melancholia offers the paradox of an intention to mourn that precedes and anticipates the loss of the object" (20).

There are clear resonances here between Morton's description of ecological elegy and Agamben's description of melancholia as anticipatory mourning. However, Agamben goes further in that he joins writers like Nicolas Abraham and Julia Kristeva in arguing that at the same time that the melancholic wants to conserve the (never) lost object by "encrypting" or "incorporating" it in the ego, this desire to conserve the object is often conjoined with the desire to destroy it. The reason for this, Agamben argues, is that the melancholic builds her/his identification around objects such as nature *tout court* that cannot be delimited or possessed. In *Black Sun*, Kristeva names the impossible object of melancholic desire "the Thing." She describes it as an unrepresentable and ungraspable "supreme Good" that haunts her dreams and drives her desire (13). Because the Thing is an unstable, ungraspable, and ultimately frustrating amalgam of memory, imagination, and desire, the melancholic seeks to stabilize it and control it by symbolically destroying it. In other words, it can exist for the melancholic *only* as something that has been lost or destroyed. Agamben nicely sums up the situation: "the withdrawal of melancholic libido has no other purpose than to make viable an appropriation in a situation in which none is really possible. From this point of view, melancholy would not be so much the regressive reaction to the loss of the loved object as the imaginative capacity to make an unobtainable object appear as if lost [. . .] melancholy succeeds in appropriating its object only to the extent that it affirms its loss [. . .]" (20).

This detour through melancholia gives us one possible answer to Lampman's puzzling use of the verb *must* as opposed to *will* or *might* when describing the fate of Canada's forests. As a poet whose work often revolves around making antimodernist contrasts between the alienating city and spiritually nourishing nature, Lampman provides abundant textual evidence of his close self-identification with nature and his melancholic vacillation between symbolically destroying and conserving nature. Many of his poems begin with a figuration of urban life and capitalist modernity as a ruined world, as sites of the traumatic loss of self and nature. Only once the speaker destroys nature in these poems can he then come to repossess it, to be at one with it. "Life and Nature," for example, begins with him entering the sterile city which is empty but for the mournful sounds of a church organ: "A sound of some great burden / That lay on the world's dark breast, / Of the old, and the sick, and the lonely, / And the weary that cried for rest" (139). As he wanders through the desolate, funereal, and alienating space of the city, the poet's psyche takes on its character. He becomes "Like one distracted or mad. / 'Oh, Life! Oh, Life!' I kept saying, / And the very word seemed sad" (139). His alienation and melancholy only end once he leaves the city and lies down "on the earth's quiet breast" (139). To take another example, the sonnet "On the Companionship with Nature" begins with a critique of the murderous capitalist-extractive relationship to nature but is then festooned with sexual imagery, speaking to his desire to "be much with Nature," to "be with her wholly at all hours / With the fond lover's zest," and maternal/filial imagery that identifies the poet and nature as "children of one common birth" who share "Kinship and bond with this diviner clay" (258–59). To go back to Lampman's *must*, it would seem that in order to for this poetic fusion with nature to occur, it must first be made to disappear.

In this way, ecological elegy seems to merge with taxidermy. As Pauline Wakeham writes in *Taxidermic Signs*, "although taxidermic modes of representation purport to engage in the work of preservation, these technologies ironically encode the threat of extinction upon the objects they frame, thereby prophesying the future death of bodies that are supposedly doctored to transcend the force of time" (18). Taxidermy is among several prominent "conservation" technologies, including the photograph, the herbarium, and the diorama, that gained increased prominence in the late nineteenth century. These technologies of the melancholic gaze always place their viewers in an ambiguous temporality: the serene past of an imagined and idealized unity with the object, the frozen present of the object, and a future filled with dread and anxiety. As I've written elsewhere about the diorama, this dread comes from the fact that these technologies were often expected to preserve something of the "natural environment" of animal species or cultural "ways of life" that their makers assumed were doomed to extinction (Hodgins, "Haunted Dollhouses" 106). In a similar vein, Christian Metz has described the snapshot as "an instantaneous abduction of the object out of the world into another kind of time. [. . .] [W]ith each photograph, a tiny piece of time brutally and forever escapes its ordinary fate, and thus is protected against its own loss" (140).

Some of the most important cultural historiography produced since the early 1990s has tracked how much of what became the iconic texts, narratives, images, sacred places, and cultural institutions of twentieth-century English Canada emerged out of this melancholic/taxidermic urge to preserve the traces of what were anticipated to be vanishing cultures or nature that developed during the Victorian period (cf. Bentley, *Mnemographia*; Dawn; Francis; Jasen; Jessup; McKay; O'Brian and White). As Carl Berger has detailed, the dominant philosophy of history in late-Victorian English-Canadian intellectual culture was a virulent and racist strain of historical determinism that asserted the inevitability of the global spread of a Northern European-dominated, industrially based, primarily urban, politically liberal, technologically, scientifically, and culturally sophisticated, Christian and capitalist civilization. In the face of the Anglo-American juggernaut, it was believed, untouched wilderness and all other ways of life were doomed to imminent extinction (Berger, "True North" and *Sense of Power*; Grace; Mackey).

This belief in the inevitability of the extinction of the other is ubiquitous in the art and literature of the late nineteenth and early twentieth centuries, with the result that, from Duncan Campbell Scott's "Onondaga Madonna" to Emily Carr's totem poles, the semi-mournful and semi-triumphant tones of imperialist nostalgia resonate throughout the early post-Confederation canon. In *Dark Vanishings*, Patrick Brantlinger borrows Patricia Rae's notion of "proleptic elegy"—a genre of "consolatory writing produced in anticipation of sorrow" (Rae 247)—to explain, in ways that parallel Morton's account of ecological elegy, how mourning and triumphalism often coexisted in the colonial imagination. He argues that proleptic elegies composed for vanishing Indigenous peoples or nature were the Janus-face to the epic, the conventional nation-founding genre which celebrates the nation's subjugation of its others. According to Brantlinger, both epic and proleptic elegy framed the present as one in which nature and Indigenous peoples "were and remain presences disturbing the process of national unification and identification" (4) and the future as one in which "new white colonies and nations arise as savagery and wilderness recede" (3). However, a poetic division of labour existed in which the proleptic elegy was tasked with the job of sentimentally mourning the various others who must vanish before modernity and the triumphant nation.

The discourse of "imminent vanishing" also gave rise to a whole industry of cultural preservation dominated by what James Clifford called "the salvage paradigm" (121). While Ian McKay's exploration of

East Coast folkloric collecting practices has most notably demonstrated its potential for extension into other preservation practices, the salvage paradigm has generally been used in Canada to discuss salvage ethnology. As Andrew Nurse explains, salvage ethnology was premised on the assumption that "[i]nteraction with white culture caused authentic aboriginal cultures to decay as elements of these cultures fell into disuse or were abandoned by aboriginal people themselves in favor of newer cultural adaptations imported from white sources. The task of the salvage ethnographer was to preserve the remnants of rapidly vanishing cultures to reconstruct authentic 'prehistoric' native cultures" (444). To return to Lampman, perhaps this is what explains his uncontrollable urge to collect a few golden lady's slippers. Perhaps he just saw himself as a salvage herbalist and his description of the destruction of the more public stand of wildflowers confirmed his sense that while, like the forests, the lady's slippers too must be destroyed, they could at least be preserved in his herbarium.

ANAMNESIS, OR, UNFORGETTING

As we have seen, in spite of his own urge to preserve, Lampman was highly suspicious of the collecting efforts of others to the point that he vowed to keep his lady's slippers hidden from public view. In much of Lampman's poetry, poetically enhanced vision is identified as the key faculty for the legitimate collection, preservation, and remembrance of lost nature. The short poem "Why Do Ye Call the Poet Lonely?", for example, most clearly expresses his sense that the poet can see what the so-called "ordinary person" cannot: "Why do ye call the poet lonely, / Because he dreams in lonely places? / He is not desolate, but only / Sees, where ye cannot, hidden faces" (11). In this short poem, Lampman trots out two of the most enduring tropes of the Western poetic and philosophical tradition. Extending from Plato's theory of the Forms to our contemporary obsession with transgression, trauma, and disaster, there is an enduring identification in Western high culture of the rhythms, routines, and concerns of so-called "ordinary" adult life and so-called "mainstream society" with a forgetting that produces somnolence and blindness.

The solution to this blindness is to "open people's eyes," to shake them out of their amnesia through a refocalization of vision. As the above poem suggests, the poet/artist/philosopher is given special pride of place in the project of collective anamnesis (unforgetting). First of all, he is figured as someone who retreats from the busy-ness and practical orientation of "ordinary society" and everyday life to "dream." This withdrawal from the everyday allows the poet to see "where ye cannot." Western artists and philosophers have developed several major strategies of artistic anamnesis in hopes of enlightening the somnolent majority. The sleepwalkers can be confronted with the sublime and the shocking, drawn into a kind of Blakean microscopic that reveals the world in a grain of sand, troubled by parodies, pastiches, and other *mésalliances* that violate their normal expectations of the organization of social, cultural, and physical space and time or they can be frustrated by the interplay of the excessive, the opaque, and the undecidable. In doing so, the artists and the philosophers seek to position themselves as vehicles of vision *and* cultural memory, replacing the clergy as the only status group that is capable of entering the sacred world and grasping its mysteries.

As "Why Do Ye Call the Poet Lonely?" reveals, the success of this hostile takeover depended heavily upon the (re)construction of a hierarchy of vision in which only those who have the courage, imagination, and sensibility to tarry in "desolate" places are able to really see. This assumption of the existence of a hierarchy of viewers can also be seen in the last of the two quotes from "At the Mermaid Inn" that I cited earlier. Lampman's insistence on keeping the stand of lady's slippers secret but still granting himself the authority to pick them doubly reinforces his privileged status. On the one hand, because he was chosen to be initiated into the secret, he is able to use his membership in the exclusive club of "authorized knowers" in the pages of his herbarium as well as those of "At the Mermaid Inn." On the other hand, in order to maintain and protect the cultural capital that comes with knowing "the secret," this mediation can never be direct but must instead be an interplay of transparency and opacity, mystery and revelation (Lessl 185). In refusing to reveal the site of the golden lady's slippers but in permitting himself to partake of its mysteries and delights, Lampman reinforces a hierarchy of gazers *and* rememberers with himself as poet/priest placed at the top.

It could also be argued that his desire to keep to himself the sight of this stand of native flowers mirrors the "positional competition" that drives tourism. The logic of positional competition works as follows: in the same way that the priest gains cultural capital by having a privileged access to some sort of extra-human "reality," the would-be sophisticated tourist/romantic gazer gains status through securing access to natural areas and exotic cultural locales that are typically inaccessible to less knowledgeable or adventurous travellers (Jessup 156). Perhaps even more cynically, it could be argued that in guarding the secret, Lampman was not just following the logic of consumer capitalism, he was following that of extractive capitalism. As Peter Thompson and I have argued elsewhere, the romantic gaze is often the Janus-face of an "extractive gaze" (Hodgins and Thompson 394). The latter reduces the natural and human world to what Heidegger called a "standing-reserve" of inert matter that exists to be dug up, collected, recombined, divided and sub-divided, engineered, and bought and sold at will. The romantic gaze, as we have already seen, works by initially disavowing the extractive—by honouring nature as a space of spiritual revelation and renewal. In doing so, however, it also ends up reducing nature to a resource—in this case, a "spiritual," "artistic," or "poetic" resource that reproduces the same proprietary, ethical, and epistemic relationship between the willing and desiring subject and "natural resources" (Hodgins and Thompson 395). In keeping the golden lady's slippers secret, therefore, it could be argued that Lampman was protecting his poetic resources in the same way that a gold-miner might protect his own discovery.

CONCLUSION

Maybe this is all too simple, too neat, and far too cynical. Much as the suspicious nature of cultural theory might push us to view him as a melancholic and/or crypto-capitalistic hoarder, the fact remains that Lampman would have been a daily witness to the incessant and remorseless assault on nature in the years that he lived in late-Victorian Ottawa. For most of the nineteenth century, the major industry in Ottawa was forestry and lumber milling. By the time that he arrived in Ottawa in 1883, the eastern half of the Ottawa Valley had been completely stripped of old-growth forests and the Ottawa River was highly polluted by sawdust, industrial effluents, raw sewage, and household garbage (Gwyn 39–40, 54–58; Taylor 97, 106). Furthermore, in a period of unrestrained resource capitalism, multiple attempts by the local citizens to restrain the very wealthy and well-connected mill-owners were rejected by Parliament (McLaren 222–23). Finally, during the years in which Lampman lived in the city, Ottawa was a boomtown whose population had nearly quadrupled from 27,400 in 1881 to 101,000 in 1901 (Lampman arrived in 1883 and died in 1899). For many ecologically minded Ottawans like Lampman, the city's rapid expansion must have been akin to watching nature disappear before their very eyes. One palpable indication of the imminent death of nature for many in this period was the rapid decline of the passenger pigeon. Eradicated from the Ottawa Valley by 1890, it is estimated that 4 billion of them were killed across North America between 1850 and 1914 (the year that the last one was spotted) to feed the mushrooming urban population (Jenkins 149).

Furthermore, the traumatic character of this daily experience of the loss of nature would have been amplified in light of some of the intellectual developments of the time. Lampman was a fixture in a vibrant late-Victorian Ottawa intellectual and cultural club scene which brought together many of the prominent Canadian scientists, jurists, writers, and historians of the period (most of whom were civil servants). As the "brains" behind the nascent Canadian nation-state, many members of this scene shared Lampman's ambivalence towards a Canadian economy based on extraction and a Canadian culture based on collection. While the more culturally oriented members of this scene like Scott read into Darwin the racist philosophy of history discussed above, his naturalist friends like James Fletcher (the chief Dominion Botanist and Entomologist with whom he would take regular evening strolls) also discussed and understood his larger point that the survival of species of flora and fauna was highly dependent upon a sensitive and complex web of relationships. This new understanding of the sensitivity of natural habitats, to take one example, led several other Ottawa-based scientists who travelled in his circles (Connor 80) to articulate the relationship between deforestation, loss of habitat, soil erosion, and, yes, climate change by the late nineteenth century (cf. Morgan 11; Macoun 3).

Lampman, therefore, was certainly not alone in believing that, failing government protection, Canadian wilderness was at risk of disappearing, and his daily experience seemed to confirm that belief. In other words, he probably had good reason to be depressed and angry about environmental despoliation and popular and elite complicity in that process. Still, it's a long way from *will* or *is likely to* to the *must* of his 10 June 1893 "At the Mermaid Inn" contribution. This long way forces upon us many undecidable and unanswerable questions: Should he be remembered as one of Canada's earliest environmental advocates or as yet another melancholic poet who turned away from life to identify with an unobtainable object? Was he simply someone whose desire to possess that which he loved required preserving it by killing it, or a man of his time whose imagination was constrained by his uncritical acceptance of a deterministic philosophy of history? Perhaps his melancholy comes from that philosophy's nostalgia for impossible lost objects such as an unspoiled nature or the authentic noble savage that existed only as a product of that philosophy. Unfortunately for us, we can only guess at the answers based on one simple word: *must*, a word that, like both memory and imagination, is at once forceful and vague.

• ◆ •

CHAPTER 14

Under Other Skies: Personal and Cultural Memory in E. Pauline Johnson's Nature Lyrics and Memorial Odes

Jesse Rae Archibald-Barber

The poems of E. Pauline Johnson, or Tekahionwake, cover a broad range of personal experiences, historical perspectives, and heroic figures, many of which relate to the connection between personal and cultural memory. In her nature lyrics, Johnson explores the power of personal memory to overcome feelings of isolation and give meaning to the transience of existence. Johnson's abundant use of sensuous imagery also provides an alternative to the Canadian colonial view of Indigenous nature as hostile or savage. In this way, her lyrical poems provide a more unifying, rather than divisive, sense of Canadian life, which forms the basis for an exploration of cultural memory in her memorial odes where she honours fallen heroes as part of the basis of a shared national consciousness. Through this connection between personal and cultural memory, Johnson offers a positive representation of Canadian society by encouraging a reconciliation of the conflicts between Aboriginal peoples and English Canadians.

More specifically, Johnson reflects on the legacy of colonialism by offering intertextual critiques of some early English-Canadian poets, including Isabella Valancy Crawford, Charles G.D. Roberts, and Oliver Goldsmith. Several of their poems romanticize, marginalize, or even exclude First Nations presence, but Johnson resists this kind of cultural amnesia by developing a more inclusive recollection of the foundations of Canadian identity. To this end, Johnson often considers divergent perspectives simultaneously to achieve a balanced negotiation between cultures, conveying a more open understanding of the political and spiritual conflicts than do her contemporaries. Indeed, Johnson goes beyond her contemporaries by mirroring their own canonical authority against them.

NATURE LYRICS: TRANSCENDENCE AND IMMANENCE

Expressing a widely held view of memory in the late nineteenth century, in his seminal essay "Memory," Ralph Waldo Emerson states that memory "holds together past and present, beholding both, existing in both, abides in the flowing, and gives continuity and dignity to human life" (64). In this sense, personal memory provides the basis of identity, informs experience, and allows one both to inhabit and transcend the present moment. At the same time, because of the transient and fluid nature of existence, identity cannot be based on memory alone, as it must contend with immediate experience, which does not allow one to retain a detached, transcendent perspective.

Johnson addresses both this power and failure of transcendence through memory in several poems. For example, in "Re-Voyage" (1891), the speaker attempts to reach back across time to connect with an absent lover and recreate a cherished experience. Alone in her canoe, she asks, "[w]hat of the days when we two dreamed together?" (l. 1):

> Have you no longing to re-live the dreaming,
> Adrift in my canoe?
> To watch my paddle blade all wet and gleaming
> Cleaving the waters through?
> To lie wind-blown and wave-caressed, until
> Your restless pulse grows still? (ll. 13–18)

Although the speaker is "[a]drift," she does not find nature to be a place of fear or loss, for with her imagination she is able to restore the sense of her lover's "pulse." With this assurance, she knows that her absent lover "[w]ould toss the world away to be but lying / Again in my canoe" (l. 27). The speaker has returned to the place in nature where they shared the experience, and through her lyric she transcends her solitude and recreates her past love from memory. By the end of the poem, however, Johnson acknowledges that the demands of life do not allow one to remain in a transcendent reverie, as the speaker is suddenly forced back to her present solitary struggle on the river:

Ah me! my paddle failed me in the steering
Across love's shoreless seas;
All reckless, I had ne'er a thought of fearing
Such dreary days as these,
When through the self-same rapids we dash by,
My lone canoe and I. (ll. 31–36)

The speaker must still contend with the same dangers, or "rapids," in life
as before, but the transient nature of existence, symbolized by the swift-
flowing river, does not allow her to dwell in nostalgia, and she concedes
that her lost love cannot be recovered.

. Johnson reveals that although memory can provide consolation for
separation and lost love, one cannot avoid the sudden immersion in reality. Thus, in essence, there is an acknowledgement of the failure of transcendence through memory in this lyric. This failure, though, allows the
speaker to come to terms with the difficult realities of the temporal flow
of life. Human existence is linear and has an end that cannot be known
in the present, as that present moment irrevocably disappears into the
past. However, with metaphors of the canoe and the rapids, her response
to the failure of transcendence is not to surrender herself, but to take
charge of her whole being uninhibitedly in the living moment, leading
her to discover the consolation of self-love and self-determination. Thus,
despite the solitary flow of her journey, the speaker still shows that human life cannot simply be reduced to a linear process, for the very reason
that individuals persist in "re-voyaging" to past ideal experiences.

Nonetheless, although lyrical poetry can help one to recreate a personal memory, Johnson further acknowledges the pressing temporal aspect of the present in many other poems, most notably in "The Song My
Paddle Sings" (1892), in which the speaker finds fulfillment in the passing
moment rather than in its transcendence. Again, the speaker is alone in
nature, but this time the absent lover she calls for is the "West wind" (l. 1),
though she knows she cannot conjure it no matter how she uses her words:
"I stow the sail, unship the mast: / I wooed you long but my wooing's past"
(ll. 10–11). Unlike the speaker in "Re-Voyage," she does not attempt to
leave her present reality, nor does she lament her solitary condition:

August is laughing across the sky,
Laughing while paddle, canoe and I,

Drift, drift,
Where the hills uplift
On either side of the current swift. (ll. 19–23)

By finding comfort in the present moment, the speaker realizes that fulfillment happens not beyond nature or time, but in the sensuous flow of
life. She is ready when "the river runs swifter" (l. 29), finding excitement
in its sudden changes and threats:

Be strong, O paddle! Be brave, canoe!
The reckless waves you must plunge into.
Reel, reel,
On your trembling keel,
But never a fear my craft will feel. (ll. 39–43)

Here, the metaphors of the canoe and the rapids convey the surrender
of herself to a total immersion in the living moment. In this poem, experience is found in the present and not in the memory of a lost past;
or rather, one's memory of the past is continually reshaped by present
experience. Returning to Emerson's connection between memory and
identity, it is in this sense that he acknowledges how memory changes
with new experiences: "The Past has a new value every moment to the
active mind" (64). Transcendence becomes an act of consciousness as
it interacts with natural phenomena, and thus personal memory is not
detached from immediate experience: "Memory is not a pocket, but a
living instructor" (65).

This view of memory informs Johnson's understanding of the spiritual aspect of human life and how one remembers those who have died,
again not as detached from nature but as still inhabiting present experience. In "The Happy Hunting Grounds" (1889), Johnson depicts a popular version, at the time, of a First Nations view of the afterlife.[1] Providing
an idealized reflection of the Canadian landscape, the speaker does not
base her vision on the transcendence of nature, but rather infuses the life
world with a sense of the eternal, where all that has passed still inhabits
the present: "Into the rose gold westland, its yellow prairies roll, / World

---

1   "The Happy Hunting Grounds" was recited when Johnson's ashes were laid to rest in Stanley
     Park near Siwash Rock (Gray 393).

of the bison's freedom, home of the Indian's soul" (ll. 1–2). In the consolatory aspect of her vision of the afterlife, there is not the slightest trace of
absence or loss; there is no death, as identity is fully preserved from one
world to the other, a world that abounds with all that the departed found
joyful in life. The plenitude of life fulfills itself and resonates with an eternal sense of the good. Significantly, the speaker acknowledges how this
infusion of the natural world with consolatory value contrasts with the
traditional Christian consolation of heavenly transcendence:

> Surely the great Hereafter cannot be more than this,
> Surely we'll see that country after Time's farewell kiss.
> Who would his lovely faith condole?
> Who envies not the Red-skin's soul[?] (ll. 21–24)

The Native afterlife provides a spiritual reassurance like the Christian
heaven, as the memory of all things is idealized and projected into an
eternal realm; it differs, however, in that it is not a realm that is separate from nature or personal experience. Johnson uses memory in this
context not to transcend the present moment in nature, but to reflect a
spiritual immanence that runs throughout nature and unites all beings
and things.

However, the last rhetorical question of the passage complicates her
view of a Native afterlife, as what follows it supports many colonial assumptions about the fate of the "Red-skins" implicit at the time: "O! dear
dead race, my spirit too / Would fain sail westward unto you" (ll. 27–28).
Like many early English-Canadian poets, Johnson romanticizes the loss
of Indigenous cultures, a colonial practice that became integral to the image of Canada during Confederation.[2] However, Johnson includes here an
ironic critique, as the primary symbolic assumptions of her lyric suggest

---

2 It must be restated here that the type of afterlife Johnson depicts is a popular and stereotypi-
cal view, as First Nations beliefs are diverse and often oppose Johnson's depiction. As Friesen
explains: "Native North Americans have frequently been the target of frivolous talk about es-
chatology with mention of the phrase 'happy hunting ground.' The phrase has been invented by
non-Natives as a parallel to the Christian version of heaven, the abode of the deceased who lived
justly. [. . .] In fact, in traditional First Nations' theology there was no clear line of demarcation
between human beings and the spirit world. It was quite possible for spirits to contact human
beings and affect their daily activities. The human world was permeable by spirit-beings who
entered the human domain and left at will. Some tribes also believed in reincarnation, that is,
some people could die and return to the human world in another form" (Friesen 135).

that a Native Canadian sense of immanence in nature contains something that Christian transcendence in heaven lacks: "The angels' songs are less divine / Than duo sung twixt breeze and pine" (ll. 15–16). The speaker does not simply fly to a transcendent saviour's arms for consolation; she does not devalue the natural world, but finds in it an immanent spiritual presence resounding with the full plenitude of life. Nonetheless, we find a consolation based on a contradiction that the poem cannot clearly re-solve: the poem is both empowering, as it sees the Indigenous sense of the afterlife as more consoling than the Christian notion of heaven, and prob-lematic, as it conveys a romanticized version of the afterlife that reinforces along the way assumptions about the fate of First Nations cultures. In her critique, Johnson unavoidably marginalizes what she privileges.

One can more clearly see Johnson's difficult position by contrasting her vision of the afterlife with Isabella Valancy Crawford's "The Camp of Souls" (1880). Like Johnson, Crawford uses Native imagery to ro-manticize the afterlife, but, unlike Johnson, she draws a distinct division between life and the afterlife and reflects Indigenous nature as hostile and redeemable only in death. The speaker is a spirit returning in his canoe to the Canadian forests from the realm of the dead in the Native cosmological and spiritual universe. The "far camp" is a peaceful "spirit land" (l. 22), where "no warrior wind / Rushes on war trail" (ll. 37–38). Here Crawford shares Johnson's view of the afterlife as a place of greater harmony beyond the colonial conflicts of the land. However, the differ-ence is that Crawford's view of the afterlife is not an idealized continua-tion of nature, but rather a refuge from a forest filled with "leaf-scalps of tall trees mourning behind" (l. 39). Although the speaker romanticizes nature and loves to return "to the forests and camps of earth" (l. 50), the lifeworld is nonetheless a place filled with violence, war trails, and the "paint of death" (l. 44). Only in an afterlife far from this world is Indigenous nature remembered as peaceful.

Johnson's response to this view of Indigenous nature lies in her emphasis on how remembrance occurs in the present temporal flow of nature. In "The Death Cry" (1895), Johnson assumes a spiritual es-sence that survives death, as the voice of the dead is recreated not in a far spirit realm, but in the ongoing present moment. The poem ad-dresses the issues of war and violence depicted in Crawford's poem, fo-cusing on the perspective of the Native warrior "in the crisis of hot strife" (l. 7). Johnson even goes beyond Crawford in depicting Indigenous nature with dark imagery, as she describes the "[m]oonless" (l. 1) lands of "northern Canada" (l. 2) as permeated with violence, where the "law is blood for blood" (l. 13) in the "depths of forest gloom" (l. 31). Johnson shows how the warrior is surrounded on every side by the death cry, as death pierces every moment of the temporal flow of nature. This is not the joyful reflection of life and the afterlife that Johnson depicts in "The Happy Hunting Grounds." However, Johnson maintains her consolatory view which redeems individual death, as the death cry of the Mohawk warrior "float[s] with the waters, and 'tis passed / from mouth to mouth" (ll. 26–27). The speaker finds a kind of beauty in the death cry, as an ancient way of communicating and remembering the passing of a life. She transforms the purely sensual sound of the death cry into something that transcends its own fleeting nature, where in the moment "all is still as death" (l. 18). Since the warrior remains "unmoved" (l. 28), Johnson finds a way to unify the transcendent and the temporal aspects of memory, as she abstracts the individual death to a point of stillness where "death itself seems dead" (l. 19). In this sense, death is not an end, but the past continues to inhabit the present, as the memory of the dead is recreated beyond physical death. For Johnson, the Indigenous voice preserves the individual's life as an ongoing verbal memorial that is continuously passed on from one warrior to another.

Johnson's nature lyrics show her Romantic sensibilities in turning to nature to overcome isolation and give meaning to loss. However, although the Romantic lyric promises the power of transcendence, she then has to negotiate the problem of being merely human, bound to the present flow of life. In response, she emphasizes immanent principles, embracing the temporal flow of life rather than its transcendence, thereby finding beauty in the Canadian landscape rather than hostility. In this way, her lyrical poems provide a more unifying, as opposed to divisive, personal memory of Canadian life. This emphasis on unity in her nature lyrics becomes central to her memorial odes, as her form of cultural memory aims to overcome the colonial image of Aboriginal peoples as disappearing cultures.

MEMORIAL ODES: POLITICAL DIVISION AND UNITY

Johnson's representation of cultural memory in her memorial odes is informed by her mixed heritage as both English and Mohawk. Not surprisingly, the way she negotiated her identity between cultures met with both praise and criticism. On the one hand, Carole Gerson and Veronica Strong-Boag point out, "[i]n the high age of Anglo-Saxon imperialism and patriarchy she was [. . .] a figure of resistance, simultaneously challenging both the racial divide between Native and European, and the conventions that constrained her sex" ("Paddling" 3). On the other hand, Johnson received criticism for her pro-British nationalism as unavoidably reinforcing the colonial system she ostensibly protests.[3] Terry Goldie sums up this problematic status: "The canon of Canadian Native literature might make her a minor early hero, the only popular Native writer between the mid-nineteenth century and the mid-twentieth. It is more likely, however, to see her as an embarrassment, another early figure who conformed all too easily to the beads and buckskins" (382). The conformity that Goldie refers to is how, for instance, during recitals of her poetry, Johnson would perform the first half of her show dressed in buckskin, and then return to the stage in late-Victorian dress (see Gray 159–60). Ironically, it is not so much Johnson's late-Victorian lady persona as it is her "Mohawk Princess" guise that is seen as assimilating Native imagery to English forms. The criticism is that her work fulfills colonial expectations and makes it easier for Canadians to stereotype the Indian as Other. However, Gerson and Strong-Boag contend that this cultural ambiguity is itself part of her significance: "By claiming and expressing the sensibilities of both Aboriginal margin and European centre, Johnson ultimately confounds the simple dichotomies that underpin Western consciousness" (5). It is because of Johnson's double perspective that her work envisions a reconciliation between First Nations and Canadians in the decades following Confederation.

The importance of Johnson's inclusive approach to memorialization can be seen more clearly by first examining Charles G.D. Roberts's "Canada" (1886), a canonical reference point in early English-Canadian literature that excludes Aboriginal cultures. Evoking a sense of urgency about defining a national consciousness, Roberts uses heroic memorial

---

3   See Tanis MacDonald's essay in this book on Joan Crate's commemoration of Pauline Johnson in her poetry collection, *Pale as Real Ladies*, for a further discussion of these contradictions in the reception of Johnson's performances and writings.

motifs to structure his vision of Canadian identity.[4] Several stanzas convey vignettes that recall important though violent events in Canadian history, "attest[ing] in burning song and psalm / How here thy heroes fell!" (ll. 31–32). Canada is a nation that was born on the "battle's brunt" (l. 33), and Roberts laments the loss of Canadian "sons" (44) who have died establishing the country. He further laments the loss of soldiers who have been killed in the "blood-red folds" (l. 20) of imperial wars across the "world" (l. 19): your "sons await thy call" (l. 44), "some in exile, some / With strangers housed, in stranger lands,—/ And some Canadian lips are dumb / Beneath Egyptian sands" (ll. 45–48). However, Roberts does not dwell in mourning the soldiers' deaths, but instead honours them by envisioning a transcendent sense of nationhood in the form of a great revelation: "dream not thou! / Wake, and behold how night is done" (ll. 53–54). To come fully into being, Canada must awake from the night of its colonial past and "Burst" into nationhood like "the uprising sun!" (l. 56). Here one can see that whereas personal memory is based on lived present experience, cultural memory is more selective and representative of a particular view of the past. Thus, while Roberts's representation of Canada's founding is filled with promise, the problem here is that it is a form of cultural memory that forgets Aboriginal presence in Canadian history. Alternatively, Johnson makes the reconciliation of First Nations and English Canada essential not only to preserving cultures, but also to sharing a national identity.

In "The Re-interment of Red Jacket" (1884), Johnson commemorates Red Jacket, or Sagoyewatha, a Seneca orator and chief who supported the British during and after the American Revolution.[5] Following the tradition of funeral elegies, the poem includes eulogistic descriptions of the achievements of the deceased and depictions of the burial ceremony. While the speaker acknowledges Red Jacket for his heroic stature and deeds in battle, she remembers him more for his intellectual and persuasive powers:

4   As Fred Cogswell explains: "While a young man, Roberts became a convinced Canadian nationalist and remained so until his death. Equally strong was his conviction of the primary role of literature in creating the mythos and ethos upon which a country's unity depended" (195).

5   Red Jacket died in 1830, but in 1885 his body was moved from its original burial place. The poem is essentially a heroic elegy that Johnson wrote for the occasion, and it was included in the literature that commemorated the ceremony (Gray 90).

The keenest flint or stone
That barbed the warrior's arrow in its flight,
Could not outreach the limit of his might
That he attained alone. (ll. 17–20)

The speaker also praises Red Jacket for the sacrifices he made to unify his people in the name of freedom and peace. Red Jacket's life has ended, but his influence continues on throughout Canadian history. Thus, instead of mourning his death, the speaker finds a deeper consolation, as each side must "forgive" (l. 45) on terms of mutual respect, rather than on terms of conquest and surrender. Johnson conveys this reconciliation in the poem by the praise she gives the "paler race" (l. 6) who honour the "dusky chief" (l. 3) with a "Christian burial" (l. 12). Thus, tropes of family alliance underlie the funerary occasion of the poem: she sees the Christian burial of the chief as a symbolic adoption that provides the basis for co-operation when both sides come together to memorialize a shared loss.

It is this sense of adoption and memorialization that trauma and memory theorist Gabriele Schwab sees as essential to the reparation of conflicts between colonizing and colonized peoples: "A politics of mourning that is mindful of the question of justice and responsibility must be grounded in a politics of memory, of inheritance, and of generations" (149). For genuine reparation to begin, "the descendants of both victims and perpetrators must take over" the task of mourning the dead, and the most effective way to do this is through adoption, whether literal or symbolic: "Dehumanizing the enemy as a people is, in fact, what prepares the ground for turning warfare into genocide. Adoption, by contrast, works with a different logic according to which, as human beings, friend and enemy become interchangeable" (146). However, returning to Johnson's memorial ode, the adoption of Red Jacket through a Western burial is a complicated issue, for it can be seen as a compromise that puts English Canadians in an unequal paternal position.

As the values of Red Jacket's identity are incorporated into a traditional Christian framework, the re-interment of his body is also a symbolic assimilation of an Aboriginal leader into the Christian belief system. Indeed, the literal moving of his bones is ironic, as he was a notoriously "staunch traditionalist" who "opposed the introduction of white ways into Indian customs" (Keenan 188). At the same time, from Johnson's double perspective, and given the double interment of the body, it must be remembered that Red Jacket had already, in some senses, adopted the English himself, and this inversion is symbolic on a larger historical scale as well. Red Jacket is a figure who held onto his traditions, while his desire for his people's autonomy through alliance with the English shows him to be a shrewd leader, ambassador, statesman, and peacemaker. Because it takes great effort and sacrifice on both sides to keep uneasy relations from erupting into open hostility, the poem, in honouring Red Jacket, attempts to find reconciliation for colonial conflicts and losses with a consolation based on mutual respect.

As Schwab maintains, despite the difficulties of overcoming past trauma and violent histories, adoption and memorialization are necessary to "breaking the cycle of violence, revenge, and retribution" (147). Indeed, Johnson uses the adoption trope so that both sides remember the loss of the same "son" and honour his legacy so that a lasting peace can ensue. This sense of a shared loss is what gives Johnson's memorialization a more inclusive unity than that of her contemporaries. As we saw in "Canada," Roberts uses the figure of the "uprising sun" for Canadians alone. However, in the final words of "The Re-interment of Red Jacket," Johnson modifies this solar trope and calls out to the "rising nation of the west" (l. 41) as a way to unite Canadian and Aboriginal peoples and compensate for both cultures' losses. Traditionally, the West is the place of the setting sun, symbolizing death and the passage to the afterlife. Here, Johnson transforms it into a symbol for the dawn of a new political and cultural identity.

Earlier poets than Johnson or Roberts had begun to articulate this kind of transcendent trope for Canadian nationhood. In "The Rising Village" (1825), Oliver Goldsmith creates the image of early colonial Canada as "the wonder of the western skies" (l. 558); however, he is totally one-sided in his reflection on Canada's past, describing Aboriginal peoples as savages who terrorize and threaten the peaceful settlement of the land:

> Behold! the savage tribes, in wildest strain,
> Approach with death and terror in their train;
> No longer silence o'er the forest reigns,
> No longer stillness now her pow'r retains;
> But hideous yells announce the murd'rous band,
> Whose bloody footsteps desolate the land. [. . .] (ll. 81–86)

Fig 2.1. First Contact diorama featuring Anthony Henday's meeting with the Chief of the Blackfoot tribe. Courtesy of Royal Alberta Museum, Ethnology.

Fig 4.5. Welcome to Pine Point. Photo taken from the production ©2010. Courtesy National Film Board of Canada.

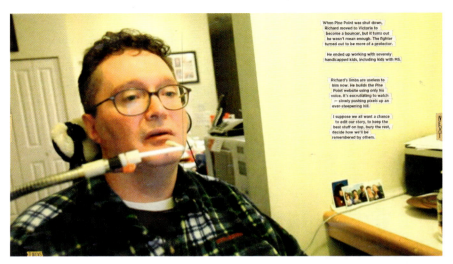

When Pine Point was shut down, Richard moved to Victoria to become a bouncer, but it turns out he wasn't mean enough. The fighter turned out to be more of a protector.

He ended up working with severely handicapped kids, including kids with MS.

Richard's limbs are useless to him now. He builds the Pine Point website using only his voice. It's excruciating to watch — slowly pushing pixels up an ever-steepening hill.

I suppose we all want a chance to edit our story, to keep the best stuff on top, bury the rest, decide how we'll be remembered by others.

NEXT

Fig 4.6. Welcome to Pine Point. Photo taken from the production ©2010. Courtesy National Film Board of Canada.

#3
The townsite is still there.

Roads are surreally intact, 40-year-old crosswalk paint defiantly holds on, but there's little else. The roads are lined with nothing, as though a suburb was about to be built.

A while back someone found a basement that had somehow escaped burial.

You pull back an old sheet of plywood, crawl through a hole – and you're standing in the basement of the Pine Point Hotel.

There are cleaning supplies, a room full of receipts and pay stubs, hallways with peeling paint, empty chairs. Then you return to the surface and the hotel disappears.

PREV

I had noticed that Pine Pointers often feel a distinct need to be 'the last person to...' At least 4 claim the final drink in the hotel bar.

While I was down there, I had a beer, just because.

Sorry...

NEXT

Fig 4.7. Welcome to Pine Point. Photo taken from the production ©2010. Courtesy National Film Board of Canada.

The speaker's consolation to the colonists is that the Natives will soon disappear, "[t]o seek their prey beneath some other skies" (l. 108). Thus, for Goldsmith, as for Roberts, the transcendent trope of nationhood is one that functions only for Canadian settlers, while Aboriginal peoples are displaced to the point of exclusion. In Goldsmith's view, once Natives are removed from the poem, and from history, then Canada will rise into nationhood. Johnson's vision, however, recognizes that for the country to fully rise, cultures must mutually acknowledge and forgive each other's wrongs, to reach a peaceful resolution of differences.

Johnson further develops her inclusive form of cultural memory in "'Brant,' A Memorial Ode" (1886), in which she also responds to the kind of exclusionary sentiments found in Goldsmith's poem. Joseph Brant, or Thayendanega ("He who sets or places together two bets"), was a Mohawk chief who, like Red Jacket, supported the British during the American Revolution.[6] Emphasizing this alliance, Johnson draws on the prejudices of the early poets and uses their canonical authority against them, specifically with sun and sky imagery and through the anglocentric consolation for loss. The sun indeed shines on "Young Canada," with both hope and lament:

> Young Canada with mighty force sweeps on
> To gain in power and strength, before the dawn
> That brings another era; when the sun
> Shall rise again, but only shine upon
> Her Indian graves, and Indian memories.
> For as the carmine in the twilight skies
> Will fade as night comes on, so fades the race. (ll. 1–7)

Recalling the colonial sentiment of the age, Johnson first depicts the new "era" of Canada as one that rises on "Indian graves." Although Johnson laments the loss of Aboriginal cultures, she makes it clear that this should not lead to their exclusion from Canadian history, by reminding Canadians that the "plumes" (l. 13) and "glories" (l. 15) of

---

6   Unlike Red Jacket, though, Brant was more loyal to the British and much more aggressive in his military action against the Americans. Brant even censured Red Jacket for not providing enough resistance to the Americans (Keenan 187).

the nation would not exist "without allegiance from thy Indian son" (l. 14). However, Johnson's view here faces the same problem of assimilation as in "The Re-interment of Red Jacket." She elevates Aboriginal values, but again it is a process that gives English Canada a paternal position of authority and reinforces the prevailing colonial ethos that views Aboriginal peoples as a "fading race." Johnson recognizes this, though, as her use of this imagery here critiques this kind of colonial rhetoric. Thus, by the end of her memorial ode, Johnson realigns the metaphor of family relations from one of adoption to one of a "common Brotherhood" (l. 17). Canada need not be hierarchical, divisive, or exclusionary, but rather it has the promise to be a country where cultures rise together on equal terms.

Although many heroic elegies may glorify the warrior's death in battle, Johnson finds in the deaths of these heroic subjects an image that can embody peace, unity, and freedom. Johnson praises Brant's life as representative of an ideal vision of the unity of Canadian and First Nations societies. She encourages Canadian recognition of Aboriginal peoples, and a mutual respect for each other's loss, in order to achieve a peaceful political unity on which to base a new Canadian identity. If either culture's sense of heritage is lost, then Canadian identity as a whole cannot emerge and stabilize. Hence, this idea of unity is not something unrealizable, but is already the essential condition that comprises the origin of Canada. The significance of memorializing leaders like Red Jacket and Brant is that they recall how the Haudenosaunee Confederacy and the British were already united in the consolidation of the Canadas after the American Revolution. It is this past unity that threatens to die, if left unremembered. Thus, though the great chiefs have died, their burial ceremonies do not represent the death of the old unity, but rather their commemoration represents the continual rebirth of that unity in the present.

Recalling her views of immanence in her nature lyrics, Johnson's point is not that the individual continues to live after death, but that an idea he or she embodied persists as a presence and manifests itself throughout history. Subsequently, at the end of "'Brant,' A Memorial Ode," she embeds an intertextual critique of Goldsmith's view that Aboriginal peoples will remove themselves from Canada's history by "seek[ing] their prey beneath some other skies." Rather, with the promise of Brant's memory, Johnson assures Aboriginal peoples that there is "no cause for us to rise / To seek protection under other skies" (ll. 29–30). This reversal and modification of Goldsmith's line critiques the imperial ethos of the early English-Canadian poets and points to a new vision of society as one not based on the dominance of one culture over the other. As a country that must create a spiritual and political ethos that has no previous historical model, Canada is now a world where cultures rise together—the ideal cultural memorial for all forms of colonial loss.

CONCLUSION

Johnson's memorial odes offer a representation of cultural memory that is more inclusive than that of her contemporaries. She confronts the racial and gender conflicts of her time and advocates equality and cultural unity as the basis for a stable Canadian society. Moreover, while recognizing that the lyrical form may not soothe personal pain, Johnson actively engaged in testing the limits of poetry, bending it toward a social function. Although she sees the failure of traditional Western promises of personal transcendence, which reveals a disconnection between Canadian and Aboriginal forms of memory, she nonetheless utilizes her mixed heritage in her memorial odes to reconnect cultures. The kinds of transcendent symbols used by the early English-Canadian poets are ultimately exclusionary, as they fail to include Aboriginal presence. Because of her double perspective, Johnson sees memorialization not as something that transcends history, but as something immanent or continually recreated within it. When she does use the transcendent images of the rising sun or the western sky, she modifies them to embody a form of cultural memory that includes Aboriginal presence. In this way, Johnson evokes a desire to bring together disparate peoples, and her poetry encourages Canadian and Aboriginal peoples to move beyond the legacy of colonialism. This is all the more significant, for she wrote her poems during the founding decades of the country—a point to be remembered as Canadian society moves forward today.

CHAPTER 15

•◆•

Indigenous Diasporas and the Shape of Cultural Memory: Reframing Anahareo's *Devil in Deerskins*[1]

Sophie McCall

In the preface to Anahareo's memoir, *Devil in Deerskins: My Life with Grey Owl*, Grant MacEwan writes that "it is a matter of the highest personal gratification that Grey Owl will return in [these] pages" (Anahareo, *Devil* vi). For decades Anahareo's life and work in both her bestselling memoir, *Devil in Deerskins*, published in 1972, and in her earlier book, *My Life with Grey Owl*, published in 1940, have been understood *in relation to* Grey Owl's. More recently, interest has been sparked about Anahareo herself, whose mother, Mary, was an Algonquin woman from the Pikwàkanagàn First Nation on Golden Lake, and whose father's parents came from Oka on Mohawk territory before settling in Mattawa, Ontario (Gleeson, "Blazing" 289). This paper reconstructs this Indigenous history of diaspora through an attentive reading of Anahareo's and her descendants' personal and collective memories, and analyzes the shape of memory itself as it is constructed, revised, and transformed in Anahareo's two published works. My interest in Anahareo's work is part of a larger collective project among scholars of Indigenous literature to construct a longer genealogy of Indigenous writing and storytelling than sometimes is assumed, particularly in light of well-intentioned celebrations of the so-called "renaissance" since the 1990s.[2] In comparing Anahareo's two publications, I

---

1   Some portions of this chapter were first published in the Afterword to Anahareo's *Devil in Deerskins: My Life with Grey Owl* (University of Manitoba Press, 2014). Permission to republish this material is gratefully acknowledged.

2   By "renaissance" I am referring to the explosion of published writings by Aboriginal authors in the 1990s, particularly by small presses like Theytus Books, Women's Press, and Fifth House. While the positive effects of opening up the Canadian literary market to new Indigenous voices are self-evident, such an emphasis on the "emergence" of Aboriginal literature in the 1990s risks obscuring older, out-of-print, or generically divergent texts.

demonstrate how her textual construction of memory impacts her editing choices as she revises, adds, deletes, and rearranges her stories in the 1972 volume. The zone of memory becomes a site of struggle as she negotiates, through the act of (re)writing, relationships of power, conflicting desires, and entrenched patterns of representation. A recurring image in both of Anahareo's texts is one of boxes: packing crates, chests, trunks, and other containers function metaphorically as storage devices for remembrances. These boxes, containing objects with personal, even secret, meanings, are simultaneously travelling cases that help constitute a transportable sense of diasporic Indigenous identity while maintaining a sense of rootedness through stories, skills, and knowledge. The paradoxical function of the boxes—sealed but openable, materially present yet movable—is tied to Anahareo's efforts to modulate the range of meanings that her life story generates, narrated as it is through a series of journeys.

The relationship between memory, place, and subjectivity is the focus of much scholarly debate, though the articulation of that relationship is contentious when comparing settler, Indigenous, and diasporic histories. In settler discourses, as Margery Fee and others have argued, establishing the legitimacy of the settler nation depends upon the production of memory-saturated landscapes and the assertion of a one-to-one relationship between land, story, and nation—a correlation characteristic of Romantic-nationalist ideology.[3] For Aboriginal peoples, the historical effect of Romantic nationalism in settler contexts has been the appropriation of their stories, occurring concurrently with the expropriation of their land and the suppression of their languages and cultures.[4] In diasporic studies, scholars have focused on the challenges facing displaced communities whose sense of connection between memory, place, and belonging has become severed or warped, and later recreated in the "new" land.[5] For example, Kirsten McAllister's *Terrain*

3   Discourses of Romantic nationalism assert that a people's sense of nationhood emerges from sharing a common land, language, and set of stories or mythologies about themselves and their territories. See Fee; Willmott.
4   Keeshig-Tobias makes clear the cost of settler discourses of Romantic nationalism on Aboriginal peoples by drawing attention to a continuum between various forms of appropriation—of voice, stories, authorship, spiritual knowledge, cultural artifacts, language, land, resources, and governance. See also Maracle.
5   See Kim for an excellent discussion of the contested conceptual ground concerning memory, displacement, and homeland undergirding theories of diaspora as articulated by scholars such as Hirsch (*Family*); Safran; Boyarin and Boyarin; and Tölölyan. See also Hirsch and Spitzer; and Kuhn and McAllister.

of Memory: A Japanese Canadian Memorial Project, a study of camps in British Columbia where Japanese Canadians were held during the Second World War, explores how landscapes marked by displacement and erasure can be transformed "into a constantly changing valley of remembrance" (18) through the "collective cultural activity" of memory work (6). For communities that have been uprooted as a result of political violence, creating memories "in the present, at the present site of the past," is vital to overcome what can be a debilitating sense of postmemory (Hirsch and Spitzer 138). The phenomenon of postmemory is often associated with second-generation survivors living in the diaspora who "grow up dominated by narratives that preceded their birth" and "whose own belated stories are evacuated by the stories of the previous generation shaped by traumatic events that can neither be understood nor recreated" (Hirsch, qtd. in Kuhn and McAllister, Introduction 4).

Although questions of postmemory have been explored and applied extensively to diasporic communities, they have not been as predominant in the context of Indigenous studies. Indeed, Indigenous literature is rarely interpreted through a theoretical lens of diaspora, since diaspora's emphasis on displacement risks re-inscribing a narrative of cultural loss and of eradication from the landscape that Indigenous scholars and writers vigorously have challenged. Emphasizing a narrative of displacement risks ignoring or underplaying how Indigenous peoples have maintained connections to land, culture, and story in ongoing and meaningful ways.[6] One critic in Indigenous studies who has explored the relationship of memory, place, and "the overwhelming pressures of diaspora" on Indigenous peoples is Cree scholar Neal McLeod. McLeod argues that "a collective memory emerges from a specific location, spatially and temporally, and includes such things as a relationship to land, songs, ceremonies, language and stories. [. . .] to tell a story is to link, in the moments of telling, the past to the present" (McLeod, "Coming" 17). Because Indigenous peoples have contended with both "spatial" and "ideological" forms of diaspora, "it is through memory, which is located in the landscape, that people are able to situate themselves in the world" (17). McLeod suggests that a return to those remembered landscapes creates the conditions by which the

---

6 For more discussion on the tensions and potential incommensurabilities between Indigenous studies and diaspora studies, see Clifford ("Diasporas"); Maracle; Eigenbrod; and McCall.

process of alienation from stories and territories may be reversed and the memories reclaimed. He implies that a process of repatriation re-establishes the connections between Indigenous story, land, and nation. Anahareo's case presents both opportunities and challenges to this aim of repatriation because her family history, upbringing, and extensive travels underline the necessity to take into consideration the persistence of memory-based notions of belonging that are only tenuously tied to an "original" landscape, nation, and language. Anahareo described herself as Mohawk, as do her descendants,[7] even though the family has both Mohawk and Algonquin ancestry. However, her memories were not located in Mohawk landscapes, and she did not have or cultivate an ongoing relationship with land-based Mohawk communities. Instead, she strongly identified with a notion of a portable past in the form of passed-down stories, skills, and objects—particularly objects held in various types of travelling cases.

Anahareo's upbringing in Mattawa, Ontario, about four hundred and fifty kilometres from Mohawk ancestral territories in and around Kanesatake, Quebec, was shaped by the systemic forces of colonial displacement affecting Indigenous peoples across the Americas that McLeod describes. Anahareo was born Gertrude Bernard in 1906 in Mattawa. When she was four years old her mother died, and Anahareo and her siblings were split up and placed under the care of relatives. Anahareo's one-year-old brother went to live with her maternal grandmother, her sister Johanna and brother Edward went to North Bay to live with Aunt Kate, and Anahareo herself was raised by her grandmother on her father's side, Catherine Papineau Bernard (Anahareo, *Devil* 36). According to Anahareo's narration of her family history in *Devil in Deerskins*, an account which cannot be fully substantiated by corroborating historical records, Catherine's grandfather was Naharrenou (the inspiration for Anahareo's name)[8] and Catherine's father was Kanistonou; both were revolutionary leaders who used guerilla warfare tactics against settlers

---

7   Katherine Swartile, Anahareo's daughter, explained to me that she calls herself Mohawk (not Indigenous, Native, Aboriginal, etc), following her mother's example (Swartile).

8   It is likely that Anahareo, in discussion with Grey Owl, came up with the name *Anahareo*, a variation of *Paharomen Nahareo*, which was translated as "Flaming Leaf" from the Mohawk language; however, there is no evidence that *Paharomen Nahareo* means anything in any language. Gleeson suggests that as Anahareo's great-grandfather was John Anenha Nelson, he was the most likely origin of the name (Gleeson, "Blazing" 299–300; 49n).

who lived in and around the town of Oka (33). Sometime during or after the War of 1812, Kanistonou, his wife, and their newborn son were killed by soldiers (35). Their daughter Catherine was taken to Montreal when she was still a baby and raised by nuns. As a young woman she rejoined her people, met her relations for virtually the first time, and learned the Mohawk language. But due to the poverty and lack of opportunity on the reserve, she left with her husband and settled north of Belleville (36).[9] After living there for twenty-five years and raising a family of eleven, they were "forced to move off the land that they had cleared" since at that time Aboriginal people "were unable to own property" (36). They travelled northwest, far from existing roads, and eventually settled on the Ottawa River in Mattawa. Mattawa is a town (like many other Canadian towns) that is sharply divided along racial and class lines. Although Anahareo's family lived in Mattawan, one of the wealthier, predominantly Euro-Canadian neighbourhoods within Mattawa, the Bernards mostly socialized and interacted with people living in an area derogatorily referred to as "Squaw Valley" (today simply called "the Valley"), populated by a diverse group of mostly Catholic, mixed-blood, working-class families with Cree, Anishinaabe, and Algonquin ancestry (Gleeson, "Blazing" 289). Squaw Valley was on the other side of town from where most of the Euro-Canadian families lived and away from where most businesses, churches, and schools were located (289).

In spite of the fact that Anahareo was born and raised far from Mohawk territory, that her grandmother was raised in a convent from a young age, and that Anahareo had little or no contact with her family's ancestral territory, language, or land-based communities, like McLeod, she affirms the power of recovery—of "'coming home' through stories" (McLeod 20). Anahareo's texts confirm McLeod's analysis that the process of alienation through the "overwhelming pressures of diaspora" is never complete. In both texts, Anahareo is sustained by the stories she learned from her father and grandmother, stories that, in McLeod's

---

9   Gleeson's account, which is based on archival and genealogical research as well as interviews with some of Anahareo's relatives, differs significantly from Anahareo's. According to Gleeson, Anahareo's Grandmother Catherine was an Algonquin woman who was born in 1833 in Oka. She was raised in a convent boarding school where she spoke French exclusively. She married a Mohawk man, John Bernard Nelson, whose parents disapproved of their son's marriage to an Algonquin woman; as a result of this disapproval, the couple decided to leave the community (Gleeson, *Anahareo* 2). It is possible that Catherine learned Mohawk from her husband (Gleeson, Email).

words, "act as the vehicles of cultural transmission by linking one generation to the next" (31). In other words, it would be a mistake to assume that Anahareo's upbringing was severed from the intergenerational conveyance of traditional practices and knowledge. Although rarely read in this way, Anahareo's texts contain much fascinating information about how she maintained her connection to Mohawk knowledge, particularly through her grandmother's teachings. Her grandmother passed on to Anahareo her knowledge of plants, medicine, family history, and craftsmanship through her own writings, oral history, and daily use of traditional skills: "Grandmother taught me to sew, bead, make deerskin mitts and moccasins, embroider, crochet, knit, tan hides, and make soap. She taught me, too, the lore of medicinal herbs" (Anahareo, *Devil* 37). Anahareo's flair for tanning, beading, and making clothes is evident in photographs of her and Grey Owl in their fashionably cut jackets, moccasins, and her signature riding pants. In both of her autobiographies, Anahareo nonchalantly describes her creative labours, while photographs of her handiwork reveal her exceptional skill (see Figure 15.1). In *Pilgrims of the Wild*, Grey Owl describes her feel for cloth and her unfussy, almost gestural expertise:

> with a pair of scissors in her mouth and a pencil in her hand, she suspended the cloth against her body, where it was held by a stiff breeze that was blowing, and marking the outline where the wind shaped the goods against her form, proceeded to cut them out. I stood by in rather apprehensive silence and viewed the apparent slaughter of this very excellent material, for which I had paid a very excellent price, but out of which there was presently constructed [. . .] one of the best fitting and most elegant looking pair of breeches anyone could wish for. (Grey Owl 44–45)

For both Grey Owl and Anahareo, clothing was one means by which to craft a sense of self that did not match their upbringing. But more importantly for Anahareo, the practice of sewing, beading, and tanning connects her to her grandmother and her teachings. Throughout *Devil in Deerskins*, as she pursues activities such as gathering herbs, making clothes, or smoking fish, Anahareo recalls lessons she had learned from her grandmother and acknowledges the debt she owes: "All that she taught me has been of great value to me through the years. Even now,

15.1 "Anahareo in a fringed and beaded moosehide jacket, circa 1931." Courtesy of Glenbow Museum, PA-3947-138.

15.2 "Anahareo in Victoria, British Columbia, around the time of the publication of *Devil in Deerskins*, 1972." Courtesy of Glenbow Museum, PA-3947-57.

there is seldom a day goes by that I don't think of her. [. . .] In fact Archie tired of my always telling him how Grandma would have done this or that" (*Devil* 37).

It is Grandmother Catherine's trunk that establishes Anahareo's fascination with boxes and their potential not only as mnemonic spaces containing traces of the past, but also as imaginative spaces within which to create a self that is not tied to one place. Anahareo writes: "I loved her huge trunk, full of souvenirs and momentos [sic], each one telling a story of romance, tragedy, or adventure" (37). Boxes and stories are closely connected, as are boxes and writing, sharing a function both as depositories for the past and as prompts for creating new subjectivities. Along with the trunk, Anahareo also describes the role that her grandmother's handwritten book played in her early life, describing it as "an immense book all written in her hand with a quill" (37). The book, a living document that was continually updated by her grandmother, was primarily made up of translations from the French into Mohawk of "prayers, history, and little anecdotes" and decorated "[a]long the margins" with images of "vines, leaves, [. . .] birds, and [. . .] flowers" (37). Both the trunk and the book are grounded in memory yet transportable. In spite of Anahareo's family's experience with multiple displacements—through conflicts with settler populations, loss of ancestral territory, religious schooling, loss of language, property laws, and other colonial regulatory systems—the traditions continue, adapt, and are renewed with the help of these storage devices whose function greatly exceed that of "storage."

More than the care and love she gave to Anahareo before she died when Anahareo was a teenager, Grandma Catherine provided a vital cultural bridge to Anahareo's sense of her family's past. Indeed, without her grandmother, Anahareo would never have been able to reconstruct her family's history of displacement and renewal. Grandma, through her own writings, as well as through her example of learning the Mohawk language as an adult, is strongly associated with a notion of writing as the basis for forging an identity and maintaining a connection to the past. Writing itself is not defined solely in Eurocentric, script-centric terms; it is also connected with storytelling as conveyed through sewing, beading, and other expressions of material culture. According to *Devil in Deerskins*, since Catherine was taken to the convent as a child, the only way she knew of her family history was because her mother, whom she names Mary Robinson,[10] reportedly had attached a letter to her wrist. In this letter, rolled up and sealed, Robinson had sketched out her daughter's ancestry: "I imagine it was because of the important looking document that was attached to Grandma's wrist, and the fact that she was part white, that she was taken to the convent instead of to Oka" (35). Whether this story is factually accurate is not as important as the "space" that this writing creates for Anahareo's conception of her self: the story underlines the transportability of writing, as well as writing's *ability to transport* history and identity. Wrapped up and sealed for future readers, the document is a box of sorts, a scroll with vital information on the bearer's past that will have repercussions far into the future.

Boxes are mentioned repeatedly in both Anahareo's texts and in Grey Owl's, and both writers emphasize their usefulness, beauty, and suitability for a peripatetic life. Grey Owl shares Anahareo's love of a good packing crate, and Anahareo reports that his breadbox, grub box, and fold-up stove were particularly treasured items (until they were destroyed by their pet beavers' teeth). In *Pilgrims of the Wild*, Grey Owl writes that the beaver would "promptly eat their way out of every thing we tried to keep them in, so that they had me busy providing boxes which lasted, if they were good, one night" (60). In both of her texts, Anahareo mentions several times a particular trunk of Grey Owl's that had been in transit for over a year. Each time the pair arrived at a location where the trunk was supposed to be, they would learn that the trunk had been shipped somewhere else, and so the chase continued. As Anahareo and Grey Owl cover substantial distances across Ontario, Quebec, and New Brunswick, later moving on to Manitoba, Saskatchewan, and Alberta, the crate acts as a talisman leading them ever onwards in their travels.

What attracts both Anahareo and Grey Owl to trunks and crates of all kinds is their paradoxical function as an "open secret" since they are both lockable and accessible. In *My Life with Grey Owl*, Anahareo describes what they found in the missing trunk once they finally caught up with it in Doucet, Quebec. Among the many objects in this trunk were bones of beloved animals, now passed on, "cones and stones from places

10 In *Devil in Deerskins*, Anahareo writes that her great-grandmother was Mary Robinson, a White woman who was captured by the Mohawk people some years before the War of 1812, eventually becoming Kanistonou's wife. Gleeson states that there is no direct evidence to support the story of Mary Robinson. However, it is possible she, or someone like her, lived in an earlier generation (Gleeson, *Anahareo* 228–29).

[they had] known," cloth, and more than ten pounds of photographic negatives (*My Life* 164). These objects assert an indissoluble link between memory, object, and place; and yet their placement in a travelling case suggests a continuous process of dis-placement and re-placement. Some of the objects from this trunk were then transferred to a "box of memories" Anahareo shared with Grey Owl, kept in an honoured place on a shelf they called their "altar":

> After Archie and I had quit roaming the country and were together at Beaver Lodge, Archie made a shelf especially for our box of memories, and we called it our altar. [. . .] On the last visit I made to Ajawaan since Archie died I found Beaver Lodge stripped of every thing but our altar. Whoever cleared the cabin, thinking it wasn't worth taking, left it there. It wasn't left in its proper place, but was carelessly (ruthlessly, to me) thrown into a dark cubby-hole. They probably needed the box for packing purposes. I gathered every bit that was there and placed it all in a tin bread box. [. . .]
>
> Right now from where I am writing I can see that box. Next summer Shirley Dawn, our daughter, will take it back to Ajawaan and bury it at the foot of her father's grave and plant a tree over it. (165–66)

To cite the work of Marianne Hirsch and Leo Spitzer in another context, the box of memories enables a dual process of both "re-plac[ing] [. . .] history into the landscape" and "displac[ing]" that history and carrying it elsewhere (Hirsch and Spitzer 153).[11] Such a dual process is critical for Anahareo in crafting an Indigenous diasporic subjectivity that is both grounded and transportable. It is a different process from the one suggested by Neal McLeod, in which Indigenous communities overcome the debilitating effects of colonial diasporic displacement by returning to a landscape to rediscover stories, memories, and a sense of cultural

---

11 Hirsch and Spitzer are writing about their momentous voyage to present-day Ukraine to visit the site of a concentration camp in which Hirsch's parents narrowly escaped being imprisoned. In considering the significance of their desire to carry away with them a piece of rubble from this camp that has virtually disappeared from both official records and the collective memory of local residents, Hirsch and Spitzer write: "[i]nstead of leaving a marker of our visit [as appropriate in Jewish mourning traditions], we carried a fragment of the place *away with us*. If through our fleeting presence there we could not hope to *re-place* its history into the landscape, we made a gesture to *displace* it" (Hirsch and Spitzer 153). Anahareo is both re-placing and displacing her history in new and old landscapes.

continuity. In contrast, Anahareo simultaneously is conserving memories and embedding them within new landscapes through her travels.

In addition to her familial history of displacement, another factor that makes determining Anahareo's "home community" problematic is that Gertie Bernard was a rebel who did not always see eye-to-eye with her Catholic, working-class community. Anahareo, who says about herself that she "wasn't cut out to follow a conventional life," began skipping school and hanging out in the forests following the death of her grandmother (*My Life* 2). After Anahareo met Grey Owl at age nineteen, she decided to forgo her education in Toronto at Loretto Abbey, a Roman Catholic boarding school, which was to be paid for by a wealthy tourist Anahareo had met while she was working as a waitress at a resort, and instead accompany Grey Owl into the bush (Anahareo, *Devil* 10). Even though they had separate cabins, her unchaperoned stay with Grey Owl for several weeks resulted in a near-permanent rift with her family. Furthermore, throughout her adult life she travelled extensively across Canada working as an independent prospector—an unusual though not unheard-of occupation for a woman at the time (Gleeson, "Blazing" 296). For all of these reasons—her family's uprooting from traditional territories, her fierce sense of independence, her loss of contact with her family from age nineteen to forty-nine, and her wandering, unconventional adult life—Anahareo's home community is not a place but rather is located within the memories of her immediate descendants.[12]

Part of the reason why Anahareo has been somewhat overlooked as an early Indigenous woman writer—*My Life with Grey Owl* is (to my knowledge) the first published, book-length memoir or life narrative by an Indigenous woman author in Canada[13]—is her family's diasporic history. In a critical biography of Grey Owl, Donald B. Smith describes Anahareo as a "town bred Indian" (79), a phrase that evokes questions of authenticity that for so long have marginalized Indigenous peoples who are mixed race, non-status, or urban, and that remains blind to people's ongoing attachments to ancestral lands, culture, knowledge, and

---

12 This point was made clear to me in conversation with her daughter, Katherine, who stated that Anahareo's "home community" should be understood primarily as her family—her children and grandchildren (Swartile).

13 A possible exception is Mourning Dove, an Okanagan woman who wrote her autobiography in the 1930s. However, it was not published until 1990 as *Mourning Dove: A Salishan Autobiography*, under the editorship of Jay Miller.

language (Lawrence 1–3). For Grey Owl, authenticity debates have fu-elled his long-term notoriety, but for Anahareo and other Indigenous writers these same debates historically have contributed to their margin-alization in public and scholarly discourses.[14] Ironically, before the expo-sure of Grey Owl's family background, it was Anahareo who was perhaps made to feel un-Indian because of her diasporic Indigenous history, and it was Grey Owl who increasingly owned a sense of "Indianness."

Anahareo's continual negotiation of her sense of herself in relation to dominant discourses of indigeneity is revealed in the telling addi-tions, deletions, and changes she made to the 1972 *Devil in Deerskins* in comparison to the 1940 *My Life with Grey Owl*. The differences be-tween the two texts also show how the process of remembering is em-bedded in relationships shaped by power, desire, and dominant patterns of representation. At certain points in her narrative, Anahareo implies that at times she was obliged to engage in a struggle for control over the narrative with Grey Owl. For example, in responding to Grey Owl's probing questions concerning her family history of diaspora in *Devil in Deerskins*, Anahareo writes: "I found these questions of Archie's too cold and concise to answer" (*Devil* 33). Anahareo's reluctance to respond to Grey Owl's questioning provides potential insight into the repeated trope of the box in Anahareo's texts. When Anahareo describes the careless handling of her and Grey Owl's precious "box of memories" by an un-known third party who packed up Beaver Lodge after Grey Owl's death (as cited above), Anahareo implies that part of the importance of the box is its function in maintaining the beloved objects' hermeneutical in-tegrity. Grey Owl's and Anahareo's life stories are not easily pried open, and I would submit that the proliferation of boxes in Anahareo's writing underlines her desire to maintain a degree of authority over the interpre-tation of her stories.

The "box of memories"—what it contains, what spills out, and what is carefully reclaimed—is implicated in the process of editing that Anahareo engaged in as she revised the 1940 text for the 1972 publica-tion. Possibly because of pressures from the publisher Lovat Dickson, who asked her not to speak of the controversy concerning Grey Owl's

---

14 See Carlson and Fagan for an excellent discussion of how discourses of authenticity, combined with the Indian Act's label of "halfbreed," contributed to the public's misperception of Henry Pennier, a Stó:lō storyteller, writer, and language teacher (xiv-xx). See also Lawrence.

background, Anahareo grew to dislike her first book and took to check-
ing it out from libraries across the country and ripping out the first
chapter (Swartile; Gleeson, *Anahareo* 179). Like many other Indigenous
texts from this time period (and continuing into the 1990s), Anahareo's
book was subject to condescending editing procedures that were at the
same time disavowed.[15] For example, in the preface to *My Life with Grey
Owl*, written anonymously in the voice of a literary and historical authority figure, Anahareo is cast within the mould of the Indian Princess,
a "strange, fascinating creature of the wilds" (Anahareo, *My Life* viii).
This introductory piece presents as comical and surprising an image of
Anahareo "walk[ing] across the drawing-room floor of an English home
to greet someone, as self-possessed as though she walked across a glade
in the forest towards a camp fire" (viii). Although the preface states that
"Anahareo tells her story in her own words," and that "[n]o attempt has
been made to 'improve' her narrative" (vii), the preface itself, unsigned
yet assertive, establishes the voice of the editor as a critical gatekeeper in
bringing about the narrative's publication and dissemination.

In the late 1960s and early 1970s, Anahareo meticulously rewrote
the book by hand with the help of her first daughter, Dawn, whose father was Grey Owl, publishing the bestseller, *Devil in Deerskins*, in 1972.
Her daughter Katherine, about ten years younger than Dawn, remembers her mother and sister writing at the table, assiduously re-using the
backs of old envelopes so as not to waste paper (Swartile). One key difference between the two books is the addition of detailed information
on Anahareo's diasporic Mohawk/Algonquin family history in the 1972
publication. The 1940 text implies that Anahareo's family, described as
Iroquois, originated from the regions surrounding Mattawa and west
of Lake Superior. No mention is made of her family's long trek from
Mohawk to Anishinaabe/Algonquin territories. At times, the legendary sparks that animated the relationship between Anahareo and Grey
Owl flew over this issue of Indigenous diasporic history. Looking closely
at the differences between Anahareo's two books reveals that the question of an Indigenous diasporic subjectivity became a point of contention between them. In the 1940 text, Anahareo cites Grey Owl's opinion

---

15 Before the 1970s, very few Aboriginal storytellers or writers were able to publish their work
   under their own names. Mourning Dove's autobiography, written in the 1930s and published in
   1990 under the editor Jay Miller's name, is a case in point (see note 13).

on "town raffs," a category that Grey Owl contrasts sharply with a more Romantic idea of land-based Indigenous peoples (*My Life* 137). For Grey Owl (as for Anahareo), the ideal Indian is embodied in the figure of Papati, a Cree chief who continued traditional practices of living on the land in spite of colonial incursions on his people's territory (122).[16] Anahareo, reporting Grey Owl's opinion, writes: "'Papati's main fight with his people is trying to keep them from being town raffs. He is afraid that they will forget that they are Indians and trappers whose work is that of a man, and will become flunkies. And there the old fellow's right, because I have seen Indians leave the woods and become tramps in no time at all'" (137). Anahareo does not verbally respond to Grey Owl's negative judgment of the feminized, urban "flunkies," but her internal commentary reveals a degree of annoyance: "I listened to Archie without a word. I couldn't have put one in edgewise even if I had wanted to, the way he rambled on" (137). In the 1972 text, she more explicitly critiques Grey Owl's dismissal of town-based Aboriginal communities by carefully outlining how, when, and for what reasons her grandmother ended up settling in Mattawa, far from Mohawk territories. The episode suggests that at least part of Anahareo's motivation for (re)writing her book was to offer her own unique perspective on events that had been described in particular ways by Grey Owl in his texts.

The emphasis on Anahareo's ongoing sense of connection to her Mohawk and Algonquin heritage in the 1972 text reflects a more general shift away from discourses of assimilation, which were largely accepted in the 1940s, and toward discourses of Native self-determination, which became emergent in the late 1960s and early 1970s in Canada, generating Aboriginal people's renewed sense of pride in tribal histories. In the 1972 text, Anahareo is more outspoken and more analytical on questions of land rights, animal rights, and Aboriginal rights; in the 1940 text her emphasis lies on creating a picture of life in the bush as an opportunity to live outside of restrictive social conventionalities, well suited to people like herself and Grey Owl who share a "free and adventurous spirit" (12). While there is no doubt that Anahareo was someone who defied the social norms of her time, she herself was caught up against Indian policy that affected her on a daily basis. When she split permanently from Grey

---

16 According to Donald B. Smith, Papati was Ignace or Nias Papaté, the Chief of the Grand Lake Victoria and Lac Simon bands (80; 255n).

Owl in 1936, she was pregnant (Gleeson 305). In this time period, as a result of government legislation and pressures from the Church, police were authorized to arrest Aboriginal single mothers (or White women with mixed-race children) who had no visible means of support (see Sangster; Demerson). Though Anahareo was not arrested, a teacher, Wilna Moore, convinced Anahareo to place her second daughter, Anne, in a Salvation Army residence for children of unwed mothers (Gleeson, "Blazing" 305). Anne stayed at the home until she was three, at which point Anahareo agreed to allow a Euro-Canadian, Calgary-based family to adopt her. As Gleeson points out, although Moore, along with the authorities, "appeared sympathetic to Anahareo's unfortunate situation, their judgements and actions were clearly grounded in notions of moral and racial superiority" (306). Writing *My Life with Grey Owl* around the time that Anne was living in the residence, Anahareo comments on the paradoxical effects of the imposition of colonial policy on Aboriginal peoples: "We are free to do anything we like, move anywhere we will, and enjoy the protection of the law. But we take advantage of none of these things, except the last. And to tell the truth we spend perhaps more time avoiding penalties for breaking the law than seeking its protection" (*My Life* 1–2). In both books, Anahareo documents the devastating effects of colonial incursion, including the shrinking of Aboriginal people's land base, the destruction of forests, inhumane trapping practices, the lack of respect for the lives of animals, and the enormous loss of life due to smallpox and tuberculosis (diseases that disproportionately affected Aboriginal communities).

Anahareo's representation in the popular press, the book market, and other communication outlets, as for many other Aboriginal women of her time, was continually threatened by dominant images of the "squaw" and the "Indian Princess"—and yet Anahareo never missed an opportunity to use those same circuits of communication to create a more complex picture of herself. Indeed, she embraces the identity of her title, "devil in deerskins," defying its negative connotation and reclaiming the identity of a fierce, independent woman whose life is not ruled by restrictive social customs. The title is also a tribute to Grey Owl, and she reports that he had always meant to write a book with the same title: "'once they've read The Devil In Deerskins—that's what I'm going to call it—they'll never read another line from me [. . .] it's about me—things that even you don't know, and will never know; at least, not from me [. . .] it won't be published until I'm dead'" (Anahareo, *Devil* 175–76). By using the same title, Anahareo is asserting her feelings of identification with Grey Owl: both invent identities for particular purposes, both question imposed social scripts, and both reject the restrictive religious framework within which they were raised. But accompanying this intimate sense of recognition, there remains a gap. Anahareo writes that when she finally discovered that Grey Owl was English, "I had the awful feeling for all those years I had been married to a ghost" (187). As a ghost, Grey Owl remains a mystery, something other than is known, like a devil; but Anahareo is careful to show that the appellation applies equally to herself: "As the story unfolded, there was more about myself than there was about Archie, so, appropriately enough, I decided to call it *Devil in Deerskins*" (180).

In honour of her consistent opposition to homogenizing images of Aboriginal women widely circulated at the time, her surviving family members have taken an active role in determining how, by whom, and for what purposes Anahareo's image is represented and circulated. Their concerns are in response to historical precedents, such as Anahareo's tendency to vandalize library copies of her first book and her disgust with the portrayal of herself and Grey Owl following the revelation of Grey Owl as a "fraud" and a bigamist. In the 1999 film *Grey Owl*, directed by Richard Attenborough, Anahareo is recast in her original 1940s role as a "strange, fascinating creature of the wilds" combined with a 1950s-inspired persona of the helpless yet sexy damsel-in-distress whose dependence on Grey Owl reaffirms his central importance. These and other representations have given Anahareo's family little confidence in the publishing and filmmaking industries. However, this is not necessarily a negative situation, as it offers an opportunity to open up a frank discussion with the family concerning the ethics of editing Indigenous texts and the potential for crafting collaborative practices. If *Devil in Deerskins* is republished, its success will be measured by the revitalization of this important text not only in academic discussions, but also in larger conversations concerning Indigenous cultural production in Canada.

CHAPTER 16

•◆•

Yours to Recover: Mound Burial in Alice Munro's "What Do You Want to Know For?"

Shelley Hulan

In August 1995 I left St. John's, Newfoundland, for London, Ontario, to begin graduate studies in English at the University of Western Ontario. I travelled across the Cabot Strait and the Tantramar, through Shield country into Quebec and Northeastern Ontario, until Highway 401 brought me to *terra incognita*. The smug (I thought) rolling productive farmland and enormous barns were as foreign to me as the heat and cheap red peppers. Unbelievably, this once-alien landscape has now become home. I feel for it the love that "home" requires for the saying. But I would not feel this love had it not been for the fiction of Alice Munro, which has permanently altered my view of a place I once found completely foreign. As impossible as it was for me to see anything but settled surfaces during that first pass through the Toronto–London corridor, now it is equally impossible for me to see those surfaces without the strata of time and event that Munro's work, repeatedly intervening between me and the Southwestern Ontario landscape, gives them.

These strata fascinate me along with many other Munro readers. They do not thrill all Munro's narrators, who sometimes opine that there is nothing left to dig for. "I have written about it and used it up," says the narrator of "Home" (*View* 300). The depletion she describes refers to her store of childhood memories accumulated in the Southwestern Ontario community to which she returns only to visit her father. Memories anchor Munro's fictional world. As in "Home," they often emanate from first-person narrators who resemble Munro herself. Specific autobiographical markers vary from story to story. None of her "I-narrators" ever completely duplicates the real-life Alice Munro, and most critics read them as fictional characters communicating fictional recollections (Osachoff 63). Yet this semi-autobiographical presence opens her stories to interpretations as something other than fiction. Similarities between the events and characters of "Home" and certain events and people in Munro's own life convince her literary biographer closely to identify this particular story's first-person narrator with its author, a genuinely autobiographical "I" recounting true life experiences (Thacker 6–8). The possibility, though never the certainty,[1] of a fully autobiographical "I" implies that the narrative may also present a nonfictional Southwestern Ontario and with it, an invitation to search for the "documentary moment" of the past in its unfabricated being, to paraphrase one of Paul Ricoeur's definitions of history (254).

In this essay I examine history and memory as represented in "Home" and "What Do You Want to Know For?," adjacent chapters in Munro's 2006 collection *The View from Castle Rock*. By *memory* I mean both the personal memories that the first-person narrators relay in these stories and cultural memory, usefully glossed by Aleida Assmann as the past that a society chooses to remember (with help from its media and institutions) after events have vanished from living recall (*Cultural Memory and Western Civilization* 6). The latter appears in the recollections and reminders that the narrators receive from other Southwestern Ontario characters. These two stories sever the "documentary moment" of history from memory, making possible a counter-memory of the region that the narrator alone cannot negotiate. Explaining the concept of counter-memory in "Nietzsche, Genealogy, History," Michel Foucault warns against "the theme of history as reminiscence or recognition" (385), his choice of words suggesting that homologies of the two privilege the past that the researcher finds most familiar. Dividing them, on the other hand, stakes no claim that either memory or history guarantees access to a truer or authentic past. Rather, it enables an approach to past matters that resists the oversights and false generalizations that their fusion facilitates. Counter-memory attempts to recover what memory, conflated with history, conspires to forget.

It seems unlikely that any person researching the history of a place to which remembrance closely ties her could sustain this division, and the narrators of these stories never do. Their activities and reflections emphasize the Southwestern Ontario past of the Euro-settler community

---

1   In this essay, I contend that the potential encounter with this autobiographical "I" in Munro's work draws attention to, and invites readings of, its non-fiction elements. I do not contend that the narrators of "Home" and "What Do You Want to Know For?" are the author herself.

that produced them. The task of forging a counter-memory falls to readers who may choose to recover the traces of another past detectable in these narratives.

In my case, a will to indigenize writing about Southwestern Ontario informs my effort to find and follow these traces in Munro's stories. I take the term *indigenize* from Len Findlay's contention that humanities researchers have a primary responsibility to seek out the foundational contributions to knowledge, in Canada and worldwide, that Indigenous peoples have made from the beginning of time (368–70). Documents (everything from works of fiction to archival fonds) may well obstruct efforts to do so given the literally deleterious effect that centuries of suppression and concealment have had on the textual as well as the physical presence of Indigenous peoples in invaded lands; as Findlay points out, the Eurocentric doctrine of "*terra nullius* (*empty land*)" (369, emphasis in original) continues to portray pre-Contact Canada as devoid of history, culture, and technology (369–70).[2] Challenging that doctrine begins with the conscious effort to discern the ubiquitous signs of First Peoples' activities both before and after various European arrivals in North America. Among other possibilities, indigenizing one's research means attempting to recover First Nations' central place in the history, and role in the formation, of cultures before and after Contact.

Surprisingly, given the number and occasional prominence of references to First Nations in Munro's *oeuvre*, the voluminous criticism that has grown up around her work communicates almost no awareness of these references, let alone analysis of them. In "Alice Munro's Heritage Narratives" Coral Ann Howells remarks of Munro's "Meneseteung" that "native prehistory is acknowledged in [the title,] the indigenous name for the Maitland River" in Southern Ontario (7). Statements such as this one and Sabrina Francesconi's that "[t]he retracing of Indian place names recognises the historical importance of and gives political dignity to the First Nations" (para. 18) overstate the extent to which a lone word, even a word originating in an Indigenous language, can recognize First Nations in a story that empties the signifier as far as possible of every historical association it has with its language and culture of origin: the story's researcher-narrator transforms *Meneseteung* from the Ojibwa name for

---

2   Findlay explains the fiction of *terra nullius* as land virtually unpopulated and "empty of any social organization" as Europeans understood it (369).

the Sowesto river renamed the Maitland into the "hopeful sign" of art's liberating self-referentiality for the woman at the centre of her research, the nineteenth-century small-town poet Almeda Roth. *Meneseteung* becomes, too, a metaphor for the failed literary ambitions she attributes to Roth, ambitions she imagines Roth fulfilling with a long poem of the same name. What this story's narrator never acknowledges, however, is the Nation whose word it is.

This dearth of attention to the use of First Nations referents in Munro's stories is the more remarkable given that they appear in her work from the publication of "Walker Brothers Cowboy," the first story in Munro's first collection *Dance of the Happy Shades*. Two pages into it, the narrator's father explains to her how a glacier carved the Great Lakes out of the midwestern plain millions of years ago. "I try to see that plain before me, dinosaurs walking on it," she ruefully admits, "but I am not able even to imagine the shore of the Lake when the Indians were there, before Tuppertown" (3). Ironically, the narrator's use of "Indian" fatally compromises her claim that she cannot imagine the region's Aboriginal inhabitants, since the term perpetuates the European explorer fantasies of finding a western route to Asia that generated the name in the first place. Whether she thinks she is or not, she is "imagining the Indian."

While the narrator invokes the First Nations only to dismiss them for allegedly lying beyond her visualizing capacity, her reference to them establishes that pre-settler Sowesto is not "empty land." It is, however, a land represented by a narrator who follows her admission of a First Nations presence in the region with an immediate erasure of it, a paradox in need of a reading strategy that moves beyond *terra nullius*, since the narrator acknowledges that the land was occupied and yet denies that occupation in the same sentence. Pointing out that grand "legal fiction[s]" such as *terra nullius* tend exclusively to underwrite settler-nationalist narratives' linear triumphalist plot, Bain Attwood argues that settler nations' local stories of events in specific communities emphasize instead "the struggle to legitimize possession and dispossession in settler societies" as "more complicated and contested than many have tended to allow" (190), often by foregrounding the simultaneity of settler efforts to find and forget the Indigenous presence in the lands they invade.

"'Meneseteung', the first harvest of an interest in the nineteenth-century history of Southwestern Ontario that culminates in *The View from Castle Rock*" (Ware, "'And They May Get it Wrong, After All'" 67), aptly demonstrates Attwood's axiom, its narrator alluding to a First Nations presence on the shores of Lake Huron only to subordinate that presence completely to the needs of the story she tells about Roth. When the use of an Ojibwa word in an English-language narration inserts an unmistakable trace of the Ojibwa into a story that otherwise ignores the longstanding relations between that Nation and the region where the story events take place, it asks a question about the word's historical meaning that only readers can explore, since the narrator does not. The narrative's foray into the use of names to recover a regional history also warns that even the strongest-seeming signs of First Nations presences can be turned into vehicles of their symbolic removal. As in "Walker Brothers Cowboy," the "Meneseteung" narrator's imagination engineers the turn, for the history she recovers blurs into an invention of Almeda that embroiders significantly upon the sparse archival record. Her embroidery includes a reference to "Indians"—"Champlain and the naked Indians," whom Almeda envisions as she contemplates her great unwritten poem (70)—that literally strips the Indigenous presence she imagines to a negligible minimum, a minimum she adds to a "popular [. . .] belief" about Champlain's visit to the area that she earlier called "untrue" (52). Classifying that belief as false, however, does not alter the fact that she uses it in a context (her own research and the speculative interventions she makes in it) that has already rubbed away the line between history and fiction.

In two ways, the 1974 and 2006 versions of "Home" incorporate a fused acknowledgement and excision of First Nations similar to the one that Attwood situates in local stories. The 1974 version manifests the conflict as a difficulty that the story's supposed author (and I-narrator) has positioning herself in relation to a hometown community she views both from the inside and the outside, a difficulty she expresses in an italicized passage that departs from the story-in-progress to comment metacritically upon it:

A problem of the voices, the way people talk, how can it be handled? [. . .] My own attitude, too; complicated and unresolved. [. . .] A friend of mine who worked for the national radio network told me about a program they had made, in a village near my home, getting the natives to talk, give their opinions on something, I forget what, and he said how delightful it was, how quaint—he probably did not use that word—and how real.

Then I was angry at him, though it was not his fault, just as I am angry
at them. I did not want that done to them. [. . .] Not out of love. It is not
love I would compel for them, but respect. (142)

This aside asserts the I-narrator's insider understanding of local people, a
comprehension she sees as contrasting sharply with that of her friend at
the national broadcasting corporation. But her choice of the term *native*
instead of *Indian*, the term that the characters in her story use to refer
to local Indigenous people, also distances her from these other voices,
revealing an uncertainty about naming First Nations that sets her apart
from the Euro-settler community she tries to depict.[3]

The 2006 "Home" excises this italicized commentary and revises the
following dialogue to make the first-person narrator a participant in a
conversation about two neighbours that she merely witnesses in the 1974
version:

> "I don't know," says Harry. "They say he still thumps her good when he
> takes the notion. [. . .] Her being part Indian might have something to
> do with it. [. . .] They say the Indians thump their women every once in
> a while and it makes them love 'em better."
>
> I feel obliged to say, "Oh, that's just the way people talk about
> Indians," and Irlma—immediately sniffing out some high-mindedness
> or superiority—says that what people say about the Indians has a lot of
> truth to it, never mind. (295)

The narrator's response to Harry reiterates the same concern over au-
thentically portraying First Nations seen in the italicized passage of
1974, but changes the iterative vehicle from a comment that expresses
authorial anxiety outside the story-in-progress to a conversation that incorporates that anxiety into the narrative's live dialogue, where the narrator articulates it within a settler discourse structured upon denigrating
stereotypes of First Nations. Not unlike the local stories Attwood describes, that discourse combines an imagined First Nations ("Indians")
with the successful effort to forget them, as Irlma's swift intervention

---

3   *Native* may, of course, also refer to long-term local residents of any origin, but the proximity of
     this passage to the Harry-Irlma exchange and the narrator's subsequent visit to Joe and Peggy
     Thoms, the targets of Harry's gossip, suggests that it refers to Indigenous peoples in this instance.

demonstrates. Irlma's policing of her stepdaughter's reply endorses the derogatory stereotype ("what people say about the Indians has a lot of truth to it") and closes the subject to debate ("never mind"), fusing the invention and erasure of First Nations and pre-empting the critique of the stereotype threatened by the narrator's objection. The narrator's acquiescence to Irlma shows her complicity in this discourse. Although she "feel[s] obliged" to object to Harry's comment, she does not pursue the matter after her stepmother tells her to drop it. Once reminded of them, she recognizes and seems to accept the conversational norms of the settler community in which she grew up. Her memory and her compliance go hand in hand.

The next chapter, "What Do You Want to Know For?," combines another return to familiar Sowesto places with an investigation of local history similar to the one in "Meneseteung." A pair of differences separates the two stories. In contrast to "Meneseteung" (and the other stories discussed above), "What Do You Want to Know For?" includes no specific First Nations names, or indeed any references to First Nations. Second, although "What. . ." emplots an amateur researcher's efforts to recover part of the local past, the researcher-narrator rejects imagination as thoroughly as her "Meneseteung" counterpart embraces it, refusing to supplement the facts that documentary evidence (unsatisfactory) and fieldwork (limited) yield her. This refusal holds at least the potential for splitting the atom of First Nations' invention and erasure fused so well via the "Meneseteung" narrator's willingness to create her subject when scant research findings leave the picture of Almeda incomplete. "What Do You Want to Know For?" seems unlikely to separate the two, however: as she pursues answers about two graves in a disused Sullivan Township cemetery, this narrator looks only at sources derived from Grey County's Euro-settler population.

The objects of this narrator's investigation, a "large, unnatural mound blanketed with grass" (316) and another, smaller crypt in the same cemetery (325), protrude among the other graves. The narrator and her husband notice the first because they feel sufficiently "possessive about this country" to "try not to let anything get by us" (316). That sense of ownership also prompts them to carry maps from Putnam and Chapman's authoritative *Physiography of Southern Ontario* in their car for easy consultation as they travel the local countryside. To some extent, their learning about the different soil strata and deposits that shape the region is its own reward. "But," the narrator adds, "there is always more than just the keen pleasure of identification. There's the fact of these separate domains, each with its own history and reason, its favorite crops and trees and weeds [. . .] each with its special expression, its pull on the imagination. [. . .] It's the fact you cherish" (322).

This idea of the independence, rather than the pliability or instrumentality, of information as its most attractive feature recurs in the narrator's research on the Sullivan sites, when she turns a visit to a local university's Regional Reference Room into an opportunity to emphasize the value of information for its own sake as opposed to the purposes it may serve the researcher: "It is difficult to make [. . .] requests in reference libraries because you will often be asked what it is, exactly, that you want to know, and what do you want to know it for? [. . .] If you are doing a paper, a study, you will of course have a good reason, but what if you are *just interested*?" (326, emphasis in original). Accepting that mere curiosity receives scant respect when advanced as a research rationale, she still asserts it as her reason, describing a ruse she has deployed in similar situations—"say[ing]" she is "doing a family history" (326)—to deflect the librarians' putative demand for a more specific purpose.

This emphasis on unalloyed curiosity as her sole motive calls to mind Ricoeur's distinction in *Memory, History, Forgetting* between the writer of fiction and the writer of history, who share common narrative strategies but have different end goals for their representations of past time. Whereas writers of fiction solicit readers' "'willful suspension of disbelief'" (Coleridge qtd. in Ricoeur) and immersion into "an unreal universe," writers of history strive to recover "a world of events that actually occurred" and lay the evidence for that past world before an uncompromising audience determined to accept no substitutes (261). Their and their readers' sole motive is to reconstruct this "'real'" past (Ricoeur 262), whatever it was. While that past remains forever elusive, their conviction that recovery is possible obligates them to adopt a relentlessly skeptical attitude towards all theses on history and, by extension, the evidence marshalled to their support. Unlike readers of fiction, who may be tempted and encouraged to identify with a first-person narrator's perspective, readers of history adopt a critical distance from the makers of the historical theses they may dispute.

By naming two real Sullivan-area family crypts and a published text, "[a]n old soft-covered history of the township" (329) that readers can consult for themselves,[4] "What Do You Want to Know For?" invites an evaluation of the narrator's efforts as genuine historical research. Readers who choose to undertake that evaluation soon find reason to doubt the information she gives them, for the same passage that declares her allegiance to curiosity-driven research compromises that declaration by revealing that she has ruled out one line of inquiry before beginning her search. That line of inquiry emerges as she considers what to write on the request form she must complete in order to access Reference Room materials. After "family history," her first choice, she offers another reason, *"research for paper concerning survival of mound burial in pioneer Ontario"* (326, emphasis in original). Instantly dismissing the idea, she claims she "didn't have the nerve" to write it down: "I thought they [the reference librarians] might ask me to prove it" (326). Amusing enough to include in her story, this second option strikes her as too implausible to merit more than a passing smile. Yet by briefly acknowledging a mound burial history that she will not explore, the narrator also inserts it into her text, where skeptical readers of history might pick it up as an object of interest.

Readers may question the second reason's alleged implausibility given one of the narrator's earlier descriptions of the gravesites at the centre of her inquiry, which uses exactly the terms she now rejects. She and her husband venture that the smaller crypt is "something like mound burial" in "pre-Christian" Europe (325). The phrase *mound burial* indicates a way of doing things rather than a specific burial mound. Her later, joking use of the phrase in the Regional Reference Room likewise suggests a general practice rather than a particular site, with the repetition of *survival* strengthening that reading by echoing the earlier scene ("Something that had survived in Central Europe from pre-Christian times?" [325]) and reproducing its sense of an ongoing custom rather than a single act. Moreover, a custom that *survives* in "pioneer Ontario" is a custom that *precedes* pioneers' arrival; repetition of *survival*, then, draws attention to the burial practices that pre-date settlers, potentially opening the narrator's inquiry to a whole different population and acknowledging that population's pre-settler habitation of the area.

---

4   The book as described closely resembles *The History of Sullivan Township 1850–1975*, by the Sullivan Historical Society.

The strangely unsettled semantics of the narrator's little joke thus catch her in the act of imposing a peculiar restriction of her own, naming a possible investigative angle on her subject that she has no intention of taking. Clearly, curiosity does not carry her everywhere an investigation of mound burial in Southwestern Ontario might.

As skeptical readers of history, readers might wish to look into the matter that this narrator rules out. What does a search for information about the survival of mound burial in pioneer Ontario offer? A simple keyword query on "mound" and "burial" in the London Public Library in London, Ontario,[5] turns up several monographs. Most, starting with the first on the list,[6] concern pre-settler-era burial mounds in central North America. Mainly archaeological studies undertaken since the mid-nineteenth century, the older publications easily outnumber more recent ones. These studies focus on the human-made tumuli that Europeans encountered upon arriving on the continent. They frequently describe their excavation and inventory their contents. The evident age of these built objects, often covered with mature trees—Euro-settler "experts" date the mounds as far back as several millennia BCE—swiftly changed the topic of interest from the mounds themselves to debates over the identity of their creators. Mid-Victorian scholarship favoured the view that the "mound-builders" were the ancestors of the Indigenous peoples living on the continent when Europeans arrived. By the late nineteenth century, however, a new theory emerges of the mounds as relics of an extinct race whom the First Nations had displaced. Reiterated in countless monographs and scholarly journals and disseminated to a larger reading public via popular newspapers and magazines, this new thesis led to claims that no ancestral connection of any kind had ever obtained between this dead race and living Aboriginal peoples. Ostensibly concentrated on the examination of data gathered from the mounds, mound-building studies fostered a pseudo-scientific discourse that inculcated an idea of contemporary First Nations as interlopers who had violently decimated a population more sophisticated in technological skill and culture and much closer in both terms to more recent transatlantic migrants. Proof of this fundamental separateness lay in the alleged absence of knowledge among

5   Simple keyword search conducted at the main branch of the London Public Library, London, Ontario, on 14 November 2012.
6   W.A. Kenyon's *Mounds of Sacred Earth: Burial Mounds of Ontario*.

First Nations living near the mounds of their provenance or of the skills this ancient people possessed. "[E]ven the oldest red man could give no history" of "these wonderful remains," proclaimed the Rev. William J. Smyth in 1886 (3), while to George Bryce, "the continual occurrence of pottery in the [Manitoba] mounds shows that the mound-builders were potters [. . .] none of the tribes [presently] inhabiting the district have any knowledge of the art of pottery" (13). Sweeping inductions followed: Europeans, such "experts" argued, were the natural heirs of this more sophisticated extinct civilization: "The white man but arrived upon the scene to succeed the farmer, the metal worker and the potter, who had passed away so disastrously, and to be the avenger of the lost race, in driving before him the savage red man" (Bryce 17).

The pseudo-scientific discourse that men such as Bryce and Smyth developed could never attempt a disinterested path to the continent's past. Using the mounds, they invented a history that confirmed what they wished to believe, and reading their work today presents a cautionary tale about how quickly scholars can trick themselves into fabricating the facts they think they find. A little further reading also illuminates the counter-arguments that quickly challenged the "lost civilization" idea and its transparent attempt to disinherit the continent's First Peoples. But the narrator never confronts the discourse, hears the caution, or discovers how central First Nations–Euro-settler relations have been to the subject of mounds on the continent, for she never looks into the possibility opened to her by the research question she decides not to ask.

This cursory search in a Sowesto public library shows, too, that an amateur researcher who really wants to learn more about "survival of mound burial in pioneer Ontario" will find the gates of knowledge wide open. No reference librarian can block them, and in fact, no librarian ever *does* prevent this narrator from looking for information. She narrows her own search when she abandons her unasked question. As that question demonstrates, offering a reason for one's research can expand its horizons, not just shrink them, increasing the chances of approaching the documentary moment that the narrator's faithfulness to history would suggest she wants to approach.

Self-imposed restrictions continue to define her search after she leaves the Regional Room, as information gleaned there from a book on local churches leads her to an assortment of settler families. Discussions with these informants produce the family name of the crypt, Mannerow (another fact found in *The History of Sullivan Township*, which is available in at least one Southwestern Ontario library[7]), and the address of the last surviving family member, whom she visits. The visit may be read as another assertion of the documentary moment's motivating force for her; witnesses to the past personify a direct access to matters that may otherwise be lost to history, and visiting the Mannerow home indicates her desire to hear whatever testimony to the crypts the last of the Mannerows can offer. But when the prospective witness's wife prevents her from seeing him on the grounds that he is too ill for visitors, the narrator readily acquiesces. Instead, Mrs. Mannerow tells her what *she* knows about the two vaults, including a hearsay account of the last time one of the crypts was opened, a story the narrator may not have heard had she not travelled to the Mannerow home. Much of Mrs. Mannerow's information, however, comes from the published history of Sullivan Township on which the narrator's other informants also depend.

Given the determination suggested in the narrator's travelling to see the Mannerows, her rapid abandonment of all hope of speaking to a witness while standing on his doorstep and her acceptance of Mrs. Mannerow as a valid substitute seems sharply at odds with the fidelity to history that has seemed so clearly to distinguish her from her "Meneseteung" counterpart. This is not the resignation to necessity one might associate with being turned away from an elderly, sick informant such as Mr. Mannerow. On the contrary, the narrator embraces her conversation with Mrs. Mannerow, finding in it an appropriate coda to her efforts. She sees that coda in Mrs. Mannerow's pleasant countenance as she explains that no one knows why her husband's family buried their dead in the crypts: "She smiles at me with a sociable sort of perplexity, [. . .] As if to say, it's beyond us, isn't it? A multitude of things, beyond us. Yes" (339). The narrator had in fact begun to feel the end of her inquiry was at hand when she entered the Mannerow yard, observing that she has lost her drive to inquire further: "what has been so compelling is drawn now into a pattern of things we know about" (336). Perhaps the Mannerow garden generates this thought, for she finds the yard very familiar from her own memories and experiences. More than the Mannerows' tastes alone, this garden speaks to her of an entire community, a community for which

---

7   Available at the University of Guelph Library.

she, the narrator, speaks confidently as she defines it through its insiders and outsiders:

> I look around at the bright beds of annuals and a rose of Sharon bush and a little black boy sitting on a stump with a Canadian flag in his hand. There are not so many little black boys in people's yards as there used to be. Grown children, city dwellers, may have cautioned against them—though I don't believe that a racial insult was ever a conscious intention. It was more as if people felt that a little black boy added a touch of sportiness, and charm. (336)

One of the most striking things about this astonishing passage is the narrator's assumption that her audience will know the figure in the garden is a statue, as if it should be obvious that she does not refer to a live Black child. The race of the *living* characters in the story has been implied, never stated, but thanks to these characters' constant references to the German, Dutch, and English settlers in the region to whom they have past and present connections, there is little doubt as to the group's homogeneousness.

The narrator's defence of such statues as benignly lending "a touch of sportiness, and charm" to the scene positions her squarely among the people whose feelings she describes, a local who has seen these figures in many gardens and who has heard the objections that may, she thinks, have led to a reduction in their numbers. Attributing this interpretation of the statue's meaning not to herself or the Mannerows in particular but to "people" in general, she signals an empathy with feelings common to a larger, racially exclusive community, a community that either does not know or does not care (for example) about the nineteenth-century dispossession and displacement of Black settlers who had lived in Grey County for many decades (see *Speakers for the Dead*). The questions the narrator could ask but doesn't always determine the history she accesses; her silence derives from the same deference to local customs and ways of speaking that Irlma invokes to censor her stepdaughter in "Home."

And it is to a First Nations past that these scenes most often tacitly advert. The narrator's insistence in "What Do You Want to Know For?" that the past ought to be found, not made, offers readers opportunities to glimpse a First Nations history that she herself cannot see despite her anti-speculative approach, a past rendered invisible to her by the terms through which she chooses to inquire into it. Those terms fabricate Southwestern Ontario's history not through the narrator's imagination but through her purge of the queries that could lead to a fuller disclosure of a non-European regional past. The readers-of-history to whom she addresses this story have a different duty of recovery, one that pursues these unasked questions about the Sowesto histories she does not name.

CHAPTER 17

•◆•

Romancing Canada in Bestsellerdom: The Case of Quebec's Disappearance

Dennis Duffy

The Easter weekend of 1918 (28 March–1 April) found Quebec City the site of "one of the most violent civil disturbances in Canadian history, causing important destruction of property and about 150 casualties" (Auger 504). The anti-conscription riots were the high point of French Canada's resistance to the 1917 Military Service Act, the climax of a process involving Quebec's bitter alienation from the wartime fervour of the rest of Canada. Some months before, a future prime minister, Mackenzie King, who would later prove to be an expert in finessing his way through a conscription crisis in the next war, wrote to a New York paper that anglophone Canada discerned "in the Quebec attitude nothing but disloyalty" (Granatstein and Hitsman 69–70). The Québécois had been commonly viewed as "slackers" for years; the Quebec riots heated to a flash point for anglophone Canada's distrust and even hatred that seemed close to a "cold" civil war (Amy Shaw 32; Willms 11–12). Even as prudent and prominent a public personage as J.W. Dafoe had written to a friend that "the only known race of white men to quit" needed to be taught a lesson, that "a solid Quebec without power" might produce "a return to reason along the banks of the St. Lawrence" (letter to T. Coté 15 January 1918; Granatstein and Hitsman 82). The act bringing in conscription had been proclaimed by a Union government that ran "one of the few [federal elections] in Canadian history deliberately conducted on racist grounds" (Granatstein and Hitsman 78).[1] Pulpit and press alike viewed the Quebec resistance as disloyal and even treasonous. In the manner of an imperial authority choosing to divide and conquer, the military units chosen to reinforce the helpless local

---

1   Present-day usage would probably substitute *ethnocentric* for *racist*.

civil power came from anglophone regions of the nation, lest local units might display sympathy with the dissidents.

What we might now view as the usual suspects rose as potential conspiratorial players: Bolsheviks, German agents, American war resisters (Auger 536–37). Soon after the suppression of the riots, Amy Scott wrote to her husband, the Canadian Corps' best-loved chaplain, Canon Frederick Scott, who was stationed at the front, that a new front had opened at home. She added the rebellious Irish and even devout Catholics to the enemies' list: "Sinn Feiners, Bolsheviks, and French Canadians" provide "a shocking example of the hatred that the French bear to British Rule. Their Church has sown the seeds of disloyalty ever since the war began" (Scott). It would take until 1919 for what functioned in a quiet Canadian manner as an occupation force to retire permanently from Quebec City, leaving behind a legacy of distrust for which Canada "for generations to come [. . .] would pay the price" (Desmond Morton 102).

The 1917 anti-conscription riots, I contend, stand as a manifestation of a cultural process of alienation, making it possible for a bestselling Canadian novel (Mazo de la Roche's *Jalna* [1927]) to proffer a vision of Canada in which Quebec and the French fact play no significant role. The well-attested postwar surge in anglophone Canadian nationalism— resting as it did upon a war effort that many in Quebec had resisted—had in fact erased a contemporary Quebec from a significant portion of the Anglo-Canadian literary imagination.

Two novels—Canadian in their authorship, setting, and themes— played significant roles in the Anglo-American literary market during their respective eras. Both Sir Gilbert Parker's *The Seats of the Mighty* (1896) and Mazo de la Roche's *Jalna* (1927) became bestsellers in the adult fiction market (rather than in the "juveniles" stream in which L.M. Montgomery played so prominent a role) of their day. Both widely read novels confirmed that Canadian material could be shaped into the stuff of transatlantic popularity in adult fiction. The former, a historical novel, the second, set in the present-day of its publication, placed sexual passion, with its alternations of attraction and repulsion, at the centre of their plotting. In exploiting this dynamic, they resembled the majority of bestseller fiction. Yet their mutual linkage of erotic drive with the expression of a national vision gave these two differing works (the one a costume drama, the other the beginning of what turned out to be a family saga) a degree of kinship. Each, however, conveys a very different imaginative national vision. Parker's novel deals with the integration of differing historical entities (colonial Canada and New France) within a single Euro-Canadian culture and nation-state. De la Roche's *Jalna*, on the other hand, sets itself within a wholly autonomous *British* Canada, itself nearly devoid of any trace of a French-Canadian element in its nature or origins. My initial brief recounting of the facts of Easter 1918 does not submit those facts as a cause of Quebec's absence from de la Roche's romance. I present the event instead as a dramatic example of a historical and cultural process enabling the dismissal of Quebec from a widely popular imaginative vision of Canada. My concern here lies not with the causes lying behind that imaginative dismissal, but with the fact of that vacuum as it shapes the world of *Jalna*.

Tracing the extent to which Jalna fences off Quebec from its environs heightens our understanding of the gulf that had opened in anglophone Canadian sensibilities. What had proven possible at one time—a strongly imperialist imaginative evocation of Canadian nationhood widely appealing to a reading public—seems to have passed by the date of *Jalna*'s appearance. What was once unimaginable in bestsellerdom— the disappearance of the French fact from any imaginative presentation of Canadian nationhood—had sprung into being, the result of a nationalist imagination that could flourish within an exclusively Anglo-Canadian setting.

I. LOVE AND WAR

Love and war, Mars and Venus, seem such abiding narrative staples that tracing their usage in *The Seats of the Mighty* seems redundant. *Jalna* contents itself with Venus alone, with Mars relegated to the background as a distant conflict that once preoccupied the novel's romantic lead. The co-habitation of love and war in *Seats*, however, lends a particular flavour to that fiction that throws into relief the idiosyncratic nature of sexual passion as it drives events in *Jalna*.

From its inception at the hands of Sir Walter Scott (*Waverley* 1814), the historical novel melded the quest for a new historical destiny with the (male) pursuit of a beloved. Edward Waverley's romantic quest for Rose Bradwardine sets a pattern followed by historical fiction in Canada from *Wacousta* to *Kamouraska*: the erotic quest is also the quest to realize a historical destiny. The linkage between the romantic quest and the social one places eros into a role that extends beyond the purely symbolic and affective. Parker—as an early critic of his fiction observes—thrusts his obscure hero into a significant role in the imperial struggle that concluded with the British conquest of New France (Fridén 47).

Historical events seem to spiral and form a causal, teleological progression. The conquest of the fortress of Quebec leads to the conquest of New France, leading in turn to the establishment of a British North America. A fragment of this political construct will then survive the British defeat in the American Revolutionary War. This result culminates finally in the establishment of a Canada whose existence within a British imperial structure is confirmed and celebrated by Parker's novel and its audience. This apostolic succession of events, in actual fact, as every student of history understands, is itself a construct that begs any number of questions and imposes a single-minded metanarrative of design rather than happenstance upon the shifting events it purports to describe. Yet that version of historical narrative that looms behind *Seats*—a narrative shared by the readers of its time—at once justifies and explains the nature of the romantic quest that occupies the centre stage of the novel.

By revealing to General Wolfe the little-known, lightly guarded footpath leading to the Plains of Abraham, Robert Moray offers Wolfe the key to the conquest of the fortress of Quebec. He thus serves as a linchpin in the historical narrative that enfolds the novel and allows the fiction to claim a relevance extending beyond the belles-lettristic.[2] In "working up" a personal narrative (a memoir of Major Robert Stobo) that had been brought to his attention by a Montreal antiquarian, and by deriving his title from a scriptural passage proclaiming the overturning of the established hierarchy and the coming reign of the lowly, Parker implicitly claims for his novel the authority of a historical meditation, of a significance greater than an entertaining imaginative narrative based on historical fact.[3]

---

2   I have written on *Seats* in another context (Duffy, *Sounding* 13–17). In view of the numerous editions of the novel, I have supplied references to chapters rather than to pages. What is now the most widely and easily available edition of the novel can be found online: http://archive.org/stream/gp56w/gp56w10.txt

3   The account of Stobo's role in the fall of Quebec that first came to Parker's attention is found in Le Moine. Stobo's memoir itself has also been published. The scriptural passage occurs in Luke 1:52.

This inflation allows Parker to hold his audience even as he stretch-es the boundaries of sexual and ethical behaviour as depicted within a high-minded historical romance. Parker represents his heroine Alixe's sexuality as compelling and even aggressive. Dancing in (improbable) disguise before a group of the hero's dissolute enemies, Alixe's sexual magnetism rather than her choreography compels the drunken gather-ing's notice: "I must have wound these men up to excitement beyond all sense, for they would not be dissuaded, but swarmed toward the dais where I was [. . .]" (Ch. XIX). Oscar Wilde's scandalous Salome would not make her appearance until nine years after *Seats*, in 1905. However justified by Alixe's pure-hearted concern for her endangered beloved, her compelling, sexualized intervention in affairs of state anticipates this appearance of a new sort of romantic heroine. Her forceful sexual-ity is matched by the transgressive ethical musings of Moray. He is far from the naive hero whose intervention in history comes about as the result of a kind of sleepwalking. Moray recognizes the implications of his every act, ever-ready with a rationalization for the killing of enemy sentries, the deceits that he practises on those who trust him, and the dishonourable nature of his violation of the terms of a prisoner of war by his work as a spy.

Though Parker's chief written historical source was himself bothered by Moray's moral slipperiness, Parker displays it without commentary (Le Moine 57–58). On a number of occasions, Moray relies on a mix-ture of "they started it" and "what choice had I?" to see himself and his skeptical reader through. Whether rationalizing his role as a spy while on parole, or killing two enemy sentries, or killing a former jailer who had befriended him, Moray retains his moral aplomb (Ch. VI; XXII; XXVIII). Exalting romantic love becomes the way to bridge any ethical gap. As Moray observes, "[T]here comes a time when a man has a right to set all else aside but his own personal love and welfare, and to me the world was now bounded by just so much space as my dear Alixe might move in" (XI). Because the dance is performed for love, Alixe's erotic dis-play to secure her lover's well-being fails to diminish her wholesomeness. She remains, finally, an object—rather than a provoker—of male sexual desire. Moray's violence also avoids any linkage with amorality, because his actions adhere to the same code. Love conquers all, even the controls that morality imposes upon sexuality and violence. Romantic conquest leads inexorably to Britain's conquest of Quebec.

Paradoxically, this straining against the bounds of morality works in the service of a moral goal. New France falls, Moray prophesies, on account of the immorality of its leadership.

> I foresaw a strife, a complication of intrigues, and internal enmities which would be (as they were) the ruin of New France. I saw, in imagination, the English army at the gates of Quebec, and those who sat in the seats of the mighty, sworn to personal enmities—Vaudreuil through vanity, Bigot through cupidity, Doltaire by the innate malice of his nature—sacrificing the country; the scarlet body of British power moving down upon a dishonoured city, never to take its foot from that sword of France which fell there on the soil of the New World. (XIV)

There can be little doubt that he is speaking as well for Parker in this moralizing.[4] Callousness and corruption unite Quebec with Versailles: François Bigot, the corrupt Intendant, and the King's powerful mistress, Madame de Pompadour (the novel's villain, Doltaire, works in her service), together represent a system incapable of a successful response to Britain's offensive.

In thus moralizing military victory, Parker's novel continues along a path set by another Anglo-Canadian novelist. William Kirby's 1877 *Le chien d'or/The Golden Dog* also tailors New France into its garb of an unwilling participant in the making of British North America. Parker's title inverts the facts in order to label the superior British forces as the underdogs overturning the "mighty" of New France. Mary Jane Edwards, editor of the definitive version of Kirby's novel, cites archival evidence in noting that Parker wrote to Kirby of his admiration for the unwieldy novel, and sought to bring it to the attention of a British publisher (xc–viii).[5] So he should have, for Parker's moralism about Quebec's fall derives from Kirby's, as does his creation of a female foil to his heroine and his employment of Gothic motifs in his setting.[6]

---

4 Parker's biographer asserts that writer and character are one in their "self-righteousness and [. . .] inclination to justify expediency on moral grounds" (Adams 157).

5 Ironically, the success of *Seats* provoked Boston publisher L.C. Page's interest in Kirby's usage of material similar to Parker's. The result was an abridgement—read, mutilation—of *The Golden Dog* more severe than any other (Edwards lxxvi).

6 Kirby's moralistic explanation for the fall of New France occupies much of Chapter 39 of the novel, especially 461–63. The Gothic has appeared in historical fiction since its inception at the hands of Scott; I mention Kirby, however, as a more proximate source of such motifs for Parker.

Unlike Parker's highly sexualized account, Kirby's account of New France's fall proved tepid in its treatment of passion. The heroine Amélie enters the convent following the irreparable split from her impetuous lover, who dies later, elsewhere and not for love. *Seats*'s annexation of the moral high ground for the triumphant imperial Canada that Parker himself embodied rests upon passion for both plot and message, as passion fuses with national destiny. Moray is the triumphant, dashing hero, who will stop at nothing to secure his mate. The object of his passion, however, is no mere passive observer. As we have noted, she actively seeks to protect Moray from his deadly enemies, even as she doggedly resists the wiles of the villain. Here is a robust story whose interpretation of Canada's settlement any audience could grasp. Canada functioned as an amalgam of two founding traditions, with the masculinist role played by the British conqueror. His conquest of a space, however, has not given him a rapacious control over the woman representing that space. He has instead melded with her in a union based upon mutual attraction. Their coming together is a blending of equals, with each maintaining their own sphere of power. We may now look upon that notion of a heterosexual relationship and its power dynamics with a far more jaundiced eye than did Parker's original audience, but we cannot ignore the importance of the national vision asserted in the novel.

For Alixe and Moray's union asserts a principle vital in the symbolic structure of any social formation, whether family, religion, or nation-state. The principle of continuity runs throughout all of these and other groupings. Modern Canada as depicted imaginatively by Parker consists of a single foundation: the entities of British North America and New France. Canadian history is a single stream, Canadian political and cultural realities a single construct. One imperial fragment falls victim to another empire. Integrated within that victorious empire, the one-time fragment remains fused even when that empire is itself later fragmented by a rebel colony. Yet that remaining, loyal fragment—Canada—retains its own unity, with a continuous history resulting from the earlier fusion. If historical memory resembles genealogy, then the family tree has long since been fused into one. The two imperial entities are no longer autonomous and discrete, but one in any historical schema imposed upon Canadian space.

A late-Victorian historical potboiler *Seats* may seem today. Yet it presents a sustained treatment of the origins and destiny of the Euro-Canadian nation whose foundation rests upon the defeat of one empire by another, and whose continuation depends upon collaboration and assimilation rather than subjugation and force. The sexual passion that rests at the heart of this imaginative representation of that union is fully sublimated, tamed by the institution of patriarchal marriage. Roger Burlingame, a historian of the Scribner publishing house, chooses Parker's work as an exemplar of a lowering of literary merit and a slippage in the quality of public taste in the ranks of the top sellers that the firm issued. Where Barrie and Kipling had once reigned, Parker, Wm. J. Locke, and Mrs. Humphry Ward held sway (132). However accurate this may appear in the assignment of strictly aesthetic and belles-lettristic ranking, the fact remains that Parker presented his audience with a coherent imaginative account of Euro-Canada's origins that is marked by inclusivity and continuity. Parker's historical bestseller mythically anneals the two once-contending imperial forces. The romance integrates the Laurentian space of central Canada within the matrix of a single nation-state, as represented by a sexual union. When we turn our attention to the next novel of Canadian origin and setting, Mazo de la Roche's *Jalna*, we find there a present-day Canada content in an exclusivist, anglophone nationalism in which the French role seems a remote and barely relevant aside.

II. LOVE WITHOUT WAR

Does a Canadian novelist have to present a national vision? Must a domestic chronicle set in the present-day of its appearance reflect cultural preoccupations in the manner of a historical romance? Of course not. Yet *Jalna*'s Canadian setting does play a major role in the lives and possibilities that its characters experience, and *Jalna* exploits that setting in fashioning its theme. De la Roche did not set her novel in some vaguely defined continentalist neighbourhood; *Jalna*'s sense of homeland rests within a specifically Canadian space. That Canadian space is also marked by its incorporation of British-Canadian usages and values. From the style of table silver, to the Whiteoak family's descent from a British officer couple, to the male lead Renny's adherence to his wartime regiment, the *Jalna* series embodies a Canada highly resistant to American influence.[7] Yet this Canada barely acknowledges the existence of Quebec, itself one of the most distinctively non-American of entities on the nation's

---

7   Detailed treatment of this aspect of *Jalna* can be found in Hammill.

political and cultural map. *Jalna*'s very Canadian-ness is single-minded rather than complex. Any sense of Canadian settler nationhood's heterogeneity is muted. The estate and the tribal family that occupy it function quite comfortably in their insularity. This imaginative aplomb reflects that of a larger group of people in the culture of anglophone Canada, an absence of concern for francophone Canadians marking the chasm that the Great War tore open within Canada.

The property of Jalna, functioning both as realistically conceived imaginative setting and as symbolic homeland, stands as the great, good place of the Anglo-Canadian imagination of its day. Its creator, who lived more than a bit of her life in England and whose adopted children came from there, nonetheless delighted in the fact of "Old Quebec" (Givner 60). Her title for a Quebec City reminiscence/travel guide, *Quebec: Historic Seaport* (1944), discloses where her interest in the province resided—in its past rather than in the Quebec of de la Roche's lifetime. One of the Whiteoak family members in a later volume of her series reads from Kirby's *Golden Dog* while visiting the Citadel in Quebec (*Whiteoak Heritage* X), an *hommage* to Kirby's romanticization and moralization of Quebec's past. Quebec as a historical artifact formed a part of this character's sense of nationhood, yet its prosaic, twentieth-century descendant held no interest or relevance to the author's vivid sense of nationhood.

Jalna's Canada is populated by the Whiteoaks. They fill the Jalna property in the manner of a current university residence—each one with his, her, or their own room with a common dining and living room. Their doings bubble along like a tea urn perpetually roiling with appetite, sexual and alimentary. Substituting "samovar" for "tea urn" conveys the particular qualities of this Canadian family. Chekhov's characters also appear to live in elastic houses that hold any number of new arrivals and servants. They also share an obsessive interest in each other's doings. Their ritualized meals are marked by tensions and revelations indicating shifts in action. Meals advance the plot, and lay bare familiar stances and attitudes that underlie the unchanging nature of the company at the table. Where the Whiteoaks differ from their Russian counterparts is in the absence of ideas in their frequent encounters and discussions. Let the provincial Russians yearn for the delights of the capital, let them envision the graces and perils of an era to come, let them regret lost opportunities and loves. The Whiteoaks instead squabble over hierarchy and emotional territory; they lament the misadventures of the character under consideration; they then speculate upon the outcome of whatever rivalries occupy the domestic scene.

Sexual desire and curiosity provide a substitute for the atmosphere that ideas generate. Biographer Joan Givner has surmised that the physical facts of heterosexual coupling were likely unknown and never experienced by de la Roche herself. However convincing that speculation in fact, when it came to imaginary narrative, de la Roche still managed to infuse the Jalna household with seething sexual desire. Chief among those concerns roiling the Whiteoaks of Jalna are the romantic engagements involving their members; these intrigues usually involve one brother coveting and at times winning another's wife (Givner 49–50, 51). Such an entanglement drives both *Jalna*'s plot and its symbolic action. For the dreamy, poetical brother Eden's pursuit and capture of the American Alayne Archer while in New York fulfills two goals. It first of all introduces an "alien" (de la Roche's term) viewpoint, a perspective from which to delimit the characters and reinforce their Canadianness, so strange to a foreigner. Then Alayne's appearance also moves the story along as its focus turns to the patriarch Renny's attempt to wrest the newcomer away from his brother.

If sexual appetite drives the story, the alimentary provides us with a genteel reinforcement to sex. Gran Whiteoak controls the family's capital, whose components, provenance, and exercise are never made clear. This fairy-tale pot of gold embodies Gran's control, but her conduct is marked by an insatiable hunger for sweets and kisses. *Jalna* concludes with Gran's celebration of her hundredth birthday, as she garners the physical signs of affection from a new granddaughter-in-law: "From that hug she gathered new vitality. Her arms grew strong" (Ch. XXVI).[8] Those hugs and caresses follow an abortive embrace on the part of Renny and Alayne. As he manfully renounces temptation, and breaks the bond uniting him with his brother's wife, Alayne beseeches him to renew their touch: "'Again,'" she implores, anticipating Gran's use of the same word in the novel's final moment. No less appetitive in its depiction of the characters' drives than *Seats*, *Jalna* restricts those drives to the assimilating family and their domain. The Whiteoaks absorb and ingest; this marks a significant departure from the integrative nationalist vision of *Seats*.

---

8   The many editions of *Jalna* render the use of chapter references more accessible to readers than page numbers.

Gran's vitality marks all the Whiteoaks as Alayne experiences them. His rivalrous brother Renny may view Eden's poetic pursuits as somehow unmanly, but Eden in Manhattan fears resembling "[a] Canadian backwoodsman." His poetic allegiances are Canadian: he has published a volume of "genius," *Under the North Star*, which he wrote "a thousand miles from nowhere." He is at work on a long poem, *The Golden Sturgeon* (an echo of Kirby's *The Golden Dog*), and contemplates another "about Americans." His self-deprecating mention of his location while writing *Under the North Star*, followed by his announcement of a new poem on a topic described in vague and general terms ("the Americans"), discloses the emotional distance that separates him from New York (IX). Alayne views Eden as a bundle of contradictions, which nonetheless mark him as Canadian—outdoorsy, rustic—in her eyes: "[A] stammering, sunburned, egotistical young Canadian with not too good an education," who is nevertheless "a suddenly wooden and un-demonstrative young Britisher." Both parties to this attitudinal transaction engage in national stereotypes: the family views Alayne as a "rich American girl of fiction," and Alayne of course is costumed as the Statue of Liberty in a Christmas charade (XI; XX).9 While Alayne finds Jalna a "backwater," she cannot resist its "pungent vitality" and thrills to its wilderness tales (XVI, XV). Her late father a historian of the Revolutionary War, Alayne discovers in herself an affinity for the United Empire Loyalists (X). Bookish, fastidious in her reading tastes, a reader for an old-line publisher, she nonetheless succumbs to Renny's attractions as the "very spirit of the woods and streams" (X).

Throughout, Alayne oscillates between feelings of alienation and integration. At first applying to herself the Keatsian epithet of "Ruth—amid the alien corn," she immediately counters this with the conviction that "she should not feel that [the Whiteoaks] were alien. It was a lovely land. The language was her own" (XIII). Her integration within the Whiteoak ménage and their homeland is signified in the recurrence of the word *alien* toward the novel's end. After the Christmas charade that saw her costumed as Liberty, she beholds a winter landscape embodying her conversion to a new homeland:

---

9   The fact that her last name is "Archer," and that the Whiteoaks view her as an American heiress, discloses that while the Whiteoaks may never have read Henry James, their author did.

The pines and hemlocks, clothed in the somber grandeur of their winter foliage, threw shadows of an intense, translucent blueness. And in
the hard bright intensity of the northern ether, every smallest twig was
bitten against its background as though with acid. *An atmosphere hate-
ful to those who see it in alien loneliness, but of the essence and goodness
of life to the native born.* (XXI; emphasis mine)

Jalna thus outlines a process of cultural conversion. Employing the familiar tropes of the Canadian true North, resting upon a boreal nationalism
familiar enough in post-Confederation Canadian nationalist writings,
de la Roche wrote a pastoral novel.[10] Here the girl from the rarefied city,
site of the American literary marketplace that the novelist had sought
to break into, finds herself transformed into a figure within a peculiarly
Canadian scene.[11] De la Roche saved the final outcome of Alayne and
Renny's affair (a divorce from Eden; remarriage to Renny) for the next
novel in the series that she had probably not yet planned at the time of
Jalna's creation, but the union between the chthonic Anglo-Canadian
and the deracinated American is predictable at the conclusion of *Jalna*.

What can be more germane to a variety of Canadian nationalism
than a character whose deepest yearnings, imaginative and sexual, sever
her American ties and bring her into the heart of a vital, enduring, and
emotionally authentic family? Alayne's first unimpeded sight of Renny
occurs while she is immersed within the erotic languor of an Indian summer afternoon: "[t]he earth, after all its passion of bearing, was relaxed in
passive and slumberous contentment. Its desires were fulfilled, its gush-
ing fertility over" (XIII). Juxtapose this passage—which continues with
Alayne's initial glimpse of a Renny who resembles the "[r]ed and rayless
sun"—with the winter landscape that I cited earlier. A kind of Lawrentian
modernism emerges, a contrast to the geographical Laurentian theme of
Seats. That is, the high-born lady succumbs to the lure of the rugged
masculinity of the guardian spirit of a more authentic and elemental way
of life. She comes to disregard the all-too-cultivated attractions of her
husband in favour of the compelling drive of the would-be lover. Small
wonder that a novel as replete with near-domesticated passion as *Jalna*

---

10 For the cult of the true North, see Berger 128–33.
11 For a discussion of the sources and implications of the British squirearchical social and house-
    hold order that de la Roche concocts, see Duffy, *Gardens* 76–91, and Fellows.

quickly acquired the applause of a reading public, answering that appro-
bation with further instalments of a racy yet restrained saga.

Within so erotic a climate, the attractions of a brief Quebec past for
the Whiteoaks appear pale indeed. Quebec and its garrison first drew
Captain Philip Whiteoak from his service with the *raj* in India (location of the original Jalna) to Canada. Unfortunately, Quebec, for all "its
freedom from the narrow conventionalities of the Old World, combined
with a grace of living bequeathed by the French," nonetheless held "far
too many French [. . .] to be congenial to an English gentleman." Where
the city's church bells lured his wife to "those Roman churches," making
Philip fear that "she would under such influence become a papist [. . .,]
the fertile southern shore of [Lake] Ontario" beckoned him with "the
welcome here that people of your consequence *merit*" (II; emphasis in
original).

At the age of forty-eight, de la Roche was an experienced professional writer when *Jalna* won Little, Brown's *Atlantic* prize for the best
novel manuscript submitted to them in 1927. Her two previous novels,
and numerous stories and "juveniles" that she had published, had not
made use of a metaphorized Canadian setting in the manner of *Jalna*.
A mature popular writer, de la Roche expressed in *Jalna's* pages a more
intense national thematic than any she had heretofore written. Setting
and theme were at once national and nationalist, with her version of
Canadian pastoral establishing her country as a vivid, enduring, and
above all authentic alternative to the American metropolis. Of interest,
then, is *Jalna's* relegation of Quebec to a dim background location, a kind
of North American depot that passes the founder of the Whiteoak dy-
nasty along to the genuine seat of quasi-pastoral simplicity and vitality.
Why this disappearance of Quebec from her exaltation of Canada's superiority to the republican south?

De la Roche had invented for herself a distinguished French royalist
ancestry, one that her cousin and lifelong companion, Caroline Clement,
shared and even embroidered upon (Givner 2–3). Kirby had found the
moral of his story in what he viewed as Quebec's loyalty. Loyal to its
French heritage, it logically followed that sentiment in refusing to join in
the American Revolution and in its resistance to American invasion during the War of 1812 (Kirby 748–49). De la Roche herself venerated what
she viewed as a Loyalist tradition and outlook throughout her fiction,

as critics have attested (Duffy, Fellows). Yet that tradition, fundamentally British in its attachment to imperial institutions, did not necessarily exclude Quebec, as Kirby's and Parker's novels attest. *Jalna*'s imaginative projection of Canada's nature reveals that by 1927, the inclusion of Quebec, its origins, history and nature, was no longer considered integral to an imaginary memorialization of Canada.

But how could a bestselling author, whose work would come to be taken as an imaginative realization of the very fact of Canada, relegate Quebec to a historic footnote in its evocation of the nation's significance? A host of fan letters, from Canada and elsewhere, preserved among the de la Roche papers residing in the University of Toronto's Fisher Library, attest more dramatically than any critic just how potent the author's vision of Canada appeared to her wide readership. *Jalna* exploded on the anglophone literary scene during a period marked by a surge in "Canadian cultural nationalism that would influence Canada's cultural institutions for generations to come" (Litt 34). De la Roche's Canadian publishers rode this wave when promoting her work (Panofsky 78–79). *Jalna*'s downplaying of Quebec and the French fact demonstrates just how distant the union between Gilbert Parker's one-time couple had grown.

De la Roche's grasp of contemporary affairs could be personalized, moralistic, and infantile, as revealed in her account of the Great Depression: "Canada had done nothing to deserve [the Depression]. She had been good; she had been loyal; she had spilled her own blood when there was fighting to be done; and had minded her own business afterwards. Especially the family at Jalna did not deserve it. They had upheld the old traditions in the province. They had stood by Jalna and stuck by each other. So they reasoned, and looked at one another baffled" (de la Roche, *Master* VIII). Such bafflement, however, does not mark a skilled popular writer's understanding of what had taken place in the imagery of Anglo-Canadian nationalism. A new civic cult had arisen. Mackenzie King had served as its national acolyte, while observing in the House of Commons that the Vimy Ridge battlefield had been transmuted into "one of the world's great altars [. . .] consecrated and hallowed ground" (King). That new Canadian sacred space had no room for Quebec. The new Canada's boundaries were co-terminous with Canada's role in the Great War, from which Quebec, in the new social mythology, had been excluded itself.[12] *Jalna* reflects this exclusion. A profound irony had arisen. The imperialist vision typified by Parker had founded itself upon an inclusive vision of a complex, dualist Canadian nationality. That vision in fact contained a wider range of linguistic and cultural possibilities than an independent, war-begotten, and exclusivist national map had been able to accommodate. Subsequently, the collective memory that was based on the centrality of the Great War as a foundation for Canadian nationalism, a Great War from which Quebec has absented itself except as an irritant to the anglophone project, created a great blank in the nation's imaginative cartography. The Conscription Crisis and the sundering between national attitudes that it represents had their fictional fallout.

---

12 See the essay by Marissa McHugh in Chapter 18 of this volume, "Collective Memory, Cultural Transmission, and the Occupation(s) of Quebec: Jean Provencher and Gilles Lachance's *Québec, Printemps 1918*," which explores Québécois resistance to the nationalist Great War narrative.

CHAPTER 18

•–•

Collective Memory, Cultural Transmission, and the Occupation(s) of Quebec: Jean Provencher and Gilles Lachance's *Québec, Printemps 1918*

Marissa McHugh

English Canada's preferred memory of the Great War has been dominated by accounts that envision the War as a foundational—even mythic
event—that transformed Canada from colony to nation. In particular,
1918, the year of the War's end, largely represents a victorious time when
Canadian soldiers distinguished themselves overseas, earning Canada
international recognition and stimulating a wave of patriotism on the
home front. Since the War's end, countless historical and fictional accounts of the War have appeared in English Canada, celebrating the War
as seminal to the development of a mature Canadian nation-state and
identity. While this commemoration focuses on Canada's significant
gains in and as a result of the War, it forgets the way in which the War
and, namely, the 1918 Easter Riots, divided English and French Canada.
Historian Jean Provencher and theatre practitioner Gilles Lachance's play
Québec, Printemps 1918, written in the aftermath of the 1970 October
Crisis, recalls this forgotten history and, in doing so, unsettles Canada's
preferred memory of the War as a consolidating event. At the same time,
it utilizes the memory of the Riots to enable communal mourning and
to construct and solidify an emergent Québécois national identity in opposition to that of English Canada.

I. REMEMBERING, FORGETTING, AND THE FORMATION OF IDENTITY

English Canada's and Quebec's active remembering and selective forgetting of aspects of the Great War attests to the constructed nature of memory. In particular, it demonstrates memory's relationship with identity by
pointing to the way in which memory creates and/or sustains identity.
Memory and identity, as John R. Gillis explains, occupy "parallel lives"

(3), and their interconnectedness "alert[s] us to the fact that the notion of identity depends on the idea of memory, and vice versa. The core meaning of any individual or group identity [. . .] is sustained by remembering; and what is remembered is defined by the assumed identity" (3). Gillis also makes evident, however, that identity is not only intrinsically connected to remembering but also to forgetting (3). This process is particularly evident at a national level, as Brian S. Osbourne explains: "[n]ational cohesion [. . .] requires a sense of collective awareness and identity that is promoted through a sense of mutual historical experience. [. . .] The orchestration of such collective remembering—and, if necessary, *collective amnesia*—constitutes the crucial underpinning of national-state identities" (41; emphasis added). This "forgetting," which Benedict Anderson identifies as "characteristic amnesias" (204), "is not the result of accident or omission, but is a largely concerted process, intended, on some level, to reconcile the collective memories of a group with a particular version of group identity" (Johnston 11). Gillis defines this "concerted process" as the basis of "'memory work'" (3), and he argues that memory functions "like any other kind of physical or mental labor, embedded in complex class, gender and power relations that determine what is remembered (or forgotten), by whom, and for what end" (3; see also Confino 1393).

II. ENGLISH CANADA'S "USABLE PAST"

What has become evident in recent years is that the preferred English-Canadian memory of the War is intrinsically linked to national identity and that this memory-identity continuum is predicated upon a selective remembering of the gains of the War. English Canadians have long remembered the War as a nation-building event, one which enabled Canada to earn international recognition, to acquire a degree of political autonomy, and to develop a distinct cultural identity. This pervasive remembering of the War as Canada's "coming of age," as several contemporary Canadian historians attest, has remained the dominant means of assessing and understanding the War. Jeffrey A. Keshen points to the enduring quality of this association, noting that "[t]here [. . .] persists the picture of soldiers who, through their extraordinary bravery, won the hardest and most important battles [. . .] and thus emerged a singular and heroic force in transforming Canada from colony to nation" (xvii). Jonathan F. Vance adds to this assumption, arguing that "Canada's progress from colony to nation by way of Flanders, an interpretation born in the earliest days of the war, has become the standard method of judging the impact of 1914–1918" (10).

Vance points to the genesis of this understanding of the War, which he identifies as "a mythic version of the events of 1914–1918" (3) focused on the War's "positive outcomes" (9). He suggests this "mythic" remembering had an intrinsic connection with mourning and that bereaved Canadians found it "appealing because it filled needs. For some people, it was consolatory; for others, it was explanatory" (9). Ultimately, he argues that it was constructed and embraced because it rendered the War serviceable and infused the extensive number of human sacrifices with use-value. As he explains, "[i]n remembering the war, Canadians were concerned first and foremost with utility: those four years had to have been of some use. The war had to be recalled in such a way that positive outcomes, beyond the defeat of German aggression, were clear. In short, the mythic version existed to fashion a usable past out of the Great War" (9).[1] This "usable past," as Vance explains, was then disseminated by "historians [. . .] happy to aid and abet this process by articulating a vision of the war as a nation-building event of signal importance" (10).

Evidently, many English-Canadian historical accounts remember the War in celebratory terms and point to its role in national development. George W. Brown's 1942 *Building the Canadian Nation*, for example, suggests the War enabled "further advances on the road to nationhood" and earned Canada "recogni[tion] by Britain as a partner" (503). Considering that *Building the Canadian Nation* was a high-school textbook for over ten years and "sold about 600,000 copies" (Igartua 110), it is likely that Brown's representation would have reached many Canadians, contributing to the accumulating mythos of the War in the Canadian imaginary. Not surprisingly, one finds echoes of these opinions in later works, which attest to the way in which the War came to be

---

1   The phrase *usable past* comes from literary critic Van Wyck Brooks's 1918 essay "On Creating a Usable Past." Brooks called for Americans to piece together aspects of their past into a cohesive whole that would be beneficial in the present. Lois Parkinson Zamora builds on Brooks's discussion, noting that Brooks's use of the term "'[u]sable' implies the active engagement of a user or users, through whose agency collective and personal histories are constituted. The term thus obviates the possibility of innocent history, but not the possibility of authentic history when it is actively imagined by its user(s). What is deemed usable is valuable; what is valuable is constituted according to specific cultural and personal needs and desires" (ix).

further understood as a foundational moment. Pierre Berton, for one, envisions the War as "a searing experience and also a turning point" contributing to Canadian national maturity. He suggests that "Canada entered the war as a colony, emerged as a nation," and "grew up as a result of that war" (Foreword 8). In *Tapestry of War*, Sandra Gwyn argues that "it is the Great War that marks the real birth of Canada" (xvii). She also suggests that Canada's significant contributions to the War effort enabled this "birth": "our blood and our accomplishments transformed us from colony to nation" (xvii).

While these accounts serve as a means to remember the international recognition Canada earned as a result of the nation's extensive contribution to the War effort,[2] they are deeply problematic, for they exclude the experiences of many Canadians, especially those at home, and they fail to acknowledge the extent to which the War divided the nation, in particular English Canada and Quebec.[3] The conscription debate and the resulting Military Service Act (1917), which required that all Canadian men between the ages of twenty and thirty-five enlist, for example, created significant tension between pro-War English Canada and anti-conscription Quebec. Though there is some scholarship on this crisis, its culmination, the Easter Riots of 1918, a "war" in Quebec that left four Quebec civilians dead at the hands of the English-Canadian military, remains largely unknown. As Martin Auger explains, "[a]side from Jean Provencher's *Québec sous la loi des mesures de guerre 1918* [. . .] no studies of the Easter Riots or their aftermaths exist in both the English- and French-language literature" (505). Auger also notes that the limited "[k]nowledge of the riots stems [. . .] from general studies of Canada's conscription crisis" (505).

---

2   In 1917, British Prime Minister David Lloyd George invited Prime Minister Robert Borden to the Imperial War Conference. George recognized Canada's significant sacrifice and realized that he could not ask Borden to invigorate recruitment campaigns without offering him a place in the Imperial War Cabinet and a voice in war affairs (Granatstein and Morton, *Canada* 92). Borden seized this opportunity and proposed Resolution IX, which called for the "'full recognition of the Dominions as autonomous nations of an Imperial Commonwealth'" ("Extracts" 2373). The resolution passed, granting the dominions "'an adequate voice in foreign policy and in foreign relations'" and ensuring they would be consulted "'in all important matters of common imperial concern and for such necessary concerted action founded on consultation as the several Governments may determine'" ("Extracts" 2373).

3   Vance notes that "[f]our years of battle [. . .] did not create a single nationalism, but strengthened the two nationalisms of French and English Canada; both societies gained a greater appreciation of their separate identities from the experience of war" (10).

The Riots initially erupted in Quebec City in response to the Dominion Police's presence and their violent enforcement of the Military Service Act. Protests began on Thursday, 28 March 1918, after two Dominion Police constables arrested Joseph Mercier (a central character in *Québec, Printemps 1918*) and roughly forced him into custody because he could not immediately produce his exemption papers. A crowd witnessed the mistreatment of Mercier and revolted against it, assaulting police stations and sacking pro-conscription newspaper offices. By Friday evening, approximately fifteen thousand people had assembled within the streets of Quebec City. The Robert Borden government then invoked the War Measures Act, suspending *habeas corpus* and fully occupying Quebec with English-speaking troops. These "troops were [. . .] free to intervene at any time, anywhere in the city, without the approval of the civilian authorities, and to use whatever force necessary" (Auger 511). Over the weekend, soldiers "patrolled the streets on foot, horseback, and in motorized vehicles, and stood guard at strategic locations. Machine guns were placed at several locations around the city" (Auger 517).

Easter Monday ended in a bloody battle, which affirmed the strength of pro-conscription English Canada over Quebec. The military expected that the numerous city placards, newspaper articles, and religious sermons, urging the populace to remain safely within their homes, would quell unrest (Elizabeth Armstrong 228–29; Wade 764). Quebec civilians, however, disregarded these warnings and continued to assemble. The military, as Provencher recalls, thus undertook drastic, violent measures to finalize the conflict (*Québec sous la lois* 110). This particular brutality provoked the Quebec population, inciting them to take up arms against the military (110). The military retaliated against this civilian ambush (Wade 764–65), firing back at civilians, and the "[c]avalry charged the mob with drawn swords, while infantry picked off the snipers" (Wade 765). This and the military's ensuing violence left four civilians dead and numerous people injured. Fearing further bloodshed, Quebec ceased all forms of protest. Borden, however, feared a potential civil war in Quebec; thus he ordered troops to remain stationed throughout the city until the War's end.

The cause of the collective amnesia that followed the riots in Quebec City is difficult to determine. What is evident, however, is that this extensive forgetting took place at a time when grieving English Canadians were demonstrating a significant desire to remember the War years as a time of nation-building and cultural consolidation. While English Canadians appear to have willingly and concertedly engaged in a process of forgetting, Quebecers also appear to have demonstrated a reticence to speak publicly about their traumatic experience of this localized instance of warfare in its immediate aftermath. This silence, enabling Canada's erasure of the past, however, was short-lived, and Provencher unearthed the history of the Riots in the context of 1960s and 1970s intra-Canadian politics, destabilizing the English-Canadian mythic memory of the War as a nation-building event.

III. QUEBEC'S "USABLE PAST"

In 1968, Provencher discovered a coroner's report that had been conducted in the aftermath of the Riots. This little-known report, including the testimonies of civilians, police officers, and military personnel, concludes that the government was responsible for the four civilian deaths and recommends that the families of the victims receive indemnity. Despite this verdict, the government rejected this official interpretation of events and refrained from any form of apology. Provencher adapted the report into a book, which was published in 1971 as *Québec sous la loi des mesures de guerre 1918*. This treatise continues to be the only book-length study of the Riots, and though it has not been translated into English, it remains a seminal commentary on Quebec, Canada, and the War.

The book also functions as an independence manifesto, a testimony and judgment on Canada's relation to Quebec past and present. It returns not only to 1918 to recover history but also to comment upon the October Crisis of 1970, when the War Measures Act was, once again, invoked. Considering that the October Crisis took place only a year prior to the publication of *Québec sous la loi des mesures de guerre 1918*, it is likely that Provencher's experience of the Crisis shaped his perception of the war measures in 1918. As Maurice Halbwachs explains, "[e]ven at the moment of reproducing the past our imagination remains under the influence of the present social milieu" (49). Certainly, Provencher had a strong interest in the Crisis, as his 1974 historical treatise *La grande peur d'Octobre '70* attests. This book carefully details the chronology of the Crisis—in a similar structural manner to *Québec sous la loi des mesures de guerre 1918*—during 5–25 October.

The roots of the Crisis, however, date back to the 1960s when a coalition of revolutionary separatists formed the Front de libération du Québec (FLQ). This group sought independence from Canada as well as a means to end "200 years of 'Anglo-Saxon' violence against the Quebec people" (Torrance 35). Throughout the 1960s, the FLQ and the independence movement steadily gained momentum, and, in April of 1970, the Parti Québécois won seven seats in the Quebec National Assembly. For the FLQ, however, this was not a radical enough means to ensure Quebec's independence. Thus, on 5 October 1970, they abducted the British trade commissioner, James Cross, and Quebec's minister of labour and immigration, Pierre Laporte. Prime Minister Pierre Elliott Trudeau's government responded swiftly, and, on 7 October, the Dominion Police began conducting raids and making arrests (Bélanger, "Chronology"). Trudeau stationed the army in Ottawa in order to protect government officials, deployed soldiers in Quebec, and invoked the War Measures Act. By 18 October, government officials had arrested approximately five hundred people and conducted numerous unsanctioned searches. Though government forces attempted to target nationalists and activists, all Quebecers were subject to abuse. Nick Auf der Maur recalls the "indiscriminate" nature of the arrests, noting that "[e]verybody was up for grabs" (113). Certainly, the suspension of basic rights applied to all Quebec residents—in the same manner as it had in 1918. Provencher's historical treatise thus "had a certain resounding importance" (Provencher, Preface), as it pointed to an earlier instance of Quebec's occupation.

Initially, Provencher had no intention of adapting the coroner's report or the historical treatise into a play-script, and he had little experience in the theatre. Thus, when Paul Hébert, artistic director of Théâtre Le Trident in Quebec, confessed to Provencher that he "dreamed of reproducing on stage the coroner's report" and felt that this reproduction could not be completed without Provencher's historical expertise, Provencher was somewhat reticent (Provencher, Preface). By the end of the summer of 1973, however, with the help of Hébert and Lachance, Hébert's vision was realized. The play premiered at the Théâtre Le Trident in Quebec in October and November of 1973, a time of "remarkable [theatrical] growth" in Quebec (Hébert 28) as well as of historical recovery[4] and cultural consolidation in the province. Approximately seventeen hundred

---

4   In 1978, Quebec adopted the licence plate slogan "Je me souviens," a gesture affirming their commitment to recovering the past and retaining it within public consciousness.

18.1 13 October 1973 Advertisement in *Le Soleil* for *Québec, Printemps 1918*.

people attended the performance (Provencher, Preface), and the play was further disseminated in Quebec after its publication by Éditions L'aurore (1974).

Le Soleil's coverage of the play stressed its importance in Quebec and illustrated that it functioned as more than a means of theatrical entertainment. An article on the play, published before its premiere (29 September 1973), noted that the play was a "reconstitution d'un drame de l'histoire québécoise" and that it unearthed "des pages trop peu connues de notre histoire" (37). It also predicted the audience's role in the production and, seemingly, in the future dissemination of history: "[c]'est le 11 octobre prochain que le public découvrira, lui, son rôle" (37). After the production opened, a 11 October 1973 review celebrated it for commemorating the deceased: "[c]e soir débute au Trident la réhabilitation des victimes de 1918" (52). The second review in *Le Soleil* (13 Oct. 1973) called attention to the play's important recovery of unrecorded, forgotten history: "[c]ette histoire-là, on ne l'a pas encore écrite et trop de gens l'ont déjà oubliée." What is most interesting about this review, however, is its suggestion of the way in which the recovered history resonated with the audience:

> les dialogues entendus, les faits relatés, les événements reconstitués appartiennent eux, à la réalité, à un passé pas tellement éloigné, a l'histoire. Et parce que l'on peut toujours, 55 ans plus tard, reconnaître des répliques, comparer des climats qui ont conduit à un drame au cours duquel quatre hommes innocents sont tombés sous les balles des forces de l'ordre, on est embarrassé. (36)

While *Le Soleil*'s coverage of the play focuses on its important commemorative and informative function in 1973, Chris Young's master's thesis "'Sous les balles des troupes fédérales': Representing the Quebec City Riots in Francophone Quebec (1919–2009)" illustrates that the play, coupled with Provencher's historical treatise, "profoundly revive[d] the story of the Quebec City riots" (59) and led to a wealth of memory work on the subject. As he explains, "[s]ince Provencher published his work, [. . .] the story of the Quebec City riots has been frequently represented in texts, documentaries, and public commemorations" (83). He notes that "Quebec's francophone historians [. . .] have parroted Provencher's works" and that "Provencher's account of the riots has greatly influenced how the event has been portrayed" in a variety of post-1973 media (119).

IV. *QUÉBEC, PRINTEMPS 1918*

The play, a courtroom drama, recalls Quebec's distinct experience of the War, selectively remembering aspects of the Easter Riots in the context of the October Crisis in order to highlight Quebecers' distinctness from English Canadians. The play, entirely composed of testimonies, calls attention to the unethical treatment of Quebecers by English-Canadian officials, figuring English Canadians as a deadly, invasive force attempting to repress and/or annihilate Quebecers and Québécois culture. In remembering a cruel, unjust "war" waged against innocent Québécois civilians, it suggests the extent to which the invasion of Quebec (both in 1918 and, consequently, in 1970) sharply divided the nation into two distinct factions: oppressive English Canadians and peaceful Quebecers. This revisionary commemoration also functions as a means to consolidate Quebecers in a shared act of remembering the occupation(s) of Quebec.

The play opens with the testimony of Joseph Mercier, the young man who was brutally arrested and detained by the Dominion Police for failing to produce his exemption papers. Mercier affirms that he had been legally excused from military duty; however, on Easter Thursday, he failed to carry his exemption papers with him (61). He testifies that officers immediately dismissed his explanation and denied him the right to make a telephone call—despite his insistence that it would yield his papers: "I told them, 'Let me phone.' But they wouldn't. I said, 'Look, you can go stand by the phone with me. I can't get away.' But they wouldn't" (62). Mercier also calls attention to the officers' aggression: "they called soldiers to take me away. Five of them. They grabbed me. I couldn't even touch the ground" (62). While this account suggests the officers' animosity toward Quebecers in the context of the conscription crisis, it also brings to mind the violence inflicted on many Quebecers in the wake of the 1970 invocation of the War Measures Act. At the same time, it implicitly functions as a critique of the English-Canadian officials' judgment in both time periods, particularly of their ability to discern actual and significant threats, for neither Mercier nor many arrested civilians in 1970 were dangerous.[5]

The play's focus on the military's arrival after the invocation of the War Measures Act and the figuration of the military as dismissive of Québécois life, however, most evocatively contributes to the play's polarization of English Canadians and Quebecers. The play characterizes the military as ruthless, controversially implying that they poorly articulated the Riot Act in order to legitimate their ensuing martial attack.[6]

---

5 In 1970, the military arrested over five hundred Quebecers and did not convict any of them (Denis Smith xiii).
6 If a group of twelve or more people do not disband after a lawful authority reads the Riot Act, then they are committing a criminal offence and are subject to violence and arrest. *Québec, Printemps 1918* and *Québec sous la lois des mesures de guerre 1918* both suggest that the military did not properly issue the Riot Act before they fired on civilians.

In Municipal Police Sergeant Isidore Caouette's testimony, he attests that despite having been on patrol on Easter Monday, he at no point heard the Riot Act read (116). This seems plausible considering Major George Robert Rodgers' earlier testimony. Rodgers reveals that Captain Haughton recited the Riot Act "[n]ear Place Jacques-Cartier. [. . .] [a] short time after nine" and that the protestors dispersed. "Almost a half-mile distant and two hours later," however, soldiers opened fire on civilians (96)—though the Act was not reread (98). These facts suggest that many of the gathered civilians would not have been cognizant that their presence on the streets defined them as a military threat. They also intimate Provencher and Lachance's understanding of English-Canadian forces as a threatening, deadly force, evidently committed to the repression of Quebecers.

The play's depiction of Quebec City as a war-ravaged space in the aftermath of the salvo further points to the military's characterization as such, while also evoking the martial climate of 1970 Quebec.[7] The testimony of Père Isidore Evain, for example, memorializes Quebecers as martyr-like figures, "fleeing" from their persecutors and lying prostrate in the streets (100). As Père Evain recalls in an elegiac, funereal tone, after navigating through crowds of retreating civilians, he located Joseph-Edouard Tremblay, who "was suffering a great deal," and he "gave him the consolations of [his] ministry" (100). He then recovered the "lifeless" body of Alexandre Bussières and "administered conditional absolution" (100). He also attests to the military's devaluation of Québécois life, noting that while he was "caring for the wounded," soldiers continued to fire at [fleeing] civilians (101). When he requested they cease fire, a soldier justified the continued assault, explaining, "'[w]e have orders to fire at any head we see in the street'" (101).

The soldiers, as the play implies by including the testimony of the pathologist Albert Marois, were not only intent on frightening and repressing their perceived enemy but also in significantly and permanently wounding the Québécois national body. Though Marois hesitates to make any final conclusions, his testimony suggests that Quebecers were subject to premeditated cruelty. From his examination of Honoré Bergeron,

---

7   Jason R. Burke notes that "[f]our decades after the October Crisis of 1970, images of the Canadian military occupying the streets of Ottawa, Montreal and Quebec City remain potent" (335).

he dutifully testifies, "I make no absolute claim that they used explosive or malleable bullets. But the wound which I observed did not seem to me to have been made by the ordinary bullets used by the Army. [. . .] An ordinary bullet could not have produced the wounds which I have described" (104–105). Marois' suggestion is that Bergeron was shot with a bullet of "malleable texture"—that is, with a bullet typically reserved "for big game hunting" (105). This type of bullet opens to carve a large wound channel within the prey and is strictly forbidden within the army. Marois testifies that he also discovered wounds of this nature on the corpses of Georges Demeule and Bussières, further confirming his suspicions of foul play (106). Lachance and Provencher highlight this portion of the coroner's report in order to suggest that soldiers illegally tampered with military bullets, perhaps even prior to their invasion, as a means of inflicting the maximum injury possible upon their victims.

Though Marois cannot confirm whether Tremblay died of an explosive bullet wound, as he did with the other deceased, he notes that the military could have prevented Tremblay's death. As Marois explains, Tremblay's "wounds were not mortal," and a simple ligature would have ensured his survival (105). Tremblay, however, received no medical assistance and "died of a hemorrhage caused by the rupture of the popliteal artery" (105). Marois also insists that the military misapprehended Tremblay, Bergeron, Demeule, and Bussière: he "found no objects that might be considered offensive arms" (106) or indication that the deceased were engaged in anti-conscription machinations. It thus remains uncertain whether these deaths had any political purpose—other than affirming English Canada's dominance over Quebec. Demeule, for one, was only fourteen years old—neither old enough to vote or enlist. After being shot in the right lung and in his liver, he painfully hemorrhaged on home terrain, with his death doing little to quell the riots, to encourage Quebecers to enlist, or to strengthen the War effort.

What the play therefore implies is that the "war" within the War involved not only the persecution of a tangible enemy but also the French language and, consequently, Québécois culture. The playwrights point to this secondary dimension of the War by representing the military as an imperialist force, hostile to French speakers, and by implicitly gesturing to language tensions in Quebec in the past and in their present. For Quebecers in the early 1910s, these tensions were brought to the fore with the passing of Regulation 17, a 1912 law disallowing French-language instruction after grade two in Ontario schools (Granatstein and Hitsman 27; E. Armstrong 139). Within the play, the testimony of Père Evain serves as a means to capture this tension, aggravated by the conscription crisis, while enabling Provencher and Lachance's representation of the military as a deadly, anglocentric force. Père Evain, for example, recalls that the military only issued warnings to French-speaking Quebecers in English, conscious that they would not be understood (102). They shouted "'[h]ands up'" (102), and, as Père Evain painfully recalls, the civilians "did not understand. They were Canadiens. [. . .] so—the policeman and I would cry out in French, telling them to get out and they would run" (102). This horrific depiction of events would have resonated with many of the play's audience members and readers, considering that, in post-1960s Quebec, "the unifying component of the Quebec nation was the French language" (Bélanger, "Quebec Nationalism") and that during the October Crisis many experienced bodily harm and/or fear of cultural disintegration at the hands of the military.

While the play focuses on the repression of Quebecers and Québécois culture, it also functions as a platform for the commemoration of forgotten and/or unfavourably remembered "rioters." To achieve this end, the playwrights privilege the public grievances of several widows, who openly affirm the moral qualities of the deceased. Madame Honoré Bergeron, for example, "*is visibly grief-stricken*" as she begins her testimony, and she remains "*on the edge of tears*" throughout the proceedings (67), imbuing the courtroom with a funereal atmosphere. Defence attorney Major George Barclay, however, questions whether the public should join in Madame Bergeron's sorrow. He asks, "[w]as your husband sober, Madame?" (67), hinting that Bergeron might not have been an upstanding citizen worthy of public and communal mourning. Madame Bergeron, however, retaliates by affirming her husband's virtuous character. "*Visibly offended*," she assures the court (and audience) that her "husband did not drink" and that he "was sober and in good health" (67). Her testimony comes to resemble a eulogy, undermining the military's representation of her late husband as a violent protestor. As she recounts, he only left the house because he wanted to locate his children and bring them to safety (67). The courtroom setting thus offers Madame Bergeron a means to challenge the assumption that her husband was a disreputable drunk rioter who either wandered into the streets incoherently or set out to disturb the peace.

This testimony also serves as a means to invert the military's conception of Bergeron as a war target rather than a human life. In Judith Butler's *Frames of War*, she argues that certain lives, namely those "framed" as the enemy in war discourse, come to be conceived purely as threats to the valuable lives of a given citizenry. Their lives are "construed as instruments of war or pure vessels of attack," and "they are already deprived of life before they are killed, transformed into inert matter or destructive instrumentalities" (xxix). In a sense, these "vessels of attack" are devoid of life because they are not "grievable": "[o]nly under conditions in which the loss would matter does the value of the life appear. Thus grievability is a presupposition for the life that matters. [. . .] Without grievability there is no life, or, rather, there is something living that is other than life" (14–15). Because the military considered Bergeron as "ungrievable," they did not recognize him as (having been) a living subject and did not report his death. As Madame Bergeron attests, he simply disappeared from existence:

> [S]omeone came to tell me that my husband had been arrested by the spotters. I began to try to find him. [. . .] I was under the impression my husband was in the military prison. I did the same thing Wednesday but I didn't get any news. It was Thursday, that afternoon, someone asked me to go to Monsieur Moisand, the keeper of the morgue. [. . .] There, I identified my husband. It was only then that I learnt he died. *She breaks into tears.* (67–68)

Regina Bussières similarly recounts the military's dismissal of her husband's life: "I was told he'd been arrested by the spotters. My father and my father-in-law tried to find out where he was. [. . .] but they couldn't find him" (69). After three days of searching, she finally "found out he had died" and "was asked to go identify him at the morgue" (69). Whereas the military would have respectfully reported the death of a fallen soldier overseas, this measure was not extended to these French-Canadian families.[8] The play thus suggests that for the military, the Quebecer was akin to an overseas enemy, a subject devoid of life; in doing so, it powerfully

---

8   Claude Bélanger points to the military's dehumanization of Quebecers in 1970: "[i]t was difficult for family members to find out about those arrested and to get in touch with them. Sometimes, people were held incommunicado for days" ("Chronology")

emblematizes the conflict as a war on home soil and explains the erasure of "ungrievables" from English-Canadian collective memory.

The widows' testimonies therefore serve as a means to reconstitute the deceased's humanity in a public forum. Their expressions of grief, however, not only enable the commemoration of the casualties of this conflict but also serve as a means to acknowledge the widows' (and Quebecers') shared experience of trauma and to illustrate the consolidating effect of communal mourning. After Madame Bussières' testimony, "*Madame Bergeron rises to meet her*" and "*helps her to her seat*," and there is a profound "*silence*" in the courtroom (69). While this affirms the assembly/audience's awareness of the women's profound sorrow as well as the significant social-domestic damage engendered by their losses, it also functions as a formal moment of silence, uniting Quebecers in a communal act of remembrance and commemoration.

This moment in the play is particularly powerful, for it enables the play's continued function as a "site of memory" and, consequently, as a "site of mourning," enabling both personal and communal reparation. After the War, as Jay Winter argues, "sites of memory" (and, in particular, "[w]ar memorials") "were places where people grieved both individually and collectively" (*Sites* 79). While the trial would have afforded several of the bereaved to name and mourn those fallen in the conflict, communal healing after the Riots (and in the immediate aftermath of the October Crisis) was not performed on a far-reaching public scale until the appearance of the play. This might explain why the play, a "site of memory" countering traditional, stigmatizing depictions of Quebecers and acknowledging Quebec's collective trauma in the aftermath of occupation, was so widely attended in 1973.

Though there appears to have been only one subsequent production of *Québec, Printemps 1918* (at the Palais Montcalm in Quebec City in 2000) (Young 119), the play nevertheless remains of significant importance in Québécois collective memory. Certainly, the play, along with Provencher's book, influenced the representation of the Easter Riots in historical works and documentary films (Young 86–91, 93–104). Provencher and Lachance's work, however, also inspired the creation of two notable monuments in Quebec City. Young notes that "[b]y the mid 1970s, a few years after Provencher published his two works, the *Société nationale des Québécois* led a movement to commemorate the riots," and

"[o]n July 1st, 1978, [. . .] a group of Quebecers attended the unveil-
ing of a small plaque in Quebec City's Lower Town," which listed the
names of the deceased (106). In 1998, a larger, more attention-grabbing
monument, bearing the title of the play, was erected at the intersection
of Saint-Vallier, Saint-Joseph, and Bagot in Quebec City (where English-
Canadian soldiers were stationed during the Riots). This commemorative statue selectively remembers the Riots in much the same way as the
play—as its engraved history of the event makes abundantly clear—and

18.2 Aline Martineau's *Québec, Printemps 1918.* Used with permission of Aline Martineau.

18.3 Aline Martineau's *Québec, Printemps 1918.* Used with permission of Aline Martineau.

it echoes traditional war monuments, naming and honouring the deceased, remembering the occupation, and offering Quebecers a place for communal mourning.

The statue, however, is also indicative of the playwrights' (particularly Provencher's) historical legacy in Quebec. Young concludes, after an interview with Louis Bélanger, the civil servant who petitioned for the monument and assembled its committee (which included Provencher), that "Provencher's work [. . .] ultimately inspired this public remembrance" (85). The statue therefore suggests Provencher and Lachance's function as "'social agents,'" a term Winter employs to designate those "who do the work of remembrance" (*Remembering* 136). Winter notes that without these "'social agents,'" "collective memory would not exist" (136). Certainly, the statue's representation of Quebecers as innocent victims of English-Canadian wartime brutality appears to derive directly from Provencher and Lachance's work. This suggests that their resuscitation of history contributed to a "'fictive kinship'" (Winter 137) between Quebecers in the past and present. "'[F]ictive kin,'" as Winter also explains, are those who "share the imprint of history on their lives," and it is the people within these communities that "are the key agents of remembrance" (136). The monument, as well as the yearly commemoration at this "site of memory," therefore illustrates the play's function as a consolidating device, uniting members of a "fictive kinship" in a shared history of English-Canadian invasion, especially in the wake of the October Crisis. The play is worthy of further attention, however, not only because of its continued role in the formation of Québécois identity but also because it unsettles the mythic English-Canadian collective memory of the War by calling attention to its divisive effects in 1918 and, by extension, in the post-1970 context. This is particularly important as Canadians approach the War's 2014 centennial anniversary. What remains to be determined is the effects of the play's destabilizing representation of history in the wake of the extensive commemorative celebrations that are to come.

PART IV

·◆·

The Compulsion
to Remember:
Trauma and Witnessing

CHAPTER 19

•◆•

Under Surveillance: Memory, Trauma, and Genocide in Madeleine Thien's *Dogs at the Perimeter*

Robyn Morris

Angkar was all powerful.
Angkar never slept because the
Centre consisted of every one
of them, watching and
listening, reporting and
punishing. Everywhere you
are, there is the Centre.
Madeleine Thien, *Dogs at the Perimeter* 104

INTRODUCTION

The increase in human-induced atrocities such as genocide, intern-ment, war, and terrorist acts in the late twentieth and early twenty-first centuries, and the literary engagement with the aftermath of such acts upon the individual, family, community, and nation as depicted in con-temporary diasporic Asian writing, requires urgent study. Madeleine Thien's fictional examination of the Cambodian genocide in *Dogs at the Perimeter* (2011) is part of an emerging literary focus in Asian diasporic writing centring on issues of trauma and memory, disappearance, and surveillance.[1] Marianne Hirsch writes that research and theorizing about the workings of memory, trauma, and second-generation acts of trans-fer are moving outside of Holocaust studies to also include American slavery, the Vietnam War, and South African apartheid ("Generation"

---

1   See also Kim Echlin's *The Disappeared* (London: Abacus, 2009), Dionne Brand's *What We All Long For* (Toronto: Knopf, 2005), Alice Pung's *Her Father's Daughter* (Sydney: Black, 2011), and Vaddey Ratner's *In the Shadow of the Banyan* (New York: Simon & Schuster, 2012). Excerpts from *Dogs at the Perimeter* by Madeleine Thien (copyright 2011) are reprinted by permission of McClelland & Stewart.

104).[2] Writing that explores issues of memory, and, to use Dominick LaCapra's term, the "acting out" (*Writing History* 142) or transference of trauma, is a timely intervention in cultural and political discussion, particularly in the context of debates about whether the experience of trauma should, or should not, reflect policies on human rights and the perception and reception of refugees in particular countries of relocation. Thien's *Dogs at the Perimeter*, set in both Cambodia and Montreal, examines the suppression and recollection of trauma by a child survivor of the Cambodian genocide under the Khmer Rouge[3] and invites the wider, non-Cambodian transnational community to listen and respond with empathy to stories of Cambodian refugees. Thien's writing connects the past and present, emphasizing that cultural memory is subject to both self-suppression and revision.

Dogs at the Perimeter makes visible what is largely an invisible genocide; one that should resonate in contemporary cultural consciousness as an "enduring perpetual concern" (Jill Bennett 149). Thien notes the potential cultural impact of her fiction, stating that: "my work runs counter to the idea expressed by Cambodia's Prime Minister, Hun Sen: [who states] 'we should dig a hole and bury the past and look ahead to the 21st Century.'"[4] The novel contests this notion of "digging a hole" in its examination of how a child's experience of genocide has been suppressed and then re-remembered thirty years later in the adult narrator's life. The child, Janie, is adopted by Canadian parents, but her past hovers in her Canadian present. This experience is for Janie, to use Cathy Caruth's description of trauma stories, "unbearable" (7) . This is, significantly, a dual "unbearability" related to both "the nature of the event and the nature of its survival" (*Caruth,* Unclaimed 7). As Janie notes, she is indeed haunted:

---

2   As Paul Williams writes, "The elimination of many aspects of material life, a key phase of the Khmer Rouge revolution, meant that few reminders of the following three years and eight months survived. Money, markets, wages, and private property were abolished; universities, schools, banks, cultural institutions, government buildings, and places of worship were smashed; the use of foreign and minority languages was criminalised; religious practices and education were prohibited; families were disbanded" (234). This practice resulted in the deaths of nearly two million people, between a quarter to a third of the country's population.
3   The Khmer Rouge regime (officially named the Democratic Kampuchea DK) was headed by Pol Pot (born Saloth Sar). Its leaders were known as Angkar or the Organisation.
4   www.memorytheatre.tumblr.com/writing (accessed 2 July 2012).

> Night after night I tried to bring back the ones I had left behind. In the mornings when I opened my eyes, I saw only bare walls. Everything, the good and the selfish, the loved and the feared had taken refuge inside me. Thirty years later and still I remembered everything. (Thien 147)

On the verge of a breakdown which is precipitated by the disappearance of her friend and mentor Dr. Hiroji Matsui, Janie finds that she is no longer able to suppress the memories of the death and starvation of her loved ones. The narrator's recounting of both her experience and that of her brother Sopham's enforced role as a Khmer Rouge interrogator, of her mother's descent into starvation and madness, of witnessing her father being herded into a truck with other men that was taking them to the forest to be "educated," and her witnessing Sopham's drowning at sea when the boat on which they finally flee Cambodia is overtaken by Khmer pirates, enables us, as readers, to "listen to another's wound" (Caruth 7). Janie's "wound" is the memory of her experience of genocide. As these memories begin to overwhelm her consciousness in her Canadian present, we become aware that the experience of trauma has familial, communal, national, and international repercussions.

Thien's narrativizing of the lived experiences in the Cambodian Killing Fields in *Dogs at the Perimeter* urges a reassessment of the psychological, physical, and emotional impact of the genocide on survivors. As Janie recalls of her childhood experience of horror in Cambodia, "There was a memory at the edges of my consciousness but with great force of will, I manage to avert with my eyes" (Thien 37). Janie lives with what Gabrielle Schwab terms "haunting legacies—things hard to recount or even to remember, the results of a violence that hold an unrelenting grip on memory yet is deemed unspeakable" (1). Writing that speaks to both older and younger generations about refugees or "boat people," through narrations of first-hand experience or a second-generation re-telling of trauma, is culturally important in evoking empathic communal and national responses to claims for refugee status.[5] The act of writing therefore, has the possibility to become an act of empathic witnessing.

---

5   Marianne Hirsh defines such texts as "postmemorial fiction" characterized by an "attempt to represent the long-term effects of living in close proximity to the pain, depression and dissociation of persons who have witnessed and survived massive historical trauma" (2008 12).

As Jill Bennett argues, "For the memories of past subjects to be made vital—that is 'living'—in the full sense, they must in some way be inherited, opened up to empathic connection through their reembodiment in present imagination" (132). Thien's novel creates an "empathic connection" between reader and text, representing a real past in a fictionalized present and this has the possibility of prompting a readership not familiar with such horror to reassess their knowledge and beliefs of immigrant "otherness." As Judith Butler, referring to September 11, 2001, in the United States notes, "if we are interested in arresting cycles of violence to produce less violent outcomes, it is no doubt important to ask what, politically, might be made of grief besides a cry for war" (xii). In a lengthy interview, Thien indicates the pedagogical basis of her novel, acknowledging that despite occurring less than forty years ago, the Cambodian genocide hovers at the periphery of international consciousness:

> it's one of those genocides that seems to be known at the basic level—when you say "Khmer Rouge," people know—but after that, there's not a lot of knowledge. So how do you write about the aftermath or how do you write about Cambodia post-that or how do you write about Cambodian refugees if what they went through stays invisible? (Colbert 5)

Thien assumes a form of authorial ethics or "responsibility" and significantly begins her novel with the epigraph "tell the gods what is happening to me," taken from another haunting legacy of the Cambodian genocide, Haing Ngor's memoir, *Survival in the Killing Fields* (1987), which recounts years of deprivation, death, and hardship. Ngor's story emerged after he achieved international fame with his Oscar-winning performance as Best Supporting Actor in the 1984 film *The Killing Fields*. Ngor states in his Introduction that his performance as the fictional character Dith Pran in the film was "a matter of taking on a new identity and convincing others of it. [. . .] Waiting for the envelope to be opened and the winner announced, I was excited but my heart was at peace. Whatever happened I would accept because I knew my best performances were over before I left Cambodia. And the prize there was much greater" (Ngor 6). Using a similar trope, Thien explores the notion of performativity as a survival mechanism through an examination of the differing ways in which Janie and Sopham react to the daily threat of death and surveillance of self in their new lives under the Khmer Rouge regime. The trauma of Janie's two years in the Killing Fields is constantly played out in what she calls "the theatre of my mind" (Thien 24), and Sopham is described as "concealing himself like a stem overlaid with branches" (101), suggesting how lives under threat from starvation, disease, and torture initiate a reinvention of the self in order to survive.

SURVEILLANCE, POWER, AND GENOCIDE

The Prologue of *Dogs at the Perimeter* introduces the thematics of surveillance; of being seen and not seen, of performance and facades, with the seemingly benign statement that, "in a world of constant surveillance and high security, it is still remarkably easy to vanish" (Thien 1). There is, however, nothing benign, as is gradually revealed in the narrative, about the "disappearance" of over two million people following the Khmer Rouge takeover. Angkar, or the ubiquitous "Organisation," as the new regime was called, utilized the power of political and self-surveillance to brutal and horrific effect. This is a practice that could be aligned with what Nicolas Mirzoeff defines as "visuality's aura of authority" (479). The act of looking is a major structuring and ordering device of "normality,"[6] and, if "seeing is believing," as the saying goes, then, in Cambodian society after 17 April 1975, perceptions of "normality" were effectively blurred or obliterated. John Berger writes that "Seeing comes before words. The child looks and recognizes before it can speak" (7). However, Berger qualifies this statement, noting that

> there is also another sense in which seeing comes before words. It is seeing which establishes our place in the surrounding world; we explain the world with words but words can never undo the fact that we are surrounded by it. The relation between what we see and what we know is never settled. Each evening we *see* the sun set. We *know* that the earth is turning away from it. Yet the knowledge, the explanation never quite fits the sight. (7; italics in original)

---

6   Anne Cranny-Francis notes that early feminist critics emphasize the many ways in which the "normal" body was assumed to be male and suggests that this construction "is also a technology for maintaining the social dominance of a particular discursive positioning: Anglo, middle class, masculine, heterosexual and youthful to middle aged" (9).

This gap between knowledge and sight becomes a central area of investigation in *Dogs at the Perimeter*. The surveillance processes used by the Khmer Rouge regime to prevent mass insurrection following its evacuation of the entire city of Phnom Penh can be understood as an extreme and deadly example of panoptic vision.

In his essay "The Eye of Power," Michel Foucault equates vision with power, using as an example Bentham's model of the Panopticon, an architectural model in which institutionalized subjects can be observed within their cells from a single and centrally placed observation tower (*Power/Knowledge* 148). Based on a reversal of the dungeon theory, in which darkness is central to controlling the individual, panoptic vision derives its knowledge of the individual through surveillance from above. Control and power are maintained when the subject under surveillance internalizes the gaze and begins to police and categorize their own behaviour. The difference between seeing and being seen throughout the Cambodian genocide is based on inequitable power relations, and the domination of an entire country by the Khmer Rouge is perpetuated through both an external and internal surveillance of the self: "Angkar was all powerful. Angkar never slept because the Centre consisted of every one of them, watching and listening, reporting and punishing. Everywhere you are there is the Centre" (Thien 104). Identifying, maintaining, and surveying the division between the "April 17 people" (Thien 79), those who had been expelled from the cities, and the "pure, true Khmer" (79), the uneducated peasant class, is central to the race- and class-based polemics that underwrites the Khmer Rouge mandate. The all-seeing, all-pervasive, and fearful power of the invisible Angkar operates much like the all-seeing eye in Rene Magritte's "The False Mirror." Commenting on this painting, Arthur Kroker observes that

> Everything works within and under the suffocating gaze of the mirrored eye. Magritte's universe is one of terror. [. . .] There is no frontal oppression; no sovereign authority of a father-figure whose function is the incantation of the eternal "no." Instead, the terrorism of the world as a pure sign-system works at the symbolic level: a ceaseless and internal envelopment of its "subjects" in a symbolics of domination. (83)

Vision is used by the Khmer Rouge regime as a controlling device of identity, resulting in an internalization and tacit acceptance of the individual's loss of authority. This is indeed a false mirror, and the internalization of this form of terrorism is twofold. It results, for the individual, in a ceaseless surveillance of the physical self and concomitant surveillance of the psychological self. In this sense, "the projection of an inferior or demeaning image on another can actually distort and oppress, to the extent that the image is internalised" (Charles Taylor 37). This is the philosophical debate at the core of *Dogs at the Perimeter* and its extended engagement with the dehumanizing effects of genocide perpetuated by a relentless surveillance of people's lives and behaviour and an effacement of their cultural and familial ties. As such, Angkar insisted that the time after 17 April 1975, be known as Year Zero.

The result, for those who managed to survive, is a shared cultural memory of brutality. The act of being forced to witness torture and the deaths of family and friends accords the authority of the visual a macabre, psychological oppression. Shortly after their removal from Phnom Penh, Janie and her brother are forced to watch the strangulation of an elderly man, a former hotel manager, who is accused of betraying the regime because of his occupation and education: "My mother tried to turn our faces away but Kosal [the leader of their co-operative] rebuked her. [. . .] He told us to pay attention, to learn from this man's example. He said we must make ourselves strong and self-sufficient, we must never rely on anyone else, we must be clean inside because purity was strength" (Thien 83). This form of witnessing reinforces the fear that a similar fate awaits any who come to Angkar's attention. It effectively represses any physical or verbal dissent and it is this "foreclosure of critique [which] empties the public domain of debate and democratic contestation itself, so that debate becomes the exchange of views among the like-minded and criticism, which ought to be central to any democracy, becomes a fugitive and suspect activity" (Butler xx). The horror of witnessing mass killings by starvation and torture causes Janie and Sopham to retreat from reality and to invent new selves. Janie states that

> The Khmer Rouge had taught us how to survive, walking alone, carrying nothing in our hands. Belongings were slid away, then family and loved ones, and finally our loyalties and ourselves. Worthless or precious, indifferent or loved, all of our treasures had been treated the same. (39)

The novel is a search or recovery of this disappeared self, and upon the eventual death of her mother, Janie, then eleven years of age, writes that she was "fearful that Angkar would see my pain, [so] I hid in the forest. I asked myself how I had disappeared and why I could not remember the moment, the act" (125). In Canada, thirty years after this event, Janie continues to feel this same loss of self: "Someone says my Canadian name. Janie. [. . .] I look everywhere for Janie. There are no trees, no forest anywhere to keep the light from falling through" (64). Cathy Caruth, drawing on the work of Freud's *Beyond the Pleasure Principle* and *Moses and Monotheism*, defines trauma as an "accident" (6), an unexpected experience that is endured but not fully processed by the victim when it occurs. Trauma narratives do "not simply represent the violence of a collision but also convey the impact of its incomprehensibility. What continues to haunt the victim [. . .] is not only the reality of the violent event but also the reality of the way that its violence has not yet been fully known" (6). Janie's debilitating breakdown is the result of trying to suppress her memories of trauma for over three decades. She also understands that these memories will never be severed from her "self" for they have made her the person she is in the present: a researcher, wife, and mother. Janie states that she needed a repository in her mind that could hold "the things I needed to keep but that I could not live with. If such a library, a memory theatre, existed, I could be both who I was and who I had come to be" (147). The past and present collide, resulting in debilitation of the self for Janie.

As painful as Janie's breakdown is, the articulation of the historical act of genocide in literature could provide a prompt for Canadian and indeed world citizens to engage in a process of psychological reassessment or looking within. This would enable individuals to recognize the trauma of the transcultural citizen who has endured a forced dislocation. As Mirzoeff suggests, in the looking exchange "you find both the other and yourself. It means requiring the recognition of the other in order to have a place from which to claim a right and to determine what is right" (474). The right to look for victims in the Cambodian genocide is both taken from and used against Janie. The leader of her rural co-operative further instructs the relocated and "impure" city people on how to behave:

> we must abandon our diseased selves, we had to cut loose our dreams, our impurities, our worldly attachments. To pray, to grieve the missing,

to long for the old life, all these [are] forms of betrayal, Memory sick-
ness Kosal called it. An illness of the mind. (79)

This use of metaphors of disease and moral cleanliness and mantras such
as "Let us dignify the unlettered and eradicate the learned" (103) are
indicative of the regime's determination to use language as another controlling device of behaviour (see Marston). This worked to obliterate any
familial or cultural ties to the past, reducing the individual to an isolated
self. It is for this reason that we are never told Janie's birth name and we
only know her in Cambodia as Mei, the name she has been given by the
Khmer Rouge. Renaming becomes another Khmer Rouge tactic of obliteration and subterfuge surveillance. Sopham is renamed Rithy, and Janie
is told by a leader in her village that "If you want to be strong you have
to become someone else. You have to take a new name," which is both an
effacement of the former self and a performance to ensure survival (93).
Names, extracted under torture, were also used by the Khmer Rouge as
way of tracing perceived enemies of the regime. Assuming a new name
could be understood as an act of self-preservation enabling the former
"impure" individual to disappear from one's familial origins and therefore from Angkar's all-pervasive sight.

Janie and her brother's stories are underpinned by a narrative of
covertness, and both realize that in order to survive one needs to enact
a resistance of subterfuge. As a torturer and interrogator, Rithy understands that in order to survive "he must cleave his soul" (106). He
extracts stories and falsified confessions with the aim of dehumanizing
the individual, but in doing this, Rithy's right to an innocent childhood is obliterated along with his sense of self: "Rithy existed and survived. He waited and kept his hand and his face impeccably clean but
inside, there was someone else, a boy who watches, who had no need
for language, who saw everything but never spoke" (113). Rithy understands both the power of language and the safety of silence. His
cleansing of his hands with water after the repeated violence he enacts in the torture cells enables him to distance himself psychologically
from the event. His eventual death at sea by drowning can be read in
two ways. Firstly, this is the ultimate "cleansing" and it symbolically
restores Rithy to his innocent, pre-genocide self. It could, however, indicate Thien's understanding of the problematics of citizenship. How
would multicultural Canada embrace an individual such as Rithy who

is a known child perpetrator of violence? Thien's engagement with the trauma of genocide, and with the effects or wounds inflicted upon children totally ill-equipped to deal with such visceral and psychological horror, urges a reassessment of both the physical and emotional impact of the genocide on survivors. They are, as Felman writes about survivors of the Jewish Holocaust, "neither its perpetrators nor its most immediate and most devastated victims, but its historical *onlookers*; it *witnesses*" (96).

The forced biographies which Rithy extracts from his victims who arrive at the prison blindfolded and tied with rope, and which the Documentation Centre of Cambodia, located in Phnom Penh, now uses to help families trace those who disappeared, are artifacts of and witnesses to a sustained suppression of human rights. They operate as engravings and a grave, for the interrogator's role is to "trace all lines to the enemy, to lay bare the networks of connections and then to follow this taint to every corner of the country" (107). The regime also systematically photographed these prisoners, removing their blindfolds and subjecting them to the glare of the flashbulb before leading them to the torture cells. The brutal efficiency of the Khmer Rouge regime was that it used the oppressed and the persecuted to participate in and hasten the demise of themselves, their family, their community, and their nation. Torture is bound up with writing and surveillance, but this is a story that cannot be told in all its truth. These biographies are confessions of torture, and they resonate symbolically as performances or scenes of power and control that are hidden from sight. Rithy is an eight-year-old murderer, one of the regime's faceless interrogators who "were pulling truth from the bleakest corners, they were the hands and eyes of Angkar" (106). The biographies, then, are both evidence of torture and a performance of oppression. Janie notes:

> Every person, no matter their status with the Khmer Rouge, had to dictate their life story or write it down. We had to sign our names to these biographies, and we did this over and over, naming family and friends, illuminating the past. My little brother and I were only eight and ten years old, but, even then, we understood that the story of one's life could not be trusted, that it could destroy you and all the people you loved. (25)

While testimonies are most normally associated with the truth, these biographies encourage us to reflect on the nature of truth and the link between an "illuminated" past or cultural memory. The act of telling, recording, listening, and responding is chilling in that these biographies were never meant for other family members to remember a life but were recorded for the purposes of further genocidal action. The Cambodian testimonies, written or narrated under extraordinary conditions, including torture and impending death of family members, are simultaneously individual while functioning as stories of an imploding nation. They narrate the life of the individual but they are written only because of coercion and are therefore linked inextricably to the reality of an otherwise unspeakable horror and violence that was occurring outside of the torture chamber, and across the whole of Cambodia.

Human-induced catastrophes, such as the Cambodian and Rwandan genocides, 9/11, and the Bali bombings are beginning to be "witnessed" in literature. The importance of such literary engagement is not simply to evoke an empathic response from the reader but to promote, as Anne Kaplan writes, a better "understanding of injustices—that an injustice has taken place—rather than focussing on a specific case. [. . .] Art that invites us to bear witness to injustice goes beyond moving us to identify with and help a specific individual, and prepares us to take responsibility for preventing future occurrences" (Kaplan 23). The narrativizing of how an entire city is force-marched to the countryside, placed in agrarian communities where children and adults worked from dawn until darkness, and fed watery broth with a few grains of rice, and where disappearances or torture by anyone suspected of betraying the ideals of Angkar became regular occurrences, evokes, for this reader at least, a politics of discomfort.

Thien's writing is characterized by two cultural or political affects. Firstly, by what Dominick LaCapra terms "empathic unsettlement," which he defines as

The study of traumatic events poses especially difficult problems in representation and writing both for research and for any dialogic exchange with the past which acknowledges the claims it makes on people and relates it to the present and future. Being responsive to the traumatic experience of others, notably of victims, implies not the appropriation of their experience but what I would call *empathic unsettlement*, which should have stylistic effects, or more broadly, effects in writing which cannot be reduced to formulas or rules or method. (*Writing History* 41; emphasis added)

The second is what Jill Bennett, with resonances of LaCapra's notion of "unsettlement," terms a "politics of empathy" (Bennett 151). In examining Thien's novel, a critical question underpinning one's analysis is whether the trauma that is invoked has more to do with the experience of having survived genocide than with the experience of violent, sustained, and daily encounters with death. As Janie states, "I remembered arriving in Canada, my stomach clenched, ashamed that I had lived yet terrified of disappearing. Chance had favoured us but chance had denied so many others" (21). The politics of trauma as fictionalized by Thien is not so much a case of to look or not to look back—but of finding a balance, for the traumatized subject and for the family, community, and nation they are part of. Thien's work is compelling for the way in which it signals an acceleration away from the current and popularized tradition of writing the immigrant story as a geographical move from hardship to a place of prosperity and peace. She refuses to emphasize the story of geographical transition as the dominant trope of memorialization. Instead, Thien places an emphasis on the notion of transculturality. The memory of the destruction of Janie's family and Cambodian culture is suppressed as she grows up in Canada, embracing its lifestyle, attending university, marrying a Canadian citizen, and, for over thirty years, giving a performance of a non-traumatized self. Thien's novel, however, is not a happy immigrant story. Janie does break down under the weight of her memories, and it is this which makes it so politically compelling. Commenting on fiction by immigrant, ethnic, and Native writers in a Canadian context, Fred Wah writes that in the process of textualizing an experience such as trauma, "for some writers this entails an alignment with mainstream and traditional strategies while for others the tactics of refusal and reterritorialisation offer a more appropriate poetics" (51).

In this sense, Thien employs a "tactics of refusal," for her novel is critically aware in its examination of the role of literature in its exploration of the link between a personal memory of a historical atrocity and the transcultural citizen. Judith Butler argues that although images of war atrocities "might act on us" (68), they do not "produce ethical pathos" (69). Drawing on Sontag's work, Butler notes that viewing such photographs produces only a momentary response to the horror, "the pathos conveyed by narrative forms, by contrast 'does not wear out'" (69). This is the mobilizing or affective role of *Dogs at the Perimeter*. Thien's novel is part of an increasing literary engagement with a largely unphotographed genocide. The novel's importance for cultural memory is not, as Rosemary Buikema in reference to J.M. Coetzee's *Disgrace* argues, "in the way a literary work informs a reader about a historical context, but certainly also in what it generates as a literary event" (188).[7] If reading stories, as either fiction or memoir, about acts of human rights violations can mobilize individual and collective empathic responses, compelling readers to rethink assumptions about refugees, about coercion, and about the need for humankind to resist and take responsibility for such acts, then this is the potential power of literature. What Thien's novel makes clear is that trauma cannot be totally suppressed or erased but needs to be understood by the person who is subject to the traumatic experience, by the second generation living closely to it, and by the nation in which people such as the fictionalized Janie have sought refuge from persecution. The attempt, by the Khmer Rouge, to eradicate cultural memory by creating Year Zero fails because of Janie's return to both her happy and her horrific past. The novel moves our understanding of the trauma of genocide beyond memories internalized by the individual into that of the cultural, which potentially renders the writing of trauma a political act.[8] Thien uses a fictional depiction of witnessing to suggest how the trauma of the Cambodian genocide shapes individuals and communities. Arguably, the act of reading about a traumatic memory involving a horrific past has the potential to impact the future through a form of affective cultural inheritance, enabling what Bennett describes as its "reembodiment in present imagination" (132).

7   A well-known example would be Joy Kogawa's much-lauded *Obasan*. The publication of this book, the first by a Japanese Canadian, prompted consciousness-raising about human rights abuses enacted through internment. The book became a powerful catalyst for social change.
8   Jill Bennett ascribes a similar political phenomenon to the depiction of trauma in art (150–53).

CHAPTER 20

•◆•

"I didn't want to tell a story like this": Cultural Inheritance and the Second Generation in David Chariandy's *Soucouyant*

Farah Moosa

David Chariandy's *Soucouyant* (2007) raises important questions about cultural memory, inheritance, and second-generation immigrant Canadians. In the opening of Chariandy's novel, an unnamed second-generation Canadian protagonist, the son of an Afro-Trinidadian mother and an Indo-Trinidadian father, returns to his mother Adele's Scarborough, Ontario, home after being away for two years. Unable to deal with Adele's degeneration due to her early-onset dementia and unable to listen to her endlessly repeat fragments from a traumatic event that occurred during her childhood in Trinidad, the protagonist tries to find solace in central Toronto at age seventeen. Adele does not intend to reveal the hidden truths of her past, truths she had repressed but forgets to forget in her condition, and pieces of her story slip out over time, becoming retold almost compulsively. What interests me is how the protagonist's decision to leave his mother is prompted not only by the difficulty of living with a parent with dementia, but by his need to escape from the repetition of her stories, a need that, at times, seems to exceed his desire to escape from the content and meaning of the stories themselves. Though Adele mainly refers to the event in which she mistakenly caused a terrible fire during the Second World War American occupation of Trinidad in the guise of an encounter with a *soucouyant* (a vampiric spirit from Caribbean folklore), and though the protagonist senses that this figure also intimately connects him with his cultural and familial past, he is haunted by what becomes its palpable presence in his life through overexposure, and so he wants to forget about it. Yet,

Acknowledgements: My thanks to Donald Goellnicht, Lorraine York, Daniel Coleman, and the editors of this volume for their thoughtful comments on earlier drafts of this paper.

as Chariandy tells Kit Dobson, "[o]bviously, because Adele is now forgetting her past in Trinidad, the burden of memory is thrust upon her Canadian-born and raised son" ("Spirits" 813). *Burden* signals both the protagonist's responsibility to adequately remember his cultural and familial past as a performer of cultural memory for Adele, as well as the weight of this task, a weight that contributes to his desire to forget. I use the term *performer* in light of Mieke Bal, Jonathan Crewe, and Leo Spitzer's belief, expressed in *Acts of Memory* (1999), that "cultural recall is not merely something of which you happen to be a bearer but something that you actually *perform*, even if, in many instances, such acts are not consciously and wilfully contrived" (Bal vii). For the protagonist, the performance of cultural memory is in tension with his own capacity to engage in such work, a situation that is complicated by a sense of filial duty to know, understand, and remember the past as Adele's condition worsens and by the fact that her story is traumatic.

In this paper, I explore the significance of the protagonist's predicament as well as the emplacement of the spectral figure of the soucouyant in his life. What becomes clear in a reading of Chariandy's novel is the centrality of the soucouyant to the novel's themes of cultural memory and generational identity. Subtitled "A Novel of Forgetting," the book attends not only to individual processes of remembering and forgetting associated with Adele's condition and the larger historical forgetting of the American occupation of Trinidad and its effects on the local population alongside the twin legacies of the slave trade and indentured labour, but also the push–pull between memory and forgetting that can characterize diasporic subjectivities in a Canadian setting.[1] I examine how Chariandy mobilizes the soucouyant as a way to demonstrate the complex cultural legacies that are inherited, consciously and unconsciously, by second-generation Canadians from their birthplace and ancestral homeland, legacies that may create tension between the desire to remember and

---

1 For a study of what Trinidadians have called the "American occupation" of Trinidad, see Harvey Neptune. On 2 September 1940, the British colony of Trinidad became conscripted into the Allied cause when British prime minister Winston Churchill and American president Franklin Roosevelt signed a bases-for-destroyers deal under which the United States was allowed to build naval and air bases on several British West Indian islands in exchange for fifty destroyers. The largest military installations were put in Trinidad, and the American presence of upwards of twenty-five thousand troops in an island of just under half a million people deepened internal struggles among a diverse and divergent populace. Neptune characterizes the occupation (1941–47) as a time of "epochal" change in the island's history (1).

to forget. Furthermore, I argue that, in *Soucouyant*, Chariandy asks the difficult questions of when, how, and to what extent it is productive for second-generation diasporic subjects to remember and re-imagine diasporic histories, especially where traumatic histories are concerned. Paul Connerton draws attention to our general valorization of memory and undervaluing of forgetting, noting that, in common belief, "remembering and commemoration is usually a virtue and [. . .] forgetting is necessarily a failing" (59). Unravelling the different types of acts that fall under the term *to forget*, Connerton suggests that in individual cases where remembering creates "too much cognitive dissonance," certain "small acts of forgetting" may be desirable or even necessary because "[w]hat is allowed to be forgotten provides living space for present projects" and allows new memories to form (63).[2] Bearing in mind Connerton's discussion, I suggest that what is at stake for the protagonist is this need for a "living space."[3]

I

Chariandy demonstrates how the diasporic past haunts his protagonist through the prevalence of the soucouyant. As Dobson observes, there seems to be "something deliberately layered or palimpsestic about how the figure [. . .] appears in the book" (810). Appearing in both the formal elements of the text, as well as in various reincarnations throughout the narrative, the soucouyant is ever-present. The novel opens with an epigraph: *"Old skin, 'kin, 'kin, / You na know me, / You na know me . . ."* (n.p.). This is the song that a soucouyant croons to the skin she wears as a disguise by day if she returns from her nightly activities to find that someone in her village has filled it with salt in order to make it unwearable for her. If the soucouyant accidentally puts on the skin, it will burn

---

2   These types of forgetting, which have various agents, functions, and values, include "repressive erasure; prescriptive forgetting; forgetting that is constitutive in the formation of a new identity; structural amnesia; forgetting as annulment; forgetting as planned obsolescence; forgetting as humiliated silence" (Connerton 59).

3   In an article on the registers in which cultural memory is performed in *Soucouyant*, Jennifer Bowering Delisle also addresses how the protagonist is overwhelmed by Adele's memories; however, my analysis is distinct from Delisle's due to its focus on the tension between memory and forgetting in *Soucouyant* as well as on the significance of forgetting for second-generation Canadian diasporic subjects. Delisle argues that cultural memory is performed as "inherited trauma or 'postmemory,' diasporic histories, national mythologies, and powerful nostalgias" in Chariandy's novel (3).

her; if she does not wear it, she will either burn when she is exposed to sunlight or she may be identified and punished by other villagers. The soucouyant is a feared creature, for though "[s]he lives a reclusive but fairly ordinary life on the edge of town" as an old woman by day, "at night she'll shed her disguise and travel across the sky as a ball of fire," hunting an unsuspecting sleeper in order to suck his or her blood (*Soucouyant* 135). If an individual wakes up tired, pale, or with a "tell-tale bruise or mark," he or she may have been visited by a soucouyant (135). Giselle Liza Anatol provides a helpful genealogy of the soucouyant, suggesting that notions of the vampire in Victorian England might have influenced early documentation about the figure as vampires were likely familiar to the Europeans who travelled to the Caribbean and recorded oral stories about the soucouyant (39). Such notions, Anatol indicates, may have also resulted in the creation of a Caribbean soucouyant that is usually female, unlike its West African counterpart, the Akan figure of the *obayfo*, which is a male or female figure that sheds its skin and becomes a ball of fire (40, 41). However, the French origin of the word *soucouyant* shows that the legend may have been influenced by French oral traditions as well. Most significantly, as Chariandy indicates, the word *soucouyant* (and presumably, by extension, the legend) is likely "intimately familiar" to "residents and first-generation immigrants from specific Caribbean islands like Trinidad" ("Spirits" 810). By titling his novel *Soucouyant* and using the spirit's song as its epigraph, Chariandy demonstrates how, for the protagonist, cultural memories of the diasporic past are distant and yet intimately close.

In "Spirits," Chariandy himself speaks to these concerns:

> I wanted my title to suggest that the protagonist of the novel, a second-generation Caribbean immigrant based in Canada, was engaging with a cultural legacy that seemed, at least on the surface, to be attached to a very different space, a legacy that seemed, at times, to be remote, other-worldly, and spectral, and yet hauntingly present at the same time. The soucouyant functioned for me as a means to explore the language and "ghosts" of precisely such a "remote" cultural legacy. (811)

By placing the spectral figure of the soucouyant in Scarborough, Chariandy indicates how the "language and 'ghosts'" of the protagonist's diasporic past, including histories of colonial violence and their trickle-down effects, form an integral part of his present. Avery Gordon, in *Ghostly Matters* (2008), suggests that "[h]aunting and the appearance of specters or ghosts is one way [. . .] we are notified that what's been concealed is very much alive and present, interfering precisely with those always incomplete forms of containment and repression ceaselessly directed toward us" (xvi). For Gordon, "haunting, unlike trauma, is distinctive for producing a something-to-be-done" (xvi). In the protagonist's case, this "something-to-be-done" involves remembering his mother and late father's past in Trinidad in a way that allows him to find a balance between the desire to remember and to forget. Indeed, as I will discuss later, *soucouyant* is the word that the protagonist unconsciously mumbles in his sleep and that contributes to his decision to return to Adele once he is made aware of his utterances (Chariandy, *Soucouyant* 32). *Soucouyant*, in this instance, also signals "what's been concealed" by the protagonist in his attempt at forgetting the past by leaving home—his own cultural past. Daniel Coleman lends further insight into the figure of the soucouyant in Chariandy's novel, suggesting that "if we read for the trace of the remote cultural legacy that Chariandy gestures towards in the [above] statement," it places Adele's history and memory "alongside, if not directly within, a long-held set of community beliefs and ritualistic practices" (63). Coleman's observation draws attention to the multiple and layered meanings the soucouyant holds for the protagonist, including connections between the seemingly spectral diasporic and the personal, familial, cultural, and spiritual realms.

Chariandy also makes clear the haunting presence of the soucouyant in his protagonist's life through the handwritten script that appears above each of the six chapters in the novel. Drawn by artist Cindy Mochizuki, each chapter number is preceded by script that illustrates the protagonist's older brother's attempts at spelling the word *soucouyant*. For instance, the first chapter begins with a backward letter *s*, the crossed-out segment *so*, and finally the segment *su* (7). The second chapter begins with a mostly indecipherable scribbled-out attempt to spell out the first syllable of the word *soucouyant* and then a crossed-out second attempt alongside the first: *sooucy* (37). By the sixth chapter, the word is spelled almost correctly: *soucouyan* (173). Only the silent *t* is missing, a spelling error which, in its intimation that subjects who are not entirely familiar with the word may forget about the letter, gestures towards the idea that the figure will always retain a mysterious quality for second-generation subjects. Though the older brother's attempts to spell the word *soucouy-ant* generally become more accurate from chapter to chapter, the error points toward his futile attempts to grasp the figure by spelling her name.[4] In these ways, the book demonstrates how the protagonist and his brother grew up with the shadowy presence of the soucouyant and the diasporic past she represents or embodies while also highlighting the fragmentary nature of their knowledge. As Chariandy suggests, the soucouyant offered a way "to explore a particular generational condition, a particular state of sensing but not really knowing one's origins, and, consequently, a particular process of exploring one's origins without easy recourse to official meanings or narratives" ("Spirits" 811). In the protagonist's case, this generational condition, a second-generation diasporic subjectivity, is complicated not only by the limits of official narratives which offer imperial perspectives on or touristic versions of Trinidad, as evidenced by the history books and a travel guidebook ordered by a well-intentioned community librarian named Mrs. Cameron, but by Adele's repression of her memories and the ways in which they resurface.[5]

Adele's repressed memories of the traumatic fire, together with her condition, result in the protagonist learning about his familial past not only in fragments, but often in sudden and accidental ways, giving him little or no time to mentally prepare for the stories that he is to be told. Recounting a conversation he had with Adele as her dementia worsened, the protagonist says: "Mother never deliberately explained to me her past, but I learned anyway. Of lagahoos, and douens, and other specters of long-ago meaning. 'Soucouyant,' Mother said aloud to herself one day. 'I saw one in the morning. A morning thick with burnt light. I walking a narrow path of dirt, you see, my ankles painted cool by wet grasses . . .'" (23). This passage indicates how the protagonist learned about various Trinidadian spirits in the same breath as he heard his mother's story about her encounter with a soucouyant, a story which covers over her

---

4   In a note in her essay on fictional Canadian Alzheimer's narratives, Wendy Roy reads the script headings differently, suggesting that "Chariandy's book focuses on [Adele's] loss of lexical ability by labelling each chapter with a failed attempt to spell *soucouyant*" (59, note 4).

5   For instance, the travel book Mrs. Cameron orders is published by a cruise-ship company and features a full-colour illustration of "a black man playing a steel pan, an impossibly huge smile on his face" (Chariandy, *Soucouyant* 136–37). The protagonist encounters the word *soucouyant* in a glossary at the back, amidst words like *saga boy* and *sorrel*, leading him to cynically conclude: "My history is a travel guidebook. My history is a creature nobody really believes in. My history is a foreign word" (137).

memory of the fatal fire, leaving him to sort through, piece together, and contextualize various narratives. As Chariandy's readers learn by the end of the novel, when Adele was a child, she and her mother were forcibly moved from the village of Chaguaramas to Carenage when the American military bases were established in Trinidad. Due to the dislocation, Adele's mother had to work as a prostitute in order to support herself and Adele. During a confrontation with some soldiers, Adele's mother was soaked with a waste pail of solvents and gasoline, and without realizing that she had been splashed with some of the liquid herself, Adele, in a mixture of panic, confusion, and rebellion, lit a flame on her mother's sleeve with the lighter a soldier had presented to her earlier, setting them both on fire. The context of Adele's actions demonstrates that she is in many ways a victim of colonial forces; however, her guilt has become internalized and the memory repressed until her condition results in her saying "aloud to herself one day" that which she never meant to voice (23).

Though Adele did not plan to speak about her traumatic past, this silence is also consistent with her and her late husband Roger's general silence about their diasporic past since they immigrated to and met in Canada. Thinking about his parents' relationship in 1960s Toronto, the protagonist says, "They are here now, and they have almost no interest in their respective pasts" (73). Adele and Roger's lack of interest in their past seems rooted in a desire to distance themselves from their difficult memories of it, as well as in their hope for a better life in Canada. Although Roger has not experienced a direct trauma, he is haunted by his diasporic history, as the sign of the soucouyant, a "pin-prick beauty mark on the back of his wrist," suggests (25). Roger has inherited the legacies of indentured labour in the Caribbean, for his Tamil ancestors were brought from Madras (now Chennai) to work on plantations. Thus, he remembers that his ancestors' narratives included "[h]ushed stories of desperate flights, of cutlasses and sweat. Bodies broken in the canefields" (79). He also knows that they were Tamil, for his grandfather could speak the language (79). Yet he remembers little else about his ancestral heritage, save for certain "surviving rituals of belief" from Madras, like the fire coal walking done "by his grandfather and men of his generation on certain obscure days" and some songs, such as the beginning of the Tamil folk lullaby he often hums: "*Araaroo ariraroo . . .*" (79). Roger's characterization of the lullaby as "'just a scrap of something gone" indicates that, for him, the diasporic past is painful due to the losses involved with the transatlantic migration, losses made worse by the fact that when his ancestors migrated, "it didn't involve circumstances that anyone had thought important to remember and pass on" (79). Roger's past, along with Adele's condition, further highlights the responsibility the protagonist has as a performer of cultural memory for his family, as well as the weight of this endeavour.

II

In a key passage on the tension between memory and forgetting in the novel, the protagonist states:

> I'll explain it this way. During our lives, we struggle to forget. And it's foolish to assume that forgetting is altogether a bad thing. Memory is a bruise still tender. History is a rusted pile of blades and manacles. And forgetting can sometimes be the most creative and life-sustaining thing that we can ever hope to accomplish. The problem happens when we become too good at forgetting. When somehow we *forget* to forget, and we blunder into circumstances that we consciously should have avoided. This is how we awaken to the stories buried deep within our sleeping selves or trafficked quietly through the touch of others. This is how we're shaken by vague scents or tastes. How we're stolen by an obscure word, an undertow dragging us back and down and away. (32)

The protagonist's point that forgetting is not "altogether a bad thing" and may, in fact, be "creative and life-sustaining" is significant, for it allows him to intimate that a forgetting of the past—as well as a remembering of it—has its place. As Chariandy states, "[f]orgetting is perhaps how we first survive a traumatic event," carefully noting that he is referring to "the forgetting of the subject who endures trauma, not the forgetting of those who deny the traumas of others" ("Spirits" 813). Adele engages in this type of forgetting in her childhood due to the traumatic fire. Roger, too, "has learned to live through forgetting," for his ancestral history, "due to the oppression associated with caste, race, and wealth, could not easily have been remembered" ("Spirits" 814). Chariandy's references to memory as "a bruise still tender" and history as "a rusted pile of blades and manacles" reinforces the idea that forgetting can be beneficial, for it points toward the potential painfulness of cultural memory. The images of the rusted blades and manacles evoke the legacies of indentured labour and the transatlantic slave trade. Yet Chariandy's reference is canny, for it draws attention to the significance of forgetting while at the same time reminding his readers about these histories and legacies. In this way, Chariandy gestures towards a space for individual acts of forgetting at times when the past is too painful, without actually forgetting larger histories. These individual acts, to borrow Connerton's language, might best be described as "small acts of forgetting," for they are not complicit with dominant forms of power (63).

Through the protagonist's meditation, Chariandy also considers the value of forgetting for second-generation diasporic Canadian subjects. As the protagonist's use of the pronoun *we* in the passage shows, he includes himself in this discussion. Indeed, by leaving Adele, the protagonist was engaging in a project of forgetting, for Toronto allowed him to find his "anonymity in a series of rent-by-the-week rooms" and "under-the-counter jobs" (30). In addition, the protagonist also "met others who were fleeing their pasts, the discontents of nations and cultures, tribes and families" (30). Yet, as the ironic undertone in his reference to various discontents shows, such a project cannot (and should not) be entirely successful. Connerton's discussion of "forgetting that is constitutive in the formation of a new identity" (the third type of forgetting he outlines and under which "small acts of forgetting" are included) is helpful for my analysis (62). In this type of forgetting, Connerton says, "[t]he emphasis [. . .] is not so much on the loss entailed in being unable to retain certain things as rather on the gain that accrues to those who know how to discard memories that serve no practicable purpose in the management of one's current identity and ongoing purposes" (63). Bearing in mind Connerton's discussion, I suggest that while Chariandy's protagonist left home due to his need for a "living space," Toronto only offers him a temporary respite because he cannot simply discard the cultural memories he has inherited from Adele through an absence; these memories are a part of his "current identity and ongoing purposes."

Soucouyant also indicates the impossibility or implausibility of a total forgetting through its discussion of intergenerational transmission. The passage appears in the Toronto scene in which the protagonist's friend wakes him up because, in his sleep, he has been saying what his friend hears as "sookooya" (32). *Soucouyant* functions as the "obscure word" that influences or, rather, symbolically drags the protagonist in an undertow, away from his respite and back towards Adele after two years away. Drawing on Marianne Hirsch's concept of "postmemory," Jennifer Bowering Delisle points out that in the last few lines of the passage, the protagonist himself becomes the subject of the narrative: "Stories, we are told, can be 'trafficked' simply though touch, and the mother's trauma, represented by the memory of the soucouyant, has been transmitted to the son, surfacing in these unbidden corporeal responses" (5). Hirsch defines postmemory as "the relationship that the 'generation after' bears to the personal, collective, and cultural trauma of those who came be-fore—to experiences they 'remember' only by means of the stories, im-ages, and behaviors among which they grew up" (Generation 5). She also notes that "these experiences were transmitted to them so deeply and affectively as to *seem* to constitute memories in their own right" (5). Delisle's observation draws my attention to the multiple ways in which the protagonist has inherited and cannot avoid (and yet has become too close to) his mother's stories. As Hirsch puts it, "[t]o grow up with over-whelming inherited memories, to be dominated by narratives that pre-ceded one's birth or one's consciousness, is to risk having one's own life stories displaced, even evacuated, by our ancestors" (5).

The ways in which Adele's stories impinge on the protagonist's psy-chological space are evident in his response to her soucouyant story and her questions about the fire. In a scene in which Adele traces the "lacy script" along her chin and then looks at her newly returned son, her "face a question" about these scars whose origin she cannot remember, the protagonist explains: "'Chaguaramas [. . .]. There was a fire. Your chin was cut and an old woman healed you with cobwebs'" (35). His straight-forward explanation, which skips over Adele's role in the fire, indicates his awareness of the things Adele usually mentions in her own retelling of this story—the village, the fire, the chin cut on a rock, and an old healer who used cobwebs to soothe the burns—for he has heard it many times.[6] Yet as the protagonist's unwillingness to mention Adele's role in the fire shows, he may be protecting not just his mother, but himself, from her story. Furthermore, though Adele asks him about the cobwebs as she tries to remember what they were used for, the protagonist replies:

---

6   See Adele's telling of the same story during the protagonist's youth for comparison. Adele begins her narrative after the fire has already been set, when her mother "'loss she skin at the military base in Chaguaramas'" (Chariandy, *Soucouyant* 24).

"'It doesn't matter, Mother. It happened long ago. A faraway place'" (35). His response shows his own desire to cast aside the difficult past by trying to locate it in another time and place.

In another scene, the protagonist cuts off his mother's retelling of her soucouyant story, losing patience with her, for it is a story he has heard often. The protagonist states:

> "It happen . . ." she begins, "It happen one fore-day morning when the sun just a stain on the sky. When the moon not under as yet. Me, I was a young girl running from home. Running 'pon paths so old that none could remember they origin. My ankle paint cool, cool by the wet grasses. I run and stumble into a clearing with an old mango knotting up the sky with it branch. The fallen fruit upon the ground. They skin all slick and black. The buzz of drunken insect. . . ." (45)

Without letting her finish her sentence, the protagonist says: "'You saw a soucouyant, Mother'" (45). This prompts Adele to shout, "'*Child? Is I* telling this story or is *you*?'" (45). The chorus-like quality of Adele's narrative, together with the protagonist's impatient response, signals how, for him, the story of the soucouyant has become a tale as familiar as an old song. Furthermore, this particular narrative also becomes a kind of chorus in the text, one a reader might look forward to coming across precisely for its familiar song-like quality, which includes visual imagery and figurative language. In this way, Chariandy uses literary language to indicate to his readers how Adele's story may elicit the opposite response in his protagonist.[7] As the protagonist knows, the soucouyant Adele believes she came across is in fact her mother, who, like the soucouyant, became a ball of fire.

The above passage appears as the last in a series of "very difficult moments" that the protagonist notes he experienced with Adele upon his return (42). In recounting these moments, the protagonist moves from the relatively mundane to the painful. For instance, he first notes how "Mother might accuse [him] of stealing the avocado 'pear' that was ripening in the fruit bowl when there was never one there to begin with" (42). Next, he mentions how Adele pulled a steak knife on him when she

---

7   For a detailed discussion of various textual mediums and the transmission of trauma, see Hirsch's *The Generation of Postmemory.*

feared he was a dangerous stranger, leaving him to wonder whether, "[i]f she were to act, would she understand the result? The red oil leaking from the young man's body" (43). He also mentions the moment when he and Adele have "fun together for the first time since [his] return" by dancing together and hugging "warmly," until his mother "kisses [him] passionately on the mouth," forcing him to "jerk violently free" (44). Lastly, he refers to her stories. As the protagonist's discussion indicates, Adele's endless storytelling is painful for him, perhaps even more painful than his mother's mistakenly placed kiss.

Chariandy draws further attention to the value of forgetting in the scene in which the protagonist notices an underlined passage in a well-worn copy of Friedrich Nietzsche's 1874 essay, *On the Advantage and Disadvantage of History for Life*: ". . . *it is possible to live with almost no memories, even to live happily as the animal shows; but without forgetting it is quite impossible to live at all. Or, to say it more simply yet: there is a degree of insomnia, of rumination, of historical sense which injures every living thing and finally destroys it, be it a man, a people or a culture . . .*" (54). The protagonist knows little about Nietzsche save for the fact that he is a philosopher, a "'*German* philosopher,'" and uses these facts to try and impress Meera, the book's owner and another second-generation charac-ter in the novel (54). Meera received the book in a box of random titles from the protagonist's older brother and seems to have little interest in indulging the protagonist's attempt at conversation. Yet Chariandy's use of the intertextual reference is noteworthy, for it outlines Nietzsche's perspec-tive on the significance of forgetting, especially where injury is involved. Connerton classifies Nietzsche's perspective as "forgetting as annulment," a type of forgetting which "flows from a surfeit of information" (64). This "surfeit of information" that the protagonist experiences is exemplified by the consequences of his overexposure to Adele's history and stories—he becomes overwhelmed to the point of wishing for an escape from his aging mother. Though the protagonist returns to his mother and takes good care of her, he again harbours the thought that, somewhat like Adele, he is "also losing [himself], going [his] own way," and may need to leave again (132).

III

At the end of *Soucouyant*, readers learn that the protagonist recounted the story of his mother's diasporic past to her before he left for Toronto. The protagonist begins his narrative by stating: "There was once a girl named

Adele. She was the sort of girl who always seemed to be elsewhere" (180). Drawing on Bal's claim that "[t]o enter memory, the traumatic event of the past needs to be made 'narratable'" (Bal x), Delisle points out that through this fairytale-like framing, the protagonist attempted to make Adele's story narratable, as he used what he imagined to be a safe mode (the third person) to communicate to his mother a traumatic past (Delisle 7). Cathy Caruth explains how a traumatic event "cannot become, as [Pierre] Janet says, a 'narrative memory' that is integrated into a completed story of the past," since trauma is likely encoded in the mind differently from other memories (153). By starting his mother's story with an account of her everyday life before the fire and ending it in the old healer's home, the protagonist intuitively integrates Adele's trauma as best as he can. He also tries to show Adele the moment at which he believes her memory dissociates.[8] Reminding Adele about how she ran away from her mother's pained laughter after she made an unfair accusation against her, he mentions the "sound that chases [her] as she flees the house and runs through the streets of Carenage. Then farther still, outside the village, along a path so old that none could remember its origins . . ." (190). At this point, the protagonist seems to believe, Adele is en route to the military base where her mother will soon appear. Yet as Adele's interruption of her son's narrative with her own soucouyant story at precisely the same moment, along with her ultimate discounting of his narrative as "'some old nigger-story,'" indicates, their exchange is not wholly successful (194).

Before he leaves Adele, the protagonist says: "'Please listen to me, Mother. Please believe me. I didn't want to sadden you or betray the spell. I didn't want to tell a story like this. I just wanted you to realize that I knew. That I was always close enough to know. That I was your son, and I could hear and understand and take away . . .'" (195). As his pleading implies, he "didn't want to tell a story like this," not only because it is a difficult story for a child to have to tell a parent, but because it is a difficult story for him to have inherited and to have to carry with him. Thus, he wants Adele to listen, to believe, to know that he told a story "like this,"

---

8   Bessel van der Kolk and Onno van der Hart explain that while Sigmund Freud and others have used the concepts of repression and dissociation, repression "reflects a vertically layered model of mind: what is repressed is pushed downward, into the unconscious" (168). Dissociation, instead, "reflects a horizontally layered model of mind" in which a subject's memory "is contained in an alternative stream of consciousness, which may be subconscious or dominate consciousness" (168).

as he senses that it will help them both heal from the trauma that Adele has experienced and that has been transmitted to him. Like Adele, the protagonist is in need of a listener for his story.

A fellow second-generation diasporic subject who "grew up in the shadows cast by [Adele's] house," Meera is an ideal listener for the protagonist (154). Meera's relationship to Adele's history is what Hirsch calls an "affiliative" form of postmemory, a "result of contemporaneity and generational connection with the literal second generation" (36).[9] Notably, the protagonist's account of the story he told Adele is framed by his interactions with Meera. Noticing a reference to the soucouyant in one of the protagonist's older brother's notebooks when she helps the protagonist pack up Adele's house, Meera says to him: "'That's an evil spirit, isn't it? A soucouyant?'" (172). Her question goes unanswered for an "unknowable length of time," prompting Meera to state to him: "'You don't have to tell me the story'" (172). Though the protagonist says "'I know,'" and the chapter closes with his words, the final chapter of the novel opens with the story of how Adele "saw a soucouyant" (173). As the novel's structure implies, Meera, too, is one of the protagonist's listeners, for he tells her the story he told Adele. In the novel's closing, the protagonist also relates his own memories of his and Adele's trip to Carenage when he was young. After he recounts the memory that is most precious to him, Meera replies with her own intimate gesture, touching the protagonist's face and saying: "'Eyestache'" (196). *Eyestache* is Adele's word for *eyebrow*, a word that is familiar to those who know her best, including the protagonist, his family, and Meera, as well as Bohdan, an autistic Eastern European boy that Adele took care of while his mother was at work. As Meera knows, Adele often said "eyestache" as she gently traced the eyebrows of those she cared about. In this way, Meera helps the protagonist reclaim his personal memories, memories that were lost when the past—and sometimes the present—felt too painful. Furthermore, she helps him carry forward Adele's story. Meera's sharing of this story is significant, as it draws attention to the alliances that can be formed between second-generation diasporic subjects as they negotiate the uneasy terrain between memory and forgetting, and together with Bohdan's memory of Adele, it reminds us that various individuals and communities can share or participate in memory work.

---

9   For a detailed discussion of Meera and cultural memory, see Delisle.

IV

Though Chariandy's *Soucouyant* explores the limits of remembering for second-generation Canadian immigrant subjects, it does so without participating in or condoning larger acts of forgetting. Chariandy draws attention to Canada's histories of racism, from Adele's arrival in 1960s Toronto "through a scheme that offered landed status to single women from the Caribbean after a year of household work" (47–48) to the unique forms of racism experienced by the protagonist, his brother, Meera, and Bohdan in an officially multicultural Canada in both institutional and non-institutional settings. Chariandy also acknowledges Canada's settler-colonial history, for his protagonist "learn[s] about the 'Toronto Purchase' of land from three Mississauga chiefs in 1787" from Mrs. Cameron, "but also how no document describing a neighbouring 'Scarborough Purchase' has ever come to light (103)."[10] In addition, Chariandy gives his readers a sense of the imperial perspectives on wartime Trinidad in what Dobson refers to as "a more official tone or discourse of history" towards the end of the novel ("Spirits" 812), thereby indicating how the unofficial stories of everyday individuals, like the fictional Adele and her mother, were left undocumented. As these acts of remembering show, Chariandy's novel remains critically aware in its discussion of cultural memory.

Soucouyant engages in an ethics of remembering, showing how second-generation diasporic subjects can productively remember the diasporic past in ways that account for the cultural legacies of their birthplace and ancestral homeland as well as the capacity of each individual subject to engage (or not engage) with aspects of these legacies. Through his protagonist, Chariandy not only shows the complex cultural legacies that second-generation Canadian subjects inherit and the ways in which they inherit them, but he also demonstrates that remembering must be done in ways that do not disrupt one's own psyche or the psychological spaces of others. In these ways, past injustices are not elided or forgotten, while, to borrow Chariandy's closing words in "The Fiction of Belonging," second-generation subjects can live "ethically and soulfully" (828).

---

10 See Kit Dobson's *Transnational Canadas* on Chariandy's intertextual reference to Susanna Moodie's 1852 memoir *Roughing It in the Bush* for further discussion on this subject.

CHAPTER 21

•◆•

Confronting the Legacy of Canada's Indian Residential School System: Cree Cultural Memory and the Warrior Spirit in David Alexander Robertson and Scott B. Henderson's *7 Generations Series*

Doris Wolf

I often begin my teaching of young people's texts on Canada's residential school legacy by showing a short clip from the CBC Digital Archives entitled "'A New Future' for Children at James Bay Residential School." First televised on 13 March, 1955, on *News Magazine*, a CBC weekly news television series, it foregrounds smiling residential school children in Moose Factory, Ontario, who appear to be thriving emotionally, intellectually, and physically under the tutelage of caring and competent teachers. With a happy Disney-like soundtrack playing in the background, the overall impression of the school and the system of which it was part conveyed in this brief two-minute and thirty-seven- second broadcast is one of legitimacy and success. If I judge from the reactions of my students, I might feel fairly confident saying that many Canadians today, non-Aboriginal as well as Aboriginal, would view this footage with a degree of skepticism that seemed unavailable to its implied mainstream viewers half a century ago. Prime Minister Stephen Harper's 2008 apology to former students of Canada's Indian residential schools, for instance, has brought heightened national awareness to the devastating impact of the federally financed, often church-run residential school system on the Aboriginal children who attended them. Yet, even following Harper's well-publicized and widely broadcast apology, the Truth and Reconciliation Commission of Canada (TRC)[1] has discovered a continued mainstream resistance to learning a

---

1   The TRC was established in 2008 under the Indian Residential Schools Settlement Agreement to create a historical record and promote public awareness of the Indian residential school system. For a full version of the Commission's mandate and activities to date, see both its *Interim Report* and its website (www.trc.ca).

fuller version of the past that it warns in its *Interim Report*, published early in 2012, "will cause many Canadians to see their country differently" (25). Unlike truth and reconciliation commissions in other parts of the world which have typically emerged out of regime changes or as part of peace accords, Canada's was established in response to litigation by survivors and not public concern for past injustices. "This means," writes Kim Stanton, "that the TRC will be faced with the need to prompt Canadians to invest in and take ownership of a process they did not instigate" (4). As TRC commissioners reveal in their report, they have met with a number of roadblocks in carrying out their mandate, including the failure of some federal government and church officials in passing on all promised relevant documents pertaining to the schools (16) and "huge challenges in raising awareness, among non-Aboriginal Canadians" (9).

If, as Marita Sturken maintains, "Cultural memory is a field of cultural negotiation through which different stories vie for a place in history" ("Tangled Memories" 1), then the challenges faced by the TRC in accomplishing all of its mandate, which calls as much for reconciliation between Aboriginal and non-Aboriginal Canadians as within Aboriginal families, underscore the power of hegemonic narratives in recuperating possible sites of contestation. The political stakes, Sturken reminds us, are large: "The debates over what counts as cultural memory are also debates about who gets to participate in creating national meaning" (12). With an eye on reforming the national symbolic, the TRC in its Vision Statement connects the revelation of "the truth about residential schools" to the creation of "a renewed sense of Canada that is inclusive and respectful" (*Interim Report* 2). Yet, the question raised by my students' skeptical reactions to the 1955 broadcast is this: What, precisely, does this truth entail in a post-apology climate? As Stanton surmises, "In Canada, the factual truth about IRS may be publicly available" (7). Yet, while the dominant narrative today may allow that abuses, often horrific, occurred within the schools, what remains missing is a full understanding of them "as one attempt at obliterating the Indigenous cultures in what is now Canada" (Stanton 7). As Stanton outlines and the TRC emphasizes with its focus not only on survivors but on those left behind and on the generations that follow, what Canadians still need is a fuller understanding of IRS's systemic aspects, its assimilationist goals, and its long-term consequences. Although in general a better understanding of residential schools and their impacts may exist in Aboriginal communities,[2] all Canadians, the TRC emphasizes, need to learn more through public-education campaigns and in-school educational efforts (7).

This chapter explores David Alexander Robertson and Scott B. Henderson's *7 Generations Series*, a four-book graphic novel series aimed at a grade 9–12 audience, which grapples with Canada's residential school history. Endorsed by the Chair of the Truth and Reconciliation Commission, Justice Murray Sinclair,[3] published by Highwater Press, a trade imprint of educational publisher Portage & Main Press, and supported by a comprehensive Teacher's Guide written by Niigaanwewidam James Sinclair, a professor of Native Studies at the University of Manitoba, this series might well be integrated into high-school curricula as part of an in-school effort to help counter the myth "that IRS was akin to a bad boarding school" (Stanton 7). To explore the possibilities of this series in connecting truth-telling and national revisioning, I take up Cree scholar Neal McLeod's concept of Cree narrative memory, which he defines as a large, intergenerational, collective memory informed by Cree narrative (8). McLeod writes, "The activity and process of these narratives challenge the hegemony of the mainstream discourse, which has often been conflated with notions of 'progress' that have ultimately undermined Cree narrative memory and been used as a tool of conquest" (18). Told in four parts, *Stone, Scars, Ends/Begins,* and *The Pact,* the series focuses on Edwin, a Plains Cree teenager living in Winnipeg in 2010, who must come to understand his father's experiences as a residential school survivor in order to overcome his own sense of despair and hopelessness for the future. As his mother tells him stories of his family's past, she seeks to help her son and save his life by reconnecting him to Cree collective memory. Beginning with pre-Contact times, she focuses on the story of a warrior named Stone, so that all the stories about the devastating impact of colonization on the Plains Cree which follow are framed within the emancipatory power of the warrior ethic and spirit.

If one of the chief struggles of Cree narrative memory is, as McLeod says, the discordance and conflict between ancient memory and the

---

2 Stanton refers to a poll conducted for Indian Residential Schools Resolution Canada and the Truth and Reconciliation Commission in 2008 which reveals that the IRS system is generally better known in Indigenous communities and that six in ten Canadians were unable to cite any long-term consequences of the IRS system (see footnotes 40 and 45).

3 His endorsement appears on the back cover of the last book in the series, *The Pact.*

experience of modernity and colonialism, then the warrior story as it is told here becomes a present-day manifestation of the past that offers to heal this rift. Borrowing from McLeod's work on memory and Kanien'kehaka scholar Taiaiake Alfred's on contemporary warrior societies and the restoration of the warrior ethic as the basis for regenerating Indigenous identities and struggles against colonialism, I examine the ways in which *7 Generations* challenges old ideas of Canada as a settler nation and insists instead on radical change for Aboriginal peoples as related to land, rights, and sovereignty. This challenge imputes different responses from and roles for Aboriginal and non-Aboriginal readers. An Aboriginal educator teaching First Nations issues to high-school students in British Columbia remarks, "when our cultures are being taught [it] is personal. [. . .] it touches us emotionally . [. . .] That stuff is our lived experience, it's our lived history, it's our parents' lived history and our grandparents' lived history" (qtd. in Rachel Mason 139). Through an identification with Edwin who comes to understand the past in increasingly complex ways, Aboriginal readers might come to contextualize their own individual and personal histories within much longer and larger histories of colonization and empowerment. As Justice Sinclair remarks, "reconciliation is about respect . . . and self-respect is where it starts" (back cover, *The Pact*). For non-Aboriginal readers such as myself, confronting these contextualized histories can disrupt any sense of complacency we might have that Canada's apology to residential school survivors marks a closure—a sense that we already know enough—when it fact it should serve to initiate a new beginning marked by our own efforts at reconciliation based in a sense of shared history and mutual respect.

SPIRITUAL AND SPATIAL EXILE: THE INTERGENERATIONAL IMPACT OF RESIDENTIAL SCHOOLS

The disclaimer on Highwater Press's website that warns the content of *7 Generations* may be disturbing to some readers underscores the potential power of the graphic narrative form in conveying the past. The two middle books of the series take up two histories that their intended high-school audience may encounter in the school system: *Scars* is based on the smallpox epidemic that swept the prairies in 1870–71 and *Ends/Begins*, the book on which I am focusing in this section, on the residential school system that existed in Canada for more than a century. Both use text and image to emphasize how the experience of colonization was systemic, personal, intergenerational and, significantly, genocidal. At the beginning of *Scars,* Lauren, Edwin's mother, opens her story about White Cloud, an adolescent Cree boy orphaned by the ravages of the disease, by locating it in the larger historical dispossession of the Plains Cree: "In many ways, it was the end of our way of life as a people. The end of the time we called paradise" (4). Her words are borne out visually throughout the book through its many gruesome images of people dying or dead from smallpox, their bodies marked by the disease's most visible symptom, its pustules. Yet, it is through the main character White Cloud's experience of the epidemic that the book moves the reader beyond understanding smallpox in terms of its technologies of dissemination and warfare and high body count. The close-ups of his sad face as he encounters death again and again or the long shots of him alone in the distance surrounded by empty landscape emphasize the horrific reality of losing family, community, and way of life. At the end of the book, the authors visually juxtapose White Cloud's scars from smallpox to Edwin's from cutting or attempted suicide in order to emphasize the continued effects of a dispossession that began long ago.

End/Begins builds on the notion of a lost paradise initiated in *Scars* and also uses the power of the graphic narrative to represent history as lived and living. Set in the mid-1960s, this book recounts the residential school experience of James, Edwin's father, and his younger brother, Thomas, who is sexually abused and dies at the school they are forced to attend. Told by James to Edwin, the narrative opens by foregrounding the closeness of the brothers as they run and play together outside in the fields near their home. On the panels that show their happiness, we read the voice-over of their grandfather who warns the boys, ". . . The white people are numerous. There are too many of them. / They are like birds in the autumn that blacken the sky. / Our people are now scattered leaves on the ground, fallen from what we once knew" (6). This page foreshadows the events to come. At one point Thomas, who is about ten years old, stumbles and falls down a hill while James, who looks to be in his midteens, is playfully chasing him; later Thomas dies when he falls trying to run away from the school with James close on his heels trying to stop him. In two of the panels, one of Thomas's legs is notably darker than any other image on the page. When we see the priest who abuses him on the next page, his dark clothing immediately connects him to Thomas in ominous ways. Throughout the book, which is rendered in black and white like the rest of the series (only the covers are in colour),[4] both the priest and nuns stand out with their imposing body language and dark clothing as they move among the children with stern or, often even more frighteningly, with impassive faces. These images are contrasted with the forlorn faces and vulnerable body language of the children, who tend to be portrayed in lighter-coloured clothing. The use of light and dark horror iconography to suggest good and evil imposes a moral judgment on the people in power. The priest hardly speaks and the nuns never, thereby emphasizing the power of the system to control through fear and intimidation.

Told from James's perspective, part of the story's effectiveness in portraying both boys lies in the initial silence around Thomas's experiences at the school. As one of the older boys, James does not attend classes but performs hard physical labour outdoors all day so that the only glimpses he has of Thomas are at meal times. "And sometimes he wasn't even at dinner," James recounts, "At the time, I didn't know where he could be. / He never told me either" (14). Numerous images highlight a sense of imposed distance between the boys. In one panel, we see Thomas from the back, standing at a window watching James rake leaves. Initially, our perspective is with Thomas looking at his older brother who is a small figure in the distance (20). In the next panel, we shift to viewing Thomas from outside. The close-up of his face that readers witness gives us a sense that we are privy to something that James is not from his more distant vantage point: the intense sadness conveyed in Thomas's expression and sense of helplessness and longing intimated in how he presses his palm against the window. On the same page, we see James at dinner, glancing sideways at an empty chair. The chair fills its own panel so that James's puzzlement and distress over his younger brother's absence is intensified. Twice we see Thomas crawl into James's bed looking for comfort, shaking in fear, and whispering, "I want to go home" (15, 21). Told retrospectively, James clearly intimates what has been happening to Thomas out of sight, but his emphasis on his lack of knowledge at the time enhances the dramatic tension of the story.

---

4   Highwater has recently published a full-colour compilation of the series, entitled *7 Generations: A Plains Cree Saga*. My work here is based on the original series, which published each book separately and, except for the covers, in black and white.

The book's crisis occurs when James finally discovers the reason for Thomas's frequent absences and fear: the priest has been sexually abusing him. Throughout the book, the priest is a frightening figure, whose eyes are almost always hidden by the glare of his glasses so that he appears as a menacing, soulless creature. The scenes of his sexual violation of Thomas employ a narrative and graphic strategy that relies on creating a tension between saying and not saying, showing and not showing, to underscore the horror of what Thomas goes through. For example, the priest's violation of him on his first night at the residential school is portrayed across a two-page spread (18–19). On the left side, seven panels depict the priest slowing opening the door, waking Thomas, and leading him from his dorm room. In this way, Henderson slows down the sense of time in order to increase the reader's sense of foreboding. The opposing page uses five frames to depict the bathroom where the priest takes Thomas under the pretext of giving him a bath (see Figure 21.1). As he leads Thomas to the room, removes his pyjama top, and begins to shut the door, he says, "You see, you're a dirty boy. / So we're going to clean you. / And you'll be better for it" (19). The two frames absent of people are the most menacing of all: one portrays the bathtub full of water, waiting, with a barred window in the background, and the other, the last and largest on the page, the closed door. Our perspective in this last frame is from the dark hallway outside. We see only the glow of the bathroom light framing the door; we know what is happening, but do not want to see more.

The full power of *End/Begins* lies in revealing how James's and Thomas's experiences lead to a spatial and spiritual exile that extends into the present. Defining spatial exile as the removal of an Indigenous group from its lands, and spiritual exile as the alienation of a group from its stories (55), Neal McLeod emphasizes how they were concurrent processes: "Spiritual exile was the internalization of being taken off the land. A central manifestation of this was the residential school system, which was established as a way of 'educating' and assimilating Indigenous people" (58). Literally removed from the landscape in which they initially run and play freely, the brothers find themselves in a place of marked contrast: the institutional and indoor settings of a rigid and frightening residential school. This spatial exile carries over into the next generation for Edwin, who, in both of the book's other time frames, 1994 when he is a toddler and 2010 when he is a teenager, moves in a cityscape defined

21.1 David Alexander Robertson and Scott B. Henderson's *Ends/Begins*, 19. Portage and Main Press. Used with permission.

by poverty and alienation. Physical dislocation is both a manifestation and a source of the spiritual exile that clearly haunts both father and son. James's sense of guilt over failing to protect his brother leads him to turn to alcohol to escape his inner turmoil, which in turn becomes directly and dramatically responsible for his desertion of Lauren and Edwin. The book is framed by a traumatic event that occurs in 1994 when James is intoxicated while he is supposed to be watching Edwin. James leaves the front door of the house open, and Edwin is almost killed by a car when he wanders onto the street to play. James's reaction to the near miss is to punish Edwin. The image that depicts James standing over his son, hand with belt raised, ready to strike (see Figure 21.2) parallels the one in which he walked in on the priest abusing Thomas (see Figure 21.3). The similarity between the priest's and James's stances visually enacts the intergenerational consequences of the residential school experience. Edwin's attempted suicide in the first book of the series, which we now know through events in Book III, is directly connected to his father's abandonment of him after this near abuse, and reveals the next generation's spiritual exile.

21.2 David Alexander Robertson and Scott B. Henderson's *Ends/Begins*, panel on p. 30. Portage and Main Press. Used with permission.

21.3 David Alexander Robertson and Scott B. Henderson's *Ends/Begins*, panel on p. 26. Portage and Main Press. Used with permission.

WARRIOR CULTURE: AN ECHO FROM THE PAST, A NEW VISION OF THE FUTURE

To counter the negative intergenerational impact of his father's residential school experience, Edwin is offered a story of empowerment which originates in traditional Plains Cree warrior culture. Warrior culture as it is represented in *7 Generations* becomes a specific manifestation of McLeod's concept of Cree narrative memory and in this way holds great promise for Edwin if he can come to hear and internalize it in the present. McLeod theorizes Cree narrative memory as collective memory carried forward through generations in oral stories:

> Collective memory is the echo of old stories that links grandparents with their grandchildren. In the Cree tradition, collective narrative memory is what puts our singular lives into a larger context. Old voices echo; the ancient poetic memory of our ancestors finds home in our individual lives and allows us to reshape our experience so that we can interpret the world we find ourselves in. (11)

The echo metaphor is crucial to McLeod's conceptualization of intergenerational linkages, and it is grounded in the names of both ancestors and places (18). The idea of the echo of old stories that connects generations in ongoing ways is crucially embedded in the *7 Generations* series through the story of Stone, a Plains Cree warrior who lived at the beginning of the nineteenth century and is Edwin's ancestor. Stone, too, is an example of ongoing history, although of a different, more positive kind than the colonial histories that I discussed in the previous section. Part of the power of this story is in challenging mainstream understandings of Cree narratives as mythological and pre-historical and thus lower status. As McLeod writes, "Colonial powers, mainstream historians, and academics have often thought of Indigenous 'lived' memory as myth" (18). As Edwin comes to understand traditional Cree warrior society as lived and historical rather than mythical, he simultaneously learns to see his own connection to this past in ways that can transform his life in the present.

Lauren is the one who tells her son the warrior story that becomes the primary intergenerational echo of strength and resilience in the series. That Book 1, *Stone*, comprises this story makes sense from a chronological viewpoint: Stone is the first representative of the seven generations that the series covers, and Edwin is the last. More so, however, it grounds Edwin, who at the beginning of Book I is lying in a hospital bed after taking an overdose of pills, in an image of the past that evokes a strong version of Aboriginal identity. The story Lauren recounts to her son is distinctly male, a choice that suggests her understanding of what Aboriginal writers such as Sakej Ward and Kim Anderson have underscored in their assessment of the current climate of exile for Aboriginal peoples: that Aboriginal men have often experienced a greater crisis of identity and have found it more difficult than women to define their roles in contemporary society (in McKegney, "Warriors" 241–42). At the outset of the book, Stone is beginning his journey to become a man, and specifically a warrior, through the formal rites of passage this entails in Plains Cree culture. Beginning with the vision quest and culminating in the Thirst Dance, with other steps such as the buffalo hunt in between, Lauren's story traces Stone's progress toward becoming a warrior.[5] The main challenge Stone faces is his intense grief over the death of his older brother, which might have led him into a kind of spiritual exile had he not been so grounded in his place and community. His visit to the Calling River—a place that will become significant in the last book of the series for both James and Edwin—puts him back on the right path as a warrior, husband, and future father (18–20). The idea that Edwin should learn from Stone's experiences of sorrow and strength is foregrounded through the juxtapositions between the two young men that lie at the centre of the book. Literalizing McLeod's notion of echo in Cree narrative memory, Robertson and Henderson employ visual echoes across two spreads (14–15; 16–17) through the format of the panels (number, placement, and size) and the characters' similar body positions and facial expressions (see Figures 21.4 and 21.5). Although the words on these pages tell very different stories of past and present, the images create parallels between the young men to represent how Edwin comes to embody the memory of his ancestor in ways that become more and more powerful as the series progresses.

The echo metaphor is also literalized in *7 Generations* through the eagle-shaped stone amulet that Stone finds during his vision quest and that comes to be passed down through the generations. As Lauren says in *Scars* when she gives it to Edwin, "It has the power of our culture within it. / It will help **you** on your journey of healing" (26). The healing had already begun in the first book when Edwin came to understand that the traditional warrior of his people had not even been accorded the status of myth in mainstream history and culture but had been eradicated and replaced with the image of a bloodthirsty savage. Still resonating strongly in contemporary media, art, film, and literature, this historical image, as Sam McKegney argues in "Warriors, Healers, Lovers, and

---

5   See Niigaanwewidam James Sinclair's Teacher's Guide for the *7 Generations Series* for a guided reading of these Plains Cree rites of initiation. Sinclair's Guide repeatedly draws attention to and calls for a tribally specific understanding of the series.

21.4 David Alexander Robertson and Scott B. Henderson's *Stone*, panels on p. 14. Portage and Main Press. Used with permission.

21.5 David Alexander Robertson and Scott B. Henderson's *Stone*, panels on p. 15. Portage and Main Press. Used with permission.

Leaders," helped justify colonial expansion and act as evidence for colonialism's success: "The bloodthirsty warrior, although perhaps admirable in his fearlessness and compelling in his hypermasculine violence, provides [. . .] the foil for colonial conquest: he's the perfect enemy who, in defeat, solidifies the masculinity of his conqueror" (259). We see that Edwin believes this stereotype when he says to Lauren in the middle of *Stone*, "I thought we used to be savages" (21). The remaining three books in the series portray the struggles of subsequent generations of men in Edwin's family to retain the spirit and power invested in the Plains Cree warrior tradition in a post-Contact society that worked hard to eradicate it. Closer in historical time to *Stone*, Book II portrays how after much struggle and despair, White Cloud ultimately uses the strength represented by the amulet to survive what Lauren calls "one of the dark times in our history" (28). However, almost one hundred years later, Book III reveals how the incessant onslaught of colonialism has so worn away at Cree society and culture that James's experience of the residential school system results in his complete disconnection from the warrior spirit. Before James leaves for school, he gives the eagle amulet to Lauren as a symbol of his commitment to her and for safe keeping. For years, Lauren is entrusted with the responsibility to look after it, but it is out of place both in terms of familial lineage and gender until she gives it to Edwin. Yet, at the conclusion of *Ends/Begins*, Edwin gives the amulet back to his father so that James can continue healing himself, a process that has been happening outside of our view but which we learn began with Edwin's attempted suicide. The amulet and the echoes of warrior culture it represents can now pass through successive generations in the way that was intended.

Although the series ends with Edwin still waiting his turn for the amulet, it is clear he will not do so passively. The last image of Edwin in Book IV mirrors an early one of Stone in Book I, so that Edwin is depicted as being solidly on the path of a warrior. Edwin kneels in a posture of strength as visions of the past are ripped from his chest (*The Pact* 30), just like Stone knelt during his vision quest, and images of his past and future were ripped from his chest (*Stone* 9). Both of these scenes evoke the final trial Stone underwent to become a warrior: the "Making of a Brave" ceremony which is part of the Thirst Dance (25–26), so that we are reassured that Edwin will eventually arrive at this point just like his ancestor did two centuries before. The intertextual allusions between the covers of *The Pact* and *Stone* have already hinted at this positive outcome: on the cover of *Stone*, Edwin is kneeling in a despondent posture, eyes closed, facing right, while Stone stands ready for battle behind him, an icon of strength; on the cover of *The Pact*, Edwin is now upright, running toward the left side of the page, so that his body position is evocative of Stone's on the first cover: both have their left legs and right arms in a forward position and their mouths are set in a similar, determined line. Although Edwin's eyes are still closed and his head is down on this last cover, suggesting he might not yet have the confidence of Stone, he is nonetheless closer to his ancestor's spirit than when he began. His parents, smaller figures in the background, frame him, their hands stretched toward each other, so that Edwin is grounded in a sense of a reconciled family that bodes well for all of them. James's character, before and after his spiritual transformation, has deconstructed another prominent mainstream stereotype of Aboriginal men, the drunken absentee.[6] First contextualized as a product of colonial history, his alcoholism is now literally refused as he reconciles his past. This change allows the family to move forward although Edwin's new-found strength is not dependent on it.

I want to conclude by locating the final scene of *The Pact* at the Calling River where Stone regains his spiritual strength after his brother's death and where Edwin gives his father the amulet and comes himself to embody a more hopeful future. This is also where James and Thomas play before going to residential school. By grounding their contemporary protagonist in a sense of place, Robertson and Henderson ask that their use of the Plains Cree warrior figure be read as deeply political and not simply cultural. Kristina Fagan outlines how criticism of Aboriginal literature in Canada has tended to be culturalist, that is, overly concerned with how texts by Aboriginal writers represent identifiable external symbols of their culture and far less concerned with how they portray specific political topics such as land ownership, law, and governance. As Fagan writes, "In a context of Aboriginal nationalism, indeed, focusing on markers of 'culture' can allow people to avoid dealing with the underlying principle of nationhood and its concrete consequences" ("Tewatatha:wi" 14). Edwin's location on traditional lands at the end connects his struggles to larger ones of Aboriginal nationalism. While "being home" for McLeod means "to dwell in the landscape of the familiar, of collective memories," and "stands in opposition to being in exile," it ultimately "means to be a nation, to have access to land, to be able to raise your own children, and to have political control" (54). Similarly, for Taiaiake Alfred, who has done the most sustained work on contemporary warrior societies in Indigenous communities in the Canadian context, "Comprehending warrior societies as they actually exist among Indigenous people is impossible without considering them in the context of the larger struggle of Indigenous peoples to

---

6   McKegney discusses how the bloodthirsty warrior and drunken absentee represent alternative pathways of degeneration from the noble savage image that has long been a popular stereotype of Indigenous men in the settler imaginary (256).

survive as nations of people with their lands, cultures, and communities intact" ("Warrior Societies" 2). Grounded in a restoration of a spiritual and cultural foundation for Onkwehonwe (original peoples), the people who take on this battle become Alfred's vision of the new warrior: "The warrior's first battle is with himself or herself; having fought that battle his or her responsibilities are extended to immediate family and other human beings. The warrior takes action to change the conditions that cause suffering for the people in both the immediate (self-defence) and long-term (self-determination) sense" (*Wasáse* 86–87). This conceptualization of the contemporary warrior stands in stark contrast to how the media has represented Indigenous warriors as misguided malcontents who have taken Canadian law into their own hands (Alfred, "Warrior Societies" 23–24). The resurgence of the warrior spirit that readers witness in Edwin works to deconstruct this criminalization of the contemporary warrior in ways that parallel how the story of Stone deconstructed the traditional warrior as bloodthirsty savage earlier. It also fundamentally locates Edwin's struggle in contemporary political struggles over sovereignty.

The depiction of the warrior spirit in *7 Generations* with its connection to politics and not simply culture has radical implications for Aboriginal and non-Aboriginal readers, although in different ways. With its intergenerational focus, the series emphasizes reconciliation within Aboriginal families. Edwin forgives his father at the end of Book IV and finds empowerment in the new warrior spirit. In this way, he becomes a representative of Alfred's powerful conception of the seventh generation: "We are the prophetic Seventh Generation; if we do not find a way out of the crises, we will be consumed by the darkness, and whether it is through self-destruction or assimilation, we will not survive" (*Wasáse* 31). The series ends with hope. As James says to Edwin, "The Elders say what was done to us will touch us for 7 generations / So, too, the healing we do now will mend our people over that time" (28). The strongest implied readership of the series, Aboriginal youth, and I would argue perhaps even more specifically, young Aboriginal men, become part of this vision and may be inspired by Edwin to take on a similar role.[7] But

---

7   As we can see in the quotation in the previous paragraph, in *Wasáse*, Alfred includes both men and women in his conception of the new warrior. Robertson and Henderson's warriors in *7 Generations* are conceptualized as more specifically male, although Lauren is clearly a strong figure who did wear the stone amulet for years.

non-Aboriginal readers also have a role, though more implicit. Again, turning to Alfred: "If non-indigenous readers are capable of listening, they will learn from these shared words, and they will discover that while we are envisioning a new relationship between Onkwehonwe and the land, we are at the same time offering a decolonized alternative to the Settler society by inviting them to share our vision of respect and peaceful coexistence" (*Wasáse* 35). Although I am not sure that Alfred would see the TRC as a body that can effect this change, I think the series embodies the possibility of reconciliation between Aboriginal and non-Aboriginal Canadians grounded in a new vision of Canada. By positing portrayals of the systemic and long-term impacts of colonization against a tribally specific understanding of Aboriginal empowerment, *7 Generations* profoundly alters our understanding of past and present.

CHAPTER 22

•◆•

Recovering Pedagogical Space: Trauma, Education, and *The Lesser Blessed*

Robyn Green

According to Stanley Cohen, reconciliation processes are designed to perform a "symbolic recognition of what is already known but was officially denied" (qtd. in Moon 72). In Canada, reconciliation processes have been critiqued for using residential schooling as a synecdoche for colonialism, which can obscure the asymmetrical political and economic relationship between the settler state and Indigenous peoples (see Henderson and Wakeham; Simpson). In light of this, Courtney Jung's assertion that Canada remains a "non-transitional" society may trouble the potential for ethical and just reconciliatory outcomes (218). While the politics of reconciliation may not play out directly in Richard Van Camp's novella, *The Lesser Blessed*, the narrative provides a site in which these politics may be interrogated through the romance formed between the novel's protagonist, Larry Sole, and the object of his affections, Juliet Hope. Throughout this narrative, Van Camp not only reveals the intergenerational trauma of residential schooling but documents ongoing systemic disparities that continue to racialize and colonize Indigenous peoples in institutional settings. Using *The Lesser Blessed* as a point of departure, I argue that the assimilative logics embedded in residential school policy did not cease upon the official closure of these schools and are still felt by many First Nations students in the school system today. This chapter asks: How are mainstream educational policies and practices situated alongside the residential school legacy in *The Lesser Blessed*? In what ways does Van Camp's novella challenge and critique the settler society's conceptualization of Indigenous–settler reconciliation?

This essay will respond to these questions in three sections. Section I provides a history of the Indian Residential School system (IRS) in Canada, focusing specifically on how these policies were enacted in the North. *The Lesser Blessed* can be described as a coming-of-age story narrated by a male protagonist, Larry Sole,[1] but it is important to note that while the IRS system is not the subject of Van Camp's text, the protagonist's experience is exemplary of its intergenerational legacy. Also explored is reconciliation as a contested concept that is both actively embraced and refuted by a myriad of actors. Section II examines the concept of *trauma*, which is generally understood as a psychological affliction that can reify Western constructions of discrete individual subjectivity. Yet, the novella reveals colonial violence as a process of residual and emergent practices that constitute the "trans/historicity" of traumatic experience (Van Styvendale 206–208). Using the trans/historical as a temporal frame, I counter the assumption that colonialism is an era of separate and unrelated practices (often presented later as "mistakes"). Section III outlines how trauma(s) experienced by Van Camp's protagonist that occur at different temporal moments are often connected through specific educational *spaces*. The author aptly situates intrusive memories of the past to coincide with incidents of contemporary violence and bullying to transpire almost exclusively within Larry's high school.

This chapter utilizes a spatial analysis to elucidate Van Camp's structural critique of colonial institutions in the North as a way to demonstrate how cultural memory and policy become imbricated. Cree scholar Jo-Ann Episkenew's work, *Taking Back Our Spirits*, demonstrates a need for interdisciplinary analysis of Indigenous literatures as a means to situate texts within the infrastructure of colonial policies enacted by the settler state (16). In light of this, this chapter argues that *The Lesser Blessed* demonstrates a link between the legacy of the IRS system and the current educational system that incorporates neglectful teachers, segregated classrooms, and contemptuous racist attacks among students. Van Camp addresses epistemic violence and the structural barriers that Indigenous students continue to face, suggesting that these inequalities have yet to be reconciled in contemporary Canada despite the centrality of education and pedagogy to the redress process.

---

1   While the novella lacks first-hand observations of residential schooling found in other novels, such as Johnston's *Indian School Days*, Alexie's *Porcupines and China Dolls*, or Highway's *Kiss of the Fur Queen*, the adolescent protagonist is repeatedly confronted by the intergenerational legacy of residential schooling. For another example of this characterization of the residential school legacy, see Eden Robinson's protagonist Lisamarie Hill in *Monkey Beach*.

I. TO RECONCILE RESIDENTIAL SCHOOLING

Residential schooling—enacted through a set of principles embedded in the Indian Act (1876)—resulted in the removal of over 150 thousand children from their homes, communities, and families to be placed in "educational" institutions. Residential schools were under-funded and under-staffed, which resulted in inadequate guardianship, low standards of living, and remedial curricula (see Chrisjohn; Furniss; Agnes Grant; Milloy; and Woolford). Children who attended these schools experienced neglect, physical violence, and sexual abuse at the hands of their caretakers and were subjected to a curriculum replete with assimilationist logic that demonized Indigenous epistemologies and practices (Green 132). As an institutionalized form of "cognitive imperialism" (Battiste 192–93), residential schooling not only adversely affected individual students but was designed to shatter familial and community relationships as elder and parental authority were undermined through the imposition of Western systems of knowledge and language. From the outset, these schools were a predominant colonial tool "to coerce Indian people to obey the dictates of the empire" as "[b]oth churches and colonial officials agreed that Indians would be less likely to engage in hostile and disruptive acts if their children remained in the custody of the schools" (Episkenew 47). Canada's Northern region (Yukon and Northwest Territories) saw a disproportionately high number of children removed from their homes. Just as residential schooling in the South began to recede, the number of removals in the territories escalated (Milloy 239), leaving intergenerational effects of residential schooling to be acutely felt in many Northern communities today.[2]

Since Prime Minister Stephen Harper's apology in 2008, the legacy of residential schools has largely been associated with Indigenous–settler *reconciliation*,[3] yet the framework upon which a reconciled Canada is to be built remains highly contested. Part of the debate arises from the definition of the term, Maaka and Fleras suggest: "Reconciliation

---

2   The height of residential schooling in Southern Canada was in the early 1930s; however, as John Milloy suggests, "As the nation moved north, further penetrating the homelands of Aboriginal communities, a whole new tier of schools was created, beginning in 1955" (239).

3   In 2007, the Indian Residential School Settlement Agreement (IRSSA) was finalized, resulting in compensation for survivors as well as monies for health support, a Truth and Reconciliation Commission, and commemoration activities.

has become a core phrase in righting historical wrongs. Both indigenous peoples and central authorities make repeated references to reconciliation, but mean something different by it, with the result that they literally end up talking past each other" (Maaka and Fleras 289). In light of this, the concept of reconciliation is often met with trepidation and reproach by both parties. According to Henderson and Wakeham, "[r] econciliation's more abstract resonances of overcoming differences lend the term to cooptation by governments seeking to cleanse the national image through more symbolic measures" (15). While the emphasis on symbolic measures undermines efforts for decolonization, the political and economic purchase this term has recently brought to the Harper government is particularly worrisome.[4] Official definitions of reconciliation have been deployed as a form of "moving on" and "never again" by the settler state, which resemble a global rhetoric that addresses intergroup conflict resolution in lieu of a commitment to decolonization. Leanne Simpson, in her book *Dancing on Our Turtle's Back*, warns that "[i]f reconciliation is focused only on residential schools rather than the broader set of relationships that generated policies, legislation and practices aimed at assimilation and political genocide, then there is a risk that reconciliation will 'level the playing field' in the eyes of Canadians" (21). Framing colonialism as a bounded historical policy engenders a perception among many Canadians that "post-reconciliation, Indigenous peoples no longer have a legitimate source of contention" against the settler state (Simpson 22). In light of this, Kanien'kehaka scholar Taiaiake Alfred dismisses reconciliation "as a process and a concept [that] is not compelling" (152) and thereby focuses on *resurgence* and *restitution* as more apt goals for Indigenous peoples. Reconciliation is now assumed to be the ultimate goal for Indigenous peoples, but this supposition is considered largely problematic given these critical interventions.

---

4   In another project, I have traced ways in which the Indian Residential School Settlement Agreement (IRSSA) has been utilized for Conservative ideological purposes. In the summary of Aboriginal Affairs and Northern Development Canada (AANDC), the IRSSA is said to be "a touchstone towards building a new relationship with Aboriginal peoples based on reconciliation and healing for past injustices, and strengthening Aboriginal governance and self-government" (AANDC website). Yet, Conservative gains in the area of reconciliation consist of orchestrating the First Nations Financial Transparency Act. This highly controversial Act, constructed to make bands more "transparent and accountable," places First Nations governments under further scrutiny, generates further intervention in communities, and destabilizes a movement towards self-government guaranteed by the treaties and the Constitution.

In *The Lesser Blessed*, reconciliation can be explored through the relationship forged between Larry Sole, the protagonist of Dogrib (now known as Tlicho) descent, and Juliet Hope, his White classmate. Juliet is often described in both affectionate and lustful terms throughout the novella, but it is her "purity" that Larry often refers to:

> But, alas, enough of her ass. It's really her face I want to talk about. Juliet Hope was white and pure. [. . .] Her skin was perfect, not like mine. No blemishes, no greasy forehead, no cracks or lizard skin. There was only her, Juliet. And I adored her seven dreams deep. (Van Camp 27)

Larry goes on to say later that "I think in another life I was a great Dogrib hunter who had Juliet in my sights. She was a white caribou, pure. I believe I let her go out of respect and awe" (29). Juliet's "perfect" skin serves as a foil to Larry's "lizard" skin as he embodies his traumatic experience through extensive scarring acquired from past events. Larry's description of Juliet creates a binary between an awkward and unpopular youth and the woman he adores. Yet, while allusions to her whiteness are consistent, references to her purity are not, as her reputation for being "easy" is revealed throughout the novella. In fact, her character is pathologized through references to her as a carrier of "disease." This character's complexity should be duly noted so that the intimate relationship between Larry and Juliet is not read solely as an allegory for the politics of reconciliation. Juliet appears as a friend, muse, confidante, and lover to the protagonist and is integral to facilitating Larry's acts of disclosure. The reference to Juliet alludes to Shakespeare's star-crossed lovers whose romance is torn asunder by two warring families. In this novella, however, the two characters are separated instead by histories of violence, colonization, and injustice. Van Camp's allusion to Juliet is where the similarities between the two narratives end, as the "glooming peace" central to *Romeo and Juliet*'s conclusion is replaced by a hopeful prospect. Yet, despite its sanguine tone, Van Camp's conclusion remains ambivalent due to the couple's hurried estrangement. This juxtaposition may be aligned with Indigenous conceptualizations of healing that can be used to critique Western piecemeal approaches to reconciliation. In short, I ask whether the irreconcilable estrangement of Larry and Juliet at the novel's conclusion could be indicative of the systemic inequalities between Indigenous peoples and settlers that are carefully mapped throughout this text.

II. CIRCLING THE DRAIN: TRAUMA AND TIME IN *THE LESSER BLESSED*

The concept of trauma has become synonymous with the history of residential schooling as this term is circulated by both Indigenous peoples and settlers to describe survivors' experience. Yet Trauma Studies, as an interdisciplinary scholarly field, is highly contested.[5] Predominantly, the term *trauma* is associated with an individualized disorder labelled "post-traumatic stress disorder" (PTSD) that has been deployed (and popularized) in both clinical and literary disciplines.[6] This disorder elicits a wide spectrum of symptoms usually initiated by a shocking past event experienced by an individual that is then iteratively relived in the present. Indigenous scholars and practitioners, however, have been critical of this limited diagnostic frame. For example, Eduardo Duran uses the term *soul wound* instead to suggest that a "wounding that is sustained by the collective culture has an impact on the psyches of individuals in the society" (20). Similarly, "historic trauma transmission" (HTT) describes the intergenerational and collective impact of trauma within Indigenous communities. As Cynthia Wesley-Esquimaux and Magdalena Smolewski explain,

> Hidden collective memories of this trauma, or a collective non-remembering, is passed from generation to generation, as are the maladaptive social and behavioural patterns that are symptoms of many

---

5   Trauma Studies emerged as an interdisciplinary field that engages with major strands of Western thought. As Roger Luckhurst points out in *The Trauma Question*, the discrete categories can be formed from four main theoretical classifications: the Frankfurt School, post-structuralism (Hartman; Felman), psychoanalysis (Caruth; Leys), and feminism (Herman; Laura Brown). The former three categories deal primarily with the experiences of Holocaust survivors and the harrowing task of "disclosure." Feminist scholars engage with the experiences of incest survivors alongside a systemic critique of patriarchy, which makes this field more sensitive to the pursuit of social justice. A field of postcolonial trauma studies has also emerged in response to the epistemological limitations of the trauma analyses produced by Western theoretical framings (see Rothberg; Visser).

6   Psychoanalytic frameworks have been repeatedly contested by literary and Indigenous critics because they fail to account for Indigenous epistemologies (see Visvis; Fagan). The pathologization of Indigenous survivors has also been critiqued for emphasizing and creating victim subjectivities of residential school survivors (see Chrisjohn and Young). Akin to this view, Episkenew suggests that "Colonialism is sick; under its auspices and supported by its mythology, the colonizers have inflicted heinous wounds on the Indigenous population that they set out to civilize" (11).

social disorders caused by historic trauma. There is no "single" historic trauma response; rather, there are different social disorders with respective clusters of symptoms. (iv)

While the concept of trauma is deployed to describe residential school experience, discourses of healing are frequently circulated to respond to this experience (Henderson and Wakeham 16) and often become conflated with the concept of reconciliation (Green 135). The misappropriation of both trauma and healing is potentially harmful, as responsibility for recovery is placed on the individual. The Royal Commission on Aboriginal Peoples offers a decolonized definition of this term:

> Healing, in Aboriginal terms, refers to personal and societal recovery from lasting effects of oppression and systemic racism experienced over generations. Many Aboriginal people are suffering not simply from specific diseases and social problems, but also from a depression of spirit resulting from 200 or more years of damage to their cultures, languages, identities and self-respect. (109)

Akin to this view, Patricia Monture-Angus states that negotiations with the federal government have often been arduous "because part of what Aboriginal people seek, the right to heal, is not considered by all a self-governing function" (27), since Indigenous conceptualizations of healing generally carry holistic responses to the injuries caused by colonization.

Arguably, Van Camp's text may demonstrate "the power of literature both to heal Indigenous people from postcolonial traumatic stress response and to cure the settlers from the delusions learned from their mythology" (Episkenew 15). Trauma is explored at the margins of the narrative through memory and flashback, which provide a testament to historical inequity that unfolds into the lived experience of an adolescent intergenerational survivor in the North. The protagonist's pursuit of romance (situated at the forefront of the narrative) as a means of intimacy and disclosure demonstrates a present consistently haunted by the past. As the audience is privy to the protagonist's first-person narration, they are also plagued by Larry's intrusive memories that disrupt a teleological unfolding of the past. As Fagan notes, "Larry uses his abilities as a storyteller to express and understand his traumatic past. The past is gradually revealed through his stories, as well as through fragmentary flashbacks, and we must struggle to put together Larry's horrific history" ("Weesageechak" 212). The text reads like a patchwork chronicle of anxiety, romance, and violence. Van Styvendale's concept of *trans/historical* trauma can help elucidate the text as it "gestures toward a trauma that takes place and is repeated in multiple epochs and, in this sense, exceeds its historicity, conventionally understood as its singular location in the past" (204). However, this novella should not simply be read as an example of traumatic repetition introduced through flashbacks and nightmares, which in Western psychoanalytic theory is theorized as a pronounced struggle to synchronize chronological events.[7] Laguna Pueblo critic Paula Gunn Allen suggests that "when an Indian writes a chronological tale, it is a tale of colonization and death. That's what is going to happen. Nothing else *can* happen to an Indian in a chronological time frame. [. . .] But in this other structure ['anachronicity'], what's happening is we're beginning to develop a structural mode that will enable us to affirm life and to talk about who we really are, as well as who we imagine ourselves to be" (qtd. in Madsen 126).[8] Moreover, Athabaskan scholar Dian Million's *felt theory* elucidates how trauma narratives disclosed by Indigenous women "transformed the debilitating force of an old social control, *shame*, into a social change agent," thereby invalidating the pathological frame imposed by settlers by "creat[ing] a context for a more complex 'telling'" of residential school history (54). In light of this, I read Van Camp's novel from its end because the intricacies of the novella's conclusion are deeply entwined with the violence at its opening.

---

7   Madsen argues that resistance to the linear rejects the imposition of psychoanalytic labels such as *repetition* to Indigenous literary forms. She also suggests that Gunn Allen's concept of *circling* and the psychoanalytic concept of *repetition* may have commonalities but remain different epistemological positions (126–7). Indigenous critics insist that Indigenous worldviews should not be reduced to cultural or folk discourses that are subsumed under, likened to, or "explained" by Western theories and knowledge frameworks. I am reminded of Armand Ruffo's assertion that "Indigenous peoples have their own, long-standing 'ways of knowing' and to simply categorize them in Western terms is to dismiss thousands of years of traditional knowledge and indeed to perform a new act of colonization and conquest" ("Exposing" 95).

8   This quote is taken from a 1983 interview with Paula Gunn Allen in the literary journal MELUS. In this interview she describes the pitfalls of *synchronicity* in Indigenous narratives or narratives *about* Indigenous peoples (see Ballinger and Swann). A prominent example of the linear frame is used by Robert Alexie in his novel *Porcupines and China Dolls* to narrate the history of colonization in Gwi'chin territory. In his introductory chapter, Alexie relays a history of the Blue People, which details acts of dispossession and the imposition of residential schooling. The chapters that follow, however, do not utilize the same teleological frame to depict this legacy.

Despite Larry's intimate friendship and sexual union with Juliet Hope, she departs the Northwest Territories for a new life in Alberta due to her pregnancy by Larry's best friend, Johnny Beck. Van Camp ends the narrative with the following passage:

> I said, "Rest."/ I said, "Sleep."/ I said, "Die."/ And I wept because I knew I had someone / someone to remember my name/ someone to cry out my name / someone to greet me naked in snow / someone to mourn me in death / to feel me there / in my sacred place / and I wept because I did not belong to anyone / I was not owned / not with mate / but I smiled too knowing this because I knew my life was still unwrapped / I would in time / find one to call my own / mine to disappear in / to be [. . .] (118–19)

This passage is central to the novella as it is linked specifically to two previous passages and in turn fixes the present to the past. The repetition of the language in this passage at other moments in the text represents a connection between two forms of institutionalized education situated within a larger frame of colonization. Firstly, the words *to be* (articulated in English at the end) are emphasized at the beginning of the text in Mlle. Savoie's classroom at the Fort Smith high school. Larry and his fellow classmates "were going through the six stages of rigor mortis, droning on and on about the verb être, which means 'to be.' It didn't mean a damn thing to me, but I had it down pat: 'Je suis, tu es, il est, elle est, nous sommes, vous êtes, ils sont, elles sont'" (11). The French language is only mentioned twice in the text: in this classroom and during his father's drunken rages. Larry notes that "My dad stood over my mom. He had called me out of my room. He was holding a yellow broom. He was speaking French. He had learned it in the residential schools. He never talked about what happened there, but he always talked French when he drank" (58). The scene that follows demonstrates his father's cruelty and sexual violence as Larry is forced to witness the rape of his mother. The memory of residential schools is situated within Larry's memory of his own abuse at the hands of his father and blurs the distinction between individual, collective, and historic trauma, thus illustrating the overlapping and far-reaching impact of colonization.

Secondly, the concluding passage can also be read as a re-articulation of one used previously in the novella. While the passage is not identical, its similarity is unmistakable:

> And we wept because we knew we had no one. No one to remember our names, no one to cry them out, no one to greet us naked in snow, to mourn us in death, to feel us there, in our sacred place. We wept because we did not belong to anyone. I cried too for what had to happen. Our shadows were black. Mine was the only one with fire it its eyes. (79)

This passage is situated in a moment when Larry is reminded of his culpability in an arson that resulted in the horrific maiming of himself and his younger cousins. While sitting within the "snuffhouse" shack, Larry and his cousins sniff gasoline as they weep softly and separately about the abuse and neglect they have endured at the hands of their parents. McKegney states that "Larry and his cousins are wounded by isolation; they have 'no one' because they have been abandoned by their parents, the broader community, and the Canadian nation, leaving no dynamic relational space in which to negotiate empowered identities (masculine or otherwise)" (McKegney, "Beautiful Hunters" 211). To demonstrate this, Van Camp's narrative defies linear narration and could instead be read as "a process of circling, recording sensation and fragmented thought," where the narrative unfolds "in such a way as to permit the gradual accumulation of meaning by key symbols" (Madsen 126). Through the repeated passages, the novella circles back through historical and contemporary events that appear outside a conventional chronological frame; this temporal frame highlights the correlation between the legacy of residential schooling and the intergenerational transfer of trauma to subsequent generations. Each of these passages demonstrates how intimate and individual experiences are fixed to the imposition of colonial policies on the individual. To further explore the ambivalence of the novella's ending, I draw on Cecil White Hat, who states that

> for Native people, the trauma continues. There hasn't been an end. It is seen in the racism Native people face every day, and in the ignorance of the dominant society. It is especially seen in the school systems, the

mental and chemical health systems, and in the lack of appropriate resources which are culturally meaningful. (qtd. in Wesley-Esquimaux
and Smolewski 55)

While Van Camp's narrative remains ambivalent, the translation of *to be*
to English from the original French (a language marked by both residential schooling and the contemporary high school setting) demonstrates
some semblance of transformation and perhaps alludes to a more hopeful conclusion.

III. EDUCATING LARRY: WHERE IS THE NORTH?

Michael Rothberg's contribution to the special issue of *Studies in the
Novel* endorses trauma theory that highlights the "collective, spatial and
the material (instead of the individual, temporal and linguistic)" (228).
Rothberg emphasizes the consideration of space as integral to opening
up trauma theory to account for collective and historic experience, as
opposed to relying solely on Freudian constructs that underline individual and event-specific experiences. This is important in considering
the legacy of residential school trauma in Van Camp's novella. Michelle
Balaev suggests that "descriptions of the geographic place of traumatic
experience and remembrance situate the individual in relation to a larger
cultural context that contains social values that influence the recollection of the event and the reconfiguration of the self" (149). Similarly,
Legat points out that "temporality" in Tlicho culture "is an aspect of the
places where events, and therefore, stories reside" (34). While temporal
analyses of traumatic experience can aid in conceptualizing collective
effects, the spatialization of trauma explores specific material origins and
outcomes of these experiences which can be helpful in revealing the om-
nipresence of the settler state.

Educational space is introduced early by Van Camp as he dedicates a
section of his novella to the description of a specific teacher, Mr. Harris.
The narrator describes him as a "blown-human tire," but he also reveals
that "There was this cool thing about him: his index finger. I watched it.
It was actually a magic wand that cast the spell of human blush around
the room. Whoever he'd point to, they'd blush. He'd point to me, I'd
blush" (8). While the source of Larry's ignominy is never revealed, the
relationship between student and teacher is built on asymmetrical authority maintained by the practice of public shaming. This is reflected in

a scene that takes place between Mr. Harris and Johnny Beck, in which Johnny's dysfunctional family life is publicly revealed and he is labelled a "social misfit" by Mr. Harris (10). Later, during a school assembly, Juliet outbids Mr. Harris, who is attempting to purchase Johnny as a "slave" to enact revenge for repeated attempts to resist his disciplinary behaviour. As Juliet is crowned victorious, Larry notices the teacher's absence and reflects, "[b]ut there were no teachers left. They'd waddled off to the staff room to bloat and stink and die" (28). Given Mr. Harris's propensity to degrade his students publicly, it is no accident that Van Camp ensures that he and other faculty are portrayed as embodiments of decay and decomposition. This subversive tactic demonstrates how "patriarchal white sovereignty as a regime of power deploys a discourse of pathology as a means to subjugate and discipline Indigenous people to be extra good citizens," but these "tactics and strategies" are what constitute pathological behaviour (Moreton-Robinson 63). Furthermore, the educational terrain of the North is presented as alien, since Mr. Harris (and other teachers) insist on having their children educated "down South" instead of at Larry's high school (Van Camp 8). This alludes to violence that is enacted "whenever people feel the need to draw the line between the civilized and uncivilized" (Razack, qtd. in Philipose 72). The division between the Northwest Territories and the "South" spells out not only a material and economic divide, but an epistemological one that builds on a binary established through the lens of White privilege.

Larry's experience of violence in the novella is highly spatialized—often occurring at the high school—which gestures to a continuum of epistemic and symbolic violence in the contemporary school system that replicates the violence of residential schools already haunting the narrative. For Larry, high school is the site of verbal torments and beatings by Jazz the Jackal, which are accompanied by a laissez-faire and almost permissive attitude by Mr. Harris. Van Camp describes how Larry is racially bullied and how Jazz taunts him: "Hey Dogrib. [. . .] They're having a sale on Lysol down the street. I seen your mom passed out in a ditch. I fucked her for fifteen bucks" (45). The high school is often depicted as a site of violence as Larry witnesses a fight between Johnny and Darcy in which "there were about thirty guys—Chipewyn, Cree, Slavey, Inuit and white—with their arms locked to form a huge human circle so nobody in the ring could escape until it [the physical fight] was all over. If whoever was fighting tried to escape, they'd be kicked back into the ring" (19). Larry later reveals that a White student named Darcy McManus had given him a concussion the previous year during an attack so violent he could have pressed charges. Accordingly, "conceptualizations of place might take direction from considerations of the body, or indeed that the body is a politicized place unto itself," meaning that "the body is the more intimate of places while simultaneously embodying crucial sites of political, economic, and cultural struggles" (de Leeuw 342). Episodes of bullying are present throughout the novella, with Jazz beating Larry mercilessly at a dance.[9] Johnny, who has become a de facto protector for Larry, looks on, but neglects him as he receives a concussion from Jazz's beating. In his unconscious state, Larry remembers the violence perpetrated against him by his father and the subsequent patricide he later commits (yet this is relayed earlier in the novella). The bullying that Larry receives in the present becomes tied to events that have occurred in the past through the act of remembering.

In light of Van Camp's rather dark characterization of educational spaces and teachers, where is the ideal pedagogical space in *The Lesser Blessed*? Million states that "even after looking at the tactical spectrum of colonization, from economic disenfranchisement to confinement on reserves and their effects on Indigenous autonomy, Canadian Indigenous peoples often cite their effective colonization as the social dismemberment of families" (3). Larry has two primary caregivers in the novella, his Tlicho mother and her often estranged partner, Jed, who is of Slavey descent.[10] Larry lives with his mother, who, coincidentally, is described as "busy" because she is studying to become a teacher. While their relationship is characterized by deep silences, she insists that he spend time with Jed as he instructs Larry in hunting and in Dene histories. In light of this, Fagan suggests that Larry is able to negotiate his traumatic experiences through Jed's instruction in Dene stories (213). In the novella, after receiving a severe beating from Jazz, Larry finds himself in the hospital accompanied by his mother and Jed where he joins their arms to form a "triangle." McKegney observes that "[t]he triangle is 'perfect' because none of the three attempts to assert her or his will over the others; they

---

9   It is unclear in the novella whether the dance takes place on school grounds or at a community centre.

10 The term *Slavey* is rarely used except in the description of the North Slavey and South Slavey language groups. The North Slavey Nations are now referred to as Sahtu and the South Slavey Nations are now known as Deh Cho.

gain strength through commitment to balance and harmony" (217). This scene is profoundly moving as familial relationships eroded by residential schooling begin to stabilize, and it is within this family unit that a consummate pedagogical space of *home* and *family* resurges. Moreover, it is the romantic relationship between Larry's mother and Jed that remains consistent, as opposed to the relationship between Larry and Juliet.[11]

Chrisjohn and Young suggest that "the use of education as a weapon of oppression has largely been concealed" (62). Residential schools were actually a form *de-education* that "consisted of purging the knowledges from Indigenous societies, knowledges that were housed in the collective oral narratives, and replacing them with imperial knowledge" (Episkenew 25). De Leeuw suggests that residential schools "ensured First Nations students, from the moment they set eyes upon the places of their 'education,' were spatially disoriented in a place designed to exclude and expunge Indigeneity" (345). Yet, Van Camp's text not only depicts an interpersonal legacy of residential schooling, it attends to larger structural questions of education, violence, and racism. The novella opens with Larry reflecting that "the sad thing about our school was that we were so far behind the system. It's true, and as a result, the students in our school were baby birds falling to their deaths while the school was guilty of failure to breathe" (8).

In *Sharing Our Successes*, David Bell consolidates various policy reports to list First Nations' educational goals.[12] As part of a reconciliation strategy, these goals would be reflected in both First Nations communities and within the mainstream school system. Recommendations include (though not exclusively): "Aboriginal control of education, school courses in Aboriginal Studies, training and hiring of Aboriginal teachers, inclusion of parents and elders in the education of Aboriginal children,

---

11 Earlier in the novel, Larry places the relationship between his mother and Jed alongside his relationship with Juliet as he draws hearts containing the couples' names in the snow. Beside Jed and "Mom's" heart Larry writes "True Love Forever," while beside his and Juliet's, he writes "True if Destroyed" (29).

12 Some key documents include: National Indian Brotherhood Education Committee, *Indian Control of Indian Education* (Ottawa: National Brotherhood, 1969); Assembly of First Nations, *Tradition and Education: Towards a Vision of Our Future* (Ottawa: AFN, 1989); Department of Indian Affairs and Northern Development, *MacPherson Report on Tradition and Education: Towards a Vision of Our Future* (Ottawa: DIAND, 1991); Royal Commission on Aboriginal Peoples, "Education," Final Report, *Volume 3: Gathering Strength* (Ottawa: Royal Commission on Aboriginal Peoples, 1996).

and Aboriginal language instruction" (Bell 33). While these proposals have been reiterated frequently, the implementation of curricular or pedagogical change has been glacial and, in some cases, virtually ignored. Jurisdictional complexity and obstructionist government policy (at both federal and provincial levels) continue to sideline these recommendations in favour of short-term fixes.

While First Nations control over education is still highly contested, comprehensive land claims in the North have extended First Nations authority considerably. In 1990, the Dogrib (Tlicho) Nation held a meeting to discuss educational outcomes for children and youth. Conducted entirely in the Dogrib (Tlicho) language, community members showed great concern that schools were staffed by people from the south and only Anglo teaching techniques were utilized (see Martin). A 1972 speech by Tlicho Elder Jimmy Bruneau reflects this position: "I have asked for a school to be built [. . .] on my land [. . .] and that school will be run by my people, and my people will work at that school and our children will learn both ways, our way and the whitemen's way" (Bell 62). In the formulation of curriculum, "Dene elders stated unequivocally and repeatedly that education and the curriculum must teach children survival, survival not only of the Dene people and their language and way of life, but survival of all living beings and the world in which they live" (Chambers 141). Supporting this, Legat suggests there is an agreement between Elders and scholars that the "Dene have remained open to new ways" whereas Anglo-Canadians have not, "leading to the creation of government policies that are controlling and inflexible, designed to limit the ability to think for oneself" (32). Highlighting community and parental involvement in pedagogy and curriculum, Western epistemologies and methodologies are positioned as secondary to Tlicho pedagogy, language, and epistemology. Instruction in Tlicho language, culture, and history is central to the curriculum on Tlicho territory, yet the territorial government's curriculum still extends its reach into most other school boards whereby many members of the Dene Nation are subject to Westernized pedagogy.[13] However, the Tlicho

13 Eurocentric curriculum still prevails in the North, despite opposition, and the Northwest Territories has adopted the curricular guidelines from the province of Alberta. However, it is important to note that the Northwest Territories was the first provincial or territorial government to construct and implement curriculum that documents the history of residential schooling. This was announced at a March 2011 conference in British Columbia hosted by the Truth and Reconciliation Commission of Canada.

First Nation Land Claim, settled in 2003, is an example of the expansion of rights and governance in educational jurisdiction.

CONCLUSION

In February 2012, Justice Murray Sinclair, Chief Commissioner of the Indian Residential School Truth and Reconciliation Commission, stated that the "education system was the vehicle for inflicting generations of abuse and pain on aboriginal [sic] people in Canada so it must also be the vehicle for redemption" (Theodore). While Commissioner Sinclair's optimistic statement may offer important insight into a possible strategy for ensuring the success of Indigenous–settler reconciliation in Canada, Assembly of First Nations leader Shawn A-in-chut Atleo warns that settler governments (both federal and provincial) continue to ignore and violate treaty obligations to First Nations peoples, particularly in the crafting of education policy and the delegation of necessary funds to sustain on-reserve education. The neglect of First Nations education and the subsequent right to govern curriculum and resources has resulted in reduced funding and lower graduation rates for First Nations students (Toesing). These facts call into question the state's commitment to First Nations education and the process of reconciliation. While residential schooling was not successful in undermining the cultural integrity of First Nations peoples, much damage was done to the transmission of knowledge and culture through language. Yet, *The Lesser Blessed* highlights pedagogical figures who re-enact this suppression via language instruction and the spread of historical narratives. Despite the horror of the residential schools legacy, Van Camp's text resists deploying a victimized subjectivity for its protagonist. The conclusion suggests the failure of reconciliation due to the ongoing structural inequities faced by an intergenerational survivor. While Larry is able to disclose his painful past to Juliet, he gains some comfort, but ultimately the romance between the Indigenous student and his White classmate is unattainable. It is the reconstituted family unit and the growing knowledge of his language and culture (epistemologies and histories directly targeted by the IRS) that ultimately gesture towards a robust form of healing.

PART V

·◆·

Cultural Memory
in a Globalized Age

CHAPTER 23

•-•

"I have nothing soothing to tell you": Dionne Brand's *Inventory* as Global Elegy[1]

Alexis Motuz

*[. . .] Monday, February 28th, one
hundred and fourteen, Tuesday, August 16th, ninety
Wednesday September 14th, one hundred and eighty-
two, Friday November 18th, eighty
these were the bloodiest days in one year,
in one place*

*there are atomic openings in my chest
to hold the wounded,*

*besides the earth's own
coiled velocities, its meteoric elegance,
and the year still not ended, [. . .]*

Dionne Brand, *Inventory* 100

Although the elegy has long functioned as a memorial, its purpose has traditionally been to offer consolation and compensation to mourners, to allow them to move on and, paradoxically, to forget: "the best way to forget the dead [is] by giving them a quiet grave [. . .] first to remember them. Only a past that has been genuinely recollected can also be forgotten" (David Shaw 216). Written amid ongoing genocides, wars, and human rights abuses, Dionne Brand's postmodern elegy, *Inventory* (2006), forbids such forgetting.

Brand presents an unnamed speaker who attempts to respond ethically to the ongoing global violence by taking an inventory of the death

1   This research was supported by a Social Sciences and Humanities Research Council Doctoral Fellowship. I am grateful to Tanis MacDonald and Carol Louise for their comments. Excerpts from *Inventory* by Dionne Brand (copyright 2006) are reprinted by permission of McClelland & Stewart.

and devastations to which she bears witness at the window of the television. Throughout her long poem, Brand draws our attention to the ways in which mainstream media emotionally distances viewers from the events they communicate. While these media bring geographically distant events into our living rooms, the hourly influx of dissociated visual images both emotionally distances and overwhelms viewers, creating in them a feeling of helplessness and apathy that leads to cultural amnesia.

To re-sensitize readers to global violence, Brand uses visceral imagery to translate abstracted and highly mediated images of the dead and dying into intimate terms. Brand contrasts the impersonality of the news media—signified in the above passage by dates and body counts—with the intimacy of the actual loss: "there are atomic openings in my chest / to hold the wounded" (100). These openings gesture to minute but multiplicitous spaces between atoms in all matter which, by dismissing our conception of the body as a clearly defined and closed space, blur the boundaries between one body and another and leave room for the ecocritical interpretation that we are all interconnected. At the same time, with its allusion to the atomic bomb, these "atomic openings" intimate the enormity and significance of global violence as well as the impossibility of knowing, or even accounting for, its innumerable victims. This incomprehensibility provides the central paradox of Brand's elegy: the ethical necessity and yet the impossibility of mourning mass death.[2] Rather than attempt to make sense of this devastation, Brand acknowledges its incomprehensibility and focuses instead on garnering an affective response from her readers that might connect them with the world's dead and foster remembrance. Unable to account for each individual, the speaker expresses her devastation by opening the intimate space of the chest—location of the heart, passions, and symbolically all feeling—to acknowledge these unnamed and unknowable wounded. Her inability to mourn these dead is exacerbated by the scale and continuation of global violence: these atrocities account for only "one place [. . .] and the year still not ended." While this statement seems to signal the introduction of another devastating list, the speaker instead turns directly to the reader:

---

2   In "Witness to the Body Count: Planetary Ethics in Dionne Brand's *Inventory*," Cheryl Lousley situates this paradox within the postcolonial tradition: "The gesture toward making a comprehensive recording of fact, while simultaneously marking its impossibility, is characteristic of the postcolonial long poem" (37–38).

I have nothing soothing to tell you,
that's not my job,
my job is to revise and revise this bristling list,
hourly (100)

Reversing the roles set out in the traditional elegy—in which the ele-gist undertakes the work of mourning and guides the reader through a trajectory beginning with lament and ending with consolation[3]—Brand reconsiders the role of the poet-witness by claiming for herself the "job" of informer and not of deliverer. She positions her readers as compli-cated witnesses—witnesses who are themselves implicated in the very acts they grieve—and shifts to them the burden of mourning. In doing so, Brand has her readers consider the ethical impossibilities of mourn-ing mass death in the globalized and heavily mediated society of twenty-first-century North America.

Despite having been shortlisted for a Governor General's Literary Award, the Trillium Book Award, and the Pat Lowther Memorial Award, *Inventory* has received little in-depth critical attention.[4] As a postmod-ern elegy that effectively highlights the impediments to postmodern mourning and yet overcomes readers' apathy, Brand's poem deserves more critical attention. In her postmodern elegy, Brand draws attention to the ways in which highly mediated forms of witnessing by communi-cations media both make possible and simultaneously undermine grief; despite these challenges, she fulfills the role of the contemporary elegist of maintaining "ongoing affectionate relations with the dead" (Zeiger 63). Throughout her elegy, Brand draws on the physical and emotional responses she elicits from readers to create a sense of connection to, and responsibility for, the world's dead. I argue that this ethical connection stands in for the "affectionate relations" made impossible by the con-ditions of postmodern mourning. Brand maintains this connection through her subversions of the elegiac genre that prompt ongoing en-gagement with the dead and continued remembrance.

---

3   For an in-depth critical study of the conventions of the traditional elegy, see Peter Sacks's *The English Elegy: Studies in the Genre from Spenser to Yeats*. For an in-depth reading of the contem-porary Canadian elegy, see Priscila Uppal's *We Are What We Mourn* and Tanis MacDonald's *The Daughter's Way*.

4   *Inventory* has been the focus of only three articles to date; see Brydon, Lousley, and Barrett.

Drawing on current scholarship on the role of media in cultural memory-making, the first section of this essay considers *Inventory* as indicative of the difficulties posed to mourning by the mainstream media. In the second section, I analyze how Brand uses embodied imagery to affectively re-mediate conventional news media and connect readers intimately with the dead, thus forming the basis of an ethical response from readers. In the third section, I examine how, as an example of the postmodern elegy, *Inventory* subverts conventional elegiac expectations to foster ongoing remembrance of the dead.

MEDIA AND MEMORY

In *Mediation, Remediation and the Dynamics of Cultural Memory*, Astrid Erll and Ann Rigney describe the relationships between media and memory-making. Media of all forms—"spoken language, letters, books, photos, films"—function, they suggest, "as instruments of sense-making [that] mediate between the individual and the world" and that "provide frameworks for shaping both experience and memory" (1). In our increasingly globalized world, we depend more than ever on news media to communicate to us world events (Erll 9). This news media—their stories and images—circulate among us to form the common understanding and cultural memory of the represented events. In "Conflicts of Memory in a Media Age," Andrew Hoskins argues that this increasing reliance on mass media representations for our understanding of world events has effected a "collapse of memory" (*Televising War* 6). He argues that our memory provides us with visual images that represent events and that help us call to mind their surrounding contexts and this makes visual images "vital to memory" (4). While the media supplies us with images, the repetition of these images and their similarity to one another conflates individual representations and causes them to become disconnected from the events they represent. The result is that these dissociated images come to *stand in* for our *understanding* of the event, and remembering becomes replaced with the ability to "call up a picture" (Sontag, qtd. in Hoskins 12), thereby resulting in amnesia of the event itself (12). In "Cannibalizing Memory in the Global Flow of News," Barbie Zelizer takes Hoskins's "collapse of memory" a step further to expose how the mediation of local experience by global news flows leads to a "cannibalization" or erasure of local memory. She points to the fundamental "misfit between the work of memory and that of mediation" (27) and argues that the local experience required for memory-making is erased by news delivery systems that privilege "the uniform over the differentiated, form over content" (28) and "the simple over the complex" (30). She explains that "when memory moves into global flows of news, it by definition loses some of its locality" (28), and, consequently, it "loses the starting point so central to memory work" (28). As a result, the actualities of local events are replaced by Western media's own definitive interpretations of them (29).

Examining the mnemonic stages that play to Western media's need for "mnemonic certainty," Zelizer argues that while these stages make the West's global news stories "accessible, understandable, and formulaic" (29), they forfeit accuracy. As an example of the erasure of local experience, Zelizer cites how in 1993, during a series of famines in Africa, Kevin Carter's famous photo of a small starving Sudanese girl being tracked by a vulture (32) was used to represent famines across the continent. This "signal image" erased local experience by displacing the particular social, political, and environmental factors contributing to each individual famine. Zelizer concludes that what gets communicated by global news flows "are strategic associations rather than a regard for the local experiences so central to memory work" (33). Whereas for Hoskins, the image becomes dissociated from the narrative it aims to represent, in Zelizer, a single image is used to represent multiple unique circumstances, thus displacing the local narrative in the process of media production; this results in the erasure of local experience and the prevention of memory rather than its collapse. For both Hoskins and Zelizer, however, the effect is that engagement is deflected and memory erased. In "Journalism as an Agent of Prospective Memory," in which Keren Tenenboim-Weinblatt argues that open news stories "can take the form of a *to-do list*" for intended actions (216), the displacement of the particularities of these local experiences undermines our ability either to respond appropriately or to prevent such events from happening again. Hoskins further complicates the use of images as initiators of an ethical response from viewers by pointing out that although "one of the principal justifications espoused for the display and publication of 'disturbing' images is that they act precisely to prevent amnesia" (11), the affective power of an image no longer depends on the extent of suffering depicted, but on the context of its mediation: "[A]udiences treat images of death very differently according to their mediated context and also their familiarity with those similar images, rather than against any standard of suffering" (9). Thus, even those images that do attempt to represent local circumstances are undermined by their mediated contexts.

The difficulty of engaging with the events portrayed by the global media stems not only from the context but also from the conditions of representation. As Margaret Gibson argues in her sociological study "Death and Mourning in Technologically Mediated Culture," although media technology is "designed to over-come the actual corporeal and geographical distance of a representation," viewers are always aware that they are "experiencing proximity at a distance" (417). This perceived distance undercuts viewers' emotional connection to represented subjects and results in many of these news stories having "a short-term impact on psyche and emotions." Add to this the "fast flows of imagery, talk and sounds," and viewers' ability to process the consequences of represented atrocities is undermined: viewers become, instead, "bodies and psyches absorbing and deflecting stories and emotions within fractions of time" (418).

In *Inventory*, Brand addresses how pervasive media shape our experience and our memories of events by exposing how form and content of the media dehumanize both viewers and represented subjects. Inscribing the harmful effects of mediated experiences as violence on the body, Brand presents images of bodies as consumed and/or fragmented as symbolic of our own fragmented subjectivities and relationships: she writes "screens lacerate our intimacies" (5). Because the screen only allows viewers to watch at a remove, it renders engagement through the proximate senses impossible. Able only to see and listen to what is reported, viewers remain disconnected from represented subjects, rendering our increasingly globalized world an affectively distanced and "distancing planet" (10). This distance, combined with the saturating, real-time broadcasts that implicate us as vicarious witnesses to global atrocities, produces in audiences the passive complicity that Brand criticizes and attempts to re-mediate in *Inventory*.

MEDIATION AND REMEDIATION

Brand's opening poem lays bare a history of global injustice and establishes what is to be mourned at the beginning of the twenty-first century: namely, the apathy of society toward ongoing global violence. The speaker opens by making reference to an undefined "we" which resurfaces throughout the poem: she laments,

We believed in nothing

the black-and-white american movies
buried themselves in our chests,
glacial, liquid, acidic as love. (3)

As in her description of "atomic openings in [her] chest / to hold the wounded" (100), Brand draws on the intimacy of the chest—the location of the heart and the symbolic space in which we store our beliefs and passions—to show the extent to which our bodies and minds are occupied by the media. By shifting the agency from *us* to the mediated images—*they* "buried *themselves* in *our* chests" (emphasis added)—Brand emphasizes the extent to which we enable the media to objectify us through our own passive consumption. Believing in "nothing," rather than developing our own beliefs and values, we have created a void into which the American mainstream media has inserted its own ideals and its depictions of a simplified "black-and-white" world. While this world offers an escape, it neither helps us cope with real-life complexity nor offers us the consoling warmth or the sense of groundedness potentially offered by personal beliefs; rather, they are "glacial, liquid, acidic." That these movies are "acidic as love" highlights the capacity of both these movies and love to consume the self. Love is acidic but reformative in that it painfully challenges our conception of self and corrodes individualistic tendencies so that we develop the vulnerability and take on the sacrifice necessary for relationship and community. By contrast, these movies are painfully acidic in their alienation—"their love stories never contained us, / their war epics left us bloody" (5)—they corrode relationship and consume rather than foster one's humanity.

Although she criticizes the media for its dehumanizing effects, Brand is careful not to position her readers as helpless victims: we are complicit in the making of this unjust world and in our own self-objectification. After drawing attention to the long history of injustices she inherits—"the homicides of Indians"; "the forests we destroyed"; "the orange clad criminals" in Guantanamo Bay—the speaker admits her own and our responsibility: "we did all this and more" (7). She points out how, as witnesses, we admit "blindfolds" (7) and willingly eschew our ethical responsibilities; instead we adopt journalistic discourses that justify our lack of response by reinforcing binaries between "us" and "them": "we do not deserve it [. . .] they hate our freedom" (27). In passively consuming these discourses, we have "tender[ed] / our own bodies into dreamery" (3) and so numbed ourselves to human suffering: now, we are "dead on our feet" performing "acts of ventriloquism" (4).

Even while she criticizes North Americans for their collective amnesia and their apathy, she reminds readers of how, while the media invites us to mourn these mass deaths, it simultaneously makes this mourning impossible. "Half the mind is atrophied in this" (9), she writes, referring to the effects of the overwhelming amount of reported violence. She highlights the dehumanization of represented subjects by showing that what we see is not starving people but instead fragmented subjects —"the broken fingers, pricked and bruised, / misformed ribs and the famished babies" —to which, try as we might, we cannot relate and which, despite this, become fodder "for the world's most famous photos" (6). Unable to respond and exhausted by our attempts, we have "succumbed / headlong in effusive rooms / to the science-fiction tales of democracy" (8) and turned to "the unremitting malls of all desires" (9) because their advertisements promised us relief and happiness, even though we could feel "our hungers, / nibbling our own hearts to red pits" (10). Acknowledging the dehumanizing effects of both media representation and its consumption, she writes: "no wonder, no wonder, / every evening falls on axioms" (9), thereby recognizing the difficulty of addressing the complexity of our world and acting ethically within it.

Against this apathetic and disconnected culture, Brand envisions an alternative way of life that is politically engaged and based on active, passionate response to others, and the shared bodily experiences of singing, dancing, and aging. In contrast to her earlier images of destruction—"the homicides of Indians" and "the suicides inside us" (3)—she inserts images of hope, love, and tenderness. She asks us to imagine "how would it truly be to have danced / with Celia Cruz, unsmiling" or "to have seen Che / Guavara as an old man on television" (10–11). Drawing on historical figures, she reminds us of the intimacy and connection to others that we have lost through our past and present passive choices and our consumption of mediated culture. She cites "Te recuerdo Amanda" by Victor Jara and she asks us to consider what it would have been like to sing, instead, about the rain in a lover's hair (*la lluvia en el pelo*) or "to have never heard 'Redemption Song,' so hoarse, at all" (11). Invoking sensual experiences between couples, she contrasts the intimacy of might have been—the overwhelming "compassion" that would have "made jails extinct"—with the alienation of our current disconnected and highly mediated culture.

Along with these alternative cultures that show what we have lost, Brand offers personal experiences with "Others" as a means to re-mediate the distant and disconnected images of the global atrocity presented by the mainstream media. Revealing how sensory apprehension breaks down barriers between one body and another, Brand depicts individuals as connected to or disconnected from the world depending on their ability to sense the world around them. Focusing specifically on the proximate senses of taste and touch, she draws attention to the ways in which these senses require an openness and vulnerability toward the "Other." Both senses depend on the contact between bodies and the crossing of internal and external boundaries: taste, for example, requires bringing an external object into the vulnerable and intimate internal space of the mouth; touch requires contact that allows the warmth and pressure of one body to pass through the external boundary of the skin to receptors below. Brand's re-mediations establish a sense of intimacy with faraway "Others" that removes the distance otherwise created by mainstream mediated representations.

In "IV ii," the speaker describes an intimate exchange with a silversmith who calls her "Cousin." In a word that is "a soft meeting and a love" (58) and "that [. . .] is more than father sister brother / mother" (59), she experiences the intimacy of a human connection which leaves her feeling as if she "needed nothing [. . .] other than the time we'd spent" (60). After leaving the market, the speaker expresses her yearning for intimate connection, stating, "I wanted to go back, take / his hand, eat from it." The speaker's yearning not only to bridge the physical space by taking the silversmith's hand, but to break down the physical borders between them by eating and taking nourishment from it, communicates the extent to which she longs to open herself and be vulnerable to this stranger. Although the speaker desires such a relationship, she recognizes that this word is "a warning and a lie" since such intimacy between a tourist and a local would be constructed, would be out of place considering the socio-economic differences between them: "that was, would be, another life" (58). These embodied images, which eliminate physical distance and cross internal–external bodily borders to create intimacy, also express the speaker's desire to eliminate the more abstract geographical, political, and ideological boundaries that separate "us" from "them." Although it is "a warning and a lie," the speaker dwells on the silversmith's address *cousin* which, unlike *sister* or *mother*, recognizes affiliation without depending on the sameness of blood, experience, or ideology and thus welcomes difference, "clasping what is foreign whole" (59). By describing her longing for connection and yet drawing attention to the impossibility of such a connection in our current society, Brand highlights the intimate and meaningful connection with others that we have lost through our past and present choices and our consumption of mediated culture.

Brand's project in writing this inventory is to counter the sense of detachment and the accompanying apathy created by the media and to incite readers to respond ethically to global injustice. Surrounded by those who "carry umbrellas against the drizzled rain of evidence" (40), and the "children whose hearing's / been ruined already by the noise" (71), Brand writes,

> If they're numb over there, and all around her,
> She'll gather the nerve endings
> spilled on the streets, she'll count them like rice grains
> she'll keep them for when they're needed. (30)

To communicate the urgency of her project, Brand has her speaker-witness isolate the nerve endings and so remove any barriers between viewers and the outside world. In doing so, she removes the possibility of numbness and so obliges us to feel, then choose whether to act or to continue in our apathy.

Through her visceral imagery, Brand figuratively gather[s] our nerve endings and exposes us to the realities of global violence. In contrast to abstracted notions of "the abrupt density of life gone out" or the "bundles of plump / corpses" (21), Brand re-humanizes distant others and makes understandable what the media depicts as the "unrealities of faraway islands." Her imagery breaks down barriers between poet, speaker-witness, and reader and engenders in us an affective response to ongoing injustice. As the speaker "listens, each hour, each night" (29) and bears witness to "what is never shown" (31), she composes "a letter, / an account of her silence, / its destination all the streets" (34). Her third-person descriptions of the speaker spill into first-person narrations so that when she writes,

all I can offer you now though is my brooding hand,
my sodden eyelashes and the like,
these humble and particular things I know,
my eyes pinned to your face (37)

readers think the speaker is addressing the dead and suggesting, in typical elegiac fashion, that her words and images will keep them alive: "understand, I will keep you alive like this." Two stanzas later, however, she explicitly addresses readers, stating, "take this letter, put it on your tongue" (37), an image that shows that she wants her nourishing words to be received intimately, tasted, and incorporated into readers' bodies as visceral knowledge.

That these affective bodily responses are highly intimate but also nearly universal, allows them to establish a connection between readers, the poet-speaker, and the re-mediated subject. In "Global Intimacies," Diana Brydon writes that Brand's embodied imagery "shifts the terrain from the personal (with its focus on the autonomous individual as separate from others) to the intimate (that is, to the co-constitutions of subjectivity, image, word, and world and to a self developing through relation)" (997). In *Inventory*, these relations take on a new physicality where exchanges through the proximate senses depict an intimacy that generates in readers an affective response and a sense of connection to, and responsibility for, the world's dead. In elegiac terms, Brand's embodied imagery shifts the terms of relation from the *personal* "affectionate relations with the dead" normally described by the elegist (Zeiger 63), to the *impersonal* yet paradoxically *intimate affective* relations between readers and the dead that open up the possibilities for mourning and remembrance.

POSTMODERN ELEGY

Despite the challenges offered by postmodern mourning—the mourners' complicity, the multiplicity of loss, and the highly mediated forms of witnessing offered by communications media which make possible and simultaneously undermine grief—Brand fulfills the role of the contemporary elegist of maintaining "ongoing affectionate relations with the dead" (Zeiger 63). Having elicited an affective response from readers, Brand draws on this response to create an ethical connection to the dead that stands in for the "affectionate" relations made impossible by the conditions of postmodern mourning. Brand then maintains these affective relations by refusing to offer any formal or aesthetic closure. Both by refusing to offer consolation and by continuing her record beyond the ending of the text, Brand forces readers to remain engaged with her inventory and the grief it provokes. In so doing, she fosters remembrance, or at least a continued acknowledgement, of the dead.

Memory theorist Ann Rigney highlights the connection between closure and forgetting when she writes, "[t]o bring remembrance to a conclusion is de facto already to forget" and notes that, "[w]hile putting down a monument may seem like a way of ensuring long-term memory, it may in fact turn out to mark the beginning of amnesia" (Koselleck, qtd. in Rigney 345). Because a marked conclusion provides a sense of closure to one's grief that permits mourning and moving on, Brand leaves her elegy incomplete. She not only refuses to offer her elegy as a monument by which to forget the dead, but she reminds us that bodies continue to pile up.

As "the wars' last and late night witness" (21), Brand's speaker keeps readers attuned to atrocities as they occur—"here is the latest watchful hour / —twenty-seven in Hillah, three in fighting in / Amariya, two by roadside bombing [. . .] *twenty seven* again, twenty-seven—" (23)—and she highlights both that this violence is ongoing—"enough numbers still to come so twenty" (26)—and the rapidity with which bodies accumulate: "this time / forty, / then in Milan twenty-four [. . .] all one hundred or so in one week" (72). Although she intersperses these body counts with moments of beauty and tempered hope to remind us of what ought to be fought for—"river song and bird song and / wine naturally" and "the surface of the earth, how it keeps springing back, / for now" (89)—she complicates these images by showing that we are in the process of destroying our only sources of consolation. The poet-speaker asks "where's their sweet life of green oranges, / of plums and dates, of papayas ripening," evoking sensual and comforting images of nourishment and plenty, only to then interrupt the comfort evoked by accusing us with our complicity: "forget it, we can't speak of nature in that breath any more, / the earth is corroding already with cities" (40). Subverting the conventional elegiac trope of invoking images of pastoral renewal to offer consolation to mourners, she rejects them as both inadequate and inappropriate given our current ecological crisis: "Let us not invoke the natural world, it's ravaged like any battlefield" (42). Likewise, she refuses religious consolations because faith-based explanations might prevent her listeners from engaging directly with world issues: "don't pray it only makes things worse, I know, / think instead of what we might do" (34).

By refusing the consolation and closure that would allow readers to mourn the dead and move on, Brand creates a post-postmodern elegy that forbids forgetting. Concluding her inventory by stating, "I have nothing soothing to tell you, / that's not my job," Brand subverts elegiac convention by positioning her readers as witnesses and complicated mourners—mourners who are themselves complicit in allowing the very acts they grieve—and bestowing on them the onus for ethical response. She maintains the affective relations with the dead by continually reminding readers that the tally is rising. "Revis[ing] and revis[ing] this bristling list / hourly" (100)—a job which, as the lack of a period indicates, continues beyond the text—the speaker connects the completion of her inventory/*Inventory* with the end of global violence and shows the necessity of keeping the poem, like the reader's grief, open-ended: this grief is all we have by which to acknowledge the dead.

Situated midway through her *Inventory*, Brand's elegy for Marlene Green juxtaposes a succinct, personal consolatory elegy against Brand's own impossible task of re-membering the dead. Contrasting the speaker's lack of personal knowledge of the mass dead with her intimate and detailed lament for the death of political activist Marlene Green, Brand emphasizes the practical difficulties and ethical tensions inherent in mourning mass death.

Brand's elegy for Green follows a conventional elegiac trajectory moving from lament to consolation and incorporates familiar tropes such as a procession of mourners and nature's union in mourning. It opens,

> The day you left the air broke
> into splinters,
> all night before the tree outside
> held its breath. (61)

In contrast to the dead who "disappea[r] in / the secret seas of living rooms here" (39), the whole human and non-human world responds in grief to Green's death—"the newspapers whimpered unread." Even those unaware of her death felt her absence: "old lovers, unknowing, staggered /

in doorways" (61). Brand's speaker proclaims that rivers and cities the world over *ought* to mourn Green's death—"the Layou, the Niger, the St. Lawrence / should weep now," "this city should spring hibiscus / in late winter." She declares, "we should call storms, / our grief will dry lakes," to express the extent to which her world is overturned by Green's death. Moving from grief to idealization, Brand positions Green as a saviour who, in her wisdom and leadership, could help to reclaim and re-mediate the world: "You knew the world" (61),

> you would [. . .]
> [. . .] tell us [. . .]
> how we could dilute bitter things
> and acrid cities; how
> to strain sorrow through our hands. (62)

Brand then completes the traditional elegiac trajectory by offering consolation in the hope that contact will be renewed—"will you send word / in letters, in goldenrod leaflets"—and concludes with hope renewed, "till then Marlene, / we will fix petals of you to our eyes" (62). By adhering to the structural and tropic conventions of the traditional elegy, Brand's elegy for Green reveals the potential force of the traditional elegy when used within the appropriate context—a personal lament for an individual. The detail she knows about Green's life allows her to mourn the individual; this same lack of detail in Brand's postmodern elegy makes such mourning impossible.

In the postmodern context, traditional elegiac discourse fails, and any attempt to elegize the mass dead is fraught with ethical tensions. The speaker is faced with the dilemma of desiring to make memorable the lives of the dead, to re-humanize them and thus prevent their simply being "add[ed] up" (52), and knowing that it is impossible to recognize each individual death in an ever-mounting death toll. Against the abstractness of "numbers so random, / so shapeless" (26), Brand's speaker writes "this figure, eight hundred every month / for the last year, and one hundred / and twenty in a brutal four days," and concludes, "things, things add up" (52)—a phrase which, in its simplicity, exemplifies our inability to grasp the magnitude of our loss and leaves us to make sense of how, and to what, this abundance of violence adds up, or even if it does "add up." She strives to render loss comprehensible by describing absence in material terms: "Consider the obliteration of four restaurants / the disappearance of sixty taxis each with one passenger / or four over-crowded classrooms" (78). Faced with the "impossibility of names" (78), she takes an inventory of the anonymous dead and records where and how they died—"five by suicide bomb in Kirkuk, five / by suicide in Shorgat, one [. . .]" (23). Constrained by time, space, language, and the urgency of her project, the speaker reduces each dead to a single "trium-phant" detail (29) but cannot capture the complexities of their individ-ual lives. The speaker thus risks essentializing the dead in order to bear witness to their deaths, all the while knowing that such "triumphant" details are not enough.

Anita Helle's, Alicia Ostriker's, and Tanis MacDonald's work on American and Canadian women's elegies opens up a variety of ethical questions about the role and responsibility of the postmodern poetic witness and the ethics of the elegiac genre that Brand's work addresses. In "Elegy as History," Anita Helle points to the history of the elegy as a genre for individuating loss and asks how far the genre can be opened up to mourn a mass dead (51). Situating contemporary elegiac women's writing within a historical context, she argues that the rhetorical power of the women's elegy begins this work by deviating from the tradition of individualizing grief to offer "politically conscious constructions of ele-giac purpose" (53). While Helle concerns herself with poems that "pres-ent an intimate relation to singular deaths as symptoms of larger-scale, global, historical disaster" and thus focuses on the personal relationship between the elegist/speaker-witness and a single, known, individual who stands in for the whole, Brand's postmodern elegy strays further from individuation to address mass death and the effects of mediation on memory and memorialization directly. In this context, Brand's speaker acts as what Ostriker defines in "Beyond Confession" as a "postmodern witness": one who rejects "master narratives of loss and mourning" and incorporates postmodern linguistic strategies such as "employing frag-mentation" and "refusing the pretence to coherence of mourners and witnesses" (35). In *The Daughter's Way*, MacDonald confirms that "the female-written elegy tends to refuse resolution rather than invite it" (15), but she also explores a further complication all postmodern elegies face: in secular Western society in which Christianized notions of consolation may be "puzzling," "incomprehensible," or, as we saw for Brand, "unap-pealing," "how does the elegist resist languishing in melancholia" (36) and "how can female resistance to consolation [. . .] be recuperated as a constructive force?" (218). By refusing to offer consolation, Brand opens up a space for her readers to engage constructively with global injustice so that her elegy gains ethical force through its resistance to consolation. While Ostriker's postmodern witness "preserv[es] the link, complexly, between affect and moral accountability" (35), Brand tests this link by providing readers with an affective recognition of their accountability to which *they* choose the direction and mode of response.

Brand's final image "there are atomic openings in my chest / to hold the wounded" (100), brings the poem full circle, replacing "the black-and-white American movies" (3) with the re-mediated dead and emphasizing the progression of affect in both the speaker and readers. The speaker's desire to "hold the wounded" expresses her yearning to overcome the distance and borders between herself and these "Others" and so establish the intimacy necessary to mourn them. Such intimacy, however, is impossible, as the image suggests. Since the dead are an anonymous multitude that continues to add up, they must necessarily remain unknown. Unable to recollect and elegize them, the speaker must take up the "job" of keeping readers attuned to ongoing violence, gathering the dead and holding them in her "bristling list" to be acknowledged.

In "V xi," Brand writes that "perfection, deep / at its source [. . .] isn't power" but "immaculate possibility" (79); by leaving her inventory open-ended and her readers unconsoled, Brand opens up the "possibility" for ethical remembrance. Subverting conventional elegiac tropes, she highlights our need to memorialize the dead even as she reminds us that traditional mourning practices cannot hold in the postmodern context. In denying her readers consolation, Brand shifts to them the burden of mourning and makes them consider the ethical impossibilities of mourning mass death in the globalized and heavily mediated society of twenty-first-century North America. Her "impossible" elegy overcomes the obstacles to postmodern mourning not by offering the "soothing" consolation that fosters forgetting, but by maintaining grief and suggesting that ethical memorialization must occur beyond the text: it depends on readers taking up ethical action.

CHAPTER 24

·◆·

Now and Then: Dionne Brand's
What We All Long For, the Desire to Forget,
and the Urban Archive

Joel Baetz

But in the city I long for men complete
their origins.
Dennis Lee, *Civil Elegies* (29)

History hovers over the four main characters in Dionne Brand's *What We All Long For*, and, at first, they don't know it.[1] Tuyen, Carla, Oku, and Jackie begin the novel as eager and self-induced amnesiacs, who imagine that the city is aggressively contemporary and an obvious antidote to the recent and distant pasts that chase them. What these decidedly urban citizens long for is to "disappear their origins" (Brand, *Map* 63). What they long for is to escape from home lives that are burdened with memories of unfamiliar people, distant places, and different experiences. What they long for is a city that will (choose your metaphor) distance them from domestic rituals of commemoration, sever their ties to their parents and their "nostalgic comparisons" (Brand, "Dionne" 71), or dispense with the "heterogeneous baggage" they carry downtown (Brand, *What We All Long For* 5). But what they get is a version of Toronto that is full of second-hand clothing,[2] old photographs, older habits, recurring nightmares, familiar haunts, unacknowledged memorials, and repurposed artifacts. Brand's Toronto is part-archive, part-palimpsest, a site in

---

1   My opening line recalls Brand's response to a question about the historical nature of *At the Full and Change of the Moon*: "It [history] penetrates the rest of the book, and it hovers over the rest of the book. [. . .] I was really [. . .] interested in the twentieth century descendents [sic] and how history hovers over them, whether they want to or not, whether they know it or not, whether they like it or not" (Brand, "At the Full" 24). Excerpts from *What We All Long For* by Dionne Brand (copyright 2005) are reprinted by permission of McClelland & Stewart.

2   The second-hand clothing store owned by Jackie is suggestively named *Ab und Zu*, which she translates as "now and then" (133).

which its cosmopolitan citizens are constantly confronted by the pasts—personal and cultural—that they long to forget.

Ever since *What We All Long For* was published, reviewers have been eager to celebrate the novel for its celebration of Toronto's general diversity.[3] Taking their cue from Tuyen's momentary excitement about the beautiful and hopeful "polyphonic" quality of a multilingual, multicultural, multiracial urban environment, these reviewers celebrate a version of the city that they long for—and not the one (or at least not the only one) that appears on the pages of Brand's novel. Sure, the Toronto that appears in *What We All Long For* is diverse in almost every way. There are "Bulgarian mechanics, there are Eritrean accountants, Colombian café owners, Latvian book publishers, Welsh roofers, Afghani dancers, Iranian mathematicians, Tamil cooks in Thai restaurants, Calabrese boys with Jamaican accents," and so on (5). There are "Sikhs in Fubu, Portuguese girls in DKNY, veiled Somali girls in Puma sneakers, Colombian teenagers in tattoos" (213). The catalogues of countries and cultures are hard to miss, and there is an obvious (and momentary) thrill experienced by Tuyen, Carla, Oku, and Jackie when they share in the excitement of the World Cup celebrations or when they come in contact with the various flavours, languages, sights, and experiences of a multicultural city.

I have no doubt that Brand's renditions of the thrill and beauty of Toronto's diversity are some of the most moving in the novel and some of the best in contemporary literature; I fully agree with David Chariandy on this matter. But I also believe that the recurring, even singular, celebration of the novel's rendition of Toronto's diversity runs the risk of oversimplifying Brand's expansive rendition of urban matters. The dangers are, I think, twofold. One, the recurring celebration tends to occlude the novel's general suspicion of the challenges of multiculturalism. The novel is less a straightforward rendition of Global Toronto, and more a diligent examination of the benefits and frustrations that come with such a high degree of diversity. Any benefit that the characters experience is temporary or restrained, qualified by a moment of misapprehension or aggravation or suspicion or hatred. Whether it's the boutique multiculturalism

---

3   Michael Buma has already pointed out this early interpretation of the novel; it was "widely hailed in the popular press as [. . .] an expression of the urban, multicultural, and cosmopolitan "new" realities of Canadian society and space" (13). And he is right; what he doesn't mention, though, is that a number of these celebrations hinge on a single declaration by Tuyen about the "polyphonic" quality of the city.

(as Stanley Fish would call it) that greets Cam and Tuan's Vietnamese restaurant, the "things [. . .] [that] were unknowable, unshareable" between even the closest neighbours (38), the warnings from old women that "you have to be careful when you speak" (149), the obvious and brutal racism of the police, or the disjointed and unfinished conversations (full of pauses, misdirections, and unspoken motivations), Brand's city foregrounds not only the continual pleasures of coming in contact with different people from different places, but also the obvious challenges and failures that come with it. The city is full of unbridgeable gaps—linguistic, socio-economic, generational, and so on—between people who live in such close proximity to one another.[4]

Two, if we see the novel only as a tribute to urban diversity, we are likely to mistake this version of Toronto for a venue for the consideration and formulation of new and alternative identities and experiences. In his very thoughtful "'Struggle Work': Global and Urban Citizenship in Dionne Brand's *What We All Long For*," Kit Dobson suggests that "transformative, open modes of being seem readily available to the generation of children born in the city" (96). And to make that point, Dobson catalogues the openness that each of the characters discovers. Indeed, the article's watchword is "open." Carla "comes to embrace an open-ended future" (99); Oku "looks to open boundaries"; Jackie maintains "an openness towards difference" (101); and the city itself is a site "for being that is open" (89). My reading of the novel is far more pessimistic. I'm not convinced that the city is as liberating or as open as all of the characters believe it to be. They want a Toronto that provides a venue for the discovery (to use Brand's and Dobson's formulation) of a way of being that is notably different from the one that they have seen at home. They want to liberate themselves from the suffocating histories that burden their parents (or their relationship with them). But they never really find that release, that openness, that liberation. Even Tuyen recognizes the impossibility of complete freedom, on some level. She leaves her home to escape her family and their devotion to their long-lost son. She is eager to distance herself "as far as possible from the unreasonableness, the

---

4 Quy's beating is further evidence of these unbridgeable gaps (or the misapprehensions that Brand mentions at the end of the remarkable first chapter). Unable to speak English, Quy can't tell Jamal to just let him go. "He realizes," Brand writes, "that they want the car, and he says, 'Take the fucking car' in Vietnamese, but no one understands him" (*What* 317).

ignorance, the secrets, and the madness of [her] parents" (19). But in her art, on the street, in her mind, "here they were—her family—returning again and again" (149).

THE HISTORY OF URBAN HISTORIES

A few years ago, in the *National Post*, Barbara Kay announced that the bulk of Canadian literature is "virtually unreadable"; it all tells the same story. There are so many historical novels that they are "jumbled together in memory as feminized paeans to a sepulchral past, mired in poetically lyrical, but navel-gazing narrative stasis." Her complaints would be more shocking if they hadn't already been articulated, in slightly different forms, by a number of other vocal (and mistaken) critics. Russell Smith, Stephen Henighan, and a handful of others have all lamented the number of historical novels that are written, marketed, celebrated, and read every publishing season. Scan any national bestseller list in the past two decades or so, and you're bound to see that it's dominated by historical novels. And for a small but vocal group, that is a problem. The popularity of historical novels is a symptom of a flagging (and politically correct) Canadian culture more interested in righting/writing past wrongs than identifying and exploiting contemporary experience, a function of the liberal guilt felt by the book-buying public who take pleasure in reading about past social inequities because they are safely confined to a world they have left behind, or a sign that we produce generally timid writers who are more interested in the next paycheque than a contribution to a culture of experimentation. Or so the complaints go.

They're right, sort of. There is an inordinate number of Canadian historical novels. Just a passing understanding of the Canadian publishing industry (or even a quick glance at a year's publishing catalogues, the national-award shortlists, or your local bookstore's shelves) proves that point. But where they go wrong is in their tendency to homogenize the national interest in historical literature. It's more widespread—and decidedly more varied—than any of them realize. Our literary interest in the past isn't confined to the historical novel. The long poems and lyrics and graphic novels that this volume of essays talks about are already good evidence of that fact. Canadian literature—poetry, prose, and drama—is populated by amateur and professional historians who think about the past, its substance and value, its durability and accessibility. For some years now (culminating with Herb Wyile's *Speculative Fictions*), we have been preoccupied with the histories that take shape within the sharply defined limits of a recognizable genre. But the truth is that our historical literature is more varied than that. To be sure, there are more than a few meticulously researched historical novels that describe a range of domestic chores (just as Russell Smith says there are) on a distant prairie farm; but there are also memoirs of fading television stars, long-form elegies for a dead brother, and—yes—novels about the city.

Our historical literatures don't all tell the same story. One of the ideas that lurks at the edges of these condemnations (which would be easy to ignore if they didn't appear so frequently and so publicly) is that our historical literatures are almost always fantasies of rural preservation or nostalgia which obscure our contemporary urban culture.[5] These condemnations posit a false binary between rural historical literature and urban contemporary literature that simply does not stand up to the briefest scrutiny. Even a partial catalogue of the historical literatures that begin and end in a Canadian city is enough of a reminder. From Hugh MacLennan's *Barometer Rising* (which grants Halifax an historical depth even as some of the characters refuse to acknowledge it) to Raymond Souster's *A Local Pride* (which offers retrospective lyrical meditations on personal and communal landmarks in Toronto)[6] to Dennis Lee's *Civil Elegies* (which preserves a defeatist, even absent history, as Toronto's most authentic) to Michael Turner's *Kingsway* (which treats the urban thoroughfare as a palimpsest of past experiences, scratched out yet still visible) to Rawi Hage's *Cockroach* (which positions Montreal as a kind of archive of diasporic longings for home): Canadian writers are routinely committed to identifying and dramatizing the cultural memories that are accessible but overlooked

---

5 There is a long line of Canadian historical novels that celebrate decidedly rural locales and mythopoeia. That tradition begins in the nineteenth century, runs through Mazo de la Roche's *Jalna* series, continues with Margaret Laurence's *The Diviners*, and finds contemporary expression in Ami McKay's *The Birth House* or Michael Crummey's *Galore* (to name only a few). The critics who lament the popularity of the historical novel in Canada often mistake this tradition as the only tradition. For instance, Andrew Pyper, in his polemic and entertaining identification of critical prejudices in Canadian criticism, sets rural histories against urban contemporary fiction (and, in doing so, reifies the kind of bias he is trying to challenge): "[T]o this day the ratio of midlife crises, marital affairs, and multigenerational, 'regional,' family sagas in our literature to tales of urban dwellers under the age of forty stands at roughly 100:1" ("High Anxiety" 91–92). The distinction is subtle but apparent; to write about the city is to write about the present; to write about the rural (here coded as "regional") is to write about the past.

6 For a full discussion of Souster's Toronto, see Cain.

in our urban spaces. Rather than reifying the Wordsworthian city—a rendition of urban space that remains distant from the deep primordial origins available in rural climes—our urban literatures are frequently (though not exclusively) intent on treating the urban space as decidedly historical in orientation. They expose the hidden histories and cultural memories and primordial origins—embedded in street names and city squares and memorials and gentrifying corners—of an urban geography that we thought we knew or, really, have only ever seen as a disruption of a national identity that has been for far too long predicated on a deep and abiding connection with nature.[7]

TORONTO, THE ARCHIVE

If Brand's version of Toronto has been misread, it's for one very good reason. The four main characters believe wholeheartedly in the city's ability to liberate them from the personal histories they find so restrictive. All of them—Tuyen, Carla, Jackie, and Oku—have faith that they can escape their home lives (most of which are marked by a reverence for past diasporic journeys). After all, that faith is what first brings them together and brings them downtown:

> Most days they smoked outside school together, planning and dreaming their own dreams of what they would be if only they could get out of school and leave home. No more stories of what might have been, no more diatribes on what would never happen back home, down east, down the islands, over the South China Sea, not another sentence that began in the past that had never been their past. (47)

This passage is crucial for a couple of reasons. First (and less importantly), it puts on display the novel's most striking stylistic feature. Note the sonic and structural repetition. It starts with "dreaming their own dreams"; then moves into the "what they would be," "what might have

---

7   Even some of the historical novels that reach back to a rural past aren't simple or straightforward escapist fantasies. They don't deny the existence or the legitimacy of any contemporary (read: urban) worlds. Instead, they identify and amplify the connections between rural past and urban present. Of course, the most striking iteration is Ondaatje's *In the Skin of a Lion*, but there are less obvious examples. *Fall on Your Knees*, for instance, isn't only about a quaint early-twentieth century Cape Breton town. The novel stages a transnational journey from New Waterford to New York. Lily's story gives Anthony—newly located in New York—his rural roots.

been," "what would never happen" conditional phrasing; then ends with the "down east" and "down the islands" and "the past that had never been their past" section.[8] On a sentence level, this repetition serves as a reminder, not of the so-called poetic potential of Brand's novel but of its core idea about the past. It is almost always carried forward. And that structural and sonic repetition is our first, if subtle, indication that the characters' dismissals of their pasts are delusional. The dismissals are, at best, ironic; the long catalogue of what they do not have or do not want is also a testament to what is always there: their families' histories.

Second (and more importantly), the passage identifies the kinds of histories these characters are trying to forget. Generally, it is their parents' histories that they long to escape. Tuyen wants to leave behind her family's constant memorialization of an absent brother, and leaves the excessive archive that is their suburban home, where everything—from the carpet to the citizenship documents—is wrapped in plastic or duplicated. Oku wants to leave behind the "old-time lessons" (83) from an overbearing "old school" father who dreams of back home (87). Jackie wants to forget her parental history of violence.[9] And Carla is determined to leave behind the ghosts that haunt her life: the obvious one in the form of her brother (nicknamed Ghost) and the figurative one in the form of her mother.

More specifically, it's their parents' diasporic histories that they are trying to forget. Almost all of their parents are immigrants (or at least almost all are new to Toronto), and Tuyen, Jackie, Carla, and Oku are all trying to escape the burden of thinking about the "back home" and "back then" that their parents remember. The children are trying to resist the nostalgia that marks their parents' existence or trying to ward off the

---

8   Elsewhere that repetition appears as the more recognizable anaphora (which, helpfully, translates to "carrying back"). I'm thinking of the final section of the first chapter, which describes the kind of personal detritus that falls on the sidewalks of the city: "after they've emerged from the stations, after being sandpapered by the jostling and scraping that a city like this does, all the lives they've hoarded, all the ghosts they've carried, all the inversions they've made for protection, all the scars and marks and records for recognition" (5).

9   Jackie's desire to forget (and its apparent failure) appears when she resists Oku's advances on the streetcar. She dismisses him because his "Hook a brother up" reminds her of her father. It carries with it the "same mix of desire and revulsion, the same feeling in that train car of warmth and insecurity, damage and seduction" (91). (I thank Denise Lefebvre for pointing out that passage.) Or as Jackie puts it later: "With Oku, she was on that train [the same train that brought her mother and father to the city], liquid and jittery and out of control" (101).

harmful effects of some of their diasporic journeys.[10] That dismissal of the parents' diasporic legacies gets full expression early in the novel:

> They all [. . .] felt as if they inhabited two countries—their parents' and their own—when they sat dutifully at their kitchen tables being regaled with how life used to be "back home," and when they listened to inspired descriptions of other houses, other landscapes, other skies, other trees, they were bored. They thought that their parents had scales on their eyes. Sometimes they wanted to shout at them, "Well you're not *there!*" [. . .] Each left home in the morning as if making a long journey, untangling themselves from the seaweed of other shores wrapped around their parents. Breaking their doorways, they left the sleepwalk of their mothers and fathers and ran across the unobserved borders of the city, sliding across ice to arrive at their own birthplace—the city. They were born in the city from people born elsewhere. (21)

The tentativeness of the passage is striking; the "as if" positions their attempt to leave as a delusion, a simple fantasy, a mere longing.[11] More remarkable, though, is their willfulness to separate themselves from their parents and reattach to a less imposing, less demanding urban environment. In the city, they can—temporarily—avoid those mentions of elsewhere (whether it's Vietnam or Halifax or Jamaica or Woodbridge) and dismiss them with a wave of the hand and a simple "Anyways" (19). In her essay "Past Lives," Marianne Hirsch offers the term *postmemory* to

---

10 Carla is the most challenging to think about in these terms, in part because Brand says so little about Derek and Angie's relationship outside of their struggles in the apartment on Wellesley Street. But the description of Angie is at least suggestive. To be with Derek, she had to leave behind her Italian-Canadian family; by coming downtown, "good or bad she had crossed a border" (106).

11 That tentativeness recurs throughout the novel, usually to throw suspicion on the possibility that the characters in particular, or Torontonians in general, have access to fresh, new identities. Note, for instance, the similar "as if" repetition (nearly anaphoric) to describe Binh and Tuan's devotion to the city: "Cam and Tuan expected much from them. As if assuming a new blood had entered their veins; as if their umbilical cords were also attached to this mothering city" (67). Note, too, the vocabulary of appearances and trickery in the description of spring (and all of its connotations of fresh possibilities) that appears in the first chapter: "New lives can be started, or at least spring is the occasion to make it seem possible. No matter how dreary yesterday was, all the complications and problems that bore down then, now seem carried away by the melting streets. At least the clearing skies and the new breath of air from the lake, both, seduce people into thinking that" (2).

describe "the experience of those who grow up dominated by narratives that preceded their birth, whose own belated stories are displaced by the stories of the previous generation, shaped by traumatic events that can neither be fully understood nor re-created"; it is a kind of "secondary, or second-generation, memory" that tries to bridge the unbridgeable temporal and spatial gaps (662).[12] That term is helpful here because it positions all four characters as reluctant sufferers of postmemory; at least early on in the novel, postmemory is an affliction to be cured or a burden to be cast off. And for that, they all turn to the city—or believe that in the city they can hide from these discomfiting histories.

The long-form catalogue of the characters' desires to forget (or to see the city as a place where life can "disappear like that" [183]) is valuable because it reminds us of two distinct but related ideas: one, the intensity of Tuyen's, Jackie's, Oku's, and Carla's desires to forget their parents' (diasporic) pasts; and, two, the ease with which we can misread the text of Brand's city (by mis-taking the characters' longings for the city's actuality). Indeed, these desires are only ever ironic in Brand's novel, and the longings of the characters can only be read as self-protecting delusions. They testify to the absence of such a possibility—something that we're told from the very beginning. In the novel's opening chapter, we're reminded that the city is always a historical site, even if it is ignored by the people who live there: "Name a region on the planet and there's someone from there, here. All of them sit on Ojibway land, but hardly any of them know it or care because that genealogy is willfully untraceable except in the name of the city itself" (4). That brief allusion to Toronto's longstanding wilful ignorance of its native origins is just one of the ways that we are reminded that Brand's city has historical depth.[13] In that passage, the city is an easily dismissed family tree or (even) an unrecognized palimpsest. Elsewhere, the metaphors are different, but the motivation is the same. The city doesn't wipe away personal and cultural memories; it collects them. It inspires memory—whether you want it to or not. The

---

12 I want to thank Professor Elicia Clements for pointing me in the direction of Hirsch's essay. Credit goes to Professor Christine Kim, too, whose "Racialized Diasporas, Entangled Postmemories, and Kyo Maclear's *The Letter Opener*" offers a full accounting of the importance of Hirsch's postmemory to diasporic narratives.

13 For a full discussion of Toronto's history of forgetting/erasure of its native origins, see Victoria Freeman's "'Toronto Has No History!': Indigeneity, Settler Colonialism, and Historical Memory in Canada's Largest City."

street lights become reminders of dead parents; the buildings preserve traces of their former owners; parks inspire recollections of old arguments. Even the garbage that gathers on every street—the metaphorical baggage that spills out with every step or the literal "general debris" (11) that gathers in Tuyen's room (the "mess of wood rails and tree stumps, twigs and rope" [14]) and reappears in the city's alleyways "like old habits" ("the plastic bags, popcans," "the mess of bottles and old shoes and thrown away beds" [11])—is a sign of the city's historical orientation. In these instances, the city becomes an archaeological site in the middle of a dig, all of its artifacts uncovered and ready to be examined. Or, as Michael Sheringham puts it, "[o]ne of the city's archives is its detritus: hieroglyphic blobs of gum splattering the sidewalk, runic streaks and crevices on pavements or blank facades, encampments of bottle banks, hoppers for supplements to supplements and household non-desiderata" (1). And Brand's Toronto is an archive of thrown-away objects. It is also an archive of stories about first-generation diasporas that the second generation struggles to resist.

It is a struggle, and the characters fail to resist; they fail to forget. And for a moment the city becomes an irresistible archive, one that puts on full display your personal and cultural memories that you can't help but acknowledge. The past has never quite passed in this novel. Carla can't pedal fast enough to escape the Ghost that haunts her; instead she makes "a new vow to remember Angie [her mother]" (315). So, too, with Oku and Jackie: much to her chagrin, Jackie's relationship with Oku recalls her mother's relationship with her father;[14] and Oku's conversation with Jackie's father suggests his new-found understanding, if not acceptance, of the role of paternal figures (if not the significance of his own father). This acceptance of the past (or at least the realization of its importance) occurs for Tuyen when she discovers Quy. His appearance spurs Tuyen's new-found loyalty (a hallmark of these final chapters) to her own parents. He is the absent past, suddenly made present. He is the embodiment of the losses (now restored) that occurred on their trip from Vietnam. He is a corporeal reminder of where they came from and what it cost them, and a reminder for Tuyen that she can't

---

14 Moreover, Oku unearths Jackie's "loyalty" to her family; she "hadn't left Alexandra Park" and maintains an obvious "faithfulness" to her parents (265).

escape her diasporic inheritance. He has, after all, been there from the very beginning (of the novel).

It is tempting to stop here, with the city positioned as an irresistible archive, one that helps the second generation discover and honour the history of the first. That interpretation, though, would provide the characters with a sense of closure that doesn't really exist. They would learn the value of their parents' past and search out ways to recover it (even if, according to Hirsch's formulation, that recovery would be obviously fictional). They would no longer suffer from postmemory and work to cure it; they would embrace it. They would become creators of postmemorials, objects or events or records designed to preserve or transmit the pasts which they weren't a part of. But all of that doesn't happen.

The most potent events of the novel's final chapters—Quy's beating and Tuyen's finalization of her plans for the art installation built around the *lubaio*—indicate the failure of postmemorial work. These two events establish the characters' (particularly Tuyen's) desire to recover the past (whatever has been lost or longed for on the various diasporic journeys) and her failure to do so. In the novel, the spatial and temporal gaps appear to be too big to cross.

Moments before Quy is beaten, carjacked outside of his parents' suburban home, Tuyen believes that she can create a postmemorial; "[t]hey [Binh and Tuyen] must [. . .] translate now the years between that man and their parents. They must stand between them to decode the secret writing of loss and hurt" (307). This ambivalent formulation of Tuyen's postmemorial work (the translation) is a neat repetition of Hirsch's definition; Tuyen wants to recover or transmit a past she was not a part of, and recognizes that her efforts will be mediated. Or to put it another way, Tuyen wants to recover the past, but will only be able to offer a translation, a kind of decoding and recoding. But Brand's description of Quy's beating suggests the impossibility of this postmemorial work:

His mouth is full of the brittle, rusty taste of blood, and the sky looks like the sea that first morning on the *Dong Khoi*. And he leans his head as he had over the side of the boat, longingly, and Bo and Ma are finally running out of a doorway, running toward him, and the road between them is like water, and they both grab him as they should have and his mouth splits open and all the water spills out. (317)

The issue here is not whether Quy lives or dies. Such intensely figurative language makes it impossible to decide. What is crucial is the way the description suggests the desire and failure to connect with the past. "[T]he water spills out" is a suggestive phrase that hints at the loss of the past; it is an image of entropy or disappearance or erasure, and suggests that the past cannot be recovered or transmitted. It has been washed away, and Tuyen's hoped-for postmemorial (in this case, the translation) never appears.

The apparent difficulty of postmemorial work appears again in Tuyen's art installation. Throughout the novel, Tuyen works and reworks an art project, one that is formulated in its earliest stages as a record of urban memory. Making use of a *lubaio*—a kind of signpost used "long ago" (16) and a product of what Tuyen calls "ancient Chinese-Vietnamese shit" (16) which she constructs out of repurposed "railway ties" (15)—this art installation is immediately connected to the past. Its expressed intention is twofold: to record "[m]essages to the city" and "to reclaim" (17). Exactly what Tuyen wants to reclaim is not immediately obvious, but the subsequent descriptions of the project—namely as a record of longing—clarify the matter. It is the memories of first-generation immigrants that she wants to recover. In the final draft of the project's plans, Tuyen says that

> She felt comforted by their [hers and Quy's] commonality, the same commonality that had made her so uneasy most of her life; it had made her long to be unexceptional. Yet, here was their specialness now carried between them to the door of the house, the recognitive gaze of an exception cherished through all this time. Wasn't that what her art was all about in the end? She had a vision of the cloth on the wall in her apartment, the scores of scribbled longings, then she felt for the photographs of Quy still stuffed in her bag. She would make tiny copies of the image, yes, and insert them among the records of longing in her installation. She would take photographs of the people of the city too, and sprinkle them throughout. She would need a larger space for the installation, three rooms really, very high ceilings. In the middle of each room a diaphanous cylindrical curtain, hung from the ceiling, that the audience could enter. At the centre of one cylinder would be the *lubaio* with all the old longings of another generation. She would do something with the floor here too, perhaps rubble, perhaps sand, water. In

another cylinder there would be twelve video projections, constantly changing, of images and texts of contemporary longing. [. . .] The last cylinder would be empty, the room silent. What for? (308)

We'll never know. After positioning her installation as a postmemorial—it seeks and finds the connections to the past that it also obviously fabricates—Tuyen's description trails off with crucial uncertainty. This passage is only the description of a postmemorial that she wants to create but doesn't. These are the blueprints for a monument that she cannot or does not build—and by not realizing that vision, Tuyen suggests the postmemorial's insufficiency or impossibility. She longs for connection (between the first and second generations, between the first generation and their longings, which are almost always about back home or down east)—but cannot find it.

In Roland Barthes's famous essay on urban semiology, he proposes that the city is a text, one that can be and must be read by its citizens. The "most important thing," he says, is to "multiply the readings of the city" (201). Tuyen, Jackie, Oku, and Carla all turn out to be bad readers of urban semiology. They misinterpret the Toronto that appears in *What We All Long For*, and believe the city can isolate them from the diasporic longings and legacies that define their home lives. Brand's Toronto is an archive of daydreams and memories and genealogies that are wilfully ignored. To stand anywhere in the city is not to stand in the centre of the universe (as most Torontonians imagine) but to stand at the end of an always developing history. And yet when Tuyen, Jackie, Oku, and Carla discover that the city seethes with memories, they remain completely out of reach, unrecovered and unrecoverable. The characters eventually discover a Toronto that makes the completion of their origins possible (in almost the very same way that Dennis Lee's *Civil Elegies* says it is); it becomes possible, in Tuyen's mind for instance, that she could engage in the kind of postmemorial work that transmits her family's and her generation's traumatic pasts, despite their obvious distances. And yet she cannot seem to take full advantage of that possibility. The city is an archive that is present but inaccessible, unrealized but longed for.

CHAPTER 25

Haunted/Wanted in Jen Sookfong Lee's *The End of East*: Canada's Cultural Memory Beyond Nostalgia

Eva Darias-Beautell

In *Specters of Marx*, a work that strives to bring the *spirit* of Marxism back into the political and ideological arena, Jacques Derrida talks about a notion of *hauntology* that may "replace" ontology in that it defines a process of return of suppressed knowledge (hence the tropes of spectres/ghosts) that constantly suspends ontological certainties (10). Hauntology is tied to memory and historicity, on one end, and to a notion of future justice, on the other, for the project involves the recognition of a politics of memory that can effect social and historical transformation. Here Derrida brings forth "the messianic" to express a radical possibility and an openness towards the future: "an alterity that cannot be anticipated. Awaiting without horizon of the wait, awaiting what one does not expect yet or any longer, hospitality without reserve, welcoming salutation accorded in advance to the absolute surprise of the *arrivant*" (65). As a politically meaningful project, the messianic's potential power stems from the in-between spaces between Self and Other, opening a "horizon of *transformation*, the horizon of *differance*, the horizon of *catachresis* as a hitherto unexplored *possibility*" (Lai 499). It is this allusion to the terrain of the "not yet" that marks, I believe, the full potential of the spectral trope for the analysis of literature and cultural memory.

This essay focuses on the metaphoric possibilities of *hauntology* as trope in relation to the production of cultural memory in Canada, and provides a discussion of these issues in two main parts. I will begin by describing a deconstructive approach to the notion of cultural memory that relies on a complex interrelation between remembering and forgetting, presence and absence. A literary hauntology would demand the analysis of the ghostly traces of the past that return to problematize, but also potentially to enrich, the text's present. I will argue that in their implicit emphasis on the need to rearticulate Canadian culture's relationship to otherness, recent critical work and fiction hint at a hauntological mechanism, delineating a process of construction of tradition and culture that is "a productive opening of meaning rather than a determinate content to be uncovered" (Colin Davis 376). The second part of this essay will read Jen Sookfong Lee's *The End of East* (2007) in this context as a case in point. This novel, about three generations of a Chinese-Canadian family in Vancouver, has been invariably discussed in the context of the Chinese-Canadian culture it describes. I suggest that by shifting the critical focus towards the novel's effective/affective inscription of cultural memory, Lee's text can be read *hauntologically* in modes that take the discussion away from the merely ethno-literary and into complex processes of cultural formation that exceed and transcend multiculturalist expectations and transform the shape and location of Canada's collective imaginary.

HAUNTED/WANTED: A LITERARY HAUNTOLOGY

"The history that is remembered reinforces an individual's or a group's self-image," writes Aleida Assmann in "Remembrance as a Resource for Legitimation": "What we remember therefore, is not based on what actually happened, but on what we later can and wish to tell a story about. What is and is not remembered from the past ultimately depends on who needs the story and for what purpose." With this simple statement, Assmann articulates the main axes of cultural memory: namely, that there is a gap between historical facts and cultural memory, the question of accuracy being subordinate to what is emotionally significant for the individual and the community; secondly, that cultural memory is both an individual and a collective endeavour that is maintained and transmitted through art and communal rituals; thirdly, that it has a social and political function and thus serves a particular ideology. Cultural memory is frequently tied to national identity, for it is bolstered by institutions that administer and endow certain events with cultural significance within the nation's history and project that significance onto its present everyday life. It is therefore a necessarily changing discourse composed, Jan Jansen explains, of "functional" as well as "storage" elements: "While the 'inhabited' functional memory stands for all the active components of cultural memory, the 'uninhabited' storage memory also contains all the disordered elements of the past whose meaning has not (yet) been determined" (Jansen).

As a glance at some of the recent critical work on the field in Canada will reveal, it is precisely that intrinsic need for constant revision and transformation—the endless trickling of the hitherto uninhabited memory into the state-sanctioned versions of it—that makes of cultural memory a highly contested area: to remember is to forget, and cultural memory is necessarily a never-ending process, as much about including as it is about excluding. In "Jane Rule and the Memory of Canada," for instance, Richard Cavell lays out the basis of a theory of queer cultural memory, arguing that sexuality is crucial to any understanding of nationhood and that the individual act of memory cannot be "transposed seamlessly onto the memory of the community, let alone that of the nation—historically, nations have often sought to forget what individuals cannot help but remember, at times breaking communities in order to rupture memory" (160). Cavell's analysis of Jane Rule's novels in this context shows the potential of queer theory to transcend the sexual denotation by introducing an ethics of alterity that denies the completion of cultural/sexual identities, national or otherwise.

Given the ongoing questioning of the nation-state as a valid social, economic, and political structure, the nation, as the site of production of collective imagination within it, is also often placed under erasure. But, while some critics have decreed the death of the nation as a useful cultural paradigm, most seem to opt for keeping the category as a working framework of cultural analysis, for, as Adam Carter claims, "[t] he nation informs and is assumed by, *haunts,* even those theoretical positions which would most radically eliminate it" (91; see also Kertzer, *Worrying* 37–61). There is an immensely imaginative potential implied in the notion of cultural haunting. That recent discussions of memory in Canada have often drawn on hauntology appears, then, as no coincidence, for such combination of theme and perspective has become a critical challenge.

As editors of the special issue of the *University of Toronto Quarterly* on this theme, Marlene Goldman and Joanne Saul set out to probe such potential, "to explore past histories, and to examine the empowering and provocative uses of haunting in contemporary Canadian cultural expressions" (647). Although confining their study to those cases in which there is an *actual* appearance of ghosts, that is, to Canadian texts in which haunting is somehow explicit and foregrounded, their interest in its metaphoric possibilities to define Canada's cultural memory is manifest: "How does living with ghosts entail a politics of memory, of inheritance, and of mourning that continues to shape Canadian literature and visual culture?" (645). Significantly, they also attend to the function of ghosts as traces of the nation's cultural anxiety, diasporic dissonance, or suppressed histories:

> "Home" as a constant has become less of a given, and more and more people are "unhomed"—often forced to exist in a kind of liminal space traditionally associated with the ghost. The sense of "neither here nor there" experienced (albeit in profoundly different ways) by the traveller, immigrant, migrant, and refugee can all be related to the in-between space of the ghost. This may explain why various theories of postcolonialism and diaspora that take as their starting point the movements of people, the dispossession of people, and the clash of disparate cultures make use of the image of the ghost to capture the in-betweenness of the displaced. (Goldman and Saul 648–49)

A hauntology of cultural memory of the kind sketched here would focus on those in-between spaces that may open a horizon of transformation. It would look at the palimpsestic traces of historical silences as ghosts that haunt the nation's memory, and would as such constitute an effective tool "to break down the symmetry and duality of self/other, inside/ outside" (Goldman and Saul 654). The dispossession of the Indigenous peoples of Canada, the forced displacement of Japanese Canadians during and after the Second World War, or the Exclusion Act against the Chinese-Canadian community, just to mention some of the most controversial chapters in Canada's history, have broken down the logic of the nation's hegemonic narrative. How ghostly or unhomely is the place that these episodes occupy in the collective imaginary? What is the status in the national canon of the texts that have represented these events? Attention to these questions would reveal the exclusionary bias of certain forms of cultural memory and introduce "the question of the event as question of the ghost" (Derrida 10).

As an example of such clashing palimpsestic evidence, Jonathan Kertzer claims that the metaphor of transplanting describes well the growth of Canadian literature: "Imagery of organic process is compelling in the double sense that it imposes itself on us, so that we use it without question; and that it conveys comforting assumptions about the relation between literature, spirit and place" ("Genius" 76). Yet that same imagery has proven wanting when applied to the relationship of Canadians of non-European origins to the land, and much has been written in recent years that places and then dismantles such a connection in the origin of settler narratives (see Ty, "Revising"). As I will show later, in novels such as Jen Sookfong Lee's *The End of East*, the characters' inability to fit in or feel at home parallels their repeated failures at gardening, their unsuccessful agricultural ventures, ghostly traces of the dissonance between the dream of Gold Mountain, and the drudge of their real lives. In that context, a hauntological approach to the transplanting myth would unearth the buried narratives that dismantle its discursive structure.

Studying Canada's literary texts from the perspective of the repressed or suppressed forms of nation narration thus reveals a challenging picture, opening the possibility for cultural recuperation and initiating a move both backward towards a historical revision and forward towards a *messianic* vision of the national culture in the Derridean sense discussed above. In the first place, a reading of this kind would imply, as Joel Baetz has argued in his analysis of Ann-Marie MacDonald's *Fall on Your Knees*, "a direct and open challenge to the assumptions about Canada's cultural absence" (63), for texts often act as ghosts "haunting those who believe that Canada is a blank space and scaring them into recognition of the diverse richness of our past, the false exclusivity of our written history, and the potentiality of an inclusive present" (63). Drawing on Sigmund Freud's theory of the uncanny, Baetz succeeds in explaining "how and why in *Fall on Your Knees* the buried haunt the living; the missing are never lost but eventually recovered. Their recovery makes a diverse future possible" (63). More importantly in the context of this essay, looking at the many cases of cultural haunting in Canadian literature reopens the question of canonicity and repositions critical discourses about collective memory. Whereas narratives of racial erasure and discrimination in Canada appear in this light as "reminders of a forgotten, often violent, past," cultural haunting especially disturbs identity affiliation and the processes of canon formation, thereby turning these narratives into "manifestations of a potentially pluralistic present or a possible and nearly-arrived future" (Baetz 66; see also Brogan 5–21).

It is that emphasis of cultural haunting on a return to what has been settled that Chung-Hsiung Lai associates with the "thrownness of being in the multicultural condition":

> The past and the repressed, I contend, are just like traces of a palimp-sest, which, in the process of re-writing the subject, are constantly be-ing thrown and transformed as *disturbances* of a full presence in the name of justice; *a* simulacrum of absence disrupts *the* simulacrum of a full presence, a *haunting* of the repressed cultural identities under-mines the fixed and dominant sense of belonging to the ego-guided culturalism. (Lai 498)

For Lai, there is an implicit connection between hauntology and the sub-ject in the multicultural condition, whose discursive possibilities often involve "the repressed Other [writing] back in the form of hauntological thrownness" (502). There is no escape and no closure for this haunto-logical subject: "It forever *re-turns*, *re-enters* and *re-writes*" (502). The self-conscious troping of spectrality in literature may disrupt in this way state-sanctioned forms of cultural memory. In Canada, this entails a dis-tinction between what Roy Miki sees as "culture," a commodified item controlled by the nation-state, and "the cultural," or specific individual instances of production of culture. Miki initially argues that "the cul-tural" could function as an effective counter-discourse to "culture," since "operating out of the material exigencies of daily lives," it is "unpredict-able in the multiple affects generated in subjects who process them" (2). However, he continues, the critical potential of the cultural is often being co-opted by the very official discourses it wishes to oppose, and ends up being absorbed by the logics of profitability. It is essential to enact critical practices that reveal these contradictions and are vigilant to the changing strategies of appropriation of cultural difference by state ideology and the literary market.

CANADA'S CULTURAL MEMORY BEYOND NOSTALGIA

In the remaining part of this essay, I wish to offer a brief reading of Jen Sookfong Lee's *The End of East* (2007) as a case in point. Despite this novel's relative success in the literary market, it has received little critical attention outside of what Eleanor Ty and Christl Verduyn have called an "auto-ethnographic" reading. This seems deeply at odds with the novel's at-times poignant critique of master narratives of the nation, such as multicultural tolerance, immigrant success, or the coherence of White colonial settlements. In fact, as Mark Diotte has argued in his exceptional study of labour in the literature of British Columbia, *The End of East* disturbs "the dominant, perhaps hegemonic, male dominated, racially-biased labour narrative of British Columbia—a narrative that despite its often blatant sexism and racism, maintains a strong presence in twenty-first century British Columbia" (2). The analysis of the modes in which Lee's novel contests that master narrative, one "predicated on the colonial ideology and settler economy of British Columbia" (2), is beyond the scope of this essay, although the study of the intersections between such a form of nation narration and the gender and racialization processes associated with it would certainly yield insightful results. My point is that shifting the critical focus would open new possibilities for reading diasporic literature in Canada outside critically sanctioned forms. A look at *The End of East*'s inscription of cultural memory through spectrality, for example, would take the reader in promising directions. In what follows, I discuss the novel's hauntological troping of the relationship between East and West, China and Canada, Vancouver's Chinatown and Vancouver, as paradigmatic of a process of construction of cultural memory in diasporic texts that rewrites and reopens the question of the collective imaginary.

Moving back and forth between China and Canada, first- and third-person narrators, past and present, *The End of East* tells the story of Seid Quan's family since his arrival in Canada in 1913 on board a boat full of Chinamen who "had read letters that other men from their villages sent home describing the beautiful land, the generosity of the white men, the fortunes they were making" (15; excerpts from *The End of East* reprinted by permission of Knopf Canada). After years of hard work and immense loneliness, Seid Quan manages to bring from China first his only son, Pon Man, and then his wife, both of whom have by then grown apart and fail to develop a meaningful personal bond with him. The story begins as Sammy, Seid Quan's granddaughter and the novel's narrator in the present, returns to Vancouver, dragging a failed relationship and an unfinished degree from Montreal, to take care of her aging mother, Siu Sang, an embittered Hong Kong bride brought to Canada in order to marry Pon Man, with whom she has five daughters and no son. The narrative is initially (and typically) framed within the terms of Sammy's own need to see through a cryptic family history, to be able to read her grandfather's silence and his refusal to forget. As she finds Seid Quan's yellowed papers and photographs, Sammy wonders what this will to remember may have meant for her grandfather. Central to the narrative impulse is her own position as a reluctant cultural mediator with the mission to throw light on the dark recesses of the family's history; "I am looking at a beginning and an end, and a myriad of possibilities for the body in between" (7). Siu Sang's odd burning of Seid Quan's personal belongings in the backyard of the family house in East Vancouver symbolically triggers the search as it sets the story in the appropriate ghostly tone: "The remains of my grandfather's life floating through the air and into our noses and mouths, no heavier than useless flakes of skin" (11). Later, Seid Quan's ghost will follow the narrator in her walk through Stanley Park and the West End, aptly lodging the story with Hamlet's dilemma in obeying the exhortation of his father's ghost and trapping Sammy in the in-between space associated with the spectre: "I do not turn, knowing that once I look directly at him, his gaze will hold me until he is ready to let me go, until I've done exactly what he wants and he rests, allowing me to do the same" (13).

The novel has been invariably praised for its gripping portrait of life in twentieth-century Vancouver's Chinatown, and critics have agreed that the story is bold, accomplished, and evocative. "*The End of East*," reads the blurb on the publisher's webpage, "sets family conflicts against the backdrop of Vancouver's Chinatown—a city within a city where dreams are shattered as quickly as they're built, and where history repeats itself through the generations" (Publisher's blurb). Typically, the critical language echoes the melodramatic tone associated with family sagas and Chinese opera, emphasizing themes of "loneliness," "obligation," and "desire" (Publisher's blurb). In her review of the novel, Tara Lee complains that "while the prose is raw and the creative energy evident, Lee's novel stays within conventional and claustrophobic narrative territory." That is so because the story "offers no alternative to the East/West opposition that it continually invokes. Canada and China are oceans apart, and the characters who are both Chinese and Canadian are lonely and adrift in identity confusion." Lee admits that *The End of East* succeeds in locating the family story within "a history of social and legislated racism. [. . .] The pervasive sense of entrapment comes from a historical context that prevented Chinese Canadians from breaking out of a ghettoized Chinatown existence." Yet she insists that the novel stays within that ghettoized sense of identity and thus fails to articulate any positive mode of cultural belonging in Canada.

Whether by means of reproducing certain multicultural expectations or by trying to escape them, it is common to see critics replicate the very discursive entrapment that they accuse the novel of building. Tara Lee's opinion that the text does not provide an alternative to the East/West opposition that it plays with seems to stem from the particular binary frame that it intends to overthrow: East/West, China/Canada. So does Cherie Thiessen's complaint that "[h]appiness and dreams are not part of life's plan for this immigrant family, and that's part of the problem. If one looks continually backward when in a new place, how can she see where she is? The End of East should naturally become the beginning of West, but in the Chan family, this is never allowed to happen." No emphasis has been placed on the possibility that the novel undoes the structure of such expectations by proposing a very different reading of its own title. Its suggestion that "the end of East" is "where the West begins" (Lee, *The End* 33) does not necessarily imply a relation of opposition between the terms involved, but rather defines, I would suggest, the inevitable hauntological relationship between East and West as well as between the metaphoric spaces invoked by these signs.

In fact, I would further claim that the trope of spectrality works to prevent a straightforward reading of novel's title. The specific geographic locations haunt the bodies of the characters through the sense of smell. Thus, when Seid Quan first arrives in Vancouver in 1913, he is aware of his own dirtiness: "he can smell the boat on his own skin, the salty, rancid odour of cured fish, other men's hair oils, rotting wood" (Lee, *The End* 14). For him, however, this particular boat smell is not identified with China but with the concrete material conditions of labour movements between China and Canada. It is that smell that interferes with the immigrants' initial hope for success: "*I cannot imagine that this will be all right*" (14). By means of an extended spectral logic, the following scene identifies the city of Vancouver with the smell of the arriving Chinamen:

> [Seid Quan] looks out toward the city and sees the mountains, dark blue and hazy behind the wood frame buildings, which appear dirty and brown, larger manifestations of the smell on his skin. He fears that the stink will be mistaken for the smell of China, but he does not know

how to say that there would be no smell if Canada never was, if the boats were not so full of desperation, men trading one kind of poverty for another. (14)

The trope of spectrality is also used to describe Sammy's own relationship with Vancouver Chinatown, a specific cultural location within the city invariably identified in the novel with a stink of "rotten produce, like a thick soup" (169). When Sammy moves to Montreal, she is convinced that Montrealers could smell the stink in her skin, "durian and rain-soaked cardboard boxes—leaking out of my pores" (11). Yet, in this case, the haunting acts as a connecting sign, endowing the body with a sense of *groundedness*, however bittersweet. That is so because, by forcing the subject to return to the spatial location that haunts her, Vancouver Chinatown, spectrality inspires a new *event-ness*: it reconnects Seid Quan, who "could navigate every bump and turn automatically" (234), and whose face, when in Toronto, "is always turned West" (240), with his granddaughter, the sidewalks of Chinatown "deeply lodged" in her body, tilting her "walk just so" (12). A hauntological approach disturbs in this way the binary opposition between East and West while it allows, in looking at the elements of a previously silenced body of knowledge, for the recuperation of a family history and, with it, for the rewriting of the nation's cultural memory.

In an interview, Jen Sookfong Lee herself talks about "this idea that there is back home and there is Canada. [. . .] You don't look for meaning in Canada. [. . .] We have this idea that home must be somewhere else." Conversely, she expresses the sense of emptiness that marked her visit to China, how meaningless an experience it was for her: "It wasn't until I started sort of digging around in Chinatown [. . .] that I started feeling like this is where I'm supposed to look" (J.S. Lee, Interview). It could be said that *The End of East* is about the death of that diasporic fantasy, for the construction of cultural memory, although travelling back and forth between China and Canada, is firmly rooted in relation to the specific cultural location of Vancouver Chinatown. Whereas romanticization and embellishing techniques are explicitly avoided, the return being to the "messy beginnings," to the alleys of "sagging power lines and trails of urine," Sammy's project is unfailingly grounded in that urban space, "an uncut diamond in the back of my mind—shining dully, its glow persistent and unflagging" (243).

At the same time, Chinatown is articulated by means of a double movement—of East towards West; of West towards East—that precludes the renunciation of either identitary location. This results in an alternative form of historical memory that veers away from the nostalgic (the *end* of East) and opens into a messianic possibility: that is, "a matter of thinking another historicity," or "another opening of event-ness as historicity that permitted one not to renounce, but on the contrary to open up access to an affirmative thinking of the messianic and emancipatory promise as promise" (Derrida 74–75). If hauntology, as Derrida believes, defines that spectral relationship between presence and absence (East and West), "how to comprehend in fact the discourse of the end or the discourse about the end?" (Derrida 10). There is no place for nostalgia in this *event-ness* since it contains the condition of its own spectral return.

In that context, the spatialization of cultural memory makes sense in as much as Chinatown becomes in its turn haunted by other Vancouver spaces and vice versa, an extended pivotal move that seems paramount to the text's project of transgression of essentialist or multiculturalist identities. I would argue that *The End of East* appears haunted by the spectral space defined by multiculturalism, but manages to break the symbolic enclosure of Chinatown through different strategies. In the first place, the text questions and refigures the "Chineseness" of Chinatown in both spatial (East/West) and ethnic terms (Chinese/Canadian). Secondly, it expands the physical location by pushing the boundaries of Chinatown into other urban spaces that haunt Chinatown and are haunted by it in an endless referential movement. Thirdly, its engagement with memory and historicity in the process of production of "the cultural" in Canada transforms hegemonic forms of nation narration, probing their limits and "returning" them for further scrutiny.

A telling moment of that logic of the return can be found, symbolically, in the novel's approach to gardening. As Seid Quan walks along False Creek in Vancouver in the early twentieth century, he is shocked to discover the shacks where the old Chinamen, left-behind railway workers, live like human debris, "the gaping holes in the walls, the small plots of limp vegetables growing in the muck. He feels the failure in the air, almost as thick as the smell of the human waste being used as manure" (Lee, *The End* 19). The failure to grow healthy vegetables symbolizes the limits of hospitality in the new country and signifies the distance between Seid Quan and the less successful immigrant Other, who occupies the ghostly space of the unwanted. Later on, we learn that his son Pon Man keeps a vegetable and flower garden, a practice that he unconsciously associates with the family's social and economic improvement and their moving out of Chinatown. Spatial mobility is not only linked to climbing up the social scale. It also implicitly promises the transcendence of the subject's ethnicity:

> [Pon Man] cannot go back there, immerse himself in the workings of Chinatown, the place he knows so intimately. Even now, he is sure that, if he were blindfolded, he could find his way among the alleys and streets just by his sense of smell, by the dips of the pavement under his feet. He is no longer a Chinatown boy—he is an accountant with a house on the East Side. He tends a flower garden. He loves his car. (204)

But the evident haunting of his own repressed history undermines the illusion of ethnic transcendence, and the return of his ghostly (unwanted) memories seems to suspend the certainty of his new life. Fittingly, the garden turns brown and weedy after his death (223). When Siu Sang, "never a gardener to begin with" (223), and then Sammy return to the *idea* of that garden towards the end of the novel, the approach is much more self-conscious. Here, it is through the metaphor of gardening that the text seems to comment on the history of discrimination against Chinese Canadians and their resilience: "In the back, I pause to run my hands over the sprouting beans. 'Even if we wanted to stop them from growing, we couldn't,'" writes Sammy (228). A sign of the characters' physical and psychological instability, gardening haunts the family's everyday life with its ups and downs; and so does the text seem haunted by its mythic signification within the national imaginary. In its emphasis on affective histories and its reach towards the future, the narrator's mnemonic project supports a politics of memory that may enact cultural and social transformation. The trope of gardening serves, in this context, to express the possibilities of that haunting that comes back from the past but also reaches forth into an open future:

> The soil feels like warm flesh in my hands, as if I am freeing a long-lost, living person from years of layers of dirt. I pull out buttercups from around the base of the daffodils my father once planted, which have,

somehow, survived years of neglect to return every spring, their blossoms bobbing in the wind, perennially cheerful even in rain or fog.

When I finish, I lie down on the lawn. Muddy water seeps through my jeans and sweater, but it doesn't matter. I squint into the sky, watch clouds floating in from the north. My eyes close and I fall asleep, the spade in my hands. (228–29)

In their emphasis on the need to acknowledge these open processes of cultural formation, recent criticism and fiction in Canada are promoting an ontological shift. This consists of a gradual move towards a messianic notion of culture, entailing "the promise of a future to come" and "a desire for emancipation from the present" (Joseph 98). If, as Mark Mason maintains, Derrida's hauntology involves an attempt "to unsettle the present and subvert and alienate us from any/all settled temporalities/chronologies [. . .] via the positive use of the concepts of repetition and anachrony" (493), the approach to Canada's cultural memory as haunted space becomes a welcome step toward a politics of literary and cultural hospitality that may effect social and historical change.

CHAPTER 26

•◆•

Rethinking Postcolonialism and Canadian Literature through Diasporic Memory: Reading Helen Humphreys's *Afterimage*

Jennifer Andrews

What is an afterimage? A term of the 1870s [. . .] it is a memory that impresses or burns itself upon the mind's eye.
Karin Cope, Review of *Afterimage* 35

There has been much effort made over the previous three decades to locate English Canada's place in postcolonial studies, to situate what has been often called a "Second World" literature within the wider scope of the field, and to mobilize texts to illustrate crucial aspects of this complex and often contradictory set of relationships within a specifically English-Canadian context. At the conclusion of her provocative 2001 article, "Can the Canadian Speak? Lost in Postcolonial Space," Cynthia Sugars wonders whether "a Canadian can speak (internationally) at all" and suggests that it may be most productive to return to the title of Rudy Wiebe's short story, "Where is the Voice Coming From?" (144–45). Wiebe begins his narrative with the statement that "The problem is about the story" (712), and goes on to recount the marginalization of Native peoples in the Prairie museum built to record the encounter between Almighty Voice and the Northwest Mounted Police, which proves inadequate to the task of relaying a story which not even Wiebe can translate. As Wiebe demonstrates, there are crucial gaps in the construction of a dominant Canadian cultural imaginary that, given the current federal government's commitment to reshaping national history, may never be recovered. It is this need to attend to the (un)official memories of the past which arises in a slightly different form in Helen Humphreys's millennial novel, *Afterimage*, a text that though located in Britain also speaks to the subjects of Canadian history, geography, and national identity in ways that appear peripheral but emerge as quite central over the course of the narrative, precisely because of Canada's complex status as a "settler-invader" nation. In particular, fictional perspectives on Canada, like those put forth in Humphreys's novel, offer a crucial site for probing the power of diasporic memory for a nation that continues to be shaped by its own (post)coloniality.

Written by Humphreys, an English-born White female Canadian writer, *Afterimage* may seem an unlikely text from which to rethink post-colonialism and Canadian literature through the construction of shared or disparate cultural memories at this juncture. *Afterimage* has received virtually no critical attention since its publication; there is scant mention of Canada in it, and the novel does not focus on a visibly ethnic or racial minority population.[1] But the novel is fundamentally concerned with gaps in memory, dreams that attempt to recover fading memories, and the efforts made to memorialize the experience of diasporic displace-ment and childhood loss through the creation of maps, photographs, and objects of remembrance that also function as visual markers of colonial conflict. Moreover, Humphreys overtly positions her novel as conversant with colonial and postcolonial perspectives by invoking and rewriting two key texts in that field of study: Charlotte Bronte's *Jane Eyre* and Jean Rhys's *Wide Sargasso Sea*. Set in rural England circa 1865, *Afterimage* explores how the lives of Isabelle and Eldon Dashell, a wealthy and privi-leged British woman and her middle-class husband, are changed forever by the arrival of a young Irish maid, Annie Phelan, who escaped the Great Famine as a girl. The novel offers a nuanced exploration of the structures of race, gender, and class as they pertain to "insider-outsiders of the nation" (Bannerji 37), by considering not only English–Irish rela-tions but also the imaginative domain of the Northwest Passage, on the eve of Canadian Confederation.

Humphreys's narrative begins by focusing on the relationship be-tween Isabelle, who is a photographer and Annie. Influenced by the visual power of Julia Margaret Cameron's revealing Victorian portraits of her real-life maids, Mary Hillier and Mary Ryan (who herself fled the Irish potato famine as a child), Humphreys explores the aristocratic

---

1   Certainly Irish racial stereotypes abound in nineteenth- and twentieth-century British and Canadian cartoons, often depicting "brutish Irish peasants with prognathous faces," which im-plied a lack of intellectual development based on physical features (Cumming 8); such racist depictions were part of British and Canadian efforts to claim moral superiority over the Irish.

Isabelle's desire to control Annie's image, her history, and by implication, her cultural memories. The impulse to frame and contain Annie, however, is complicated by the fact that she arrived in England as a young girl and thus possesses few memories of her homeland. Moreover, the presence of Eldon Dashell, Isabelle's husband and a cartographer who wants to create his own maps of the world—particularly the coast of Canada—brings another dimension to the novel by creating an intricate palimpsest of visual and verbal cultural constructs around how one sees and memorializes people and places (whether in the form of maps or photographs). I want to suggest that the novel actually addresses Wiebe's question—literally and figuratively—in significant ways, by suspending itself between postcolonial and post-colonial readings that strategically embody the complexities of Canada through its metaphorical links with both England and, by implication, Ireland.[2] In doing so, *Afterimage* can be read as re-envisioning Canada's place on the international scene and making a significant contribution to explorations of what constitutes Canadian cultural memories, especially for diasporic, and specifically, displaced Irish populations.

As Sugars notes, Canada may occupy a place between the old world and new, but has in recent years been "lost in post-imperial space" because it lacks the international cachet of places such as India, Africa, and Ireland, the primary colonized "Other" in *Afterimage* (115). Moreover, when Canadians return to Northrop Frye's famous question about Canada—"Where is here?"—a query that necessitates speaking, Sugars puts it, "from [a] Canadian geographical (and psychological) space," those who are abroad can often make sense of such a question only by re-phrasing it to reflect a different positioning; as a result, "Where is here?" soon becomes "Where is there?" from a British perspective, reasserting Canada as peripheral on the international scene (124). While Sugars quite rightly urges an examination of how "the subject is placed within any particular instance of postcolonial discourse," in order to consider the question of, in Martina Michel's words, "Where am I coming from?"

---

2   See Boehmer, who explains that *"postcolonial* literature is that which critically scrutinizes the colonial relationship" and "must be distinguished from the more conventional hyphenated term *post-colonial*, which [. . .] [is a] period term designating the post–Second World War era" (3). In other words, while the hyphenated term suggests that colonialism can be chronologically located in the past, *postcolonialism* insists that colonialism is an ongoing phenomenon and thus demands continued scrutiny.

rather than just "Who am I?" (143), Humphreys physically relocates the focus of her novel from Canada to Britain to metaphorically explore both the British tendency to "'Other" the postcolonial subject within the British national cultural imaginary, through the erasure or repression of memories, and the ways in which romantic textualizations of Canadian space reflect much more about the colonial speaker than about the object of his or her attention. In particular, *Afterimage* probes the question of "whose imagination is advanced as the national imaginary"[?] (Bannerji 24). Humphreys's novel traces Annie's efforts to re-imagine her future in ways that critically reinvigorate and complicate how we understand Canada by prioritizing memory—however hazy—in defiance of "national forgettings" (Cho, "Diasporic Citizenship" 109), including the legacy of Canadian racism against Irish immigrants.

The histories of Ireland and Canada certainly cannot be equated; Ireland fought for independence, becoming a model for other colonized countries such as India, whereas Canada did not pursue political resistance through force but wanted to end colonial dependence.[3] Yet Humphreys's use of Annie Phelan in *Afterimage* is also explicitly intertextual in its invocation and refashioning of the youthful Miss Canada, as epitomized by Canadian J.W. Bengough's nineteenth-century political cartoons in the form of a young, female Ireland (notably much different from the small, hairy, and noisily defiant Irish man, held in Mrs. Britannia's arms along with a pitchfork in Figure 26.1) (Cumming 9). This slippage combines traditional perceptions of Ireland as female land (which is intended to ensure Catholic control over female reproduction within the state) with the newly Confederate Canada's status in Bengough's cartoons of the same era as a young, naive woman vulnerable to the predatory American dandy, and who must be protected by the wise, older Mrs. Britannia (Figure 26.2); thus the novel becomes a doubled narrative of colonial struggle for control of which country's political, economic, and cultural memories will dominate. Paradoxically, Canada became "the main destination for large parties of women sent from the Irish workhouses" after the Great Famine, displacing Australia's previous dominance in this role (McLean and Barber 135). The impoverished circumstances and lack of education of these women made them especially vulnerable to racism, conflicts with employers, and in some instances, sexual exploitation, as is portrayed in

---

3   See Boehmer 213.

Margaret Atwood's *Alias Grace*, though Atwood, as McLean and Barber note, makes no direct links between the young woman's "Irish emigrant background to [. . .] [her] sense of [. . .] identity and her treatment as a domestic servant" (134).

Afterimage functions differently from *Alias Grace* by foregrounding the relationship between the young Annie Phelan and her past exploitation, and by placing her in a more privileged domestic position than

HOW IT MAY END.

Britannia.—O, IF HE'S RIGHT YOU'LL HAVE TO GIVE IN ; AND IF YOU'RE RIGHT YOU'LL HAVE TO GIVE IN ; SO DON'T BOTHER ME ABOUT YOUR FISHERY TROUBLES. DON'T YOU SEE I'VE GOT MY HANDS FULL?

Miss Canada.—WELL, MAMMY, IF THAT'S HOW YOU FEEL, DON'T YOU THINK I'D BETTER JUST MARRY HIM AND GET RID OF HIM?

26.1 J.W. Bengough, "How It May End," *Grip*, 29 May 1886. From Carmen Cumming, *Sketches from a Young Country: The images of* Grip *Magazine*.

A PERTINENT QUESTION.

MRS. BRITANNIA.—"IS IT POSSIBLE, MY DEAR, THAT YOU HAVE EVER GIVEN YOUR COUSIN JONATHAN ANY ENCOURAGEMENT?"

MISS CANADA.—"ENCOURAGEMENT! CERTAINLY NOT, MAMMA. I HAVE TOLD HIM WE CAN *NEVER* BE UNITED."

26.2 J.W. Bengough, "A Pertinent Question." *Diogenes*, 18 June 1869.

that of Atwood's Grace Marks. Humphreys's novel begins with the arrival of young Annie at the Dashell's English estate after her previous mistress dies, leaving her penniless. In an ironic twist on Annie's favourite novel, *Jane Eyre*, a classic in postcolonial studies precisely because of its colonizing treatment of those women who are deemed to be "Other," the young Irish woman, who believes herself to be an orphan, having been raised in a British workhouse, joins the staff not as a governess but a servant. Despite Annie's lack of formal schooling, she can read and write and is curious about the world. She captures Isabelle's attention because of her looks and her ability to engage with and visibly convey emotional states, soon becoming her mistress's photographic muse.

Annie's mistress, Isabelle, is a daughter of privilege who has produced three stillborn babies with her middle-class husband. These losses suggest a lack of individual and perhaps national fecundity as a result of her class-crossing marriage and fuel her efforts to reject the traditional role of a dutiful wife. Instead, Isabelle takes solace in her exploration of the pioneering art of photography, a medium that, as she puts it, "is supposed to see what she sees" (21). Damned by a male neighbour, who is a successful painter, because she is a woman and thus perceived to be lacking the proper soul to be a real artist, Isabelle is determined to create images that she (and the world) will value. And Annie becomes the means to do so, eventually enabling Isabelle to win a gold medal for photography at the Dublin Exposition, an event that paradoxically was created to demonstrate Irish progress and innovation at a time when the country was still trying to recover from the Famine of 1845 and the subsequent economic ruin of the labouring classes. Notably, Isabelle wins for a series of photographs she has taken of Annie posing as various figures of virtue, including Grace, Humility, and Faith.

Isabelle, however, is not the only one to become enchanted by this figurative melding of Ireland and Canada, as embodied by Annie. Her husband, Eldon, who dreams of being an explorer in the New World, cultivates an intellectual friendship with the maid whose interest in reading, involvement in photography, and fascination with maps locates her literally and figuratively between husband and wife. In an effort to share his cartographic knowledge of Ireland, Eldon even shows Annie a map of her Irish homeland while lamenting the impact of industrialization on the art of mapping. For him, the wonder of maps lies in their siren call of "*Trust me*," and the fact that even when one is in an unknown place, the map can tell you, in his words, "*This* is where you are. This is what it looks like. Never mind that you don't recognize anything" (47; my emphasis). The inevitable inaccuracies of such maps and the cartographer's imprint of his own vision are the elements that he sees as fundamental to producing a successful—meaning emotionally compelling—map. But Eldon is certainly not altogether free of imperialist aspirations or the romance of conquering, or being conquered by, the natural elements as he eventually reveals to Annie: he is fascinated by the ill-fated Franklin expedition, particularly by those who went in search of Franklin afterward, an obsession Eldon is convinced saved him from a terrible childhood illness. As Annie soon learns, the third Franklin expedition marks the convergence of several important events, personally and historically: Annie's birth, Eldon's childhood illness, and the departure of Franklin to find a passage from the Atlantic to the Pacific north of the Dominion of Canada.

In their introduction to *Rites of Return*, Marianne Hirsch and Nancy K. Miller caution against a simplistic "celebration of rootlessness," as manifested through Isabelle and Eldon's shared fascination with Annie Phelan. Rather Hirsch and Miller insist upon the necessity of exploring the "persistent power of nostalgia" and "the magnetism of the idea of belonging," even while casting "a critical eye on the obsession with roots" (5), which Humphreys accomplishes by juxtaposing the voices and perspectives of the Dashells with Annie's own vision. Not surprisingly, Hirsch and Miller insist that "the desire for 'home' and for the concreteness and materiality of place and connection" also requires a commitment to undertake "carefully contextualized and differentiated practices of witness, restoration of rights, and acts of repair" (5), strategies that insist upon making distinctions between and among individuals and their experiences. Hirsch and Miller also work to reconfigure the concept of diaspora as traditionally "masculinist, patriarchal, and heteronormative" by insisting that more attention be paid to "the multiplicity of roots and the lateral, extrafamilial connections queering structures of kinship" (6), which become especially critical to the survival of those like Annie whose labour excludes the possibility of a stable heterosexual family as part of her future. And as *Afterimage* unfolds, the complexity of diasporic cultural memories becomes increasingly apparent, particularly as Annie asserts herself as a subject in her own right, who possesses imaginative map-making and photographic skills, and in turn refuses to respect the dominant patriarchal and heterosexual frameworks of nationhood.

For Annie, the stories of the Franklin expedition and his disappearance perversely resonate with the dreams and memories of her own familial losses, which are slowly fading away despite her sustained efforts to recall them. As she explains to Eldon, her family was part of a British public works project designed to give purpose and an income to working-class Irish families who were impoverished by the Great Famine: "My parents worked on a road that went nowhere. [. . .] No one could ever walk down it expecting to get to the next village" (51). Instead, the labour required for road-building killed Annie's parents, creating a void in her memories that fuels a desire to know about her past and the need to forge a sense of belonging in the absence of any tangible links to her Irish family and heritage. In an effort to subvert the dominant colonial narrative of *Jane Eyre*, in which Ireland and the New World (as represented by the West Indies) figure, Humphreys can be read as parodically invoking and revising Bronte's novel through Annie's dreams and memories. For example, just before her marriage to Rochester is exposed as a sham because of the existence of a Caribbean-born first wife, Bertha Mason, Jane Eyre describes to Rochester the content of a fortuitous dream, in which Jane follows her master/fiancé down a winding "unknown road" (284) burdened with a crying, small child that impedes her ability to catch Rochester's attention. In *Afterimage*, while out walking a country road *with* a purpose between the estate and the village, Annie describes to Eldon the repetitive power of the dream that disrupts her nocturnal slumber, which consists of featureless workers noisily building a road but never enables her to see the faces of those she most longs for: "I never see my parents, don't know what they would have looked like" (51). When read in conjunction with one another, Jane's dream brings to light the material reality of Annie's family struggle to survive a situation of colonial exploitation, complete with a crying, starving infant, one that is perceived by the English as needy and requiring the proper guidance and discipline to mature.

But Jane Eyre's subsequent dream, which also occurs just before Bertha's existence is publicly revealed, complicates this colonial dynamic even further, as Jane describes the dreary ruins of Thornfield Hall, her arrival with the heavy babe in arms which tries to strangle Jane as she climbs a stone wall in an effort to spot the disappearing Rochester, and eventually leads to the baby falling, a dream that recalls the Dashells' lack of fecundity and their mistaken presumption that Annie can serve as a surrogate bond between them. Indeed, *Afterimage* opens with the visual panorama of Annie's arrival at the Dashell house. Having just re-read *Jane Eyre*, the young woman explicitly parallels the decrepit state of Thornfield Hall with the estate of her new employer and in a rare moment of self-indulgence, wishes that she "could just keep walking down this lane, that the house would keep appearing around every bend. She needs more time than this to arrive here fully. The moment she enters that house, [. . .] all of her imaginings of this will stop and what is real will fill that space completely" (8). For Annie the power of the imagination as fuelled by what she reads offers a tangible, if temporary, escape from the few fading memories she possesses of her own childhood, particularly her mother. As Humphreys's narrator explains: "Annie's mother is a story. Her mother is a far-off feeling that she sometimes falls out of when she wakes. She has nothing real left to her from that life. Only stories and the dream of her two brothers hovering above her like spent breath" (51). Annie's precarious memories echo and complicate the story of *Jane Eyre* by reminding readers that the desire for roots must be weighed against nationalist quests for rootedness which rely on territorial practices that relegate those who are not deemed to be part of the cultural imaginary of a country to the margins—or insist upon finding ways to incorporate them into the national agenda (as Isabelle does through her photographs of Annie fulfilling the role of a number of ill-fated female figures, including Guinevere and Ophelia).

Moreover, in "The 'Irish Concern' in *Jane Eyre*," Susan Kroeg has argued that this Bronte novel is explicitly and implicitly concerned with Ireland's complex status as an unacknowledged British colony that "occupies the liminal space between foreign and domestic" (7). Kroeg suggests that Rochester, in particular, can be read as embodying Irish racial stereotypes because of his quick temper, dark skin colour, and simian build. Given Kroeg's approach, the maternal dream scenes in *Jane Eyre* offer further parallels between *Afterimage* and Bengough's cartoon (Figure 26.1), in which Mrs. Britannia tells Miss Canada that she has no choice but to surrender her virginity to Sam Slick because the mother country has her "hands full" with the noisily defiant bearded Irish baby (Cumming 9). This trio of texts, when juxtaposed, highlights the powerfully racist and sexist clichés that were cultivated and perpetuated about Britain, Ireland, and Canada as part of the colonial project. If Mrs. Britannia—in the form of Jane—is preoccupied by the screaming male Irish man-baby Rochester, Miss Canada becomes a conduit for the memories of an Irish baby girl, namely the now-grown Annie Phelan who refuses to forget.

In *Afterimage*, Eldon and Annie's shared interest in the Franklin expeditions marks the only overt reference to Canada (other than the surveyor's map of the Canadian wilderness that Eldon admires), but it also provides a turning point for Annie's negotiation of her diasporic status through memory and dreaming. While the newspaper coverage of the expeditions fuelled Eldon's imagination during a period of child-hood illness when he was confined to his bed and continues to shape his map-making efforts, he admits to Annie that he is no explorer: "I am the man who copies out journeys of other men" (143). These words reveal Eldon's frustration with the changing field of map-making in an era of increased imperial focus, which as a result has led his publisher to reject Eldon's proposal to create an imaginative map of the world that cultivates a visceral reaction in viewers in favour of a theme map that will point "the way to emeralds and rubies in Africa" (103).

Britain's increasing concern with the material gains of colonization is represented in *Afterimage* by the catalogue of possessions the Irish explorer Francis McClintock provides in *The Voyage of the "Fox" in the Arctic Seas*, a book Eldon shares with Annie, as McClintock, funded by Franklin's widow to find her husband, attempts to reconstruct the last weeks of the ill-fated expedition. Eldon's estrangement from his wife, a gulf that has emerged after the multiple stillbirths, leads him to cultivate an intellectual and emotional relationship with Annie which is cemented through their animated discussions of books, particular-ly those about the Franklin expedition and its aftermath. As a result, Annie finds herself learning about the colonial voyages, and particu-larly McClintock's efforts to track Franklin's fate. Annie is most struck by McClintock's detailed description of the detritus the crew left behind, including a sled weighing over "fourteen hundred pounds. [. . .] loaded down with unnecessary items such silk handkerchiefs, teaspoons, din-ner knives, [and] needle-and-thread cases" and a lifeboat filled with chocolate, tea, a Bible, prayer book, and a copy of Irish writer Oliver Goldsmith's *The Vicar of Wakefield*, which paradoxically satirizes the English sentimental novel (149).

Eldon even lends Annie Goldsmith's text, a story that Annie reads explicitly mindful of the struggles faced by Franklin's dying crew. She speculates that the novel, with its ever-optimistic vicar whose life and family are torn apart during the narrative but who refuses to give up hope, must have offered something for these starving men to cling to by insisting that they "*Read* [. . .] *anguish into patience*" (157). This novel by an Irish author, coupled with Jane Franklin's unwavering faith in the potential for there to be "survivors" of her husband's expedition and McClintock's powerful account of his discoveries, leads Annie to recognize that she is evidence of her family's existence and an important source of alternative cultural memories that demand nurturance (150). Unlike the absurd plethora of colonial artifacts that litter the Arctic landscape, Annie's family valuables—her mother's "silver locket [and] [. . .] wedding ring"—are gone, having been sold to pay for the young girl's passage to England (50). Yet Annie draws parallels between the slow and painful deaths of Franklin's crew, who were thought to have, in the words of one Inuit woman, fallen "down and died as they walked along," with the fate of her own starving family (149). While Franklin's men may have left notes buried under cairns of rocks to document their slow demise, a record that McClintock adds to by describing everything that his crew has discovered during their voyage, Annie recognizes that she is the "cairn" of her family, a living testament to their existence (149), a realization that motivates her to return to Ireland to discover if any of her family members survived.

In the meantime, though, Annie becomes Eldon's saviour when she rescues him, literally, from a voyage gone wrong; in a parodic repetition of the miseries of the Franklin expedition, Eldon dons frozen boots and (with Annie's help) replays on the grounds of the Dashell estate the experience of the dying crew, only to eventually be dragged by her back into the house when he starts to go into shock from the cold. In a poetic gesture, Annie builds a cairn in the backyard and writes a note to record their failed expedition, functioning as McClintock to Eldon's Franklin but with a critical difference. Here, the British captain is saved by his Irish crew. During this process, Annie realizes that "praying is waiting for something better to happen. Salvation means rescue" (161). She rejects the evangelical passivity that she has been schooled in since arriving in England in favour of action and realizes the possibility that narratives, including her own, can be altered by not merely memorializing the past but engaging with it differently. Even Eldon, while recovering from this performative re-enactment in front of a roaring fire, laments the lame efforts of the British to claim the world for themselves, stating, "We thinking we're gods, [. . .] Going all over the world. Exploring. Discovering. And there we are, appearing to the native people, either lost or staggering down to die. What pathetic souls they must think us" (164). In this context, Annie serves as both the sensible servant and the perceptive observer—she recognizes the genocidal dimensions of having starving Irish men, women, and children dig roads without purpose, and questions the logic of Franklin's crew's collection of class-conscious objects on a trip into the barren wilderness in the name of English righteousness. When Eldon expresses his gratitude, however absurd, for Annie's rescue of him, she seizes the opportunity to explore the possibility of her family's survival. Having "by accident, really heard" her request, Eldon agrees to contact the county clerk in the district of her birthplace to discover if there are indeed people who can share their memories of the Phelan family (164). As Humphreys suggests, the ability to recognize and re-frame colonial dynamics remains highly fraught in a household where the suppression of memories and desires is essential to the continuation of the patriarchal family unit and nation as a group of citizens dedicated to building a domestic and international imperial power.

Through her desire to create her own individual and cultural memories, Annie comes to understand and resist what Linda McDowell has called the "quiet violence of traditional geographical" and, in this instance, photographic practices, which attempt to fix "the Other," a goal which Annie understands is ultimately impossible (234). Isabelle, as part of her efforts to resist becoming a traditional affluent mistress of her estate, seeks Annie's help to escape the loneliness of her life and becomes intrigued with the young housemaid's perspective on the world. As part of this experimentation with subverting class and gender norms, Isabelle asks Annie to pose as Sappho, lounging in a bathtub and then, in a moment of intimacy, hands the camera over to Annie so that she can take Isabelle's portrait. Annie, frustrated by her fragmented childhood memories of her mother and the realization that that she can never know "what she looked like, and if Annie looks like her," decides to "push against" the imagined pain of her mother's labours on the road to nowhere and take a photograph of Isabelle that captures her "defiant gaze" (95). In doing so, Annie plays with the frame of the photograph, focusing the lens closely on Isabelle's face and thus breaking the conventions of the era which favoured formal portraiture of whole bodies, stiffly posed (embodied by the *cartes de visite* that were typically awkward images of middle- and working-class people who could only afford a single photo shoot once in their lifetime). The result is an image that inspires Isabelle to alter her own photographic techniques but also threatens her already strained relationship with her husband, who sees the portrait and immediately tears up the photo, chastising Isabelle for not conducting herself properly: "You are the mistress of this house. Act like it. Keep the maid in the position she belongs. Maids are maids. [. . .] They are not artists or friends" (105). In an eerie echo of the sudden departure of Isabelle's childhood friend, Ellen, when the two women reached puberty, Eldon's insistence upon the maintenance of household rules—specifically for upper-class women—and the need to avoid fraternizing with maids epitomizes an instance of what Homi Bhabha has famously called the ambivalence of "colonial mimicry" (86). For Eldon, Annie's ability to convey the "gentle feeling" of Isabelle's gaze threatens the sanctity of the colonial project, even though Eldon repeatedly articulates his own uncertainty about British imperialism.

As Annie grows increasingly motivated to find out more about her family and intrigued by "[t]he sudden possibility of a new story of them" (172), she also recognizes Isabelle's inability to perceive Annie as more than a muse despite her belief that becoming a maid, like Annie, will enable her to escape the lingering pain of her stillborn children, the resulting sexual estrangement from her husband, and the disappearance of her childhood friend, Ellen: "Isabelle could never be Annie. To be me, thinks Annie, to really be me, is to not be in control of the moment. I don't know what is going to happen. She [Isabelle] does" (175). Paradoxically, one night, Isabelle finds Annie in the now-abandoned nursery room of the house that the maid uses to secretly read books, and in a moment of mutual vulnerability, Isabelle laments the fact that her success as a photographer cannot outweigh her inability to produce living children. Annie, who is moved by Isabelle's assertion that her maid is "the only person in the world who truly cares for me," takes a chance and kisses her mistress, breaking, if only momentarily, the fixed patterns of class and race hierarchies that ensure English control over the Irish (205). But the mutual passion of the moment is halted by the sudden singeing of Annie's hair by a candle, and this queer expression of alternative cultural memories is immediately denied by Isabelle, who in an effort to displace one version of the past for another, tells Annie, "This didn't happen. [. . .] Remember that" (206). Isabelle's attempts to erase hidden cultural memories of nation that do not ensure the sanctity and fecundity of Britain are countered by Annie's passion for Isabelle and her increasing confidence that she can "become [. . .] someone who acted" (209), and thus has the capacity to create new cultural memories of her own making.

Shortly after, an accidental fire breaks out on the estate and Annie rushes to save the local bell-ringer's son, Gus, who has been hired by

Isabelle to pose for her Madonna series as Jesus; the young boy, costumed in heavy wings, gets stuck on the second floor, arms ablaze until Annie throws a mattress out the window and sends him down to safety. Isabelle, who has been busy in the darkroom despite all of the outside noise, appears just in time to watch the boy fall to the ground and laments the fact that she has missed "the perfect photograph," explaining, "This is what she has always feared. That she will not be able [. . .] to create an image as pure and true as this. That what she does isn't really about life, about living. It is about holding onto something long after it has already left" (247). In contrast, for Annie, Gus's flight serves two purposes; the shape of his faux wings and body are "almost the shape of a country," but also he reminds her of her lost Irish brother, a possibility that further motivates her to travel back to Ireland, especially after she discovers that Eldon has died in the fire (231). Moreover, Gus's tumble to the mattress while wearing wings can be read as a parodic refiguring of the death of a parrot named Coco in *Wide Sargasso Sea*, Jean Rhys's rewriting of *Jane Eyre* from Bertha's (Antoinette's) perspective. In *Wide Sargasso Sea*, the French-speaking Coco, known because he constantly asks "Qui est là?" or "Who is there?", plunges to his death because the English master of the household has clipped his wings, and thus he is unable to escape the plantation fire set by revolting Jamaican workers. In *Afterimage*, however, the lower-class British boy, posing as divine, is rescued by an Irish servant girl, and his plunge to safety becomes a moment of revisioning for both Annie and Isabelle.

The only one who does not survive the house fire at the conclusion of *Afterimage* is Eldon, the romantic map-maker, who stays in the house to search for Annie, and in doing so concludes that he is undertaking his own journey of survival, like Franklin's men, to help those who may be lost. He even asserts just before collapsing from smoke inhalation, "*I am here*" (232), claiming his position as an explorer, albeit a domestic one. The last chapter of Humphreys's novel, aptly named "Cosmographia Universalis" ("World Map"), alludes to Eldon's resting place after the fire, when Isabelle places him on top of his study desk covered in maps. When the doctor arrives and removes the body, Isabelle sees her husband's final legacy:

> . . . the map he was lying on has become a blotter for the ink of his dissolving body. His flesh has divided counties and formed tiny islands in

the sea. The seepage from his body has permanently altered the maps beneath him. [. . .] New bays and, further inland from the coast of Ireland, a darker shading to the landscape. On the map under that one, an early survey of the Great Lakes in the Dominion of Canada, Eldon's body has oozed plasma into the basin of Lake Superior, completely changing the course of the northern shore. And on the map under that, the Arctic Circle spreads out to join hands with Greenland. Like strata in a bluff, Isabelle peels the maps one from the other to see how they have changed, how they have revealed themselves. He has been granted his wish. Eldon Dashell has been on a journey. He has made his map of the world. (239–40)

In "Remapping the Body/Land," Catherine Nash emphasizes the problematic relationship between maps, bodies, and cultural memories, particularly with respect to female bodies. The fulfillment of Eldon's wish on his deathbed is disturbingly ironic. Annie, in particular, does not pay attention to the maps he has created in death but instead makes a point of taking Eldon's secretly stashed *cartes*, commercial portraits taken without Isabelle's knowledge of him standing with his hand resting on a globe, holding the very territory that has kept him alive and inspired since boyhood. Annie also writes a final note to store under the backyard cairn made for their expedition, in which she states *"I have gone on"* (243), and insists that Isabelle take a last portrait of the young maid as herself, an act that Isabelle cannot complete; as Annie puts it, "Isabelle Dashell has looked so hard at Annie Phelan and has never once seen her at all" (246). Unwilling to remain like Eldon, who imagined going all kinds of places and yet never did, Annie seizes the opportunity to cultivate and nurture her own cultural memories by visiting her homeland of Ireland, to experience the "where of here" and examine the literal roots of her own voice.

Humphreys's novel is instructive on several fronts—Annie exemplifies the intricacies of a colonized diasporic subject who has only ever known the British cosmopolitan centre and is eager to deconstruct both the righteousness of British rule over Ireland and explore the realities of Irish social and political life. And her positioning provokes the question stressed by Michel, of not just "where am I?" but "where am I coming from?" (Sugars 143). *Afterimage* is about the imperfections of colonial vision and memory, and its postcolonial revisionings in the case of

Annie, a discussion that in this novel seems to be politically resonant only if it takes place on the colonizer's turf. Moreover, Sugars' suggestion that "the overarching signifier of Canadianness which so many English readers seek is a phantom" (143) is particularly true of Annie if one reads her as also embodying the young, naive Miss Canada, to be sheltered and protected by Isabelle's Mrs. Britannia, who wishes to shape her colonial offspring to suit her own purposes. As Humphreys suggests, the problem of seeking out an afterimage, as Isabelle repeatedly does through photographs and her readings of Eldon's maps, is that she misses capturing the immediacy of the image altogether or ends up fashioning the ghosts she sees to suit a pre-established ideal. In doing so, she is blind to Annie's resolute desire to form her own identity based on her individual and collective memories of a colonized homeland that the young Irish woman needs to explore first-hand. Finally, if Antoinette (Bertha) in Rhys's *Wide Sargasso Sea* operates as a ghost in her husband's English household, who seems on the road to self-destruction and even death by fire, Annie is the reverse; she understands the structures of imperialism and is potentially well equipped to undermine them upon her return to Ireland. She already possesses her own store of cultural memories and has learned to value their preciousness. Then the question becomes not only "Where is the voice coming from?", as Wiebe poignantly points out, but "Who and where is there?" Perhaps it is only when Canadian stories go abroad, particularly to Britain as Humphreys's novel does, and re-write narratives of colonialism that Canada can once again posit itself as a critical site from which to revision the complexities of postcolonialism through the cultivation and refashioning of cultural memories that include diasporic populations and their distinctive experiences.

CHAPTER 27

·◆·

Transnational Memory and
Haunted Black Geographies: Esi Edugyan's
The Second Life of Samuel Tyne

Pilar Cuder-Domínguez

This essay draws from memory studies in locating Esi Edugyan's first novel, *The Second Life of Samuel Tyne* (2004), within the practice of memory work. This novel undertakes an excavation of the history of Black people in Alberta, thus performing an intervention into Canadian cultural memory designed to bring to light Black memories and experience. By "cultural memory" I understand the dynamic processes of remembering and forgetting that preserve or erase social symbols, meanings, and practices within the shared past of a community (Erll 6–12), in this case the Canadian nation-state. Moreover, my essay subscribes to the view that cultural memory is a political field within which different stories struggle for their place in history (Hua 199). Because Edugyan's approach to Canadian cultural memory in the novel relies heavily on the transnational trajectories of Black subjects, her revision entails the incorporation of what is inescapably a transnational memory. As John Sundholm suggests, this transnational memory "is not anti-national, but non-national and ambivalent, taking into account the increased mobility, due to immigration/migration, dual citizenship, circulation of labour force, not to mention all those numerous historical events that have shaped new nations and altered state boundaries."

The essay also draws from the fields of geography and cultural studies in order to read the fictional space of Aster as a paradigmatic "third-space" that brings together the three dimensions of spatiality (perceived space), historicity (imagined space), and sociality (lived space) (Soja 70), thus fruitfully exploring the matrix of space from both a historical and a social perspective. It is my purpose throughout this essay to show how Edugyan's *The Second Life of Samuel Tyne* challenges the perceived whiteness of Western Canada by re-inscribing a historical Black presence that is full of discontinuities and erasures, thus attesting to what Vernon has called "the difficulty of finding an adequate 'home' for prairie blackness" (67). While her inspired creation of the fictional northern Albertan town of Aster was drawn from archival history concerning Black immigration to the Amber Valley, Edugyan has inserted into this newly whitened space a family of Ghanaian immigrants who must again negotiate local racist resistance to their arrival as well as tensions with former Black settlers. Therefore, Aster constitutes a kind of "Black geography" as defined by Katherine McKittrick and Clyde Woods, that is, one bearing "a history of brutal segregation and erasure" (4). Moreover, in showcasing several waves of Black migration, the novel also enacts the geography of Paul Gilroy's "Black Atlantic," which he describes as a crisscrossing of historical arrivals and departures, and thus as a flowing network of cultural influences within the framework of the Black diasporas in the West. The first part of the essay will describe historical evidence regarding the presence of Black people in Western Canada and its representation in Edugyan's fiction. Next, because "the quest for memory is the search for one's history" (Hua 198), it will turn to the complex representation of memory as both forgetting and remembering, pausing to consider the conceptualization of the Tyne house as a site of memory in Pierre Nora's sense of the term, that is, as a placeholder for the memories of Black Albertans.

"HAUNTED BY LACK OF GHOSTS"

The title of Northrop Frye's famous essay cited above was inspired by the last line in Earle Birney's poem "Can. Lit.": "It's only by our lack of ghosts we're haunted" (qtd. in Frye 478). In it, Frye identified Canadian poetry's defining traits, among others the themes of loneliness and alienation, silence and absence. "Haunting" is a suitable concept to bring to bear on a reading of *The Second Life of Samuel Tyne* for several reasons, perhaps most prominently for its Gothic aesthetic.[1] Ghosts and ghostliness have also been used to signify the lack of home or the disconnection between past and present homes in diasporic contexts, as Radhakrishnan points out: "The diasporic/ethnic location is a 'ghostly' location where

---

1   Sugars and Turcotte have provided an illuminating account of Gothic haunting in Canadian literature in their introduction to *Unsettled Remains* (vii–xxvi). See also Marlene Goldman and Joanne Saul's introduction to a special issue of *University of Toronto Quarterly* (645–55).

the political unreality of one's present home is to be surpassed only by the ontological unreality of one's place of origin" (175). Vernon, perhaps with added urgency, has formulated a similar idea for Black writing in Western Canada: "The sense of home as a fraught space haunts black prairie cultural production. Like black writers in other regions of Canada, black prairie authors must constantly negotiate the erasure of their history in both the official accounts of the region and in the national and regional imaginaries" (67). For writers such as Edugyan, then, literature becomes the medium of remembrance, for as Erll and Rigney have remarked, "collective memories are actively produced through repeated acts of remembrance using both a variety of media and a variety of genres" (112), outstandingly among them literature. In conversation with Wayde Compton and Karina Vernon, Edugyan has admitted that, having grown up in 1970s and 1980s Alberta, in which there seemed to be very few Black people, the discovery of the existence of historical Black settlements in the province fascinated her and became the novel's main spur (Compton, Edugyan, and Vernon).

Although the presence of scattered Black people in the prairies can be traced back to the late nineteenth century, the arrival of large numbers, coming from the south, was delayed until the early 1900s. Mensah records that approximately 300 Black people from Oklahoma settled in Alberta in 1910, many of them in a northern community originally known as Pine Creek and later named Amber Valley. He stresses the hard beginnings of the settlement: "As usual, they were promised good farmlands but, upon arrival, were given poor land and had to create farms from dense bush and swamps with rudimentary implements" (51). To these hardships were added the petitions and town-council resolutions passed throughout the prairies variously advocating the total exclusion of Black people from the area, or at least the limitation of new arrivals, or even their segregation. These resolutions encountered such strong support that medical inspections were used to turn away Black immigrants at the border, and information meant to discourage them was widely circulated, stressing how the climate was allegedly particularly harsh for Black people. Most infamously, the city of Edmonton banned Black people altogether in 1911 (Mensah 52).

These Black pioneers are represented in *The Second Life of Samuel Tyne* by the Porters, the only Black family remaining in Aster by 1968, when the novel starts. Saul Porter stands for what is known as the "first"

African diaspora, that is, those Black people struggling with the legacy of slavery. He came with his father from Oklahoma looking to escape post–Civil War segregation and systemic racism in the United States: "It was not being able to read that kept the vote from us in Oklahoma, sent us north in the first place. We always been the bottom of the pecking order. No respect" (163). Furthermore, Porter embodies the living memory of the Black pioneers, orally transmitting the story of how his father Harlan, born in Georgia, went west when the Civil War gave him his freedom, moving across Kansas, Utah, and Oklahoma, but thirty years later "things weren't any easier. Good for nothing but barbers and bootblacks—if your luck was buttered, you became a porter" (164). These migration trajectories within the wide space of the United States paved the way for the transnational route that would send the family north, answering the call of the "Last Best West" to become ranchers and farmers. On arrival they found a brutal land and neighbours that despised them and campaigned against their presence. Ironically, even disenfranchised groups in the area such as women and francophones sent petitions against them to the federal government. However, what Porter most eloquently describes is "the gift of close-knit community" (166); as his memory idealizes the lost all-Black settlement, he looks back with nostalgia from a time when the line of its founders has all but become extinguished. Saul Porter is the exceptional Black presence in what is otherwise a completely White northern Albertan rural landscape. Interestingly, his presence is completely invisible for many pages. Although his actions are indirectly felt or talked about from the beginning of the narrative, Saul's interaction with other characters is delayed until midway through the novel (123), a device that casts a veil of mystery on his actions and motivations. The result is that his motives become especially hard for the main character, Samuel Tyne, to fathom.

In contrast to the Porters, the Tynes stand for the "new" or contemporary African diaspora, that is, those waves of immigrants arriving in the New World since the late nineteenth century. Paul Zeleza has distinguished three main waves: colonization, decolonization, and structural adjustment. Samuel Tyne and his wife Maud would fall into the first of the three waves, which according to Zeleza includes those students who went abroad to study and stayed, many seamen, and others whom immigration regimes in the host countries allowed to become citizens (36). The Tynes consistently refer to their country of origin with the colonial name of "Gold Coast."[2] Samuel comes from a wealthy cocoa farming family, and he left for Great Britain to study on a grant, later arriving in post–Second World War Canada alongside "[w]ar brides, Holocaust survivors, refugees of every skin [. . .] seeking new lives in a quieter country" (8). His only remaining connection to the old country is his dislike of Western food, a clock marking Ghanaian time, and family letters requesting more money or berating him for failing to return home and do his bit for his country. Samuel's is a diasporic location, "one of painful, incommensurable simultaneity: the [. . .] past as countermemory and memory (depending upon one's actual generational remove from one's 'native' land) coexists with the modern or the postmodern present within a relationship that promises neither transcendence nor return" (Radhakrishnan 175). Even within this wave of migration one can find stark differences based on class and gender. Maud Tyne's rejection of the ancestral country is even stronger than Samuel's. Unlike her husband's privileged background as a chieftain's son, Maud's childhood was marked by the absence of her mother, who died at childbirth, and by her father's regular beatings. She eventually left Ghana for Canada as a nanny to a family of missionaries returning home. Whereas Samuel arrived as an educated man who obtained a comfortable position in the civil service, Maud's only heirloom was her father's curse. While Samuel was supported by his Uncle Jacob during the first hard months, Maud was impoverished and utterly alone, living in the basement of churches. There she practised reading aloud from the New Testament, "enunciating to shave her origins from her voice. By the time she met Samuel, only her tribal marks, still visible under face powder, gave her away" (21).

Edugyan establishes another powerful contrast between the Tynes' colonial, assimilationist attitudes and a representative of the decolonization diaspora: Saul Porter's second wife, Akosia, a Ghanaian who, having arrived in Canada after the struggles for independence, takes exception to the name "Gold Coast." She is also outraged to find out that the Tyne children are unable to speak any Ghanaian language because Samuel and Maud speak only English at home, and she accuses them of killing their

---

2   According to Mensah, Ghanaians constitute one of the leading sources of Black Africans in Canada. They are heavily concentrated in Ontario, the hub of their settlement being Toronto, but there are other sizable Ghanaian populations in Montreal, Vancouver, Ottawa-Hull, and Edmonton, in that order (111–18).

heritage (168). In other words, Edugyan has painted a complex picture of Black people in Alberta, torn apart not only by the different chronologies of migration and their own transnational trajectories, but also by diverse identity features. As Anh Hua observes: "There are always power struggles within diasporic communities, disjunctures produced by the diverse intersectional experiences of gender, class, sexuality, ethnicity, age, generation, disability, geography, history, religion, beliefs, and language/dialect differences" (193).

At the same time, the experiences of everyday racism of these later Black diasporas are remarkably similar. The Canadian-born Tyne children, Yvette and Chloe, try on headscarves to hide their hair because they are "tired of being black" and of being bullied at school in Edmonton (27–29), while their guidance counsellor complains to Maud that "their speech is pretty sluggish, not very clear. Though I suppose we're just not used to the accent" (23). Maud herself, with all her careful enunciation exercises, is the target of similar comments at Aster's town-hall meeting (95), and she has to put up with the racist views on immigration held by their neighbour Ray Frank, although she permits herself an occasional taunt: "Aren´t your ancestors foreigners, if you go way back?" (133–35). Maud´s struggle to belong is reinforced by the White female friendships she forms, first in Calgary with Ella Bjornson and in Aster with Eudora Frank. These church-going pillars of middle-class decency prevent her from taking a single step away from utter conformity, even to the extent of nipping in the bud any new friendship she may make. In turn, Maud unsuccessfully tries to perform the same role for Akosia, who resists all attempts to erase her difference and merge into the mainstream.

Nevertheless, Maud and Samuel's attempt to assimilate, to blend in, is constantly thwarted by their twin daughters' unpredictable and contradictory behaviour. Yvette and Chloe embody doubleness, that is, the ways migrants are pulled in opposite directions: on the one hand, the desire to belong, to be and look the same as everybody else, and on the other, the equally strong compulsion to hold on to what makes them different. The girls constantly perform these diametrically opposed attitudes, for instance when Yvette asks her mother to buy her new clothes, similar to those their White guest Ama Ouillet wears, and then Chloe cuts them to shreds (90–92). Their knack for appearing and disappearing turns them into ghostly presences in the novel, most often only felt by their effects. Their more destructive behaviour surfaces when they feel threatened by other people's animosity, for instance when Yvette sets fire to the old diner in response to the hostile stares of its patrons, that had made her walk out of there earlier: "'I hate that,' said Yvette, trembling. 'Even though this town used to be all black, everywhere you go they stare at you'" (85). In Andrea Davis's words, it is the teenage bodies of the twins that "are made to bear the scars of cultural displacement and racism" (44).[3] There seems to be critical consensus in attributing the impact of a racist society as well as emotional neglect as the main causes for the twins' psychosis, although for Brenda Cooper it also relates to African beliefs on the unnatural condition of twins, conveyed as well in the pervasive Magic-Realist atmosphere and Gothic features of the novel (60).[4] Edugyan herself has admitted to using Gothic or Magic-Realist conventions in her portrayal of the twins due to her literary influences at the time of writing, even though she has also stated that "every element of the twins' behavior is based in some measure in reality" (Compton, Edugyan, and Vernon), specifically on two famous cases of twins in California and Wales.[5] Diana Brydon, however, emphasizes the postcolonial condition's dual allegiances as the root of the novel's aesthetics, and states that for that reason "Edugyan's novel is based on a true story of disorientation, suffering and loss, where magic [. . .] retains its capacity to terrify" ("Global Friction" 7). One may conclude that Edugyan has managed to depict the intricate trajectories of Black bodies across national and transnational borders without obliterating their distinctive historical features while using Gothic features that help convey how they are haunted by the past. The next section will turn to the literary inscription of Black memory on this Canadian space.

"WE SPEAK SO MUCH OF MEMORY BECAUSE THERE IS SO LITTLE OF IT LEFT"

Pierre Nora's famous dictum cited above (7) captured the guiding principle of his work, that industrialization has done away with the traditional

---

3   However, Davis downplays the importance of the theme of racism in the novel, claiming that it is only "a subtle subtext" (44).

4   Some recent fiction by Black British women writers also features oddly behaved twins of West African ancestry. See my essay "Double Consciousness in the Work of Helen Oyeyemi and Diana Evans."

5   For more information on these famous cases, see Davis (43–44).

way of life and brought about the collapse of collective memory. Faced with this acceleration of history, societies need to turn to memory props, sites of memory (*lieux de mémoire*) to replace the real environments of memory that we have lost (*milieux de mémoire*). This notion is particularly appropriate in relation to Black memory, because Black bodies and lives have historically been subjected to invisibility, erasure, and active or passive forgetting. Seldom have Black people's experiences been the subject of historical record and study,[6] and traditional lifestyles were long ago disrupted or altogether suppressed as a result of slavery and repeated displacement. Toni Morrison has insisted on the weight that memory carries in her fiction, describing her job as "ripping that veil drawn over 'proceedings too terrible to relate'" (302). Consequently, memory in Morrison's writing becomes an antidote to historical amnesia, a statement that might be extended to a large number of Black writers, and one that would perfectly fit Edugyan's endeavour in this novel as well.

In *The Second Life of Samuel Tyne* the tensions surrounding Black presence in the White Canadian prairies are played out in terms of memory, forgetting, and space. The town of Aster that the Tynes encounter in the late 1960s bears hardly any trace of its remarkable Black history. The three remaining landmarks of Black spatiality are the two pioneers' homes (those belonging to the Tynes and to the Porters), located in the outskirts (and therefore neatly demarcating Black spaces from White), and the stone wall. This latter construction physically reminds Aster citizens of a past of mutual distrust and fear, because they believe it was built by the original Black families for protection against racist attacks. Like the Black population of Aster, which dwindled after the Second World War, the wall and the houses have suffered the erosion of time. The wall is now reduced to scarcely two inches, "a skirt of parched rock at the river's edge" (33), while the Tyne house is described as "famished" in the novel's opening sentence, and compared to its late owner Jacob Tyne in "its thinness, its severity, its cheerless decay" (1).

Yet, the Tyne house embodies Aster's rich history as the container of the memories of its many dwellers, therefore metaphorically standing for Alberta, or even for the Canadian nation-state. It was once among Aster's

---

6   I have argued elsewhere that Black-Canadian fiction has mostly taken over the task of recording Black Canadians' lives from historians. See my essay "The Racialization of Canadian History."

most salient architectural features, cutting "a splendid figure against the town's purple dusk" (34). As a boarding house run by an old widow, it became a safe haven for weary travellers who were guided there by the beacon of its ostentatious, screeching weathervane. In order to accept more boarders, the widow decided to partition the rooms by building more walls, a beautiful spatial metaphor for the historical construction of an inclusive Canadian citizenship that changes shape to accommodate new arrivals. However, the walls have crumbled into piles of rubbish, and those times are long past when Jacob Tyne comes along and buys it. Samuel is warned that Aster's town authorities had designs to appropriate the house and convert it into a heritage site. This attempted act of memorialization implies that the Black population is seen as a thing of the past, and has been very much consigned to oblivion: it simultaneously asserts their past existence and their current absence. The arrival of the Tyne family thwarts the town's project and revives the Black community, but, as mentioned above, at the cost of rekindling past antagonisms and igniting some new ones.

Those altercations take place in and around the pioneer houses, which stand very close, separated by some fields. Ownership of these fields is a matter of dispute between Saul Porter and Samuel Tyne, another feature that articulates what McKittrick names "the where of blackness" because "[b]lack diasporic struggles can also be read [. . .] as geographic contests over discourses of ownership" (3). In this novel ownership of the land is an act of Black self-validation, underpinning the momentous trajectory from being owned to owning things, and specifically for both diasporic families it is the key to assert Black diasporic subjectivity and their right to belong. However, this kind of Black self-affirmation is always fragile, based on archival evidence and historical documents notoriously beyond Black people's reach. In the novel, this issue is suggested by the fact that Jacob Tyne's will is mysteriously missing. Saul Porter declares that the old man granted him his lands in gratitude for looking after him in his final years. Their neighbour Ray Frank also covets those lands to expand his property and experiment with new seeds, and he happens to be one of Aster's town officials by whom Jacob's will has allegedly been misplaced. Thus, the land becomes the source of friction between White and Black Albertans, and seemingly unimportant acts of intrusion on what Samuel considers his own place become the cause of increasing irritation, as surface signals of the undergoing tug of war. Samuel finds the Porter ladder leaning on his house and resents that trespass, or the Tyne family notice "their" lawn has been mowed without their knowledge; later, trees are cut.[7]

Porter's claim over the land doubly upsets Samuel, on the one hand because he finds it hard to believe that Jacob, always so respectful of family hierarchy, might have deprived his own blood of their rightful legacy, and on the other because he is reminded that he neglected his own duties towards his uncle, who had worked so hard to support him for many years. Samuel is haunted by Jacob's lingering presence in the house: "In the room of prayer mats, Samuel imagined Jacob kneeling, slow with age, and wondered if he'd been the subject of any of those prayers. In the ancient study [. . .] he pictured the old man sitting to write him a letter and being so respectful of Samuel's peace that he set the task aside with great moral resolve" (65). Even the mattress where Samuel and Maud sleep carries "the smell of fevers and old age" (70). Thus, involuntary memories of Jacob, their life together, and their later estrangement are triggered regularly by the place itself and by various little objects left behind by Jacob, some of which are flaunted by Saul Porter to Samuel's vexation.[8]

Accordingly, Jacob is another ghostly presence in the novel, all the more real because guilt over having neglected Jacob is compounded by Samuel's painful awareness that he failed to perform the proper funeral rituals for his uncle, a sin for which Akosia Porter upbraids him:

> Anyone who thinks himself above grieving has something wrong with him. Moving to another country does not exempt you from a proper burial and the forty days' libation. Your uncle was a good, good man, deserving of his final rest. Do you think you are not bringing punishment against yourselves? Do you think we sleep in comfort knowing he has not received his proper rest? (122)

Strictly speaking, one might argue that Samuel's omission represents the kind of forgetting that Paul Connerton defines as deriving from the construction of a new identity, that is, the ability "to discard memories that

---

7 Again in this context, the invisibility of the agent of these actions strengthens the Gothic atmosphere.

8 By involuntary memories I am referring to those awakened by sensorial impressions like the famous episode of Proust's madeleine, attesting to the fact that "the body can play a crucial role in resurrecting the past" (Whitehead 106).

serve no practical purpose in the management of one's current identity
and ongoing purposes" (63). A new set of memories often demands letting go of others. Yet, the narrative makes clear that even as he strives
after his dream of ownership and entrepreneurial success, Samuel is falling apart by letting go of his Ghanaian identity, and this fracture is mir-
rored in the twins' growing psychosis, whom Samuel is shocked to find
violently beating each other in utter silence (222). Although too late for
the twins, the rift is repaired towards the end of the novel, when Samuel
performs the ceremonial libation for Maud "and belatedly for Jacob, asking the ancestors to put them to peaceful rest. Jacob could finally stop
wrestling and be blessed by his angel" (265).

However, before that happens, the conflict between the Porters and
the Tynes (and, in the sidelines, the Franks) comes to a head when the
twins allegedly set the Porter house on fire. The Tynes are ostracized and
forced to institutionalize Yvette and Chloe and to share their home with
the Porters, while the disputed fields are bought by Ray Frank in a move
that reasserts White ownership of the land. In the last chapters, Aster's
remaining Black citizens have to learn the way towards reconciliation.
The house becomes a claustrophobic space in which they are forced to
live together in resentful poverty. However, small acts of kindness and
re-memory bring them closer over the years. This happens first between
Samuel and Maud, who are finally united in their grief and guilt over
the twins. Eventually, it happens as well between the Tynes and Porters.
Maud and Akosia cook together, Maud giving in to using their mother
tongue, which she had rejected out of hurt. Samuel helps Akosia raise
her children after the deaths of their spouses. In a way, they have become a single family, reenacting once more the close-knit community
Saul Porter used to reminisce about. The reestablishment of tradition
and these acts of re-memory repair the tear in the fabric of collective
memory caused by diaspora, suturing the disruption.

Consequently, the house is invested with a number of symbolic
meanings in connection to Black-Canadian history. It is a true *lieu de
mémoire*, that is, a site "where memory crystallizes and secretes itself"
(Nora 7). By means of this lived space (but also a contested as well as a
hybrid one, according to Soja's formulation of a "thirdspace"), Edugyan
engages in the reconstruction and re-vision of a Black cultural memory,
proving that spatiality is "crucial to the activity of remembering, and
seems as important as temporality to both its conceptualization and its

practice" (Whitehead 10). One can concur with Davis as to the import of Edugyan's fiction, insofar as the insertion of Black families into "the whiteness of the Canadian prairies represents a kind of spatial transgression, a critical disruption of the construction of Canadian cultural and national identity as primarily white and British" (33). However, it is important to stress that, despite its Magic-Realist aesthetic, the novel does not transmit a feeling of nostalgia for an idealized Black community. On the contrary, the realism of the novel's ending, with the eventual dispersal of the Black families of this rural area of northern Alberta, as they variously drift towards the cities, their ancestral country, or simply their graves, suggests that Edugyan is performing here an act of critical memory. Realistic is also the overall rendering of the hardships of the Black settlement and the unattainability of the dream of success for many of them, so that most often "black Canada is lived as invisibility" (McKittrick 96). It is precisely that invisibility that Edugyan has masterfully managed to redress for Black Albertans in *The Second Life of Samuel Tyne*.

Works Cited

Aboriginal Affairs and Northern Development. "Key Priorities at Aboriginal Affairs and Northern Development." Ottawa: Aboriginal Affairs and Northern Development, 2012. Web. 28 Nov. 2012.

Abraham, Nicolas. *L'écorce et le noyau*. Paris: Flammarion, 1978.

Acoose, Janice. *Iskwewak–kah'ki yaw ni wahkomakanak/ Neither Indian Princesses Nor Easy Squaws*. Toronto: Women's Press, 1995. Print.

Adams, John Coldwell. *Seated with the Mighty: A Biography of Sir Gilbert Parker*. Ottawa: Borealis, 1979. Print.

Agamben, Giorgio. *Homo Sacer: Sovereign Power and Bare Life*. Stanford: Stanford UP, 1998. Print.

———. *Stanzas: Word and Phantasm in Western Culture*. Minneapolis: U of Minnesota P, 1993. Print.

Agnew, Vanessa. "Introduction: What Is Reenactment?" *Criticism* 46.3 (2004): 327–39.

———. "History's Affective Turn: Historical Reenactment and Its Work in the Present." *Rethinking History* 11.3 (2007): 299–312. Print.

——— and Jonathan Lamb, eds. *Settler and Creole Reenactment*. Houndmills: Palgrave Macmillan, 2009. Print.

Aichorn, August. "The Transference." Aaron Esman, ed. and introd. *Essential Papers on Transference*. New York: New York UP, 1990. 94–109. Print.

Al Purdy A-Frame Association. Save Al Purdy's House, 2012. Web. 23 Oct. 2012.

Alexie, Robert Arthur. *Porcupines and China Dolls*. Penticton: Theytus, 2009. Print.

Alfred, Taiaiake, and Jeff Corntassel. "Being Indigenous: Resurgences against Contemporary Colonialism." *Government and Opposition* 40.4 (2005): 597–614. Print.

———. *Wasáse: Indigenous Pathways of Action and Freedom*. Peterborough: Broadview, 2005. Print.

——— and Lana Lowe. "Warrior Societies in Contemporary Indigenous Communities." Toronto: Ontario Ministry of the Attorney General, n.d. Web. 12 May 2012.

Anahareo. *Devil in Deerskins: My Life with Grey Owl*. Toronto: new press, 1972. Print.

———. *My Life with Grey Owl*. London: Peter Davies, 1940. Print.

Anatol, Giselle Liza. "A Feminist Reading of Soucouyants in Nalo Hopkinson's *Brown Girl in the Ring* and *Skin Folk*." *Mosaic* 37.3 (2004): 33–50.

Anderson, Benedict. *Imagined Communities: Reflections on the Origin and Spread of Nationalism*. 1983. London: Verso, 2006. Print.

Anderson-Dargatz, Gail. *The Cure for Death by Lightning*. 1996. Toronto: Vintage Canada, 1997. Print.

———. *Turtle Valley*. Toronto: Knopf, 2007. Print.

Appadurai, Arjun. *Modernity at Large: Cultural Dimensions of Globalization*. Minneapolis: U of Minnesota P, 1996. Print.

APTN National News. APTN Television Inc. 10 Dec. 2012. Print.

Aquin, Hubert. "The Cultural Fatigue of French Canada." *Selected Essays by Hubert Aquin*. Ed. Anthony Purdy. Edmonton: U of Alberta P, 1988. 19–48. Print.

———. "The Politics of Existence." *Selected Essays by Hubert Aquin*. Ed. Anthony Purdy. Edmonton: U of Alberta P, 1988. 8–18. Print.

Armitage, Kevin. "Bird Day for Kids: Progressive Conservation in Theory and Practice." *Environmental History* 12.3 (2007): 528–51. Print.

Armstrong, Elizabeth H. *The Crisis of Quebec, 1914–1918.* Toronto: McClelland and Stewart, 1974. Print.

Armstrong, Jeannette. "Aboriginal Literatures: A Distinctive Genre within Canadian Literature." *Hidden in Plain Sight: Contributions of Aboriginal Peoples to Canadian Identity and Culture.* Ed. David R. Newhouse, Cora Vaygeur, and Dan Beavon. Toronto: U of Toronto P, 2005. 180–86. Print.

——— and Lally Grauer, eds. *Native Poetry in Canada: A Contemporary Anthology.* Peterborough: Broadview, 2001. Print.

Assmann, Aleida. *Cultural Memory and Western Civilization: Functions, Media, Archives.* Cambridge: Cambridge UP, 2011. Print.

———. "Remembrance as a Resource for Legitimation." Feb. 2008. Web. 9 Jan. 2013.

Assmann, Jan. "Collective Memory and Cultural Identity." Trans. John Czaplicka. *New German Critique* 65 (1995): 125–33. Print.

"Attawapiskat Members Issue Demands to De Beers." *Wawatay News* 9 Feb. 2009. Web. 1 Apr. 2013.

Attwood, Bain. "The Batman Legend: Remembering and Forgetting the History of Possession and Dispossession." *Storied Communities: Narratives of Contact and Arrival in Constituting Political Community.* Ed. Hester Lessard, Rebecca Johnson, and Jeremy Webber. Vancouver: U of British Columbia P, 2011. 189–210. Print.

Auf der Maur, Nick. "'Everybody was up for grabs." *Trudeau's Darkest Hour: War Measures in Time of Peace: October 1970.* Ed. Guy Bouthillier and Édouard Cloutier. Montreal: Baraka, 2010. 111–20. Print.

Auger, Martin F. "On the Brink of Civil War: The Canadian Government and the Suppression of the 1918 Quebec Easter Riots." *Canadian Historical Review* 89.4 (2008): 503–40. Print.

Bachelard, Gaston. *The Poetics of Space.* Trans. Maria Jolas. New York: Orion, 1964. Print.

Badman, Derek A. Rev. of *White Rapids*, by Pascal Blanchet. *MadInkBeard.* 3 Dec. 2007. Web. 23 May 2012.

Baetz, Joel. "Tales from the Canadian Crypt: Canadian Ghosts, the Cultural Uncanny, and the Necessity of Haunting in Ann-Marie MacDonald's *Fall on Your Knees.*" *Studies in Canadian Literature* 29.2 (2004): 62–83. Web. 21 Jan. 2013.

Bailey-Dick, Matthew. "The Kitchenhood of All Believers: A Journey into the Discourse of Mennonite Cookbooks." *Mennonite Quarterly Review* 79.2 (April 2005): 153–79. Print.

Bal, Mieke. "Introduction." *Acts of Memory: Cultural Recall in the Present.* Ed. Mieke Bal, Johnathan Crewe, and Leo Spitzer. Hanover: UP of New England, 1999. vii–xvii. Print.

Balaev, Michelle. "Trends in Literary Trauma Theory." *Mosaic: Journal for the Interdisciplinary Study of Literature* 41.2 (2008): 149–66. Print.

Baldwin, Andrew, Laura Cameron, and Audrey Kobayashi. "Introduction: Where is the Great White North? Spatializing History, Historicizing Whiteness." *Rethinking the Great White North: Race, Nature, and the Historical Geographies of Whiteness in Canada.* Vancouver: U of British Columbia P, 2011. 1–15. Print.

Ball, David P. "'Educational Apartheid' Remains Despite New School at Attawapiskat." *Windspeaker* 1 Aug. 2012: 24. Print.

Ballinger, Franchot, and Brian Swann. "A MELUS Interview: Paula Gunn Allen." *MELUS* 10.2 (1983): 3–25. Print.

Bannerji, Himani. "Geography Lessons: On Being an Insider/Outsider to the Canadian Nation." *Dangerous Territories: Struggles for Difference and Equality in Education.* Ed. Leslie G. Roman and Linda Eyre. New York: Routledge, 1997. 23–42. Print.

Barbeau, Marius. *Indian Days in the Canadian Rockies*. Toronto: Macmillan, 1923. Print.
———. *The Downfall of Temlaham*. Toronto: Macmillan, 1928. Print.
Barbour, Douglas. *Visions of My Grandfather*. Ottawa: Golden Dog, 1977. Print.
Barrett, Paul. "'There are atomic openings in my chest / to hold the wounded': Intimacy, the Body and Transnational Solidarity in Dionne Brand's *Inventory*." *Canadian Women and Multiculturalism* 27.2/3 (2009): 100–06. Print.
Barthes, Roland. *Camera Lucida: Reflections on Photography*. New York: Hill and Wang, 1981. Print.
———. "Semiology and Urbanism." *The Semiotic Challenge*. Trans. Richard Howard. New York: Hill and Wang, 1988. 191–201. Print.
———. "Toward a Psychosociology of Contemporary Food Consumption." Counihan and Van Esterik 20–27. Print.
Battiste, Marie. "Maintaining Aboriginal Identity, Language and Culture," *Reclaiming Indigenous Voice and Vision*. Ed. Marie Battiste. Vancouver: U of British Columbia P, 2000. 192–208. Print.
Beachy, Kirsten. "Gelächterkuchen: Mennonite Girls Can Read (With Recipes!)" *Mennonite Life* 66 (2012): n. pag. Web. 5 April 2013.
Bélanger, Claude. "Chronology of the October Crisis, 1970, and its Aftermath." *Quebec History*. Marianopolis College, 23 Aug. 2000. Web. 10 Dec. 2012.
———. "Quebec Nationalism." *Quebec History*. Marianopolis College, 23 Aug. 2000.Web. 10 Dec. 2012.
Belasco, Warren. *Food: The Key Concepts*. New York: Berg, 2008. Print.
Bell, David. *Sharing Our Successes: Ten Case Studies in Aboriginal Schooling*. Kelowna: Society for the Advancement of Excellence in Education, 2004. Print.
Bemrose, John. "A Poet for the Ages." Rev. of *Reaching for the Beaufort Sea*, by Al Purdy. *Maclean's* 7 Feb. 1994: n. pag. *LexisNexis*. Web. 28 Nov. 2012.
Benjamin, Walter. "The Work of Art in the Age of Mechanical Reproduction." *Illuminations*. Trans. Harry Zohn. New York: Harcourt, Brace, 1968. 211–44. Print.
Bennett, Donna, and Russell Brown, eds. *An Anthology of Canadian Literature in English*. 3rd ed. Toronto: Oxford UP, 2010. Print.
———, eds. *A New Anthology of Canadian Literature in English*. Toronto: Oxford UP, 2002. Print.
Bennett, Jill. *Empathic Vision: Affect, Trauma, and Contemporary Art*. Stanford: Stanford UP, 2005. Print.
Bentley, D.M.R. *Canadian Architexts: Essays on Literature and Architecture in Canada, 1759–2006*. London: Canadian Poetry Press, 2009. Print.
———. "Conclusion, Retrospective, and Prospective." Lynch et al. 239–46. Print.
———. *Mnemographia Canadensis: Essays on Memory, Community, and Environment in Canada, with Particular Reference to London, Ontario*. 2 vols. London: Canadian Poetry Press, 1999. Print.
Berger, Carl. "Writings in Canadian History." *Literary History of Canada: Canadian Literature in English: Volume Four*. 2nd ed. Ed. W.H. New. Toronto: U of Toronto P, 1990. 293–332. Print.
———. *The Sense of Power: Studies in the Ideas of Canadian Imperialism, 1867–1914*. Toronto: U of Toronto P, 1970. Print.
———. "The True North Strong and Free." *Nationalism in Canada*. Ed. Peter Russell. Toronto: McGraw-Hill, 1966. Print.
Berger, John, and Jean Mohr. *Another Way of Telling*. New York: Pantheon, 1982. Print.

Berry, Susan, and Jack Brink. *Aboriginal Cultures in Alberta: Five Hundred Generations.* Edmonton: Provincial Museum of Alberta, 2004. Print.

Berton, Pierre. Foreword. *To Mark Our Place: A History of Canadian War Memorials,* by Mark Shipley. Toronto: NC Press, 1987. 7–8. Print.

Berzensky, Steven (a.k.a. Mick Burrs). *The Names Leave the Stones: Poems New and Selected.* Regina: Coteau, 2001. Print.

Bhabha, Homi. *The Location of Culture.* London: Routledge, 1994. Print.

Bidini, Dave. "Writer in Residence; A Visit to Al Purdy's Home Stirs Up More Than a Few Old Ghosts." *National Post* 31 Oct. 2009: n. pag. *Proquest.* Web. 7 Nov. 2012.

Blair, Sara. "Cultural Geography and the Place of the Literary." *American Literary History* 10.3 (1998): 544–67. Print.

Blanchet, Pascal. Interview with Michael C. Lorah. 17 Jan. 2008. *Newsarama.* Reposted at *Drawn & Quarterly.* 18 Jan. 2008. n. pag. Web. 22 May 2012.

———. *White Rapids.* 2007. Trans. Helge Dascher. Montreal: Drawn & Quarterly, 2010. Print.

Boehmer, Elleke. *Colonial and Postcolonial Literature.* Oxford: Oxford UP, 1995. Print.

Boire, Gary. "How Long is Your Sentence?: Classes, Pedagogies, Canadian Literatures." *Home-Work: Postcolonialism, Pedagogy & Canadian Literature.* Ed. Cynthia Sugars. Reappraisals ser. 28. Ottawa: U of Ottawa P, 2004. 229–44. Print.

Bollas, Christopher. *The Shadow of the Object: Psychoanalysis of the Unthought Known.* New York: Columbia UP, 1987.

Bolter, Jay David, and Richard Grusin. *Remediation: Understanding New Media.* Cambridge: MIT P, 1999. Print.

Bowering, George. "A Happy, Makeshift Vision." *Cottage Life* May 2011: 55+. Print.

Boyarin, Daniel, and Jonathan Boyarin. "Diaspora: Generation and the Ground of Jewish Identity." *Critical Inquiry* 19 (1993): 693–725. Print.

Boyarin, Jonathan, ed. *Remapping Memory: The Politics of Timespace.* Minneapolis: U of Minnesota P, 1994. Print.

Brand, Dionne. *A Map to the Door of No Return.* Toronto: Doubleday, 2001. Print.

———. "At the Full and Change of CanLit: An Interview with Dionne Brand." Interview with Rinaldo Walcott and Leslie Sanders. *Canadian Woman Studies* 20.2 (2000): 22–26. Print.

———. "Dionne Brand on Struggle and Community, Possibility and Poetry." Interview with Pauline Butling. *Poets Talk: Conversations with Robert Kroetsch, Daphne Marlatt, Erin Mouré, Marie Annharte Baker, Jeff Derksen, and Fred Wah.* Ed. Pauline Butling and Susan Rudy. Edmonton: U of Alberta P, 2005. 63–87. Print.

———. *Inventory.* Toronto: McClelland and Stewart, 2006. Print.

———. *What We All Long For.* Toronto: Random House, 2005. Print.

Brant, Beth. *Writing as Witness: Essays and Talk.* Toronto: Women's Press, 1994. Print.

Brantlinger, Patrick. *Dark Vanishings: Discourse on the Extinction of Primitive Races, 1800–1930.* Ithaca: Cornell UP, 2003. Print.

Bringhurst, Robert. *A Story Sharp as a Knife: The Classical Haida Mythtellers and Their World.* Lincoln: U of Nebraska P, 1999. Print.

Brockwell, Stephen. "Ingredients for Certain Poems by Al Purdy." Lynch et al. 9–12. Print.

Brogan, Kathleen. *Cultural Haunting: Ghosts and Ethnicity in Recent American Literature.* Charlottesville: UP of Virginia, 1998. Print.

Bronte, Charlotte. *Jane Eyre.* Oxford: Oxford UP, 1988. Print.

Brooks, Van Wyck. "On Creating a Usable Past." *The Dial* 64.7 (11 Apr. 1918): 337–41. Print.

Brown, George W. *Building the Canadian Nation*. Toronto: J.M. Dent, 1942. Print.

Brown, Laura S. "Not Outside the Range: One Feminist Perspective on Psychic Trauma." *Trauma: Explorations in Memory*. Ed. Cathy Caruth. Baltimore: Johns Hopkins UP, 1995. 100–12. Print.

Brown, Russell. "'Perhaps He'll Fall': Rereading the Poetry of Al Purdy." *Essays on Canadian Writing* 49 (1993): 59–84. Print.

Bryce, George. *The Mound Builders*. Winnipeg: Manitoba Free Press, [1885?]. Early Canadiana Online. Web. 26 Feb. 2014.

Brydon, Diana. "Dionne Brand's Global Intimacies: Practising Affective Citizenship." *University of Toronto Quarterly* 76.3 (2007): 990–1006. Print.

———. "Global Friction, Alberta Fictions." "The Prairies in 3-D: Disorientations, Diversities, Dispersals." University of Manitoba, Sept. 2007. Web. 24 April 2013. Cited with the author's permission.

——— and Marta Dvořák, eds. *Crosstalk: Canadian and Global Imaginaries in Dialogue*. Waterloo: Wilfrid Laurier UP, 2012. Print.

Buikema, Rosemary. "Literature and the Production of Ambiguous Memory." *European Journal of English Studies* 10.2 (2006): 187–97. Print.

Buma, Michael. "Soccer and the City: The Unwieldy National in Dionne Brand's *What We All Long For*." *Canadian Literature* 202 (2009): 12–27. Print.

Burke, Jason R. "Conflict in Cities and the Struggle for Modernity: Toward an Understanding of the Spatiality of the October Crisis." *Cahiers de géographie du Québec* 53.150 (Dec. 2009): 335–49. Print.

Burke, Kenneth. *Language as Symbolic Action: Essays on Life, Literature, and Method*. 1966. Berkeley: U of California P, 1968. Print.

Burlingame, Roger. *Of Making Many Books: A Hundred Years of Reading, Writing and Publishing*. New York: Scribner's, 1946. Print.

Buss, Helen M. *Repossessing the World: Reading Memoirs by Contemporary Women*. Life Writing ser. Waterloo: Wilfrid Laurier UP, 2002. Print.

Butler, Judith. *Frames of War: When is Life Grievable?* London: Verso, 2010. Print.

Cabajsky, Andrea, and Brett Josef Grubisic, eds. *National Plots: Historical Fiction and Changing Ideas of Canada*. Waterloo: Wilfrid Laurier UP, 2010. Print.

Cain, Stephen. "Mapping Raymond Souster's Toronto." *The Canadian Modernists Meet*. Ed. Dean Irvine. Ottawa: U of Ottawa P, 2005. 59–75. Print.

Campbell, Maria. Interview with Hartmut Lutz. *Contemporary Challenges: Conversations with Canadian Native Authors*. Ed. Hartmut Lutz. Saskatoon: Fifth House, 1991. 41–65. Print.

Canadian Charter of Rights and Freedoms, Part I of the Constitution Act, 1982, Appendix II. 23 Nov. 2011. Web. 10 Dec. 2012.

Careless, J.M.S. "'Limited Identities' in Canada." *Canadian Historical Review* 50.1 (1969): 1–10. Print.

Carlson, Hans M. *Home is the Hunter: The James Bay Crees and Their Land*. Vancouver: U of British Columbia P, 2008. Print.

Carlson, Keith Thor, and Kristina Fagan. "Introduction to the 2006 Edition." *'Call Me Hank': A Stó:lō Man's Reflections on Logging, Living, and Growing Old*, by Henry Pennier. Ed. Keith Thor Carlson and Kristina Fagan. Toronto: U of Toronto P, 2006. xiii–xxxix. Print.

Carter, Adam. "Kingdom of Ends: Nation, Post-Nation and National Character in Northrop Frye." *English Studies in Canada* 29.3-4 (September/December 2003): 90–115. Print.

Caruth, Cathy. Introduction. *Trauma: Explorations in Memory.* Ed. Cathy Caruth. Baltimore: Johns Hopkins UP, 1995. 3–12. Print.

———. *Unclaimed Experience: Trauma, Narrative, and History.* Baltimore: Johns Hopkins UP, 1996. Print.

Castells, Arnau Gifreu. "Differences between Linear and Interactive Documentaries." *I-Docs.* 12 Dec. 2011. Web. 24 Sep. 2012. Print.

Cavell, Richard. "Jane Rule and the Memory of Canada." *Unruly Penelopes and the Ghosts: Narratives of English Canada.* Ed. Eva Darias-Beautell. Waterloo: Wilfrid Laurier UP, 2012. 157–82. Print.

"Ce soir débute au Trident la réhabilitation des victimes de 1918." *Le Soleil* 11 Oct. 1973: 52. Print.

de Certeau, Michel. *The Practice of Everyday Life.* Trans. Steven Rendall. Berkeley: U of California P, 1984. Print.

———. *The Writing of History.* New York: Columbia UP, 1988. 1973. Print.

Chafe, J.W, and Arthur R. M. Lower. *Canada: A Nation, and How It Came To Be.* Toronto: Longmans Green, 1948. Print.

Chakrabarty, Dipesh. "Minority Histories, Subaltern Pasts." *Postcolonial Studies* 1.1 (1998): 15–29. Print.

Chambers, Cynthia. "A Topography for Canadian Curriculum Theory." *Canadian Journal of Education/Revue Canadienne de L'éducation* 24. 2 (1999): 137–50. Print.

Chariandy, David. "'The Fiction of Belonging': On Second-Generation Black Writing in Canada." *Callaloo* 30.3 (2007): 818–29. Print.

———. *Soucouyant.* Vancouver: Arsenal Pulp, 2007. Print.

———. "Spirits of Elsewhere Past: A Dialogue on *Soucouyant.*" Interview with Kit Dobson. *Callaloo* 30.3 (2007): 808–17. Print.

———. Rev. of *What We All Long For. New Dawn: Journal of Black Canadian Studies* 1.1 (2006): n. pag. Web. 2 Oct. 2012.

Cho, Lily. "Diasporic Citizenship: Contradictions and Possibilities for Canadian Literature." *Trans. Can. Lit.: Resituating the Study of Canadian Literature.* Ed. Smaro Kamboureli and Roy Miki. Waterloo: Wilfrid Laurier UP, 2007. 93–110. Print.

———. *Eating Chinese: Culture on the Menu in Small Town Canada.* Toronto: U of Toronto P, 2010. Print.

Chow, Rey. *The Protestant Ethnic and the Spirit of Capitalism.* New York: Columbia UP, 2002. Print.

Chrisjohn, Roland, and Sherri L. Young. *The Circle Game: Shadows and Substance in the Indian Residential School Experience in Canada.* Penticton: Theytus, 1997. Print.

Clifford, James. "Diasporas." *Routes: Travel and Translation in the Late Twentieth Century.* Cambridge: Harvard UP, 1997. 244–77. Print.

———. "Four Northwest Coast Museums: Travel Reflections." *Exhibiting Cultures: The Poetics and Politics of Museum Display.* Ed. Ivan Karp and Steven D. Lavine. Washington: Smithsonian Institution P, 1991. 212–54. Print.

———. "The Others: Beyond the Salvage Paradigm." *Third Text* 3.6 (1989): 73–78. Print.

Cloutier, Richard. *Pine Point Revisited.* 2 Aug. 2012. Web. 24 Sep. 2012.

Coates, Ken. "Writing First Nations into Canadian History: A Review of Recent Scholarly Works." *The Canadian Historical Review* 81.1 (2000): 99–114. Print.

Cogswell, Fred. *Charles G.D. Roberts and His Works.* Toronto: ECW, 1983. Print.

——— and Jo-Anne Elder, trans and eds. *Unfinished Dreams: Contemporary Poetry of Acadie.* Fredericton: Goose Lane, 1990. Print.

Colbert, Jade. "Speak, Memory—Madeleine Thien Interview." *The Varsity* [U of Toronto] 132.19 (27 Feb. 2012): 1–26. Web. 25 Apr. 2013.

Coleman, Daniel. "Epistemological Crosstalk: Between Melancholia and Spiritual Cosmology in David Chariandy's *Soucouyant* and Lee Maracle's *Daughters are Forever*." *Crosstalk: Canadian and Global Imaginaries in Dialogue*. Ed. Diana Brydon and Marta Dvořák. Waterloo: Wilfrid Laurier UP, 2012. 53–72. Print.

Colombo, John Robert. *Canadian Literary Landmarks*. Willowdale: Hounslow, 1984. Print.

Compton, Wayde, Esi Edugyan, and Karina Vernon. "Black Writers in Search of Place." *The Tyee* 28 Feb. 2005. Web. 23 April 2013. Print.

Confino, Alon. "Collective Memory and Cultural History: Problems of Method." *American Historical Review* 102.5 (1997): 1386–1403. Print.

Connerton, Paul. "Seven Types of Forgetting." *Memory Studies* 1.1 (2008): 59–71. Print.

Connor, Carl. *Archibald Lampman: Canadian Poet of Nature*. 2nd ed. Ottawa: Borealis, 1977. Print.

Constitution Act, 1982, Schedule B to the Canada Act, 1982. U.K., 1982, c. 11. 23 Nov. 2012. Web. 8 Nov. 2012.

Cook, Ramsay. "Canadian Centennial Celebrations." *International Journal* 22.4 (1967): 659–63. Print.

Cook, Terry. "What Is Past Is Prologue: A History of Archival Ideas Since 1898, and the Future Paradigm Shift." *Archivaria* 43 (Spring 1997): 17–63. Print.

Cooley, Dennis. "Documents in the Postmodern Long Prairie Poem." *History, Literature, and the Writing of the Canadian Prairies*. Winnipeg: U of Manitoba P, 2005. 175–211. Print.

Cooper, Arnold. "Changes in Psychoanalytic Ideas: Transference Interpretation." Esman, Aaron, ed. and introd. *Essential Papers on Transference*. New York: New York UP, 1990. 511–28. Print.

Cooper, Brenda. "Diaspora, Gender and Identity: Twinning in Three Diasporic Novels." *English Academy Review* 25.1 (2008): 51–65. Print.

Cope, Karin. Rev. of *Afterimage. Antigonish Review* 126 (Summer 2001): 33–36. Print.

Corrivault, Martine. "'Québec, printemps 1918': le jeu conscient de l'ambiguité." *Le Soleil* 13 Oct. 1973: 36. Print.

Counihan, Carole, and Penny Van Esterik, eds. *Food and Culture: A Reader*. 2nd ed. New York: Routledge, 2007. Print.

Cranny-Francis, Anne. *The Body in the Text*. Melbourne: Melbourne UP, 1995. Print.

Crate, Joan. *Foreign Homes*. London: Brick, 2001. Print.

———. "Negative of You," "Shawnandithit (Last of the Beothuks)," "The Blizzard Moans My Name." *Canadian Literature* 124/125 (1990): 16–18. Print.

———. *Pale as Real Ladies: Poems for Pauline Johnson*. London: Brick, 1991. Print.

Crawford, Isabella Valancy. *Collected Poems*. Toronto: U of Toronto P, 1973. Print.

Crozier, Lorna. *Angels of Flesh, Angels of Silence: Poems*. Toronto: McClelland and Stewart, 1988. Print.

———. "The Edge of the Page: A Response to Barry McKinnon's *I Wanted to Say Something*." *Essays on Canadian Writing* 18–19 (1980): 106–11. Print.

———. *Inventing the Hawk*. Toronto: McClelland and Stewart, 1992. Print.

Cruikshank, Julie. *Do Glaciers Listen? Local Knowledge, Colonial Encounters, and Social Imagination*. Vancouver: U of British Columbia P, 2005. Print.

Cuder-Domínguez, Pilar. "Double Consciousness in the Work of Helen Oyeyemi and Diana Evans." *Women: A Cultural Review* 20.3 (2009): 277–86. Print.

———. "The Racialization of Canadian History: African-Canadian Fiction, 1990–2005." *National Plots: Historical Fiction and Changing Ideas of Canada*. Ed. Andrea Cabajsky and Brett Josef Grubisic. Waterloo: Wilfrid Laurier UP, 2010. 113–29. Print.

Culhane, Dara. *The Pleasure of the Crown: Anthropology, Law and First Nations*. Vancouver: Talon Books, 1998. Print.

Cultural Memory Group. *Remembering Women Murdered by Men: Memorials across Canada*. Toronto: Sumach, 2006. Print.

Cumming, Carman. *Sketches from a Young Country: The Images of* Grip Magazine. Toronto: U of Toronto P, 1997. Print.

Davey, Frank. "Al Purdy, Sam Solecki, and the Poetics of the 1960s." *Canadian Poetry: Studies, Documents, Reviews* 51 (2002): 39–57. Print.

Davies, Rosamund. "Digital Intimacies: Aesthetic and Affective Strategies in the Production and Use of Online Video." *Ephemeral Media: Transitory Screen Culture from Television to YouTube*. Ed. Paul Grange. London: BFI/Palgrave Macmillan, 2011. 214–27. Print.

Davis, Andrea. "Black Canadian Literature as Diaspora Transgression: *The Second Life of Samuel Tyne*." *Topia* 17 (2007): 31–49. Print.

Davis, Colin. "Hauntology, Spectres and Phantoms." *French Studies* 59.3 (2005): 373–79. Print.

Dawn, Leslie. *National Visions, National Blindness: Canadian Art and Identities in the 1920s*. Vancouver: U of British Columbia P, 2006. Print.

Dawson, Carrie. "The Importance of Being Ethnic and the Value of Faking It." *Postcolonial Text* 4.2 (2008): 1–10. Print.

de la Roche, Mazo. *Jalna*. Toronto; Macmillan, 1927. Print.

———. *The Master of Jalna*. Toronto: Macmillan, 1933. Print.

———. *Whiteoak Heritage*. Toronto : Macmillan, 1940. Print.

De Leeuw, Sarah. "Intimate Colonialism: The Material and Experienced Places of British Columbia's Residential Schools." *Canadian Geographer* 51.3 (2007): 339–59. Print.

Delgamuukw v. British Columbia, 1991 CanLII 2372 (BC SC), [1991]. Web. 20 Oct. 2013.

Delgamuukw v. British Columbia, 1997 CanLII 302 (SCC), [1997] 3 SCR 1010. Web. 20 Nov. 2012.

Delisle, Jennifer Bowering. "'A bruise still tender': David Chariandy's *Soucouyant* and Cultural Memory." *ARIEL* 41.2 (2010): 1–21. Print.

Demerson, Velma. *Incorrigible*. Waterloo: Wilfrid Laurier UP, 2004. Print.

Derksen, Jeff. *Annihilated Time: Poetry and Other Politics*. Vancouver: Talonbooks, 2009. Print.

Derrida, Jacques. *Archive Fever: A Freudian Impression*. Trans. Eric Prenowitz. Chicago: U of Chicago P, 1996. Print.

———. *Specters of Marx: The State of the Debt, the Work of Mourning, and the New International*. Trans. Peggy Kamuf. New York: Routledge, 1994. Print.

Devlin, Tom. Email to author. 13 Nov. 2009. Print.

Dinius, Oliver J., and Angela Vergara, eds. *Company Towns in the Americas: Landscape, Power, and Working-Class Communities*. Athens: U of Georgia P, 2011. Print.

———. Introduction. *Company Towns in the Americas: Landscape, Power, and Working-Class Communities*. 1–20. Print.

Diotte, Mark. "Labour and Literature in the 'West Beyond the West.'" Diss. U of British Columbia, March 2012. Web. 28 Jan. 2014.

"Directory of Federal Heritage Designations." *Parks Canada*. Government of Canada, 15 Mar. 2012. Web. 23 Oct. 2012.

Dobbs, Kildare. "Remembering Al Purdy." *Descant* 135 (2006): 22. Print.

Dobson, Kit. "'Struggle Work': Global and Urban Citizenship in Dionne Brand's *What We All Long For.*" *Studies in Canadian Literature.* 31.2 (2006): 88–104. Print.

———. *Transnational Canadas: Anglo-Canadian Literature and Globalization.* Waterloo: Wilfrid Laurier UP, 2009. Print.

Douglas, Kate. *Contesting Childhood: Autobiography, Trauma and Memory.* New Brunswick: Rutgers UP, 2010. Print.

Dragland, Stan. "An Open Letter." Vermeersch, *Al Purdy* 18–19. Print.

Duffy, Dennis. *Gardens, Covenants, Exile: Loyalism in the Literature of Upper Canada/ Ontario.* Toronto: U of Toronto P, 1982. Print.

———. *Sounding the Iceberg: An Essay on Canadian Historical Novels.* Toronto: ECW, 1986. Print.

Dunley, Kathleen. "Pascal Blanchet's *White Rapids* and the Sense of History." *The Comics Grid: Journal of Comics Scholarship.* 26 May 2011. n. pag. Web. 22 May 2012.

Duran, Eduardo. *Healing the Soul Wound: Counseling with American Indians and Other Native Peoples.* New York: Teachers College P, 2006. Print.

Edugyan, Esi. *The Second Life of Samuel Tyne.* London: Virago, 2004. Print.

Edwards, Elizabeth. "Photographs as Object of Memory." *The Object Reader.* Ed. Fiona Candlin and Raiford Guins. New York: Routledge, 2009. 331–42. Print.

Edwards, Mary Jane. Introduction. *Le Chien d'or The Golden Dog*, by William Kirby. Montreal: McGill-Queen's UP, 2012. xix–clxxii. Print.

Eigenbrod, Renate. "Diasporic Longings: (Re)Figurations of Home and Homelessness in Richard Wagamese's Work." Kim, McCall, and Baum Singer 133–51. Print.

Emerson, Ralph Waldo. "Memory." *Natural History of Intellect and Other Papers.* Boston: Houghton Mifflin, 1921. 61–82. Print.

Episkenew, Jo-Ann. *Taking Back Our Spirits: Indigenous Literature, Public Policy, and Healing.* Winnipeg: U of Manitoba P, 2009. Print.

Epp, Marlene. "Memories of Sauerkraut and Zwieback: Foodways in the Mennonite Diaspora." *Rhubarb* 26 (2010): 33–40. Print.

———. "The Semiotics of Zwieback: Feast and Famine in the Narratives of Mennonite Refugee Women." *Sisters or Strangers? Immigrant, Ethnic, and Racialized Women in Canadian History.* Ed. Marlene Epp, Franca Iacovetta, and Frances Swyripa. Toronto: U of Toronto P, 2004. 314–40. Print.

Erll, Astrid. *Memory in Culture.* Trans. Sara B. Young. Palgrave Macmillan Memory Studies. Houndmills: Palgrave Macmillan, 2011. Print.

——— and Ansgar Nünning, and Sara B. Young, eds. *A Companion to Cultural Memory Studies.* New York: Walter de Gruyter, 2008. Print.

——— and Ann Rigney. Introduction. *Mediation, Remediation, and the Dynamics of Cultural Memory.* Ed. Astrid Erll and Ann Rigney. Berlin: Walter de Gruyter, 2009. 1–11. Print.

Esman, Aaron, ed. and introd. *Essential Papers on Transference.* New York: New York UP, 1990. Print.

——— "Extracts from Minutes of Proceedings of the Imperial War Conference, 16 April 1917, on the Constitution of the Empire." *World War I: A Student Encyclopedia.* Ed. Spencer C. Tucker and Priscilla Mary Roberts. Santa Barbara: ABC-CLIO, 2005. 2373–74. Print.

Fagan, Kristina. "Tewatatha:wi: Aboriginal Nationalism in Taiaiake Alfred's *Peace, Power, Righteousness: An Indigenous Manifesto.*" *American Indian Quarterly* 28.1/2 (2004): 12–29. Print.

————. "Weesageechak Meets the Weetigo: Storytelling, Humour, and Trauma in the Fiction of Richard Van Camp, Tomson Highway, and Eden Robinson." *Studies in Canadian Literature* 34.1 (2009): 204–26. Print.

Fanon, Frantz. *Black Skin, White Masks*, trans. Charles Lam Markmann. New York: Grove, 1967.

Farrar, Margaret. "Amnesia, Nostalgia, and the Politics of Place Memory." *Political Research Quarterly* 64.4 (2011): 723–35. Print.

Faulkner, Joanne. "Negotiating Vulnerability through 'Animal' and 'Child': Agamben and Rancière at the Limit of Being Human." *Angelaki* 16.4 (Dec. 2011): 73–85. Print.

Federman, Mark, and Derrick De Kerckhove. *McLuhan for Managers: New Tools for New Thinking*. Toronto: Viking, 2003. Print.

Fee, Margery. "Romantic Nationalism and the Image of Native People in Contemporary English-Canadian Literature." *The Native in Literature*. Ed. Thomas King, Cheryl Calver, and Helen Hoy. Toronto: ECW, 1987. 15–33. Print.

Fellows, Jo-Ann. "The 'British Connection' in the Jalna novels of Mazo de la Roche: The Loyalist Myth Revisited." *Dalhousie Review* 56 (Summer 1976): 283–90. Print.

Felman, Shoshana, and Dori Laub. *Testimony: Crises of Witnessing Literature, Psychoanalysis, and History*. London: Routledge, 1992. Print.

Findlay, Len. "Always Indigenize! The Radical Humanities in the Postcolonial University." 2000. *Unhomely States: Theorizing English-Canadian Postcolonialism*. Ed. Cynthia Sugars. Peterborough: Broadview, 2004. 367–82. Print.

Fish, Stanley. "Boutique Multiculturalism, or Why Liberals Are Incapable of Thinking About Hate Speech." *Critical Inquiry* 23.2 (1997): 378–95. Print.

Foucault, Michel. *The Archaeology of Knowledge and the Discourse on Language*. Trans. A.M. Sheridan Smith. New York: Pantheon, 1972. Print.

————. *Language, Counter-Memory, Practice: Selected Essays and Interviews*. Ed. Donald F. Bouchard. Trans. Donald F. Bouchard and Sherry Simon. Ithaca: Cornell UP, 1977. Print.

————. "Nietzsche, Genealogy, History." Trans. Donald F. Brouchard and Sherry Simon. *Aesthetics, Method, and Epistemology*. Trans. Robert Hurley, et al. Ed. James D. Faubion. New York: New Press, 1998. 369–91. Print.

————. *Power/Knowledge: Selected Interviews & Other Writings, 1972–1977*. Ed. and trans. Colin Gordon, et al. New York: Pantheon/Harvester, 1980. Print.

Francesconi, Sabrina. "Negotiation of Naming in Alice Munro's 'Menesteung'." *Journal of the Short Story in English* 55 (2010): n. pag. Web. 17 Oct. 2012.

Francis, Daniel. *The Imaginary Indian*. Vancouver: Arsenal Pulp, 1992. Print.

Freeman, Victoria. "'Toronto Has No History!': Indigeneity, Settler Colonialism, and Historical Memory in Canada's Largest City." *Urban History Review* 38.2 (2010): 21–35. Print.

Frenette, Brad. "Pascal Blanchet's 'Poetic Conception.'" *Brad Frenette: Writing and Miscellany*. 15 Mar. 2010. N. pag. Web. 22 May 2012.

Freud, Sigmund. *An Autobiographical Study*. London: Hogarth, 1946. Print.

————. "The Dynamics of Transference." *The Standard Edition of the Complete Psychological Works of Sigmund Freud, 1856–1939*. Volume 12. Trans. James Strachey. London: Hogarth, 1964–1974. 97–108. Print.

————. *Fragment of an Analysis of a Case of Hysteria. The Standard Edition of the Complete Psychological Works of Sigmund Freud, 1856–1939*. Volume 7. Trans. James Strachey. London: Hogarth, 1964–1974. 3–112. Print.

———. "An Outline of Psychoanalysis." *The Standard Edition of the Complete Psychological Works of Sigmund Freud, 1856–1939*. Volume 23. Trans. James Strachey. London: Hogarth, 1964–1974. 141–205. Print.

———. *Studies in Hysteria*. New York: Nervous and Mental Disease Monographs, 1936. Print.

Fridén, Georg. *The Canadian Novels of Gilbert Parker: Historical Elements and Literary Technique*. Upsala: Upsala Canadian Institute, 1953. Print.

Friesen, John W. *Aboriginal Spirituality and Biblical Theology: Closer than You Think*. Calgary: Detselig, 2000. Print.

Froese Tiessen, Hildi. "Homelands, Identity Politics, and the Trace: What Remains for the Mennonite Reader?" *Mennonite Quarterly Review* 87 (Jan 2013): 11–22. Print.

———. "Mennonite/s Writing: State of the Art?" *Conrad Grebel Review* 26.1 (Winter 2008): 41–49. Print.

Frow, John. "From '*Toute la mémoire du monde*: Repetition and Forgetting.'" *Theories of Memory: A Reader*. Ed. Michael Rossington and Anne Whitehead. Baltimore: Johns Hopkins UP, 2007. 150–56. Print.

Frye, Northrop. "Haunted by Lack of Ghosts: Some Patterns in the Imagery of Canadian Poetry." 1977. *Northrop Frye on Canada*. Ed. Jean O'Grady and David Staines. Toronto: U of Toronto P, 2003. 472–92. Print.

Furniss, Elizabeth. *Victims of Benevolence: Discipline and Death at the Williams Lake Indian Residential School, 1891–1920*. Williams Lake: Cariboo Tribal Council, 1992. Print.

Fuss, Diana. *The Sense of an Interior: Four Writers and the Rooms that Shaped Them*. New York: Routledge, 2004. Print.

Gagan, David, and Herbert Mays. "Historical Demography and Canadian Social History: Families and Land in Peel County, Ontario." *Canadian Historical Review* 54.1 (1973): 27–47. Print.

Gallant, John, and G. (Seth) Gallant. *Bannock, Beans, and Black Tea: Memories of a Prince Edward Island Childhood in the Great Depression*. Montreal: Drawn & Quarterly, 2004. Print.

Gallery Tour. Exploring Alberta—Discovering the World: Syncrude Gallery of Aboriginal Culture. 14 March 2006. Royal Alberta Museum. Web. 31 May 2012.

Gerson, Carole. "'The Most Canadian of All Canadian Poets': Pauline Johnson and the Construction of a National Literature." *Canadian Literature* 158 (1998): 90–107. Print.

———. *A Purer Taste: The Writing and Reading of Fiction in English in Nineteenth-Century Canada*. Toronto: U of Toronto P, 1989. Print.

——— and Veronica Strong-Boag. *Paddling Her Own Canoe: The Times and Texts of E. Pauline Johnson, Tekahionwake*. Toronto: U of Toronto P, 2000. Print.

——— and Veronica Strong-Boag, eds. *E. Pauline Johnson: Tekahionwake: Collected Poems and Selected Prose*. Toronto: U of Toronto P, 2002. Print.

Gibson, Margaret. "Death and Mourning in Technologically Mediated Culture." *Health Society Review* 16 (2007): 415–24. Print.

Gillis, John R., ed. *Commemorations: The Politics of National Identity*. Princeton: Princeton UP, 1994. Print.

———. "Memory and Identity: The History of a Relationship." Introduction. *Commemorations: The Politics of National Identity*. Ed. John R. Gillis. Princeton: Princeton UP, 1994. 3–24. Print.

Gilroy, Paul. *The Black Atlantic: Modernity and Double Consciousness*. London: Verso, 1993. Print.

Givner, Joan. *Mazo de la Roche: The Hidden Life*. Toronto: Oxford UP, 1990. Print.

Gleeson, Kristin. *Anahareo: Wilderness Spirit*. Tucson: Fireship, 2012. Print.

———. "Blazing Her Own Trail: Anahareo's Rejection of Euro-Canadian Stereotypes." *Recollecting: Lives of Aboriginal Women of the Canadian Northwest and Borderlands*. Ed. Sarah Carter and Patricia A. McCormack. Edmonton: Athabaska UP, 2011. 287–311 Print.

———. Email to Sophie McCall. 27 April 2013. Web.

Godard, Barbara. "The Politics of Representation: Some Native Canadian Women Writers." *Canadian Literature at the Crossroads of Language and Culture: Selected Essays by Barbara Godard, 1987–2005*. Ed. Smaro Kamboureli. Edmonton: NeWest, 2008. 109–59. Print.

Goldie, Terry. "Fresh Canons: The Native Canadian Example." *English Studies in Canada* 17.4 (1991): 373–84. Print.

Goldman, Marlene. *DisPossession: Haunting in Canadian Fiction*. Montreal: McGill-Queen's UP, 2012. Print.

——— and Joanne Saul. "Talking with Ghosts: Haunting in Canadian Cultural Production." *University of Toronto Quarterly* 75. 2 (2006): 645–55.

Goldsmith, Oliver. "The Rising Village." *Early Long Poems on Canada*. Ed. D.M.R. Bentley. London: Canadian Poetry, 1993. 199–216. Print.

Gordon, Avery. *Ghostly Matters: Haunting and the Sociological Imagination*. Minneapolis: U of Minnesota P, 2008. Print.

Goyette, Linda. "Still Waiting." *Canadian Geographic* 130.6 (Dec. 2010): 48–64. *Academic Search Premier EBSCO Host*. Accessed 20 Nov. 2012.

Grace, Sherrill. *Canada and the Idea of North*. Montreal: McGill-Queen's UP, 2001. Print.

Granatstein, J.L., and J.M. Hitsman. *Broken Promises: A History of Conscription in Canada*. Toronto: Oxford UP, 1977. Print.

Granatstein, J.L., and Desmond Morton. *Canada and the Two World Wars*. Toronto: Key Porter, 2003. Print.

Grant, Agnes. *No End of Grief: Indian Residential Schools in Canada*. Winnipeg: Pemmican, 1996. Print.

Grant, Shelagh. *Polar Imperative: A History of Arctic Sovereignty in North America*. Toronto: Douglas & McIntyre, 2010. Print.

———. *Sovereignty or Security: Government Policy in the Canadian North, 1936–1950*. Vancouver: U of British Columbia P, 1988. Print.

Gray, Charlotte. *Flint and Feather: The Life and Times of E. Pauline Johnson, Tekahionwake*. Toronto: Harper Collins, 2002. Print.

Green, Robyn. "Unsettling Cures: The Possibilities and Limitations of the Indian Residential School Settlement Agreement." *Canadian Journal of Law and Society* 27.1 (2012): 129–48. Print.

Gregory, Derek. "Interventions in the Historical Geography of Modernity: Social Theory, Spatiality and the Politics of Representation." *Place/Culture/Representation*. Ed. James Duncan and David Ley. London: Routledge, 1993. 272–313. Print.

Grey Owl. *Pilgrims of the Wild*. 1934. Ed. Michael Gnarowski. Toronto: Dundurn, 2010. Print.

Griffiths, Alison. *Shivers Down Your Spine: Cinema, Museums, and the Immersive View*. New York: Columbia UP, 2008. Print.

Gunnars, Kristjana. *Settlement Poems I*. Winnipeg: Turnstone, 1980. Print.

———. *Settlement Poems II*. Winnipeg: Turnstone, 1980. Print.

Guth, Gwendolyn. "Good People." Lynch et al. 137–41.

Gwyn, Sandra. *The Private Capital.* Toronto: McLelland and Stewart, 1984. Print.

———. *Tapestry of War: A Private View of Canadians in the Great War.* Toronto: HarperCollins, 1992. Print.

Hacking, Ian. "Memory Sciences, Memory Politics." *Tense Past: Cultural Essays in Trauma and Memory.* Ed. P. Antze and M. Lambek. London: Routledge, 1996. 67–87. Print.

Hagan, William T. "Archival Captive—The American Indian." *The American Archivist* 41.2 (1978): 135–42. *The Society of American Archivists.* 03 Mar. 2010. Web. 7 June 2012.

Halbwachs, Maurice. *The Collective Memory.* 1950. Trans. Francis J. Ditter and Vida Yazdi Ditter. Introd. Mary Douglas. New York: Harper Colophon, 1980. Print.

———. *On Collective Memory.* Ed. and trans. Lewis A. Coser. Chicago: U of Chicago P, 1992. Print.

Hale, Alice K., and Sheila A. Brooks, eds. *The Depression in Canadian Literature.* Themes in Canadian Literature ser. Toronto: Macmillan, 1976. Print.

Hammill, Faye. "The Sensations of the 1920s: Martha Ostenso's *Wild Geese* and Mazo de la Roche's *Jalna.*" *Studies in Canadian Literature* 28.2 (2003): 74–97. Print.

Harris, Kenneth B., and Frances M. P. Robinson. *Visitors Who Never Left: The Origin of the People of Damelahamid.* Vancouver: U of British Columbia P, 1974. Print.

Harris, Michael, ed. *The Signal Anthology: Contemporary Canadian Poetry.* Montreal: Véhicule, 1993. Print.

Hartman, Geoffrey H. "On Traumatic Knowledge and Literary Studies." *New Literary History* 26.3 (1995): 537–63. Print.

Harvey, David. *The Condition of Postmodernity: An Enquiry into the Origins of Cultural Change.* Oxford: Blackwell, 1989. Print.

Hayden, Dolores. *The Power of Place: Urban Landscapes as Public History.* Cambridge: MIT P, 1995. Print.

Haywood, Ian. *The Making of History: A Study of the Literary Forgeries of James Macpherson and Thomas Chatterton in Relation to Eighteenth-Century Ideas of History and Fiction.* London: Fairleigh Dickinson UP, 1986. Print.

Hébert, Chantal. "The Theater: Sounding Board for the Appeals and Dreams of the *Quebecois* Collective." *Essays on Modern Quebec Theater.* Ed. Joseph I. Donohoe and Jonathan M. Weiss. East Lansing: Michigan State UP, 1995. 27–46. Print.

Heidegger, Martin. "The Thing." *The Object Reader.* Ed. Fiona Candlin and Raiford Guins. New York: Routledge, 2009. 113–23. Print.

Heldke, Lisa. *Exotic Appetites: Ruminations of a Food Adventurer.* New York: Routledge, 2003. Print.

Helle, Anita. "Elegy as History: Three Women Poets 'By the Century's Deathbed.'" *South Atlantic Review* 61.2 (1996): 51–68. Print.

Henderson, Jennifer, and Pauline Wakeham. "Colonial Reckoning, National Reconciliation? Aboriginal Peoples and the Culture of Redress in Canada." *English Studies in Canada* 35.1 (2009): 1–26. Print.

Hendrix, Harald. "From Early Modern to Romantic Literary Tourism: A Diachronical Perspective." *Literary Tourism and Nineteenth-Century Culture.* Ed. Nicola J. Watson. Houndmills: Palgrave-Macmillan, 2009. 13–24. Print.

———, ed. *Writers' Houses and the Making of Memory.* New York: Routledge, 2008. Print.

Henighan, Stephen. "Court Jester." *Geist.* n.d, n. pag. Web. 2 Oct. 2012.

Herman, Judith Lewis. *Trauma and Recovery: From Domestic Abuse to Political Terror.* London: Pandora, 1994. Print.

Highway, Tomson. *Kiss of the Fur Queen*. Toronto: Doubleday Canada, 1998. Print.

Hill, Tom, and Trudy Nicks, eds. *Turning the Page: Forging New Partnerships Between Museums and First Peoples*. 2nd ed. Ottawa: Assembly of First Nations and the Canadian Museums Association, 1992. Print.

Hirsch, Marianne. *Family Frames: Photography, Narrative, and Postmemory*. Cambridge: Harvard UP, 1997. Print.

———. "The Generation of Postmemory." *Poetics Today* 29.1 (2008): 103–28. Print.

———. *The Generation of Postmemory: Writing and Visual Culture After the Holocaust*. New York: Columbia UP, 2012. Print.

———. "Maternity and Rememory: Toni Morrison's *Beloved*." *Motherhood and Representation*. Ed. Donna Bassin, Margaret Honey, and Meryle Kaplan. New Haven: Yale UP, 1994. 92–110. Print.

———. "Past Lives: Postmemories in Exile." *Poetics Today* 17.4 (1996): 659–86.

——— and Nancy K. Miller. "Introduction." *Rites of Return: Diaspora Poetics and the Politics of Memory*. Ed. Hirsch and Miller. New York: Columbia UP, 2011. 1–20. Print.

——— and Leo Spitzer. "'There Was Never a Camp Here': Searching for Vapniarka." Kuhn and McAllister 135–54. Print.

Hobbes, Thomas. *Leviathan*. Harmondsworth: Penguin, 1974.

Hobsbawm, Eric. "Introduction: Inventing Traditions." *The Invention of Tradition*. 1983. Ed. Eric Hobsbawm and Terence Ranger. Cambridge: Cambridge UP, 1992. 1–14. Print.

Hodgins, Peter. "The Haunted Dollhouses of Diana Thorneycroft." *Jeunesse* 3.1 (2011): 99–136. Print.

———. "Our Haunted Present: Cultural Memory in Question." *Topia* 12 (2004): 99–108. Print.

——— and Nicole Neatby, eds. *Settling and Unsettling Histories: Essays in Canadian Public History*. Toronto: U of Toronto P, 2012. Print.

——— and Peter Thompson. "Taking the Romance out of Extraction." *Environmental Communication* 5.4 (2011): 393–410. Print.

Hoffman, Eva. *After Such Knowledge: Memory, History, and the Legacy of the Holocaust*. New York: Public Affairs, 2004. Print.

Hoogland, Cornelia. Introduction to "I Am a Prophet." "Canada's Most Memorable Poems: The *LRC* Contributors' List (Part 1)." *Literary Review of Canada* (Apr. 2008). Web. 28 Jan. 2014.

Hoskins, Andrew. *Televising War: From Vietnam to Iraq*. New York: Continuum International, 2004. Print.

Hossack, Darcie Friesen. *Mennonites Don't Dance*. Saskatoon: Thistledown, 2010. Print.

Howells, Coral Ann. "Alice Munro's Heritage Narratives." *Where Are the Voices Coming From? Canadian Culture and the Legacies of History*. Ed. Coral Ann Howells. Amsterdam: Rodopi, 2004. 5–14. Print.

Hua, Anh. "Diaspora and Cultural Memory." *Diaspora, Memory and Identity: A Search for Home*. Ed. Vijay Agnew. Toronto: U of Toronto P, 2005. 191–208. Print.

Hubbard, Tasha. "Voices Heard in the Silence, History Held in the Memory: Ways of Knowing Jeannette Armstrong's 'Threads of Old Memory.'" *Aboriginal Oral Traditions: Theory Practice, Ethics*. Ed. Renée Hulan and Renate Eigenbrod. Halifax: Fernwood, 2008. 139–53. Print.

Humphreys, Helen. *Afterimage*. Toronto: HarperCollins, 2000. Print.

Hurley, Mary C. *Aboriginal Title: The Supreme Court of Canada Decision in* Delgamuukw v.

British Columbia. 1998. Parliament of Canada. Library of Parliament. 2000. Web. 21 Oct. 2013.

Huyssen, Andreas. "Present Pasts: Media, Politics, Amnesia." *Public Culture* 12.1 (2000): 21–38.

Iacovetta, Franca, Valerie J. Korinek, and Marlene Epp, eds. *Edible Histories and Cultural Politics: Towards a Canadian Food History.* Toronto: U of Toronto P, 2012. Print.

Igartua, José E. "The Genealogy of Stereotypes: French Canadians in Two English-Language Canadian History Textbooks." *Journal of Canadian Studies/Revue d'études canadiennes* 42.3 (Fall 2008): 106–32. Print.

Innis, Harold A. *The Bias of Communication.* 1951. Toronto: U of Toronto P, 1982. Print.

Ipellie, Alootook. "People of the Good Land." *The Voice of the Natives: The Canadian North and Alaska.* Ed. Hans-Ludwig Blohm. Ottawa: Penumbra, 2001. 19–31. Print.

Jackson, Emily. "Efforts to Save Poet Al Purdy's Ontario Home Stall." *Toronto Star* 10 Mar. 2012. *The Star.com.* Web. 23 Oct. 2012.

Jackson, Marni. "Saving a Purdy A-Frame—and Other Cultural Edifices." *Globe and Mail* 5 Apr. 2012. *The Globe and Mail.com.* Web. 23 Oct. 2012.

Jansen, Jan. "Cultural Memory." Jan. 2008. Web. 9 Jan. 2013.

Jasen, Patricia. *Wild Things: Nature, Culture and Tourism in Ontario, 1791–1914.* Toronto: U of Toronto P, 1995. Print.

Jenkins, Keith. *The Postmodern History Reader.* London: Routledge, 1997. Print.

Jenkins, Phil. *An Acre of Time.* Toronto: MacFarlane, Walter & Ross, 1996. Print.

Jessup, Lynda. "The Group of Seven and the Tourist Landscape in Western Canada." *Journal of Canadian Studies* 37.1 (2002): 144–71. Print.

Jiles, Paulette. "Night Flight to Attiwapiskat." *Celestial Navigation: Poems.* Toronto: McClelland, 1984. Print.

———. "Night Flight to Attiwapiskat." *An Anthology of Canadian Literature in English.* Rev. ed. Ed. Russell Brown, Donna Bennett, and Nathalie Cooke. Toronto: Oxford UP, 1990. 670–71. Print.

———. *North Spirit: Travels Among the Cree and Ojibway Nations and Their Star Maps.* Toronto: Doubleday, 1995. Print.

———. *Song to the Rising Sun: A Collection.* Vancouver: Polestar, 1989. Print.

Johnson, E. Pauline. *Collected Poems and Selected Prose.* Ed. Carole Gerson and Veronica Strong-Boag. Toronto: U of Toronto P, 2002. Print.

———. *Flint and Feather: The Complete Poems of E. Pauline Johnson (Tekahionwake).* Markham: PaperJacks, 1972. Print.

———. *Legends of Vancouver.* 1911. Vancouver: Kessinger, 2004. Print.

———. "A Strong Race Opinion: On the Indian Girl in Modern Fiction." *The Globe* 22 May 1892. Rpt. *E. Pauline Johnson: Tekahionwake: Collected Poems and Selected Prose.* Ed. Carole Gerson and Veronica Strong-Boag. Toronto: U of Toronto P, 2002. 177–83. Print.

Johnston, Basil. *Indian School Days.* Toronto: Key Porter, 1988. Print.

Johnston, Sasha. "Slavery, Abolition, and the Myth of White British Benevolence." Diss. U of British Columbia, 2009. Web. 28 Jan. 2014.

Joseph, Jonathan. "Derrida's Spectres of Ideology." *Journal of Political Ideologies* 6.1 (2001): 95–115. Print.

Jung, Courtney. "Canada and the Legacy of the Indian Residential Schools: Transitional Justice for Indigenous People in a Nontransitional Society." *Identities in Transition:*

Challenges for Transitional Justice in Divided Societies Ed. Paige Arthur. Cambridge: Cambridge UP, 2010. 217–50. Print.

Kamboureli, Smaro. "The Culture of Celebrity and National Pedagogy." *Home-Work: Postcolonialism, Pedagogy, and Canadian Literature*. Ed. Cynthia Sugars. Ottawa: U of Ottawa P, 2004. 35–55. Print.

———. *Scandalous Bodies: Diasporic Literature in English Canada*. Don Mills: Oxford UP, 2000. Print.

Kaplan, E. Anne. *Trauma Culture: The Politics of Terror and Loss in Media and Literature*. New Brunswick: Rutgers UP, 2005. Print.

Kay, Barbara. "Unreadably Canadian." *National Post* 15 July 2009: n. pag. Web. 31 May 2013.

Keenan, Jerry. *Encyclopedia of American Indian Wars: 1492–1890*. New York: Norton, 1997. Print.

Keeshig-Tobias, Lenore. "Stop Stealing Native Stories." *Borrowed Power: Essays on Cultural Appropriation*. Ed. Bruce Ziff and Pratima V. Rao. New Brunswick: Rutgers UP, 1997. 71–73. Print.

Kelman, Suanne. "Terrific First Novel Includes Recipes." *Globe and Mail* 8 June 1996: C24. Print.

Kent, John. "The Editor's Address to the Public." *The Canadian Literary Magazine* 1.1 (Apr. 1833): 1–2. Print.

Kenyon, W.A. *Mounds of Sacred Earth: Burial Mounds of Ontario*. Royal Ontario Museum Archaeology Monograph 9. Toronto: Royal Ontario Museum, 1986. Print.

Kertzer, Jonathan M. "Genius Loci: The Ghost in Canadian Literature." *Canadian Literature* 130 (1991): 70–89. Print.

———. *Worrying the Nation: Imagining a National Literature in English Canada*. Toronto: U of Toronto P, 1998. Print.

Keshen, Jeffrey A. *Propaganda and Censorship During Canada's Great War*. Edmonton: U of Alberta P, 1996. Print.

Kilbourn, Russell J.A., and Eleanor Ty, eds. *The Memory Effect: The Remediation of Memory in Literature and Film*. Waterloo: Wilfrid Laurier UP, 2013. Print.

Kim, Christine. "Racialized Diasporas, Entangled Postmemories, and Kyo Maclear's *The Letter Opener*." Kim, McCall, and Baum Singer 171–89. Print.

———, Sophie McCall, and Melina Baum Singer, eds. *Cultural Grammars of Nation, Diaspora, and Indigeneity in Canada*. Waterloo: Wilfrid Laurier UP, 2012. Print.

King, Thomas. "Introduction." *All My Relations: An Anthology of Contemporary Canadian Native Fiction*. Ed. Thomas King. Toronto: McClelland and Stewart, 1990. ix–xvi. Print.

———. *The Truth about Stories: A Native Narrative*. Toronto: Anansi, 2003. Print.

King, William Lyon Mackenzie. House of Commons. 30 June 1928, 1443. Print.

Kirby William. *Le Chien d'or/The Golden Dog*. Ed. Mary Jane Edwards. Montreal: McGill-Queen's UP, 2012. Print.

Klassen, Pamela. "What's Bre(a)d in the Bone: The Bodily Heritage of Mennonite Women." *MQR* (Apr. 1994): 229–47. Print.

Kogawa, Joy. *Obasan*. Toronto: Lester & Orpen Dennys, 1981. Print.

Kristeva, Julia. *Black Sun: Depression and Melancholia*. New York: Columbia UP, 1989. Print.

Kroeg, Susan. "The 'Irish Concern' in *Jane Eyre*." *Women's Writing* 14.1 (2007): 70–90. Print.

Kroetsch, Robert. "On Being an Alberta Writer." 1983. *Canadian Literature in English: Texts and Contexts*. Vol. II. Ed. Laura Moss and Cynthia Sugars. Toronto: Pearson/Penguin, 2009. 327–31. Print.

Kroker, Arthur, and David Cook. *The Postmodern Scene: Excremental Culture and Hyper-Aesthetics*. New York: St Martin's, 1988. Print.

Kuhn, Annette, and Kirsten Emiko McAllister. "Locating Memory: Photographic Acts—An Introduction." Kuhn and McAllister 1–17. Print.

———, eds. *Locating Memory: Photographic Acts*. New York: Berghahn, 2006. Print.

Lacan, Jacques. *The Ethics of Psychoanalysis, 1959–1960*. Book VII of *The Seminar of Jacques Lacan*. Ed. Jacquest-Alain Miller. Trans. Dennis Porter. London: Routledge, 1992. Print.

———. "Presence of the Analyst." Esman, Aaron, ed. *Essential Papers on Transference*. New York: New York UP, 1990. Print. 480–91.

LaCapra, Dominick. "History and Psychoanalysis." *Critical Inquiry* 13.2 (1987): 222–51.

———. *Writing History, Writing Trauma*. Baltimore: John Hopkins UP, 2001. Print.

———. *Prosthetic Memory: The Transformation of American Remembrance in the Age of Mass Culture*. New York: Columbia UP, 2004. Print.

Lahji, Nadir. "The City in the Traumatic Scene of Modernity." *Architectural Theory Review* 7.1 (2002): 103–16. Print.

Lai, Chung-Hsiung. "Re-Writing the Subject: The Thrownness of Being in the Multicultural Condition." *Canadian Review of Comparative Literature* 30.3–4 (2003): 495–503. Print.

Lampman, Archibald. *At the Mermaid Inn: Wilfred Campbell, Archibald Lampman, Duncan Campbell Scott in* The Globe *1892–93*. Toronto: U of Toronto P, 1979. Web. 3 Aug. 2012.

Landsberg, Alison. "Prosthetic Memory: Total Recall and *Blade Runner*." *Cyberspace/Cyberbodies/Cyberpunk: Cultures of Technological Embodiment*. London: Sage, 1995. Print.

———. *The Poems of Archibald Lampman*. Ed. Duncan Campbell Scott. Toronto: George Morang, 1900. Print.

LaRochelle, Raymond. "L'histoire du Rapide-Blanc et RB Station." *Le Rapide-Blanc*. n.d. Web. 22 May 2012.

Laurence, Margaret. *The Diviners*. Toronto: McClelland and Stewart, 1974. Print.

Lawrence, Bonita. *"Real" Indians and Others: Mixed-Blood Urban Native Peoples and Indigenous Nationhood*. Vancouver: U of British Columbia P, 2004. Print.

Le Goff, Jacques. 1992. *History and Memory*. Trans. Steven Rendall and Elizabeth Claman. New York: Columbia UP. Print.

Le Moine, J.M. "Major Robert Stobo." *Maple Leaves*. 4th series. Quebec: Augustin Coté, 1873. 55–73. Print.

Leblanc, Raymond. "Acadie." *Cri de terre: poèmes 1969–71*. Moncton: Éditions d'Acadie, 1972. 41. Print.

———. "Projet de pays: Acadie-Québec." *Cri de terre: poèmes 1969–71*. Moncton: Éditions d'Acadie, 1972. 45. Print.

Lee, Dennis. "Cadence, Country, Silence: Writing in Colonial Space." 1973. *Canadian Literature in English: Texts and Contexts*. Vol. II. Ed. Laura Moss and Cynthia Sugars. Toronto: Pearson/Penguin, 2009. 470–76. Print.

———, ed. *The New Canadian Poets: 1970–1985*. Toronto: McClelland, 1985. Print.

———. *Civil Elegies*. 1972. Toronto: Anansi, 1994. Print.

———. "Till the House Was Real." Introduction. Vermeersch, *Al Purdy* 11–17. Print.

Lee, Jen Sookfong. *The End of East*. Toronto: Knopf, 2007. Print.

———. Interview with Craig Rintoul. *The End of East*. Web. 22 Jan. 2013.

Lee, Tara. Review of *The End of East*. *Quill and Quire* (March 2007): Web 12 Jan. 2013.

Lefebvre, Henri. *The Production of Space*. Trans. Donald Nicholson-Smith. Oxford: Blackwell, 1991. Print.

Legat, Allice. *Walking the Land, Feeding the Fire: Knowledge and Stewardship among the Tlicho People*. Tucson: U of Arizona P, 2012. Print.

Leighton, Mary Elizabeth. "Performing Pauline Johnson: Representations of 'the Indian Poetess' in the Periodical Press, 1892–95." *Essays on Canadian Writing* 65 (1998): 141–64. Print.

Lessl, Thomas. "The Priestly Voice." *Quarterly Journal of Speech* 75.2 (1989): 182–97. Print.

Lévy, Pierre. *Cyberculture*. Trans. Robert Bononno. Minneapolis: U of Minnesota P, 2001. Print.

Lewis, Tanya. "Eating Identity: Food and the Construction of Region in *The Cure for Death by Lighting* and *Fall on Your Knees*." *Essays on Canadian Writing* 78 (2003): 86–109. Print.

Leys, Ruth. *Trauma: A Genealogy*. Chicago: U of Chicago P, 2000. Print.

Litt, Paul. "The War, Mass Culture, and Cultural Nationalism." *Canada and the First World War: Essays in Honour of Robert Craig Brown*. Ed. David Mackenzie. Toronto: U of Toronto P, 2005. 323–49. Print.

"Loblaw Reports Third-Quarter Profit of \$189M." *The Star* Online. 17 Nov. 2009. Web. 16 Feb. 2011.

"Loblaws Backs Off Lawsuit against Bathurst Coach." CBC News Online. 8 Jan. 2010. Web. 12 Jan. 2010.

Locke, John. *An Essay Concerning Human Understanding*. Ed. Roger Woolhouse. New York and London: Penguin, 1997. Print.

Logan, Robert. *The Fifth Language: Learning a Living in the Computer Age*. Toronto: Stoddart, 1995. Print.

Longacre, Doris Janzen. *More-with-Less: Recipes and Suggestions by Mennonites on How To Eat Better and Consume Less of the World's Limited Food Resources*. 25th ed. Waterloo: Herald, 2000. Print.

Lousely, Cheryl. "Witness to the Body Count: Planetary Ethics in Dionne Brand's *Inventory*." *Canadian Poetry* 63 (2008): 37–58. Print.

Lowenthal, David. "Identity, Heritage, and History." *Commemorations: The Politics of National Identity*. Ed. John R. Gillis. Princeton: Princeton UP, 1994. 41–57. Print.

———. *The Past Is a Foreign Country*. Cambridge: Cambridge UP, 1985. Print.

———. *Possessed by the Past: The Heritage Crusade and the Spoils of History*. New York: Free Press, 1996. Print.

Luckhurst, Roger. *The Trauma Question*. London: Routledge, 2008. Print.

Lynch, Gerald, Shoshannah Ganz, and Josephene T.M. Kealey, eds. *The Ivory Thought: Essays on Al Purdy*. Ottawa: U of Ottawa P, 2008. Print.

Lyon, George W. "Pauline Johnson: A Reconsideration." *Studies in Canadian Literature* 15.2 (1990): 136–59. Print.

Maaka, Roger, and Augie Fleras. *The Politics of Indigeneity: Challenging the State in Canada and Aotearoa New Zealand*. Dunedin: U of Otago P, 2005. Print.

Macalpine, Ida. "The Development of the Transference." Esman, Aaron, ed. *Essential Papers on Transference*. New York: New York UP, 1990. 188–220. Print.

MacDonald, Heidi. "Doing More with Less: The Sisters of St. Martha (PEI) Diminish the Impact of the Great Depression." *Acadiensis: Journal of the History of the Atlantic Region* 33.1 (2003): 21–46. Print.

MacDonald, Tanis. *The Daughter's Way: Canadian Women's Paternal Elegies*. Waterloo: Wilfrid Laurier UP, 2012. Print.

Mackey, Eva. *The House of Difference*. Toronto: U of Toronto P, 2002. Print.

MacKendrick, Louis K., ed. *Al Purdy Issue.* Spec. issue of *Essays on Canadian Writing* 49 (1993): 1–222. Print.

Macoun, John. "The Forests of Canada and their Distribution." *Transactions of the Royal Society of Canada, Section 4.* 1894. 3–20. Web. 3 Aug. 2012.

Madsen, Deborah L. "Of Time and Trauma: The Possibilities for Narrative in Paula Gun Allen's *The Woman Who Owned the Shadows.*" *Transatlantic Voices: Interpretations of Native North American Literatures.* Ed. Elvira Pulitano. Lincoln: U of Nebraska P, 2007. 111–28. Print.

Maillet, Antonine. *Pélagie: The Return to Acadie.* 1979. Trans. Philip Stratford. Fredericton: Goose Lane, 2004. Print.

———. *La Sagouine.* Trans. Luis de Céspedes. Toronto: Simon & Pierre, 1979. Print.

Mandel, Eli. *Out of Place: Poems.* Erin: Press Porcepic, 1977. Print.

———. "Writing West: On the Road to Wood Mountain." *Another Time.* Erin: Press Porcepic, 1977. 91–102. Print.

Maracle, Lee. "Oratory on Oratory." *Trans.Can.Lit: Resituating the Study of Canadian Literature.* Ed. Smaro Kamboureli and Roy Miki. Waterloo: Wilfrid Laurier UP, 2007. 55–70. Print.

Margalit, Avishai. *The Ethics of Memory.* Harvard UP, 2002. Print.

Mark, Charles. "List of crests of House of Wiget with narrative summaries." 1923. Marius Barbeau Fonds. Canadian Museum of Civilization, Gatineau. B5, B-F-63.14–15, Northwest Coast Files. 2–28.

Marlatt, Daphne. *Steveston.* Vancouver: Talonbooks, 1974. Print.

Marston, John. "Metaphors of the Khmer Rouge." Ed. May Ebihara. *Cambodian Culture Since 1975.* New York: Cornell UP, 1994. 105–18. Print.

Marte, Lidia. "Foodmaps: Tracing Boundaries of 'Home' Through Food Relations." *Food & Foodways* 15 (2007): 261–89. Print.

Martin, Jim, ed. *Strong Like Two People: The Development of a Mission Statement for the Dogrib Schools.* Rae: Dogrib Board of Education, 1989. Print.

Marty, Sid. *Tumbleweed Harvest.* Wood Mountain: Sundog, 1973. Print.

Marx, Karl. *Grundrisse.* Trans. Martin Nicolaus. London: Penguin, 1973. Print.

——— and Friedrich Engels. *Selected Correspondence.* Trans. Dona Torr. London: International Publishers, 1934. Print.

Mason, Mark. "Historiospectography? Sande Cohen on Derrida's *Specters of Marx.*" *Rethinking History* 12.4 (2008): 483–514. Print.

Mason, Rachel. "Conflicts and Lessons in First Nations Secondary Education: An Analysis of BC First Nations Studies." *Canadian Journal of Native Education* 31.2 (2008): 130–53. Print.

McAllister, Kirsten. *Terrain of Memory: A Japanese Canadian Memorial Project.* Vancouver: U of British Columbia P, 2010. Print.

McCall, Sophie. "Diaspora and Nation in Métis Writing." Kim, McCall, and Baum Singer 21–42. Print.

McCalman, Iain. "The Little Ship of Horrors: Reenacting Extreme History." *Criticism* 46.3 (2004): 477–86. Print.

——— and Paula A. Pickering, eds. *Historical Reenactment: From Realism to the Affective Turn.* Houndsmills: Palgrave Macmillan, 2010. Print.

McCue, Harvey. "Native Culture and the Recording of History." *The Place of History: Commemorating Canada's Past/Les lieux de la mémoire: la commemoration du passé du Canada.* Ottawa: Royal Society of Canada, 1997. 93–96. Print.

McDaniel, Susan, and Wendy Mitchinson. "Canadian Family Fictions and Realities: Past and Present." *Family Fictions in Canadian Literature*. Waterloo: U of Waterloo P, 1988. 11–25. Print.

McDowell, Linda. *Gender, Identity and Place: Understanding Feminist Geographies*. Minneapolis: U of Minnesota P, 1999. Print.

McKay, Ian. *The Quest of the Folk: Antimodernism and Cultural Selection in Twentieth-Century Nova Scotia*. Montreal: McGill-Queen's UP, 1994. Print.

McKegney, Sam. "'Beautiful Hunters with Strong Medicine': Indigenous Masculinity and Kinship in Richard Van Camp's *The Lesser Blessed*." *Canadian Journal of Native Studies* 29.1&2 (2008): 203–27. Print.

———. "Warriors, Healers, Lovers, and Leaders: Colonial Impositions on Indigenous Male Roles and Responsibilities." *Canadian Perspectives on Men & Masculinities: An Interdisciplinary Reader*. Ed. Jason A. Laker. Don Mills: Oxford UP, 2012. 241–68. Print.

McKinnon, Barry. Email Interview with Barry McKinnon. 7 Dec. 2012.

———. *I Wanted to Say Something*. 1975. Red Deer: Red Deer College, 1990. Print.

McKittrick, Katherine. *Demonic Grounds: Black Women and the Cartographies of Struggle*. Minneapolis: U of Minnesota P, 2006. Print.

——— and Clyde Woods, eds. *Black Geographies and the Politics of Place*. Toronto: Between the Lines, 2007. Print.

McLaren, John P.S. "Tribulations of Antoine Ratte: A Case Study of the Environmental Regulation of the Canadian Lumbering Industry in the Nineteenth Century." *University of New Brunswick Law Journal* 33 (1984): 203–59. Print.

McLean, Lorna C., and Marilyn Barber. "In Search of Comfort and Independence: Irish Immigrant Domestic Servants Encounter the Courts, Jails, and Asylums in Nineteenth-Century Ontario." *Sisters or Strangers: Immigrant, Ethnic, and Racialized Women in Canadian History*. Ed. Marlene Epp et al. Toronto: U of Toronto P, 2004. 133–60. Print.

McLeod, Neal. "Coming Home through Stories." *(Ad)dressing Our Words: Aboriginal Perspectives on Aboriginal Literatures*. Ed. Armand Garnet Ruffo. Penticton: Theytus Books, 2001. 17–36. Print.

———. *Cree Narrative Memory: From Treaties to Contemporary Times*. Saskatoon: Purich, 2007. Print.

McLuhan, Marshall. *Understanding Media*. New York: McGraw-Hill, 1964. Print.

Medina, José. "Toward a Foucaultian Epistemology of Resistance: Counter-Memory, Epistemic Friction, and *Guerrilla* Pluralism." *Foucault Studies* 12 (2011): 9–35. Print.

Mensah, Joseph. *Black Canadians: History, Experiences, Social Conditions*. Halifax: Fernwood, 2002. Print.

Mercier, Laurie. "Borders Gender, and Labor: Canadian and U.S. Mining Towns during the Cold War Era." Dinius and Vergara 158–77. Print.

Metz, Christian. "Photography and the Fetish." *The Photography Reader*. Ed. Liz Wells. London: Routledge, 2003. 138–47. Print.

Meyrowitz, Joshua. *No Sense of Place: The Impact of Electronic Media on Social Behavior*. New York: Oxford UP, 1985. Print.

Michel, Martina. "Positioning the Subject: Locating Postcolonial Studies." *ARIEL* 26.1 (1995): 83–99. Print.

Mighton, John. *Half Life*. Toronto: Playwrights Canada, 2005. Print.

Miki, Roy. "Inside the Black Egg": Cultural Practice, Citizenship, and Belonging in a Globalising Canadian Nation." *Mosaic* 38.3 (2005): 1–20. Print.

Mildon, Drew. "A Bad Connection: First Nations Oral Histories in the Canadian Courts."

Aboriginal Oral Traditions: Theory, Practice, Ethics. Ed. Renée Hulan and Renate Eigenbrod. Halifax: Fernwood, 2008. 79–97. Print.

Miller, Bryan. "An Interview with Seth." Bookslut. June 2004. Web. 3 May 2013.

Miller, Jay, ed. *Mourning Dove: A Salishan Autobiography.* Lincoln: U of Nebraska P, 1990. Print.

Miller, Susan Beth. *Disgust: The Gatekeeper Emotion.* Hillsdale: Analytic, 2004. Print.

Million, Dian. "Felt Theory: An Indigenous Feminist Approach to Affect and History." *WicazoSa Review* 24. 2 (2009): 53–76. Print.

Milloy, John. *A National Crime: The Canadian Government and the Residential School System, 1879 to 1986.* Winnipeg: U of Manitoba P, 1999. Print.

Mills, P. Dawn. *For Future Generations: Reconciling Gitxsan and Canadian Law.* Saskatoon: Purich, 2008. Print.

Mirzoeff, Nicolas. "The Right to Look." *Critical Inquiry* 3 (Spring 2011): 473–96. Print.

Mitchell, Don. *Cultural Geography: A Critical Introduction.* Oxford: Blackwell, 2000. Print.

Miyoshi, Masao. "A Borderless World? From Colonialism to Transnationalism and the Decline of the Nation-State." *Critical Inquiry* 19.4 (Summer 1993): 726–51. Print.

Monture, Patricia. "What is Sovereignty for Indigenous People?" *Questioning Sociology: Canadian Perspectives.* Ed. George Pavlich and Myra Hird. Don Mills: Oxford UP, 2007. 253–65. Print.

Monture-Angus, Patricia. *Journeying Forward: Dreaming First Nations' Independence.* Halifax: Fernwood, 1999. Print.

Moon, Claire. "Healing Past Violence: Traumatic Assumptions and Therapeutic Interventions in War and Reconciliation." *Journal of Human Rights* 8.1 (2009): 71–91. Print.

Moreton-Robinson, Eileen. "Imagining the Good Indigenous Citizen: Race, War and the Pathology of Patriarchal White Sovereignty." *Cultural Studies Review* 15.2 (2009): 61–79. Print.

Morgan, J.H. *Report on the Forests of Canada.* Ottawa: MacLean, Rogers and Co., 1886. Print.

Morrison, Toni. "The Site of Memory." *Out There: Marginalization and Contemporary Cultures.* Ed. Russell Ferguson, Martha Gever, Trinh T. Minh-ha, and Cornel West. New York: The New Museum of Contemporary Art, 1990. 299–305. Print.

Morrissey, Stephen. *Family Album.* Vancouver: Caitlin, 1989. Print.

Morton, Desmond. "French Canada and War, 1868–1917: The Military Background to the Conscription Crisis of 1917." *War and Society in North America.* Ed. J.L. Granatstein and R.D. Cuff. Toronto: Thomas Nelson, 1971. 84–103. Print.

Morton, Timothy. *Ecology without Nature.* Cambridge: Harvard UP, 2007. Print.

Moses, Daniel David, and Terry Goldie, eds. *An Anthology of Canadian Native Literature in English.* Don Mills: Oxford UP, 2005. Print.

Mulvey, Laura. "Visual Pleasure and Narrative Cinema." 1975. *Visual and Other Pleasures.* Bloomington: Indiana UP, 1989. 14–26. Print.

Munce, Alayna. *When I Was Young and In My Prime.* Roberts Creek: Nightwood Editions, 2005. Print.

Munro, Alice. "Home." *74: New Canadian Stories.* Ed. David Helwig and Joan Harcourt. Kingston: Oberon, 1974. 133–53. Print.

———. "Meneseteung." *Friend of My Youth.* Toronto: McClelland and Stewart, 1990. 50–73. Print.

———. "Home." *The View from Castle Rock.* Toronto: Penguin Canada, 2006. 285–315. Print.

———. "What Do You Want to Know For?" *The View from Castle Rock.* Toronto: Penguin Canada, 2006. 316–40. Print.

————. "Walker Brothers Cowboy." *Dance of the Happy Shades*. 1968. 2nd ed. Toronto: McGraw-Hill Ryerson, 1988. 1–18. Print.

Musgrave, Susan. *Origami Dove*. Toronto: McClelland and Stewart, 2011. Print.

Nanibush, Wanda. "Love and Other Resistances: Responding to Kahnesatà:ke Through Artistic Practice." *This Is an Honour Song: Twenty Years since the Blockades*. Ed. Leanne Simpson and Kiera L. Ladner. Winnipeg: Arbeiter Ring, 2010. 165–93. Print.

Nash, Catherine. "Remapping the Body/Land: New Cartographies of Identity, Gender, and Landscape in Ireland." *Writing Women in Space: Colonial and Postcolonial Geographies*. Ed. Alison Blunt and Gillian Rose. New York: Guilford, 1994. 227–50. Print.

Negroponte, Nicholas. *Being Digital*. New York: Vintage, 1996. Print.

Neptune, Harvey R. *Caliban and the Yankees: Trinidad and the United States Occupation*. Chapel Hill: U of North Carolina P, 2007. Print.

New, W.H. *Borderlands: How We Talk About Canada*. Vancouver: U of British Columbia P, 1998. Print.

Ngor, Haing (with Roger Warner). *Survival in the Killing Fields*. London: Robinson, 1987. Print.

nichol, bp. "In Place: An Appreciation." MacKendrick 27–31. Print.

Nietzsche, Friedrich. *The Use and Abuse of History*. 2nd ed. Trans. Adrian Collins. Indianapolis: Bobbs-Merrill, 1957. Print.

NO 'XYA ' (Our Footprints). Dir. David Diamond, Hal B. Blackwater, Lois G. Shannon, and Marie Wilson. Perf. Hal B. Blackwater, Sylvia-Anne George, Sherri-Lee Guilbert, and Ed Astley. Headlines Theatre. 1987. DVD.

Nora, Pierre. "Between Memory and History: *Les Lieux de Mémoire*." Trans. Marc Roudebush. *Memory and Counter-Memory*. Spec. issue of *Representations* 26 (1989): 7–24. *JSTOR*. Web. 15 Feb. 2012.

————. "From 'Between Memory and History: *Les Lieux de Mémoire*.'" *Theories of Memory: A Reader*. Ed. Michael Rossington and Anne Whitehead. Baltimore: Johns Hopkins UP, 2007. 144–49. Print.

————, ed. *Lieux de mémoire*. 7 vols. Paris: Gallimard, 1984–1992. Print.

Norris, Ken. "What Happened to the Avant-Garde?" Rev. of *The New Canadian Poets: 1970–1985*. *Essays on Canadian Writing* 36 (1988): 110–22. Print.

Nurse, Andrew. "But Now Things Have Changed: Marius Barbeau and the Politics of Amerindian Identity, 1911–15." *Ethnohistory* 48.3 (2001): 433–72. Print.

————. "Marius Barbeau and the Methodology of Salvage Ethnography in Canada." *Historicizing Canadian Anthropology*. Ed. Julia Harrison and Regna Darnell. Vancouver: U of British Columbia P, 2006. 52–64. Print.

O'Brian, John, and Peter White. *Beyond Wilderness: The Group of Seven, Canadian Identity, and Contemporary Art*. Montreal: McGill-Queen's UP, 2007. Print.

Odell, Jonathan. "Ode for the New Year." *The Loyal Verses of Joseph Stansbury and Doctor Jonathan Odell*. Ed. Winthrop Sargent. Albany: J. Munsell, 1860. 59–60. Print.

Olick, Jeffrey K., Vered Vinitzky-Seroussi, and Daniel Levy, eds. *The Collective Memory Reader*. Toronto: Oxford UP, 2011. Print.

Olick, Kevin, and Joyce Robbins. "Social Memory Studies: From 'Collective Memory' to the Historical Sociology of Mnemonic Practices." *Annual Review of Sociology* 24 (1998): 105–40. Print.

Ondaatje, Michael. *Running in the Family*. Toronto: McClelland and Stewart, 1982. Print.

Osachoff, Margaret Gail. "'Treacheries of the Heart': Memoir, Confession, and Meditation in the Stories of Alice Munro." *Probable Fictions: Alice Munro's Narrative Acts*. Ed. Louis K. MacKendrick. Downsview: ECW, 1983. 61–82. Print.

Osbourne, Brian S. "Landscapes, Memory, Monuments, and Commemoration: Putting Identity in Its Place." *Canadian Ethnic Studies Journal* 33.3 (Fall 2001): 39–77. Print.

Ostriker, Alicia. "Beyond Confession: The Poetics of Postmodern Witness." *American Poetry Review* 30.2 (2001): 35–39. Print.

Padolsky, Enoch. "You Are Where You Eat: Ethnicity, Food and Cross-Cultural Spaces." *Canadian Ethnic Studies* 37.2 (2005): 9–31. Print.

Pannekoek, Frits. Review of "Syncrude Gallery of Aboriginal Culture, Provincial Museum of Alberta." *The Canadian Historical Review* 82.2 (2001): 348–49. Print.

Panofsky, Ruth. "Don't Let Me Do It: Mazo de la Roche and her Publishers." *International Journal of Canadian Studies* 11 (1995): 171–84. Print.

Parker, Sir Gilbert. *The Seats of the Mighty, Being the memoirs of Captain Robert Moray sometime an officer in the Virginia regiment and afterwards of Amherst's regiment*. Intro. John Coldwell Adams. Ottawa: Tecumseh, 1981. Print.

Parkinson Zamora, Lois. *The Usable Past: The Imagination of History in Recent Fiction of the Americas*. Cambridge: Cambridge UP, 1997. Print.

Peake, Linda, and Brian Ray. "Racializing the Canadian Landscape: Whiteness, Uneven Geographies, and Social Justice." *Canadian Geographer* 45.1 (2001): 180–87. Print.

Philipose, Liz. "The Politics of Pain and the End of Empire." *International Feminist Journal of Politics* 9.1 (2007): 60–81.

Phillips, Mark Salber. "What Is Tradition When It Is Not 'Invented'? A Historiographical Introduction." *Questions of Tradition*. Ed. Mark Salber Phillips and Gordon Schochet. Toronto: U of Toronto P, 2004. 3–29. Print.

Plato. "From *Theaetetus* and *Phaedrus*." *Theories of Memory: A Reader*. Ed. Michael Rossington and Anne Whitehead. Baltimore: Johns Hopkins UP, 2007. 25–27. Print.

Potter, Andrew. *The Authenticity Hoax: How We Get Lost Finding Ourselves*. Toronto: McClelland and Stewart, 2010. Print.

Pound, Ezra. "Canto LIX." *The Cantos*. 1934. New York: New Directions, 1969. 324–27. Print.

Power Play with Don Martin. CTV Television. 26 Oct. 2012.

Provencher, Jean. *La grande peur d'octobre '70*. Montreal: L'Aurore, 1974. Print.

———. Preface. *Québec, Spring 1918*. *Canadian Theatre Review* 28 (Fall 1980): 56. Print.

———. *Québec sous la loi des mesures de guerre 1918*. Trois-Rivières: Boréal Express, 1971. Print.

———. *Québec, Spring 1918*. Trans. Leo Skir. *Canadian Theatre Review* 28 (Fall 1980): 57–127.

——— and Gilles Lachance. *Québec, Printemps 1918*. Montreal: L'Aurore, 1974. Print.

Publisher's blurb. *The End of East*. Random House of Canada. Web. 21 Jan. 2013.

Purdy, Al. *Beyond Remembering: The Collected Poems of Al Purdy*. Ed. Al Purdy and Sam Solecki. Madeira Park: Harbour, 2000. Print.

———. *In Search of Owen Roblin*. Toronto: McClelland and Stewart, 1974. Print.

———. *Reaching for the Beaufort Sea*. Ed. Alex Widen. Madeira Park: Harbour, 1993. Print.

Putnam, Donald F. and L.J. Chapman. Physiography of Southern Ontario. Toronto Ontario Geological Survey, 1984.

Pyper, Andrew. "High Anxiety in the Bush Garden: Some Common Prejudices in Mainstream Canadian Criticism." *Essays on Canadian Writing* 71 (2000): 88–95. Print.

"'Québec 1918': Le Trident se fait théâtre de la vie vécue." *Le Soleil* 29 Sept. 1973: 37. Print.

Radhakrishnan, R. *Diasporic Mediations: Between Home and Location*. Minneapolis: U of Minneapolis P, 1996. Print.

Radstone, Susannah. "Memory Studies: For and Against." *Memory Studies* 1:1 (2008): 31–39. Print.

Rae, Patricia. "Proleptic Elegy and the End of Arcadianism in 1930s Britain." *Twentieth-Century Literature* 49.2 (2003): 246–75. Print.

Rajchman, John, ed. *The Identity in Question*. New York: Routledge, 1995. Print.

Ratsoy, Ginny. "Dramatizing Alterity: Relational Characterization in Postcolonial British Columbia Plays." *Embracing the Other: Addressing Xenophobia in the New Literatures in English*. Ed. Dunja M. Mohr. New York: Rodopi, 2008. 295–305. Print.

Razack, Sherene, H. "When Place Becomes Race." *Race, Space, and the Law: Unmapping a White Settler Society*. Ed. Sherene H. Razack. Toronto: Between the Lines, 2002. 1–20. Print.

Resendes, Tammy. "Collaborative Study Aims to Promote Social Change." *News@Guelph*. Web. 17 June 2012.

Rhys, Jean. *Wide Sargasso Sea*. London: Penguin Classics, 2000. Print.

Rich, Adrienne. "When We Dead Awaken: Writing as Re-Vision." *On Lies, Secrets, and Silence: Selected Prose, 1966–1978*. New York: Norton, 1995. 33–108. Print.

Richards, David Adams. "My Miramichi Trilogy: A Practising Novelist's View of the Novel in New Brunswick." *Proceedings of the 6th International Literature of Region and Nation Conference*. Ed. Winnifred M. Bogaards. Vol. II. Saint John: U of New Brunswick/ Purple Wednesday Society, 1998. 73–84. Print.

Richler, Noah. *This Is My Country, What's Yours? A Literary Atlas of Canada*. Ill. by Michael Winter. Toronto: McClelland and Stewart, 2006. Print.

Ricoeur, Paul. *Memory, History, Forgetting*. Trans. Kathleen Blamey and David Pellauer. Chicago: U of Chicago P, 2004. Print.

Rifkind, Candida. "Drawn from Memory: Comics Artists and Intergenerational Auto/biography." *Canadian Review of American Studies* 38.3 (2008): 399–427. Print.

Rigney, Anne. "The Dynamics of Remembrance: Texts Between Monumentality and Morphing." *Mediation, Remediation, and the Dynamics of Cultural Memory*. Ed. Astrid Erll and Ann Rigney. Berlin: Walter de Gruyter, 2009. 345–56. Print.

Rimstead, Roxanne. "Introduction: Double Take: The Uses of Cultural Memory." Spec. issue on "Cultural Memory and Social Identity" of *Essays on Canadian Writing* 80 (Fall 2003): 1–14. Print.

——. "'Knowable Communities' in Canadian Criticism." *Review: Literature and Arts of the Americas"* 41.1 (2008): 43–53. Print.

——. *Remnants of Nation: On Poverty Narratives by Women*. Toronto: U of Toronto P, 2001. Print.

Roberts, Charles G.D. *Selected Poems of Sir Charles G.D. Roberts*. Toronto: Ryerson, 1936. Print.

Robertson, David Alexander, and Scott B. Henderson. *Ends/Begins*. Book III. *7 Generations Series*. Winnipeg: Highwater, 2010. Print.

——. *The Pact*. Book IV. *7 Generations Series*. Winnipeg: Highwater, 2011. Print.

——. *Scars*. Book II. *7 Generations Series*. Winnipeg: Highwater, 2010. Print.

——. *Stone*. Book I. *7 Generations Series*. Winnipeg: Highwater, 2010. Print.

Robins, Kevin, and Frank Webster. *Times of the Technoculture: From the Information Society to the Virtual Life*. London: Routledge, 1999. Print.

Robinson, Eden. *Monkey Beach*. Toronto: Vintage Canada, 2001. Print.

Robinson, Frances M. P. Introduction. *Visitors Who Never Left: The Origin of the People of Damelahamid*. By Chief Kenneth B. Harris and Frances M. P. Robinson. Vancouver: U of British Columbia P, 1974. xi–xxi. Print.

Rollwagen, Katharine. "When Ghosts Hovered: Community and Crisis in a Company Town, Britannia Beach." *Urban History Review* 35.2 (Spring 2007): 25–36. Print.

Rooke, Constance. "Getting into Heaven: An Interview with Diana Hartog, Paulette Jiles, and Sharon Thesen." *Malahat Review* 83 (1988): 5–52. Print.

Ross, Malcolm, ed. *Poets of the Confederation*. Toronto: McClelland, 1960. Print.

Rothberg, Michael. "Decolonizing Trauma Studies: A Response." *Studies in the Novel* 40.1/2 (2008): 224–34. Print.

Rousseau, Jean-Jacques. *The Social Contract and Discourses*. Trans. G.D.H. Cole. N.p.: Fitzhenry & Whiteside, 1986. Print.

Roy, Wendy. "The Word is *Colander*: Language Loss and Narrative Voice in Fictional Canadian Alzheimer's Narratives." *Canadian Literature* 203 (2009): 41–61. Print.

Royal Commission on Aboriginal Peoples. "Health and Healing." *Volume 3: Gathering Strength: Royal Commission on Aboriginal Peoples Final Report*. Ottawa: Royal Commission on Aboriginal Peoples, 1996. Print.

Ruffo, Armand Garnet. "Exposing the Poison, Staunching the Wound: Applying Aboriginal Healing Theory to Literary Analysis." *Canadian Journal of Native Studies* 29.1&2 (2009): 91–110. Print.

———. "Introduction." *(Ad)dressing Our Words: Aboriginal Perspectives on Aboriginal Literatures*. Ed. Armand Garnet Ruffo. Penticton: Theytus, 2001. 5–15. Print.

———. "Poem for Esher (In Memory)." *Opening in the Sky*. Penticton: Theytus, 1994. 89. Print.

Saarinen, Oiva W. "'Single-Sector Communities in Northern Ontario: The Creation and Planning of Dependent Towns.'" *Power and Place: Canadian Urban Development in the North American Context*. Ed. Gilbert Stelter and Alan Artibise. Vancouver: U of British Columbia P, 1986. 220–64. Print.

Sacks, Peter. *The English Elegy: Studies in the Genre from Spenser to Yeats*. Baltimore: John Hopkins UP, 1987. Print.

Safran, William. "Diasporas in Modern Societies: Myths of Homeland and Return." *Diaspora* 1.1 (1991): 83–99. Print.

Sam-Cromarty, Margaret. *Souvenirs de la baie James/James Bay Memoirs*. Hull: Lettresplus, 2002. Print.

Sangster, Joan. "Native Women, Sexuality and the Law." *In the Days of Our Grandmothers: A Reader in Aboriginal Women's History in Canada*. Ed. Mary-Ellen Kelm and Lorna Townsend. Toronto: U of Toronto P, 2006. 301–35. Print.

Saul, Joanne. "'In the Middle of Becoming': Dionne Brand's Historical Vision." *Canadian Woman Studies* 23.2 (2004): 59–63. Print.

Saul, John Ralston. *A Fair Country: Telling Truths about Canada*. Toronto: Viking, 2008. Print.

Schafer, Roy. "The Interpretation of Transference and the Conditions for Loving." Esman, Aaron, ed. and introd. *Essential Papers on Transference*. New York: New York UP, 1990. 401–22. Print.

Schellenberg, Lovella, et al. *Mennonite Girls Can Cook*. Waterloo: Herald, 2011. Print.

Schwab, Gabriele. *Haunting Legacies: Violent Histories and Transgenerational Trauma*. New York: Columbia UP, 2010. Print.

Schwenger, Peter. *The Tears of Things: Melancholy and Physical Objects*. Minneapolis: U of Minnesota P, 2006. Print.

Scobie, Stephen. *A Grand Memory for Forgetting*. Edmonton: Longspoon, 1981. Print.

Scott, Amy. Letter to Frederick G. Scott, 3 April 1918. Scott Papers, McCord Museum P229 A/4. folder 31. Print.

Seager, Alan. "Company Towns." *The Canadian Encyclopedia*. Toronto: Historica Dominion, 1999. Web. 24 May 2012.

Seth. *It's a Good Life, If You Don't Weaken*. Montreal: Drawn & Quarterly, 2007. Print.

Shakespeare, William. *Romeo and Juliet*. Ed. Jill L. Levenson. Oxford: Oxford UP, 2000. Print.

Shaw, Amy. *Crisis of Conscience: Conscientious Objection in Canada during the First World War*. Vancouver: U of British Columbia P, 2009. Print.

Shaw, W. David. *Elegy and Paradox: Testing the Conventions*. Baltimore: Johns Hopkins UP, 1994. Print.

Shawana, Perry. "Legal Processes, Pluralism in Canadian Jurisprudence, and the Governance of Carrier Medicine Knowledge." *Indigenous Legal Traditions*. Law Commission of Canada, ed. Vancouver: U of British Columbia P, 2007. 114–35. Print.

Sheringham, Michael. "Archiving." *Restless Cities*. Ed. Matthew Beaumont and Gregory Dart. New York: Verso, 2010. 1–17. Print.

Sherman, Kenneth, ed. *Relations: Family Portraits*. Oakville: Mosaic, 1986. Print.

Silverberg, Mark. "The Can(adi)onization of Al Purdy." *Essays on Canadian Writing* 70 (2000): 226–51. Print.

Simpson, Leanne. *Dancing on Our Turtle's Back: Stories of Nishnaabeg Re-Creation, Resurgence, and a New Emergence*. Winnipeg: Arbeiter Ring, 2011. Print.

Sinclair, Niigaanwewidam James. "Manitoba Aboriginal Writing." Symposium on Manitoba Writing, Canadian Mennonite University, Winnipeg. 11 May 2012. Spoken.

———. *Teacher's Guide for 7 Generations Series*. Winnipeg: Portage & Main, 2011. Web. 29 Mar. 2013.

"The Skeena River Revolt." *New York Times*. 22 July 1888. Web. 10 April 2012.

Small, Caroline. "Nostalgic History: Pascal Blanchet's *White Rapids*." *The Hooded Utilitarian: A Pundit in Every Panopticon*. 10 Feb. 2011. n.pag. Web. 22 May 2012.

Smith, Denis. *Bleeding Hearts . . . Bleeding Country: Canada and the Quebec Crisis*. Edmonton: Hurtig, 1971. Print.

Smith, Donald B. *From the Land of Shadows: The Making of Grey Owl*. Vancouver: Greystone, 1990. Print.

Smith, Neil. *The Endgame of Globalization*. New York: Routledge, 2005. Print.

———. *Uneven Development: Nature, Capital, and the Production of Space*. 3rd ed. Athens: U of Georgia P, 2008. Print.

Smith, Russell. "A Contemporary Novel? There's No Such Thing." *Globe and Mail* 15 June 2011: n. pag. Web. 31 May 2013.

———. "Why Is Reading This Canadian Novel So Hard?" *Globe and Mail* 25 Aug. 2005: R2. Print.

Smith, Sidonie, and Julia Watson. *Reading Autobiography: A Guide for Interpreting Life Narratives*. 2nd ed. Minneapolis: U of Minnesota P, 2010. Print.

Smyth, Rev. William J. *Mound-Builders*. Montreal: Gazette Printing Company, 1886. Early Canadiana Online. Web 26 Feb. 2014.

Snyder, Carrie. *The Juliet Stories*. Toronto: Anansi, 2012. Print.

Soja, Edward W. *Thirdspace: Journeys to LA and Other Real and Imagined Places*. Oxford: Wiley-Blackwell, 1996. Print.

Solecki, Sam. *The Last Canadian Poet: An Essay on Al Purdy*. Toronto: U of Toronto P, 1999. Print.

Solway, David. "Standard Average Canadian." *Director's Cut*. Erin: Porcupine's Quill, 2003. 87–100. Print.

Sommer, Doris. "Attitude, Its Rhetoric." *The Turn to Ethics*. Ed. Marjorie Garber, Beatrice Hanssen, and Rebecca Walkowitz. New York: Routledge, 2000. 201–20. Print.

Spargo, Tamsin, ed. *Reading the Past*. New York: Palgrave, 2000. Print.

Speakers for the Dead. Dir. Jennifer Holness and David Sullivan. National Film Board of Canada, 2000. Film.

Spender, Dale. *Nattering on the Net: Women, Power and Cyberspace*. Toronto: Garamond, 1996. Print.

Stacey, Charles P. "Nationality: The Experience of Canada." *Historical Papers/Communications historiques* 2.1 (1967): 10–19. Print.

Stacey, Robert David. "Purdy's Ruins: *In Search of Owen Roblin*, Literary Power, and the Poetics of the Picturesque." Lynch et al. 103–18.

Staebler, Edna. *Food That Really Schmecks: Mennonite Country Cooking as Prepared by My Mennonite Friend Bevvy Martin, My Mother, and Other Fine Cooks*. Waterloo: Wilfrid Laurier UP, 2002. Print.

Stanton, Kim. "Canada's Truth and Reconciliation Commission: Settling the Past?" *International Indigenous Policy Journal* 2.3 (2011): 1–18. Print.

van Steen, Marcus. Rev. of *In Search of Owen Roblin*. *Ottawa Citizen* 2 Nov. 1974: 68. Print.

Steffler, John. "Bruckner KO'd by Uncle Al." MacKendrick 42–43. Print.

Stegner, Wallace. "The Sense of Place." *Where the Bluebird Sings to the Lemonade Springs: Living and Writing in the West*. New York: Penguin, 1993. 199–206. Print.

Stevens, Peter. *Family Feelings & Other Poems*. Guelph: Alive, 1974. Print.

Stewart, Susan. *On Longing: Narratives of the Miniature, the Gigantic, the Souvenir, the Collection*. Durham: Duke UP, 1993. Print.

[Stobo, Robert]. *Memoirs of Major Robert Stobo of the Virginia Regiment*. London: J. Skirven, 1800. openlibrary.org. Web. 15 Nov. 2012.

Stoler, Ann Laura. "Colonial Archives and the Arts of Governance: On the Content in the Form." *Archival Science* 2 (2002): 87–109. Web. 1 May 2013.

Stouck, David. *Major Canadian Authors: A Critical Introduction to Canadian Literature in English*. 2nd ed. Lincoln: U of Nebraska P, 1988. Print.

Strachey, James. "The Nature of the Therapeutic Action of Psyho-Analysis." Esman Aaron, ed. and introd. *Essential Papers on Transference*. New York: New York UP, 1990. 49–79. Print.

Sturken, Marita. "Narratives of Recovery: Repressed Memory as Cultural Memory." *Acts of Memory: Cultural Recall in the Present*. Ed. Mieke Bal, Jonathan Crewe, and Leo Spitzer. Hanover: Dartmouth College, 1999. 231–48. Print.

———. "Reenactment, Fantasy, and the Paranoia of History: Oliver Stone's Docudramas." *History and Theory* 36.4 (1997): 64–79. Print.

———. *Tangled Memories: The Vietnam War, the AIDS Epidemic, and the Politics of Remembering*. Berkeley: U of California P, 1997. Print.

Sugars, Cynthia. "Can the Canadian Speak? Lost in Postcolonial Space." *ARIEL* 32.3 (2001): 115–52. Print.

——— and Gerry Turcotte, eds. *Unsettled Remains: Canadian Literature and the Postcolonial Gothic*. Waterloo: Wilfrid Laurier UP, 2009. Print.

Suknaski, Andrew. *Wood Mountain Poems*. Toronto: Macmillan, 1976. Print.

Sullivan Historical Society. *The History of Sullivan Township 1850–1975*. Desboro: Sullivan Historical Society, 1975. Print.

Sundholm, John. "Visions of Transnational Memory." *Journal of Aesthetics & Culture* 3 (2011). DOI: 10.3402/jac.v310.7208 Last accessed 27 February 2014.

"Support for the Al Purdy A-Frame Trust." Vermeersch, *Al Purdy* 152–57.

Swartile, Katherine. Personal conversation. Kamloops. 12 June 2012.

Swift, Todd, and Evan Jones, eds. *Modern Canadian Poets: An Anthology of Poems in English*. Manchester: Carcanet, 2010. Print.

Tannock, Stuart. "Nostalgia Critique." *Cultural Studies* 9.3 (1995): 453–64. Print.

Tapscott, Don. *Growing Up Digital: The Rise of the Net Generation*. New York: McGraw-Hill, 1998. Print.

Taylor, Charles. "The Politics of Recognition." Ed. Amy Gutman. *Multiculturalism: Examining the Politics of Recognition*. New Jersey: Princeton UP, 1994. 25–73. Print.

Taylor, John H. *Ottawa: An Illustrated History*. Toronto: Lorimer, 1986. Print.

Tenenboim-Weinblatt, Keren. "Journalism as an Agent of Prospective Memory." *On Media Memory: Collective Memory in a New Media Age*. Ed. Motti Neiger, Oren Meyers, and Eyal Zandberg. New York: Palgrave Macmillan, 2011. 213–25. Print.

Thacker, Robert. *Alice Munro: Writing Her Lives*. Toronto: McClelland and Stewart, 2005. Print.

Theodore, Terri. "Education Key to Redemption of Residential School Legacy: Commission Chair." *Winnipeg Free Press*. 24 Feb. 2012. Web. 25 Feb. 2012.

Thien, Madeleine. *Dogs at the Perimeter*. Toronto: McClelland and Stewart, 2011. Print.

Thiessen, Cherie. "East Side Story." Review of *The End of East. January Magazine*. Web. 12 Jan. 2013.

Toesing, Gale. "Atleo Seeks 'Fundamental Shift' in First Nations—Federal Government Relationship." *Indian Country Network*. 3 Oct. 2011. Web. 26 Feb. 2012.

Tölölyan, Khachig. "Rethinking Diaspora(s): Stateless Power in the Transnational Moment." *Diaspora* 5.1 (1996): 3–36. Print.

Torrance, Judy M. *Public Violence in Canada, 1867–1982*. Kingston: McGill-Queen's UP, 1986. Print.

Torsen, Molly, and Jane Anderson. *Intellectual Property and the Safeguarding of Traditional Cultures: Legal Issues and Practical Options for Museums, Libraries and Archives*. Geneva: World Intellectual Property Organization, 2010. Print.

Trubek, Anne. *A Skeptic's Guide to Writers' Houses*. Philadelphia: U of Pennsylvania P, 2011. Print.

Trudeau, Pierre Elliott. "New Treason of the Intellectuals." 1962. *Federalism and the French Canadians*. Trans. Patricia Claxton. Toronto: Macmillan, 1968. 151–81. Print.

Truth and Reconciliation Commission of Canada. *Truth and Reconciliation Commission of Canada: Interim Report*. Winnipeg. 2012. Print.

Tuan, Y. *Space and Place: The Perspective of Experience*. Minneapolis: U of Minnesota P, 1977. Print.

Turkle, Sherry, ed. *Evocative Objects: Things We Think With*. Cambridge: MIT P, 2007. Print.

Ty, Eleanor. "Revising the Romance of the Land: Place in Settler Narratives by Contemporary Asian Canadian Writers." *The Canadian Mosaic in the Age of Transnationalism*. Ed. Jutta Ernst and Brigitte Glaser. Heidelberg: Universitätsverlag, 2010. 169–84. Print.

———. "Representing 'Other' Diasporas in Recent Global Canadian Fiction." *College Literature* 38.4 (2011): 98–114. Print.

——— and Christl Verduyn, eds. *Asian Canadian Writing Beyond Autoethnography.* Waterloo: Wilfrid Laurier UP, 2008. Print.

Tyler, Paul. *A Short History of Forgetting.* Kentville: Gaspereau, 2010. Print.

Underhill, Ian. *Family Portraits.* Toronto: McClelland and Stewart, 1978. Print.

Uppal, Priscila. *We Are What We Mourn: The Contemporary English-Canadian Elegy.* Montreal: McGill-Queen's UP, 2009. Print.

Van Camp, Richard. *The Lesser Blessed.* Vancouver: Douglas & McIntyre, 1996. Print.

van der Kolk, Bessel A., and Onno van der Hart. "The Intrusive Past: The Flexibility of Memory and the Engraving of Trauma." *Trauma: Explorations in Memory.* Ed. Cathy Caruth. Baltimore: Johns Hopkins UP, 1995. 158–82. Print.

Van Styvendale, Nancy. "The Trans/Historicity of Trauma in Jeannette Armstrong's *Slash* and Sherman Alexie's *Indian Killer.*" *Studies in the Novel* 40.1&2 (2008): 203–23. Print.

Vance, Jonathan F. *Death So Noble: Memory, Meaning, and the First World War.* Vancouver: U of British Columbia P, 1997. Print.

Vermeersch, Paul, ed. *The Al Purdy A-Frame Anthology.* Madeira Park: Harbour, 2009. Print.

———. "If You're Ever Down My Way, Drop in and Say Hello." Afterword. Vermeersch, *Al Purdy* 145–49.

Vernon, Karina. "Writing a Home for Prairie Blackness: Addena Sumter Freitag's *Stay Black and Die* and Cheryl Foggo's *Pourin' Down Rain.*" *Canadian Literature.* 182 (2004): 67–83. Print.

Verwaayen, Kimberley J. *Fiction Alices: Through the Looking-Glass of Post-Structuralist AutoBYography, and Four (Eight? Fifteen?) Canadian Women's Texts.* Diss. U of Western Ontario, London. 2004. Web. 20 July 2009.

Visser, Irene. "Trauma Theory and Postcolonial Literary Studies." *Journal of Postcolonial Writing* 47.3 (2011): 270–82. Print.

Visvis, Vicki. "Beyond the 'Talking Cure': The Practical Joke as Testimony for Intergenerational Trauma in Eden Robinson's 'Queen of the North.'" *Studies in Canadian Literature* 29.2 (2004): 37–61. Print.

Voth, Norma Jost. *Mennonite Foods and Folkways from South Russia.* Vol. 1. Intercourse: Good Books, 1990. Print.

Wade, Mason. *The French-Canadians,1760–1967.* Volume 2: 1911–1967. Toronto: Macmillan, 1975. 2 vols. Print.

Wah, Fred. *Faking It: Poetics and Hybridity: Critical Writing 1984–1999.* Ed. Smaro Kamboureli. Edmonton: NeWest, 2000. Print.

Wakeham, Pauline. *Taxidermic Signs: Reconstructing Aboriginality.* Minneapolis: U of Minnesota P, 2008. Print.

Wallace, Bronwen. "Lilacs in May: A Tribute to Al Purdy." MacKendrick 86–92. Print.

Ware, Tracy. "Al Purdy, Sam Solecki, and Canadian Tradition." Lynch et al. 227–38.

———. "'And They May Get It Wrong, After All': Reading Alice Munro's 'Meneseteung.'" *National Plots: Historical Fiction and Changing Ideas of Canada.* Ed. Andrea Cabajsky and Brett Josef Grubisic. Waterloo: Wilfrid Laurier UP, 2010. 67–79. Print.

Welcome to Pine Point. Dir. The Goggles. 2011. National Film Board of Canada. Web. 28 Jan. 2014.

Wesley-Esquimaux, Cynthia, and Magdalena Smolewski. *Historic Trauma and Aboriginal Healing.* Ottawa: Aboriginal Healing Foundation, 2006. Print.

White, Hayden. *The Content of Form: Narrative Discourse and Historical Representation.* Baltimore: Johns Hopkins UP, 1987. Print.

———. *Metahistory.* Baltimore: Johns Hopkins UP, 1973. Print.

White, Howard. Foreword. Vermeersch, *Al Purdy* 9. *Historic Joy Kogawa House*. Historic Joy Kogawa House, n.d. Web. 23 Oct. 2012.

White, Neil. "Creating Community: Industrial Paternalism and Town Planning in Corner Brook, Newfoundland, 1923–1955." *Urban History Review* 32.2 (Spring 2004): n. pag. Proquest. Web. 22 May 2012.

Whitehead, Anne. *Memory*. London and New York: Routledge, 2009. Print.

Whitehouse, Paul. "Seeing Red: Violence and Cultural Memory in D'Arcy McNickle's *The Surrounded*." *Dandelion* 2.1 (2011): 1–14. dandelionjournal.org Web. 30 Dec. 2013.

Whittington, Les. "Ottawa Blamed for Scuttling Plan: Minister Doesn't Back Loans in Proposal for Building 30 Homes." *Toronto Star* 11 Aug. 2012: A7. Print.

Wiebe, Rudy. *Where is the Voice Coming From?* Toronto: McClelland and Stewart, 1974. Print.

Wilbur, Richard. *The Rise of French in New Brunswick*. Halifax: Formac, 1989. Print.

Williams, Paul. "Witnessing Genocide: Vigilance and Remembrance at Tuol Sleng and Choeung Ek." *Holocaust and Genocide Studies* 18.2 (2004): 234–54. Print.

Willmott, Glenn. "Modernism and Aboriginal Modernity: The Appropriation of Products of West Coast Native Heritage as National Goods." *Essays on Canadian Writing* 83 (2004): 75–139. Print.

Willms, J.M. "Conscription 1917: A Brief for the Defense." *Conscription 1917*. Ed. Carl Berger. Toronto: U of Toronto P, 1970. 1–14. Print.

Winson, Anthony, Mustafa Koç, and Jennifer Sumner, eds. *Critical Perspectives in Food Studies*. Don Mills: Oxford UP, 2012. Print.

Winter, Jay. *Remembering War: The Great War Between Memory and History in the Twentieth Century*. New Haven: Yale UP, 2006. Print.

———. *Sites of Memory, Sites of Mourning: The Great War in European Cultural History*. Cambridge: Cambridge UP, 1995. Print.

Woolf, Virginia. *A Room of One's Own*. 1929. New York: Harcourt Brace, 1989. Print.

Woolford, Andrew. "Ontological Destruction: Genocide and Aboriginal Peoples in Canada." *Genocide Studies and Prevention* 4.1 (2005): 81–97. Print.

Wright, Patrick. *On Living in an Old Country: The National Past in Contemporary Britain*. London: Verso, 1985. Print.

Wyile, Herb. *Anne of Tim Hortons: Globalization and the Reshaping of Atlantic-Canadian Literature*. Waterloo: Wilfrid Laurier UP, 2011. Print.

———. *Speculative Fictions: Contemporary Canadian Novelists and the Writing of History*. Montreal: McGill-Queen's UP, 2002. Print.

York, Lorraine. *Literary Celebrity in Canada*. Toronto: U of Toronto P, 2007. Print.

Young, Chris. "'Sous les balles de troupes fédérales': Representing the Quebec CityRiots in Francophone Quebec (1919–2009)." M.A. thesis, Concordia U, 2009. Print.

Zamora, Lois Parkinson. *The Usable Past: The Imagination of History in Recent Fiction of the Americas*. Cambridge: Cambridge UP, 1997. Print.

Zeiger, Melissa F. *Beyond Consolation: Death, Sexuality and the Changing Shapes of Elegy*. New York: Cornell UP, 1997. Print.

Zeleza, Paul Tiyambe. "Diaspora Dialogues: Engagements between Africa and Its Diasporas." *The New African Diaspora*. Ed. Isidore Okpewho and Nkiru Nzegwu. Bloomington: Indiana UP, 2009. 31–58. Print.

Zelizer, Barbie. "Cannibalizing Memory in the Global Flow of News." *On Media Memory: Collective Memory in a New Media Age*. Ed. Motti Neiger, Oren Meyers, and Eyal Zandberg. New York: Palgrave Macmillan, 2011. 27–36. Print.

Index